Second Canadian Edition

SOCIOLOGY

A Brief Introduction

SOCIOLOGY AROUND THE WORLD

Most countries identified on this map are cited in the book, either in the context of research studies or in relevant statistical data.

15°W
0°
15°E
30°E
45°E
60°E
75°E
90°E
105°E
130°E
145°E
160°E
75°N
45°N
30°N
15°N
0°
15°S
45°S
60°S
ARCTIC OCEAN
RUSSIA
SWEDEN
NORWAY
FINLAND
ESTONIA
LATVIA
LITHUANIA
UNITED KINGDOM
DENMARK
IRELAND
THE NETHERLANDS
BELARUS
GERMANY
POLAND
UKRAINE
FRANCE
SWITZERLAND
ROMANIA
ITALY
BULGARIA
SPAIN
PORTUGAL
GREECE
TURKEY
KAZAKHSTAN
MONGOLIA
UZBEKISTAN
KYRGYZSTAN
TURKMENISTAN
TAJIKISTAN
PEOPLE'S REPUBLIC OF CHINA
N. KOREA
S. KOREA
JAPAN
MOROCCO
TUNISIA
MALTA
LEBANON
ISRAEL
SYRIA
IRAQ
IRAN
AFGHANISTAN
JORDAN
ALGERIA
LIBYA
EGYPT
SAUDI ARABIA
PAKISTAN
NEPAL
BHUTAN
INDIA
BANGLADESH
MYANMAR
LAOS
TAIWAN
PACIFIC OCEAN
MAURITANIA
MALI
NIGER
CHAD
SUDAN
UNITED ARAB EMIRATES
OMAN
YEMEN
DJIBOUTI
THAILAND
VIETNAM
CAMBODIA
PHILIPPINES
Mariana Islands
Guam
Belau
Caroline Islands
NIGERIA
CENTRAL AFRICAN REP.
ETHIOPIA
SRI LANKA
BRUNEI
MALAYSIA
LIBERIA
GHANA
TOGO
CAMEROON
EQUATORIAL GUINEA
SAO TOME AND PRINCIPE
GABON
CONGO REP.
DEMOCRATIC REPUBLIC OF THE CONGO
KENYA
SOMALIA
SEYCHELLES
TANZANIA
INDONESIA
PAPUA NEW GUINEA
ANGOLA
ZAMBIA
MOZAMBIQUE
MALAWI
INDIAN OCEAN
NAMIBIA
ZIMBABWE
BOTSWANA
MADAGASCAR
MAURITIUS
SWAZILAND
SOUTH AFRICA
LESOTHO
AUSTRALIA

Second Canadian Edition

SOCIOLOGY

A Brief Introduction

RICHARD T. SCHAEFER
DePaul University

BONNIE HAALAND
Kwantlen University College

McGraw-Hill Ryerson

Toronto Montréal Boston Burr Ridge, IL Dubuque, IA Madison, WI New York
San Francisco St. Louis Bangkok Bogotá Caracas Kuala Lumpur Lisbon London
Madrid Mexico City Milan New Delhi Santiago Seoul Singapore Sydney Taipei

The McGraw-Hill Companies

McGraw-Hill Ryerson

Sociology: A Brief Introduction
Second Canadian Edition

ISBN: 0-07-093977-2

1 2 3 4 5 6 7 8 9 10 VH 0 9 8 7 6

Executive Sponsoring Editor: James Buchanan
Managing Editor, Development: Jennifer DiDomenico
Photo Researcher: Christina Beamish
Marketing Manager: Marc Trudel
Senior Supervising Editor: Margaret Henderson
Copy Editor: Dawn Hunter
Senior Production Coordinator: Jennifer Wilkie
Composition: Bookman Typesetting Co.
Cover Design: Greg Devitt
Cover Image: images.com/Todd Davidson
Printer: Von Hoffman Press, Inc.

Library and Archives Canada Cataloguing in Publication

Schaefer, Richard T.
Sociology : a brief introduction / Richard T. Schaefer, Bonnie Haaland. — 2nd Canadian ed.

Includes bibliographical references and indexes.
ISBN 0-07-093977-2

1. Sociology—Textbooks. I. Haaland, Bonnie II. Title.

HM586.S32 2006 301 C2005-907781-6

DEDICATION

To my son, Peter

— Richard T. Schaefer

To C.A. and Z.A.
with gratitude

— Bonnie Haaland

ABOUT THE AUTHORS

RICHARD T. SCHAEFER

Growing up in Chicago at a time when neighbourhoods were going through transitions in ethnic and racial composition, Richard T. Schaefer found himself increasingly intrigued by what was happening, how people were reacting, and how these changes were affecting neighbourhoods and people's jobs. His interest in social issues caused him to gravitate to sociology courses at Northwestern University, where he eventually received a BA in sociology.

"Originally as an undergraduate, I thought I would go on to law school and become a lawyer. But after taking a few sociology courses, I found myself wanting to learn more about what sociologists studied and fascinated by the kinds of questions they raised." This fascination led him to obtain his MA and PhD in sociology from the University of Chicago. Dr. Schaefer's continuing interest in race relations led him to write his master's thesis on the membership of the Ku Klux Klan and his doctoral thesis on racial prejudice and race relations in Great Britain.

Dr. Schaefer went on to become a professor of sociology and now teaches at DePaul University in Chicago. In 2004 he was named to the Vincent DePaul professorship in recognition of his undergraduate teaching and scholarship. He has taught introductory sociology for more than 30 years to students in colleges, adult education programs, nursing programs, and even a maximum-security prison. Dr. Schaefer's love of teaching is apparent in his interaction with his students. "I find myself constantly learning from the students who are in my classes and from reading what they write. Their insights into the material we read or current events that we discuss often become part of future course material and sometimes even find their way into my writing."

Dr. Schaefer is author of the ninth edition of *Sociology* (McGraw-Hill, 2005) and of *Sociology Matters* (McGraw-Hill, 2004). Dr. Schaefer is also the author of *Racial and Ethnic Groups,* now in its tenth edition, and *Race and Ethnicity in the United States,* third edition. His articles and book reviews have appeared in many journals, including *American Journal of Sociology; Phylon: A Review of Race and Culture; Contemporary Sociology; Sociology and Social Research; Sociological Quarterly;* and *Teaching Sociology.* He served as president of the Midwest Sociological Society in 1994–1995.

Dr. Schaefer's advice to students is to "look at the material and make connections to your own life and experiences. Sociology will make you a more attentive observer of how people in groups interact and function. It will also make you more aware of people's different needs and interests—and perhaps more ready to work for the common good, while still recognizing the individuality of each person."

BONNIE HAALAND

Bonnie Haaland has been teaching sociology for more than 20 years to classes with as many as 350 students and as few as 9; to teachers, bankers, and nurses; and to new high school graduates and senior undergraduates, through various modes of instruction. Bonnie was one of the first instructors at the University of Western Ontario to teach courses by using distance education technology, which simultaneously connected clusters of students in smaller cities and towns throughout southwestern Ontario. At Western, she later coordinated a program involving distance education, overseeing the delivery of courses in such fields as chemistry, nursing, psychology, anthropology, and English. During this time, Bonnie has also been actively involved in research related to distance and continuing education, presenting papers at conferences, such as the International Congress on Distance Education in Melbourne, Australia.

In addition to teaching at the University of Western Ontario, Bonnie has taught at the University of Regina and is currently at Kwantlen University College, where she teaches introductory sociology and other undergraduate courses.

Bonnie is the author of *Emma Goldman: Sexuality and the Impurity of the State;* a co-author of *Sociology: A Brief Introduction*, First Canadian Edition and Census Update Edition; and author of articles published in Canadian and American journals. She is the recipient of the Canadian Association for University Continuing Education's Award of Excellence for her article "In Pursuit of Self: The Values of the Post-War Baby Boom Generation and the Implications for Continuing Education."

Bonnie grew up in Saskatchewan and graduated with distinction from the University of Saskatchewan with a BA, from the University of Western Ontario with a MA, and from the University of Toronto with a PhD. She currently lives in South Surrey/White Rock, British Columbia, and has a son, Jordie, who is a first-year student at the University of Victoria, studying the social sciences, arts, and humanities.

CONTENTS IN BRIEF

CONTENTS

LIST OF BOXES

Sociology in the Global Community

Research in Action

Eye on the Media

LIST OF SOCIAL POLICY SECTIONS

PREFACE

As I leave the classroom each day, I am frequently struck by how my students' lives have changed since I taught my first sociology class in the late 1970s. I can't help but notice how "connected" students seem today; how technologically savvy they appear; how their social networks, shaped and maintained fundamentally by newer communication technologies, are larger and more wide-reaching than that of other age groups. The rapidity of technological change and the diverse—and often conflicting—demands for undergraduates' time and attention are challenges with which students must contend on a daily basis. The dramatic increases in tuition costs and the increased need to hold a job while studying; the need for Internet access and currency in computer skills; the ubiquitous intrusion of the mass media and its consumer culture; and the global terrorism threat are just a few of the concerns that consume a share of students' attentions. By implication, of course, my students' challenges, to a large degree, become my challenges. Increasingly, I see my role, and more specifically the role of my discipline, as instrumental in helping undergraduates process and navigate the content of their social worlds. In this way, sociology is truly a dynamic discipline with great potential to engage learners in their social worlds not solely as actors but also as observers and interpreters. Sociology offers the opportunity to see ourselves as part of a larger entity—a friendship, a university community, a national community, a global community—and to explore diverse and often contradictory interpretations of those relationships.

To see Mills's *sociological imagination* actualized through students' ability to make the connections between the forces shaping their own lives and those shaping a friendship, a university, a nation, or the globe is a challenge and accomplishment for student and instructor alike. *Sociology: A Brief Introduction,* Second Canadian Edition, is written with that goal in mind. This text strengthens the foundation laid in the First Canadian Edition, providing compelling and relevant topics and examples that resonate with students, that are situated in a global context, and that are consistently interpreted through the lens of four theoretical perspectives. Key features of this Second Canadian Edition include the following:

- **Hot topics of Canadian and global interest.** The Second Canadian Edition covers such topics as binge drinking on university campuses, music downloading, telecommuting, global terrorism, homelessness, suburbanization and the growth of Wal-Mart, global Internet use, computer hacking, environmental justice, racial profiling, urban sprawl, same-sex marriage, post–September 11 treatment of North American Muslims, regional patterns of cohabitation, Canadian–American differences in religious beliefs, voter turnout among younger Canadians, the "greying" of Canadian society, shopping and consumer culture, the global "McDonaldization" of society, citizens' movements, media representation of minorities, the increase in nonstandard jobs, the fight against global poverty, the feminization of AIDS, the study of Canadians' sexual practices, university degrees and creditialism, gender and global rates of literacy and educational access, ethnoburbs and ethnoburbia, gender and race and occupation, and Canadian political representation.
- **Extensive updates to statistics, research, and visuals.** This edition uses the latest statistics and reports from Statistics Canada, data from the Canadian Institute of Health Information, United Nations reports, results of polls carried out by such groups as Ipsos-Reid and Leger Marketing, and data on Internet use from Global Reach. New research findings have been incorporated, drawing on the work of Canadian researchers whenever possible. In terms of pedagogical features, more than 30 percent of the boxes and 75 percent of the chapter-opening excerpts are new. Furthermore, the photo program has been revised to include current and relevant examples and illustrations for students.
- **Increased focus on providing student applications and fostering the sociological imagination.** Each

chapter of *Sociology: A Brief Introduction,* Second Canadian Edition, contains *Use Your Sociological Imagination* critical thinking sections, appropriately positioned, which foster critical thinking of the material covered in the chapter. In addition, as part of the strengthened theoretical foundation of this edition, *Applying Theory* questions have been integrated into the popular boxed features *Research in Action, Sociology in the Global Community*, and *Eye on the Media.* New *Think About It* captions accompany some figures, encouraging students' critical engagement with sociological data. Unique *Social Policy* sections continue to help students forge links between sociological theory and the world around them.

- **Stronger foundation for and more consistent treatment of sociological theory.** In response to reviewer feedback, the text has been reorganized to include more comprehensive coverage of theory at the beginning of the text, which is then built upon in each chapter. Chapter 1 contains expanded coverage of all four theoretical perspectives and postmodern perspectives. Chapter 3 includes additional coverage of the interactionist and feminist perspectives as they relate to the dominant ideology and culture. Chapter 4 contains a new section on theoretical perspectives on socialization. Chapter 5 contains a new section on feminist theories. Chapter 6 includes a new section on theoretical perspectives. Chapter 13 has new coverage of the economy from four theoretical perspectives. Chapter 15 contains additional segments on feminist and interactionist perspectives on the environment. Chapter 16 now includes the interactionist perspective on social change and social movements.
- **Integrated learning system.** The text, Online Learning Centre Web site, and *Reel Society* 2.0 CD-ROM work together as an integrated learning system to bring the theories, research findings, and basic concepts of sociology to life for students. Offering a combination of print, multimedia, and Web-based materials, this comprehensive system meets the needs of instructors and students who have a variety of teaching and learning styles.

The Plan for This Book

Sociology: A Brief Introduction, Second Canadian Edition is divided into 16 chapters that study human behaviour concisely from the perspective of sociologists. The opening chapter ("Understanding Sociology") presents a brief history of the discipline, introduces key Canadian sociologists, and explains the four basic theories and perspectives used in sociology. Chapter 2 ("Sociological Research") describes the major quantitative and qualitative research methods.

The next five chapters focus on key sociological concepts. Chapter 3 ("Culture") illustrates how sociologists study the behaviour people learn and share. Chapter 4 ("Socialization") reveals how humans are most distinctively social animals who learn the attitudes and behaviour viewed as appropriate in their particular cultures. We examine "Social Interaction and Social Structure" in Chapter 5 and the workings of "Groups and Organizations" in Chapter 6. Chapter 7 ("Deviance and Social Control") reviews how we conform to and deviate from established norms.

The next three chapters consider the social hierarchies present in societies. Chapter 8 ("Stratification in Canada and Worldwide") introduces us to the presence of social inequality, while Chapter 9 ("Racial and Ethnic Inequality") and Chapter 10 ("Gender Relations") analyze specific and ubiquitous types of inequality.

The next three chapters examine the major social institutions of human society. Marriage, family diversity, and divorce are some of the topics discussed in Chapter 11 ("The Family and Intimate Relationships"). Other social institutions are considered in Chapter 12 ("Religion and Education") and Chapter 13 ("Government and the Economy").

The final chapters of the text introduce major themes in our changing world. Chapter 14 ("Population, Aging, and Health") helps us understand the impact of these issues on Canadian society and around the world. In Chapter 15 we examine the importance of "Communities and the Environment" in our lives. Chapter 16 ("Social Movements, Social Change, and Technology") presents sociological analysis of the process of change and has a special focus on technology and the future.

CHAPTER-BY-CHAPTER CHANGES

The Second Canadian Edition has been fully updated to reflect the most recent developments in sociology and in Canada and the global society. It provides the most relevant and meaningful applications for students, including the new *Use Your Sociological Imagination* sections and the updated *Applying Theory* questions that appear in each boxed feature and Social Policy section. Below is a summary of just some of the content changes in the Second Canadian Edition.

CHAPTER 1 Understanding Sociology

- New chapter-opening excerpt from *The Urge to Splurge: A Social History of Shopping,* by Laura Byrne Paquet
- Expanded coverage of Canadian sociologists

- Stronger foundation discussion of theoretical perspectives
- Added discussion of postmodern perspectives
- Expanded coverage of "What Is Sociological Theory?"

CHAPTER 2 Sociological Research

- New chapter-opening excerpt from *Generation on Hold: Coming of Age in the Late Twentieth Century,* by James E. Côté and Anton L. Allahar
- New Sociology in the Global Community box: "Polling in Baghdad"
- New Research in Action box: "Does Hard Work Lead to Better Grades?"
- Updated data on sexual practices in Canada
- New Canadian data on education and income

CHAPTER 3 Culture

- Updated Research in Action and Eye on the Media boxes
- Expanded coverage of interactionist and feminist perspectives as they relate to the dominant ideology and culture

CHAPTER 4 Socialization

- New chapter-opening excerpt from *Deadly Persuasion: Why Women and Girls Must Fight the Addictive Power of Advertising,* by Jean Kilbourne
- Updated Sociology in the Global Community and Research in Action boxes
- Revised and updated Social Policy section
- New material from the Organisation for Economic Co-operation and Development report on child care in Canada and around the world
- New section called "Socialization: The Major Theoretical Perspectives"

CHAPTER 5 Social Interaction and Social Structure

- New Use Your Sociological Imagination questions attached to chapter opener
- New Research in Action box: "Immigrant Women's Social Networks"
- Updated material on the global AIDS crisis
- Revised Social Policy section
- New section on feminist theories

CHAPTER 6 Groups and Organizations

- New Sociology in the Global Community box: "Management, Russian Style"
- New Social Policy section on Canadian union trends and a comparison of U.S. and Canadian union activity
- Enhanced discussion of theoretical perspectives

CHAPTER 7 Deviance and Social Control

- New chapter-opening excerpt from *The Art of Intrusion: The Real Stories Behind the Exploits of Hackers, Intruders, and Deceivers,* by Kevin D. Mitnick and William L. Simon
- Revised Social Policy section on illicit drug use in Canada
- New Additional Readings

CHAPTER 8 Stratification in Canada and Worldwide

- New chapter-opening excerpt from *Nike Culture: The Sign of the Swoosh,* by Robert Goldman and Stephen Papson
- Two new Sociology in the Global Community boxes: "Slavery in the Twenty-First Century" and "Poverty and Global Inequality"
- Coverage of Leger Marketing study on wealthy or affluent Canadians
- Updated data on income and wealth in Canada
- Updated statistics on child and family poverty in Canada and recommendations for the alleviation of poverty from Campaign 2000
- Updated statistics on social assistance
- Revised Social Policy box

CHAPTER 9 Racial and Ethnic Inequality

- New chapter-opening excerpt from *The New Canada: A Globe and Mail Report on the Next Generation,* by Erin Anderssen and Michael Valpy
- New Research in Action box: "Prejudice against Arabs and Muslims in Post–September 11 America"
- New Eye on the Media box: "Racism and the Mainstream Media"
- New map depicting the First Nations Peoples of British Columbia
- New data on discrimination and unfair treatment in Canada
- Revised Social Policy section
- Rewritten and refocused sections on Aboriginal people, Asian Canadians, and white ethnic groups

CHAPTER 10 Gender Relations

- New chapter-opening excerpt on older men and cosmetic surgery from the *Vancouver Sun*
- New Sociology in the Global Community box: "The Empowerment of Women through Education"
- Expanded coverage of systemic discrimination
- Revised Social Policy section

CHAPTER 11 The Family and Intimate Relationships

- New chapter-opening excerpt on family law and technology from *The Globe and Mail*
- New coverage of the debate in Canada over same-sex marriage and Bill C-38 (Civil Marriage Act)
- Greater emphasis on family diversity in Canada
- Revised Eye on the Media box
- Revised Sociology in the Global Community box
- Revised Social policy section

CHAPTER 12 Religion and Education

- New figure on the importance of God in the lives of citizens in selected countries, showing differences between Canadians and Americans
- New coverage of debate on same-sex marriage in Canada and the religious implications
- Updated data on religious denominations in Canada
- Updated data on educational participation in Canada and globally
- Revised Research in Action box

CHAPTER 13 Government and the Economy

- New chapter-opening excerpt from *Still Counting: Women in Politics Across Canada,* by Linda Trimble and Jane Arscott
- New Sociology in the Global Community box: "Terrorist Violence"
- New Research in Action box: "Working Women in Nepal"
- New figure on the evolution of party identification in Canada
- New data on voter turnout in federal elections
- Increased coverage of gender and race occupation, and elected politics in Canada
- New coverage of the economy from four theoretical perspectives
- New coverage of women's participation in the paid labour force
- New coverage of deindustrialization of the Canadian economy and the growth of non-standard work

CHAPTER 14 Population, Aging, and Health

- New chapter-opening excerpt on the skills shortage in Canada from *Canadian Business*
- Updated data from the United Nations on the spread of HIV/AIDS and the growth of the feminization of AIDS
- Updated Sociology in the Global Community boxes
- Updated figure on the population structures of Canada and Kenya
- Revised Social Policy section on financing health care worldwide

CHAPTER 15 Communities and the Environment

- New chapter-opening excerpt from *Down to This: Squalor and Splendour in a Big-City Shantytown,* by Shaughnessy Bishop-Stall
- Updated data on urbanization rates in Canada and population concentration
- New coverage of urban sprawl
- Added discussion of interactionist and feminist perspectives on communities
- New figure on international comparison of modes of urban passenger travel
- New coverage on *ethnoburbia* and *ethnoburbs*
- Updated data on self-employed Canadians living in rural areas and small towns
- New Research in Action box: "Store Wars"
- Expanded coverage of environmental justice and Canadian research
- Added discussion of feminist and interactionist perspectives on the environment

CHAPTER 16 Social Movements, Social Change, and Technology

- New chapter-opening excerpt from *Ruling the Waves: Cycles of Discovery, Chaos, and Wealth from the Compass to the Internet,* by Debora L. Spar
- New coverage on citizens' groups in Canada
- Added discussion of interactionist perspectives
- New figure on Canadian household Internet use and additional coverage on access to Internet use in Canada
- Updated figures on global Internet usage
- Revised Social Policy section

SUPPLEMENTS

NEW! *Reel Society* Interactive Movie CD-ROM 2.0

Available on request as a separate package option with *Sociology: A Brief Introduction,* Second Canadian Edition, *Reel Society* 2.0 is a two-CD-ROM video set (with an accompanying guidebook) designed to demonstrate key topics in sociology through episodes typical of campus life. These movie scenes are augmented by a robust array of review, assessment, and reporting features.

Reel Society 2.0 is built around the learning objectives of a typical introductory sociology course. Students explore a variety of key sociological perspectives and concepts firsthand, including the conflict, functionalist, and interactionist perspectives; stratification; social mobility; the family; education; religion; and politics.

Students can follow the storyline from start to finish by using Story Mode or choose only those scenes that apply to a chapter or topic by using Study Mode. In either case, they can take advantage of several review and assessment features, including explanatory screens, a glossary, self-quizzes, and homework assignments. The Scorecard feature tracks a student's completion of CD-ROM assignments and allows the student to report it to the instructor using email and print features. Additional activities and assignments are found on the *Reel Society* Web site (**www.mhhe.com/reelsociety**).

Instructors receive their own version of the CD-ROM, which allows them to set the viewing options and choose the displayed assignments. A detailed Instructor's Manual (available on the Online Learning Centre) helps instructors to integrate *Reel Society* 2.0 into their courses.

Instructor Supplements

The **Instructor's CD-ROM** contains the Instructor's Manual, Test Bank in Rich Text Format, Computerized Test Bank, and Microsoft® PowerPoint® slides, all of which have been extensively revised to accord with the Second Canadian Edition:

- **Instructor's Manual.** The Instructor's Manual contains lecture ideas; class discussion topics; essay questions; topics for student research; and lists of audiovisual materials, additional readings, and Web sites. New to the Second Canadian Edition are in-class activities to promote student engagement.
- **Test Bank in Rich Text Format.** The Test Bank features short-answer, multiple-choice, and essay questions. Each question is accompanied by an answer and page reference in the text. Multiple-choice questions are categorized by question type.
- **Computerized Test Bank.** This flexible and easy-to-use electronic testing program allows instructors to create tests from book-specific items. It accommodates a wide range of question types, and instructors may add their own questions. Multiple versions of the test can be created and printed.
- **Microsoft® PowerPoint® Slides.** These presentations contain exhibits from the text and follow the chapter outlines of the Second Canadian Edition.

Instructor Online Learning Centre (OLC)

The Online Learning Centre (OLC) at **www.mcgrawhill.ca/college/schaefer** includes a password-protected Web site for instructors. The site offers downloadable supplements, including an Instructor's Manual, Microsoft® PowerPoint® slides, the *Reel Society* 2.0 Instructor's Manual, professional resources, and more.

CBC Videos

CBC videos are available to adopters of this textbook. As well, they are posted as streaming video on the Online Learning Centre (**www.mcgrawhill.ca/college/schaefer**).

Course Management

Visit **www.mhhe.com/pageout** to create a Web page for your course by using our resources. PageOut is the McGraw-Hill Ryerson Web site development centre. This Web-page-generation software is free to adopters and is designed to help faculty create an online course, complete with assignments, quizzes, links to relevant Web sites, and more—all in a matter of minutes.

In addition, content cartridges are available for the course management systems **WebCT and Blackboard.** These platforms provide instructors with user-friendly, flexible teaching tools. Please contact your local McGraw-Hill Ryerson *i*Learning Sales Specialist for details.

eInstruction's Classroom Performance System (CPS)

Classroom Performance System (**CPS**) is a student-response system that uses wireless connectivity. It gives instructors and students immediate feedback from the entire class. The response pads are easy-to-use remotes that engage students.

- **CPS** helps you to increase **student preparation**, **interactivity**, and **active learning** so that you can receive immediate feedback and know what students understand.
- **CPS** allows you to administer quizzes and tests and provide **immediate grading**.
- With **CPS**, you can create lecture questions that can be multiple-choice, true-false, and subjective. You can even create questions on the fly as well as conduct group activities.
- **CPS** not only allows you to **evaluate classroom attendance**, **activity**, and **grading** for your course

as a whole but CPSOnline also allows you to provide students with an immediate study guide. All results and scores can easily be imported into Excel and can be used with various classroom management systems.

CPS-ready content is available for use with *Sociology: A Brief Introduction*, Second Canadian Edition. Please contact your *i*Learning Sales Specialist for more information on how you can integrate CPS into your sociology classroom.

PowerWeb

PowerWeb extends the learning experience beyond the core textbook by offering, via the Internet, all the latest news and developments pertinent to your course, without the clutter and dead links of a typical online search.

PowerWeb offers current articles related to sociology, weekly updates with assessment tools, informative and timely world news culled by a subject expert, Web links, and more. In addition, PowerWeb provides an array of helpful learning aids, including self-grading quizzes and interactive glossaries and exercises. Contact your *i*Learning Sales Specialist to learn more about making this valuable resource available to your students.

Primis Customized Readers

An array of first-rate readings are available to adopters in a customized electronic database. Some are classic articles from the sociological literature; others are provocative pieces written especially for McGraw-Hill by leading sociologists. For more information, please contact your *i*Learning Sales Specialist.

McGraw-Hill Dushkin

Any of the Dushkin publications can be packaged with this text at a discount: *Annual Editions*, *Taking Sides*, *Sources*, and *Global Studies*. For more information, please contact your *i*Learning Sales Specialist.

Superior Service

Your **Integrated Learning Sales Specialist** is a McGraw-Hill Ryerson representative who has the experience, product knowledge, training, and support to help you assess and integrate all the supplements, technology, and services into your course for optimum teaching and learning performance. Whether it's using our test bank software, helping your students improve their grades, or putting your entire course online, your *i*Learning Sales Specialist is there to help you do it. Contact your local *i*Learning Sales Specialist today to learn how to maximize all of McGraw-Hill Ryerson's resources!

*i*Learning Services Program

McGraw-Hill Ryerson offers a unique *i*Services package designed for Canadian faculty. Our mission is to equip providers of higher education with superior tools and the resources required for excellence in teaching. For additional information visit **www.mcgrawhill.ca/highereducation/iservices**.

Teaching, Technology & Learning Conference Series

The educational environment has changed tremendously in recent years, and McGraw-Hill Ryerson continues to be committed to helping you acquire the skills you need to succeed in this new milieu. Our innovative Teaching, Technology & Learning Conference Series brings together faculty from across Canada and 3M Teaching Excellence award winners to share teaching and learning best practices in a collaborative and stimulating environment. Preconference workshops on general topics, such as teaching large classes and technology integration, are also offered. We will also work with you at your own institution to customize workshops that best suit the needs of your faculty.

Student Supplements

Student Online Learning Centre

Improve your grades! Visit the Online Learning Centre at **www.mcgrawhill.ca/college/schaefer** to access learning and study tools, such as

- Multiple-choice questions
- True-false questions
- Internet exercises
- Searchable glossary
- Interactive activities
- Internet exercises
- E-STAT
- Study to Go
- *Globe and Mail* headlines
- Streaming CBC video clips

Study Guide Now Available Online and Interactive

The Study Guide contains all the resources you need to review and apply what you've learned, and to succeed in your sociology course. It includes self-tests and understanding social policy questions for each chapter. Please contact your *i*Learning Sales Specialist for details on how to make access to this resource available to your students.

Study to Go

McGraw-Hill's Study To Go

Do you use a handheld personal digital assistant (PDA)? McGraw-Hill Ryerson's *Study to Go* application gives you the opportunity to study anytime, anywhere. And it's free for students using *Sociology: A Brief Introduction*! To download quizzes, key terms, and flashcards, visit the Online Learning Centre at **www.mcgrawhill.ca/college/schaefer.**

E-STAT

Σ-STAT

E-STAT is an educational resource designed by Statistics Canada and made available to Canadian educational institutions. Using 450 000 current CANSIM (Canadian Socio-economic Information Management System) Time Series and the most recent—as well as historical—census data, E-STAT lets you bring data to life in colourful graphs and maps. Access to E-STAT is made available to purchasers of this book, via the Schaefer Online Learning Centre, by special agreement between McGraw-Hill Ryerson and Statistics Canada. The Online Learning Centre provides additional information.

ACKNOWLEDGMENTS FROM BONNIE HAALAND

I am deeply indebted to a number of individuals at McGraw-Hill Ryerson who provided support, encouragement, and technical expertise throughout the development of this project. I wish to express my sincere thanks and appreciation to James Buchanan, Executive Sponsoring Editor; Margaret Henderson, Senior Supervising Editor; Madeleine Harrington, Senior Production Coordinator; and Dawn Hunter, Copy Editor.

A special word of thanks is owing to Jennifer DiDomenico, Managing Editor, Development. Working with Jennifer has been a pleasure that has enriched this project enormously. Her keen eye; her sharp ear; her impeccable organizational skills; and her fair, caring, and compassionate manner all combine to make her a truly outstanding editor.

I would also like to extend thanks to those instructors across Canada whose thoughtful and painstaking reviews helped to inform this text:

Salvatore Albanese, Langara College

Penny Biles, Sheridan Institute of Technology and Advanced Learning

Linda Derksen, Malaspina University College

Judith Doyle, Mount Allison University

Marissa Fleming, Georgian College

Nicole Elise Guagliano, Mohawk College

M. Morgan Holmes, Wilfrid Laurier University

Rita Isola, Capilano College

James Jackson, Humber College

Neil Jamieson-Williams, Mohawk College

Mary Knight, Durham College

David Lynes, St Francis Xavier University

Chris MacKenzie, University of British Columbia

Fred Neale, Lethbridge Community College

Tracy Nielsen, Mount Royal College

Melanie White, Trent University

Cindy Wright, Sir Sandford Fleming College

I am also indebted to many departmental colleagues at Kwantlen University College for their generosity and support. To Roger Elmes, dean of arts at Kwantlen University College, I wish to extend sincere thanks for his unwavering support and encouragement. The release of this edition will coincide with Roger's retirement and, thus, it is with regret that I say farewell to a person of remarkable character and integrity. I feel extremely fortunate to have known him, and I have been inspired by the humanity he has consistently infused into the daily activities of the institution. I will miss him greatly and know that I am not alone in expressing this sentiment.

I am also indebted to the Office of Research and Scholarship at Kwantlen University College for its support in assisting me during the final stages of this project.

To Jay and Jordie, thank you—yet again—for so graciously accepting the inconveniences and for so willingly making the sacrifices that enabled me to complete this work.

And, finally, to my students, whose reading of the First Canadian Edition lead to so many thought-provoking, critical, and practical suggestions that—in one way or another—have made their way into this Second Canadian Edition, I offer my sincere thanks.

Teaching Students to Think Sociologically

The Second Canadian Edition of *Sociology: A Brief Introduction* continues its tradition of teaching students how to think critically about society and their own lives from a wide range of sociological perspectives.

Let's be clear: There is also a New Canada out there. If Canadians can't see it themselves, they certainly pay attention when others see it on our behalf. Thus, *The Economist* magazine captured our attention in the fall of 2003 when it put on its cover a moose in sunglasses under the headline "Canada's new spirit" and went on to laud our tolerance and cultural diversity and describe our major cities as vibrant, cosmopolitan places. . . .

Our embrace of multiculturalism presents the most obvious manifestation of the New Canada. But it goes well beyond the mere fact of scores of different ethnic groups co-existing peacefully in our global cities, however notable an achievement that may represent in international terms.

Our schools ring out with the sound of different tongues, giving our children an early and ever-lasting lesson in the very Canadian balance of individual expression and social peace. The New Canada of which we speak flows from the long cherished frontier value of freedom. The New Canada is about the freedom to be who you are and still belong to the larger group. . . .

Virtually nobody under the age of 30 thinks that a similar ethnic or racial background is an important consideration in choosing a spouse—even if that means holding two separate weddings to unite the couple. . . .

Immigration died down during the Depression and the Second World War. Then, starting in the post-war period, Canada attracted a wave of skilled and semi-skilled blue-collar workers from southern Europe. Many of the children of this second wave sit proudly today in our legislatures and Parliament.

And then the third wave—the one that has so demonstrably changed the look of our cities over the past generation. Chinese, Sri Lankans, Filipinos, Sikhs, Ismailis, West Indians, North and sub-Saharan Africans—an influx that has changed our capacities but strengthened our fabric. Thanks to the education system and the media, integration occurs far faster than ever before—usually within the same generation for younger Canadians. As Queen's University professor Matthew Mendelsohn, a consultant on the New Canada series, points out, in France, Britain, Italy, the United States and elsewhere, anywhere from 30 to 50 per cent of people say that relations between ethnic groups are a problem. In Canada, just 12 per cent think so.

This process of ethnic diversification is inevitably changing our world outlook—making us less parochial in all our dealings. When you see a *pure laine* Québécois boy strolling down Rue St. Denis with his Haitian-Canadian girlfriend and their Moroccan-Canadian schoolmates, it is hard to imagine them being overly agitated about the hanging of Louis Riel. They are connected to a vibrant world, not stuck in an historical rant. *(Anderssen, Valpy, et al. 2004)* ■

194

www.mcgrawhill.ca/college/schaefer

Racial and Ethnic Inequality **195**

This excerpt from the book by Erin Anderssen, Michael Valpy, and others depicts a "New Canada" characterized as tolerant, peaceful, and culturally diverse, with vibrant cosmopolitan cities. It is a Canada, according to the authors, where people, particularly those under the age of 30, do not consider similar ethnocultural background an important consideration in choosing a mate. It is a Canada, as the authors point out, where just 12 percent of Canadians say that relations between ethnic groups are a problem, in sharp contrast to such countries as France, Britain, Italy, and the United States, where 30 percent to 50 percent of the people say that relations between ethnic groups are a problem. Despite this seemingly glowing view of ethnic diversity in Canada, patterns of inequality exist and persist, whereby some groups are systematically subjugated by the dominant groups, restricting their access to opportunity and upward mobility.

Today, thousands of people who are members of racial and ethnic minorities continue to experience the often bitter contrast between the Canadian ideal of multiculturalism and the grim realities of poverty, prejudice, and discrimination. Class, gender, and the social definitions of race and ethnicity intersect to produce systems of inequality, not only in this country but throughout the world. High incomes, a good command of French or English, and hard-earned professional credentials do not always override racial and ethnic stereotypes or protect those who fit them from the sting of racism.

What is prejudice, and how is it institutionalized in the form of discrimination? In what ways have race and ethnicity affected the experience of immigrants from other countries? What are the fastest-growing minority groups in Canada today? In this chapter we will focus on the meaning of race and ethnicity. We will begin by identifying the basic characteristics of a minority group and distinguishing between racial groups and ethnic groups. Then we will examine the dynamics of prejudice and discrimination. After considering the functionalist, conflict, feminist, and interactionist perspectives on race and ethnicity, we'll look at patterns of intergroup relations, particularly in Canada. Finally, in the social policy section, we will explore issues related to immigration worldwide. ■

Use Your Sociological Imagination www.mcgrawhill.ca/

Does Anderssen and Valpy's view of Canada match your own experiences or situation? Do you think the statistic that only 12 percent of Canadians say that relations between ethnic groups are a problem masks the everyday experiences of many Canadians who face discrimination because of their skin colour or ethnocultural identity?

MINORITY, RACIAL, AND ETHNIC GROUPS

Categories of people can often be thought of as "racial" and ethnic groups. The term ***racial group*** describes a category that is set apart and treated differently from others because of real or perceived physical differences. White, black, and Asian Canadians are all considered racial groups in Canada. It is the culture of a particular society, however, that constructs and attaches social significance to these differences, as we will see later. Unlike racialized groups, an ***ethnic group*** is set apart from others primarily because of its national origin or distinctive cultural patterns. In Canada, Italian Canadians, Jewish people, and Polish Canadians are all categorized as ethnic groups. Both types of groups are considered to be *minority groups* by sociologists, as the next section shows.

Minority Groups

A numerical minority is any group that makes up less than half of some larger population. The population of Canada includes thousands of numerical minorities, including television actors, green-eyed people, tax lawyers, and snow boarders. However, these numerical minorities are not considered to be minorities in the sociological sense; in fact, the number of people in a group does not necessarily determine its status as a social minority (or a dominant group). When sociologists define a minority group, they are primarily concerned

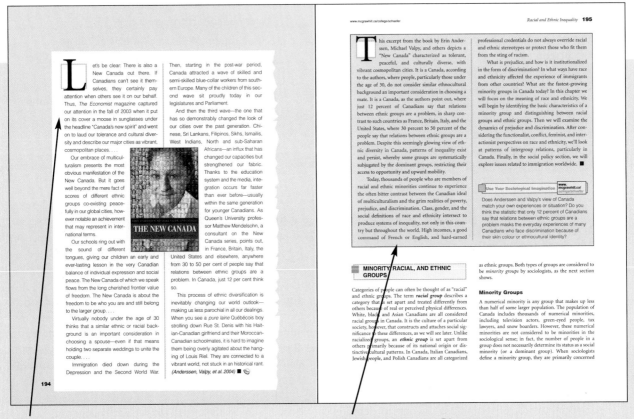

Intriguing Excerpts

Chapter-opening excerpts convey the excitement and relevance of sociological inquiry by means of lively excerpts from the writings of sociologists and others who explore sociological topics. Seventy-five percent are **new** to this edition, including Canadian selections on the history of shopping, women in politics, and urban shantytowns in Canada.

Excerpt Links to Chapters

Chapter overviews provide a bridge between the chapter-opening excerpt and the content of the chapter.

NEW! Use Your Sociological Imagination Sections

Use Your Sociological Imagination sections within each chapter pose questions designed to stimulate students' sociological imagination and help them connect major concepts and issues to their own lives. Students can respond to the questions in these sections on the Online Learning Centre and email their answers to their instructors.

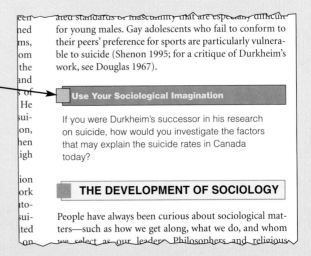

for young males. Gay adolescents who fail to conform to their peers' preference for sports are particularly vulnerable to suicide (Shenon 1995; for a critique of Durkheim's work, see Douglas 1967).

Use Your Sociological Imagination

If you were Durkheim's successor in his research on suicide, how would you investigate the factors that may explain the suicide rates in Canada today?

THE DEVELOPMENT OF SOCIOLOGY

People have always been curious about sociological matters—such as how we get along, what we do, and whom

Unique Social Policy Sections

The Social Policy sections, highly praised by reviewers of this text, provide a sociological perspective on contemporary social issues, such as the AIDS crisis, union membership and activity, and financing health care. Providing a global view of the issues, these sections are organized around a consistent heading structure and include Applying Theory questions designed to stimulate critical thinking about the issues being explored.

348 Chapter 14 www.mcgrawhill.ca/college/schaefer

health. The movement therefore has taken many forms, including organizations working for changes in the health care system, women's clinics, and "self-help" groups.

The goals of the women's health movement are ambitious, but the health care system has proved to be fairly resistant to change. Conflict theorists point out that physicians, medical schools, hospitals, and drug companies all have a vested interest in keeping women in a rather dependent and uninformed position as health care consumers. Despite an increase in the number of female doctors, women remain underrepresented in all key decision-making positions in the health care system of Canada.

The Role of Government

In 1984, the federal government's Canada Health Act became the basis for the administration of our health care system, known as *medicare*. The Act set out to ensure (in theory) that all Canadians receive access to hospital and doctors' services on the basis of need, not on the ability to pay. It also sets the conditions and criteria under which the provinces and territories receive transfer payments—payments that are then used to finance health care services in their respective jurisdictions. The principles of the Canada Health Act are as follows (Health Canada 2001):

1. *Public administration*: health care in a province or territory must be carried out by public institutions on a nonprofit basis.
2. *Comprehensiveness*: all services carried out by hospitals and doctors and deemed to be medically necessary must be insured.
3. *Universality*: all residents of a province or territory are entitled to uniform health coverage.
4. *Portability*: health coverage must be maintained when a person moves to or travels across provinces and territories or outside Canada.
5. *Accessibility*: reasonable access to necessary medical services should be available to all Canadians.

In many respects the principles of public administration, comprehensiveness, universality, portability, and accessibility represent Max Weber's idea of "ideal types"; that is, they act as abstract measuring rods against which we are able to compare our perceptions of reality. For example, most Canadians would be able to give an example of how our health care system today may not measure up to at least one of these principles. Whether the concern is waiting lists for surgery; access to specialists in remote locations; the growth of private, fee-for-service clinics; long waits in hospital emergency wards; waiting lists for specialized tests, such as MRIs; the closing of rural hospitals; the reduction of beds in urban hospitals; or the shortage of nurses nation-wide, Canadians consider the delivery of health care services a concern of top priority (Canadian Institute for Health Information 2001). Canadians living in northern or rural areas, or outside major metropolitan areas, immigrants, those with low incomes, Aboriginal persons, and people with disabilities represent some of the groups vulnerable to the so-called "crisis" in the Canadian health care system. We will look further into government's role in health care in the social policy section of this chapter.

SOCIAL POLICY AND HEALTH | Financing Health Care Worldwide

The Issue

In many developing nations of the world, health care issues centre on very basic needs of primary care. The goals established at the U.N.'s World Health Assembly in 1981 were modest by North American standards: safe water in the home or within 15 minutes' walking distance; immunization against major infectious diseases; availability of essential drugs within an hour's walk or travel; and the presence of trained personnel for pregnancy and childbirth. Although significant progress has been made in some areas, many developing countries have seen little improvement; in some places, health care has deteriorated (World Bank 1997). The focus of this social policy section, however, is on those industrialized (or developed) nations where the availability of health care is really not an issue. The question is more one of accessibility and affordability. What steps are being taken to make the available services reachable and affordable?

The Setting

The Canadian health care system, despite its flaws, is the envy of other countries. Many Americans, in particular, praise the Canadian system for its universality and accessibility. At a Canadian Medical Association conference in 1995, Dr. Theodore Marmor of the Yale School of

Sociology in the Global Community

13-2 Terrorist Violence

For people in the United States, the moment that a hijacked commercial airliner slammed into the World Trade Center on the morning of September 11, 2001, terrorism became a frightening reality—something that no longer took place only in "foreign" countries.

It was, of course, not the first terrorist attack on the United States, or even on the World Trade Center. Just six years earlier, the U.S. federal building in Oklahoma City had been truck-bombed by terrorist Timothy McVeigh, who was born and raised in the United States; 168 people died in the blast. And in 1993, terrorists had succeeded in destroying the lower levels of the World Trade Center. But the collapse of the two towers and the loss of nearly three thousand lives in 2001 seared the nation's psyche in a way the earlier attacks had not.

When letters purporting to contain anthrax spores began arriving at abortion clinics shortly after the attacks and a U.S. citizen was taken into custody by the FBI for sending them, Americans could no longer escape the fact that terrorism had become a home-grown as well as an imported phenomenon.

Such acts of terror, whether perpetrated by a few or by many people, can also be a powerful political force. Formally defined, ***terrorism*** is the use or threat of violence against random or symbolic targets in pursuit of political aims. An essential aspect of contemporary terrorism involves use of the media. Terrorists may want to keep secret their individual identities, but they want their political messages and goals to receive as much publicity as possible. Drawing on Erving Goffman's dramaturgical approach, sociologist Alfred McClung Lee has likened terrorism to the theatre, where certain scenes are played out in a predictable fashion. Whether through calls to the media, anonymous manifestos, or other means, terrorists typically admit responsibility for and defend their violent acts.

For terrorists, the end justifies the means. The status quo is viewed as oppressive; desperate measures are believed essential to end the suffering of the deprived. Convinced that working through the formal political process will not bring about desired political change, terrorists insist that illegal actions—often directed against innocent people—are needed. Ultimately, terrorists hope to intimidate society and thereby create a new political order.

Some political commentators have argued that terrorism defies definition because one person's "terrorist" is another person's "freedom fighter." To many people around the world, for example, Osama bin Laden and the terrorists who destroyed the World Trade Center were heroes. In this view of terrorism, we carry our biases into our evaluation of terrorist incidents and criticize only those perpetrated by groups who do not share our political goals.

Sociologists reject this critique, countering that even in warfare there are accepted rules outlawing the use of certain tactics. For example, civilian noncombatants are supposedly immune from deliberate attack and are not to be taken prisoner. If we are to set objective standards regarding terrorism, then we should condemn *any and all people* who are guilty of certain actions, no matter how understandable or even admirable some of their goals may be.

Applying Theory

1. Have you ever lived in a place where the threat of terrorism was a part of daily life or known someone who did? What was it like?
2. Can any goal, no matter how noble, justify terrorist activity?

Sources: Eisler 2000; Herman and O'Sullivan 1990; A. Lee 1983; Lewin 2001; McCoy and Cauchon 2001; R. Miller 1988.

Sociology in the Global Community Boxes

The Sociology in the Global Community boxes provide a global perspective on topics, such as poverty, domestic violence, and terrorism, and feature Applying Theory questions. Five boxes are completely **new** to the Second Canadian Edition.

Research in Action Boxes

Research in Action boxes present sociological findings on relevant topics, such as the relationship between students' grades and hard work, immigrant women's social networks, and the impact of Wal-Mart on communities, and they feature Applying Theory questions. Six boxes are completely **new** to the Second Canadian Edition.

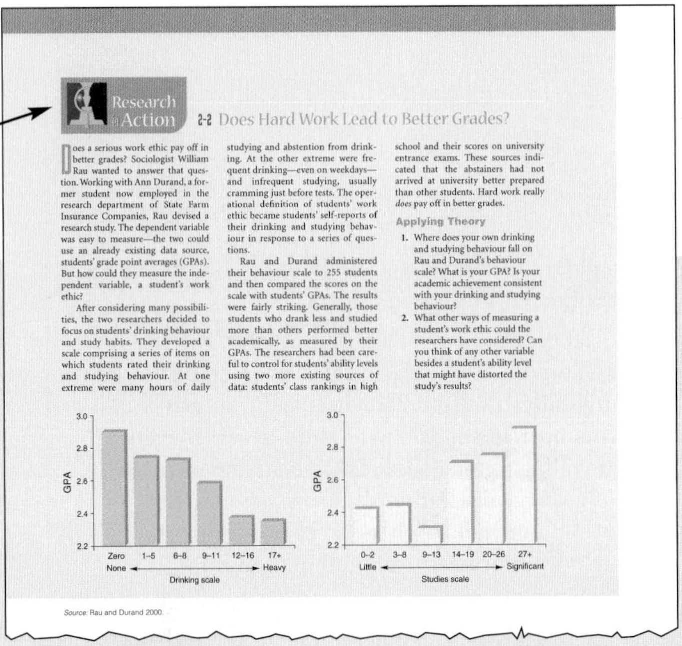

Research in Action **2-2 Does Hard Work Lead to Better Grades?**

Does a serious work ethic pay off in better grades? Sociologist William Rau wanted to answer that question. Working with Ann Durand, a former student now employed in the research department of State Farm Insurance Companies, Rau devised a research study. The dependent variable was easy to measure—the two could use an already existing data source, students' grade point averages (GPAs). But how could they measure the independent variable, a student's work ethic?

After considering many possibilities, the two researchers decided to focus on students' drinking behaviour and study habits. They developed a scale comprising a series of items on which students rated their drinking and studying behaviour. At one extreme were many hours of daily studying and abstention from drinking. At the other extreme were frequent drinking—even on weekdays—and infrequent studying, usually cramming just before tests. The operational definition of students' work ethic became students' self-reports of their drinking and studying behaviour in response to a series of questions.

Rau and Durand administered their behaviour scale to 255 students and then compared the scores on the scale with students' GPAs. The results were fairly striking. Generally, those students who drank less and studied more than others performed better academically, as measured by their GPAs. The researchers had been careful to control for students' ability levels using two more existing sources of data: students' class rankings in high school and their scores on university entrance exams. These sources indicated that the abstainers had not arrived at university better prepared than other students. Hard work really *does* pay off in better grades.

Applying Theory

1. Where does your own drinking and studying behaviour fall on Rau and Durand's behaviour scale? What is your GPA? Is your academic achievement consistent with your drinking and studying behaviour?
2. What other ways of measuring a student's work ethic could the researchers have considered? Can you think of any other variable besides a student's ability level that might have distorted the study's results?

Source: Rau and Durand 2000.

Eye on the Media Boxes

Eye on the Media boxes illustrate how the media affect, and are affected by, social trends and events. Topics include racism and the mainstream media and virtual social movements. Each box contains Applying Theory questions.

Eye on the Media **1-1 Looking at Television from Four Perspectives**

Television to most of us is that box sitting on the shelf or table that diverts us, occasionally entertains us, and sometimes puts us to sleep. But sociologists look much more deeply at the medium. Here is what they find using the four sociological perspectives.

Functionalist View

In examining any aspect of society, including television, functionalists emphasize the contribution it makes to overall social stability. Functionalists regard television as a powerful force in communicating the common values of our society and in promoting an overall feeling of unity and social solidarity:

- Television vividly presents important national and international news. On a local level, television communicates vital information on everything from storm warnings and school closings to the locations of emergency shelters.
- Television programs transmit valuable learning skills (*Sesame Street*) and factual information (CBC's *The National*).
- Television "brings together" members of a community or even a nation by broadcasting important events and ceremonies (press conferences, parades, and state funerals) and through coverage of disasters, such as the September 11, 2001, terrorist attacks on the United States.
- Television contributes to economic stability and prosperity by promoting and advertising services and (through shopping channels) serving as a direct marketplace for products.

Conflict View

Conflict theorists argue that the social order is based on coercion and exploitation. They emphasize that television reflects and even exacerbates many of the divisions of our society gender, race, ethnicity, and social class:

- Television is a form of big business in which profits are more important than the quality of the product (programming).
- Television's decision makers are overwhelmingly white, male, and prosperous; by contrast, television programs tend to ignore the lives and ambitions of subordinate groups, among them working-class people, visible minorities, Aboriginal people, gays and lesbians, people with disabilities, and older people.
- Television distorts the political process, as candidates with the most money (often backed by powerful lobbying groups) buy exposure to voters and saturate the air with attack commercials.
- By exporting *Survivor*, *Baywatch*, and other programs around the world, U.S. television undermines the distinctive traditions and art forms of other societies and encourages their cultural and economic dependence on the United States.

Interactionist View

In studying the social order, interactionists are especially interested in shared understandings of everyday behaviour. Consequently, interactionists examine television on the micro-level by focusing on how day-to-day social behaviour is shaped by television:

- Television literally serves as a babysitter or a "playmate" for many children for long periods.
- Friendship networks can emerge from shared viewing habits or from recollections of a cherished series from the past. Family members and friends often gather for parties centred on the broadcasting of popular events, such as a Stanley Cup game, the Academy Awards, or even series,
- The frequent appearance of violence in news and entertainment programming creates feelings of fear and may actually make interpersonal relations more aggressive.
- The power of television encourages political leaders and even entertainment figures to carefully manipulate symbols (through public appearances) and to attempt to convey self-serving definitions of social reality.

Feminist Views

Feminist theorists believe that gender is constructed by society; thus, television plays a major role not only in reflecting society's ideas about gender but also in constructing its own images:

- Television reinforces gender inequality through its portrayal of women as subordinate and powerless and men as dominant and powerful.
- Television objectifies women through its portrayal of women as objects to be admired for their physical appearance and sexual attractiveness.
- Television creates the false impression that all women are the same—young, white, middle-class, slim, and heterosexual.

Despite their differences, feminist theorists functionalists, conflict theorists, and interactionists would agree that there is much more to television than simply "entertainment." They would also agree that television and other popular forms of culture are worthy subjects for serious study by sociologists.

Applying Theory

1. What functions does television serve? What might be some "dysfunctions"?
2. If you were a television network executive, which perspective would influence your choice of

the subjects of inquiry, who makes the critical ethical decisions. Therefore, sociologists and other investigators bear the responsibility for establishing clear and sensitive boundaries for ethical scientific investigation.

Preserving Confidentiality

Like journalists, sociologists occasionally find themselves subject to questions from law enforcement authorities or to legal threats because of knowledge they have gained in conducting research and maintaining confidentiality. This situation raises profound ethical questions.

In 1994, Russel Ogden was a graduate student at Simon Fraser University (SFU) in British Columbia. In his research, Ogden conducted interviews with people involved in assisted suicide or euthanasia among people with AIDS. A newspaper report about the study came to the attention of the Vancouver coroner, who was already holding an inquest into the death of an "unknown female." Ogden's thesis reported that two research participants had knowledge about her death. The coroner subpoenaed Ogden to identify his sources, but he cited a promise of "absolute confidentiality" and refused to name them. This promise had been authorized by SFU's Research Ethics Board.

The coroner initially found Ogden to be in contempt of court but later accepted a common law argument that the communications between Ogden and his participants were privileged. In doing so, the coroner released Ogden from "any stain or suggestion of contempt." But Ogden's battle in coroner's court was fought without the support of his university. He sued SFU, unsuccessfully, to recover his legal costs. However, the judge condemned SFU for

As part of this neutrality, investigators have an ethical obligation to accept research findings even when the data run counter to their own personal views, to theoretically based explanations, or to widely accepted beliefs. For example, Émile Durkheim challenged popular conceptions when he reported that social (rather than supernatural) forces were an important factor in suicide. p. 8

Some sociologists believe that neutrality is impossible. At the same time, Weber's insistence on value-free sociology may lead the public to accept sociological conclusions without exploring the biases of the researchers. As we have seen, Weber was quite clear that sociologists may bring values to their subject matter. In his view, however, they must not confuse their own values with the social reality under study (Bendix 1968).

Let's consider what might happen when researchers bring their own biases to the investigation. A person investigating the impact of intercollegiate sports on alumni contributions, for example, may focus only on the highly visible revenue-generating sports of football and basketball and neglect the so-called minor sports, such as tennis or soccer, which are more likely to involve female athletes. Despite the work of Dorothy Smith and Margrit Eichler, sociologists still need to be reminded that the discipline often fails to adequately consider *all* people's social behaviour. p. 15

Theoretical Perspectives and Research Methods

The research methods that researches choose to employ in their study of social phenomena are informed and

Cross-Reference Icons

When the text discussion refers to a concept introduced earlier in the book, an icon points the reader to the page where it first appeared.

Demographic Map Program

Two kinds of maps—"Mapping Life Nationwide" and "Mapping Life Worldwide"—are featured throughout the text.

FIGURE 9-2

First Nations People of British Columbia

Mapping Life WORLDWIDE

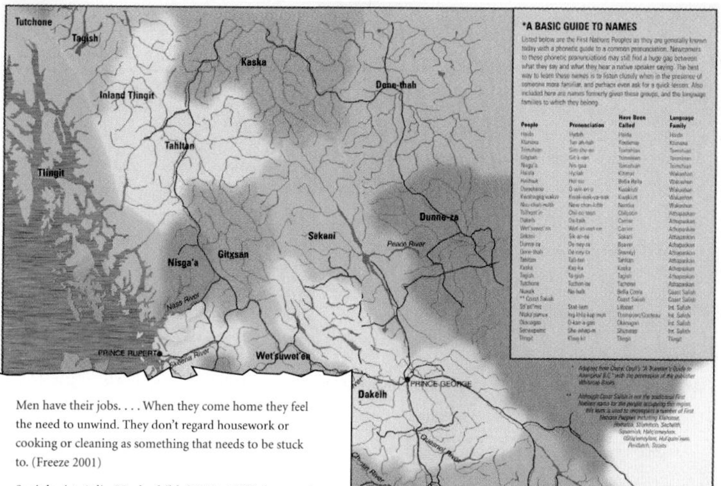

FIGURE 10-3

Percentage of People Aged 25–44 Employed Full-Time Who Are Severely Time Stressed, 1998

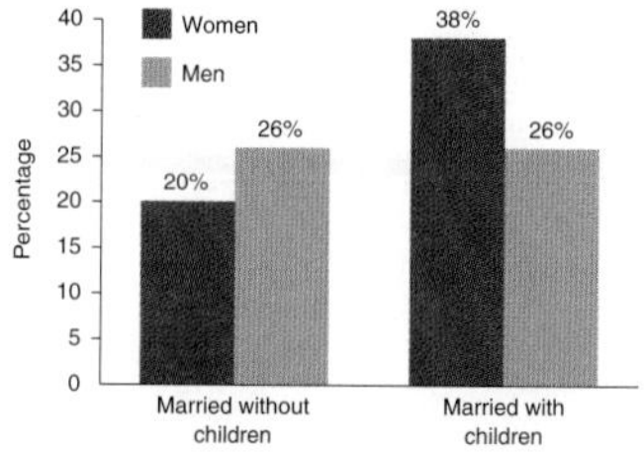

Source: Statistics Canada 2000a, p. 115.

Think about It
How might these figures be related to growing rates of depression and anxiety among working women?

industry, which provides many of the meals that women used to prepare during the day. For another, it raises

> Men have their jobs. . . . When they come home they feel the need to unwind. They don't regard housework or cooking or cleaning as something that needs to be stuck to. (Freeze 2001)

Sociologist Arlie Hochschild (1989, 1990) has used the phrase "second shift" to describe the double burden—work outside the home followed by child care and housework—that many women face and few men share equitably. On the basis of interviews with and observations of 52 couples over an eight-year period, Hochschild reports that the wives (and not their husbands) drive home from the office while planning domestic schedules and play dates for children—and then begin their second shift. Drawing on national studies, she concludes that women spend 15 fewer hours in leisure activities each week than their husbands do. In a year, these women work an extra month of 24-hour days because of the "second shift"; over a dozen years, they work an extra year of 24-hour days. Hochschild found that the married couples she studied were fraying at the edges, and so were their careers and their marriages. Juggling so many roles means that more things can go wrong for women, which contributes to stress. A study by a Harvard sociologist found that married women are 50 percent more likely than married men to complain of being in a bad mood (Kessler 1998).

With such reports in mind, many feminists have advocated greater governmental and corporate support

NEW! Think about It Caption Feature

The Think about It captions, which accompany many of the book's maps, graphs, and tables, encourage students to think critically about information presented in illustrative materials.

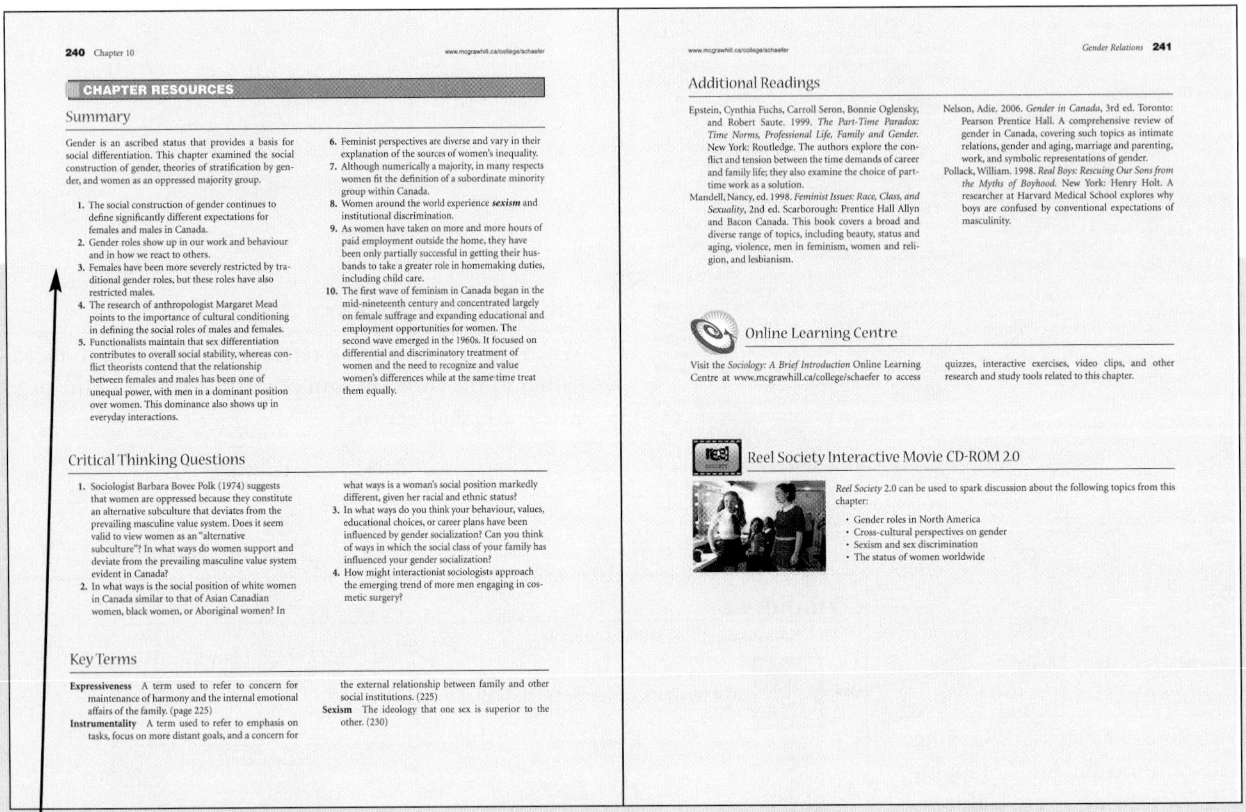
240 Chapter 10 www.mcgrawhill.ca/college/schaefer

CHAPTER RESOURCES

Summary

Gender is an ascribed status that provides a basis for social differentiation. This chapter examined the social construction of gender, theories of stratification by gender, and women as an oppressed majority group.

1. The social construction of gender continues to define significantly different expectations for females and males in Canada.
2. Gender roles show up in our work and behaviour and in how we react to others.
3. Females have been more severely restricted by traditional gender roles, but these roles have also restricted males.
4. The research of anthropologist Margaret Mead points to the importance of cultural conditioning in defining the social roles of males and females.
5. Functionalists maintain that sex differentiation contributes to overall social stability, whereas conflict theorists contend that the relationship between females and males has been one of unequal power, with men in a dominant position over women. This dominance also shows up in everyday interactions.
6. Feminist perspectives are diverse and vary in their explanation of the sources of women's inequality.
7. Although numerically a majority, in many respects women fit the definition of a subordinate minority group within Canada.
8. Women around the world experience ***sexism*** and institutional discrimination.
9. As women have taken on more and more hours of paid employment outside the home, they have been only partially successful in getting their husbands to take a greater role in homemaking duties, including child care.
10. The first wave of feminism in Canada began in the mid-nineteenth century and concentrated largely on female suffrage and expanding educational and employment opportunities for women. The second wave emerged in the 1960s. It focused on differential and discriminatory treatment of women and the need to recognize and value women's differences while at the same time treat them equally.

Critical Thinking Questions

1. Sociologist Barbara Bovee Polk (1974) suggests that women are oppressed because they constitute an alternative subculture that deviates from the prevailing masculine value system. Does it seem valid to view women as an "alternative subculture"? In what ways do women support and deviate from the prevailing masculine value system evident in Canada?
2. In what ways is the social position of white women in Canada similar to that of Asian Canadian women, black women, or Aboriginal women? In what ways is a woman's social position markedly different, given her racial and ethnic status?
3. In what ways do you think your behaviour, values, educational choices, or career plans have been influenced by gender socialization? Can you think of ways in which the social class of your family has influenced your gender socialization?
4. How might interactionist sociologists approach the emerging trend of more men engaging in cosmetic surgery?

Key Terms

Expressiveness A term used to refer to concern for maintenance of harmony and the internal emotional affairs of the family. (page 225)

Instrumentality A term used to refer to emphasis on tasks, focus on more distant goals, and a concern for the external relationship between family and other social institutions. (225)

Sexism The ideology that one sex is superior to the other. (230)

www.mcgrawhill.ca/college/schaefer *Gender Relations* 241

Additional Readings

Epstein, Cynthia Fuchs, Carroll Seron, Bonnie Oglensky, and Robert Saute. 1999. *The Part-Time Paradox: Time Norms, Professional Life, Family and Gender.* New York: Routledge. The authors explore the conflict and tension between the time demands of career and family life; they also examine the choice of part-time work as a solution.

Mandell, Nancy, ed. 1998. *Feminist Issues: Race, Class, and Sexuality*, 2nd ed. Scarborough: Prentice Hall Allyn and Bacon Canada. This book covers a broad and diverse range of topics, including beauty, status and aging, violence, men in feminism, women and religion, and lesbianism.

Nelson, Adie. 2006. *Gender in Canada*, 3rd ed. Toronto: Pearson Prentice Hall. A comprehensive review of gender in Canada, covering such topics as intimate relations, gender and aging, marriage and parenting, work, and symbolic representations of gender.

Pollack, William. 1998. *Real Boys: Rescuing Our Sons from the Myths of Boyhood.* New York: Henry Holt. A researcher at Harvard Medical School explores why boys are confused by conventional expectations of masculinity.

Online Learning Centre

Visit the *Sociology: A Brief Introduction* Online Learning Centre at www.mcgrawhill.ca/college/schaefer to access quizzes, interactive exercises, video clips, and other research and study tools related to this chapter.

Reel Society Interactive Movie CD-ROM 2.0

Reel Society 2.0 can be used to spark discussion about the following topics from this chapter:

- Gender roles in North America
- Cross-cultural perspectives on gender
- Sexism and sex discrimination
- The status of women worldwide

End of Chapter Resources

Each chapter concludes with a *Summary*, *Critical Thinking Questions*, list of *Key Terms* with definitions, and *Additional Readings* to help students review and extend their knowledge.

chapter 1

UNDERSTANDING SOCIOLOGY

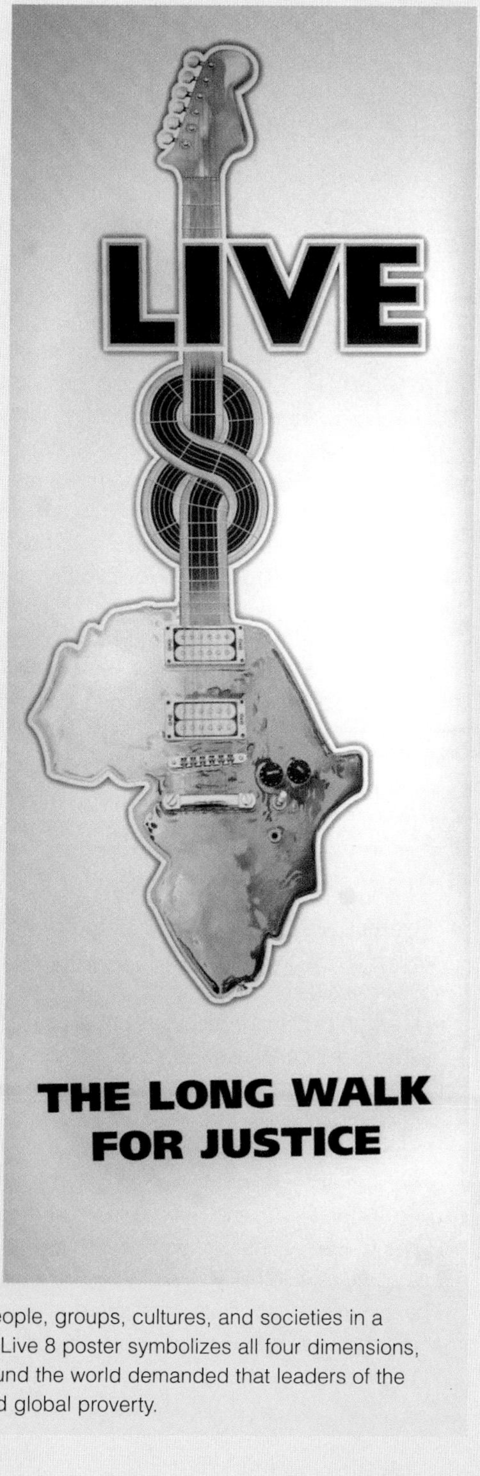

Sociology places people, groups, cultures, and societies in a global context. This Live 8 poster symbolizes all four dimensions, as citizens from around the world demanded that leaders of the richest countries end global proverty.

In the terrible days after September 11, 2001, President George W. Bush exhorted his compatriots to shop for their country. "I ask your continued participation and confidence in the American economy," he said in an address before a joint session of Congress on September 20. About six weeks later, in a speech in Atlanta, he noted with approval that despite the terrorist threat, "People are going about their daily lives, working and shopping and playing, worshiping at churches and synagogues and mosques, going to movies and to baseball games." Put this way, shopping was as noble a pursuit as praying, as much a part of American life as baseball. Shopping, it appeared, would save the U.S.A.

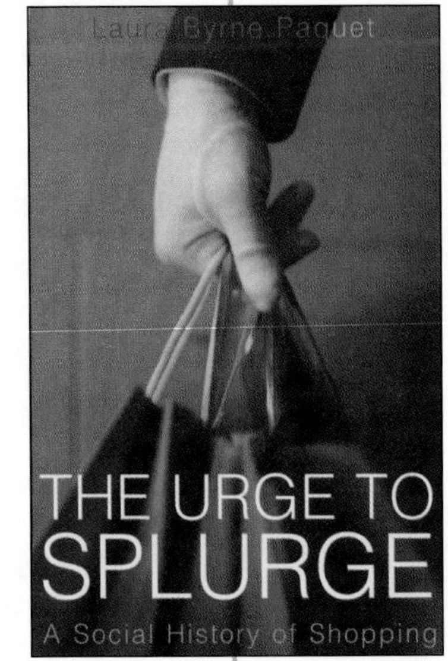

The sentiment was widely derided at the time, and it did seem a rather facile response to a cataclysmic attack. But in a way—and it pains me to admit this—Dubya was right. Love it or hate it, shopping makes the modern western economy go round.

Here's a sobering fact: in the United States, "personal consumption expenditures"—the economist's phrase for the money that individuals, not companies, spend on goods and services—is equal to roughly two thirds of the gross domestic product. If we stopped shopping, the economy as we know it really would collapse.

However, most of us probably aren't thinking about improving the country's bottom line when we head to the mall. At the most basic level, we shop because we need things: bread, a warm blanket, shingles to fix the hole in the roof.

But once we've bought the minimum number of clothes we need to protect us from the elements, and enough food to sustain us through another day in the salt mines, what keeps us going back to the cash register? When we have sensible loafers, why do we want Manolo Blahnik stilettos? Don't we realize that if we just stopped shopping, we'd have more money, more free time, less stress, and less debt?

Well, sure. But there are many reasons we shop, and very few of them have much to do with either supporting the economy or keeping ourselves fed and warm. Daniel Miller, an anthropology professor at University College London, believes that we—particularly women—shop as a way of showing love to others, particularly our families. According to *Shopping, Place and Identity*, a book he co-authored, "shopping is an investment in social relationships, often within a relatively narrowly defined household or domestic context, as much as it is an economic activity devoted to the acquisition of particular commodities."

. . . Two researchers—Cele Otnes of the University of Illinois and Mary Ann McGrath of Loyola University—have countered the "shopping as affiliation" theories with one of their own, based on their study of male shopping habits. They contend that, among men at least, shopping is all about making the best decision and getting the best deal. "[M]en who profess to enjoy shopping still typically do so in order to fulfill one entrenched tenet of the masculine code—achievement," they wrote in the *Journal of Retailing*. "We argue that in contrast to Daniel Miller's theory that women shop to express love to their families and social networks, men shop to win."

Meanwhile, medical researchers are trying to figure out whether the physical act of plunking down a credit card and carting off a new pair of shoes gives some of us an addictive rush, similar to the high that hooks gamblers and alcoholics.

There are countless other theories.... But the theory that appeals to me most is perhaps naively simplistic: we shop because, in most cultures, shopping has always been part of the way we experience the world. From the patrician haggling for pottery in the marketplaces of ancient Rome to the teenager shopping for CDs on the Internet, we have always liked to acquire things. The sentiment has stayed the same in western societies for several millennia. Only the trappings of the process have changed. ***(Paquet 2003)*** ■

What makes shopping an appropriate subject to study in sociology? Uniting all sociological studies is their focus on patterns of human behaviour. Laura Byrne Paquet's book *The Urge to Splurge: A Social History of Shopping* discusses the social history of shopping and how today, particularly in developed countries, shopping has become an activity that goes far beyond the need to acquire the daily necessities of life. Beginning her book with the words from a bumper sticker of the late twentieth century "Veni, Vidi, VISA: I came, I saw, I shopped," Paquet covers such topics as fashion victims, shopaholics, the politics of shopping, and the conflicting attitudes to shopping among consumers in such countries as Canada and the United States.

Sociologists are not concerned with what one individual does or does not do, but with what people do as members of a group or while interacting with one another, and with what that means for the individuals and for society as a whole. Shopping is, in fact, a subject that sociologists can study in any number of ways. They might, as Paquet does, examine shopping's history or its uses in different groups, regions, and cultures.

Sociology is extremely broad in scope. You will see throughout this book the range of topics sociologists investigate—from suicide to TV viewing habits, from Amish society to global economic patterns, from peer pressure to pickpocketing techniques. Sociology looks at how others influence our behaviour and how major social institutions, like the government, religion, and the economy, affect us.

This chapter will explore the nature of sociology as a field of inquiry and as an exercise of the "sociological imagination." We'll look at the discipline as a science and consider its relationship to other social sciences. We will evaluate the contributions of pioneering thinkers—Émile Durkheim, Max Weber, Karl Marx, and others—to the development of sociology. Next we will discuss a number of important theoretical perspectives used by sociologists. Finally, we will consider the ways sociology helps us to develop our sociological imagination. ■

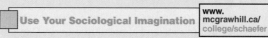

Use Your Sociological Imagination www.mcgrawhill.ca/college/schaefer

Why do you think so much emphasis is placed on material possessions in Canadian society? What do you think the slogan "shop till you drop" says about our society? Do you shop for reasons other than to buy necessities, such as food?

WHAT IS SOCIOLOGY?

Sociology is the systematic study of social behaviour and human groups. It focuses primarily on the influence of social relationships on people's attitudes and behaviour and on how societies are established and change. This textbook deals with such varied topics as families, workplaces, street gangs, business firms, political parties, genetic engineering, schools, religions, and labour unions. It is concerned with love, poverty, conformity, discrimination, illness, technology, and community.

The Sociological Imagination

In attempting to understand social behaviour, sociologists rely on an unusual type of creative thinking. C. Wright Mills (1959) described such thinking as the ***sociological imagination***—an awareness of the relationship between an individual and the wider society. This awareness allows all of us (not just sociologists) to comprehend the links between our immediate, personal social settings and the remote, impersonal social world that surrounds us and helps to shape us.

A key element in the sociological imagination is the ability to view our own society as an outsider would, rather than only from the perspective of personal experiences and cultural biases. Consider something as simple as the practice of eating while walking. In Canada we think nothing of seeing people consuming coffee or chocolate bars as they walk along. Sociologists see this as a pattern of acceptable behaviour because others regard it as acceptable. Yet sociologists need to go beyond one culture to place the practice in perspective. This behaviour is quite unacceptable elsewhere. For example, in Japan people do not eat while walking. Streetside sellers and vending machines dispense food everywhere, but the Japanese will stop to eat or drink whatever they buy before they continue on their way. In their eyes, to engage in another activity while eating shows disrespect for the food preparation, even if the food comes out of a vending machine.

The sociological imagination allows us to go beyond personal experiences and observations to understand broader public issues. Unemployment, for example, is unquestionably a personal hardship for a person without a job. However, C. Wright Mills pointed out that when unemployment is a social problem shared by millions of people, it is appropriate to question the way that a society is structured or organized. Similarly, Mills advocated using the sociological imagination to view divorce not simply as the personal problem of a particular man or woman, but rather as a societal problem, since it is the outcome of many marriages. And he was writing this in the 1950s, when the divorce rate was but a fraction of what it is today (I. Horowitz 1983).

The sociological imagination can bring new understanding to daily life. For example, in Canada, growing numbers of families are turning to food banks to provide them with daily necessities. A 1999 report on hunger, homelessness, and food bank use published by Edmonton's Food Bank and the Edmonton Social Planning Council found that 54 percent of Edmonton families using food banks live on less than $1000 per month. The majority of these families (71 percent) reported that they turn to food banks because of ongoing money shortages. Most of the families utilizing food banks (55 percent) were led by female single parents who had children under 12.

Many observers would uncritically applaud the distribution of food to the needy, but let's look deeper to offer a more probing view of these activities. In Canada, food and consumer manufacturers have joined in charitable food-distribution arrangements. For example, Food and Consumer Products of Canada (FCPC), which represents 150 Canadian corporations, formed an alliance with the Canadian Association of Food Banks (CAFB) to create the ShareGoods program. In 2004, FCPC donated $33 million to charitable causes and more than five million bags of groceries to Canadian families in need. Perhaps as a result, the focus of such relief programs is too restricted. The homeless are to be fed, not housed; the unemployed are to be given meals, not jobs. Relief efforts assist hungry individuals and families without challenging the existing social order (for example, by demanding a redistribution of wealth). Of course, without these limited successes in distributing food, starving people might assault patrons of restaurants, loot grocery stores, or literally die of starvation on the steps of city halls. Such critical thinking is typical of sociologists, as they draw on the sociological imagination to study a social issue—in this case, hunger in North America (Vladimiroff 1998).

Use Your Sociological Imagination

You attend a rock concert one night and a religious service the next morning. What differences would you see in how the two audiences behave and in how they respond to the leader? What might account for these differences?

Sociology and the Social Sciences

Is sociology a science? The term ***science*** refers to the body of knowledge obtained by methods based on systematic observation. Just like other scientific disciplines, sociology engages in the organized, systematic study of phenomena (in this case, human behaviour) in order to enhance understanding. All scientists, whether studying mushrooms or murderers, attempt to collect precise information through methods of study that are as objective as possible. These researchers rely on careful recording of observations and accumulation of data.

Of course, there is a great difference between sociology and physics, between psychology and astronomy. For this reason, the sciences are commonly divided into natural and social sciences. ***Natural science*** is the study of the physical features of nature and the ways in which they interact and change. Astronomy, biology, chemistry, geology, and physics are all natural sciences. ***Social science*** is the study of various aspects of human society. The social sciences include sociology, anthropology, economics, history, psychology, and political science.

The social sciences have a common focus on the social behaviour of people, yet each has a particular orientation. Anthropologists usually study past cultures and preindustrial societies that continue today, as well as the origins of men and women; this knowledge is used to examine contemporary societies, including industrial societies. Economists explore the ways in which people produce and exchange goods and services, along with money and other resources. Historians are concerned with the peoples and events of the past and their significance for us today. Political scientists study international relations, the workings of government, and the exercise of power and authority. Psychologists investigate personality and individual behaviour. So what does sociology focus on? It emphasizes the influence that society has on people's attitudes and behaviour and the ways in which people shape society. Humans are social animals; therefore, sociologists scientifically examine our social relationships with people.

Let's consider how the different social sciences might approach the issue of gun control. This issue began to receive increased public attention in Canada after December 6, 1987, when Marc Lepine systematically shot and killed 14 female engineering students at l'École Polytechnique in Montreal. The event became known as the "Montreal Massacre" and eventually led to stricter gun control laws in Canada in the form of registration requirements under the Firearms Act. Political scientists would look at the impact of political action groups, such as the National Firearms Association, on lawmakers. Historians would examine how guns were used over time in our country and elsewhere. Anthropologists would focus on the use of weapons in a variety of cultures as means of protection and as symbols of power. Psychologists would look at individual cases and assess the impact guns have on their owners as well as on individual victims of gunfire. Economists would be interested in how firearm manufacture and sales affect communities. Sociologists would gather data to inform policymakers. For example, they would examine data from different regions to evaluate the effect of gun restrictions on the incidence of firearm accidents or violent crimes involving firearms. They would ask: What explanations can be offered for the gender, racial, age, rural/urban, and geographic differences in gun ownership? How would these differences affect the formulation of a government policy? Sociologists might also look at data that show how Canada compares with other nations, particularly the United States, in gun ownership and use.

Sociologists put their imaginations to work in a variety of areas—including aging, criminal justice, the family, human ecology, and religion. Throughout this textbook, the sociological imagination will be used to examine Canada (and other societies) from the viewpoint of respectful but questioning outsiders.

Sociology and Common Sense

Sociology focuses on the study of human behaviour. We all have experience with human behaviour and at least some knowledge of it. All of us might well have theories about why people get tattoos, for example, or why people become homeless. Our theories and opinions typically come from "common sense"—that is, from our experiences and conversations, from what we read, from what we see on television, and so forth.

In our daily lives, we rely on common sense to get us through many unfamiliar situations. However, this commonsense knowledge, although sometimes accurate, is not always reliable, because it rests on commonly held beliefs rather than on systematic analysis of facts. It was once considered common sense to accept that Earth was flat—a view rightly questioned by Pythagoras and Aristotle. Incorrect commonsense notions are not just a part of the distant past; they remain with us today.

Common sense, for example, tells us that people panic when faced with natural disasters, such as floods, earthquakes, or ice storms. However, these particular commonsense notions—like the notion that Earth is flat—are untrue; they are not supported by sociological research. Disasters do not generally produce panic. In the aftermath of disasters and even explosions, greater social organization and structure emerge to deal with a community's problems. In Canada, for example, emergency response teams often coordinate public services and even certain services normally performed by the private sector, such as food distribution. Decision making becomes more centralized in times of disaster.

Do disasters produce panic or an organized, structured response? Common sense might tell us the former, but, in fact, disasters bring out a great deal of structure and organization to deal with their aftermath. Pictured, then Prime Minister Jean Chrétien thanks rescue workers for their effort at the World Trade Center at Ground Zero, September 29, 2001.

Like other social scientists, sociologists do not accept something as a fact because "everyone knows it." Instead, each piece of information must be tested, recorded, and then analyzed in relationship to other data. Sociology relies on scientific studies in order to describe and understand a social environment. At times, the findings of sociologists may seem like common sense because they deal with facets of everyday life. The difference is that such findings have been *tested* by researchers. Common sense now tells us that Earth is round. But this particular commonsense notion is based on centuries of scientific work upholding the breakthrough made by Pythagoras and Aristotle.

WHAT IS SOCIOLOGICAL THEORY?

Why do people commit suicide? One traditional commonsense answer is that people inherit the desire to kill themselves. Another view is that sunspots drive people to take their own lives. These explanations may not seem especially convincing to contemporary researchers, but they represent beliefs widely held as recently as 1900.

Sociologists are not particularly interested in why any one individual commits suicide; they are more concerned with the social forces that systematically cause some people to take their own lives. In order to undertake this research, sociologists develop a theory that offers a general explanation of suicidal behaviour.

We can think of theories as attempts to explain events, forces, materials, ideas, or behaviour in a comprehensive manner. Within sociology, a ***theory*** is a template containing definitions and relationships used to organize and understand the social world. A theory may have explanatory power, predictive power, or both. That is, it may help us to see the relationships among seemingly isolated phenomena and to understand how one type of change in an environment leads to others.

Émile Durkheim (1951, original edition 1897) looked into suicide data in great detail and developed a highly original theory about the relationship between suicide and social factors. He was primarily concerned not with the personalities of individual suicide victims, but rather with suicide *rates* and how they varied from country to country. As a result, when he looked at the number of reported suicides in France, England, and Denmark in 1869, he also examined the populations of these nations to determine their rates of suicide. He found that whereas England had only 67 reported suicides per million inhabitants, France had 135 per million, and Denmark had 277 per million. The question then became "Why did Denmark have a comparatively high rate of reported suicides?"

Durkheim went much deeper into his investigation of suicide rates, and the result was his landmark work *Suicide*, published in 1897. Durkheim refused to automatically accept unproven explanations regarding suicide, including the beliefs that cosmic forces or inherited tendencies caused such deaths. Instead, he focused on such problems as the cohesiveness or lack of cohesiveness of religious, social, and occupational groups.

Durkheim's research suggested that suicide, although a solitary act, is related to group life. Protestants had much higher suicide rates than Catholics did; the unmarried had much higher rates than married people did; soldiers were more likely to take their lives than civilians were. In addition, it appeared that there were higher rates of suicide in times of peace than in times of war and revolution, and in times of economic instability and recession rather than in times of prosperity. Durkheim concluded that the suicide rates of a society reflected the extent to which people were or were not integrated into the group life of the society.

Émile Durkheim, like many other social scientists, developed a theory to explain how individual behaviour can be understood within a social context. He pointed out the influence of groups and societal forces on what had always been viewed as a highly personal act. Clearly, Durkheim offered a more *scientific* explanation for the causes of suicide than that of sunspots or inherited tendencies. His theory has predictive power, since it suggests that suicide rates will rise or fall in conjunction with certain social and economic changes.

Of course, a theory—even the best of theories—is not a final statement about human behaviour. Durkheim's theory of suicide is no exception; sociologists continue to examine factors that contribute to differences in suicide rates around the world and to a particular society's rate of suicide. For example, although the overall rate of suicide in New Zealand is only marginally higher than in the United States, the suicide rate among young people is 41 percent higher in New Zealand. Sociologists and psychiatrists from that country suggest that their remote, sparsely populated society maintains exaggerated standards of masculinity that are especially difficult for young males. Gay adolescents who fail to conform to their peers' preference for sports are particularly vulnerable to suicide (Shenon 1995; for a critique of Durkheim's work, see Douglas 1967).

Use Your Sociological Imagination

If you were Durkheim's successor in his research on suicide, how would you investigate the factors that may explain the suicide rates in Canada today?

THE DEVELOPMENT OF SOCIOLOGY

People have always been curious about sociological matters—such as how we get along, what we do, and whom we select as our leaders. Philosophers and religious authorities of ancient and medieval societies made countless observations about human behaviour. They did not test or verify these observations scientifically; nevertheless, these observations often became the foundation for moral codes. Several of the early social philosophers predicted that a systematic study of human behaviour would one day emerge. Beginning in the nineteenth century, European theorists made pioneering contributions to the development of a science of human behaviour.

Early Thinkers: Comte, Martineau, and Spencer

The nineteenth century was an unsettling time in France. The French monarchy had been deposed earlier in the revolution of 1789, and Napoleon had subsequently suffered defeat in his effort to conquer Europe. Amid this chaos, philosophers considered how society might be improved. Auguste Comte (1798–1857), credited with being the most influential of these philosophers of the early nineteenth century, believed that a theoretical science of society and systematic investigation of behaviour were needed to improve society. He coined the term *sociology* to apply to the science of human behaviour.

Writing in the nineteenth century, Comte feared that the excesses of the French Revolution had permanently impaired France's stability. Yet he hoped that the systematic study of social behaviour would eventually lead to more rational human interactions. In Comte's hierarchy of sciences, sociology was at the top. He called it the "queen" and its practitioners "scientist-priests." This French theorist did not simply give sociology its name; he also presented a rather ambitious challenge to the fledgling discipline.

Scholars were able to learn of Comte's works largely through translations by the English sociologist Harriet Martineau (1802–1876). But Martineau was a pathbreaker in her own right as a sociologist. She offered insightful observations of the customs and social practices of both her native Britain and the United States. Martineau's book *Society in America* (1962, original edition 1837) examines religion, politics, child rearing, and immigration in the young nation. Martineau gave special attention to social class distinctions and to such factors as gender and race.

Martineau's writings emphasized the impact that the economy, law, trade, and population could have on the social problems of contemporary society. She spoke out in favour of the rights of women, the emancipation of slaves, and religious tolerance. In Martineau's (1896) view, intellectuals and scholars should not simply offer observations of social conditions; they should act on their convictions in a manner that will benefit society. In line with this view, Martineau conducted research on the nature of female employment and pointed to the need for further investigation of this important issue (Lengermann and Niebrugge-Brantley 1996).

Another important contributor to the discipline of sociology was Herbert Spencer (1820–1903). A relatively prosperous Victorian Englishman, Spencer (unlike Martineau) did not feel compelled to correct or improve society; instead, he merely hoped to understand it better. Drawing on Charles Darwin's study *On the Origin of Species*, Spencer applied the concept of evolution of the species to societies in order to explain how societies change, or evolve, over time. Similarly, he adapted Darwin's evolutionary view of the "survival of the fittest" by arguing that it is "natural" for some people to be rich while others are poor.

Harriet Martineau was an early pioneer of sociology who studied social behaviour both in her native England and in the United States.

Spencer's approach to societal change was extremely popular in his own lifetime. Unlike Comte, Spencer suggested that societies are bound to change eventually; therefore, no one need be highly critical of present social arrangements or work actively for social change. This position appealed to many influential people in England and the United States who had a vested interest in the status quo and were suspicious of social thinkers who endorsed change.

Émile Durkheim

Émile Durkheim made many pioneering contributions to sociology, including his important theoretical work on suicide. The son of a rabbi, Durkheim (1858–1917) was educated in both France and Germany. He established an impressive academic reputation and was appointed as one of the first professors of sociology in France. Above all, Durkheim will be remembered for his insistence that behaviour must be understood within a larger social context, not just in individualistic terms.

As one example of this emphasis, Durkheim (1947, original edition 1912) developed a fundamental thesis to help understand all forms of society through intensive study of the Arunta, an Australian tribe. He focused on the functions that religion performed for the Arunta and underscored the role that group life plays in defining what we consider religious. Durkheim concluded that, like other forms of group behaviour, religion reinforces a group's solidarity.

Another of Durkheim's main interests was the consequences of work in modern societies. In his view, the growing division of labour found in industrial societies as workers became much more specialized in their tasks led to what he called *anomie*. ***Anomie*** refers to the loss of direction that a society feels when social control of individual behaviour has become ineffective. The state of anomie occurs when people have lost their sense of purpose or direction, often during a time of profound social change. In a period of anomie, people are so confused and unable to cope with the new social environment that they may resort to taking their own lives.

Durkheim was concerned about the dangers that alienation, loneliness, and isolation might pose for modern industrial societies. He shared Comte's belief that sociology should provide direction for social change. As a result, he advocated the creation of new social groups—between the individual's family and the state—which would ideally provide a sense of belonging for members of huge, impersonal societies. Unions would be an example of such a group.

Like many other sociologists, Durkheim did not limit his interests to one aspect of social behaviour. Later in this book, we will consider his thinking on crime and punishment, religion, and the workplace. Few sociologists have had such a dramatic impact on so many different areas within the discipline.

Max Weber

Another important early theorist was Max Weber (pronounced "vay-ber"). Born in Germany in 1864, Weber took his early academic training in legal and economic history, but he gradually developed an interest in sociology. Eventually, he became a professor at various German universities. Weber taught his students that they should employ ***Verstehen,*** the German word for "understanding" or "insight," in their intellectual work. He pointed out that we cannot analyze much of our social behaviour by the kinds of objective criteria we use to measure weight or temperature. To fully comprehend behaviour, we must learn the subjective meanings people attach to their actions—how they themselves view and explain their behaviour.

For example, suppose that a sociologist was studying the social ranking of students at a high school. Weber would expect the researcher to employ *Verstehen* to determine the significance of the school's social hierarchy for its members. The researcher might examine the effects of athleticism or grades or social skills or physical appearance in the school. He or she would seek to learn how students relate to other students of higher or lower status. While investigating these questions, the researcher would take into account people's emotions, thoughts, beliefs, and attitudes (Coser 1977).

We also owe credit to Weber for a key conceptual tool: the ideal type. An ***ideal type*** is a construct, a made-up model that serves as a measuring rod against which actual cases can be evaluated. In his own works, Weber identified various characteristics of bureaucracy as an ideal type (discussed in detail in Chapter 6). In presenting this model of bureaucracy, Weber was not describing any particular business, nor was he using the term *ideal* in a way that suggested a positive evaluation. Instead, his purpose was to provide a useful standard for measuring just how bureaucratic an actual organization is (Gerth and Mills 1958). Later in this textbook, we use the concept of ideal type to study family, religion, authority, and economic systems and to analyze bureaucracy.

Although their professional careers coincided, Émile Durkheim and Max Weber never met and had little or no impact on each other's ideas. This was certainly not true of the work of Karl Marx. Durkheim's thinking about the impact of the division of labour in industrial societies was related to Marx's writings, while Weber's concern for a value-free, objective sociology was a direct response to Marx's deeply held convictions. Thus, it is not surprising that Karl Marx is viewed as a major figure in the development of sociology as well as several other social sciences (see Figure 1-1).

Karl Marx

Karl Marx (1818–1883) shared with Durkheim and Weber a dual interest in abstract philosophical issues and the concrete reality of everyday life. Unlike the others, Marx was so critical of existing institutions that a conventional academic career was impossible, and although he was born and educated in Germany, he spent most of his life in exile.

Marx's personal life was a difficult struggle. When a paper that he had written was suppressed, he fled his native land for France. In Paris, he met Friedrich Engels (1820–1895), with whom he formed a lifelong friendship. They lived at a time when European and North American economic life was increasingly being dominated by the factory rather than the farm.

In 1847, Marx and Engels attended the secret meetings in London of an illegal coalition of labour unions, known as the Communist League. The following year, they prepared a platform called *The Communist Manifesto*, in which they argued that the masses of people who had no resources other than their labour (whom they referred to as the *proletariat*) should unite to fight for the

FIGURE 1-1

Early Social Thinkers

	Émile Durkheim 1858–1917	Max Weber 1864–1920	Karl Marx 1818–1883
Academic training	Philosophy	Law, economics, history, philosophy	Philosophy, law
Key works	1893—*The Division of Labor in Society* 1897—*Suicide: A Study in Sociology* 1912—*Elementary Forms of Religious Life*	1904–1905—*The Protestant Ethic and the Spirit of Capitalism* 1922—*Wirtschaft und Gesellschaft*	1848—*The Communist Manifesto* 1867—*Das Kapital*

overthrow of capitalist societies. In the words of Marx and Engels,

> The history of all hitherto existing society is the history of class struggles. . . . The proletarians have nothing to lose but their chains. They have a world to win. WORKING MEN OF ALL COUNTRIES UNITE! (Feuer 1959:7, 41)

After completing *The Communist Manifesto*, Marx returned to Germany, only to be expelled. He then moved to England, where he continued to write books and essays. Marx lived there in extreme poverty. He pawned most of his possessions, and several of his children died of malnutrition and disease. Marx clearly was an outsider in British society, a fact that may well have affected his view of Western cultures.

In Marx's analysis, society is fundamentally divided between classes, which clash in pursuit of their own class interests. When he examined the industrial societies of his time, such as Germany, England, and the United States, he saw the factory as the centre of conflict between the exploiters (the owners of the means of production) and the exploited (the workers). Marx viewed these relationships in systematic terms; that is, he believed that an entire system of economic, social, and political relationships maintained the power and dominance of the owners over the workers. Consequently, Marx and Engels argued that the working class needed to overthrow the existing class system. Marx's influence on contemporary thinking has been dramatic. Marx's writings inspired those who were later to lead communist revolutions in Russia, China, Cuba, Vietnam, and elsewhere.

Even apart from the political revolutions that his work fostered, Marx's influence on contemporary thinking has been dramatic. Marx emphasized the *group* identifications and associations that influence an individual's place in society. This area of study is the major focus of contemporary sociology. Throughout this textbook, we will consider how membership in a particular gender classification, age group, racial or ethnic group, or economic class affects a person's attitudes and behaviour. In an important sense, we can trace this way of understanding society back to the pioneering work of Karl Marx.

Modern Developments

Sociology today builds on the firm foundation developed by Émile Durkheim, Max Weber, and Karl Marx. However, the discipline of sociology has certainly not remained stagnant over the last century. Although Europeans have continued to make contributions to the discipline, sociologists from throughout the world have advanced sociological theory and research. Their new insights have helped them to better understand the workings of society.

Charles Horton Cooley (1864–1929) was typical of the sociologists who came to prominence in the early 1900s. Cooley received his graduate training in economics but later became a sociology professor at the University of Michigan. Like other early sociologists, he had become interested in this "new" discipline while pursuing a related area of study.

Cooley shared the desire of Durkheim, Weber, and Marx to learn more about society. But to do so effectively, Cooley preferred to use the sociological perspective to look first at smaller units—intimate, face-to-face groups, such as families, gangs, and friendship networks. He saw these groups as the seedbeds of society in the sense that they shape people's ideals, beliefs, values, and social nature. Cooley's work increased our understanding of groups of relatively small size.

Sociologist Robert Merton (1968) made an important contribution to the discipline by successfully combining theory and research. Born in 1910 of Slavic immigrant parents in Philadelphia, Merton's teaching career has been based at Columbia University in New York.

Merton produced a theory that is one of the most frequently cited explanations of deviant behaviour. He noted different ways in which people attempt to achieve success in life. In his view, some may not share the socially agreed-on goal of accumulating material goods or the accepted means of achieving this goal. For example, in Merton's classification scheme, "innovators" are people who accept the goal of pursuing material wealth but use illegal means to do so, including robbery, burglary, and extortion. Merton bases his explanation of crime on individual behaviour—influenced by society's approved goals and means—yet it has wider applications. It helps to account for the high crime rates among the nation's poor, who may see no hope of advancing themselves through traditional roads to success. Chapter 7 discusses Merton's theory in greater detail.

Merton also emphasized that sociology should strive to bring together the "macrolevel" and "microlevel" approaches to the study of society. ***Macrosociology*** concentrates on large-scale phenomena or entire civilizations. Thus, Émile Durkheim's cross-cultural study of suicide is an example of macrolevel research. More recently, macrosociologists have examined international crime rates (see Chapter 7), the stereotype of Asians as a "model minority" (see Chapter 9), and the population patterns of Islamic countries (see Chapter 14). By contrast, ***microsociology*** stresses study of small groups and often uses experimental study in laboratories. Sociological research on the microlevel has included studies of how divorced men and women, for example, disengage from significant social roles (see Chapter 5); of how conformity can influence the expression of prejudiced attitudes (see Chapter 7); and of how a teacher's expectations can affect a student's academic performance (see Chapter 12).

In Canada, the work of sociologists Harold A. Innis (1894–1952) and S.D. Clark (1910–2003) established a strong foundation for the examination of Canada from a political economy perspective. Innis rejected existing interpretations of Canadian society and theorized about the relationship between the extraction of products, such as fish, timber, wheat, and hydroelectric power, and the development of the Canadian state. Innis's works, such as *A History of the Canadian Pacific Railway* (1923), *The Fur Trade in Canada: An Introduction to Canadian Economic History* (1930), *The Cod Fisheries: The History of an International Economy* (1942), and *Political Economy in the Modern State* (1946), took a historical perspective on the production of staple goods (e.g., fish, fur, and forest products) in the young Canadian economy, emphasizing the importance of communication and transportation to the development of political and economic systems. In his later research at the University of Toronto, Innis's work *The Bias of Communication* (1951) addressed the influence of the media; thus, his contribution to Canadian sociology also included modern communication theory.

S.D. Clark studied under Innis at the University of Toronto, completing his Ph.D. in 1938. At that time, Clark began his academic career teaching in the political

Although the number of women teaching sociology in Canadian postsecondary institutions has increased over the last two decades, women remain underrepresented in the profession.

science department at the University of Toronto, as a department of sociology had not yet been formed. Clark's works, such as *The Social Development of Canada* (1942), *Church and Sect in Canada* (1948), and *Movements of Political Protest* (1959), depict the struggle between the hinterlands and the cultural and financial metropolis of Canada, which results in regional conflicts, the emergence of new political parties and religions, and social movements. Clark's body of work helped to win increasing respect for sociology as a discipline in Canada, and he is credited with establishing the department of sociology at the University of Toronto in 1963.

Later, John Porter's *The Vertical Mosaic* (1965) provided a formative examination of social inequality as it relates to race, ethnicity, social class, and gender in Canada. Porter's depiction of Canadian society as a "mosaic" continues to be used in contrast to the American metaphor of the "melting pot." (These concepts will be discussed in more detail in Chapter 3). Using Canadian census data before 1961, Porter revealed the existence of a hierarchy among ethnic groups in which the charter groups—the French and British—occupied the top socioeconomic positions. The charter groups were followed by other northern Europeans (e.g., Norwegians, Swedes, Dutch, Belgians), who were then followed by Southern and Eastern Europeans (e.g., Ukrainians, Hungarians, Italians, Greeks). At the bottom of this socioeconomic hierarchy were visible minority groups, such as Chinese, blacks, and Aboriginals. Porter referred to groups that were not charter groups as *entrance groups*. These groups typically were assigned to lower-status jobs, according to the stereotypical preferences of the dominant charter groups. According to sociologist Richard Wanner (1998), "*The Vertical Mosaic* set the agenda for several streams of research, including studies of elites and the structure of power, social mobility and the role of education in the occupational attainment process, and immigrant integration and ethnic inequality."

In 1975, Patricia Marchak contributed to the foundation of Canadian sociology through the publication of *Ideological Perspectives in Canada*. In this work, Marchak examines the way in which Canadians perceive and make sense of their social world.

Marchak's work is helpful in understanding why inequality exists, why tension exists between the police and a particular ethnic group, why a labour dispute results in a lockout, or why young people demonstrate at World Trade Organization meetings. Marchak (1975) claims that people interpret such events according to ideologies, which act as "screens" through which they perceive the world. Ideologies, according to Marchak, are rarely taught explicitly; they are learned through observation, casual conversation, and example. Children learn an ideology by listening to and internalizing their parents' responses to questions, such as "Why is that family poor?" or "Why do doctors make more money than police officers?" In many cases children receive responses that, according to Marchak, represent a dominant Canadian ideology—an ideology that supports the prevailing order.

Counter-ideologies, according to Marchak, challenge the assumptions of the dominant ideology, providing alternative interpretations to views that simply reflect the interests of the dominant ruling class.

Contemporary sociology reflects the diverse contributions of earlier theorists. As sociologists approach such topics as divorce, drug addiction, and religious cults, they can draw on the theoretical insights of the discipline's pioneers. A careful reader can hear Comte, Durkheim, Weber, Marx, Cooley, and many others speaking through the pages of current research. Sociology has also broadened beyond the intellectual confines of North America and Europe. Contributions to the discipline now come from sociologists studying and researching human behaviour in other parts of the world. In describing the work of today's sociologists, it is helpful to examine a number of influential theoretical approaches (also known as *perspectives*).

The work of Patricia Marchak, which examined the ways in which Canadians make sense of their social world, contributed to the building of the foundation of Canadian society.

MAJOR THEORETICAL PERSPECTIVES

Students studying sociology for the first time may not be surprised to learn that sociologists view society in different ways. Some see the world basically as a stable and ongoing entity. They are impressed with the endurance of the family, organized religion, and other social institutions. Some sociologists see society as composed of many groups in conflict, competing for scarce resources. To other sociologists, the most fascinating aspects of the social world are the everyday, routine interactions among individuals that we sometimes take for granted. Others see the world in terms of how gender is socially constructed. These four views, the ones most widely used by sociologists, are the functionalist, conflict, feminist, and interactionist perspectives. They will provide an introductory look at the discipline. One way to think about the theoretical perspectives used by sociologists is to compare them to the wearing of a lens. A sociologist sees the social world according to the assumptions and emphases of his or her theoretical perspective, just as the wearer of a lens sees the world according to the lens's size, shape, colour, and other characteristics.

Functionalist Perspective

Think of society as a living organism in which each part of the organism contributes to its survival. This view is the ***functionalist perspective***, which emphasizes the way that parts of a society are structured to maintain its stability.

Let's examine prostitution as an example of the functionalist perspective. Why is it that a practice so widely condemned continues to display such persistence and vitality? Functionalists suggest that prostitution satisfies needs of patrons that may not be readily met through more socially acceptable forms, such as courtship or marriage. The "buyer" receives sex without any responsibility for procreation or sentimental attachment; at the same time, the "seller" makes a living through this exchange.

Such an examination leads us to conclude that prostitution does perform certain functions that society seems to need. However, this is not to suggest that prostitution is a desirable or legitimate form of social behaviour. Functionalists do not make such judgments. Rather, advocates of the functionalist perspective hope to explain how an aspect of society that is so frequently attacked can nevertheless manage to survive (K. Davis 1937).

Talcott Parsons

Talcott Parsons (1902–1979), a Harvard University sociologist, was a key figure in the development of functionalist theory. Parsons had been greatly influenced by the work of Émile Durkheim, Max Weber, and other European sociologists. For more than four decades, Parsons dominated sociology in the United States with his advocacy of functionalism. He saw any society as a vast network of connected parts, each of which helps to maintain the system as a whole. The functionalist approach holds that if an aspect of social life does not contribute to a society's stability or survival—if it does not serve some identifiably useful function or promote value consensus among members of a society—it will not be passed on from one generation to the next. Parsons viewed society as naturally being in a state of equilibrium. By "equilibrium," he meant that society tends toward a state of stability or balance. Parsons would view even prolonged labour strikes or civilian riots as temporary disruptions in the status quo rather than as significant alterations in social structure. Therefore, according to his ***equilibrium model***, as changes occur in one part of society, there must be adjustments in other parts. If this does not take place, the society's equilibrium will be threatened and strains will occur.

Reflecting an evolutionary approach, Parsons (1966) maintained that four processes of social change are inevitable. The first, *differentiation,* refers to the increasing complexity of social organization. A change from "medicine man" to physician, nurse, and pharmacist is an illustration of differentiation in the field of health. This process is accompanied by the second process, *adaptive upgrading,* whereby social institutions become more specialized in their purposes. The division of labour among physicians into obstetricians, internists, surgeons, and so forth, is an example of adaptive upgrading.

The third process identified by Parsons is the *inclusion* of groups into society that were previously excluded because of such factors as gender, race, and social class background. Medical schools have practised inclusion by admitting increasing numbers of women and visible minorities. Finally, Parsons contends that societies experience *value generalization,* the development of new values that tolerate and legitimate a greater range of activities. The acceptance of preventive and alternative medicine is an example of value generalization; our society has broadened its view of health care. All four processes identified by Parsons stress consensus—societal agreement on the nature of social organization and values (B. Johnson 1975; R. Wallace and Wolf 1980).

Manifest and Latent Functions

Your college or university calendar typically states various functions of the institution. It may inform you, for example, that the university intends to offer each student a broad education in classical and contemporary thought, in the humanities, in the sciences, and in the arts. However, it would be quite a surprise to find a calendar that declared, "This university was founded in 1895 to keep people between the ages of 18 and 22 out of the job market, thus reducing unemployment." No postsecondary institution would declare that this is the purpose of postsecondary education. Yet societal institutions serve many functions, some of them quite subtle. Postsecondary education, in fact, *does* delay people's entry into the job market.

Robert Merton (1968) made an important distinction between manifest and latent functions. ***Manifest functions*** of institutions are open, stated, conscious functions. They involve the intended, recognized consequences of an aspect of society, such as the college or university's role in certifying academic competence and excellence. By contrast, ***latent functions*** are unconscious or unintended functions and may reflect hidden purposes of an institution. One latent function of colleges and universities is to hold down unemployment. Another is to serve as a meeting ground for people seeking marital partners.

Dysfunctions

Functionalists acknowledge that not all parts of a society contribute to its stability all the time. A ***dysfunction*** refers to an element or a process of society that may actually disrupt a social system or lead to a decrease in stability.

We consider many dysfunctional behaviour patterns, such as homicide, as undesirable. Yet we should not automatically interpret dysfunctions as negative. The evaluation of a dysfunction depends on a person's own values or, as the saying goes, on "where you sit." For example, the official view in prisons in the United States is that inmate gangs should be eradicated because they are dysfunctional to smooth operations. Yet some guards have actually come to view the presence of prison gangs as functional for their jobs. The danger posed by gangs creates a "threat to security," requiring increased surveillance and more overtime work for guards (Hunt et al. 1993:400).

Conflict Perspective

In contrast to functionalists' emphasis on stability and consensus, conflict sociologists see the social world as being in continual struggle. The ***conflict perspective*** assumes that social behaviour is best understood in terms of conflict or tension between competing groups. Such conflict and change need not be violent; they can take the form of labour negotiations, gender relations, party politics, competition between religious groups for members, or disputes over the federal budget. Conflict theorists contend that social institutions and practices persist because powerful groups have the ability to maintain them. Change has crucial significance, because it is needed to correct social injustices and inequalities.

Canadian soldiers fill a manifest function by providing peacekeeping in countries around the world. Three Canadian peacekeepers guard the Canadian camp's main gate in Kabul, Afghanistan, in September 2003.

Throughout most of the twentieth century, the functionalist perspective had the upper hand in sociology in North America. However, the conflict approach has become increasingly persuasive since the late 1960s. The rise of the feminist and gay rights movements, First Nations land claims, and confrontations at abortion clinics offered support for the conflict approach—the view that our social world is characterized by continual struggle between competing groups. Currently, the discipline of sociology views conflict theory as one way, among many others, to gain insight into a society.

The Marxist View

Karl Marx accepted the evolutionary argument that societies develop along a particular path. However, unlike Comte and Spencer, he did not view each successive stage as an inevitable improvement over the previous one. History, according to Marx, proceeds through a series of stages, each of which exploits a class of people. Ancient society exploited slaves; the estate system of feudalism exploited serfs; modern capitalist society exploits the working class. Ultimately, through a socialist revolution led by the proletariat, human society will move toward the final stage of development: a classless communist society, or "community of free individuals" as Marx described it in *Das Kapital* in 1867 (see Bottomore and Rubel 1956:250).

Karl Marx viewed struggle as inevitable, given the exploitation of workers under capitalism. Marx had an important influence on the development of sociology. His thinking offered insights into such institutions as the economy, the family, religion, and government. The Marxist view of social change is appealing because it does not restrict people to a passive role in responding to inevitable cycles or changes in material culture. Rather, Marxist theory offers a tool for those who want to seize control of the historical process and gain their freedom from injustice. In contrast to functionalists' emphasis on stability, Marx argues that conflict is a normal and desirable aspect of social change. In fact, change must be encouraged as a means of eliminating social inequality (Lauer 1982).

Expanding on Marx's work, sociologists and other social scientists have come to see conflict not merely as a class phenomenon but as a part of everyday life in all societies. Thus, in studying any culture, organization, or social group, sociologists want to know who benefits, who suffers, and who dominates at the expense of others. They are concerned with the conflicts between women and men, parents and children, and urban and rural areas, to name only a few. Conflict theorists are interested in how society's institutions—including the family, government, religion, education, and the media—may help to maintain the privileges of some groups and keep others in a subservient position. Their emphasis on social change and redistribution of resources makes conflict theorists more "radical" and "activist" than functionalists (Dahrendorf 1958).

Feminist Perspectives

Feminist perspectives attempt to explain, understand, and change the ways in which gender socially organizes our public and private lives in such a way as to produce inequality between men and women.

There are as many feminist perspectives as there are social and political philosophies; they run the gamut from liberal feminism to Marxist feminism and from anarchist feminism to eco-feminism. There is no *one* feminist perspective. Feminist perspectives, which can be macro or micro, have been a major contributor to contemporary sociological theory, providing frameworks within which gender inequality can be examined, understood, and changed. Although these perspectives differ in terms of their views of the causes of and solutions to gender inequality, they share a common starting point—that is, they begin from the standpoint *of* women and advocate solutions *for* women (Lengermann and Niebrugge-Brantley 1996). The following sections provide a sample of various feminist theories, highlighting the vast diversity among them.

Liberal Feminism

Liberal feminism advocates that women's equality can be obtained through the extension of the principles of equality of opportunity and freedom. Rather than advocating structural change to the capitalist economy or attempting to eliminate patriarchy, liberal feminist approaches assume that extending women's opportunities for education and employment, for example, will result in greater gender equality. The Royal Commission Report on the Status of Women in Canada, tabled in 1970 in the Canadian House of Commons, was grounded on the principles of liberal feminism.

Marxist Feminism

Marxist feminism places the system of capitalism at fault for the oppression of women. If the capitalist economy, with its private ownership of resources and its unequal class relations, were to be replaced with a socialist system, economic inequality between the sexes would also change. Marxist feminists believe that women are not oppressed by sexism or patriarchy, but rather by a system of economic production that is based on unequal gender relations in the capitalist economy (Tong 1989).

Socialist Feminism

Gender relations, according to ***socialist feminism***, are shaped by both patriarchy and capitalism. Class and patriarchal gender relations are inextricably connected, thus equality for women implies that both the system of capitalism and the ideology of patriarchy must be challenged and eliminated. Socialist feminists, unlike Marxist feminists, who believe that the elimination of class distinctions will bring about gender equality, see patriarchy's grip in the home as well as in the public sphere (Luxton 1980).

Radical Feminism

Unlike Marxist feminist perspectives, radical feminism holds that the subordination of women will not be eradicated with the abolition of capitalism. Rather, radical feminist perspectives argue, the subordination of women occurs in all societies, regardless of whether or not they are capitalist, communist, or socialist. The root of all oppression, according to ***radical feminism***, is embedded in patriarchy (Code 1993). Some radical feminists (Firestone 1970) have based their view of women's oppression on reproduction, arguing that women's freedom from reproduction (i.e., through technological developments) will lead to their overall emancipation.

Standpoint Feminism

Standpoint feminist perspectives challenge other feminist perspectives, such as the Marxist, socialist, and radical perspectives, which attempt to lay the blame for women's oppression on one cause or source, thus suppressing the wide range and diversity of women's experiences. ***Standpoint feminism*** takes into account women's diversity (e.g., class, race, ethnicity, sexuality) and maintains that their experiences cannot be easily expressed as a single account of "women's experiences." Given the diversity and difference in women's lives, standpoint feminism acknowledges that no *one* standpoint will represent *all* women's lives (Comack 1996).

Despite their differences, feminist theories often share four elements (Jagger and Rothenberg 1984):

1. A desire to understand how gender is part of all aspects of social life
2. A belief that gender, as well as class, race, and sexuality, is socially constructed, producing inequality in the workplace, at home, in leisure activities, and in society at large
3. A belief that gender relations are not "natural," but are products of history and culture
4. An advocacy for social change

Dorothy Smith (1926–) is a Canadian sociologist whose contributions to sociology in general and feminist sociology in particular have been influential worldwide. Smith argues for a sociology that is built on the everyday experiences of women, pointing out how sociology has previously ignored these experiences. Smith's groundbreaking work, *The Everyday World as Problematic* (1987), has helped students of sociology see the everyday world from the standpoint of women.

Margrit Eichler (1942–), also a Canadian sociologist, was among the first sociologists in this country to examine the ways in which sexism can influence research in social science (A. Nelson and Robinson 1999). She examined sexist language, sexist concepts, the androcentric perspective, sexist methodology, and sexist interpretation of results (Eichler 1984:20).

The work of such sociologists as Smith and Eichler addresses the long-standing exclusion of women's standpoint in sociology, as well as sexist biases in the way in which sociological research has been conducted.

Interactionist Perspective

Workers interacting on the job, encounters in public places like bus stops and parks, behaviour in small groups—these are all aspects of microsociology that catch the attention of interactionists. Whereas functionalist and conflict theorists both analyze large-scale societywide patterns of behaviour, the ***interactionist perspective*** generalizes about everyday forms of social interaction in order to understand society as a whole. In the 1990s, for example, the workings of juries became a subject of public scrutiny. High-profile trials ended in verdicts that left some people shaking their heads. Long before jury members in the United States were being interviewed on their front lawns following trials, interactionists tried to better understand behaviour in the small-group setting of a jury deliberation room.

Interactionism is a sociological framework for viewing human beings as living in a world of meaningful objects. These "objects" may include material things, actions, other people, relationships, and even symbols.

Although functionalist and conflict approaches were initiated in Europe, interactionism developed first in the United States. George Herbert Mead (1863–1931) is widely regarded as the founder of the interactionist perspective. Mead taught at the University of Chicago from 1893 until his death. His sociological analysis, like that of Charles Horton Cooley, often focused on human interactions within one-to-one situations and small groups. Mead was interested in observing the most minute forms of communication—smiles, frowns, nodding of the head—and in understanding how such individual behaviour was influenced by the larger context of a group or society. Despite his innovative views, Mead only occasionally wrote articles and never a book. He was an extremely popular teacher, and most of his insights have come to us through edited volumes of lectures that his students published after his death. Mead continued Cooley's exploration of interactionist theory (1934, 1964a), developing a useful model of the process by which the self emerges. According to Mead, this process was defined by three distinct stages, which he called the preparatory stage, the play stage, and the game stage.

Mead is best known for his theory of the self. According to Mead (1964b), the self begins as a privileged, central position in a person's world. Young children picture themselves as the focus of everything around them and find it difficult to consider the perspectives of others. For example, when shown a mountain scene and asked to describe what an observer on the opposite side of the mountain might see (such a lake or hikers), young children describe only objects visible from their own vantage point. As people mature, the self changes and begins to show greater concern about the reactions of others. Parents, friends, teachers, coaches, and co-workers, are often among those who play a major role in shaping a person's self. Mead used the term ***significant others*** to refer to those individuals who are the most important in the development of the self. Many young people, for example, find themselves drawn to the same kind of work as their parents engage in (Schlenker 1985).

Mead uses the term ***generalized other*** to refer to the attitudes, viewpoints, and expectations of society that a child takes into account. Simply put, this concept suggests that when an individual acts, he or she considers an entire group of people. For example, a child will not act courteously merely to please a particular parent. Rather, the child comes to understand that courtesy is a widespread social value endorsed by parents, teachers, and religious leaders.

The interactionist perspective is sometimes referred to as the *symbolic interactionist perspective,* because interactionists see symbols as an especially important part of human communication. Members of a society share the social meanings of symbols. In Canada, for example, a handshake symbolizes congeniality, while a middle-finger salute signifies disrespect. However, another culture might use different gestures to convey a feeling of congeniality or disrespect.

Consider the different ways various societies portray suicide without the use of words. People in Canada point a finger at the head (shooting); urban Japanese bring a fist against the stomach (stabbing); and the South Fore of Papua, New Guinea, clench a hand at the throat (hanging). These types of symbolic interaction are classified as forms of ***nonverbal communication,*** which can include many other gestures, facial expressions, and postures.

Since Mead's teachings have become well known, sociologists have expressed greater interest in the interactionist perspective. Many have moved away from what may have been an excessive preoccupation with the large-scale (macro) level of social behaviour and have redirected their attention toward behaviour that occurs in small groups (microlevel).

Erving Goffman (1922–1982) popularized a particular type of interactionist method known as the ***dramaturgical approach.*** The dramaturgist compares everyday life to the setting of the theatre and stage. Just as actors project certain images, all of us seek to present particular features of our personalities while we hide other qualities. Thus, in a class, we may feel the need to project a serious image; at a party, we want to look relaxed and friendly.

Postmodern Perspective

More recently, sociologists have expanded their theorizing to reflect the conditions of postmodern society. A ***postmodern society*** is a technologically sophisticated society that is preoccupied with consumer goods and media images (Brannigan 1992). Such societies consume goods and information on a mass scale. Postmodern theorists take a global perspective and note the ways that aspects of culture cross national boundaries (Lyotard 1993). For example, residents of Yellowknife may listen to reggae music from Jamaica, eat sushi and other types of Japanese food, and wear clogs from Sweden.

Postmodern theorists point to this diversity in their rejection of the notion that the social world can be explained by a single paradigm. The intermingling of cultures and ideologies that characterizes the modern, electronically connected planet has led to a relativist approach. As part of just one of the debates taking place among sociologists, postmodernists reject science as a panacea, arguing that no single theory can accurately explain the causes and consequences of postmodern global society. For example, postmodern theorists suggest that there is no objective way of differentiating true beliefs from false ones, since there is a plurality of claims to truth.

The emphasis of postmodern theorists is on describing emerging cultural forms and patterns of social interaction. Within sociology, the postmodern view offers support for integrating the insights of various theoretical perspectives—functionalism, conflict theory, interactionism, labelling theory, and feminist theories. Some feminist sociologists argue optimistically that, with its indifference to hierarchies and distinctions, postmodernism will discard traditional values of male dominance in favour of gender equality. Yet others contend that despite new technology, postindustrial and postmodern societies can be expected to experience the problems of inequality that have plagued industrial societies (Ritzer 1995a; Sale 1996; Smart 1990; Turner 1990; van Vucht Tijssen 1990).

Contemporary debates in sociological theory consist of two opposing views: (1) one advocates the presence of a preexisting social structure (i.e., a "society") in which reality is represented in social institutions and culture, and (2) one that advocates that reality is socially constructed, locally, on a microlevel.

Postmodernism as a sociological approach, for example, focuses on individual action in which reality is socially constructed through a process of negotiated interaction with other individuals. In contrast, sociologists who offer the view that a social structure exists before an individual's entry into the world proceed from a macro rather than a micro perspective; consequently, they focus on how, for example, social institutions, such as the mass media, the education system, and religious organizations, have an impact on individuals. Although the debate may appear to be irreconcilably polarized between the social constructionist view of reality and the idea of a preexisting social structure, human history may be viewed dialectically—that is, individuals are creators of and, at the same time, creations of their social worlds.

The Sociological Approach

Which perspective should a sociologist use in studying human behaviour? functionalist? conflict? interactionist? feminist?

Sociology makes use of all four perspectives (see Table 1-1), since each offers unique insights into the

Table 1-1 Comparing Major Theoretical Perspectives

	Functionalist	Conflict	Interactionist	Feminist
View of society	Stable, well integrated	Characterized by tension and struggle between groups	Active in influencing and affecting everyday social interaction	Characterized by gender and inequality; causes and solutions vary
Level of analysis emphasized	Macro	Macro	Micro analysis as a way of understanding the larger macro phenomena	Both macro and micro levels of analysis
Key concepts	Manifest functions Latent functions Dysfunction	Inequality Capitalism Stratification	Symbols Nonverbal communication Face to face	Standpoint of women Political action Gender inequality Oppression
View of the individual	People are socialized to perform societal functions	People are shaped by power, coercion, and authority	People manipulate symbols and create their social worlds through interaction	Differs according to social class, race, ethnicity, age, sexual orientation, and physical ability
View of the social order	Maintained through cooperation and consensus	Maintained through force and coercion	Maintained by shared understanding of everyday behaviour	Maintained through standpoints that do not include those of women
View of social change	Predictable, reinforcing	Change takes place all the time and may have positive consequences	Reflected in people's social positions and their communications with others	Essential in order to bring about equality
Example	Public punishments reinforce the social order	Laws reinforce the positions of those in power	People respect laws or disobey them based on their own past experience	Spousal violence, date rape, and economic inequality need to be eliminated
Proponents	Émile Durkheim Talcott Parsons Robert Merton	Karl Marx C. Wright Mills	George Herbert Mead Charles Horton Cooley Erving Goffman	Dorothy Smith Margrit Eichler

Eye on the Media 1-1 Looking at Television from Four Perspectives

Television to most of us is that box sitting on the shelf or table that diverts us, occasionally entertains us, and sometimes puts us to sleep. But sociologists look much more deeply at the medium. Here is what they find using the four sociological perspectives.

Functionalist View

In examining any aspect of society, including television, functionalists emphasize the contribution it makes to overall social stability. Functionalists regard television as a powerful force in communicating the common values of our society and in promoting an overall feeling of unity and social solidarity:

- Television vividly presents important national and international news. On a local level, television communicates vital information on everything from storm warnings and school closings to the locations of emergency shelters.
- Television programs transmit valuable learning skills (*Sesame Street*) and factual information (CBC's *The National*).
- Television "brings together" members of a community or even a nation by broadcasting important events and ceremonies (press conferences, parades, and state funerals) and through coverage of disasters, such as the September 11, 2001, terrorist attacks on the United States.
- Television contributes to economic stability and prosperity by promoting and advertising services and (through shopping channels) serving as a direct marketplace for products.

Conflict View

Conflict theorists argue that the social order is based on coercion and exploitation. They emphasize that television reflects and even exacerbates many of the divisions of our society and world, including those based on gender, race, ethnicity, and social class:

- Television is a form of big business in which profits are more important than the quality of the product (programming).
- Television's decision makers are overwhelmingly white, male, and prosperous; by contrast, television programs tend to ignore the lives and ambitions of subordinate groups, among them working-class people, visible minorities, Aboriginal people, gays and lesbians, people with disabilities, and older people.
- Television distorts the political process, as candidates with the most money (often backed by powerful lobbying groups) buy exposure to voters and saturate the air with attack commercials.
- By exporting *Survivor, Baywatch,* and other programs around the world, U.S. television undermines the distinctive traditions and art forms of other societies and encourages their cultural and economic dependence on the United States.

Interactionist View

In studying the social order, interactionists are especially interested in shared understandings of everyday behaviour. Consequently, interactionists examine television on the micro-level by focusing on how day-to-day social behaviour is shaped by television:

- Television literally serves as a babysitter or a "playmate" for many children for long periods.
- Friendship networks can emerge from shared viewing habits or from recollections of a cherished series from the past. Family members and friends often gather for parties centred on the broadcasting of popular events, such as a Stanley Cup game, the Academy Awards, or even series, like *Survivor*.
- The frequent appearance of violence in news and entertainment programming creates feelings of fear and may actually make interpersonal relations more aggressive.
- The power of television encourages political leaders and even entertainment figures to carefully manipulate symbols (through public appearances) and to attempt to convey self-serving definitions of social reality.

Feminist Views

Feminist theorists believe that gender is constructed by society; thus, television plays a major role not only in reflecting society's ideas about gender but also in constructing its own images:

- Television reinforces gender inequality through its portrayal of women as subordinate and powerless and men as dominant and powerful.
- Television objectifies women through its portrayal of women as objects to be admired for their physical appearance and sexual attractiveness.
- Television creates the false impression that all women are the same—young, white, middle-class, slim, and heterosexual.

Despite their differences, feminist theorists functionalists, conflict theorists, and interactionists would agree that there is much more to television than simply "entertainment." They would also agree that television and other popular forms of culture are worthy subjects for serious study by sociologists.

Applying Theory

1. What functions does television serve? What might be some "dysfunctions"?
2. If you were a television network executive, which perspective would influence your choice of programs? Why?

same issue. Box 1-1 shows how television might look from the functionalist, conflict, interactionist, and feminist points of view.

No one approach to a particular issue is "correct." This textbook assumes that we can gain the broadest understanding of our society by drawing on all four perspectives in the study of human behaviour and institutions. These perspectives overlap as their interests coincide but can diverge according to the dictates of each approach and of the issue being studied. A sociologist's theoretical orientation influences his or her approach to a research problem in important ways.

DEVELOPING THE SOCIOLOGICAL IMAGINATION

In this book, we will be illustrating the sociological imagination in several different ways—by showing theory in practice and research in action; by speaking across race, gender, class, and national boundaries; and by highlighting social policy throughout the world.

Theory in Practice

We will illustrate how the four sociological perspectives—functionalist, conflict, interactionist, and feminist—are helpful in understanding today's issues. Sociologists do not necessarily declare "we are using functionalism," but their research and approaches do tend to draw on one or more theoretical frameworks, as will become clear in the pages that follow.

Research in Action

Sociologists actively investigate a variety of issues and social behaviour. We have already seen that such research might involve the meaning of television programs and decision making in the jury box. Often the research has direct applications for improving people's lives, as in the case of increasing the participation of blacks in Canada and the United States in diabetes testing. Throughout the rest of the book, the research performed by sociologists and other social scientists will shed light on group behaviour of all types.

Speaking across Race, Gender, Class, and National Boundaries

Sociologists include both men and women, people from a variety of socioeconomic backgrounds (some privileged and many not), and individuals from a wealth of ethnic, national, and religious origins. In their work, sociologists seek to draw conclusions that speak to all people—not just the affluent or powerful. This is not always easy. Insights into how a corporation can increase its profits tend to attract more attention and financial support than do, say, the merits of a needle exchange program for low-income, urban residents. Yet sociology today, more than ever, seeks to better understand the experiences of *all* people. In Box 1-2, we take a look at how a woman's role in public places is defined differently from that of a man's in different parts of the world.

SOCIAL POLICY THROUGHOUT THE WORLD

One important way we can use the sociological imagination is to enhance our understanding of current social issues throughout the world. Beginning with Chapter 2, which focuses on research, each chapter will conclude with a discussion of a contemporary social policy issue. In some cases, we will examine a specific issue facing national governments. For example, government funding of child care centres will be discussed in Chapter 4, Socialization; sexual harassment in Chapter 6, Groups and Organizations; and the search for shelters in Chapter 15, Communities and the Environment. These social policy sections will demonstrate how fundamental sociological concepts can enhance our critical thinking skills and help us to better understand current public policy debates taking place around the world.

Sociologists expect the next quarter-century to be perhaps the most exciting and critical period in the history of the discipline. This is because of a growing recognition—both in Canada and around the world—that current social problems *must* be addressed before their magnitude overwhelms human societies. We can expect sociologists to play an increasing role in the government sector by researching and developing public policy alternatives. It seems only natural for this textbook to focus on the connection between the work of sociologists and the difficult questions confronting the policymakers and people of Canada.

Sociology in the Global Community 1-2 Women in Public Places Worldwide

By definition, a public place, such as a sidewalk or a park, is open to all persons. Even some private establishments, such as restaurants, are intended to belong to people as a whole. Yet sociologists and other social scientists have found that societies define access to these places differently for women and men.

In some Middle Eastern societies, women are prohibited from public places and are restricted to certain places in the house. In such societies, the coffeehouse and the market are considered male domains. Some other societies, such as Malagasy, strictly limit the presence of women in "public places" yet allow women to conduct the haggling that is a part of shopping in open-air markets. In some West African societies, women actually control the marketplace. In various eastern European countries and Turkey, women appear to be free to move about in public places, but the coffeehouse remains the exclusive preserve of males. Contrast this with coffeehouses in North America, where women and men mingle freely and even engage each other in conversation as total strangers.

Although casual observers may view both private and public space in North America as gender-neutral, private all-male clubs do persist, and even in public spaces women experience some inequality. Erving Goffman, an interactionist, conducted classic studies of public spaces, which he found to be settings for routine interactions, such as "helping" encounters when a person is lost and asks for directions. But sociologist Carol Brooks Gardner has offered a feminist critique of Goffman's work: "Rarely does Goffman emphasize the habitual disproportionate fear that women can come to feel in public toward men, much less the routine trepidation that ethnic and racial minorities and the disabled can experience" (1989:45). Women are well aware that a casual helping encounter with a man in a public place can too easily lead to undesired sexual queries or advances.

Whereas Goffman suggests that street remarks about women occur rarely—and that they generally hold no unpleasant or threatening implications—Gardner (1989:49) counters that "for young women especially, . . . appearing in public places carries with it the constant possibility of evaluation, compliments that are not really so complimentary after all, and harsh or vulgar insults if the woman is found wanting." She adds that these remarks are sometimes accompanied by tweaks, pinches, or even blows, unmasking the latent hostility of many male-to-female street remarks.

Many women have well-founded fears for their safety in public places (DeKeseredy and Schwartz 1998). Gardner concludes that "public places are arenas for the enactment of inequality in everyday life for women and for many others" (1989:56).

Unlike in many countries in the developing world, the inequality experienced by breastfeeding mothers in public places in Canada has long been a topic of public debate. As of 2000, and after court challenges regarding the activity, most provincial and territorial human rights commissions supported women's right to breastfeed their babies in publics places as a human right, allowing them to breastfeed, openly, in hockey rinks, restaurants, schools, shopping malls, and so on. A Breastfeeding Friendly logo was created in Canada to be placed on the doors and walls of various public places to indicate that women are welcome to breastfeed their babies on the premises.

Applying Theory

1. How might some women be treated in a coffeehouse in Turkey? in Vancouver, British Columbia? What might account for these differences?
2. Do you know a woman who has encountered sexual harassment in a public place? How do the various feminist perspectives account for the prevalence of this harassment?

Sources: Cheng and Liao 1994; DeKeseredy and Schwartz, 1998; Gardner 1989, 1990, 1995; Goffman 1963b, 1971; Rosman and Rubel 1994.

CHAPTER RESOURCES

Summary

Sociology is the systematic study of social behaviour and human groups. In this chapter, we examined the nature of sociological theory, the founders of the discipline, theoretical perspectives of contemporary sociology, and ways to exercise the "sociological imagination."

1. An important element in the ***sociological imagination***—which is an awareness of the relationship between an individual and the wider society—is the ability to view our own society as an outsider might, rather than from the perspective of our limited experiences and cultural biases.
2. Knowledge that relies on "common sense" is not always reliable. Sociologists must test and analyze each piece of information that they use.
3. In contrast to other ***social sciences,*** sociology emphasizes the influence that groups can have on people's behaviour and attitudes and the ways in which people shape society.
4. Sociologists employ ***theories*** to examine the relationships between observations or data that may seem completely unrelated.
5. Nineteenth-century thinkers who contributed sociological insights included Auguste Comte, a French philosopher; Harriet Martineau, an English sociologist; and Herbert Spencer, an English scholar.
6. Other important figures in the development of sociology were Émile Durkheim, who pioneered work on suicide; Max Weber, who taught the need for "insight" in intellectual work; and Karl Marx, who emphasized the importance of the economy and of conflict in society.
7. In the twentieth century, the discipline of sociology is indebted to such sociologists as Charles Horton Cooley, Robert Merton, Harold A. Innis, S.D. Clark, John Porter, and Patricia Marchak.
8. ***Macrosociology*** concentrates on large-scale phenomena or entire civilizations, whereas ***microsociology*** stresses study of small groups.
9. The ***functionalist perspective*** of sociology emphasizes the way that parts of a society are structured to maintain its stability. Social change should be slow and evolutionary.
10. The ***conflict perspective*** assumes that social behaviour is best understood in terms of conflict or tension between competing groups. Social change, spurred by conflict and competition, is viewed as desirable.
11. The ***interactionist perspective*** is primarily concerned with fundamental or everyday forms of interaction, including symbols and other types of nonverbal communication. Social change is ongoing, as individuals are shaped by society and in turn shape it.
12. ***Feminist perspectives*** are varied and diverse; however, they argue that women's inequality is constructed by our society. Feminist perspectives include both micro- and macrolevels of analysis.
13. Sociologists make use of all four perspectives, since each offers unique insights into the same issue.
14. This textbook makes use of the ***sociological imagination*** by showing theory in practice and research in action; by speaking across race, gender, class, and national boundaries; and by highlighting social policy around the world.

Critical Thinking Questions

1. What aspects of the social and work environment in a fast-food restaurant would be of particular interest to a sociologist because of his or her "sociological imagination"?
2. What are the manifest and latent functions of shopping?
3. How might the interactionist perspective be applied to a place where you have been employed or to an organization you joined?
4. How could the sociological imagination be used to study the practice of shopping in North America?

Key Terms

Anomie The loss of direction felt in a society when social control of individual behaviour has become ineffective. (page 8)

Conflict perspective A sociological approach that assumes that social behaviour is best understood in terms of conflict or tension between competing groups. (13)

Dramaturgical approach A view of social interaction that examines people as if they were theatrical performers. (16)

Dysfunction An element or a process of society that may disrupt a social system or lead to a decrease in stability. (13)

Equilibrium model Talcott Parsons's functionalist view of society as tending toward a state of stability or balance. (12)

Feminist perspectives Sociological approaches that attempt to explain, understand, and change the ways in which gender socially organizes our public and private lives in such a way as to produce inequality between men and women. (14)

Functionalist perspective A sociological approach that emphasizes the way that parts of a society are structured to maintain its stability. (12)

Generalized others A term used by George Herbert Mead to refer to a child's awareness of the attitudes, viewpoints, and expectations of society as a whole that a child takes into account in his or her behaviour. (16)

Ideal type A construct or model that serves as a measuring rod against which actual cases can be evaluated. (8)

Interactionist perspective A sociological approach that generalizes about fundamental or everyday forms of social interaction. (15)

Latent functions Unconscious or unintended functions; hidden purposes. (13)

Liberal feminism The stream of feminism that asserts that women's equality can be obtained through the extension of the principles of equality of opportunity and freedom. (14)

Macrosociology Sociological investigation that concentrates on large-scale phenomena or entire civilizations. (10)

Manifest functions Open, stated, and conscious functions. (13)

Marxist feminism The stream of feminist sociological approaches that place the system of capitalism at fault for the oppression of women and hold that women are not oppressed by sexism or patriarchy, but rather by a system of economic production that is based on unequal gender relations in the capitalist economy. (14)

Microsociology Sociological investigation that stresses study of small groups and often uses laboratory experimental studies. (10)

Natural science The study of the physical features of nature and the ways in which they interact and change. (4)

Nonverbal communication The sending of messages through the use of posture, facial expressions, and gestures. (16)

Postmodern society A technologically sophisticated society that is preoccupied with consumer goods and media images. (16)

Radical feminism The stream of feminism that maintains that the root of all oppression of women is embedded in patriarchy. (15)

Science The body of knowledge obtained by methods based on systematic observation. (4)

Significant others A term used by George Herbert Mead to refer to those individuals who are most important in the development of the self, such as parents, friends, and teachers. (16)

Socialist feminism The stream of feminism that maintains that gender relations are shaped by both patriarchy and capitalism, and thus equality for women implies that both the system of capitalism and the ideology of patriarchy must be challenged and eliminated. (14)

Social science The study of various aspects of human society. (4)

Sociological imagination An awareness of the relationship between an individual and the wider society. (3)

Sociology The systematic study of social behaviour and human groups. (3)

Standpoint feminism The stream of feminism that takes into account women's diversity and maintains that no one standpoint will represent all women's lives. (15)

Theory A template through which to organize a way to view the world. (6)

Verstehen The German word for "understanding" or "insight"; used to stress the need for sociologists to take into account people's emotions, thoughts, beliefs, and attitudes. (8)

Additional Readings

Glasser, Barry, Rosanna Hertz, and Herbert J. Gans (eds.). 2003. *Our Studies, Our Selves: Sociologists' Lives and Work.* Oxford: Oxford University Press. This is a collection of 22 autobiographical essays by 12 women and 10 men from Canada and the United States, all contributing to the field of sociology.

Levin, Jack. 1999. *Sociological Snapshots 3: Seeing Social Structure and Change in Everyday Life.* Thousand Oaks, CA: Pine Forge Press. The sociological imagination is employed to look at everything from elevator culture and television soap operas to religious cults and the death penalty.

McDonald, Lynn. 1994. *Women Founders of the Social Sciences.* Ottawa: Carlton University Press. The author examines the important but often overlooked contributions of such pioneers as Mary Wollstonecraft, Harriet Martineau, Beatrice Webb, Jane Addams, and many more.

Tong, Rosemary. 1998. *Feminist Thought*, 2nd ed. Boulder: Westview Press. A second edition of her 1989 survey of feminist theory, providing comprehensive coverage of twentieth-century feminist thinking.

Online Learning Centre

Visit the *Sociology: A Brief Introduction* Online Learning Centre at www.mcgrawhill.ca/college/schaefer to access quizzes, interactive exercises, video clips, and other research and study tools related to this chapter.

Reel Society Interactive Movie CD-ROM 2.0

Exercise your imagination and step into the world of *Reel Society,* a professionally produced movie on CD-ROM that demonstrates the sociological imagination through typical scenarios drawn from campus life. In this movie you will become part of the exploits of several students and will influence the plot by making key choices for them. Through it all, you'll learn to relate sociological thought to real life through a variety of issues and perspectives. In addition to the interactive movie, *Reel Society* includes explanatory text screens and a glossary, as well as quizzes and discussion questions to test your knowledge of sociology. The CD also includes a link to the Online Learning Centre website for *Reel Society.*

Reel Society 2.0 can be used to spark discussion about the following topics from this chapter:

- The sociological imagination
- Major theoretical perspectives
- Speaking across race, gender, and national boundaries

chapter 2

SOCIOLOGICAL RESEARCH

RECENSEMENT · CENSUS
Soyez du nombre!
2001
Count Yourself In!
RECENSEMENT · CENSUS
Veuillez remplir le questionnaire et le poster.
Please complete your questionnaire and mail it.
Canada
Le 15 mai · May 15
Canada

In Canada, the census is the primary mechanism for collecting information about Canadians. The questions asked on the census reflect changing social and political patterns that reveal the dynamic nature of Canadian society.

We propose that as we moved into the most recent phase of industrial capitalism, which began in the 1950s, the coming-of-age process has become even longer, primarily because the labor of adolescents and youth is no longer needed, except in service industries. Consequently, young people have lost a "franchise." Now they participate less in the labor force, and when they do, it is in a more subservient manner. Accordingly, fewer young people have the full rights and privileges of citizenship, and they must wait longer before they are fully recognized as adults. In addition to not being able to make a meaningful contribution to the economy, young people have been forced to remain in school longer, where they are under the watchful eye of massive educational bureaucracies. . . . Today, the norm is to stay in high school, and not to do so is considered unacceptable.

This norm means that those coming of age now face the prospect of remaininç in school for a prolonged period primari' in order to attain high levels of educ tional credentials. While this may se like a trite observation, at the core of phenomenon called "credentialisr the assumption that the best way tc pare oneself for a job is through f educational training. Yet, as has argued elsewhere, for most jo amount of academic training (required is either unnecessary vant. In fact, it appears that the level of credentials is often based on the needs of the monopolistic educational system and the desire of certain occupational groups to acquire more status and wealth instead of on actual demands in the workplace. Many younger people are competing to do the same work as their parents, but they are only allowed to do it if they have attained a higher level of education. Thus, those coming of age must deal with "educational inflation"—an inflationary spiral in the number of credentials it takes to secure a good job.

. . . What emerges from this analysis of the changing educational system of advanced industrial society is that credentialism is exerting a normative pressure on the coming-of-age process—it is leading to an increasing prolongation of youth. At the same time, despite the scramble for credentials, it is obvious ...dvanced industrial economy ...university gradu-

Like all of th
questions of our
there so much crime
feed the population? S
whether or not they have a
unlike the typical citizen, the sc
ment to the use of the *scientific me*
ety. The scientific method is a syste
series of steps that ensures maximum o
consistency in researching a problem.
Many of us will never actually conduct sc
research. Why, then, is it important that we understa

When the parents of the baby boom generation stepped into their first jobs in the 1950s and 1960s, it was not uncommon for them to do that with a high school diploma and an expressed desire to work their way up the corporate ladder. In their book *Generation on Hold*, James Côté and Anton Allahar use existing sources—or complete what is called a secondary analysis—to show that today's younger generation follows a very different path for its prospects of and preparation for meaningful employment. Côté and Allahar point to the "coming-of-age" pressures that young people face as they spend more and more time (and financial resources) on advanced education.

In advanced industrial societies, or knowledge-based economies, educational credentials become increasingly important as the number of people with those credentials increases. Yet many younger people now experience what Côté and Allahar refer to as "normative cross-pressure": they end up working with little or no security or chance of upward mobility. Those who do end up with successful jobs after accumulating degrees and credentials may have done so, according to Côté and Allahar, on the basis of the added advantage of their class, gender, or race.

Effective sociological research can be quite thought-provoking. It may suggest many new questions about social interactions that require further study, such as why we make assumptions about people's intentions based merely on their gender or age or race. In some cases, rather than raising additional questions, a study will simply confirm previous beliefs and findings.

This chapter will examine the research process used in conducting sociological studies. How do sociologists go about setting up a research project? And how do they ensure that the results of the research are reliable and accurate? Can they carry out their research without stepping on the rights of those whom they study?

We will first look at the steps that make up the scientific method. Then we will look at various techniques commonly used in sociological research, such as experiments, observations, and surveys. We will pay particular attention to the ethical challenges sociologists face in studying human behaviour and to the debate raised by Max Weber's call for "value neutrality" in social science research. We will also examine the role that technology plays in research today. The social policy section considers the difficulties in researching human sexuality.

Whatever the area of sociological inquiry and whatever the perspective of the sociologist—whether functionalist, feminist, conflict, interactionist, or any other—there is one crucial requirement: imaginative, responsible research that meets the highest scientific and ethical standards. ■

Use Your Sociological Imagination www.mcgrawhill.ca/college/schaefer

Do you know anyone who holds a degree and works in an unskilled position for minimum wage? Do you think it is necessary to have an advanced degree to do jobs that many people in your parents' generation did without one?

WHAT IS THE SCIENTIFIC METHOD?

[illegible], sociologists are interested in the central [illegible] time. Is the family falling apart? Why is [illegible]? Is the world failing in its ability to [illegible]ch issues concern most people, [illegible]academic training. However, [illegible]ciologist has a commit[illegible]*thod* in studying soci[illegible]matic, organized [illegible]jectivity and [illegible]entific [illegible]nd [illegible] the scientific method? Because it plays a major role in the workings of our society. Residents of Canada are constantly being bombarded with "facts" or "data." Almost daily, advertisers cite supposedly scientific studies to prove that their products are superior. Such claims may be accurate or exaggerated. We can make better evaluations of such information—and will not be fooled so easily—if we are familiar with the standards of scientific research. These standards are quite stringent and demand as strict adherence as possible.

The scientific method requires precise preparation in developing useful research. Otherwise, the research data collected may not prove accurate. Sociologists and other researchers follow five basic steps in the scientific

FIGURE 2-1

The scientific method

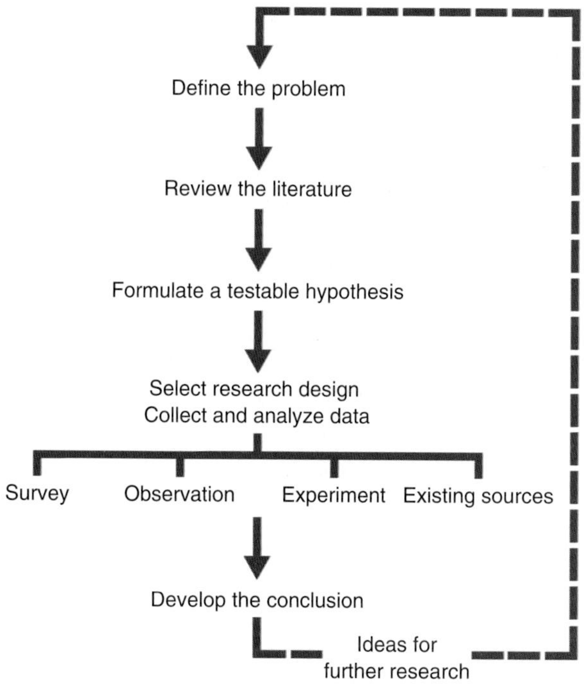

The scientific method allows sociologists to objectively and logically evaluate data they collect. Their findings can prompt further ideas for sociological research.

method: (1) defining the problem, (2) reviewing the literature, (3) formulating the hypothesis, (4) selecting the research design and then collecting and analyzing data, and (5) developing the conclusion (see Figure 2-1). We'll use an actual example to illustrate the workings of the scientific method.

Defining the Problem

Some people make great sacrifices and work hard to get a postsecondary education. Some parents borrow money for their children's tuition. Some students work part-time jobs or even take full-time positions while attending evening or weekend classes. But are these students and parents typical? Or do people whose parents have higher incomes have higher rates of university attendance?

The first step in any research project is to state as clearly as possible what you hope to investigate, that is, *define the problem.* In this instance, we are interested in knowing how parents' income relates to their children's postsecondary education. Early on, any social science researcher must develop an ***operational definition*** of each concept being studied. An operational definition is an explanation of an abstract concept that is specific enough to allow a researcher to assess the concept. For example, a sociologist interested in status might use membership in exclusive social clubs as an operational definition of status. Someone studying prejudice might consider a person's unwillingness to hire or work with members of minority groups as an operational definition of prejudice. In our example, we need to develop two operational definitions—education and income—in order to study whether parents with higher incomes have children who are more likely to attend a postsecondary institution.

It seems reasonable to assume that parents' income relates to whether their children pursue postsecondary education. But how would you go about researching this hypothesis?

Initially, we take a functionalist perspective (although we may end up incorporating other approaches). We argue that opportunities for postsecondary education are related to parents' income.

Reviewing the Literature

By conducting a *review of the literature*—the relevant scholarly studies and information—researchers define the problem under study, clarify possible techniques to be used in collecting data, and eliminate or reduce avoidable mistakes. For our example, we would examine information about the income of the parents of students in university.

The review of the literature would soon tell us that many other factors besides parents' income influence whether people attend university. And if we learn that the children of richer parents are more likely to go to college or university than are those from modest backgrounds, we might consider the possibility that these parents may also help their children secure better-paying jobs after their children get their degrees.

Formulating the Hypothesis

After reviewing earlier research and drawing on the contributions of sociological theorists, the researchers may then *formulate the hypothesis.* A ***hypothesis*** is a speculative statement about the relationship between two or more factors known as variables. Income, religion, occupation, and gender can all serve as variables in a study. We can define a ***variable*** as a measurable trait or characteristic that is subject to change under different conditions.

Researchers who formulate a hypothesis generally must suggest how one aspect of human behaviour influences or affects another. The variable hypothesized to cause or influence another is called the ***independent variable.*** The second variable is termed the ***dependent variable*** because its action "depends" on the influence of the independent variable.

Our hypothesis is that the higher their parents' income, the more likely it is that children go to university or college. The independent variable to be measured is parents' income levels. The variable thought to depend on it—attendance at a postsecondary institution—must also be measured.

Identifying independent and dependent variables is a critical step in clarifying cause-and-effect relationships in society. As shown in Figure 2-2, ***causal logic*** involves the relationship between a condition or variable and a particular consequence, with one event leading to the other. Under causal logic, being less integrated into society may be directly related to or produce a greater likelihood of suicide. Similarly, the time students spend reviewing material for a quiz may be directly related to or produce a greater likelihood of getting a high score on the quiz.

A ***correlation*** exists when a change in one variable coincides with a change in the other. Correlations are an indication that causality *may* be present; they do not necessarily indicate causation. For example, data indicate that working mothers are more likely to have delinquent children than are mothers who do not work outside the home. But this correlation is actually caused by a third

FIGURE 2-2

Causal Logic

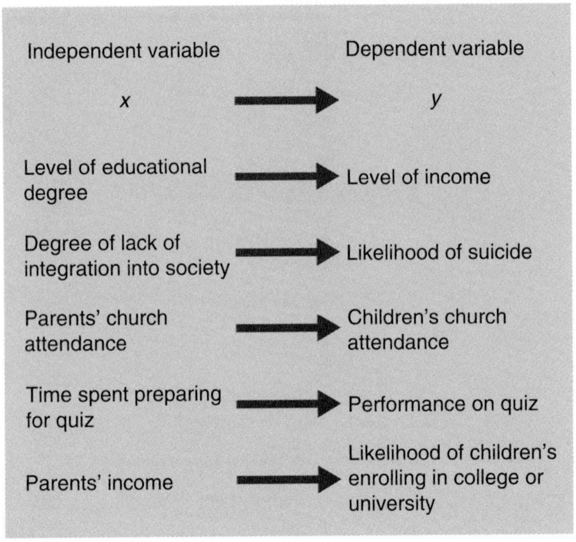

In *causal logic* an independent variable (often designated by the symbol *x*) influences a dependent variable (generally designated as *y*); thus, *x* leads to *y.* For example, parents who attend church regularly (*x*) are more likely to have children who are churchgoers (*y*).

> **Think about It**
> Identify two or three variables that might "depend" on this independent variable: number of alcoholic drinks ingested.

variable: family income. Lower-income households are more likely to have a full-time working mother; at the same time, reported rates of delinquency are higher in this income class than in other economic levels. Consequently, although having a mother who works outside the home is correlated with delinquency, it does not *cause* delinquency. Sociologists seek to identify the *causal* link between variables; this causal link is generally described by researchers in their hypotheses.

Collecting and Analyzing Data

How do you test a hypothesis to determine whether it is supported or refuted? You need to collect information, using one of the research designs described later in the chapter. The research design guides the researcher in collecting and analyzing data.

Selecting the Sample

In most studies, social scientists must carefully select what is known as a *sample.* A ***sample*** is a selection from a larger population that is statistically representative of

"And don't waste your time canvassing the whole building, young man. We think alike."

When conducting a survey, researchers must draw their sample carefully so that it is representative of the general population.

that population. There are many kinds of samples, but the one social scientists most frequently use is the random sample. In a ***random sample,*** every member of an entire population being studied has the same chance of being selected. Thus, if researchers want to examine the opinions of people listed in a city directory (a book that, unlike the telephone directory, lists all households), they might use a computer to randomly select names from the directory. This would constitute a random sample. The advantage of using specialized sampling techniques is that sociologists do not need to question everyone in a population.

Sampling is a complex aspect of research design. In Box 2-1, we consider the approach some researchers took when trying to create an appropriate sample of people during the U.S. occupation of Baghdad in 2003. Before this time, polling of public opinion had never happened. We'll also see how Gallup made use of data from the sample.

It is easy to confuse the careful scientific techniques used in representative sampling with the many *nonscientific* polls that receive much more media attention. For example, television viewers and radio listeners are encouraged to email their views on today's headlines or on political contests. Such polls reflect nothing more than the views of those who happened to see the television program (or hear the radio broadcast) and took the time, perhaps at some cost, to register their opinions. These data do not necessarily reflect (and indeed may distort) the views of the broader population. Not everyone has access to a television or radio, has the time to watch or listen to a program, or has the means or inclination to send email. Similar problems are raised by "mail-back" questionnaires found in many magazines and by "mall intercepts" where shoppers are asked about some issue. Even when these techniques include answers from tens of thousands of people, their accuracy will be far less than that of a carefully selected representative sample of 1500 respondents.

In our research example, we will use information collected in the General Social Survey (GSS) and the Survey of Consumer Finances (SCF) to examine the relationship between family income and participation in postsecondary education in Canada (Statistics Canada 2003a). The study set out to examine whether the relationship between family income and university attendance for 18- to 24-year-olds changed from 1979 to 1997. The GSS gathers data on Canadian social trends and provides information on specific policy issues. The SCF provides data on the income of Canadians and information on labour market activities.

Ensuring Validity and Reliability

The scientific method requires that research results be both valid and reliable. ***Validity*** refers to the degree to which a measure or scale truly reflects the phenomenon under study. ***Reliability*** refers to the extent to which a measure produces consistent results. A valid measure of income depends on gathering accurate data. Various studies show that people are reasonably accurate in knowing how much money they earned in the most recent year. One problem of reliability is that some people may not *disclose* accurate information, but most do.

Developing the Conclusion

Scientific studies, including those conducted by sociologists, do not aim to answer all the questions that can be raised about a particular subject. Therefore, the conclusion of a research study represents both an end and a beginning. It terminates a specific phase of the investigation, but it should also generate ideas for future study.

Supporting Hypotheses

In our example, we find that the data support our hypothesis: People whose parents have higher incomes have higher rates of postsecondary attendance.

The relationship is not perfect. Obviously, some people from families of lower incomes do attend university,

Sociology in the Global Community 2-1 Polling in Baghdad

In 2003, as the U.S. Army launched the war in Iraq, pollsters watched President George W. Bush's approval rating carefully. Such periodic measures of the public pulse have become routine in the United States, an accepted part of presidential politics. But in Iraq, a totalitarian state ruled for 24 years by dictator Saddam Hussein, polling of public opinion on political and social issues was unknown until August 2003, when representatives of the Gallup Organization began regular surveys of the residents of Baghdad. Later in the occupation, Gallup extended its survey to other areas in Iraq.

Needless to say, conducting a scientific survey in the war-torn city presented unusual challenges. Planners began by assuming that no census statistics would be available, so they used satellite imagery to estimate the population in each of Baghdad's neighbourhoods. They later located detailed statistics for much of Baghdad, which they updated for use in their sampling procedure. Gallup's planners also expected that they would need to hire trained interviewers from outside Iraq, but they were fortunate to find some government employees who had become familiar with Baghdad's neighbourhoods while conducting consumer surveys. To train and supervise these interviewers, Gallup hired two seasoned executives from the Pan Arab Research Center in Dubai.

To administer the survey, Gallup chose the time-tested method of private, face-to-face interviews in people's homes. This method not only put respondents at ease, but it also allowed women to participate in the survey at a time when venturing out in public may have been dangerous for them. In all, Gallup employees conducted more than 3400 person-to-person interviews in the privacy of Iraqis' homes. Respondents, they found, were eager to offer opinions and would talk with them at length. Only 3 percent of those who were sampled declined to be interviewed.

The survey's results are significant, since the more than six million people who live in Baghdad constitute one-fourth of Iraq's population. Asked which of several forms of government would be acceptable to them, equal numbers of respondents chose (1) a multiparty parliamentary democracy and (2) a system of governance that includes consultations with Islamic leaders. Fewer respondents endorsed a constitutional democracy or an Islamic kingdom. At a time when representatives of the Iraqi people had convened to establish a new form of government for the nation, this kind of information was invaluable.

Applying Theory

1. The 97 percent response rate interviewers obtained in this survey was extremely high. Why do you think the response rate was so high, and what do you think it tells political analysts about the residents of Baghdad?
2. What might be some limitations of this survey?

A Gallup employee interviews an Iraqi army veteran at his home in Baghdad. Pollsters had to carefully estimate the population of Baghdad's many districts, subdistricts, and neighbourhoods to obtain a statistically representative sample of respondents.

Sources: Gallup 2003; Saad 2003.

as shown in Figure 2-3. A student might earn a master's degree, for example, even though his or her parents' income was considered low.

Sociological studies do not always generate data that support the original hypothesis. In many instances, a hypothesis is refuted, and researchers must reformulate

FIGURE 2-3

University Participation Rates of 18- to 24-Year Olds by Parental Income

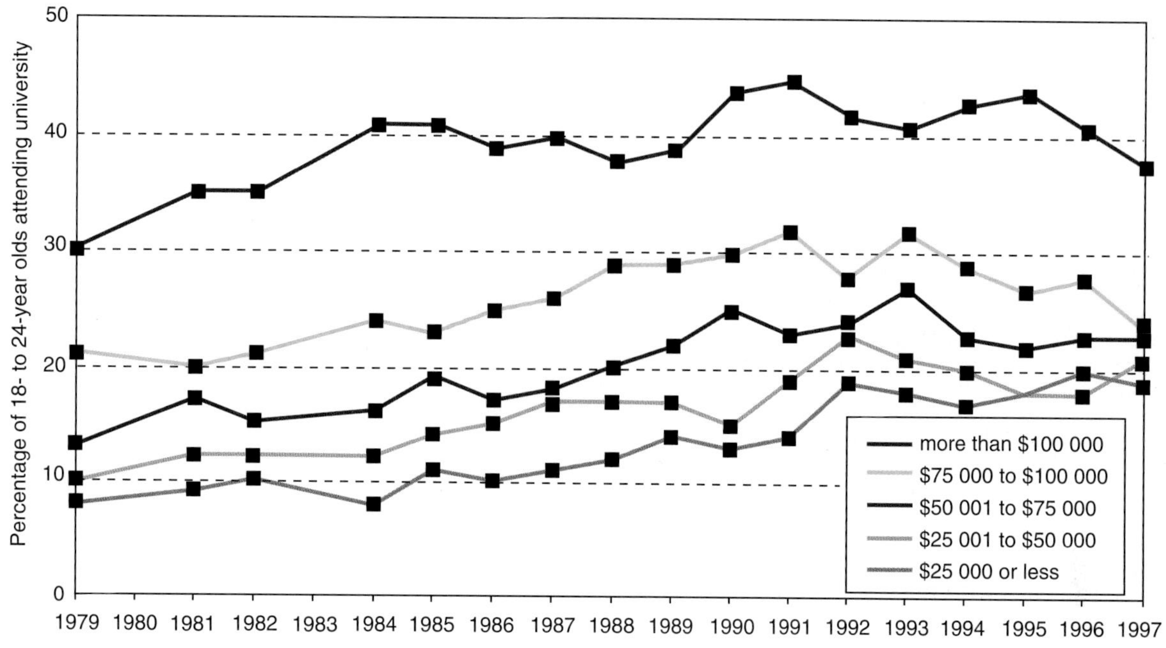

Source: Statistics Canada 2003a.

their conclusions. Unexpected results may also lead sociologists to reexamine their methodology and make changes in the research design.

Controlling for Other Factors

A ***control variable*** is a factor held constant to test the relative impact of the independent variable. For example, if researchers wanted to know how adults in Ontario feel about restrictions on smoking in public places, they would probably attempt to use a respondent's smoking behaviour as a control variable. That is, how do smokers versus nonsmokers feel about smoking in public places? The researchers would compile separate statistics on how smokers and nonsmokers feel about antismoking regulations.

Our study of the influence of parental income on education suggests that not everyone enjoys equal educational opportunities, a disparity that is one of the causes of social inequality. Since education affects a person's income, we may want to call on the conflict perspective to explore this topic further. What impact does a person's race or gender have? Do the occupations of the parents have an impact on the advanced education of their children? Do parents' occupations have an impact on their children's levels of education? Later in the text, we will more fully explore the relationship between family income and educational achievement of children, accounting for variables of gender, race, and other factors.

In Summary: The Scientific Method

Let us briefly summarize the process of the scientific method through a review of the example. We *defined a problem* (the question of whether parental income affects educational attainment). We *reviewed the literature* (other studies of the relationship between parental income and education) and *formulated a hypothesis* (the higher the parents' income the more likely their children will go to university). We *collected and analyzed the data*, making sure the sample was representative and the data were valid and reliable. Finally, we *developed the conclusion:* The data do support our hypothesis about the influence of parental income on children's attendance at a postsecondary education.

MAJOR RESEARCH DESIGNS

An important aspect of sociological research is deciding *how* to collect the data. A ***research design*** is a detailed plan or method for obtaining data scientifically. Selection

Think about It
What would constitute a less biased question for a survey on smoking?

of a research design requires creativity and ingenuity. This choice will directly influence both the cost of the project and the amount of time needed to collect the results of the research. Research designs that sociologists regularly use to generate data include surveys, field research, experiments, and existing sources.

Surveys

Almost all of us have responded to surveys of one kind or another. We may have been asked what kind of detergent we use, which political candidate we intend to vote for, or what our favourite television program is. A ***survey*** is a study, generally in the form of an interview or questionnaire, that provides researchers with information about how people think and act. Among Canada's best-known surveys of opinion are those by Ipsos-Reid and Environics. As anyone who watches the news during presidential campaigns knows, polls have become a staple of political life.

When you think of surveys, you may recall seeing many "person on the street" interviews on local television news shows. Although such interviews can be highly entertaining, they are not necessarily an accurate indication of public opinion. First, they reflect the opinions of only those people who happen to be at a certain location. Such a sample can be biased in favour of commuters, middle-class shoppers, or factory workers, depending on which street or area the newspeople select. Second, television interviews tend to attract outgoing people who are willing to appear on the air, while they frighten away others who may feel intimidated by a camera. As we've seen, a survey must utilize precise, representative sampling if it is to genuinely reflect a broad range of the population.

In preparing to conduct a survey, sociologists must not only develop representative samples, but they must also exercise great care in the wording of questions. An effective survey question must be simple and clear enough for people to understand it. It must also be specific enough so that there are no problems in interpreting the results. Open-ended questions ("What do you think of educational programming on television?") must be carefully phrased to solicit the type of information desired. Surveys can be indispensable sources of information, but only if the sampling is done properly and the questions are worded accurately and without bias.

There are two main forms of surveys: the ***interview,*** in which a researcher obtains information through face-to-face or telephone questioning, and the ***questionnaire,*** which uses a printed or written form to obtain information from a respondent. Each of these has its own advantages. An interviewer can obtain a high response rate because people find it more difficult to turn down a personal request for an interview than to throw away a written questionnaire. In addition, a skilful interviewer can go beyond written questions and "probe" for a subject's underlying feelings and reasons. However, questionnaires have the advantage of being cheaper, especially in large samples. See Box 2-2 for a discussion of one study that successfully used interviews.

Studies have shown that characteristics of the interviewer have an impact on survey data. For example, female interviewers tend to receive more feminist responses from female subjects than do male researchers, and black interviewers tend to receive more detailed responses about race-related issues from black subjects than do white interviewers. The possible impact of gender and race only indicates again how much care social research requires (D. Davis 1997; Huddy et al. 1997).

The survey is an example of ***quantitative research,*** which collects and reports data primarily in numerical form.

Field Research

Although quantitative research may make use of large samples, it can't look at a topic in great depth and detail. Many researchers prefer to use ***qualitative research,*** which relies on what is seen in field and naturalistic settings and often focuses on small groups and communities rather than on large groups or whole nations. Forms of qualitative research may include in-depth interviews.

Observation

Investigators who collect information through direct participation or by closely watching a group or community under study are engaged in ***observation.*** This method allows sociologists to examine certain behaviours and communities that could not be investigated through other research techniques.

An increasingly popular form of qualitative research in sociology today is ethnography. ***Ethnography*** refers to efforts to describe an entire social setting through extended, systematic observation. Typically, this description emphasizes how the subjects themselves view their social setting. Anthropologists rely heavily on ethnography. Much as an anthropologist seeks to understand the people of some Polynesian island, the sociologist as an ethnographer seeks to understand and present to us an entire way of life in some setting.

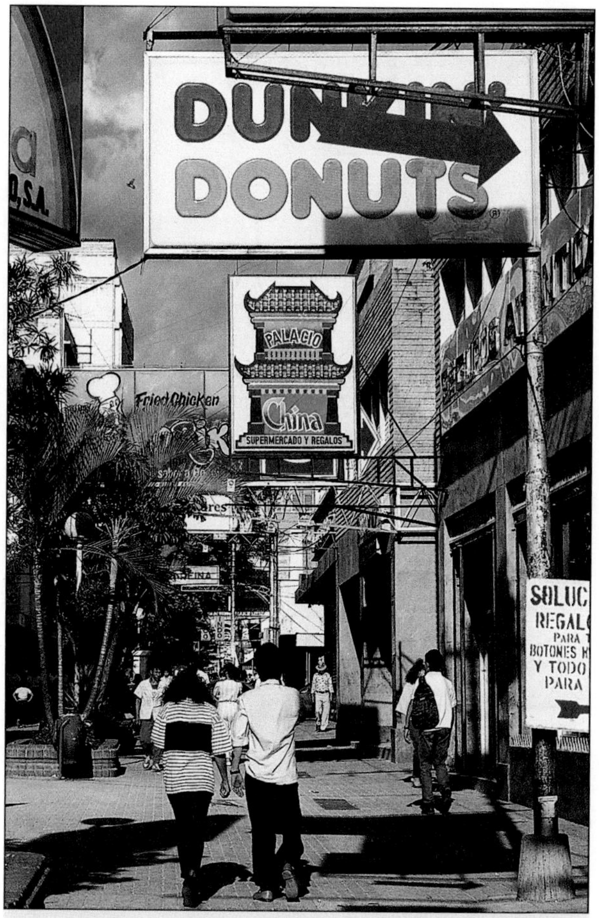

This city in Honduras in Central America provides a rich setting for observation research. An ethnographer would take note of the interplay of cultures in the everyday street life.

In some cases, the sociologist actually joins a group for a time to get an accurate sense of how it operates. This is called *participant observation.*

During the late 1930s, in a classic example of participant-observation research, William F. Whyte moved into a low-income Italian neighbourhood in Boston. For nearly four years, he was a member of the social circle of "corner boys" that he describes in *Street Corner Society.* Whyte revealed his identity to these men and joined in their conversations, bowling, and other leisure-time activities. His goal was to gain greater insight into the community that these men had established. As Whyte (1981:303) listened to Doc, the leader of the group, he "learned the answers to questions I would not even have had the sense to ask if I had been getting my information solely on an interviewing basis." Whyte's work was especially valuable, since, at the time, the academic world had little direct knowledge of the poor and tended to rely on the records of social service agencies, hospitals, and courts for information (Adler and Johnson 1992).

The initial challenge that Whyte faced—and that every participant observer encounters—was to gain acceptance into an unfamiliar group. It is no simple matter for a trained sociologist to win the trust of a religious cult, a youth gang, a poor Appalachian community, or a circle of skid row residents. It requires a great deal of patience and an accepting, nonthreatening type of personality on the part of the observer.

Observation research poses other complex challenges for the investigator. Sociologists must be able to fully understand what they are observing. In a sense, then, researchers must learn to see the world as the group sees it in order to fully comprehend the events taking place around them.

This raises a delicate issue. If the research is to be successful, the observer cannot allow the close associations or even friendships that inevitably develop to influence the subjects' behaviour or the conclusions of the study. Anson Shupe and David Bromley (1980), two sociologists who have used participant observation, have likened this challenge to that of "walking a tightrope." Even while working hard to gain acceptance from the

Research in Action 2-2 Does Hard Work Lead to Better Grades?

Does a serious work ethic pay off in better grades? Sociologist William Rau wanted to answer that question. Working with Ann Durand, a former student now employed in the research department of State Farm Insurance Companies, Rau devised a research study. The dependent variable was easy to measure—the two could use an already existing data source, students' grade point averages (GPAs). But how could they measure the independent variable, a student's work ethic?

After considering many possibilities, the two researchers decided to focus on students' drinking behaviour and study habits. They developed a scale comprising a series of items on which students rated their drinking and studying behaviour. At one extreme were many hours of daily studying and abstention from drinking. At the other extreme were frequent drinking—even on weekdays—and infrequent studying, usually cramming just before tests. The operational definition of students' work ethic became students' self-reports of their drinking and studying behaviour in response to a series of questions.

Rau and Durand administered their behaviour scale to 255 students and then compared the scores on the scale with students' GPAs. The results were fairly striking. Generally, those students who drank less and studied more than others performed better academically, as measured by their GPAs. The researchers had been careful to control for students' ability levels using two more existing sources of data: students' class rankings in high school and their scores on university entrance exams. These sources indicated that the abstainers had not arrived at university better prepared than other students. Hard work really *does* pay off in better grades.

Applying Theory

1. Where does your own drinking and studying behaviour fall on Rau and Durand's behaviour scale? What is your GPA? Is your academic achievement consistent with your drinking and studying behaviour?
2. What other ways of measuring a student's work ethic could the researchers have considered? Can you think of any other variable besides a student's ability level that might have distorted the study's results?

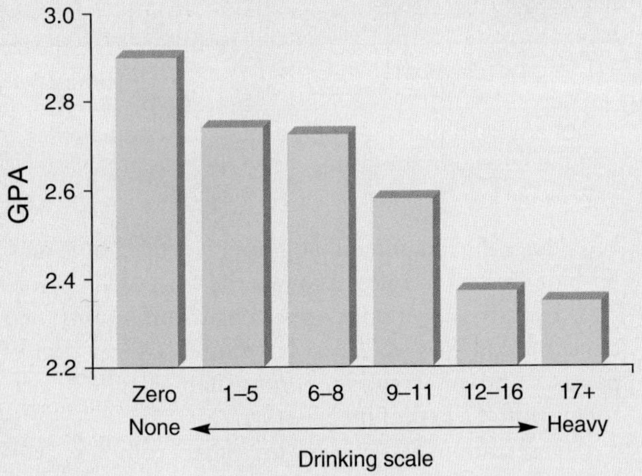

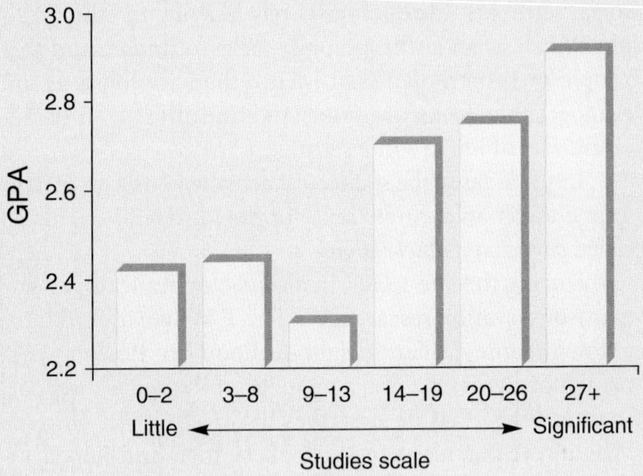

Source: Rau and Durand 2000.

group being studied, the participant observer *must* maintain some degree of detachment.

Feminist perspectives in sociology have drawn attention to a shortcoming in ethnographic research as well as other forms of sociological research. For most of the history of sociology, studies were conducted on male subjects or about male-led groups and organizations, and the findings were generalized to all people. For example, for many decades studies of urban life focused on street corners, neighbourhood taverns, and bowling alleys—places where men typically congregated. Although the insights were valuable, they did not give a true impression of city life because they overlooked the areas where women were likely to gather. Feminist perspectives attempt to redress this bias in the way in which ethnographic research was conducted. Feminist researchers also tend to involve and consult their subjects more than other types of researchers do, and they are more oriented to seeking change, raising consciousness, or trying to affect policy. In addition, feminist research is particularly open to a multidisciplinary approach, such as making use of historical evidence or legal studies as well as feminist theory (Baker 1999; Lofland 1975; Reinharz 1992).

In-Depth Interviews

In-depth interviews have the advantage of possibly revealing more than the observer or researcher can observe from the outside. In-depth interviews can be semistructured in that they may contain a specific set of questions but be flexible enough to enable participants to direct their responses to wherever they are deemed personally meaningful. In-depth interviews can also be unstructured interviews; they can be open-ended and may, therefore, not be confined to a core set of questions that the observer or researcher deems of interest or relevance. The key is that, through careful listening, the observer or researcher can uncover multiple layers of meaning in participants' responses.

Experiments

When sociologists want to study a possible cause-and-effect relationship, they may conduct experiments. An ***experiment*** is an artificially created situation that allows the researcher to manipulate variables.

In the classic method of conducting an experiment, two groups of people are selected and matched for similar characteristics, such as age or education. The researchers then assign the subjects to one of two groups: the experimental or the control group. The ***experimental group*** is exposed to an independent variable; the ***control group*** is not. Thus, if scientists were testing a new type of antibiotic drug, they would administer that drug to an experimental group but not to a control group.

Sociologists don't often rely on this classic form of experiment because it generally involves manipulating human behaviour in an inappropriate manner, especially in a laboratory setting. However, sociologists do try to re-create experimental conditions in the field. For example, they may compare children's performance in two schools that use different curricula. Another area of investigation that has led to several experimental studies in the field is an examination of police action in domestic assault cases. Emergency calls to a household where domestic violence is occurring account for a significant part of a police officer's work. Sociologists Anthony Pate and Edwin Hamilton (1992) studied cases in which officers did or did not arrest the violent suspect and then looked at the effect of the arrest or nonarrest on future incidents of assault in the household. In other words, they compared cases where no arrest was made (the control group) with incidents where the suspect was arrested (experimental group). They found that an arrest did have a deterrent effect if the suspect was employed. Pate and Hamilton concluded that although an arrest may be a sobering experience for any individual, the impact of being taken to a police station is greater if a person is employed and is forced to explain what is happening in his or her personal life to a boss.

In some experiments, just as in observation research, the presence of a social scientist or other observer may affect the behaviour of people being studied. The recognition of this phenomenon grew out of an experiment conducted during the 1920s and 1930s at the Hawthorne plant of the Western Electric Company. A group of researchers set out to determine how to improve the productivity of workers at the plant. The investigators manipulated such variables as the lighting and working hours to see what impact changes in them had on productivity. To their surprise, they found that *every* step they took seemed to increase productivity. Even measures that seemed likely to have the opposite effect, such as

Does arresting someone for domestic assault deter future incidents of violence? An experiment in Miami, Florida, studied this question by making use of control and experimental groups.

How do people respond to being observed? Evidently these employees at the Hawthorne plant enjoyed the attention paid them when researchers observed them at work. No matter what variables were changed, the workers increased their productivity every time, including when the level of lighting was *reduced*.

reducing the amount of lighting in the plant, led to higher productivity.

Why did the plant's employees work harder even under less favourable conditions? Their behaviour apparently was influenced by the greater attention being paid to them in the course of the research and by the novelty of being subjects in an experiment. Since that time, sociologists have used the term ***Hawthorne effect*** to refer to subjects of research who deviate from their typical behaviour because they realize that they are under observation (Jones 1992; Lang 1992; Pelton 1994).

Use Your Sociological Imagination

You are a researcher interested in the effect of TV-watching on the grades of school children. How would you go about setting up an experiment to measure this?

Use of Existing Sources

Sociologists do not necessarily have to collect new data in order to conduct research and test hypotheses. The term ***secondary analysis*** refers to a variety of research techniques that make use of previously collected and publicly accessible information and data. Generally, in conducting secondary analysis, researchers utilize data in ways unintended by the initial collectors of information. For example, census data are compiled for specific uses by the federal government but are also valuable for marketing specialists in locating everything from bicycle stores to nursing homes.

Sociologists consider secondary analysis to be *nonreactive*, since it does not influence people's behaviour. pp. 7–8 As an example, Émile Durkheim's statistical analysis of suicide neither increased nor decreased human self-destruction. Researchers, then, can avoid the Hawthorne effect by using secondary analysis.

There is one inherent problem, however: the researcher who relies on data collected by someone else may not find exactly what is needed. Social scientists studying family violence can use statistics from police and social service agencies on *reported* cases of spouse abuse and child abuse. But how many cases are not reported? Government bodies have no precise data on *all* cases of abuse.

Many social scientists find it useful to study cultural, economic, and political documents, including newspapers, periodicals, radio and television tapes, the Internet, scripts, diaries, songs, folklore, and legal papers, to name some examples (see Table 2-1). In examining these sources, researchers employ a technique known as

Content analysis of recent films finds this unstated message: smoking is cool. In this still from the 2001 movie *Bridget Jones's Diary,* Renee Zellweger is shown enjoying a cigarette. If the movie industry is made aware of the extent of smoking in films and the message that sends to young viewers, perhaps it will try to alter the message.

Table 2-1 Existing Sources Used in Sociological Research

Most Frequently Used Sources
Statistics Canada
Polls, such as Ipsos-Reid and Environics
Birth, death, marriage, and divorce statistics
Other Sources
Newspapers and periodicals
Personal journals, diaries, email, and letters
Records and archival material of religious organizations, corporations, and other organizations
Transcripts of radio programs
Videotapes of motion pictures and television programs
Web pages
Song lyrics
Scientific records (such as patent applications)
Speeches of public figures (such as politicians)
Votes cast in elections or by elected officials on specific legislative proposals
Attendance records for public events
Videotapes of social protests and rallies
Literature, including folklore

content analysis, which is the systematic coding and objective recording of data, guided by some rationale.

Using content analysis, Erving Goffman (1979) conducted a pioneering exploration of how advertisements portrayed women as inferior to men. The ads typically showed women being subordinate to or dependent on others or being instructed by men. They used caressing and touching gestures more than men. Even when presented in leadership-type roles, women were likely to be shown in seductive poses or gazing out into space.

Researchers today are analyzing the content of films to look at the increase in smoking in motion pictures, despite increased public health concerns. This type of content analysis can have clear social policy implications if it draws the attention of the motion picture industry to the message it may be delivering (especially to young people) that smoking is acceptable, even desirable. For example, a 1999 content analysis found that tobacco use appeared in 89 percent of the two hundred most popular movie rentals (Kang 1997; Roberts et al. 1999).

ETHICS OF RESEARCH

A biochemist cannot inject a drug into a human being unless the drug has been thoroughly tested and the subject agrees to the shot. To do otherwise would be both unethical and illegal. Sociologists must also abide by certain specific standards in conducting research—a ***code of ethics.***

The professional society of the discipline, the Canadian Sociology and Anthropology Association (CSAA), published a code of ethics in 1994. The following is a short excerpt from the CSAA's *Statement of Professional Ethics*. The complete statement is available online at http://www.csaa.ca/structure/ethics.htm:

> **Organizing and initiating research**
>
> 1. Codes of professional ethics arise from the need to protect vulnerable or subordinate populations from harm incurred, knowingly or unknowingly, by the intervention of researchers into their lives and cultures. Sociologists and anthropologists have a responsibility to respect the rights, and be concerned with the welfare, of all the vulnerable and subordinate populations affected by their work. . . .
>
> **Protecting people in the research environment**
>
> 9. Researchers must respect the rights of citizens to privacy, confidentiality and anonymity, and not to be studied. Researchers should make every effort to determine whether those providing information wish to remain anonymous or to receive recognition and then respect their wishes. . . .
>
> **Informed consent**
>
> 12. Researchers must not expose respondents to risk of personal harm. Informed consent must be obtained when the risks of research are greater than the risks of everyday life. . . .
>
> **Covert research and deception**
>
> 17. Subjects should not be deceived if there is any reasonably anticipated risk to the subjects or if the harm cannot be offset or the extent of the harm be reasonably predicted.

On the surface, these and the rest of the basic principles of the CSAA's *Statement of Professional Ethics* probably seem clear-cut. How could they lead to any disagreement or controversy? However, many delicate ethical questions cannot be resolved simply by reading the points above. For example, should a sociologist engaged in participant-observation research *always* protect the confidentiality of subjects? What if the subjects are members of a religious cult allegedly engaged in unethical and possibly illegal activities? What if the sociologist is interviewing political activists and is questioned by government authorities about the research?

Most sociological research uses *people* as sources of information—as respondents to survey questions, subjects of observation, or participants in experiments. In all cases, sociologists need to be certain that they are not invading the privacy of their subjects. Generally, they handle this by ensuring anonymity and by guaranteeing the confidentiality of personal information. However, a study by William Zellner raised important questions about the extent to which sociologists can threaten people's right to privacy.

The Right to Know versus the Right to Privacy

A car lies at the bottom of a cliff, its driver dead. Was this an accident or a suicide? Sociologist William Zellner (1978) wanted to learn whether fatal car crashes are sometimes suicides disguised as accidents in order to protect family and friends (and perhaps to collect otherwise unredeemable insurance benefits). These acts of "autocide" are by nature covert. Zellner found that research on automobile accidents in which fatalities occur poses an ethical issue—the right to know against the right to privacy.

In his efforts to assess the frequency of such suicides, Zellner sought to interview the friends, co-workers, and family members of the deceased. He hoped to obtain information that would allow him to ascertain whether the deaths were accidental or deliberate. Zellner told the people approached for interviews that his goal was to contribute to a reduction of future accidents by learning about the emotional characteristics of accident victims. He made no mention of his suspicions of autocide, out of fear that potential respondents would refuse to meet with him.

Zellner eventually concluded that at least 12 percent of all fatal single-occupant crashes are suicides. This information could be valuable for society, particularly since some of the probable suicides actually killed or critically injured innocent bystanders in the process of taking their own lives. Yet the ethical questions still must be faced. Was Zellner's research unethical because he misrepresented the motives of his study and failed to obtain his subjects' informed consent? Or was his deception justified by the social value of his findings?

The answers to these questions are not immediately apparent. Zellner appeared to have admirable motives and took great care in protecting confidentiality. He did not reveal names of suspected suicides to insurance companies, though Zellner did recommend that the insurance industry drop double indemnity (payment of twice the person's life insurance benefits in the event of accidental death) in the future.

Zellner's study raised an additional ethical issue: the possibility of harm to those who were interviewed. Subjects were asked if the deceased had "talked about suicide" and if they had spoken of how "bad or useless" they were. Could these questions have led people to guess the true intentions of the researcher? Perhaps, but according to Zellner, none of the informants voiced such suspicions. More seriously, might the study have caused the

Are some people who die in single-occupant car crashes actually suicides? One sociological study of possible "autocides" concluded that at least 12 percent of such accident victims had in fact committed suicide. But the study also raised some ethical questions concerning the right to know and the right to privacy.

bereaved to *suspect* suicide—when before the survey they had accepted the deaths as accidental? Again, there is no evidence to suggest this, but we cannot be sure.

Given our uncertainty about this last question, was the research justified? Was Zellner taking too big a risk in asking the friends and families if the deceased victims had spoken of suicide before their death? Does the right to know outweigh the right to privacy in this type of situation? And who has the right to make such a judgment? In practice, as in Zellner's study, it is the *researcher,* not the subjects of inquiry, who makes the critical ethical decisions. Therefore, sociologists and other investigators bear the responsibility for establishing clear and sensitive boundaries for ethical scientific investigation.

Preserving Confidentiality

Like journalists, sociologists occasionally find themselves subject to questions from law enforcement authorities or to legal threats because of knowledge they have gained in conducting research and maintaining confidentiality. This situation raises profound ethical questions.

In 1994, Russel Ogden was a graduate student at Simon Fraser University (SFU) in British Columbia. In his research, Ogden conducted interviews with people involved in assisted suicide or euthanasia among people with AIDS. A newspaper report about the study came to the attention of the Vancouver coroner, who was already holding an inquest into the death of an "unknown female." Ogden's thesis reported that two research participants had knowledge about her death. The coroner subpoenaed Ogden to identify his sources, but he cited a promise of "absolute confidentiality" and refused to name them. This promise had been authorized by SFU's Research Ethics Board.

The coroner initially found Ogden to be in contempt of court but later accepted a common law argument that the communications between Ogden and his participants were privileged. In doing so, the coroner released Ogden from "any stain or suggestion of contempt." But Ogden's battle in coroner's court was fought without the support of his university. He sued SFU, unsuccessfully, to recover his legal costs. However, the judge condemned SFU for failing to protect academic freedom and urged the university to remedy the situation. SFU's president responded with a written apology to Ogden, compensation for legal costs and lost wages, and a guarantee that the university would assist "any researchers who find themselves in the position of having to challenge a subpoena" (Lowman and Palys 2000).

This case points to the delicate balance researchers and sponsoring institutions must maintain between the value of research and the confidentiality of the subjects, and the threat of litigation.

Neutrality and Politics in Research

The ethical considerations of sociologists lie not only in the methods they use but also in the way they interpret results. Max Weber ([1904] 1949) recognized that personal values would influence the questions that sociologists select for research. In his view, that was perfectly acceptable, but under no conditions could a researcher allow his or her personal feelings to influence the *interpretation* of data. In Weber's phrase, sociologists must practise ***value neutrality*** in their research.

As part of this neutrality, investigators have an ethical obligation to accept research findings even when the data run counter to their own personal views, to theoretically based explanations, or to widely accepted beliefs. For example, Émile Durkheim challenged popular conceptions when he reported that social (rather than supernatural) forces were an important factor in suicide.

p. 8

Some sociologists believe that neutrality is impossible. At the same time, Weber's insistence on value-free sociology may lead the public to accept sociological conclusions without exploring the biases of the researchers. As we have seen, Weber was quite clear that sociologists may bring values to their subject matter. In his view, however, they must not confuse their own values with the social reality under study (Bendix 1968).

Let's consider what might happen when researchers bring their own biases to the investigation. A person investigating the impact of intercollegiate sports on alumni contributions, for example, may focus only on the highly visible revenue-generating sports of football and basketball and neglect the so-called minor sports, such as tennis or soccer, which are more likely to involve female athletes. Despite the work of Dorothy Smith and Margrit Eichler, sociologists still need to be reminded that the discipline often fails to adequately consider *all* people's social behaviour.

p. 15

Theoretical Perspectives and Research Methods

The research methods that researches choose to employ in their study of social phenomena are informed and guided by the theoretical perspectives they hold. Functionalist thinkers, for example, tend to value neutrality and objectivity, thus leaning toward quantitative methods, such as surveys, experiments, and secondary data analysis. Their focus is on uncovering the truth or the facts about the relationships among specified variables, according to the researchers' interpretation of the data. In response to this approach, conflict thinkers, such as Alvin Gouldner (1970) and others, have suggested that sociologists may use objectivity as a sacred justification for remaining uncritical of the dominant institutions and ruling classes of society. Unlike functionalists, conflict thinkers might employ historical analysis or engage in field research to uncover the hidden economic and political interests of a society. Again, unlike functionalists, conflict thinkers view their research as a basis for action and change.

Such research methods as ethnography and participant observation may be guided by interactionist perspectives, in which the goal of the researcher is to describe the meanings and to understand the definitions that people give to their own situations. As for feminist perspectives, no *one* research method is employed by feminist researchers, just as no *one* feminist theory exists. However, feminist researchers, like conflict thinkers, are guided by the common desire to bring about action or change through their research.

Feminist sociologist Shulamit Reinharz (1992) has argued that sociological research should not only be inclusive but should also be open to bringing about social change and drawing on relevant research by nonsociologists. Reinharz maintains that research should always analyze whether women's unequal social status has affected the study in any way. For example, a researcher might broaden the study of the impact of family income on education participation to consider the implications of participation according to gender, class, and race. The issue of the importance of value neutrality, which is often emphasized in mainstream or functional sociology, can be contrasted to feminist research, in which researchers integrate their own experiences into the research process. Reinharz (1992:262) contends that feminist researchers may use their own experiences to inform their research questions and to guide the research process; at the same time, however, feminist researchers are discussing the ways in which to "work out the tension between objectivity and subjectivity."

Computers have tremendously extended the range and capability of sociological research, from allowing large amounts of data to be stored and analyzed to facilitating communication with other researchers via Web sites, newsgroups, and email.

TECHNOLOGY AND SOCIOLOGICAL RESEARCH

Advances in technology have affected all aspects of life, and sociological research is no exception. The increased speed and capacity of computers enable sociologists to handle larger and larger sets of data. In the recent past, only people with grants or major institutional support could easily work with census data. Now anyone with a desktop computer and modem can access census information to learn more about social behaviour. Moreover, data from other countries concerning crime statistics and health care are sometimes as available as information from Canada.

Researchers usually rely on computers to deal with quantitative data, that is, numerical measures, but electronic technology is also assisting us with qualitative data, such as information obtained in observation research. Numerous software programs, such as Ethnograph and NUD*IST, allow the researcher not only to record observations, like a word processing program does, but also to identify common behavioural patterns or similar concerns expressed in interviews. For example, after observing students in a cafeteria over several weeks and putting your observations into the computer, you could then group all your observations related to certain variables, such as "club" or "study group."

The Internet affords an excellent opportunity to communicate with fellow researchers as well as to locate useful information on social issues posted on Web sites. It would be impossible to calculate all the sociological postings on Internet mailing lists or World Wide Web sites. Of course, you need to apply the same critical scrutiny to Internet material that you would use on any printed resource.

How useful is the Internet for conducting survey research? That's unclear as yet. It is relatively easy to send out or post on an electronic bulletin board a questionnaire and solicit responses. It is an inexpensive way to reach large numbers of potential respondents and get a quick return of responses. However, there are some obvious dilemmas. How do you protect a respondent's anonymity? Second, how do you define the potential audience? Even if you know to whom you sent the questionnaire, the respondents may forward it on to others.

Web-based surveys are still in their early stages. Even so, the initial results are promising. For example, InterSurvey has created a pool of Internet respondents, initially selected by telephone to be a diverse and representative sample. Using similar methods to locate 50 000 adult respondents in 33 nations, the National Geographic Society conducted an online survey that focused on migration and regional culture. Social scientists are closely monitoring these new approaches to gauge how they might revolutionize one type of research design (Bainbridge 1999; Morin 2000b).

This new technology is exciting, but there is one basic limitation to the methodology: Internet surveying works only with those who are online, who have access to the Internet. For some market researchers, such a limitation is acceptable. For example, if you were interested in the willingness of Internet users to order books or make travel reservations online, limiting the sample population to those already online makes sense. However, if you were surveying the general public about plans to buy a computer in the coming year or about their views on a particular candidate, your online research would need to be supplemented by more traditional sampling procedures, such as mailed questionnaires.

Sociological research relies on a number of tools—from observation research and use of existing sources of data to considering how the latest technology can help inform the sociological imagination. We turn now to a research study that used a survey of the general population to learn more about a particular social behaviour—human sexuality.

SOCIAL POLICY AND SOCIOLOGICAL RESEARCH: Studying Human Sexuality

The Issue

The Kaiser Family Foundation conducts a study of sexual content on American television every two years. The latest report, released in 2001, shows that more than two-thirds of all shows on TV include some sexual content, up from about half of all shows two years earlier (Figure 2-4). The study also reported that situation comedies topped the list in terms of type of television program with sexual content: 84 percent of situation comedies contained sexual content. Only one in ten programs contained references to safe sex or the possible risks of sexual behaviour. Media representations of sexual behaviour are important because surveys of teens and young adults tell us that television is a top source of information and ideas about sex for them; it has more influence than schools, parents, or peers (Kunkel et al. 2001). A recent study on Canadian broadcasting, tabled in the House of Commons in June 2003, demonstrated that the vast majority of English-language programs viewed by Canadians (aged two and older) during prime time are "foreign" (meaning, for the most part, American). Thus, it could be extrapolated that Canadians exposure to sexual content on television would be roughly equivalent to that of their American neighbours.

FIGURE 2-4

Percentage of Television Shows That Contain Sexual Content

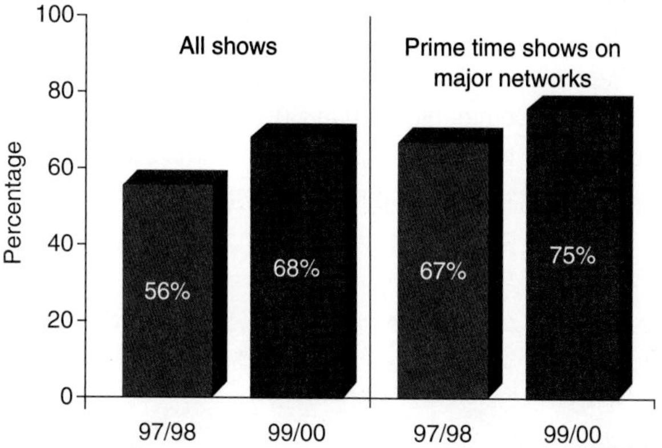

Source: Kaiser Family Foundation 2001:2.

In this age of sexually transmitted diseases, it is important to increase our understanding of human sexuality. However, it can be a difficult topic to research because of all the preconceptions, myths, and beliefs that may accompany the subject of sexuality. How can we carry out research of what might be considered a controversial and personal topic?

The Setting

Perhaps the most comprehensive study of sexual behaviour was the famous two-volume Kinsey Report prepared in the 1940s (Kinsey, Pomeroy, and Martin 1948; Kinsey, Pomeroy, and Gebhard 1953). Although the Kinsey Report is still widely quoted, the volunteers interviewed for the report were not representative of the adult population. The Kinsey Report revealed the wide range of sexual behaviours among Americans, including that 70 percent of American men had patronized prostitutes, that 92 percent of men and 58 percent of women had masturbated, and that 60 percent of men had had some form of homosexual experience before adulthood (A. Nelson and Fleras 1998). Also revealed in the report was the greater tendency for women to be bisexual (having sexual relations with both male and female partners) than exclusively homosexual.

In Canada, statistics on Canadians' sexual behaviour are collected by Statistics Canada, the primary statistical information source of the Canadian government and a major employer of sociologists. The agency's mandate is to collect, analyze, and disseminate statistical information on a broad range of subjects, including employment, health, education, agriculture, and sexual behaviour. Much of the statistical information collected by Statistics Canada about the sex lives of Canadians comes from the National Public Health Survey, the Canadian Community Health Survey, and the Canadian census. For instance, Table 2.2 shows that about 60 percent of young Canadian females who did not use a condom during their last act of sexual intercourse were sexually active by age 13 (Statistics Canada 2005a). The table illustrates that as the age of becoming sexually active increases, the percentage of condom use during last sexual encounter also increases.

Sociological Insights

The controversy surrounding research on human sexual behaviour raises the issue of value neutrality. And this becomes especially delicate when we consider the relationship of sociology to the government. The federal government has become the major source of funding for sociological research. Yet Max Weber urged that sociology remain an autonomous discipline and not become unduly influenced by any one segment of society. According to his ideal of value neutrality, sociologists must remain free to reveal information that is embarrassing to government or, for that matter, is supportive of government institutions. Thus, researchers investigating a prison riot must be ready to examine objectively not only the behaviour of inmates but also the conduct of prison officials before and during the riot.

Conflict theorists and feminists, among others, are critical of some research that claims to be objective. In turn, their research is occasionally criticized for not sufficiently addressing Weber's concern for value neutrality. In any case, maintaining objectivity may be difficult if sociologists fear that findings critical of government institutions will jeopardize their chances of obtaining federal support for new research projects.

In the United States, although the American Sociological Association's code of ethics expects sociologists to disclose all funding sources, the code does not address the issue of whether sociologists who accept funding from a particular agency may also accept their perspective on what needs to be studied. Lewis Coser

Table 2-2 Percentage of Young Canadian Females Who Had Sexual Intercourse without a Condom, According to Age of First Sexual Activity

Age at Which Became Sexually Active	Percentage Not Using Condom during Last Sexual Intercourse
13	60
14–17	46
20–24	37

Source: Statistics Canada 2005a.

(1956:27) has argued that as sociologists in the United States have increasingly turned from basic sociological research to research with application for government agencies and the private sector, "they have relinquished to a large extent the freedom to choose their own problems, substituting the problems of their clients for those which might have interested them on purely theoretical grounds." Viewed in this light, the importance of government funding for sociological studies raises troubling questions for those who cherish Weber's ideal of value neutrality in research. In Canada, the code of ethics set out by the Canadian Sociology and Anthropology Association (CSAA) states:

> Researchers must guard against the uncritical promotion of research, which in design, execution, or results, furthers the power of states, corporations, churches, or other institutions, over the lives and cultures of research subjects. . . . Researchers should be sensitive to the possible exploitation of individuals and groups.

In the funding of sociological research, the CSAA's code of ethics directly warns its members to guard against the promotion of research that furthers the power of a corporation, a government, or a church over the lives of those being studied. In addition, the code prompts sociologists to be mindful of the implications of their research and the potential for exploitation of particular individuals and groups. As we'll see in the next section, applied sociological research on human sexuality has run into barriers constructed by government funding agencies.

Policy Initiatives

In Canada, there has been willingness to research and openness toward research on such topics as same-sex relationships, condom use among teens, bisexuality, and number of sexual partners, as demonstrated by the vast number and variety of reports published by Statistics Canada. The 2001 census results, for example, were the first to provide data on same-sex relationships. It is a different story in the United States, where conservative voices in government have made government-sponsored research on the topic of sexual behaviour more difficult.

In 1987 the federal National Institute of Child Health and Human Development sought proposals for a national survey of sexual behaviour. Sociologists responded with various proposals that a review panel of scientists approved for funding. However, in 1991, led by Senator Jesse Helms and other conservatives, the U.S. Senate voted 66–34 to forbid funding any survey on adult sexual practices. Helms appealed to popular fears by arguing that such surveys of sexual behaviour were intended to "legitimize homosexual lifestyles" and to support "sexual decadence." Two years earlier, a similar debate in Great Britain had led to the denial of government funding for a national sex survey (A. Johnson et al. 1994; Laumann, Gagnon, and Michael 1994a:36).

Despite the vote by the U.S. Senate, sociologists Edward Laumann, John Gagnon, Stuart Michaels, and Robert Michael developed the National Health and Social Life Survey (NHSLS) to better understand the sexual practices of adults in the United States. The researchers raised $1.6 million of *private* funding to make their study possible (Laumann et al. 1994a, 1994b).

The researchers made great efforts to ensure privacy during the NHSLS interviews, as well as confidentiality of responses and security in maintaining data files. Perhaps because of this careful effort, the interviewers did not typically experience problems getting responses, even though they were asking people about their sexual behaviour. All interviews were conducted in person, although there was also a confidential form that included questions about such sensitive subjects as family income and masturbation. The researchers used several techniques to test the accuracy of subjects' responses, such as asking redundant questions at different times in different ways during the 90-minute interview. These careful procedures helped establish the validity of the NHSLS findings.

Today, research on human sexuality is not the only target of policymakers. Congress began in 1995 considering passage of the Family Privacy Protection Act, which would force all federally funded researchers to obtain written consent from parents before surveying young people on such issues as drug use, antisocial behaviour, and emotional difficulties, as well as sexual behaviour. Researchers around the country suggest that this legal requirement will make it impossible to survey representative samples of young people. They note that when parents are asked to return consent forms, only about half do so, even though no more than 1 percent to 2 percent actually object to the survey. Moreover, the additional effort required to get all the forms returned raises research costs by 25-fold (Elias 1996; Levine 2001).

Despite the political battles, the authors of the NHSLS believe that their research was important. These researchers argue that using data from their survey allows us to more easily address such public policy issues as AIDS, sexual harassment, rape, welfare reform, sex discrimination, abortion, teenage pregnancy, and family planning. Moreover, the research findings help to counter some "commonsense" notions. For instance, contrary to the popular belief that women regularly use abortion for birth control and that poor teens are the most likely socioeconomic group to have abortions, the researchers found that three-fourths of all abortions are the *first* for the woman and that well-educated and affluent women are more likely to have abortions than are poor teens (Sweet 2001).

The NHSLS researchers have lately moved on to other topics. One is studying adolescent behaviour in general and another is studying sexuality in China and Chicago, adding health care, jealousy, and violence to the mix of issues. The researchers hope to update the NHSLS data before too much time passes, especially now that the environment for conducting research on human sexuality has improved, and people have proved that they are more comfortable talking about sexual issues. As one of the researchers noted, "People aren't as uptight about sex as their politicians and their funders. That's good news" (Sweet 2001:13).

Applying Theory

1. When studying human sexuality, what theoretical perspective(s) would advocate high levels of objectivity and neutrality?
2. Would you be willing to participate in a study related to sexuality if you were asked?
3. For feminist researchers, what might be a major goal or purpose of any study on human sexuality?

CHAPTER RESOURCES

Summary

Sociologists are committed to the use of the scientific method in their research efforts. In this chapter, we examined the basic principles of the scientific method and study various techniques used by sociologists in conducting research.

1. There are five basic steps in the ***scientific method:*** defining the problem, reviewing the literature, formulating the hypothesis, selecting the research design and then collecting and analyzing data, and developing the conclusion.
2. Whenever researchers want to study abstract concepts, such as intelligence or prejudice, they must develop workable ***operational definitions.***
3. A ***hypothesis*** usually states a possible relationship between two or more variables.
4. By using a ***sample,*** sociologists avoid having to test everyone in a population.
5. According to the scientific method, research results must possess both ***validity*** and ***reliability.***
6. The two principal forms of ***survey*** research are the ***interview*** and the ***questionnaire.***
7. ***Qualitative research,*** which may include ***observation*** and in-depth interviews, focuses on small groups and communities.
8. When sociologists want to study a cause-and-effect relationship, they may conduct an ***experiment.***
9. Sociologists also make use of existing sources as in ***secondary analysis*** and ***content analysis.***
10. The ***code of ethics*** of the Canadian Sociology and Anthropology Association calls for objectivity and integrity in research, respect for the subject's privacy, and confidentiality.
11. Max Weber urged sociologists to practise ***value neutrality*** in their research by ensuring that their personal feelings do not influence the interpretation of data.
12. Technology today plays an important role in sociological research, whether it be a computer database or information from the Internet.
13. In Canada, much of the information about the sex lives of Canadians is collected by Statistics Canada using national public health surveys and community health surveys.

Critical Thinking Questions

1. Suppose that your sociology instructor has asked you to do a study of the issues facing Canadians today. Which research technique would you find most useful? How would you use that approach to complete your assignment?
2. Do you think you or any sociologist can maintain value neutrality while studying any group of people, such as younger Canadians?
3. Why is it important for sociologists to have a code of ethics?
4. What research method(s) do you think would produce the best results when studying the views and attitudes of the under-30 age group? Why?

Key Terms

Causal logic The relationship between a condition or variable and a particular consequence, with one event leading to the other. (page 28)

Code of ethics The standards of acceptable behaviour developed by and for members of a profession. (37)

Content analysis The systematic coding and objective recording of data, guided by some rationale. (37)

Control group Subjects in an experiment who are not introduced to the independent variable by the researcher. (35)

Control variable A factor held constant to test the relative impact of an independent variable. (31)

Correlation A relationship between two variables whereby a change in one coincides with a change in the other. (28)

Dependent variable The variable in a causal relationship that is subject to the influence of another variable. (28)

Ethnography The study of an entire social setting through extended systematic observation. (33)

Experiment An artificially created situation that allows the researcher to manipulate variables. (35)

Experimental group Subjects in an experiment who are exposed to an independent variable introduced by a researcher. (35)

Hawthorne effect The unintended influence that observers or experiments can have on their subjects. (36)

Hypothesis A speculative statement about the relationship between two or more variables. (28)

Independent variable The variable in a causal relationship that causes or influences a change in a second variable. (28)

Interview A face-to-face or telephone questioning of a respondent to obtain desired information. (32)

Observation A research technique in which an investigator collects information through direct participation or by closely watching a group or community. (33)

Operational definition An explanation of an abstract concept that is specific enough to allow a researcher to assess the concept. (27)

Qualitative research Research that relies on what is seen in field or naturalistic settings more than on statistical data. (33)

Quantitative research Research that collects and reports data primarily in numerical form. (33)

Questionnaire A printed or written form used to obtain desired information from a respondent. (32)

Random sample A sample for which every member of the entire population has the same chance of being selected. (29)

Reliability The extent to which a measure provides consistent results. (29)

Research design A detailed plan or method for obtaining data scientifically. (31)

Sample A selection from a larger population that is statistically representative of that population. (28)

Scientific method A systematic, organized series of steps that ensures maximum objectivity and consistency in researching a problem. (26)

Secondary analysis A variety of research techniques that make use of previously existing and publicly accessible information and data. (36)

Survey A study, generally in the form of interviews or questionnaires, that provides researchers with information concerning how people think and act. (32)

Validity The degree to which a scale or measure truly reflects the phenomenon under study. (29)

Value neutrality Objectivity of sociologists in the interpretation of data. (39)

Variable A measurable trait or characteristic that is subject to change under different conditions. (28)

Additional Readings

Babbie, Earl. 2003. *The Practice of Social Research*, 10th ed. Belmont, CA: Wadsworth. Covers inquiry and social research, the structuring of inquiry, types of observation, and analysis of data in qualitative and quantitative research methods.

Canadian Sociology and Anthropology Association. *Canadian Review of Sociology and Anthropology*. Montreal: CSAA. Since its inception in 1964, the *Review* has provided peer-reviewed articles and critiques on topics of sociology and anthropology. This journal provides an excellent scholarly source for research about social issues in Canada.

Ericksen, Julia A. 1999. *Kiss and Tell: Surveying Sex in the Twentieth Century*. Cambridge, MA: Harvard University Press. Evaluates the methodology of the hundreds of surveys of human sexuality conducted by sociologists and other social scientists.

Online Learning Centre

Visit the *Sociology: A Brief Introduction* Online Learning Centre at www.mcgrawhill.ca/college/schaefer to access quizzes, interactive exercises, video clips, and other research and study tools related to this chapter.

Reel Society Interactive Movie CD-ROM 2.0

Reel Society 2.0 can be used to spark discussion about the following topics from this chapter:

- The scientific method
- Neutrality and politics in research

chapter 3

CULTURE

One of many comic book stalls that line the streets near a railroad station in Bombay, India. At first glance, the comic books may look different from those in North America, but closer inspection reveals some common themes—adventure, romance, beauty, and crime.

Nacirema culture is characterized by a highly developed market economy which has evolved in a rich natural habitat. While much of the people's time is devoted to economic pursuits, a large part of the fruits of these labors and a considerable portion of the day are spent in ritual activity. The focus of this activity is the human body, the appearance and health of which loom as a dominant concern in the ethos of the people. While such concern is certainly not unusual, its ceremonial aspects and associated philosophy are unique.

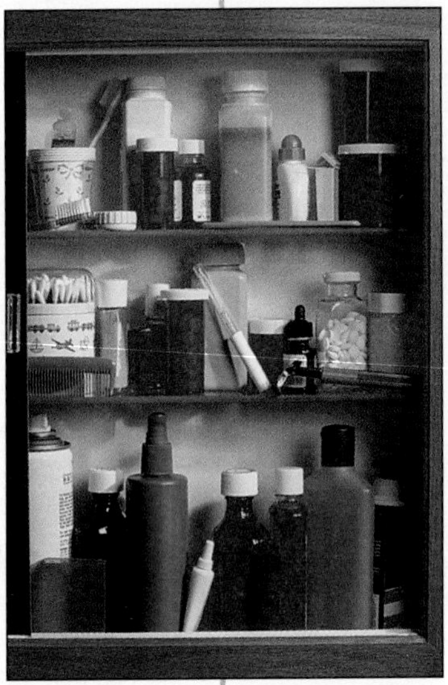

The fundamental belief underlying the whole system appears to be that the human body is ugly and that its natural tendency is to debility and disease. Incarcerated in such a body, man's only hope is to avert these characteristics through the use of the powerful influences of ritual and ceremony. Every household has one or more shrines devoted to this purpose. The more powerful individuals in this society have several shrines in their houses, and, in fact, the opulence of a house is often referred to in terms of the number of such ritual centers it possesses. . . .

While each family has at least one such shrine, the rituals associated with it are not family ceremonies but are private and secret. The rites are normally only discussed with children, and then only during the period when they are being initiated into these mysteries. I was able, however, to establish sufficient rapport with the natives to examine these shrines and to have the rituals described to me.

The focal point of the shrine is a box or chest which is built into the wall. In this chest are kept the many charms and magical potions without which no native believes he could live. These preparations are secured from a variety of specialized practitioners. The most powerful of these are the medicine men, whose assistance must be rewarded with substantial gifts. However, the medicine men do not provide the curative potions for their clients, but decide what the ingredients should be and then write them down in an ancient and secret language. This writing is understood only by the medicine men and by the herbalists who, for another gift, provide the required charm. *(Miner 1956)* ■

Anthropologist Horace Miner cast his observant eyes on the intriguing behaviour of the Nacirema. If we look a bit closer, however, some aspects of this culture may seem familiar, for what Miner is describing is actually the culture of the United States ("Nacirema" is "American" spelled backward). The "shrine" is the bathroom, and we are correctly informed that in this culture a measure of wealth is often how many bathrooms are in a person's house. The bathroom rituals make use of charms and magical potions (beauty products and prescription drugs) obtained from specialized practitioners (such as hair stylists), herbalists (pharmacists), and medicine men (physicians). Using our sociological imagination we could update the Nacirema "shrine" by describing blow-dryers, mint-flavoured dental floss, electric toothbrushes, and hair gel.

We begin to appreciate how to understand behaviour when we step back and examine it thoughtfully, objectively—whether it is "Nacirema" culture or another one. Take the case of Fiji, an island in the Pacific. A recent study showed that for the first time eating disorders were showing up among the young people there. This was a society where, traditionally, "you've gained weight" was a compliment and "your legs are skinny" was a major insult. Having a robust, nicely rounded body was the expectation for both men and women. What happened to change this cultural ideal? With the introduction of cable television in 1995, many Fiji islanders, especially girls, have come to want to look like the thin-waisted stars of *Desperate Housewives* and *The O.C.*, not their full-bodied mothers and aunts. By understanding life in Fiji, we can also come to understand our own society much better (Becker 1995; Becker and Burwell 1999).

The study of culture is basic to sociology. In this chapter we will examine the meaning of culture and society as well as the development of culture from its roots in the prehistoric human experience to the technological advances of today. The major aspects of culture—including language, norms, sanctions, and values—will be defined and explored. We will see how cultures develop a dominant ideology, and how functionalist, conflict, interactionist, and feminist theorists view culture. The discussion will focus both on general cultural practices found in all societies and on the wide variations that can distinguish one society from another. The social policy section will look at the conflicts in cultural values that underlie current debates about multiculturalism. ■

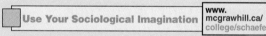

Use Your Sociological Imagination www.mcgrawhill.ca/college/schaefer

What do you think the contents of your "shrine" symbolize? Who benefits from a culture preoccupied with filling up the shrine with "charms and magical potions"?

CULTURE AND SOCIETY

Culture is the totality of learned, socially transmitted customs, knowledge, material objects, and behaviour. It includes the ideas, values, customs, and artifacts (for example, CDs, comic books, and birth control devices) of groups of people. Patriotic attachment to the game of hockey in Canada is an aspect of culture, as is national addiction to the tango in Argentina.

Sometimes people refer to a particular person as "very cultured" or to a city as having "lots of culture." That use of the term *culture* is different from our use in this textbook. In sociological terms, *culture* does not refer solely to the fine arts and refined intellectual taste. It consists of all objects and ideas within a society, including ice cream cones, rock music, and slang words. Sociologists consider both a portrait by Rembrandt and a portrait by a billboard painter to be aspects of a culture. A tribe that cultivates soil by hand has just as much of a culture as a people that relies on computer-operated machinery. Each people has a distinctive culture with its own characteristic ways of gathering and preparing food, constructing homes, structuring the family, and promoting standards of right and wrong.

Sharing a similar culture helps to define the group or society to which we belong. A fairly large number of people are said to constitute a ***society*** when they live in the same territory, are relatively independent of people outside their area, and participate in a common culture. Mexico City is more populous than many nations of the world, yet sociologists do not consider it a society in its own right. Rather, it is seen as part of—and dependent on—the larger society of Mexico.

A society is the largest form of human group. It consists of people who share a common heritage and culture. Members of the society learn this culture and transmit it from one generation to the next. They even preserve their distinctive culture through literature, art, video recordings, and other means of expression. If it were not for the social transmission of culture, each generation would have to reinvent television, not to mention the wheel.

Having a common culture also simplifies many day-to-day interactions. For example, when you buy an airline ticket, you know you don't have to bring along hundreds of dollars in cash. You can pay with a credit card. When you are part of a society, there are many small (as well as more important) cultural patterns that you take for granted. You assume that theatres will provide seats for the audience, that physicians will not disclose confidential information, and that parents will be careful when crossing the street with young children. All these assumptions reflect the basic values, beliefs, and customs of the culture of Canada.

Language is a critical element of culture that sets humans apart from other species. Members of a society generally share a common language, which facilitates day-to-day exchanges with others. When you ask a hardware store clerk for a flashlight, you don't need to draw a picture of the instrument. You share the same cultural term for a small, battery-operated, portable light. However, if you were in Britain and needed this item, you would have to ask for an "electric torch." Of course, even within the same society, a term can have a number of different meanings. In Canada, *grass* signifies both a plant eaten by grazing animals and an intoxicating drug.

DEVELOPMENT OF CULTURE AROUND THE WORLD

We've come a long way from our prehistoric heritage. We can transmit an entire book around the world via the Internet, we can clone cells, and we can prolong lives through organ transplants. The human species has produced such achievements as the ragtime compositions of Scott Joplin, the poetry of Emily Dickinson, the paintings of Vincent Van Gogh, the novels of Jane Austen, and the films of Akira Kurosawa. We can peer into the outermost reaches of the universe, and we can analyze our innermost feelings. In all these ways, we are remarkably different from other species of the animal kingdom.

The process of expanding culture has been under way for thousands of years. The first archaeological evidence of humanlike primates places our ancestors back many millions of years. About 700 000 years ago, people built hearths to harness fire. Archaeologists have uncovered tools that date back about 100 000 years. From 35 000 years ago we have evidence of paintings, jewellery, and statues. By that time, marriages, births, and deaths had already developed elaborate ceremonies (M. Harris 1997; Haviland 1999).

Tracing the development of culture is not easy. Archaeologists cannot "dig up" weddings, laws, or governments, but they are able to locate items that point to the emergence of cultural traditions. Our early ancestors were primates that had characteristics of human beings. These curious and communicative creatures made important advances in the use of tools. Recent studies of chimpanzees in the wild have revealed that they frequently use sticks and other natural objects in ways learned from other members of the group. However, unlike chimpanzees, our ancestors gradually made tools from increasingly durable materials. As a result, the items could be reused and later refined into more effective implements.

Cultural Universals

Despite their differences, all societies have developed certain common practices and beliefs, known as ***cultural universals.*** Many cultural universals are, in fact, adaptations to meet essential human needs, such as people's need for food, shelter, and clothing. Anthropologist George Murdock (1945:124) compiled a list of cultural

Cooking is a cultural universal. Both the Cambodian woman and the Moroccan women in these photos show a preference for food grilled on skewers.

universals. Some of these include athletic sports, cooking, funeral ceremonies, medicine, and sexual restrictions.

The cultural practices listed by Murdock may be universal, but the manner in which they are expressed varies from culture to culture. For example, one society may let its members choose their own marriage partners. Another may encourage marriages arranged by the parents.

Not only does the expression of cultural universals vary from one society to another, but it also may change dramatically over time within a society. Thus, the most popular styles of dancing in North America today are sure to be different from the styles dominant in the 1950s or the 1970s. Each generation, and each year for that matter, most human cultures change and expand through the processes of innovation and diffusion.

Innovation

The process of introducing an idea or object that is new to a culture is known as ***innovation***. Innovation interests sociologists because of the social consequences that introducing something new can have in any society. There are two forms of innovation: discovery and invention. A ***discovery*** involves making known or sharing the existence of an aspect of reality. The finding of the DNA molecule and the identification of a new moon of Saturn are both acts of discovery. A significant factor in the process of discovery is the sharing of newfound knowledge with others. By contrast, an ***invention*** results when existing cultural items are combined into a form that did not exist before. The bow and arrow, the automobile, and the television are all examples of inventions, as are Protestantism and democracy.

Diffusion and Technology

You don't have to sample gourmet food to eat "foreign" foods. Breakfast cereal comes originally from Germany, candy from the Netherlands, and chewing gum from Mexico. The United States has also "exported" foods to other lands. Residents of many nations enjoy pizza, which was popularized in the United States. However, in Japan they add squid, in Australia it is eaten with pineapple, and in England people like kernels of corn with the cheese.

Just as a culture does not always discover or invent its foods, it may also adopt ideas, technology, and customs from other cultures. Sociologists use the term ***diffusion*** to refer to the process by which a cultural item is spread from group to group or society to society. Diffusion can occur through a variety of means, among them exploration, military conquest, missionary work, the influence of the mass media, tourism, and the Internet.

Early in human history, culture changed rather slowly through discovery. Then, as the number of discoveries in a culture increased, inventions became possible. The more inventions there were, the more rapidly additional inventions could be created. In addition, as diverse cultures came into contact with one another, they could each take advantage of the other's innovations. Thus, when people in Canada read a newspaper, we look at characters invented by the ancient Semites, printed by a process invented in Germany, on a material invented in China (Linton 1936).

Citizens of nations tend to feel a loss of identity when they accept culture from outside. People throughout the world decry American exports, from films to language to Bart Simpson. Movies produced in the United States account for 65 percent of the global box office.

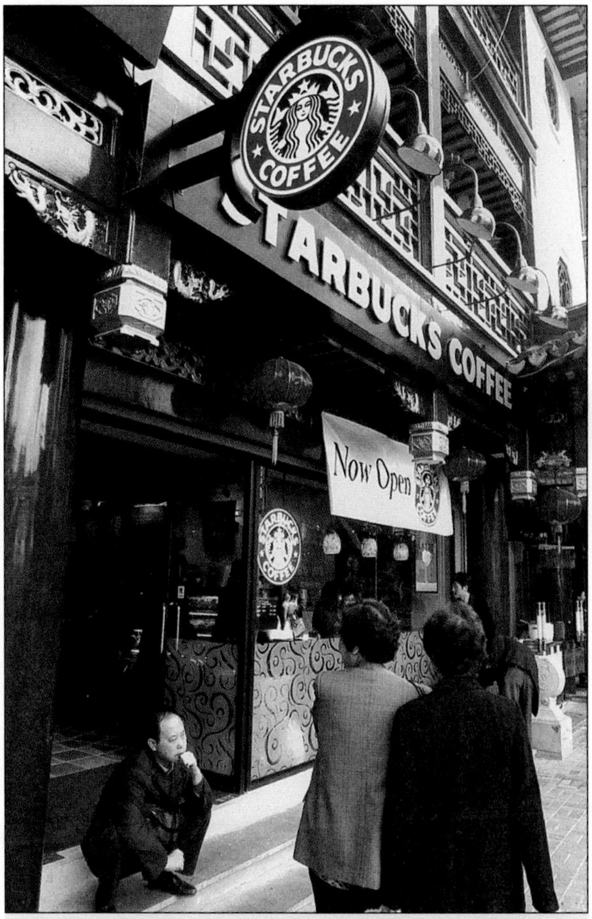

When Shanghai residents meet at Starbucks for coffee, it is in a traditional-style building, but the coffee is the same as you can order in Seattle. The spread of Starbucks to China is an example of cultural diffusion.

Magazines as diverse as *Cosmopolitan* and *Reader's Digest* sell two issues abroad for every one they sell in the United States. *The X-Files* airs in 60 countries. These examples of canned culture all facilitate the diffusion of cultural practices (Farhi and Rosenfeld 1998).

Many societies try to protect themselves from the invasion of too much culture from other countries, especially the economically dominant United States. The Canadian government, for example, requires that 35 percent of a station's daytime radio programming be Canadian songs or artists (see Figure 3-1). In Brazil, a toy manufacturer has eclipsed Barbie's popularity by designing a doll named Susi that looks more like Brazilian girls. Susi has a slightly smaller chest, much wider thighs, and darker skin than Barbie. Her wardrobe includes the skimpy bikinis favoured on Brazilian beaches as well as a soccer shirt honouring the Brazilian team. According to the toy company's marketing director, "we wanted Susi to be more Latin, more voluptuous. We Latins appreciate those attributes." Brazilians seem to agree: Before Christmas in 1999, five Susi dolls were sold for every two Barbies (DePalma 1999; Downie 2000).

Technology in its many forms has now increased the speed by which aspects of culture are shared and has broadened the distribution of cultural elements. Sociologist Gerhard Lenski has defined ***technology*** as "information about how to use the material resources of the environment to satisfy human needs and desires" (Nolan and Lenski 1999:41). Today's technological developments no longer have to await publication in journals with limited circulation. Press conferences, often simultaneously carried on the Internet, now trumpet new developments.

Technology not only accelerates the diffusion of scientific innovations but also transmits culture. Later, in Chapter 16, we will discuss the concern in many parts of the world that the English language and North American culture dominate the Internet and World Wide Web. Control, or at least dominance, of technology influences the direction of diffusion of culture. Web sites abound with the most superficial aspects of Canadian and American culture but little information about the pressing issues faced by citizens of other nations. People all over the world find it easier to visit electronic chat rooms about daytime television soaps like *All My Children* than to learn about their own government's policies on day care or infant nutrition programs.

Sociologist William F. Ogburn (1922) made a useful distinction between the elements of material and nonmaterial culture. ***Material culture*** refers to the physical or technological aspects of our daily lives, including food items, houses, factories, and raw materials. ***Nonmaterial culture*** refers to ways of using material objects and to customs, beliefs, philosophies, governments, and patterns of communication. Generally, the nonmaterial

FIGURE 3-1

What Is Canadian?

Canadians try to ward off American influence by controlling what is played on the radio. The government requires that 35 percent of a station's programming in the daytime be Canadian. But what is Canadian? A complicated set of rules gives points based on whether the artist, the composer, the lyricist, or the production is Canadian. A song that earns two points meets the government requirements. Canadian Celine Dion singing "My Heart Will Go On" would not be classified as Canadian.

Celine Dion		Lenny Kravitz
Canadian	**Nationality**	Not Canadian
"My Heart Will Go On"	**Song**	"American Woman"
Not Canadian	**Lyricist**	**Canadian**
Not Canadian	**Composer**	**Canadian**
1 point*		2 points*

**At least two points are required for music to be considered Canadian.*

Source: DePalma 1999.

culture is more resistant to change than the material culture. Consequently, Ogburn introduced the term ***culture lag*** to refer to the period of maladjustment when the nonmaterial culture is still adapting to new material conditions. For example, the ethics of using the Internet, particularly privacy and censorship issues, have not yet caught up with the explosion in Internet use and technology. Technology has a globalizing effect as diverse cultures become interconnected through the material and nonmaterial elements of its use. Technological applications, such as the Internet, provide a shared element of material culture, while the behaviours employed and attitudes acquired while participating in an online chat room contribute to shared nonmaterial culture.

Diffusion can involve a single word, like "cyber," or an entirely new orientation toward living, which may be transmitted through advances in electronic communication. Sociologist George Ritzer (1995b) coined the term "McDonaldization of society" to describe how the principles of fast-food restaurants developed in the United States have come to dominate more and more sectors of societies throughout the world. For example, hair salons and medical clinics now take walk-in appointments. In Hong Kong, sex selection clinics offer a menu of items—from fertility enhancement to methods of increasing the likelihood of producing a child of the desired sex. Religious groups—from evangelical preachers on local stations or Web sites to priests at the Vatican Television Center—use marketing techniques similar to those that sell "Happy Meals."

McDonaldization is associated with the melding of cultures, so that we see more and more similarities in cultural expression. In Japan, for example, African entrepreneurs have found a thriving market for hip-hop fashions popularized by teens in the United States. In Austria, the McDonald's organization itself has drawn on the Austrians' love of coffee, cake, and conversation to create the McCafe as part of its fast-food chain. Many observers believe that McDonaldization and the use of technology to spread elements of culture through diffusion both serve to dilute the distinctive aspects of a society's culture (Alfino, Carpeto, and Wyngard 1998; Clark 1994; Ritzer 1995b; Rocks 1999). (Cultural diffusion via the media is discussed in more detail in Chapter 4.)

Use Your Sociological Imagination

If you had grown up in your parents' generation—without computers, email, the Internet, pagers, and cell phones—how would your daily life differ from the one you lead today?

ELEMENTS OF CULTURE

Each culture considers its own distinctive ways of handling basic societal tasks as "natural." But, in fact, methods of education, marital ceremonies, religious doctrines, and other aspects of culture are learned and transmitted through human interactions within specific societies. Parents in India are accustomed to arranging marriages for their children, whereas most parents in Canada leave marital decisions up to their offspring. Lifelong residents of Naples consider it natural to speak Italian, whereas lifelong residents of Buenos Aires feel the same way about Spanish. We'll now take a look at the major aspects of culture that shape the way the members of a society live—language, norms, sanctions, and values.

Language

The English language makes extensive use of words dealing with war. We speak of "conquering" space, "fighting" the "battle" of the budget, "waging a war" on drugs, making a "killing" on the stock market, and "bombing" an examination; something monumental or great is "the bomb." An observer from an entirely different and warless culture could gauge the importance that war and the military have had on our lives simply by recognizing the prominence that militaristic terms have in our language. In the old West, words such as *gelding, stallion, mare, piebald,* and *sorrel* were all used to describe one animal—the horse. Even if we knew little of this period of history, we could conclude from the list of terms that horses were quite important in this culture. The Slave First Nations people, who live in the Northwest Territories, have 14 terms to describe ice, including 8 for different kinds of solid ice and others for seamed ice, cracked ice, and floating ice. Clearly, language reflects the priorities of a culture (Basso 1972; Haviland 1999).

Language is, in fact, the foundation of every culture. ***Language*** is an abstract system of word meanings and symbols for all aspects of culture. It includes speech, written characters, numerals, symbols, and gestures and expressions of nonverbal communication. Figure 3-2 shows where the major languages of the world are spoken.

Language is not an exclusively human attribute. Although they are incapable of human speech, primates, such as chimpanzees, have been able to use symbols to communicate. However, even at their most advanced level, animals operate with essentially a fixed set of signs with fixed meanings. By contrast, humans can manipulate symbols in order to express abstract concepts and rules and to expand human cultures.

FIGURE 3-2

Languages of the World

Mapping Life WORLDWIDE

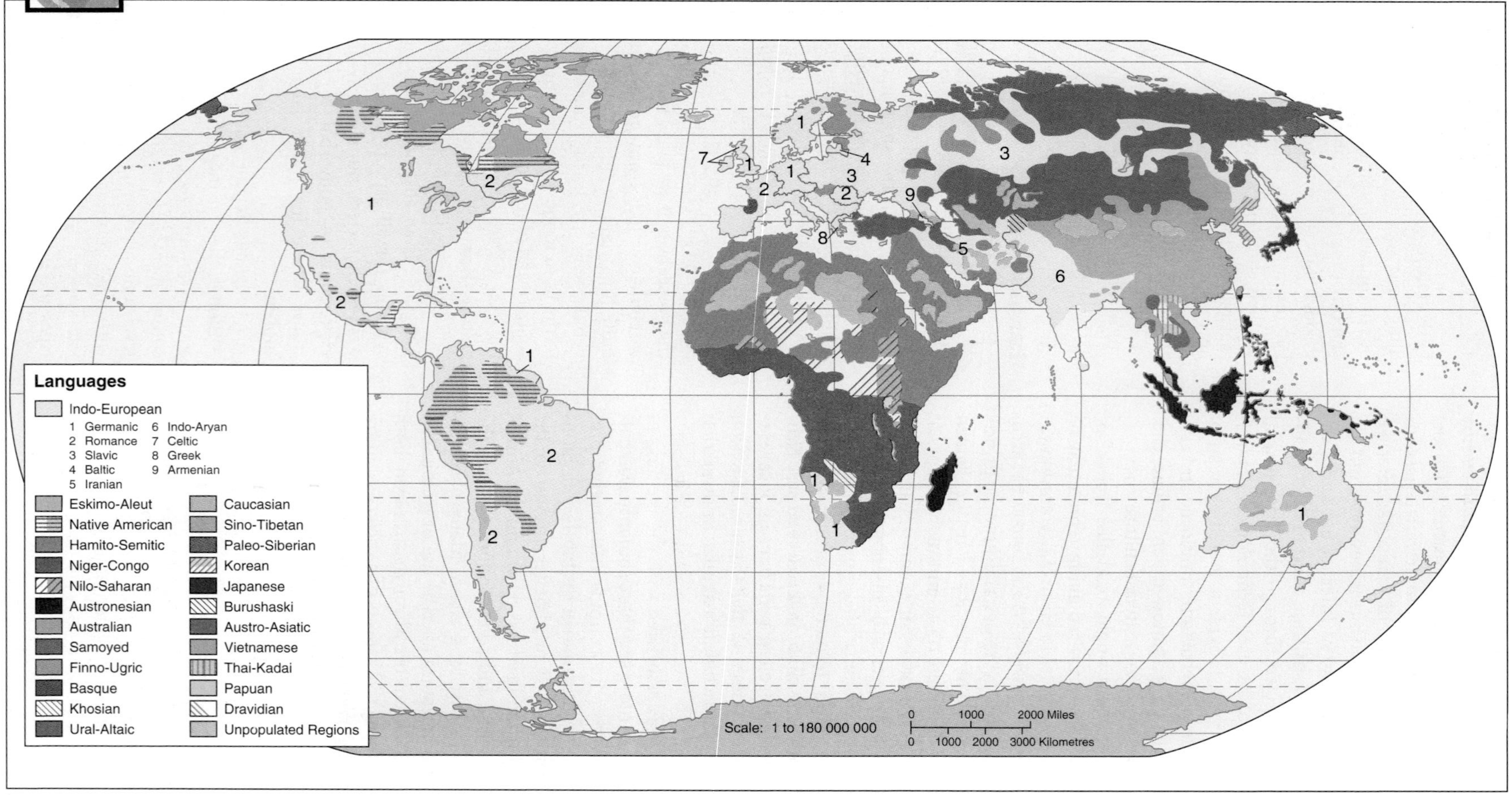

Source: Allen 2001.

Unlike some other elements of culture, language permeates all parts of society. Certain cultural skills, such as cooking or carpentry, can be learned without the use of language through the process of imitation. However, is it possible to transmit complex legal and religious systems to the next generation simply by showing how they are performed? You could put on a black robe and sit behind a bench as a judge does, but would you ever be able to understand legal reasoning without language? People invariably depend on language for the use and transmission of the rest of a culture.

Although language is a cultural universal, striking differences in the use of language are evident around the world. This is the case even when two countries use the same spoken language. For example, an English-speaking person from Canada who is visiting London may be puzzled the first time an English friend says, "I'll ring you up." The friend means "I'll call you on the telephone." Similarly, the meanings of nonverbal gestures vary from one culture to another. Whereas residents of North America attach positive meanings to the commonly used "thumbs up" gesture, this gesture has only vulgar connotations in Greece (Ekman, Friesen, and Bear 1984).

Sapir-Whorf Hypothesis

Language does more than simply describe reality; it also serves to *shape* the reality of a culture. For example, most people in the southern parts of Canada cannot easily make the verbal distinctions about ice that are possible in the Slave First Nations culture. As a result, they are less likely to notice such differences.

The ***Sapir-Whorf hypothesis,*** named for two linguists, describes the role of language in interpreting our world. According to Sapir and Whorf, since people can conceptualize the world only through language, language *precedes* thought. Thus, the word symbols and grammar of a language organize the world for us. The Sapir-Whorf hypothesis also holds that language is not a "given." Rather, it is culturally determined and leads to different interpretations of reality by focusing our attention on certain phenomena.

In a literal sense, language may colour how we see the world. Berlin and Kay (1991) have noted that humans possess the physical ability to make millions of colour distinctions, yet languages differ in the number of colours that are recognized. The English language distinguishes between yellow and orange, but some other languages do not. In the Dugum Dani language of New Guinea's West Highlands, there are only two basic colour terms—*modla* for "white" and *mili* for "black." By contrast, there are 11 basic terms in English. Russian and Hungarian, though, have 12 colour terms. Russians have terms for light blue and dark blue, while Hungarians have terms for two different shades of red.

Gender-related language can reflect—although in itself it will not determine—the traditional acceptance of men and women in certain occupations. Each time we use such a term as *mailman, policeman,* or *fireman,* we are implying (especially to young children) that these occupations can be filled only by males. Yet many women work as *letter carriers, police officers,* and *firefighters*—a fact that is being increasingly recognized and legitimized through the use of such nonsexist language (Henley, Hamilton, and Thorne 1985; Martyna 1983).

Language can also transmit stereotypes related to race. Look up the meanings of the adjective *black* in dictionaries. You will find *dismal, gloomy, forbidding, destitute of moral light or goodness, atrocious, evil, threatening, clouded with anger.* By contrast, dictionaries list *pure* and *innocent* among the meanings of the adjective *white.* Through such patterns of language, our culture reinforces positive associations with the term (and skin colour) *white* and a negative association with *black.* Is it surprising, then, that a list preventing people from working in a profession is called a *blacklist,* while a lie that we think of as somewhat acceptable is called a *white lie?*

Language can shape how we use our senses, how we see, taste, smell, feel, and hear. It also influences the way we think about the people, ideas, and objects around us. Language communicates a culture's most important norms, values, and sanctions to people. That's why the introduction of a new language into a society is such a sensitive issue in many parts of the world.

Nonverbal Communication

You know the appropriate distance to stand from someone when you talk informally. You know the circumstances under which it is appropriate to touch others, with a pat on the back or by taking someone's hand. If you are in the midst of a friendly meeting and one member suddenly sits back, folds his arms, and turns down the corners of his mouth, you know at once that trouble has arrived. These are all examples of *nonverbal communication,* the use of gestures, facial expressions, and other visual images to communicate.

We are not born with these expressions. We learn them, just as we learn other forms of language, from people who share our culture. This is as true for the basic expressions of smiling, laughter, and crying as it is for more complex emotions such as shame or distress (Fridlund, Erkman, and Oster 1987).

Like other forms of language, nonverbal communication is not the same in all cultures. For example, sociological research at the microlevel documents that people from various cultures differ in the degree to which they touch others during the course of normal social interaction.

Nonverbal communication can take many forms. Here, lowering the flag to half-mast in front of Place D'Armes in Montreal symbolizes respect and grief over the death of former Quebec Liberal leader Claude Ryan.

Norms

"Wash your hands before dinner." "Thou shalt not kill." "Respect your elders." All societies have ways of encouraging and enforcing what they view as appropriate behaviour while discouraging and punishing what they consider to be improper behaviour. ***Norms*** are established standards of behaviour maintained by a society.

For a norm to become significant, it must be widely shared and understood. For example, in movie theatres in Canada, we typically expect that people will be quiet while the film is shown. Because of this norm, an usher can tell a member of the audience to stop talking so loudly. Of course, the application of this norm can vary, depending on the particular film and type of audience. People attending a serious artistic film will be more likely to insist on the norm of silence than those attending a slapstick comedy or horror movie.

Types of Norms

Sociologists distinguish between norms in two ways. First, norms are classified as either formal or informal. ***Formal norms*** generally have been written down and specify strict rules for punishment of violators. In North America, we often formalize norms into laws, which must be very precise in defining proper and improper behaviour. Sociologist Donald Black (1995) has termed ***law*** to be "governmental social control," establishing laws as formal norms enforced by the state. Laws are just one example of formal norms. The requirements for a college or university major and the rules of a card game are also considered formal norms.

By contrast, ***informal norms*** are generally understood but they are not precisely recorded. Standards of proper dress are a common example of informal norms. Our society has no specific punishment or sanction for a person who comes to school, say, wearing a monkey suit. Making fun of the nonconforming student is usually the most likely response.

Norms are also classified by their relative importance to society. When classified in this way, they are known as *mores* and *folkways.*

Mores (pronounced "MOR-ays") are norms deemed highly necessary to the welfare of a society, often because they embody the most cherished principles of a people. Each society demands obedience to its mores; violation can lead to severe penalties. Thus, Canada has strong mores against murder and child abuse, which have been institutionalized into formal norms.

Folkways are norms governing everyday behaviour. Folkways play an important role in shaping the daily behaviour of members of a culture. Consider, for example, something as simple as footwear. In Japan it is a folkway for youngsters to wear flip-flop sandals while learning to walk. A study of Japanese adults has found that, even barefoot, they walk as if wearing flip-flops—braking their thigh muscles and leaning forward as they step. This folkway may even explain why Japan produces so few competitive runners (Stedman 1998).

Society is less likely to formalize folkways than mores, and their violation raises comparatively little concern. For example, walking up a "down" escalator in a department store challenges our standards of appropriate behaviour, but it will not result in a fine or a jail sentence.

In many societies around the world, folkways exist to reinforce patterns of male dominance. Various folkways reveal men's hierarchical position above women within the traditional Buddhist areas of southeast Asia. In the sleeping cars of trains, women do not sleep in upper berths above men. Hospitals that house men on the first floor do not place women patients on the second floor. Even on clotheslines, folkways dictate male dominance: women's attire is hung lower than that of men (Bulle 1987).

Use Your Sociological Imagination

You are a high school principal. What norms would you want to govern the students' behaviour? How might these norms differ from those appropriate for university students?

Acceptance of Norms

People do not follow norms, whether mores or folkways, in all situations. In some cases, they can evade a norm because they know it is weakly enforced. It is illegal for young Canadian teenagers to drink alcoholic beverages, yet drinking by minors is common throughout the nation.

In some instances, behaviour that appears to violate society's norms may actually represent adherence to the norms of a particular group. Teenage drinkers conform to the standards of a peer group. Conformity to group norms also governed the behaviour of the members of a religious cult associated with the Branch Davidians. In 1993, after a deadly gun battle with United States federal officials, nearly one hundred members of the cult defied government orders to abandon their compound near Waco, Texas. After a 51-day standoff, the United States Department of Justice ordered an assault on the compound and 86 cult members died.

Norms are violated in some instances because one norm conflicts with another. For example, suppose that you live in an apartment building and one night hear the screams of the woman next door, who is being beaten by her husband. If you decide to intervene by ringing their doorbell or calling the police, you are violating the norm of "minding your own business" while, at the same time, following the norm of assisting a victim of violence.

Even when norms do not conflict, there are always exceptions to any norm. The same action, under different circumstances, can cause a person to be viewed either as a hero or as a villain. Secretly taping telephone conversations is normally considered illegal and abhorrent. However, it can be done with a court order to obtain valid evidence for a criminal trial.

Acceptance of norms is subject to change as the political, economic, and social conditions of a culture are transformed. For example, under traditional norms in Canada, a woman was expected to marry, rear children, and remain at home if her husband could support the family without her assistance. However, these norms have been changing in recent decades, in part as a result of the contemporary feminist movement (see Chapter 10). As support for traditional norms weakens, people feel free to violate them more frequently and openly and are less likely to be punished for doing so.

Sanctions

Suppose that a football coach sends a 13th player onto the field. Or imagine a business school graduate showing up in shorts for a job interview at a large bank. Or consider a driver who neglects to put any money into a parking meter. These people have violated widely shared and understood norms. So what happens? In each of these situations, the person will receive sanctions if his or her behaviour is detected.

Sanctions are penalties and rewards for conduct concerning a social norm. Note that the concept of *reward* is included in this definition. Conformity to a norm can lead to positive sanctions, such as a pay raise, a medal, a word of gratitude, or a pat on the back. Negative sanctions include fines, threats, imprisonment, and stares of contempt.

Table 3-1 summarizes the relationship between norms and sanctions. As you can see, the sanctions that are associated with formal norms (those written down and codified) tend to be formalized as well. If a football coach sends too many players onto the field, the team will be penalized 15 yards. The driver who fails to put money in the parking meter will be given a ticket and expected to pay a fine. But sanctions for violations of informal norms can vary. The business school graduate who comes to the bank interview in shorts will probably lose any chance of getting the job; however, he or she might be so brilliant the bank officials will overlook the unconventional attire.

Applying sanctions entails first *detecting* violations of norms or obedience to norms. A person cannot be penalized or rewarded unless someone with the power to provide sanctions is aware of the person's actions. Therefore, if none of the officials in the football game realizes that there is an extra player on the field, there will be no penalty. If the police do not check the parking meter, there will be no fine or ticket. Furthermore, there can be *improper* application of sanctions in certain situations. The referee may make an error in counting the number of football players and levy an undeserved penalty on one team for "too many players on the field."

Table 3-1 Norms and Sanctions

	Sanctions	
Norms	**Positive**	**Negative**
Formal	Salary bonus	Demotion
	Testimonial dinner	Firing from a job
	Medal	Jail sentence
	Diploma	Expulsion
Informal	Smile	Frown
	Compliment	Humiliation
	Cheers	Belittling

Eye on the Media

3-1 Knockin' Rock—Making Music a Social Problem

In 1990, the rock group Judas Priest was sued by the parents of two boys who carried out a suicide pact. The parents claimed that the lyrics of Priest's song "Beyond the Realms of Death" encouraged the boys to opt out of life. That case was dismissed, but it symbolizes the antagonism that rock music has aroused in society, creating a cultural divide between generations.

In fact, rock music has come under attack for decades as the source of all sorts of evils—sexual promiscuity, teen pregnancy, drug use, satanism, suicide, abuse of women, and communism, to name just a few. Critics, who generally come from the religious and political right, point to the obscene lyrics of heavy metal, the anger of rap songs, the decadent lifestyles of rock artists, and the explicit movements and gestures of the performers as causes of deviant behaviour in youth.

The criticisms have had an impact. The United States Senate held hearings about obscene music, and record companies instigated voluntary labelling to alert buyers to explicit lyrics. Cities and towns have cancelled public performances of controversial rock musicians (Marilyn Manson was even paid US$40 000 *not* to play in South Carolina). In the 1950s Ed Sullivan instructed his TV camera crew to show Elvis Presley only from the waist up while he was performing. Anxious parents today attempt to monitor the music their kids buy and the music videos they watch. Rock music has been made into a social problem.

But is rock truly a social problem in that it causes undesirable behaviour? Sociologist Deena Weinstein thinks not. In her research she found "no sociologically credible evidence that rock caused sexual promiscuity, rape, drug abuse, satanism, and suicide. Indeed, there is clear evidence that it is not the cause of such behaviours" (1999). That is not to say that rock music has no part to play in these problems: according to Weinstein, rock music functions as a symbolic rebellion. It reflects the values of those who cherish the music, and these may be values that other groups in society want to inhibit. Rock music legitimizes the "disapproved" behaviours by giving them a symbolic form and making them public. Weinstein acknowledges, however, that symbols can have "complex and varied relations to behaviour."

Weinstein shows how the symbolic function of rock has changed over succeeding generations, matching the concerns and values of each youth generation. In the 1950s "rock'n'roll" expressed the rebellion of teenagers against a society conforming to respectable middle-class codes. In the 1960s rock provided an outlet for feelings of political rebellion and a desire for consciousness expansion. The 1970s and 1980s gave rise to a number of distinct styles catering to special audiences. For example, the defiance of rap music and the satanic appeals of heavy metal symbolized the alienation of marginalized youth.

In every decade, rock's detractors have tended to be the older generation—generally white, middle class, politically conservative, and religious. They are intent on preserving the cultural values they hold dear and passing these on intact and unchanged to the generations to follow. Bewildered by rapid social changes and a youth culture resisting adult authority, the older generation makes rock into a convenient scapegoat for all their own fears and failures. The result is that they are more concerned with "killing the messenger" than paying attention to the message embedded in rock's symbolic rebellion. But, as Weinstein (1999) points out, "what could be more gratifying for a young symbolic rebel than to be thought of by the adult world as really important, as really dangerous?"

Applying Theory

1. According to interactionist thinkers, what might be some of the symbolic meanings of rock music?
2. Why do you think some segments of the population object to rock music?

Sources: Weinstein 1999, 2000.

The entire fabric of norms and sanctions in a culture reflects that culture's values and priorities. The most cherished values will be most heavily sanctioned; matters regarded as less critical will carry light and informal sanctions.

Values

We each have our own personal set of standards—which may include such things as caring or fitness or success in business—but we also share a general set of objectives as members of a society. Cultural ***values*** are these collective conceptions of what is considered good, desirable, and proper—or bad, undesirable, and improper—in a culture. They indicate what people in a given culture prefer as well as what they find important and morally right (or wrong). Values may be specific, such as honouring our parents and owning a home, or they may be more general, such as health, love, and democracy. Of course, the members of a society do not uniformly share its values. Angry political debates and billboards promoting conflicting causes tell us that much. In Box 3-1 we explore how rock music reflects people's values. Those whose values conflict with the music tend to regard the music as a social problem.

Values influence people's behaviour and serve as criteria for evaluating the actions of others. There is often a direct relationship among the values, norms, and sanctions of a culture. For example, if a culture highly values the institution of marriage, it may have norms (and strict sanctions) that prohibit the act of adultery. If a culture views private property as a basic value, it will probably have stiff laws against theft and vandalism.

In a study by the federal government entitled *Citizens' Forum on Canada's Future*, conducted between November 1990 and July 1991, 400 000 Canadians were asked which values they thought of as "Canadian" values (1991:35–45).

The values that emerged included the following:

1. *Equality and fairness in a democratic society.*
2. *Consultation and dialogue.* Canadians believe that, as citizens, we value our ability to resolve problems and differences peacefully, through discussion, debate, and negotiation.
3. *Accommodation and tolerance.* Accommodation of the differences in Canadian society—ethnic, linguistic, and regional—is considered to be a value of Canadian culture.
4. *Support for diversity.* Canadians value diversity and support it as a part of what makes us Canadian.
5. *Compassion and generosity.* Caring about others, particularly those who are less fortunate, and our willingness to act to make our society more humane are values Canadians espouse.
6. *Respect for Canada's national beauty.* Preserving Canada's natural environment for future generations is a highly prized value of its citizens.
7. *Commitment to freedom, peace, and nonviolent change.* Canadians want to see their country as a leader in peacemaking and resolution of international conflicts.

People's values may differ according to such factors as their age, gender, region, ethnic background, and language. For example, a major study by Erin Anderssen, Michael Valpy, and others (2004) found that, in 2003, both older (those 31 years of age and older) and younger (those 18 to 30 years of age) Canadians valued security over salary and valued more free time over more money. When choosing a spouse, however, younger people placed far less importance on similar ethnic background than did older Canadians.

Figure 3-3 shows the difference in support for gay marriage according to the age and sex of respondents among Canadians in 2003.

FIGURE 3-3

Support for Gay Marriage by Age and Sex, 2003

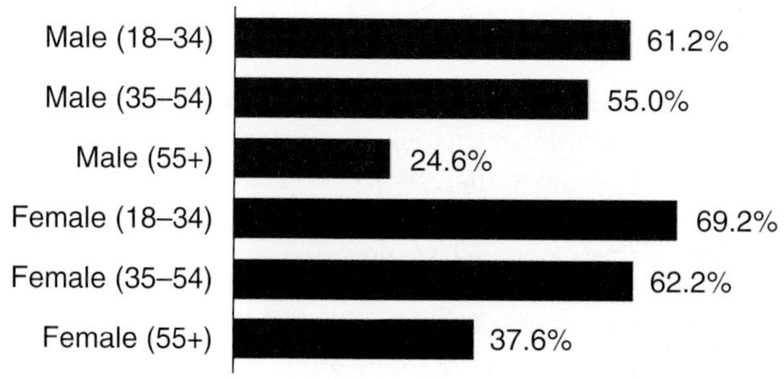

Source: Anderssen et al. 2004.

CULTURE AND THE DOMINANT IDEOLOGY: THE MAJOR THEORETICAL PERSPECTIVES

Functional Perspective

Functionalists maintain that stability requires a consensus and the support of society's members; consequently, there are strong central values and common norms. This view of culture became popular in sociology beginning in the 1950s. It was borrowed from British anthropologists who saw cultural traits as all working toward stabilizing a culture. From a functionalist perspective, a cultural trait or practice will persist if it performs functions that society seems to need or it contributes to overall social stability and consensus. This view helps explain why widely condemned social practices, such as prostitution, continue to survive. Both functionalist and conflict theorists agree that culture and society are in harmony with each other, but for different reasons.

p. 12

Conflict Perspective

Conflict theorists agree that a common culture may exist, but they argue that it serves to maintain the privileges of certain groups. Moreover, while protecting their own self-interests, powerful groups may keep others in a subservient position. The term ***dominant ideology*** describes the set of cultural beliefs and practices that helps to maintain powerful social, economic, and political interests. This concept was first used by Hungarian Marxist Georg Lukacs (1923) and Italian Marxist Antonio Gramsci (1929). In Karl Marx's view, a capitalist society has a dominant ideology that serves the interests of the ruling class. Box 3-2 illustrates that there is a dominant ideology about poverty that derives its strength from the more powerful segments of society.

p. 13

Research in Action 3-2 Dominant Ideology and Poverty

Why do we think people are poor? *Individualistic* explanations emphasize personal responsibility: Poor people lack the proper work ethic, lack ability, or are unsuited to the workplace because of problems, like drinking or drug abuse. *Structural* explanations lay the blame for poverty on such external factors as inferior educational opportunities, prejudice, and low wages in some industries. Research documents that people in Canada and the United States generally go along with the individualistic explanation. The dominant ideology in North America holds that people are poor largely because of their own shortcomings.

In a world survey assessing the causes of poverty, Canadians were asked "Why are there people in this country who live in need?" (Institute for Social Research 1994). Canadians responded with equal frequency that personal laziness and societal injustice caused poverty (31.8 percent for each reason). Such countries as Sweden, where individualistic beliefs are not as strong as in North America, responded that societal injustice far outweighed personal laziness as being the cause of poverty.

How pervasive is this individualistic view? Do the poor and rich alike subscribe to it? In seeking answers, sociologists have conducted studies of how various groups of people view poverty. The research has shown that people with lower incomes are more likely than the wealthy to see the larger socioeconomic system as the cause of poverty. In part this structural view, focusing on the larger job market, relieves them of some personal responsibility for their plight, but it also reflects the social reality that they are close to. The wealthy tend to embrace the dominant individualistic view because continuation of the socioeconomic status quo is in their best interest. They also prefer to regard their own success as the result of their own accomplishments, with little or no help from external factors.

Is the dominant ideology on poverty widespread? Yes, but it appears that the individualist ideology is dominant in Canadian society not because of a lack of alternatives, but because those who see things differently lack the political influence and status needed to get the ear of the mainstream culture.

Applying Theory

1. Does support for the dominant ideology about poverty divide along income lines among racial and ethnic minority groups? Why or why not?
2. Does your university administration have a "dominant ideology"? How is it manifested? Are there any groups that challenge it? On what basis?

Sources: Bobo 1991; Institute for Social Research 1994.

From a conflict perspective, the dominant ideology has major social significance. Not only do a society's most powerful groups and institutions control wealth and property, but they also control the means of producing beliefs about reality through religion, education, and the media. For example, if society's message, as communicated by the mass media, is to tell us that we should be consumers, this dominant ideology will help to control us and keep us in a subordinate position (while maximizing the profits of the powerful economic groups).

Neither the functionalist nor the conflict perspective alone can explain all aspects of a culture. Nevertheless, certain cultural practices in our society and others clearly benefit some to the detriment of many. These practices may indeed promote social stability and consensus—but at whose expense?

Interactionist Perspective

p. 15 Using the example of consumerism as a dominant ideology found in Canadian culture, an analysis by interactionist thinkers of the topic would differ from those of conflict thinkers and of functional thinkers. Interactionist sociologists would examine shopping, or consumer practices, from a micro perspective in order to understand the larger macro phenomenon of consumerism. Interactionist might probe consumers to discover what meaning shopping has for them or what value they attach to the activity. For example, could shopping be viewed as an activity that contributes to the economic and social well-being of Canada? Or is shopping viewed as an activity that creates a bond between child and parent as they spend time together at the supermarket selecting groceries? Someone using Goffman's dramaturgical approach (1959, 1963b, 1971) might study particular features of people's personalities that they disclose to fellow shoppers while concealing the same features from the store manager or sales assistant.

Feminist Perspectives

p. 14 Some feminist thinkers would argue that the mass media, acting as a mouthpiece for the dominant ideology, contributes to the control and marginalization of women. The mass media communicates to its readers, viewers, and listeners the message that women's value is based on their sexual attractiveness, their domestic abilities, their roles as mothers and wives, their abilities to stay fit and appear youthful, and their abilities to provide support and comfort to others (e.g., men, children, the elderly). Some feminist perspectives advocate that the mass media's portrayal of women as powerless, childlike sex objects (Graydon 2001) contributes to cultural norms, beliefs, and values that reinforce and perpetuate patriarchy as a dominant ideology.

CULTURAL DIVERSITY

Each culture has a unique character. The Inuit people of this country have little in common with farmers in Southeast Asia. Cultures adapt to meet specific sets of circumstances, such as climate, level of technology, population, and geography. This adaptation to different conditions shows up in differences in all elements of culture, including norms, sanctions, values, and language. Thus, despite the presence of cultural universals, such as courtship and religion, there is still great diversity among the world's many cultures. Moreover, even within a single nation, certain segments of the populace develop cultural patterns that differ from the patterns of the dominant society.

Aspects of Cultural Diversity

Subcultures

Residents of a retirement community, workers on an off-shore oil rig, rodeo cowboys, street gangs, goth music fans—all are examples of what sociologists refer to as *subcultures.* A ***subculture*** is a segment of society that shares a distinctive pattern of mores, folkways, and values that differs from the pattern of the larger society. In a sense, a subculture can be thought of as a culture existing within a larger, dominant culture. The existence of many subcultures is characteristic of complex and diverse societies, such as Canada.

You can get an idea of the impact of subcultures within Canada by considering the variety of seasonal traditions in December. The religious and commercial celebration of the Christmas holiday is an event well entrenched in the dominant culture of our society. However, the Jewish subculture observes Hanukkah, Muslims observe Ramadan (which falls at different times during the year, but at present is occurring during the winter months), and some people join in rituals celebrating the winter solstice.

Members of a subculture participate in the dominant culture, while at the same time engaging in unique and distinctive forms of behaviour. Frequently, a subculture will develop an ***argot,*** or specialized language, that distinguishes it from the wider society. For example, if you were to join a band of pickpockets you would need to learn what the dip, dish, and tailpipe are expected to do (see Figure 3-4).

An argot allows insiders, the members of the subculture, to understand words with special meanings. It also establishes patterns of communication that outsiders can't understand. Sociologists associated with the interactionist perspective emphasize that language and symbols offer a powerful way for a subculture to feel cohesive and maintain its identity.

Subcultures develop in a number of ways. Often a subculture emerges because a segment of society faces problems or even privileges unique to its position. Subcultures may be based on common age (teenagers or old people), region (Newfoundlanders), ethnic heritage (Indo-Canadians), occupation (firefighters), or beliefs (environmentalists). Certain subcultures,

FIGURE 3-4

The Argot of Pickpockets

Source: Gearty 1996.

such as computer hackers, develop because of a shared interest or hobby. In still other subcultures, such as that of prison inmates, members have been excluded from conventional society and are forced to develop alternative ways of living.

Interactionists contend that individuals confer meaning differently: what it means to be a successful surfer living out of a van in Tofino, British Columbia, may be quite different from what it means to be a successful Bay Street lawyer living in Toronto. Feminist perspectives might point to cultural diversity as contributing to the perpetuation of multiple layers and degrees of inequality based on gender, ethnicity, race, and class. The greater the deviation from the norms of the dominant culture, the greater the impact of inequality experienced by various subcultures.

Functionalist and conflict theorists agree that variation exists within a culture. Functionalists view subcultures as variations of particular social environments and as evidence that differences can exist within a common culture. However, conflict theorists suggest that variation often reflects the inequality of social arrangements within a society. A conflict perspective would view the challenge to dominant social norms by Quebec separatists, the feminist movement, and groups representing people with disabilities as a reflection of inequity based on ethnicity, gender, and disability status. Conflict theorists also argue that subcultures sometimes emerge when the dominant society unsuccessfully tries to suppress a practice, such as the use of illegal drugs.

Countercultures

By the end of the 1960s, an extensive subculture had emerged in North America comprising young people turned off by a society they believed was too materialistic and technological. This group primarily included political radicals and "hippies" who had "dropped out" of mainstream social institutions. These young men and women rejected the pressure to accumulate more and more cars, larger and larger homes, and an endless array of material goods. Instead, they expressed a desire to live in a culture based on more humanistic values, such as sharing, love, and coexistence with the environment.

When a subculture conspicuously and deliberately *opposes* certain aspects of the larger culture, it is known as a ***counterculture.*** Countercultures typically thrive among the young, who have the least investment in the existing culture. In most cases, a 20-year-old can adjust to new cultural standards more easily than can someone who has spent 60 years following the patterns of the dominant culture (Zellner 1995).

An example of a counterculture in Canadian history is the *Front du libération du Québec* (FLQ). In 1970, the FLQ opposed the social, economic, political, and educational institutions of the dominant culture of Quebec. Its activities included the murder of a prominent Quebec politician and the kidnapping of a British Trade Commissioner posted in Quebec. The FLQ produced a manifesto containing all of its demands, which was broadcast through public media.

"IT'S ENDLESS. WE JOIN A COUNTER-CULTURE; IT BECOMES THE CULTURE. WE JOIN ANOTHER COUNTER-CULTURE; IT BECOMES THE CULTURE..."

Cultures change. Aspects we once regarded as unacceptable—such as men wearing earrings and people wearing jeans in the workplace—and associated with fringe groups are now widely accepted. Countercultural practices are sometimes absorbed by the mainstream culture.

Culture Shock

Anyone who feels disoriented, uncertain, out of place, or even fearful when immersed in an unfamiliar culture may be experiencing ***culture shock.*** For example, a resident of Canada who visits certain areas in China and wants a local dinner may be stunned to learn that the specialty is scorpian. Similarly, someone from a strict Islamic culture may be shocked on first seeing the comparatively provocative dress styles and open displays of affection that are common in North American and various European cultures. Culture shock can also occur within the larger confines of a person's own culture. For example, a 14-year-old boy from a small town in northern Saskatchewan might feel the effects of culture shock while visiting Toronto for the first time. The speed of the traffic, the level of the street noise, and the intensity and variation of external stimuli may cause him to feel disoriented and uncomfortable with his surroundings.

All of us, to some extent, take for granted the cultural practices of our society. As a result, it can be surprising and even disturbing to realize that other cultures do not follow our way of life. The fact is that customs that seem strange to us are considered normal and proper in other cultures, which may see *our* mores and folkways as odd.

Use Your Sociological Imagination

You arrive in a developing African country as a Canadian International Development Agency (CIDA) volunteer. What aspects of this very different culture do you think would be hardest to adjust to? What might the citizens of that country find shocking about your culture?

Cultural Diversity in Canada

If a tourist were to travel across Canada for the first time, he or she would most certainly be struck by this country's diversity—diversity of region, ethnicity, race, and language. Cultural diversity, as the traveller would observe, is greatest in Canada's metropolitan areas, where the greatest number of cultural minority groups and particularly visible minority groups reside. On the basis of his or her observations of cultural diversity, the traveller might conclude that Canada is a "multicultural" society. But what does multiculturalism really mean? Does it simply describe (numerically) the variety of cultures represented in Canada?

Multiculturalism is not only a description of the reality of Canada's cultural makeup—"what is" (Fleras and Kunz 2001)—but, in Canada, it is an explicit policy set out by the government. ***Multiculturalism*** is a policy that promotes cultural and racial diversity and full and equal participation of individuals and communities of all origins as a fundamental characteristic of Canadian identity. The federal Multiculturalism Program of 1997 has three main goals (Communications Canada 2001):

1. *Identity*—fostering a society where people of all backgrounds feel a sense of attachment and belonging to Canada
2. *Civic participation*—developing citizens who are actively involved in their communities and country
3. *Social justice*—building a country that ensures fair and equitable treatment of people of all origins

Multiculturalism can also take the form of an ideology—a set of beliefs, goals, ideals, and attitudes about what multiculturalism *should be.* In embracing multiculturalism as an ideology, Canadians often compare their society's way of expressing cultural diversity with the way it is expressed in the United States (Fleras and Kunz 2001). The analogy of the "mosaic" is commonly used to describe Canada's cultural diversity, where various tiles represent distinct cultural groups that collectively form the whole. In the United States, the "melting pot" analogy represents the model of assimilation, in which Americans become more like one another, rather than distinct from one another.

Support for the "mosaic" version of Canada has been declining and shifting toward the "melting pot." Across region, age, and education levels, in 1985, 56 percent of Canadians said they preferred the "mosaic" and 28 percent the "melting pot." In 1995, only 44 percent preferred the mosaic, while 40 percent preferred the melting pot (Bibby 1995).

The ideal of multiculturalism in Canada has two desirable outcomes—the survival of ethnic groups and their cultures, and tolerance of this diversity as reflected by an absence of prejudice toward ethnic minorities (Weinfeld 1994). Multiculturalism, however, is not without its critics. Some argue that it is a divisive rather than unifying force in Canada, while others claim that it is only "window dressing," diverting attention from the real problems of ethnic and racial prejudice and discrimination (A. Nelson and Fleras 1998).

The American Influence One of the original purposes of multiculturalism was to establish a national uniqueness that would make Canadians distinct from Americans (Bibby 1990). In 1972, Prime Minister Pierre Trudeau stated that with this policy, "We become less like others; we become less susceptible to cultural, social, or political envelopment by others" (Bibby 1990:49).

The Americanization of Canada (as well as of many other countries) has lead to ***cultural imperialism***—the influence or imposition of the material or nonmaterial elements of a culture on another culture or cultures. This phenomenon is particularly relevant in the context of the global export of American culture through various forms of American mass media. Canadians have been and continue to be particularly susceptible to cultural imperialism because of geographic, economic, social, and political ties with the United States. Some organizations, such as the Council of Canadians, have an explicit mandate to protect and preserve Canada's national interests and sovereignty from forces of globalization, in which American cultural imperialism figures large.

Even though Canadians generally hold the view that Americans do not have "too much power" in our society (Bibby 1995), Canadians frequently consider Americans to be their favourite authors, TV personalities, and screen stars (Bibby 1995). Given Canadians' reliance on American culture (particularly outside Quebec) our heroes may be those that are defined by America (Bibby 1995). In 1995, when Canadians were asked to name the greatest living Canadian, 73 percent said "no one came to mind" (Bibby 1995:47). However, in 2004, in a poll sponsored by CBC television in its *Greatest Canadian* series, Canadians were asked to vote for the greatest Canadian. Tommy Douglas, the former premier of Saskatchewan and the "father of Medicare" was the winner. Feminist sociologists would draw attention to the fact that no women and only one person from a visible minority group (a man) made the list of the top ten nominees. When asked what characteristics describe Americans and Canadians, Canadians felt that the traits of confidence, patriotism, and risk-taking had greater applicability to Americans, while generosity was a trait more applicable to Canadians. As Figure 3-5 illustrates, Canadian teenagers view the description "world's best at what they do" as applicable to Americans more than they view it as applicable to Canadians (Bibby 1995). If Canadian broadcasting and publishing regulations promoting Canadian cultural content were not in place, one might wonder how much more "Americanized" our cultural preferences might be. In 1995, 64 percent of Canadians believed that "CBC television continues to play a unique role in enhancing Canadian culture" (Bibby 1995:1210).

Attitudes toward Cultural Diversity

Ethnocentrism

Many everyday statements reflect our attitude that our culture is best. We use terms such as *underdeveloped, backward,* and *primitive* to refer to other societies. What "we" believe is a religion; what "they" believe is superstition and mythology (Spradley and McCurdy 1980).

It is tempting to evaluate the practices of other cultures on the basis of our own perspectives. Sociologist William Graham Sumner (1906) coined the term ***ethnocentrism*** to refer to the tendency to assume that our own culture and way of life constitute the norm or are superior to all others. The ethnocentric person sees his or her own group as the centre or defining point of culture and views all other cultures as deviations from what is "normal."

Those Westerners who are contemptuous of India's Hindu religion and culture because of its view of cattle as sacred are engaged in ethnocentrism. As another manifestation of ethnocentrism, people in one culture may dismiss as unthinkable the mate-selection or child-rearing practices of another culture. We might, in fact, be tempted to view the Nacirema culture from an ethnocentric point of view—until we learn it is a culture similar to our own that Miner describes (see the chapter opening).

Conflict theorists point out that ethnocentric value judgments serve to devalue diversity and to deny equal opportunities. The treatment of Aboriginal children in Christian-based residential schools during the midpoint of the last century is an example of ethnocentrism that conflict theorists might point to in Canadian history. Church authorities were so convinced of the cultural superiority of their own beliefs that they set out to deny Aboriginal children the expression of theirs.

Functionalists note that ethnocentrism serves to maintain a sense of solidarity by promoting group pride. Canadians' view of our country as peaceful, safe, and relatively free from violence may create a feeling of national solidarity when comparing ourselves with our American neighbours.

Cultural Relativism

Although ethnocentrism evaluates foreign cultures by using the familiar culture of the observer as a standard of correct behaviour, ***cultural relativism*** views people's behaviour from the perspective of their own culture. It places a priority on understanding other cultures, rather than on dismissing them as strange or exotic. Unlike ethnocentrism, cultural relativism employs the kind of value neutrality in scientific study that Max Weber saw as so important.

Cultural relativism stresses that different social contexts give rise to different norms and values. Thus, we must examine such practices as polygamy, bullfighting, and monarchy within the particular contexts of the cultures in which they are found. Although cultural relativism does not suggest that we must unquestionably *accept* every cultural variation, it does require a serious and an unbiased effort to evaluate norms, values, and customs in light of their distinctive culture.

There is an interesting extension of cultural relativism, referred to as *xenocentrism.* ***Xenocentrism*** is the belief that the products, styles, or ideas of our own society are *inferior* to those that originate elsewhere (W. Wilson,

FIGURE 3-5

Applicability of Traits to Canadians and Americans

Traits Describe "Very Well" or "Fairly Well"

	ADULTS		TEENAGERS	
	Canadians	Americans	Canadians	Americans
Confident	61%	87	66%	91
Patriotic	58	92	47	89
Generous	84	53	**	**
Risk-takers	33	82	43	84
World's best	56	48	40	62

Source: Bibby 1995:49.

Dennis, and Wadsworth 1976). In a sense, it is a reverse ethnocentrism. For example, people in Canada often assume that French wine or Japanese electronic devices are superior to our own. Are they? Or are people unduly charmed by the lure of goods from exotic places? Such fascination with overseas products can be damaging to competitors in Canada. Conflict theorists are most likely to consider the economic impact of xenocentrism in the developing world. Consumers in developing nations frequently turn their backs on locally produced goods and instead purchase items imported from Europe or North America.

How people view their culture—whether from an ethnocentric point of view or through the lens of cultural relativism—has important consequences in the area of social policy concerned with multiculturalism. We'll take a close look at this issue in the next section.

SOCIAL POLICY AND CULTURE: Multiculturalism

The Issue

In 1971, multiculturalism became official government policy in Canada. It was a policy established to promote tolerance for cultural minorities, or in the words of then Prime Minister Pierre Elliott Trudeau, to "explore the delights of many cultures." Although the Canadian policy on multiculturalism provides an alternative to the American melting pot approach to cultural diversity, it has generated a great deal of conflict and faced a great deal of opposition (A. Nelson and Fleras 1998).

Much of the conflict surrounding multiculturalism stems from the variety of meanings or definitions Canadians have for the concept. The term *multiculturalism* can be used to refer to (1) the fact (what *is*, i.e., the existing complexion of Canadian society); (2) an ideology (what should be); (3) policy (what is proposed); (4) a process (what really happens); (5) a critical discussion (what is being challenged), and (6) a social movement (collective resistance) (Fleras and Elliott 1999). In general, multiculturalism can be defined as a process through which Canadians come to be engaged in their society as different from one another yet equal to one another (Fleras and Kunz 2001).

The Setting

According to Citizenship and Immigration Canada, Canada accepts more immigrants, proportional to the size of its population, than any other country in the world. One in every six residents in this country was born outside Canada. The top five sources for immigration since 1998 have been countries in Asia (Citizenship and Immigration Canada 2001). According to the 2001 census, 38 percent of Canadians declared their ethnicity to be that of "multiple origins"; that is, they declared two or more ethnic origins. Overall, multicultural minorities tend to live in Canada's large urban centres, making Vancouver, Montreal, and Toronto the most culturally diverse regions of the country. Approximately three-quarters of all immigrants who arrived in Canada between 1991 and 1996 settled in one of these three centres (Fleras and Kunz 2001).

From the standpoint of the two major sociological perspectives—conflict theory and structural-functional

Policies on multiculturalism attempt to preserve, protect, and nurture different cultural traditions in the midst of the domination of one cultural group. This boy sits outside a court hearing to decide whether he has the right to wear his kirpan, a sikh ceremonial dagger, to school.

theory—the implementation of multiculturalism as a social policy has two distinct interpretations. Conflict sociologists view multiculturalism as an attempt to "empower minorities to pursue the dual goals of ethnicity and equality" (A. Nelson and Fleras 1998:259). It is seen as an attempt to nurture, preserve, and protect different cultural traditions in the midst of domination by one cultural group. Multiculturalism policies also aim to make diversity, and the inevitable struggles that result, an accepted and welcome element of the cultural fabric of Canadian life.

Functional sociologists view culture as something that all Canadians share. It is the common values that unite and integrate us, resulting in a shared sense of identity. Therefore, according to functional thinkers, the more we diversify Canadian culture, the less we share in common; the more we hyphenate our identities (e.g., Indo-Canadian, Chinese-Canadian, Italian-Canadian, etc.) the less "Canadian" we actually become. However, both functionalist and conflict theorists have criticized multiculturalism for a number of reasons. Sociologists Fleras and Elliott (1999) argue that criticisms regarding multiculturalism can be classified into four categories:

1. Those that claim that multiculturalism is divisive and serves to weaken Canadian society
2. Those that see multicultural programs and policies as regressive, as a tool to pacify the needs and legitimate claims of the minority cultural groups
3. Those that consider the efforts of multiculturalism to be ornamental or superficial, with much form and little substance
4. Those that consider multiculturalism as a policy impractical in a capitalist society, such as Canada, where the principles of individualism, private property, profit, and consumerism prevail

Policy Initiatives

Official multiculturalism in Canada currently comes under the portfolio of Citizenship and Canadian Identity, which is in turn under the Department of Canadian Heritage. According to Fleras and Kunz (2001), policies on multiculturalism have evolved from those in the 1970s, which celebrated Canadians' differences (e.g., cultural sensitivity training programs), through those in the 1980s, which managed diversity through policies on employment equity and race relations, to those of the 1990s, with the objectives of inclusion and integration of cultural minorities. The current policies on multiculturalism encourage the full participation of all cultural groups, based on the goals of social justice. As Fleras and Kunz (2001:16) state, "Emphasis is on what we have in common as rights-bearing and equality-seeking individuals rather than on what separates or divides us." Special activities, such as Black History Month and the "Racism: Stop It!" campaign, which focus on the promotion of social justice, have been created by the federal government's multicultural programs.

Fleras and Elliott (1999) state that multiculturalism is not what divides Canada but is rather what unites us, separating us and making us distinct from Americans. They claim that multiculturalism policies focus on institutional barriers for minority groups and therefore attempt to break down the "vertical mosaic."

Applying Theory

1. What functions do you think the policy of multiculturalism serves? Do you think these functions are manifest or latent?
2. According to the assumptions of conflict thinking, how might the ideology of multiculturalism differ from the reality of living in a multicultural country?

CHAPTER RESOURCES

Summary

Culture is the totality of learned, socially transmitted customs, knowledge, material objects, and behaviour. This chapter examined the basic elements that make up a culture, social practices common to all cultures, and variations that distinguish one culture from another.

1. Sharing a similar culture helps to define the group or society to which we belong.
2. Anthropologist George Murdock has compiled a list of ***cultural universals,*** general practices found in every culture, including courtship, family, games, language, medicine, religion, and sexual restrictions.
3. Human culture is constantly expanding through ***innovation,*** including both ***discovery*** and ***invention.***
4. ***Diffusion***—the spread of cultural items from one place to another—also changes cultures. But societies resist ideas that seem too foreign as well as those that are perceived as threatening to their own values and beliefs.

5. ***Language,*** an important element of culture, includes speech, written characters, numerals, symbols, and gestures and other forms of nonverbal communication. Language both describes culture and shapes it for us.
6. Sociologists distinguish between ***norms*** in two ways. They are classified as either ***formal*** or ***informal*** norms and as ***mores*** or ***folkways.***
7. The more cherished ***values*** of a culture will receive the heaviest ***sanctions***; matters that are regarded as less critical will carry light and informal sanctions.
8. The ***dominant ideology*** of a culture describes the set of cultural beliefs and practices that help to maintain powerful social, economic, and political interests.
9. In a sense, a ***subculture*** can be thought of as a culture existing within a larger, dominant culture. ***Countercultures*** are subcultures that deliberately oppose aspects of the larger culture.
10. People who measure other cultures by the standard of their own engage in ***ethnocentrism.*** Using ***cultural relativism*** allows us to view people from the perspective of their own culture.
11. ***Multiculturalism*** is a process through which citizens come to be engaged in their society as different from one another, yet equal to one another.

Critical Thinking Questions

1. Who do you think promotes the dominant culture most rigorously?
2. Drawing on the theories and concepts presented in the chapter, apply sociological analysis to one subculture with which you are familiar. Describe the norms, values, argot, and sanctions evident in that subculture.
3. In what ways is the dominant ideology of Canada evident in the nation's literature, music, movies, theatre, television programs, and sporting events?
4. Given your understanding of culture after reading this chapter, in what way do you think the contents of bathrooms, and the activities carried out in them, reflect the culture of a given group?

Key Terms

Argot Specialized language used by members of a group or subculture. (page 61)

Counterculture A subculture that deliberately opposes certain aspects of the larger culture. (62)

Cultural imperialism The influence or imposition of the material or nonmaterial elements of a culture on another culture or cultures. (63)

Cultural relativism The viewing of people's behaviour from the perspective of their own culture. (64)

Cultural universals General practices found in every culture. (50)

Culture The totality of learned, socially transmitted customs, knowledge, material objects, and behaviour. (49)

Culture lag Ogburn's term for a period of maladjustment during which the nonmaterial culture is still adapting to new material conditions. (53)

Culture shock The feeling of surprise and disorientation that is experienced when people witness cultural practices different from their own. (62)

Diffusion The process by which a cultural item is spread from group to group or society to society. (51)

Discovery The process of making known or sharing the existence of an aspect of reality. (51)

Dominant ideology A set of cultural beliefs and practices that helps to maintain powerful social, economic, and political interests. (59)

Ethnocentrism The tendency to assume that our own culture and way of life represent the norm or are superior to all others. (64)

Folkways Norms governing everyday social behaviour whose violation raises comparatively little concern. (56)

Formal norms Norms that generally have been written down and that specify strict rules for punishment of violators. (56)

Informal norms Norms that generally are understood but are not precisely recorded. (56)

Innovation The process of introducing new elements into a culture through either discovery or invention. (51)

Invention The combination of existing cultural items into a form that did not previously exist. (51)

Language An abstract system of word meanings and symbols for all aspects of culture. It also includes gestures and other nonverbal communication. (53)

Law Governmental social control. (56)

Material culture The physical or technological aspects of our daily lives. (52)

Mores Norms deemed highly necessary to the welfare of a society. (56)

Multiculturalism A policy that promotes cultural and racial diversity and full and equal participation of individuals and communities of all origins as a fundamental characteristic of Canadian identity. (63)

Nonmaterial culture Cultural adjustments to material conditions, such as customs, beliefs, patterns of communication, and ways of using material objects. (52)

Norms Established standards of behaviour maintained by a society. (56)

Sanctions Penalties and rewards for conduct concerning a social norm. (57)

Sapir-Whorf hypothesis A hypothesis concerning the role of language in shaping cultures. It holds that language is culturally determined and serves to influence our mode of thought. (55)

Society A fairly large number of people who live in the same territory, are relatively independent of people outside it, and participate in a common culture. (49)

Subculture A segment of society that shares a distinctive pattern of mores, folkways, and values that differs from the pattern of the larger society. (61)

Technology Information about how to use the material resources of the environment to satisfy human needs and desires. (52)

Values Collective conceptions of what is considered good, desirable, and proper—or bad, undesirable, and improper—in a culture. (58)

Xenocentrism The belief that the products, styles, or ideas of our own society are inferior to those that originate elsewhere. (64)

Additional Readings

Anderssen, Erin, Michael Valpy, and others. 2004. *The New Canada: A Globe and Mail Report on the Next Generation.* Toronto: Globe and Mail/McClelland and Stewart Ltd. A portrait of a "new" Canada that is urban, ethnically diverse, secular, and media-savvy, focusing on Canadians between 20 and 29 years of age.

Bibby, Reginald. 1995. *The Bibby Report: Social Trends Canadian Style.* Toronto: Stoddart. Based on national surveys of 1975, 1980, 1985, 1990, and 1995, this book examines Canadians' values on such issues as multiculturalism, Americanization, bilingualism, and spirituality.

Dunk, Thomas W. 2003. *It's a Working Man's Town*, 2nd ed. Montreal: McGill-Queen's University Press. An examination of leisure activities of working-class males in Thunder Bay, Ontario, illustrating the importance of these activities for understanding the link between culture and consciousness.

Fleras, Augie, and Jean Lock Kunz. 2001. *Media and Minorities: Representing Diversity in Multicultural Canada.* Toronto: Thomson Educational Publishing. Fleras and Kunz analyze and assess the representation of minority groups in the mass media against a backdrop of Canada's commitment to multiculturalism.

Weinstein, Deena. 2000. *Heavy Metal: The Music and Its Culture.* Cambridge, MA: Da Capo. A sociologist examines the subculture associated with heavy metal music and efforts to curtail this subculture.

Online Learning Centre

Visit the *Sociology: A Brief Introduction* Online Learning Centre at www.mcgrawhill.ca/college/schaefer to access quizzes, interactive exercises, video clips, and other research and study tools related to this chapter.

Reel Society Interactive Movie CD-ROM 2.0

Reel Society 2.0 can be used to spark discussion about the following topics from this chapter:

- Cultural universals
- Norms

chapter 4

SOCIALIZATION

Schools can sometimes be stressful arenas of socialization. This poster informs schoolchildren in Japan that they can call a hotline and receive advice concerning stress, bullying by classmates, and corporal punishment from their teachers.

The United States is one of the few industrialized nations in the world that thinks that children are legitimate targets for advertisers. Belgium, Denmark, Norway, and the Canadian province of Quebec ban all advertising to children on television and radio, and Sweden and Greece are pushing for an end to all advertising aimed at children throughout the European Union. An effort to pass similar legislation in the United States in the 1970s was squelched by a coalition of food and toy companies, broadcasters, and ad agencies. Children in America appear to have value primarily as new customers. As an ad for juvenile and infant bedding and home accessories says, "Having children is so rewarding. You get to buy childish stuff and pretend it's for them." [America's] policy—or lack thereof—on every children's issue, from education to drugs to teen suicide to child abuse, leaves many to conclude that [America is] a nation that hates its children.

However, the media care about them. The Turner Cartoon Network tells advertisers, "Today's kids influence over $130 billion of their parents' spending annually. Kids also spend $8 billion of their own money. That makes these little consumers big business." Not only are children influencing a lot of spending in the present, they are developing brand loyalty and the beginnings of an addiction to consumption that will serve corporations well in the future. According to Mike Searles, president of Kids 'R' Us, "If you own this child at an early age, you can own this child for years to come. Companies are saying, 'Hey, I want to own the kid younger and younger.'" No Wonder Levi Strauss & Co. finds it worthwhile to send a direct mailing to seven- to twelve-year-old girls to learn about them when they are starting to form brand opinions. According to the senior advertising manager, "This is more of a long-term relationship that we're trying to explore." There may not seem much harm in this until we consider that the tobacco and alcohol industries are also interested in long-term relationships, beginning in childhood—and are selling products that can indeed end up "owning" people.

...Advertisers like to tell parents that they can always turn off the TV to protect their kids from any of the negative impact of advertising. This is like telling us that we can protect our children from air pollution by making sure they never breathe. Advertising is our *environment*. We swim in it as fish swim in water. We cannot escape it. Unless, of course, we keep our children home from school and blindfold them whenever they are outside of the house. And never let them play with other children. Even then, advertising's messages are inside our intimate relationships, our homes, our hearts, our heads.

...Advertising often sells a great deal more than products. It sells values, images, and concepts of love and sexuality, romance, success, and, perhaps most important, normalcy. To a great extent, it tells us who we are and who we should be. We are increasingly using brand names to create our identities. James Twitchell argues that the label of our shirt, the make of our car, and our favourite laundry detergent are filling the vacuum once occupied by religion, education, and our family name. *(Kilbourne 1999)* ■

Jean Kilbourne's research on the influence of advertising on women and girls reveals that advertising sells far more than just cars, jeans, detergents, teeth whiteners, shampoo, and diet programs—it sells values. In *Deadly Persuasion: Why Women and Girls Must Fight the Addictive Power of Advertising* (1999), Kilbourne points to the ways in which advertisers target children, as well as adults, arguing that their messages are ubiquitous—at school, at home, and, eventually, in our heads and hearts. Although advertising cannot *make* people buy anything, it does contribute to a climate in which our identities, values, priorities, and behaviours are framed by what and how much we buy.

Sociologists, in general, are interested in the patterns of behaviour and attitudes that emerge *throughout* the life course, from infancy to old age. These patterns are part of the process of ***socialization,*** whereby people learn the attitudes, values, and behaviours appropriate for members of a particular culture. Socialization occurs through human interactions. We learn a great deal from those people most important in our lives—immediate family members, best friends, and teachers. But we also learn from people we see on the street, on television, on the Internet, and in films and magazines. From a microsociological perspective, socialization helps us to discover how to behave "properly" and what to expect from others if we follow (or challenge) society's norms and values. From a macrosociological perspective, socialization provides for the transmission of a culture from one generation to the next and thereby for the long-term continuance of a society.

Socialization affects the overall cultural practices of a society, and it also shapes our self-images. For example, in North America, a person who is viewed as "too heavy" or "too short" does not conform to the ideal cultural standard of physical attractiveness. This kind of unfavourable evaluation can significantly influence the person's self-esteem. In this sense, socialization experiences can help shape our personalities. In everyday speech, the term ***personality*** is used to refer to a person's typical patterns of attitudes, needs, characteristics, and behaviour.

This chapter will examine the role of socialization in human development. It begins by analyzing the interaction of heredity and environmental factors. We pay particular attention to how people develop perceptions, feelings, and beliefs about themselves. The chapter will also explore the lifelong nature of the socialization process, as well as important agents of socialization, among them family, schools, peers, and the media. Finally, the social policy section will focus on the socialization experience of group child care for young children. ■

Use Your Sociological Imagination www.mcgrawhill.ca/college/schaefer

How do advertisements affect what you purchase and how much you spend? Do advertisers target girls and women more than boys and men? What do you think advertising teaches people about what is important in their lives?

THE ROLE OF SOCIALIZATION

What makes us who we are? Is it the genes we are born with? Or the environment in which we grow up? Researchers have traditionally clashed over the relative importance of biological inheritance and environmental factors in human development—a conflict called the *nature versus nurture* (or *heredity versus environment*) debate. Today, most social scientists have moved beyond this debate, acknowledging instead the *interaction* of these variables in shaping human development. However, we can better appreciate how heredity and environmental factors interact and influence the socialization process if we first examine situations in which one factor operates almost entirely without the other (Homans 1979).

Environment: The Impact of Isolation

In the 1994 movie *Nell,* Jodie Foster played a young woman hidden from birth by her mother in a backwoods cabin. Raised without normal human contact, Nell crouches like an animal, screams wildly, and speaks or sings in a language all her own. This movie was drawn from the actual account of an emaciated 16-year-old boy who mysteriously appeared in 1828 in the townsquare of Nuremberg, Germany (Lipson 1994).

The Case of Isabelle

Some viewers may have found the story of Nell difficult to believe, but the painful childhood of Isabelle was all too real. For the first six years of her life, Isabelle lived in almost total seclusion in a darkened room. She had little contact with other people, with the exception of her mother, who could neither speak nor hear. Isabelle's mother's parents had been so deeply ashamed of Isabelle's illegitimate birth that they kept her hidden away from the world. Ohio authorities finally discovered the child in 1938, when Isabelle's mother escaped from her parents' home, taking her daughter with her.

When she was discovered at age six, Isabelle could not speak. She could merely make various croaking sounds. Her only communications with her mother were simple gestures. Isabelle had been largely deprived of the typical interactions and socialization experiences of childhood. Since she had actually seen few people, she initially showed a strong fear of strangers and reacted almost like a wild animal when confronted with an unfamiliar person. As she became accustomed to seeing certain individuals, her reaction changed to one of extreme apathy. At first, it was believed that Isabelle was deaf, but she soon began to react to nearby sounds. On tests of maturity, she scored at the level of an infant rather than a six-year-old.

Specialists developed a systematic training program to help Isabelle adapt to human relationships and socialization. After a few days of training, she made her first attempt to verbalize. Although she started slowly, Isabelle quickly passed through six years of development. In a little over two months, she was speaking in complete sentences. Nine months later, she could identify both words and sentences. Before Isabelle reached the age of nine, she was ready to attend school with other children. By her 14th year, she was in sixth grade, doing well in school, and emotionally well-adjusted.

Yet, without an opportunity to experience socialization in her first six years, Isabelle had been hardly human in the social sense when she was first discovered. Her inability to communicate at the time of her discovery—despite her physical and cognitive potential to learn—and her remarkable progress over the next few years underscore the impact of socialization on human development (K. Davis 1940, 1947).

Isabelle's experience is important for researchers because it is one of few cases of children reared in total isolation. Unfortunately, however, there are many cases of children raised in extremely neglectful social circumstances. Recently, attention has focused on infants and young children in orphanages in the formerly communist countries of Eastern Europe. For example, in Romanian orphanages, babies lie in their cribs for 18 or 20 hours a day, curled against their feeding bottles and receiving little adult care. Such minimal attention continues for the first five years of their lives. Many of them are fearful of human contact and prone to unpredictable antisocial behaviour. This situation came to light as families in North America and Europe began adopting thousands of these children. The adjustment problems for about 20 percent of them were often so dramatic that the adopting families suffered guilty fears of being unfit adoptive parents. Many of them have asked for assistance in dealing with the children. Slowly, efforts are being made to introduce the deprived youngsters to feelings of attachment that they have never experienced before (Groza, Ilena, and Irwin 1999; Talbot 1998).

These children in a Romanian orphanage enjoy little adult contact and spend much of their time confined to cribs. This neglect can result in adjustment problems later in life.

Increasingly, researchers are emphasizing the importance of early socialization experiences for children who grow up in more normal environments. We now know that it is not enough to care for an infant's physical needs; parents must also concern themselves with children's social development. If, for example, children are discouraged from having friends, they will miss out on social interactions with peers that are critical for emotional growth.

Use Your Sociological Imagination

What events in your life have had a strong influence on who you are?

Primate Studies

Studies of animals raised in isolation also support the importance of socialization in development. Harry Harlow (1971), a researcher at the primate laboratory of the University of Wisconsin, conducted tests with rhesus monkeys that had been raised away from their mothers and away from contact with other monkeys. As was the case with Isabelle, the rhesus monkeys raised in isolation were fearful and easily frightened. They did not mate, and the females who were artificially inseminated became abusive mothers. Apparently, isolation had had a damaging effect on the monkeys.

A creative aspect of Harlow's experimentation was his use of "artificial mothers." In one such experiment, Harlow presented monkeys raised in isolation with two substitute mothers—one cloth-covered replica and one covered with wire that had the ability to offer milk. Monkey after monkey went to the wire mother for the life-giving milk, yet spent much more time clinging to the more motherlike cloth model. In this study, the monkeys valued the artificial mothers that provided a comforting physical sensation (conveyed by the terry cloth) more highly than those that provided food. It appears that the infant monkeys developed greater social attachments from their need for warmth, comfort, and intimacy than from their need for milk.

Although the isolation studies discussed above may seem to suggest that inheritance can be dismissed as a factor in the social development of humans and animals, studies of twins provide insight into a fascinating interplay between hereditary and environmental factors.

The Influence of Heredity

Oskar Stohr and Jack Yufe are identical twins who were separated soon after their birth and raised on different continents in very different cultural settings. Oskar was reared as a strict Catholic by his maternal grandmother in the Sudetenland of Czechoslovakia. As a member of the Hitler Youth movement in Nazi Germany, he learned to hate Jews. By contrast, his brother Jack was reared in Trinidad by the twins' Jewish father. Jack joined an Israeli kibbutz (a collective settlement) at age 17 and later served in the Israeli army. But when they were reunited in middle age, some startling similarities emerged:

> Both were wearing wire-rimmed glasses and mustaches, both sported two pocket shirts with epaulets. They share idiosyncrasies galore: they like spicy foods and sweet liqueurs, are absent-minded, have a habit of falling asleep in front of the television, think it's funny to sneeze in a crowd of strangers, flush the toilet before using it, store rubber bands on their wrists, read magazines from back to front, dip buttered toast in their coffee. (Holden 1980)

The twins also were found to differ in many important respects: Jack is a workaholic; Oskar enjoys leisure-time activities. Whereas Oskar is a traditionalist who is domineering toward women, Jack is a political liberal who is much more accepting of feminism. Finally, Jack is extremely proud of being Jewish, while Oskar never mentions his Jewish heritage (Holden 1987).

Oskar and Jack are prime examples of the interplay of heredity and environment. For a number of years, researchers at the Minnesota Center for Twin and Adoption Research have been studying pairs of identical twins reared apart to determine what similarities, if any, they show in personality traits, behaviour, and intelligence. Thus far, the preliminary results from the available twin studies indicate that both genetic factors and socialization experiences are influential in human development. Certain characteristics, such as temperaments, voice patterns, and nervous habits, appear to be strikingly similar even in twins reared apart, suggesting that these qualities may be linked to hereditary causes. However, identical twins reared apart differ far more in their attitudes, values, types of mates chosen, and even drinking habits; these qualities, it would seem, are influenced by environmental patterns. In examining clusters of personality traits among such twins, the Minnesota studies have found marked similarities in their tendency toward leadership or dominance, but significant differences in their need for intimacy, comfort, and assistance.

Researchers have also been impressed with the similar scores on intelligence tests of twins reared apart in *roughly similar* social settings. Most of the identical twins register scores even closer than those that would be expected if the same person took a test twice. At the same time, however, identical twins brought up in *dramatically different* social environments score quite differently on intelligence tests—a finding that supports the impact of socialization on human development (McGue and Bouchard 1998).

We need to be cautious when reviewing the studies of twin pairs and other relevant research. Widely broadcast findings have often been based on extremely small samples and preliminary analysis. For example, one study (not involving twin pairs) was frequently cited as confirming genetic links with behaviour. Yet the researchers had to retract their conclusions after they increased the sample from 81 to 91 cases and reclassified two of the original 81 cases. After these changes, the initial findings were no longer valid. Critics add that the studies on twin pairs have not provided satisfactory information concerning the extent to which these separated identical twins may have had contact with each other, even though they were raised apart. Such interactions—especially if they were extensive—could call into question the validity of the twin studies (Kelsoe et al. 1989).

Psychologist Leon Kamin fears that overgeneralizing from the Minnesota twin results—and granting too much importance to the impact of heredity—may lead to blaming the poor and downtrodden for their unfortunate condition. As this debate continues, we can certainly anticipate numerous efforts to replicate the research and clarify the interplay between hereditary and environmental factors in human development (Horgan 1993; Leo 1987; Plomin 1989; Wallis 1987).

Sociobiology

Do the *social* traits that human groups display have biological origins? As part of the continuing debate on the relative influences of heredity and the environment, there has been renewed interest in sociobiology in recent years. ***Sociobiology*** is the systematic study of the biological bases of social behaviour. Sociobiologists basically apply naturalist Charles Darwin's principles of natural selection to the study of social behaviour. They assume that particular forms of behaviour become genetically linked to a species if they contribute to its fitness to survive (van den Berghe 1978). In its extreme form, sociobiology suggests that *all* behaviour is the result of genetic or biological factors and that social interactions play no role in shaping people's conduct.

Sociobiology does not seek to describe individual behaviour on the level of "Why is Fred more aggressive than Jim?" Rather, sociobiologists focus on how human nature is affected by the genetic composition of a *group* of people who share certain characteristics (such as men or women, or members of isolated tribal bands). Many sociologists are highly critical of sociobiologists' tendency to explain, or seemingly justify, human behaviour on the basis of nature and ignore its cultural and social basis.

Some researchers insist that intellectual interest in sociobiology will only deflect serious study of the more significant factor influencing human behaviour—socialization. Yet Lois Wladis Hoffman (1985), in her presidential address to the Society for the Psychological Study of Social Issues, argued that sociobiology poses a valuable challenge to social scientists to better document their own research. Interactionists, for example, could show how social behaviour is not programmed by human biology but instead adjusts continually to the attitudes and responses of others.

Conflict theorists (like functionalists and interactionists) believe that people's behaviour rather than their genetic structure defines social reality. Conflict theorists fear that the sociobiological approach could be used as an argument against efforts to assist disadvantaged people, such as schoolchildren who are not competing successfully (M. Harris 1997).

Edward O. Wilson, a zoologist at Harvard University, has argued that there should be parallel studies of human behaviour with a focus on both genetic and social causes. Certainly most social scientists would agree that there is a biological basis for social behaviour. But there is less support for the most extreme positions taken by certain advocates of sociobiology (Begley 1998; Gove 1987; Wilson 1975, 1978; see also Guterman 2000; Segerstråle 2000).

SOCIALIZATION: THE MAJOR THEORETICAL PERSPECTIVES

Interactionist Perspective

We all have various perceptions, feelings, and beliefs about who we are and what we are like. How do we come to develop these? Do they change as we age?

We were not born with these understandings. Building on the work of George Herbert Mead (1964b), sociologists recognize that we create our own designation: the self. The ***self*** is a distinct identity that sets us apart from others. It is not a static phenomenon but continues to develop and change throughout our lives.

Sociologists and psychologists alike have expressed interest in how the individual develops and modifies the sense of self as a result of social interaction. The work of sociologists Charles Horton Cooley and George Herbert Mead, pioneers of the interactionist approach, has been especially useful in furthering our understanding of these important issues (Gecas 1982).

pp. 15–16

Cooley: Looking-Glass Self

In the early 1900s, Charles Horton Cooley advanced the belief that we learn who we are by interacting with others. Our view of ourselves, then, comes not only from direct contemplation of our personal qualities but also from our impressions of how others perceive us. Cooley used the phrase ***looking-glass self*** to emphasize that the self is the product of our social interactions with other people.

The process of developing a self-identity or self-concept has three phases. First, we imagine how we present ourselves to others—to relatives, friends, even strangers on the street. Second, we imagine how others evaluate us (attractive, intelligent, shy, or strange). Finally, we develop some sort of feeling about ourselves, such as respect or shame, as a result of these impressions (Cooley 1902; M. Howard 1989).

A subtle but critical aspect of Cooley's looking-glass self is that the self results from an individual's "imagination" of how others view him or her. As a result, we can develop self-identities based on *incorrect* perceptions of how others see us. A student may react strongly to a teacher's criticism and decide (wrongly) that the instructor views the student as stupid. This misperception can easily be converted into a negative self-identity through the following process: (1) the teacher criticized me, (2) the teacher must think that I'm stupid, (3) I *am* stupid. Yet self-identities are also subject to change. If the student receives an "A" at the end of the course, he or she will probably no longer feel stupid.

Mead: Stages of the Self

As mentioned in the first chapter, George Herbert Mead continued Cooley's exploration of interactionist theory, developing a useful model of the process by which the self emerges. His model was defined by three distinct stages: the preparatory stage, the play stage, and the game stage.

During the *preparatory stage,* children merely imitate the people around them, especially family members with whom they continually interact. Thus, a small child will bang on a piece of wood while a parent is engaged in carpentry work or will try to throw a ball if an older sibling is doing so nearby.

As they grow older, children become more adept at using symbols to communicate with others. ***Symbols*** are the gestures, objects, and language that form the basis of human communication. By interacting with relatives and friends, as well as by watching cartoons on television and looking at picture books, children in the preparatory stage begin to understand the use of symbols. Like spoken languages, symbols vary from culture to culture and even between subcultures. Raising an eyebrow may mean astonishment in North America, but in Peru it means "money" or "pay me," while in the Pacific island nation of Tonga it means "yes" or "I agree" (Axtell 1990).

Mead was among the first to analyze the relationship of symbols to socialization. As children develop skill in communicating through symbols, they gradually become more aware of social relationships. As a result, during the *play stage,* the child becomes able to pretend to be other people. Just as an actor "becomes" a character, a child becomes a doctor, parent, superhero, or ship captain.

Mead, in fact, noted that an important aspect of the play stage is role-playing. ***Role taking*** is the process of mentally assuming the perspective of another, thereby enabling the person to respond from that imagined viewpoint. For example, through this process, a young child will gradually learn when it is best to ask a parent for favours. If the parent usually comes home from work in a bad mood, the child will wait until after dinner when the parent is more relaxed and approachable.

"Say cheese!" Children imitate the people around them, especially family members they continually interact with, during the *preparatory stage* described by George Herbert Mead.

In Mead's third stage, the *game stage,* the child of about eight or nine years old no longer just plays roles but begins to consider several actual tasks and relationships simultaneously. At this point in development, children grasp not only their own social positions but also those of others around them—just as in a football game the players must understand their own and everyone else's positions. Consider a girl or boy who is part of a Scout troop out on a weekend hike in the mountains. The child must understand what he or she is expected to do but also must recognize the responsibilities of other scouts as well as of the leaders. This is the final stage of development under Mead's model; the child can now respond to numerous members of the social environment.

Again as discussed in Chapter 1, Mead uses the term generalized others to refer to the attitudes, viewpoints, and expectations of society as a whole that a child takes into account.

p. 16

Research in Action 4-1 Impression Management by Students after Exams

When you get an exam back, you probably react differently with fellow classmates, depending on the grades that you and they earned. This is all part of impression management, as sociologists Daniel Albas and Cheryl Albas (1988) demonstrated. They explored the strategies that post-secondary students use to create desired appearances after receiving their grades on exams. Albas and Albas divide these encounters into three categories: those between students who have all received high grades (Ace–Ace encounters), those between students who have received high grades and those who have received low or even failing grades (Ace–Bomber encounters), and those between students who have all received low grades (Bomber–Bomber encounters).

Ace–Ace encounters occur in a rather open atmosphere because there is comfort in sharing a high mark with another high achiever. It is even acceptable to violate the norm of modesty and brag when among other Aces since, as one student admitted, "It's much easier to admit a high mark to someone who has done better than you, or at least as well."

Ace–Bomber encounters are often sensitive. Bombers generally attempt to avoid such exchanges because "you ... emerge looking like the dumb one" or "feel like you are lazy or unreliable." When forced into interactions with Aces, Bombers work to appear gracious and congratulatory. For their part, Aces offer sympathy and support for the dissatisfied Bombers and even rationalize their own "lucky" high scores. To help Bombers save face, Aces may emphasize the difficulty and unfairness of the examination.

Bomber–Bomber encounters tend to be closed, reflecting the group effort to wall off the feared disdain of others. Yet, within the safety of these encounters, Bombers openly share their disappointment and engage in expressions of mutual self-pity that they themselves call "pity parties." They devise face-saving excuses for their poor performances, such as "I wasn't feeling well all week" or "I had four exams and two papers due that week." If the grade distribution in a class included particularly low scores, Bombers may blame the professor, who will be attacked as a sadist, a slave driver, or simply an incompetent.

As is evident from these descriptions, students' impression management strategies conform to society's informal norms regarding modesty and consideration for less successful peers. In classroom settings, as in the workplace and in other types of human interactions, efforts at impression management are most intense when status differentials are more pronounced, as in encounters between the high-scoring Aces and the low-scoring Bombers.

Applying Theory

1. What theoretical perspective would most likely be employed in the study of students' impression management strategies?
2. How do you think some feminist sociologists might approach the study of impression management on the part of their students?

Source: Albas and Albas 1988.

At the game stage, children can take a more sophisticated view of people and the social environment. They now understand what specific occupations and social positions are and no longer equate Mr. Sahota only with the role of "librarian" or Ms. La Haigue only with "principal." It has become clear to the child that Mr. Sahota can be a librarian, a parent, and a marathon runner at the same time and that Ms. La Haigue is one of many principals in our society. Thus, the child has reached a new level of sophistication in his or her observations of individuals and institutions.

Use Your Sociological Imagination

How has the generalized other influenced the decisions you've made?

Goffman: Presentation of the Self

How do we manage our "self"? How do we display to others who we are? Erving Goffman, a sociologist associated with the interactionist perspective, suggested that many of our daily activities involve attempts to convey impressions of who we are.

Early in life, the individual learns to slant his or her presentation of the self in order to create distinctive appearances and satisfy particular audiences. Goffman (1959) refers to this altering of the presentation of the self as ***impression management.*** Box 4-1 provides an everyday example of this concept by describing how students engage in impression management after getting their examination grades.

In examining such everyday social interactions, Goffman makes so many explicit parallels to the theatre that his view has been termed the dramaturgical approach. According to this perspective, people resemble performers in action. For example, a clerk may try to appear busier than he or she actually is if a p. 16 supervisor happens to be watching. A customer in a singles' bar may try to look as if he or she is waiting for a particular person to arrive.

Goffman (1959) has also drawn attention to another aspect of the self—***face-work.*** How often do you initiate some kind of face-saving behaviour when you feel embarrassed or rejected? In response to a rejection at the singles' bar, a person may engage in face-work by saying, "There really isn't an interesting person in this entire crowd." We feel the need to maintain a proper image of the self if we are to continue social interaction.

Goffman's approach is generally regarded as an insightful perspective on everyday life, but it is not without its critics. Writing from a conflict perspective, sociologist Alvin Gouldner (1970) sees Goffman's work as implicitly reaffirming the status quo, including social class inequalities. Using Gouldner's critique, we might ask whether women and members of minority groups are expected to deceive both themselves and others while paying homage to those with power. In considering impression management and other concepts developed by Goffman, sociologists must remember that by describing social reality, a person is not necessarily endorsing its harsh impact on many individuals and groups (S. Williams 1986).

Goffman's work represents a logical progression of the sociological efforts begun by Cooley and Mead on how personality is acquired through socialization and how we manage the presentation of our self to others. Cooley stressed the process by which we come to create a self; Mead focused on how the self develops as we learn to interact with others; Goffman emphasized the ways in which we consciously create images of ourselves for others.

Feminist Perspectives

Given the vast variety of feminist theories and the differences among them, it is not surprising that they do not all stress the importance of socialization as a key element in explaining the condition of women's lives. Some feminist theorists believe that what a society believes to be "masculine" and "feminine" is culturally imposed through systematic socialization of girls and boys, as well as women and men, according to sex. This systematic socialization takes place in the family, among peers, in the school, in the workplace, in religious organizations, and through the mass media. Liberal feminists are one such group of feminist theorists who stress the importance of avoiding this type of socialization in order to achieve equality of the sexes. Liberal feminists, who are sometimes called *equality feminists*, stress the importance of individual freedom and equality of opportunity, which for them takes place in the public or economic sphere, not the private or domestic sphere.

Thus, according to liberal feminists, institutions that socialize children and adults according to a sexual division of labour deprive girls and women of individual achievement, success, and freedom (as defined by the male-dominated public sphere).

Functionalist Perspective

p. 12 Functionalist perspectives stress the importance of consensus, stability, and equilibrium in society; therefore, socialization of society's members is essential to meets these goals. Socialization, according to functionalists, serves to ensure that the members of a given society share or buy into the basic values of that society in order to promote consensus or agreement and stability. Without high levels of agreement on the core values of society, functionalists argue that the society will become destabilized and its survival may be threatened.

Since functionalist theorists maintain that a society is analogous to a human body in which the various organs—heart, lungs, kidney, liver, and so on—work as a system to maintain the health or balance of the entire body, so must the parts of society. Such institutions as the family, schools, the state, the mass media, the legal system, and religion must function as an integrated system in which each part contributes to the functioning of the others and to that of the whole society. Here, the function of the socialization of society's members concerning basic values and goals is key, as it provides cohesion and coordination among various institutions, creating equilibrium. For example, Canada's economy, and those of many other countries, is a capitalist one based the value of competition and individual achievement. For it to function effectively and efficiently, workers must buy into the value, goal, and means of success as defined by the capitalist economy. Therefore, it becomes imperative, according to functionalists, that the family, for example, socialize its children according to the values of hard work, individual effort, and achievement; this socialization will ensure the provision of a workforce that is properly primed, ready to meet the challenges of a capitalist economy. Similarly, the education system must socialize its students with these values, as well as with the specific skills and training necessary to meet the demands of the economy.

Overall, functionalist perspectives stress the importance of maintaining the status quo. Socialization, therefore, is viewed as a way to ensure that a society's members share values, beliefs, and goals that contribute to the maintenance of society as a whole.

Conflict Perspective

Like the functionalist theorists, conflict thinkers agree that the socialization of a society's members by the major institutions (e.g., the economy, the state, the mass media) contributes to the perpetuation of the status quo. For conflict thinkers, however, this is not viewed as desirable, given the inherent inequalities of the capitalist society.

Since the capitalist society is based on the unequal distribution of power and resources, conflict thinkers advocate that the messages communicated through various forms of socialization will reflect this inequity. Karl Marx, for example, believed that the dominant ideas of a society at any given point in history will be the ideas of the dominant ruling class. Marx argued that the economic base of society (i.e., capitalism) determined the nature of the other institutions, such as the family, the education system, and the mass media, causing them also to reflect the ideas of the ruling class. For example, the mass media has often been considered by conflict thinkers as the mouthpiece of the ruling class, socializing all members of society with values and goals that reflect the economic interests of the ruling class. In this way socialization serves to ensure that the working classes continue to buy into an economic system based on the dominance and control of the ruling class. According to conflict thinkers Edward Herman and Noam Chomsky (1988), the mass media represents a propaganda model that acts to "manufacture consent" by "generating compliance" on the part of the mass population, which works for and consumes the products produced by the dominant ruling class.

Psychological Approaches

Psychologists have shared the interest of Cooley, Mead, and other sociologists in the development of the self. Early work in psychology, such as that of Sigmund Freud (1856–1939), stressed the role of inborn drives—among them the drive for sexual gratification—in channelling human behaviour. More recently, such psychologists as Jean Piaget have emphasized the stages through which human beings progress as the self develops.

Like Charles Horton Cooley and George Herbert Mead, Freud believed that the self is a social product and that aspects of personality are influenced by other people (especially parents). However, unlike Cooley and Mead, he suggested that the self has components that are always fighting with each other. According to Freud, our natural impulsive instincts are in constant conflict with societal constraints. Part of us seeks limitless pleasure, while another part seeks out rational behaviour. By interacting with others, we learn the expectations of society and then select behaviour most appropriate to our own culture. (Of course, as Freud was well aware, we sometimes distort reality and behave irrationally.)

Research on newborn babies by the Swiss child psychologist Jean Piaget (1896–1980) has underscored the importance of social interactions in developing a sense of self. Piaget found that newborns have no self in the sense of a looking-glass image. Ironically, though, they are quite self-centred; they demand that all attention be directed toward them. Newborns have not yet separated themselves from the universe of which they are a part. For these babies, the phrase "you and me" has no meaning; they understand only "me." However, as they mature, children are gradually socialized into social relationships even within their rather self-centred world.

In his well-known ***cognitive theory of development***, Piaget (1954) identifies four stages in the development of children's thought processes. In the first, or *sensorimotor,* stage, young children use their senses to make discoveries. For example, through touching they discover that their hands are actually a part of themselves. During the second, or *preoperational,* stage, children begin to use words and symbols to distinguish objects and ideas. The milestone in the third, or *concrete operational,* stage is that children engage in more logical thinking. They learn that even when a formless lump of clay is shaped into a snake, it is still the same clay. Finally, in the fourth, or *formal operational,* stage, adolescents are capable of sophisticated abstract thought and can deal with ideas and values in a logical manner.

Piaget has suggested that moral development becomes an important part of socialization as children develop the ability to think more abstractly. When children learn the rules of a game, such as checkers or jacks, they are learning to obey societal norms. Those under eight years old display a rather basic level of morality: rules are rules, and there is no concept of "extenuating circumstances." However, as they mature, children become capable of greater autonomy and begin to experience moral dilemmas as to what constitutes proper behaviour.

According to Jean Piaget, social interaction is the key to development. As they grow older, children give increasing attention to how other people think and why they act in particular ways. To develop a distinct personality, each of us needs opportunities to interact with others. As we saw earlier, Isabelle was deprived of the chance for normal social interactions, and the consequences were severe (Kitchener 1991).

SOCIALIZATION AND THE LIFE COURSE

The Life Course

Adolescents among the Kota people of the Congo in Africa paint themselves blue, Mexican American girls go on a daylong religious retreat before dancing the night away, Egyptian mothers step over their newborn infants seven times, and graduating North American students may throw hats in the air. These are all ways of celebrating ***rites of passage,*** a means of dramatizing and validating changes in a person's status. The Kota rite marks the passage to adulthood. The colour blue, viewed as the colour of death, symbolizes the death of childhood. Hispanic girls in the United States celebrate reaching womanhood with a *quinceañera* ceremony at age 15. In Miami, Florida, the popularity of the *quinceañera* supports a network of party planners, caterers, dress designers, and the Miss Quinceañera Latina pageant. For thousands of years, Egyptian mothers have welcomed their newborns to the world in the Soboa ceremony by stepping over the seven-day-old infant seven times. North American graduates may celebrate their graduation from college or university by hurling their caps skyward (D. Cohen 1991; Garza 1993; McLane 1995; Quadagno 1999).

These specific ceremonies mark stages of development in the life course. They indicate that the socialization process continues throughout all stages of the human life cycle. Sociologists and other social scientists use the life-course approach in recognition that biological changes mould but do not dictate human behaviour from birth until death.

Body painting is a ritual marking the passage to puberty among young people in Liberia in northern Africa.

Within the cultural diversity of Canada, each individual has a "personal biography" that is influenced by events both in the family and in the larger society. Although the completion of religious confirmations, school graduations, marriage, and parenthood can all be regarded as rites of passage in our society, people do not necessarily experience them at the same time. The timing of these events depends on such factors as gender, economic background, region (urban or rural area), and even when a person was born.

Sociologists and other social scientists have moved away from identifying specific life stages that we are all expected to pass through at some point. Indeed, people today are much less likely to follow an "orderly" progression of life events (leaving school, then obtaining their first job, then getting married) than they were in the past. For example, an increasing number of women in Canada are beginning or returning to postsecondary education after marrying and having children. With such changes in mind, researchers are increasingly reluctant to offer sweeping generalizations about stages in the life course.

We encounter some of the most difficult socialization challenges (and rites of passage) in the later years of life. Assessing our accomplishments, coping with declining physical abilities, experiencing retirement, and facing the inevitability of death may lead to painful adjustments. Old age is further complicated by the negative way that many societies view and treat the elderly. The common stereotypes of the elderly as helpless and dependent may well weaken an older person's self-image. However, as we will explore more fully in Chapter 14, many older people continue to lead active, productive, fulfilled lives—whether within the paid labour force or as retirees.

Use Your Sociological Imagination

What was the last rite of passage you participated in? Was it formal or informal?

Anticipatory Socialization and Resocialization

The development of a social self is literally a lifelong transformation that begins in the crib and continues as a person prepares for death. Two types of socialization occur at many points throughout the life course: anticipatory socialization and resocialization.

Anticipatory socialization refers to the processes of socialization in which a person "rehearses" for future positions, occupations, and social relationships. A culture can function more efficiently and smoothly if members become acquainted with the norms, values, and behaviour associated with a social position before actually assuming that status. Preparation for many aspects of adult life begins with anticipatory socialization during childhood and adolescence and continues throughout our lives as we prepare for new responsibilities.

You can see the process of anticipatory socialization take place when high school students start to consider which postsecondary institutions they may attend. Traditionally, this meant looking at publications received in the mail or making campus visits. However, with new technology, more and more students are using the Web to begin their educational experience. Institutions are investing more time and money in developing attractive Web sites where students can take "virtual" campus walks and hear audio clips of everything from the campus cheer to a sample zoology lecture.

Occasionally, assuming new social and occupational positions requires us to *unlearn* a previous orientation. ***Resocialization*** refers to the process of discarding former behaviour patterns and accepting new ones as part of a transition in life. Often resocialization occurs when there is an explicit effort to transform an individual, as happens in therapy groups, prisons, religious conversion settings, and political indoctrination camps. The process of resocialization typically involves considerable stress for the individual, much more so than socialization in general or even anticipatory socialization (Gecas 1992).

Resocialization is particularly effective when it occurs within a total institution. Erving Goffman (1961) coined the term ***total institutions*** to refer to institutions, such as prisons, the military, mental hospitals, and convents, that regulate all aspects of a person's life under a single authority. Because the total institution is generally cut off from the rest of society, it provides for all the needs of its members. Quite literally, the crew of a merchant vessel at sea becomes part of a total institution. So elaborate are its requirements, and so all-encompassing are its activities, that a total institution often represents a miniature society.

Goffman (1961) has identified four common traits of total institutions:

1. All aspects of life are conducted in the same place and are under the control of a single authority.
2. Any activities within the institution are conducted in the company of others in the same circumstances—for example, novices in a convent or army recruits.
3. The authorities devise rules and schedule activities without consulting the participants.
4. All aspects of life within a total institution are designed to fulfil the purpose of the organization. Thus, all activities in a monastery might be centred on prayer and communion with God (Davies 1989; P. Rose et al. 1979).

People often lose their individuality within total institutions. For example, a person entering prison may experience the humiliation of a ***degradation ceremony*** as he or she is stripped of clothing, jewellery, and other personal possessions. Even the person's self is taken away to some extent; the prison inmate loses a name and becomes known to authorities as a number. From this point on, scheduled daily routines allow for little or no personal initiative. The individual becomes secondary and rather invisible in the overbearing social environment (Garfinkel 1956).

In 1934, the world was gripped by the birth of quintuplets to Olivia and Elzire Dionne in Ontario. In the midst of the Depression, people wanted to hear and see all they could about these five girls, born generations before fertility drugs made multiple births more common. What seemed like a heartwarming story turned out to be a tragic case of Goffman's total institutionalization. The government of Ontario soon took the quintuplets from their home and set them up in a facility complete with an observation gallery overlooking their playground. Each month, 10 000 tourists paid an entry fee to view the five little "Cinderellas." When the girls left the nine-room compound, it was always to raise money for some worthwhile cause or to merchandise some product. Within their compound, even their parents and their older siblings had to make appointments to see them. A child psychiatrist responsible for their child rearing ordered they never be spanked—or hugged (to prevent the chance of infection).

After nine years, the quintuplets were reunited with their family. But the legacy of total institutionalization persisted. Sharp divisions and jealousies had developed between the five girls and other siblings. The parents were caught up in charges of doing too much or too little for all their children. In 1997 the three surviving quintuplets made public a poignant letter to the parents of recently born septuplets in Iowa:

> We three would like you to know we feel a natural affinity and tenderness for your children. We hope your children receive more respect than we did. Their fate should be no different from that of other children. Multiple births should not be confused with entertainment, nor should they be an opportunity to sell products. . . .
>
> Our lives have been ruined by the exploitation we suffered at the hands of the government of Ontario, our place of birth. We were displayed as a curiosity three times a day for millions of tourists. . . .

> We sincerely hope a lesson will be learned from examining how our lives were forever altered by our childhood experiences. If this letter changes the course of events for these newborns, then perhaps our lives will have served a higher purpose. (Dionne et al. 1997:39)

It is to be hoped that the Iowa septuplets won't find themselves in the position of the Dionne women in 1998, waging a lawsuit against the government for the way they were raised in an institutional environment.

AGENTS OF SOCIALIZATION

As we have seen, the continuing and lifelong socialization process involves many different social forces that influence our lives and alter our self-images.

The family is the most important agent of socialization in Canada, especially for children. We'll also give particular attention in this chapter to five other agents of socialization: the school, the peer group, the mass media, the workplace, and the state. The role of religion in socializing young people into society's norms and values will be explored in Chapter 12.

Family

Children in Amish communities are raised in a highly structured and disciplined manner. But they are not immune to the temptations posed by their peers in the non-Amish world—"rebellious" acts such as dancing, drinking, and riding in cars. Still, Amish families don't get too concerned; they know the strong influence they ultimately exert over their offspring (see Box 4-2). The same is true for the family in general. It is tempting to say that the peer group or even the media really raise kids these days, especially when the spotlight falls on young people involved in shooting sprees and hate crimes. Almost all available research, however, shows that the role of the family in socializing a child cannot be underestimated (W. Williams 1998; for a different view see J. Harris 1998).

The lifelong process of learning begins shortly after birth. Since newborns can hear; see; smell; taste; and feel heat, cold, and pain, they are constantly orienting themselves to the surrounding world. Human beings, especially family members, constitute an important part of their social environment. People minister to the baby's needs by feeding, cleansing, carrying, and comforting the baby.

The caretakers of a newborn are not concerned with teaching social skills per se. Nevertheless, babies are hardly asocial. An infant enters an organized society, becomes part of a generation, and typically joins a family. Depending on how they are treated, infants can develop strong social attachments and dependency on others.

Most infants go through a relatively formal period of socialization generally called *habit training*. Caregivers impose schedules for eating and sleeping, for terminating breast- or bottle-feeding, and for introducing new foods. In these and other ways, infants can be viewed as objects of socialization. Yet they also function as socializers. Even as the behaviour of a baby is being modified by interactions with people and the environment, the baby is causing others to change their behaviour patterns. He or she converts adults into mothers and fathers, who, in turn, assist the baby in progressing into childhood (Rheingold 1969).

As both Charles Horton Cooley and George Herbert Mead noted, the development of the self is a critical aspect of the early years of life. pp. 15–16 However, how children develop this sense of self can vary from one society to another. For example, parents in Canada would never think of sending six-year-olds to school unsupervised. But this is the norm in Japan, where parents push their children to commute to school on their own from an early age. In cities like Tokyo, first-graders must learn to negotiate buses, subways, and long walks. To ensure their safety, parents carefully lay out rules: never talk to strangers; check with a station attendant if you get off at the wrong stop; if you miss your stop, stay on to the end of the line, then call; take stairs, not escalators; don't fall asleep. Some parents equip the children with cell phones or pagers. One parent acknowledges that she worries, "but after they are 6, children are supposed to start being independent from the mother. If you're still taking your child to school after the first month, everyone looks at you funny" (Tolbert 2000:17).

In Canada, social development includes exposure to cultural assumptions regarding gender, class, and race. Fleras and Kunz (2001) argue that the news media tend to undermine the contributions of minority groups in Canadian society, emphasizing "their status as athletes, entertainers, or criminals, while the occasional fawning reference to minorities in position of political or economic power represents an exception that simply proves the rule" (Fleras and Kunz 2001:83). Since children are watching television at an increasingly younger age, they are increasingly susceptible to absorbing the images packaged for and by the dominant culture.

Family and Gender Socialization

Have you ever noticed when parents mention their newborn babies they may describe their daughters as "pretty," "sweet," or "angelic" and their sons as "tough," "rugged," or "strong"? Although newborn babies look much the same regardless of sex, with one noticeable exception, parents often apply cultural and social assumptions about femininity and masculinity to their

Sociology in the Global Community

4-2 Raising Amish Children

Jacob is a typical teenager in his Amish community in Lancaster County, Pennsylvania. At 14 he is in his final year of schooling. Over the next few years he will become a full-time worker on the family farm, taking breaks only for a three-hour religious service each morning. When he is a bit older, Jacob may bring a date in his family's horse-drawn buggy to a community "singing." But he will be forbidden to date outside his own community and can marry only with the deacon's consent. Jacob is well aware of the rather different way of life of the "English" (the Amish term for non-Amish people). One summer he and his friends hitchhiked late at night to a nearby town to see a movie, breaking several Amish taboos. His parents learned of his adventure, but like most Amish they are confident that their son will choose the Amish way of life. What is this way of life and how can the parents be so sure of its appeal?

Jacob and his family live in a manner very similar to that of their ancestors, members of the conservative Mennonite church who migrated to North America from Europe in the eighteenth and nineteenth centuries. Schisms in the church after 1850 led to a division between those who wanted to preserve the "old order" and those who favoured a "new order" with more progressive methods and organization. Today the old-order Amish live in about 50 communities in the United States and Canada. Estimates put their number at about 80 000 with approximately 75 percent living in three American states—Ohio, Pennsylvania, and Indiana.

The old-order Amish live a "simple" life and reject most aspects of modernization and contemporary technology. That's why they spurn such conveniences as electricity, automobiles, radio, and television. The Amish maintain their own schools and traditions, and they do not want their children socialized into many norms and values of the dominant cultures of the United States and Canada. Those who stray too far from Amish mores may be excommunicated and shunned by all other members of the community—a practice of social control called *Meiding*. Sociologists sometimes use the term "secessionist minorities" to refer to groups like the Amish who reject assimilation and coexist with the rest of society primarily on their own terms.

Life for Amish youth attracts particular attention since their socialization pushes them to forgo movies, radio, television, cosmetics, jewellery, musical instruments of any kind, and motorized vehicles. Yet, like Jacob did, Amish youth often test their subculture's boundaries during a period of discovery called *rumspringe,* a term that literally means "running around." Amish young people attend barn dances where taboos like drinking, smoking, and driving cars are commonly broken. Parents often react by looking the other way, sometimes literally. For example, when they hear radio sounds from a barn or a motorcycle entering the property in the middle of the night, they don't immediately investigate and punish their offspring. Instead, they will pretend not to notice, secure in the comfort that their children almost always return to the traditions of the Amish lifestyle. Occasionally, young people go too far. For example, in 1997 a motorcycle gang of ten Amish youth were caught selling drugs, including cocaine, in suburban Philadelphia. But cases like this are so rare that they make headlines when they happen. Research shows that only about 20 percent of Amish youth leave the fold, generally to join a more liberal Mennonite group, and rarely does a baptized adult ever leave. The socialization of Amish youth moves them gently but firmly into becoming Amish adults.

Applying Theory

1. What makes Amish parents so sure that their children will choose to remain in the Amish community? How does the growing presence of technology make this more difficult?
2. If you lived in an Amish community, how would your life differ from the way it is now? In your opinion, what advantages and disadvantages would that lifestyle have?

Source: Zellner 2001; Meyers 1992; Remnick 1998.

children from the moment of birth. Now, with the development of technologies, such as ultrasound and amniocentesis, that can reveal the sex of the fetus, parents may well begin to apply these assumptions before birth. This pattern begins a lifelong process of ***gender socialization***—an aspect of socialization through which we learn the attitudes, behaviours, and practices associated with being male or female (called ***gender roles***) according to our society and social groups within it. Our society (and various social groups, such as social classes and ethnic groups) produces ideals and expectations about gender roles, reinforcing these ideals and expectations at each stage of the life course. As we will see in Chapter 10, other cultures do not necessarily assign these qualities to each gender in the way that our culture does.

As the primary agents of childhood socialization, parents play a critical role in guiding children into those gender roles deemed appropriate in a society. Other adults, older siblings, the mass media, and religious and educational institutions also have a noticeable impact on a child's socialization into feminine and masculine norms. A culture or subculture may require that one sex or the other take primary responsibility for socialization of children, economic support of the family, or religious or intellectual leadership.

Social class may also play a role in gender socialization. Members of certain social classes may be more or less likely to engage in socialization patterns geared to traditional gender roles. Tuck et al. (1994), for example, studied gender socialization in middle-class homes with career-oriented mothers. They found these homes to be less stereotypic in terms of behaviour expectations than working-class homes. Other studies have found that working-class homes are more likely to conform to traditional or stereotypical notions of masculinity and femininity and socialize their children accordingly (A. Nelson and Robinson 2002). Daughters in a working-class family might, for example, be called on more often to help with domestic chores, such as cooking or attending to the needs of younger siblings. Sons might not be expected to help out with chores or younger children and instead might be encouraged to pursue independent activities outside the home.

Standpoint feminists support the view that the socioeconomic situation of a child's family, commingled with that child's gender, sexual orientation, race, and ethnicity, produce nongeneralizable experiences in which family contributes to the child's overall situation.

The differential gender roles absorbed in early childhood often help define a child's popularity later on. Adler and Adler (1998) give a picture of the dynamics of "in" and "out" groups among both girls and boys. Patricia Adler has found that boys typically achieve high status on the basis of their athletic ability, "coolness," toughness, social skills, and success in relationships with girls. By contrast, girls owe their popularity to their parents' status and their own physical appearance, social skills, and academic success (Adler and Adler 1998; Adler, Kless, and Adler 1992).

Like other elements of culture, socialization patterns are not fixed. The last 30 years, for example, have witnessed a sustained challenge to traditional gender-role socialization in North America, in good part because of the efforts of the feminist movement (see Chapter 10). Nevertheless, despite such changes, children growing up today are hardly free of traditional gender roles.

Interactionists remind us that socialization concerning not only masculinity and femininity but also marriage and parenthood begins in childhood as a part of family life. Children observe their parents as they express affection, deal with finances, quarrel, complain about in-laws, and so forth. This represents an informal process of anticipatory socialization. The child develops a tentative model of what being married and being a parent are like. (We will explore socialization for marriage and parenthood more fully in Chapter 11.)

School

Where did you learn the national anthem? Who taught you about the early Canadian explorers? Where were you first tested on your knowledge of your culture? Like the family, schools have an explicit mandate to socialize people in Canada—and especially children—into the norms and values of the dominant culture.

As conflict theorists Samuel Bowles and Herbert Gintis (1976) have observed, schools foster competition through built-in systems of reward and punishment, such as grades and evaluations by teachers. Consequently, a child who is working intently to learn a new

This Japanese school maintains the Japanese cultural practice of eating with chopsticks. When school lunch programs introduced the "spork" (combined plastic spoon and fork) in the late 1990s, Japanese parents raised a fuss and forced a return to the traditional chopsticks.

skill can sometimes come to feel stupid and unsuccessful. However, as the self matures, children become capable of increasingly realistic assessments of their intellectual, physical, and social abilities.

Functionalists point out that, as agents of socialization, schools fulfil the function of teaching children the values and customs of the larger society. Conflict theorists agree but add that schools can reinforce the divisive aspects of society, especially those of social class. For example, higher education in Canada is quite costly despite the existence of student aid programs. Students from affluent backgrounds have an advantage in gaining access to universities and professional training. At the same time, less affluent young people may never receive the preparation that would qualify them for the best-paying and most prestigious jobs. Moreover, conflict sociologists argue that schools tend to socialize students to emulate the dominant values of society, in preparation for them assume their places as workers in an appropriate social class. According the conflict sociologists, students are socialized by the school system to value hard work and effort, based on the belief that the most deserving students will invariably rise to the top positions. The contrast between the functionalist and conflict views of education will be discussed in more detail in Chapter 12.

In other cultures as well, schools serve socialization functions. During the 1980s, for example, Japanese parents and educators were distressed to realize that children were gradually losing the knack of eating with chopsticks. This became a national issue in 1997 when school lunch programs introduced plastic "sporks" (combined fork and spoon). National leaders, responding to the public outcry, banished sporks in favour of *hashi* (chopsticks). On a more serious note, Japanese schools have come under increasing pressure in recent years as working parents have abdicated more and more responsibility to educational institutions. To rectify the imbalance, the Japanese government in 1998 promoted a guide to better parenting, calling on parents to read more with their children, allow for more playtime, limit TV watching, and plan family activities, among other things (Gauette 1998).

School and Gender Socialization

In teaching students the values and customs of the larger society, schools in Canada have traditionally socialized children into conventional gender roles. Professors of education Myra Sadker and David Sadker (1985:54, 1995) note that "although many believe that classroom sexism disappeared in the early '70s, it hasn't."

Sadker and Sadker's research points to a gender bias in terms of the time, effort, and attention that is given to boys in the classroom, as opposed to that given to girls. For example, boys were called on more frequently by teachers to answer questions and, even when they were not directly asked to participate, boys tended to call out in class (Sadker and Sadker 1994). A study carried out in a Toronto high school classroom showed that males spoke out 75 percent to 80 percent of the time (Gaskell, McLaren, and Novogrodsky 1995).

Despite the apparent gender bias that exists in classroom participation, educators in Canada are becoming concerned that boys are lagging behind girls in academic achievement as demonstrated by girls' overrepresentation on the high school honour rolls in Ontario and British Columbia (Galt 1998). Patricia Clarke, former president of the B.C. Teachers' Federation, suggests that boys are immersed in a gender-specific culture that undervalues academic achievement and that greater attention needs to be paid to dispelling the myth that "the coolest thing to do is be stupid" (T. Holmes 2000: 11). Similar gender gaps in academic performance are being experienced in other countries, such as Britain, where girls are also academically outperforming their male classmates (Galt 1998).

Peer Group

Ask 13-year-olds who matters most in their lives and they are likely to answer "friends." As a child grows older, the family becomes somewhat less important in social development. Instead, peer groups increasingly assume the role of Mead's significant others. Within the peer group, young people associate with others who are approximately their own age and who often enjoy a similar social status.

Peer groups can ease the transition to adult responsibilities. At home, parents tend to dominate; at school, the teenager must contend with teachers and administrators. But within the peer group, each member can assert himself or herself in a way that may not be possible elsewhere. Nevertheless, almost all adolescents in our culture remain economically dependent on their parents, and most are emotionally dependent as well.

Teenagers imitate their friends in part because the peer group maintains a meaningful system of rewards and punishments. The group may encourage a young person to follow pursuits that society considers admirable, as in a school club engaged in volunteer work in hospitals and nursing homes. However, the group may encourage someone to violate the culture's norms and values by driving recklessly, shoplifting, engaging in acts of vandalism, taking drugs, and the like.

Peers can be the source of harassment as well as support. This problem has received considerable attention in Japan, where bullying in school is a constant fact of life. Groups of students act together to humiliate, disgrace, or torment a specific student, a practice known in Japan as *ijime.* Most students go along with the bullying out of fear that they might be the target some time. In some cases the *ijime* has led to a child's suicide. In 1998 the situation became so desperate that a volunteer association set up a 24-hour telephone hotline in Tokyo just for children (see the chapter opening poster). The success of this effort convinced the government to sponsor a nationwide hotline system (Matsushita 1999; Sugimoto 1997).

Peer Group and Gender Socialization

A study done in British Columbia schools points to the prevalence of bullying and some of the gender-related patterns of the activity. Approximately 10 percent to 15 percent of British Columbia students are bullies, while approximately 8 percent to 10 percent are victims (*Vancouver Sun* 2000). Researchers Debra Pepler of York University and Wendy Craig of Queen's University found that girls do more of the verbal and social bullying while boys' bullying behaviour tends to be more physical. Girls bullied boys approximately half the time, while boys primarily bullied other boys. Bullies of both sexes tended to be perceived as popular and powerful by their peer group while victims were perceived as lacking humour, having a tendency to cry easily, and deserving to be picked on. Pepler and Craig's research also showed that families of bullies tend to be permissive and display more positive attitudes toward aggression and that other students who have not yet been victimized may want to align with bullies to avoid possible bullying in the future.

Gender differences are noteworthy in the social world of adolescents. Males are more likely to spend time in *groups* of males, while females are more likely to interact with a *single* other female. This pattern reflects differences in levels of emotional intimacy; teenage males are less likely to develop strong emotional ties than are females. Instead, males are more inclined to share in group activities. These patterns are evident among adolescents in many societies around the world (Dornbusch 1989).

Mass Media and Technology

In the last 75 years, media innovations—radio, motion pictures, recorded music, television, and the Internet—have become important agents of socialization. Television, in particular, is a critical force in the socialization of children in North America. In Canada, for example, 99 percent of households own at least one television set (Withers and Brown 2001). In addition, a 1999 survey estimated that 86 percent of Canadians live in households containing a VCR and 75 percent live in households with cable TV service (Withers and Brown 2001).

This research of viewing habits revealed that, on a per capita basis, Canadians watched an average of 21.6 hours per week during the fall of 1999, the survey period. Women who were 18 years and older were the heaviest viewers (25.5 hours per week), while children (2 to 11) and teens (12 to 17) each viewed 15.5 hours per week. A Canadian feminist organization known as MediaWatch was established in 1981 to identify and monitor trends in the mass media (particularly in advertising) as they relate to the portrayal of women. Table 4-1 shows some of the ways the mass media presents a distorted view of women.

Television has certain characteristics that distinguish it from other agents of socialization. It permits imitation and role-playing but does not encourage more complex forms of learning. Watching television is, above all, a passive experience; we sit back and wait to be entertained. Critics of television are further alarmed by the programming that children view as they sit for hours in front of a television set. It is generally agreed that children (as well as adults) are exposed to a great deal of violence on television. Despite recent attention to the issue, a 1998 study showed that the situation had not changed over the last two years. Of particular concern is that 40 percent of violent incidents on television are initiated by "good" characters, who are likely to be perceived as positive role models (J. Federman 1998; L. Mifflin 1999).

Table 4-1 Distorted Viewing: The Mass Media's Treatment of Women

Objectification	Portraying women as objects that can be manipulated, bought, and sold
Irrelevant sexualization	Portraying women's bodies in a sexual way in order to attract attention and perpetuate the attitude that women's primary role is to attract male attention
Infanticization	Presenting women as childlike, coy, silly, and powerless
Domestication	Defining women in relation to their children, husbands, and family in a domestic environment
Victimization	Portraying women as victims of male brutality, inside and outside their homes

Source: Based on Graydon 2001.

Although we have focused on television as an agent of socialization, it is important to note that similar issues have been raised regarding the content of popular music (especially rock music and rap), music videos, motion pictures, video games, and Internet Web sites. These forms of entertainment, like television, serve as powerful agents of socialization for many young people around the globe. Continuing controversy about the content of music, music videos, and films has sometimes led to celebrated court battles, as certain parents' organizations and religious groups challenge the intrusion of these media into the lives of children and adolescents. In recent years, people have expressed concern about the type of material that children can access on the Internet, especially pornography.

p. 58

Finally, sociologists and other social scientists have begun to consider the impact of technology on socialization, especially as it applies to family life. The Silicon Valley Cultures Project studied families in California's Silicon Valley (a technological corridor) for ten years beginning in 1991. Although these families may not be typical, they probably represent a lifestyle that more and more households will approximate. This study has found that technology in the form of email, Web pages, cellular phones, voice mail, digital organizers, and pagers is allowing householders to let outsiders do everything from grocery shopping to soccer pools. The researchers are also finding that families are socialized into multitasking (doing more than one task at a time) as the social norm; devoting our full attention to one task—even eating or driving—is less and less common on a typical day (Silicon Valley Cultures Project 1999).

Workplace

Learning to behave appropriately within an occupation is a fundamental aspect of human socialization. In North America, working full-time confirms adult status; it is an indication to all that a person has passed out of adolescence. In a sense, socialization into an occupation can represent both a harsh reality ("I have to work in order to buy food and pay the rent") and the realization of an ambition ("I've always wanted to be an airline pilot") (W. Moore 1968:862).

Some observers feel that the increasing number of teenagers who are working earlier in life and for longer hours are now finding the workplace almost as important an agent of socialization as is school. In fact, a number of educators complain that student time at work is adversely affecting schoolwork. Will Boyce, a professor of education at Queen's University, found that the number of working high school students in Ontario is increasing (Philip 2001). Boyce discovered that 46.3 percent of high school students in Ontario were working, while in 1996 the number was 31 percent. Researchers are trying to gauge the impact on students' lives and have found that those students who work fewer than 20 hours per week often do better academically and are more involved in hobbies and sports than those students without jobs (Philip 2001).

Socialization in the workplace changes when it involves a more permanent shift from an after-school job to full-time employment. Wilbert Moore (1968:871–880) has divided occupational socialization into four phases. The first phase is *career choice,* which involves selection of academic or vocational training appropriate for the desired job. The second phase, *anticipatory socialization,* may last only a few months or may extend for a period of years. In a sense, young people experience anticipatory socialization throughout childhood and adolescence as they observe their parents at work.

The third phase of occupational socialization—*conditioning and commitment*—occurs in the work-related role. *Conditioning* consists of reluctantly adjusting to the more unpleasant aspects of one's job. Most people find that the novelty of a new daily schedule quickly wears off and then realize that parts of the work experience are rather tedious. *Commitment* refers to the enthusiastic

This boy's day doesn't end when school lets out. So many teenagers now work after school, the workplace has become another important agent of socialization for that age group.

acceptance of pleasurable duties that comes with recognition of the positive tasks of an occupation.

In Moore's view, if a job proves to be satisfactory, the person will enter a fourth stage of socialization, which Moore calls *continuous commitment.* At this point, the job becomes an indistinguishable part of the person's self-identity. Violation of proper conduct becomes unthinkable. A person may choose to join professional associations, unions, or other groups that represent the occupation in the larger society.

Occupational socialization can be most intense during the transition from school to job, but it continues through a person's work history. Technological advances may alter the requirements of the position and necessitate some degree of resocialization. Many men and women today change occupations, employers, or places of work many times during their adult years. Therefore, occupational socialization continues throughout a person's years in the labour market.

The State

Social scientists have increasingly recognized the importance of the state as an agent of socialization because of its growing impact on the life course. Traditionally, family members have served as the primary caregivers in our culture, but in the twenty-first century, the family's protective function has steadily been transferred to outside agencies, such as hospitals, mental health clinics, and insurance companies. The state runs many of these agencies or licenses and regulates them (Ogburn and Tibbits 1934).

In the past, heads of households and local groups, such as religious organizations, influenced the life course most significantly. However, today national interests are increasingly influencing the individual as a citizen and an economic actor. For example, labour unions and political parties serve as intermediaries between the individual and the state.

The state has had a noteworthy impact on the life course by reinstituting the rites of passage that had disappeared in agricultural societies and in periods of early industrialization. For example, government regulations stipulate the ages at which a person may drive a car, drink alcohol, vote in elections, marry without parental permission, work overtime, and retire. These regulations do not constitute strict rites of passage: most 18-year-olds choose not to vote, and most people choose their age of retirement without reference to government dictates. Still, the state shapes the socialization process by regulating the life course to some degree and by influencing our views of appropriate behaviour at particular ages (Mayer and Schoepflin 1989).

In the social policy section that follows, we will see that the state is under pressure to become a provider of child care, which would give it a new and direct role in the socialization of infants and young children.

SOCIAL POLICY AND SOCIALIZATION: Child Care around the World

The Issue

The rise in the number of single-parent families, increased job opportunities for women, and the need for additional family income have all propelled an increasing number of mothers of young children into the paid labour force of Canada. In 2000, almost three-fourths of women with children under the age of 16 were in the paid labour force. Who, then, is responsible for children during work hours?

For 25 percent of all preschoolers with employed parents, the solution has become day care programs. Day care centers have become the functional equivalent of the nuclear family, performing some of the nurturing and socialization functions previously handled only by family members. But how does day care compare with other forms of child care? And what is the state's responsibility to ensure high-quality care (Fields 2003; K. Smith 2000)?

The Setting

Few people in Canada or elsewhere can afford the luxury of having a parent stay at home or of paying for high-quality live-in child care. For millions of working parents, finding the right kind of child care is a challenge to parenting and to their financial responsibilities.

Researchers have found that high-quality child care centres do not adversely affect the socialization of children; in fact, good day care benefits children. The value of preschool programs was documented in a series of studies conducted in Canada by the Childcare Resource and Research Unit. Researchers found no significant differences in infants who had received extensive nonmaternal care compared with those who had been cared for solely by their parents. They also reported that more and more infants in Canada are being placed in child care outside the home and that overall, the quality of day care centres is mixed, depending on whether they were nonprofit or commercial. It is difficult, therefore, to generalize about child care. But day cares that are nonprofit have been found to be of higher quality than those run to make money (Cleveland and Krashinsky 1998).

Sociological Insights

Studies that assess the quality of child care outside the home reflect the microlevel of analysis and the interest of interactionists in the impact of face-to-face interaction. These studies also explore macrolevel implications for the functioning of social institutions, like the family. But some of the issues surrounding day care have also been of interest to those who take the conflict perspective.

In Canada, high-quality day care is not equally available to all families. Parents in wealthy neighbourhoods have an easier time finding day care than do those in poor or working-class communities. Finding *affordable* child care is also a problem. Viewed from a conflict perspective, child care costs are an especially serious burden for lower-class families. The poorest families spend 25 percent of their income for preschool child care, while families who are *not* poor pay only 6 percent or less of their income for day care.

Feminists echo the concern of conflict theorists that high-quality child care has received little government support because it is regarded as a private or personal issue, rather than a social one. Nearly all child care workers are women; many find themselves in low-status, minimum-wage jobs. The average salary of a child care worker in Canada is among the lowest of all occupational groups, and the job has few fringe benefits. Although parents may complain about child care costs, the staff members, in effect, subsidize that cost by working for low wages.

Policy Initiatives

Policies regarding child care outside the home vary throughout the world. Most developing nations do not have the economic base to provide subsidized child care. Working mothers rely largely on relatives or take their children to work. In the comparatively wealthy industrialized countries of Western Europe, government provides child care as a basic service, at little or no expense to parents.

When policymakers decide that child care is desirable, they must determine the degree to which taxpayers should subsidize it. In Sweden and Denmark, one-third to one-half of children under age three were in government-subsidized child care full-time in 2001. By contrast, in Canada, the total cost of child care typically falls on the individual family, and although the costs and options vary from urban to rural communities, informal care by friends, neighbours, relatives, and paid sitters is the most prevalent among parents who work for pay and whose children are under six years old (Baker 2001). According to the Childcare Resource and Research Unit at the University of Toronto, licensed or regulated family day care accounted for less than 14 percent of all regulated spaces in Canada in 1998 (Childcare Resource and Research Unit 2000).

There is a long way to go in making quality child care more affordable and more accessible, not just in Canada, but throughout the world. Government day care facilities in Mexico have lengthy waiting lists. In an

People in Sweden pay higher taxes than Canadian citizens, but they have access to excellent preschool day care at little or no cost.

attempt to reduce government spending, France is considering cutting back the budgets of subsidized nurseries, even though waiting lists already exist and the French public heartily disapproves of any cutbacks (L. King 1998; Simons 1997; Women's International Network 1995).

Margrit Eichler, a Canadian feminist and sociologist, proposes a "social responsibility model" for family life, endorsing the establishment and support of public day care centres (Eichler 1997). Eichler argues that the establishment and support of such centres would make good economic sense, generating jobs for day care workers and enabling mothers to work for pay. In addition, children would benefit from the social setting of the day care as well as the more individualized setting of the home. Eichler states:

> Financing does not have to come from the federal government alone. Part of it can come from municipalities, from employers, and from parents according to the ability to pay. (Eichler 1997:159–160)

A report released in 2004 by the OECD (Organisation for Economic Co-operation and Development) on child care was highly critical of the Canadian government's efforts in this area. The OECD stated that the overall funding for Canadian child care programs needs to be increased. Canada has enough regulated child care spaces for less than 20 percent of children under age six with working parents, while Denmark and the United Kingdom, for example, have 78 percent and 60 percent, respectively (OECD 2004). Forty percent of all regulated child care spaces in Canada are currently in Quebec. After years of promising funding, in late 2004, the federal government pledged $5 billion over five years for the establishment of a national child care program.

Experts in child development view such reports as a vivid reminder of the need for greater government and private-sector support for child care.

Applying Theory

1. What importance would liberal feminist thinkers place on the establishment of a national child care program for Canada? What about radical feminist thinkers?
2. If you were a conflict sociologist, how would you view the establishment of such a program in light of the overall belief in the need to eliminate social inequality?
3. What role do you think a national child care program might serve in terms of the socialization of Canadian children?

CHAPTER RESOURCES

Summary

Socialization is the process whereby people learn the attitudes, values, and actions appropriate for members of a particular culture. This chapter examined the role of socialization in human development; the way in which people develop perceptions, feelings, and beliefs about themselves; the lifelong nature of the socialization process; and the important agents of socialization.

1. Socialization affects the overall cultural practices of a society, and it also shapes the images that we hold of ourselves.
2. Heredity and environmental factors interact in influencing the socialization process. ***Sociobiology*** is the systematic study of the biological bases of social behaviour.
3. In the early 1900s, Charles Horton Cooley advanced the belief that we learn who we are by interacting with others, a phenomenon he called the ***looking-glass self.***
4. George Herbert Mead, best known for his theory of the ***self,*** proposed that as people mature, their selves begin to reflect their concern about reactions from others—both generalized others and significant others.
5. Erving Goffman has shown that many of our daily activities involve attempts to convey distinct impressions of who we are, a process called ***impression management.***
6. Socialization proceeds throughout the life course. Some societies mark stages of development with formal ***rites of passage.*** In Canadian culture, significant events, such as marriage and parenthood, serve to change a person's status.
7. As the primary agents of socialization, parents play a critical role in guiding children into those ***gender roles*** deemed appropriate in a society.
8. Like the family, schools in Canada have an explicit mandate to socialize people—and especially children—into the norms and values of our culture.

9. Peer groups and the mass media, especially television, are important agents of socialization for adolescents.
10. We are most fully exposed to occupational roles through observing the work of our parents, of people whom we meet while they are performing their duties, and of people portrayed in the media.
11. The state shapes the socialization process by regulating the life course and by influencing our views of appropriate behaviour at particular ages.
12. As more and more mothers of young children have entered Canada's labour market, the demand for child care has increased dramatically, posing policy questions for nations around the world.

Critical Thinking Questions

1. Should social research in such areas as sociobiology be conducted even though many investigators believe that this analysis is potentially detrimental to particular groups of people?
2. Drawing on Erving Goffman's dramaturgical approach, discuss how the following groups engage in impression management: athletes, students, university instructors, parents, physicians, politicians.
3. How would functionalists and conflict theorists differ in their analyses of socialization by the mass media? How would they be similar?
4. Do you think that media socialize the members of our society to be consumers, first and foremost? Why?

Key Terms

Anticipatory socialization Processes of socialization in which a person "rehearses" for future positions, occupations, and social relationships. (page 80)

Cognitive theory of development Jean Piaget's theory explaining how children's thought progresses through four stages. (78)

Degradation ceremony An aspect of the socialization process within total institutions, in which people are subjected to humiliating rituals. (80)

Face-work The efforts of people to maintain the proper image and avoid embarrassment in public. (77)

Gender roles Expectations regarding the proper behaviour, attitudes, and activities of males and females. (82)

Gender socialization An aspect of socialization through which we learn the attitudes, behaviours, and practices associated with being male and female according to our society and social groups within it. (82)

Impression management The altering of the presentation of the self to create distinctive appearances and satisfy particular audiences. (76)

Looking-glass self A concept that emphasizes the self as the product of our social interactions with others. (74)

Personality In everyday speech, a person's typical patterns of attitudes, needs, characteristics, and behaviour. (71)

Resocialization The process of discarding former behaviour patterns and accepting new ones as part of a transition in life. (80)

Rites of passage Rituals marking the symbolic transition from one social position to another. (79)

Role taking The process of mentally assuming the perspective of another, thereby enabling a person to respond from that imagined viewpoint. (75)

Self A distinct identity that sets us apart from others. (74)

Socialization The process whereby people learn the attitudes, values, and behaviours appropriate for members of a particular culture. (71)

Sociobiology The systematic study of biological bases of social behaviour. (74)

Symbols The gestures, objects, and language that form the basis of human communication. (75)

Total institutions Institutions that regulate all aspects of a person's life under a single authority, such as prisons, the military, mental hospitals, and convents. (80)

Additional Readings

Adler, Patricia A., and Peter Adler. 1998. *Peer Power: Preadolescent Culture and Identity.* New Brunswick, NJ: Rutgers University Press. Using eight years of observation research, sociologists discuss the role of peer groups and family as they relate to popularity, social isolation, bullying, and boy–girl relationships.

Danesi, Marcel. 2003. *Forever Young: The "Teen-Aging" of Modern Culture.* Toronto: University of Toronto Press. Danesi uses five years of interviews with adolescents and their parents to illustrate the "forever young" mentality and how the mass media exploit this mentality for economic purposes.

Goffman, Erving. 1959. *The Presentation of Self in Everyday Life.* New York: Doubleday. Goffman demonstrates his interactionist theory that the self is managed in everyday situations in much the same way that a theatrical performer carries out a stage role.

Graydon, Shari. 2001. "The Portrayal of Women in Media: The Good, the Bad and the Beautiful." Pp. 179–195 in *Communications in Canadian Society*, 5th ed., edited by Craig McKie and Benjamin D. Singer. Toronto: Thomson. Graydon outlines the mass media's role (with special attention to advertising) in constructing images and ideals of women in our society.

Pollack, William. 1998. *Real Boys: Rescuing Our Sons from the Myths of Boyhood.* New York: Henry Holt. A clinical psychologist looks at the disenchantment experienced by so many boys because their true emotions are kept hidden.

Online Learning Centre

Visit the *Sociology: A Brief Introduction* Online Learning Centre at www.mcgrawhill.ca/college/schaefer to access quizzes, interactive exercises, video clips, and other research and study tools related to this chapter.

Reel Society Interactive Movie CD-ROM 2.0

Reel Society 2.0 can be used to spark discussion about the following topics from this chapter:

- Agents of socialization
- Socialization as a lifelong process

chapter 5

SOCIAL INTERACTION AND SOCIAL STRUCTURE

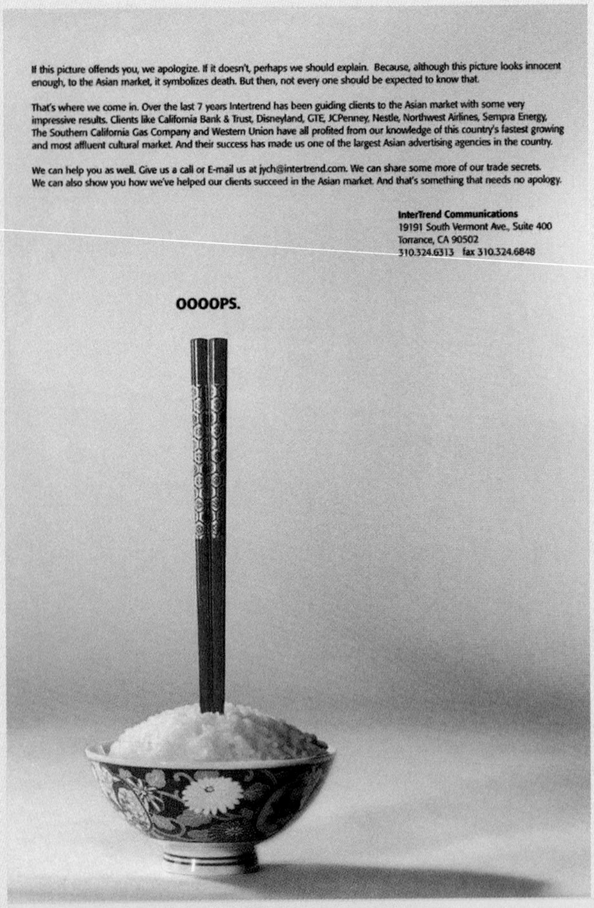
If this picture offends you, we apologize. If it doesn't, perhaps we should explain. Because, although this picture looks innocent enough, to the Asian market, it symbolizes death. But then, not every one should be expected to know that.
That's where we come in. Over the last 7 years Intertrend has been guiding clients to the Asian market with some very impressive results. Clients like California Bank & Trust, Disneyland, GTE, JCPenney, Nestle, Northwest Airlines, Sempra Energy, The Southern California Gas Company and Western Union have all profited from our knowledge of this country's fastest growing and most affluent cultural market. And their success has made us one of the largest Asian advertising agencies in the country.
We can help you as well. Give us a call or E-mail us at jych@intertrend.com. We can share some more of our trade secrets. We can also show you how we've helped our clients succeed in the Asian market. And that's something that needs no apology.
InterTrend Communications
19191 South Vermont Ave., Suite 400
Torrance, CA 90502
310.324.6313 fax 310.324.6848
OOOOPS.

In our social interaction with other cultures, it is important to know what social rules apply. In Japan, for example, it is impolite to leave your chopsticks sticking up in the rice bowl—a symbol of death for the Japanese and an insult to their dead ancestors. This poster was created by an advertising agency that promises to steer its North American clients clear of such gaffes in the Asian market.

The quiet of a summer Sunday morning in Palo Alto, California, was shattered by a screeching squad car siren as police swept through the city picking up college students in a surprise mass arrest. Each suspect was charged with a felony, warned of his constitutional rights, spread-eagled against the car, searched, handcuffed and carted off in the back seat of the squad car to the police station for booking.

After being fingerprinted and having identification forms prepared for his "jacket" (central information file), each prisoner was left isolated in a detention cell to wonder what he had done to get himself into this mess. After a while, he was blindfolded and transported to the "Stanford County Prison." Here he began the induction process of becoming a prisoner—stripped naked, skin searched, deloused, and issued a uniform, bedding, soap and towel. By late afternoon when nine such arrests had been completed, these youthful "first offenders" sat in dazed silence on the cots in their barren cells.

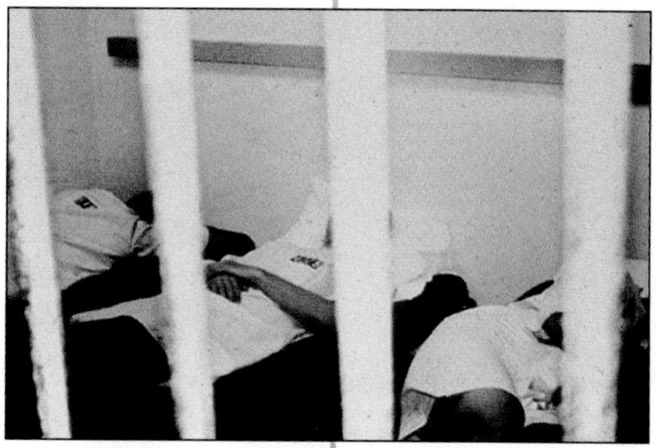

These men were part of a very unusual kind of prison, an experimental or mock prison, created by social psychologists for the purpose of intensively studying the effects of imprisonment upon volunteer research subjects. When we planned our two-week long simulation of prison life, we were primarily concerned about understanding the process by which people adapt to the novel and alien environment in which those called "prisoners" lose their liberty, civil rights, independence and privacy, while those called "guards" gain social power by accepting the responsibility for controlling and managing the lives of their dependent charges. . . .

Our final sample of participants (10 prisoners and 11 guards) were selected from over 75 volunteers recruited through ads in the city and campus newspapers. . . . Half were randomly assigned to role-play being guards, the others to be prisoners. Thus, there were no measurable differences between the guards and the prisoners at the start of this experiment. . . .

At the end of only six days we had to close down our mock prison because what we saw was frightening. It was no longer apparent to most of the subjects (or to us) where reality ended and their roles began. The majority had indeed become prisoners or guards, no longer able to clearly differentiate between role playing and self. There were dramatic changes in virtually every aspect of their behaviour, thinking and feeling. In less than a week the experience of imprisonment undid (temporarily) a lifetime of learning; human values were suspended, self-concepts were challenged and the ugliest, most base, pathological side of human nature surfaced. We were horrified because we saw some boys (guards) treat others as if they were despicable animals, taking pleasure in cruelty, while other boys (prisoners) became servile, dehumanized robots who thought only of escape, of their own individual survival, and of their mounting hatred for the guards. ***(Zimbardo et al. 1974:61, 62, 63; Zimbardo 1972:4)*** ■

In this study directed and described by social psychologist Philip Zimbardo, university students adopted the patterns of social interaction expected of guards and prisoners when they were placed in a mock prison. Sociologists use the term ***social interaction*** to refer to the ways in which people respond to one another, whether face to face or over the telephone or on the computer. In the mock prison, social interactions between guards and prisoners were highly impersonal. The guards addressed the prisoners by number rather than name, and they wore reflector sunglasses that made eye contact impossible.

As in many real-life prisons, the simulated prison at Stanford University had a social structure in which guards held virtually total control over prisoners. The term ***social structure*** refers to the way in which a society is organized into predictable relationships. The social structure of Zimbardo's mock prison influenced how the guards and prisoners interacted. Zimbardo (2004:546) notes that it was a real prison "in the minds of the jailers and their captives." Accordingly, in the case of the Stanford prison experiment, the social structure of the prison and the social interactions within the prison are linked in a dynamic manner. Through interactions with others, both prisoners and guards attach meaning to their actions, which serve to build a form of social structure. Social structure, therefore, can be patterns of social relationships that people create through the meanings they attach to others' actions; social structure becomes something that is constructed through meaningful interactions with others.

Zimbardo's simulated prison experiment, first conducted more than 30 years ago, has subsequently been repeated (with similar findings) both in the United States and in other countries. In fact, the British Broadcasting Company (BBC) in 2002 created a reality-based television program called *The Experiment* that tried to re-create the mock prison experiment, over the objections of Zimbardo and other scholars. Fortunately, the presence of TV cameras mitigated the harsh treatment of prisoners.

The closely linked concepts of social interaction and social structure are central to sociological study. Sociologists scrutinize patterns of behaviour to understand and accurately describe the social interactions of a community or society and the social structure in which they take place. Who determines how we should behave with one another? Is it possible to redefine or change that "social reality"? How do we get our social roles, and how do they affect our interactions?

This chapter begins by considering how social interaction shapes the way we view the world around us. We will focus then on the five basic elements of social structure: statuses, social roles, groups, social networks, and social institutions. Groups are important because much of our social interaction occurs in them. Social institutions, such as the family, religion, and government, are a fundamental aspect of social structure. We will contrast the functionalist, conflict, interactionist, and feminist approaches to the study of social institutions. We will also examine the typologies developed by Ferdinand Tönnies and Gerhard Lenski for comparing modern societies with simpler forms of social structure. The social policy section will consider the AIDS crisis and its implications for social institutions throughout the world. ■

Use Your Sociological Imagination www.mcgrawhill.ca/college/schaefer

If you had been selected to be a guard in the Stanford prison experiment, what meaning do you think the actions of the prisoners might have had for you? In what way do you think social reality was being constructed in the Stanford prison experiment?

SOCIAL INTERACTION AND REALITY

When someone shoves you in a crowd, do you automatically push back? Or do you consider the circumstances of the incident and the attitude of the instigator before you react? Chances are you do the latter. According to sociologist Herbert Blumer (1969:79), the distinctive characteristic of social interaction among people is that "human beings interpret or 'define' each other's actions instead of merely reacting to each other's actions." In other words, our response to someone's behaviour is based on the *meaning* we attach to his or her actions. Reality is shaped by our perceptions, evaluations, and definitions.

These meanings typically reflect the norms and values of the dominant culture and our socialization experiences within that culture. As interactionists emphasize, the meanings that we attach to people's behaviour are shaped by our interactions with them and with the larger society. Consequently, social reality is literally constructed from our social interactions (Berger and Luckmann 1966).

Defining and Reconstructing Reality

How do we define our social reality? As an example, let us consider something as simple as how we regard tattoos. Even as recently as a few years ago, many people in Canada considered tattoos as something "weird" or "kooky." We associated them with fringe countercultural groups, such as punk rockers, bike gangs, and skinheads. A tattoo elicited an automatic negative response among many people. Now, however, there are so many tattooed people, including society's trendsetters and major sports figures, and the ritual of getting a tattoo has become so legitimized, the mainstream culture regards tattoos differently. At this point, as a result of increased social interactions with tattooed people, tattoos look perfectly at home to us in a number of settings.

The ability to define social reality reflects a group's power within a society. In fact, one of the most crucial aspects of the relationship between dominant and subordinate groups is the ability of the dominant or majority group to define a society's values. Sociologist William I. Thomas (1923), an early critic of theories of racial and gender differences, recognized that the "definition of the situation" could mould the thinking and personality of the individual. Writing from an interactionist perspective, Thomas observed that people respond not only to the objective features of a person or situation but also to the *meaning* that the person or situation has for them. For example, in Philip Zimbardo's mock prison experiment, student "guards" and "prisoners" accepted the definition of the situation (including the traditional roles and behaviour associated with being a guard or prisoner) and acted accordingly.

As we have seen throughout the last 40 years—through movements to bring about greater rights for members of such groups as women, the elderly, gays and lesbians, and people with disabilities—an important aspect of the process of social change involves *re*defining or *re*constructing social reality. Members of subordinate groups challenge traditional definitions and begin to perceive and experience reality in a new way. For example, in 1985 Rick Hansen began a two-year journey, circling the world in his wheelchair to raise awareness and money for people with spinal cord injuries. After being injured in an automobile accident that left him paralyzed at the age of 15, Rick Hansen became a world-class athlete, winning international wheelchair marathons and world championships, and competing for Canada in the Olympic Games. Continually breaking down stereotypes of people with disabilities, today he is the father of three daughters, the president and CEO of the Rick Hansen Man In Motion Foundation, an active environmentalist, and an athlete who enjoys fishing, pilates, tennis, kayaking, and sit skiing.

Viewed from a sociological perspective, Rick Hansen was redefining social reality by challenging ways of thinking and terminology that restricted him and other people with disabilities.

Rick Hansen wheeled around the world to raise money for spinal cord research 20 years ago and founded the Man In Motion Foundation. Rick represents a new, proactive attitude among Canadians who have disabilities that is breaking down stereotypes.

Negotiated Order

As we have just seen, people can reconstruct social reality through a process of internal change, taking a different view of everyday behaviour. Yet people also reshape reality by *negotiating* changes in patterns of social interaction. The term ***negotiation*** refers to the attempt to reach agreement with others concerning some objective. Negotiation does not involve coercion; it goes by many names, including *bargaining, compromising, trading off, mediating, exchanging, "wheeling and dealing,"* and *collusion.* It is through negotiation as a form of social interaction that society creates its social structure (Strauss 1977; see also Fine 1984).

Negotiation occurs in many ways. As interactionists point out, some social situations, such as buying groceries, involve no mediation, while other situations require negotiation. For example, we may negotiate with others regarding time ("When should we arrive?"), space ("Can we have a meeting at your house?"), or even assignment of places while waiting for concert tickets. In traditional societies, impending marriage often leads to negotiations between the families of the husband and wife. For example, anthropologist Ray Abrahams (1968) has described how the Labwor people of Africa arrange for an amount of property to go from the groom's to the bride's family at the time of marriage. In the view of the Labwor, such bargaining over an exchange of cows and sheep culminates not only in a marriage but also in the linking of two clans or families.

Although such family-to-family bargaining is common in traditional cultures, negotiation can take much more elaborate forms in modern industrial societies. Consider postsecondary financial aid programs. From a sociological perspective, such programs are formal norms (reflected in established practices and procedures for granting aid to college and university students). Yet the programs undergo revision through negotiated outcomes involving many interests, including foundations, banks, the admissions office, and the faculty. On an individual level, the student applicant will mediate with representatives of the school's financial aid office. Changes in the individual situations will occur through such negotiations (Maines 1977, 1982; J. Thomas 1984).

Negotiations underlie much of our social behaviour. Because most elements of social structure are not static, they are subject to change through bargaining and exchanging. Sociologists use the term *negotiated order* to underscore the fact that the social order is continually being constructed and altered through negotiation. ***Negotiated order*** refers to a social structure that derives its existence from the social interactions through which people define and redefine its character.

We can add negotiation to our list of cultural universals because all societies provide guidelines or norms in which negotiations take place. The recurring role of negotiation in social interaction and social structure will be apparent as we examine the major elements of social structure (Strauss 1977).

ELEMENTS OF SOCIAL STRUCTURE

Social structures are relatively organized patterns of social relationships that contain and enable human conduct; they are durable but are capable of change over time. We can examine social relationships in terms of five elements: statuses, social roles, groups, social networks and technology, and social institutions. These elements make up social structure just as a foundation, walls, and ceilings make up a building's structure. The elements of social structure may be, in part, developed through the lifelong process of socialization described in Chapter 4. In addition, human beings create the elements of social structure through a dynamic process involving meaningful interaction (Fleras 2003).

Statuses

We normally think of a person's "status" as having to do with influence, wealth, and fame. However, sociologists use ***status*** to refer to any of the full range of socially defined positions within a large group or society—from the lowest to the highest position. Within our society, a person can occupy the status of prime minister of Canada, fruit picker, son or daughter, violinist, teenager, resident of Alberta, dental technician, or neighbour. A person can hold a number of statuses at the same time.

Ascribed and Achieved Status

Sociologists view some statuses as *ascribed,* while they categorize others as *achieved* (see Figure 5-1). An ***ascribed status*** is "assigned" to a person by society without regard for the person's unique talents or characteristics. Generally, this assignment takes place at birth; thus, a person's racial background, gender, and age are all considered ascribed statuses. These characteristics may be socially constructed as biological in origin and are significant mainly because of the *social* meanings they have in our culture. Conflict theorists are especially interested in ascribed statuses, since these statuses often confer privileges or reflect a person's membership in a subordinate group. The social meanings of race and ethnicity, gender, and age will be analyzed more fully in Chapters 9, 10, and 14.

In most cases, we can do little to change an ascribed status. But we can attempt to change the traditional constraints associated with such statuses. For example, the Canadian Association of Retired Persons—an activist

FIGURE 5-1

Social Statuses

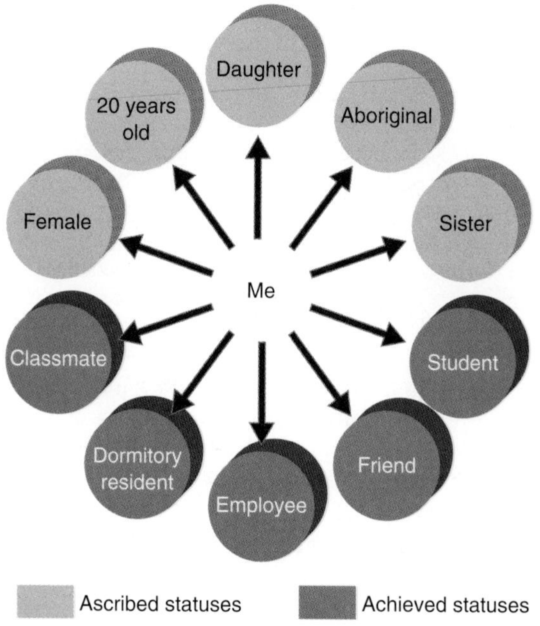

Think about It

The young woman in this figure—"me"—occupies many positions in society, each of which involves distinct statuses. How would you define *your* statuses? Which have the most influence in your life?

political group founded in 1984 to work for the rights of older people—have tried to modify society's negative and confining stereotypes of the elderly (see Chapter 14). As a result of their work and that of other groups supporting older citizens, the ascribed status of "senior citizen" is no longer as difficult for millions of older people.

An ascribed status does not necessarily have the same social meaning in every society. In a cross-cultural study, sociologist Gary Huang (1988) confirmed the long-held view that respect for the elderly is an important cultural norm in China. In many cases, the prefix "old" is used respectfully: calling someone "old teacher" or "old person" is like calling a judge in North America "Your Honour." Huang points out that positive age-seniority distinctions in language are rare in North America; consequently, we view the term *old man* as more of an insult than a celebration of seniority and wisdom.

Unlike ascribed statuses, an ***achieved status*** comes to us largely through our own efforts. Both "bank president" and "prison guard" are achieved statuses, as are "lawyer," "pianist," "convict," and "social worker." You must do something to acquire an achieved status—go to school, learn a skill, establish a friendship, invent a new product. For example, obtaining a master's degree, which results in greater financial and employment rewards, would be an example of an achieved status. As we see in the next section, our ascribed status heavily influences our achieved status. Being male, for example, decreases the likelihood that a person would consider being a child care worker.

Master Status

Each person holds many different and sometimes conflicting statuses; some may connote higher social positions, and some, lower positions. How, then, do others view someone's overall social position? According to sociologist Everett Hughes (1945), societies deal with inconsistencies by agreeing that certain statuses are more important than others. A ***master status*** is a status that dominates others and thereby determines a person's general position within society. For example, Arthur Ashe, who died of AIDS in 1993, had a remarkable career as a tennis star; but at the end of his life, his status as a well-known personality with AIDS may have outweighed his statuses as a retired athlete, an author, and a political activist. Throughout the world many people with disabilities find that their status as "disabled" is given undue weight, which overshadows their actual ability to perform successfully in meaningful employment (see Box 5-1).

Our society gives such importance to race and gender that they often dominate our lives. These ascribed statuses frequently influence achieved status. Lee Williams, a long-serving porter for Canadian National Railway, was denied advancement into more senior positions because of racism (Manitoba Human Rights Commission 2004). Williams challenged the lack of opportunity for advancement of black railway workers under the Fair Employment Act and won his case; this allowed him and other black workers to move up the ranks to assume higher achieved status within the corporation. In Canada, ascribed statuses of race and gender can function as master statuses that have an important impact on a person's potential to achieve a desired professional and social status.

Social Roles

What Are Social Roles?

Throughout our lives, we acquire what sociologists call *social roles*. A ***social role*** is a set of expectations for people who occupy a given social position or status. Thus, in Canada, we expect that cab drivers will know how to get around a city, that receptionists will be reliable in handling phone messages, and that police officers will

Sociology in the Global Community

5-1 Disability as a Master Status

When the Canadian Transportation Agency ordered VIA Rail to make the passenger rail cars it had purchased several years ago accessible to people with disabilities, VIA responded by mounting a legal challenge. Passengers with disabilities were effectively excluded from using VIA's trains.

Throughout history and around the world, people with disabilities have often been subjected to cruel and inhuman treatment. For example, in the early twentieth century, people with disabilities were frequently viewed as subhuman creatures who were a menace to society. In Japan more than 16 000 women with disabilities were involuntarily sterilized with government approval from 1945 to 1995. Sweden recently apologized for the same action taken against 62 000 of its citizens in the 1970s.

Such blatantly hostile treatment of people with disabilities generally gave way to a *medical model,* which views people with disabilities as chronic patients. Increasingly, however, people concerned with the rights of people with disabilities have criticized this model as well. In their view, it is the unnecessary and discriminatory barriers present in the environment—both physical and attitudinal—that stand in the way of people with disabilities more than any biological limitations do. Applying a *human rights model,* activists emphasize that those with disabilities face widespread prejudice, discrimination, and segregation. For example, some provinces and territories do not fund basic devices, such as wheelchairs.

Drawing on the earlier work of Erving Goffman, contemporary sociologists have suggested that society has attached a stigma to many forms of disability and that this stigma leads to prejudicial treatment. People with disabilities frequently observe that people without disabilities see them only as blind, wheelchair users, and so forth, rather than as complex human beings with individual strengths and weaknesses, whose blindness or use of a wheelchair is merely one aspect of their lives. A review of studies of people with disabilities disclosed that most academic research on the subject does not differentiate gender, thereby perpetuating the view that a disability overrides other personal characteristics. Consequently, disability serves as a master status.

Without question, people with disabilities occupy a subordinate position in Canada. The first International Day of Persons with Disabilities was declared by the United Nations in 1992 and advocates from around the world continue to lobby for the adoption of an international convention on disability rights. Women and men involved in this movement are working to challenge negative views of disabled people and to modify the social structure by reshaping laws, institutions, and environments so that people with disabilities can be fully integrated into mainstream society.

The effort to overcome the master status is global in nature. Despite a regulation in China that universities may not reject students because of a physical disability, many universities do just that. In fact, in the last five years, the dozens of universities in Beijing alone have accepted only 236 students with *any* kind of disability, however minor. It appears that bias against those with disabilities runs deep in China, and many universities use a mandate to nurture physical development as an excuse to keep them out.

Kenya's constitution outlaws discrimination on the basis of many characteristics, including race, sex, tribe, place of origin, creed, and religion, but not on the basis of disability. The African nation of Botswana, however, has plans to assist those with disabilities, most of whom live in rural areas and need special services for mobility and economic development. In many countries, disability rights activists are targeting issues essential to overcoming master status and to being a full citizen; these issues include employment, housing, education, and access to public buildings.

Applying Theory

1. How would interactionist perspectives differ from conflict positions when it comes to the study of disabilities?
2. What emphases would feminist thinkers be most likely to bring to the study of disabilities?

Sources: Albrecht et al. 2001; Goffman 1963a; Murphy 1997; *Newsday* 1997; Ponczek 1998; Rosenthal 2001; Shapiro 1993; Willet and Deegan 2000.

take action if they see a citizen being threatened. With each distinctive social status—whether ascribed or achieved—come particular role expectations. However, actual performance varies from individual to individual. One secretary may assume extensive administrative responsibilities, whereas another may focus on clerical duties. Similarly, in Philip Zimbardo's mock prison experiment, some students were brutal and sadistic guards, but others were not.

Roles are a significant component of social structure. Viewed from a functionalist perspective, roles contribute to a society's stability by enabling members to anticipate the behaviour of others and to pattern their own actions accordingly. Yet social roles can also be dysfunctional by restricting people's interactions and relationships. If we view a person *only* as a "police officer" or a "supervisor," it will be difficult to relate to this person as a friend or neighbour.

Role Conflict

Imagine the delicate situation of a woman who has worked for a decade on an assembly line in an electrical plant and has recently been named supervisor of the unit she worked in. How is this woman expected to relate to her longtime friends and co-workers? Should she still go out to lunch with them, as she has done almost daily for years? Is it her responsibility to recommend the firing of an old friend who cannot keep up with the demands of the assembly line?

Imagine you are a journalist walking down this alley as you witness the mugging going on here. What do you do? Try to stop the crime? Or take a picture for your magazine? This was the role conflict that Sarah Leen, a professional photographer, experienced when she stopped to change a lens and take a picture of this scene. At the same time, Leen felt fear for her own safety. People in certain professions—among them, journalism—commonly experience role conflict during disasters, crimes, and other distressing situations.

Role conflict occurs when incompatible expectations arise from two or more social positions held by the same person. Fulfilment of the roles associated with one status may directly violate the roles linked to a second status. In the example above, the newly promoted supervisor will most likely experience a sharp conflict between her social and occupational roles.

Role conflicts call for important ethical choices. So, the new supervisor will have to make a difficult decision about how much allegiance she owes her friend and how much she owes her employers who have given her supervisory responsibilities.

Another type of role conflict occurs when individuals move into occupations that are not common among people with their ascribed status. Male preschool teachers and female police officers experience this type of role conflict. In the latter case, female officers must strive to reconcile their workplace role in law enforcement with the societal view of a woman's role, which does not embrace many skills needed in police work. And although female police officers encounter sexual harassment, as women do throughout the labour force, they must also deal with the "code of silence," an informal norm that precludes their implicating fellow officers in wrongdoing (Fletcher 1995; Martin 1994).

Use Your Sociological Imagination

If you were a male nurse, what aspects of role conflict would you need to consider? Now imagine you are a female professional boxer. What conflicting role expectations might that involve? In both cases, how well do you think you would handle role conflict?

Role Strain

Role conflict describes the situation of a person dealing with the challenge of occupying two social positions simultaneously. However, even a single position can cause problems. Sociologists use the term ***role strain*** to describe the difficulty that arises when the same social position imposes conflicting demands and expectations.

In the chapter opening example, social psychologist Philip Zimbardo unexpectedly experienced role strain. He initially saw himself merely as a professor directing an imaginative experiment in which students played the roles of either guard or inmate. However, he soon found

Police officers may face role strain when they try to develop positive community relations but still maintain an authoritative position.

that as a professor, he was also expected to look after the welfare of the students or at least not to endanger them. Eventually he resolved the role strain by making the difficult decision to terminate the experiment early. Twenty-five years later, in a television interview, he was still reflecting on the challenge of this role strain (CBS News 1998).

Role Exit

Often, when we think of assuming a social role, we focus on the preparation and anticipatory socialization that a person undergoes for that role. This is true if a person is about to become an attorney, a chef, a spouse, or a parent. Yet, until recently, social scientists have given less attention to the adjustments involved in *leaving* social roles.

Sociologist Helen Rose Fuchs Ebaugh (1988) developed the term ***role exit*** to describe the process of disengagement from a role that is central to a person's self-identity and reestablishment of an identity in a new role. Drawing on interviews with 185 people—among them ex-convicts, divorced men and women, recovering alcoholics, ex-nuns, former doctors, retirees, and transsexuals—Ebaugh (herself a former nun) studied the process of voluntarily exiting from significant social roles.

Ebaugh has offered a four-stage model of role exit. The first stage begins with *doubt.* The person experiences frustration, burnout, or simply unhappiness with an accustomed status and the roles associated with this social position. The second stage involves a *search for alternatives.* A person unhappy with his or her career may take a leave of absence; an unhappily married couple may begin what they see as a temporary separation.

The third stage of role exit is the *action stage* or *departure.* Ebaugh found that the vast majority of her respondents could identify a clear turning point that made them feel it was essential to take final action and leave their job, end their marriage, or engage in another type of role exit. Twenty percent of respondents saw their role exit as a gradual, evolutionary process that had no single turning point.

The last stage of role exit involves the *creation of a new identity.* Many of you participated in a role exit when you made the transition from high school to university. You left behind the role of offspring living at home and took on the role of a somewhat independent student

This college student in India decorated his dorm room with photos of beautiful women and fast cars. They may signify his attempt to create a new identity, the final stage in his exit from the role of high school student living at home.

living with peers in a dorm. Sociologist Ira Silver (1996) has made a study of the central role that material objects play in this transition. The objects that students choose to leave at home (like stuffed animals and dolls) are associated with their prior identities. They may remain deeply attached to these objects but do not want them to be seen as part of their new identities at university. The objects they bring with them symbolize how they now see themselves and how they want to be perceived. CDs and wall posters, for example, are calculated to say, "This is me."

Even though you may not be totally sure whom you are "talking" to online, the Internet has added a massive new dimension to social interaction.

Groups

In sociological terms, a ***group*** is any number of people with similar norms, values, and expectations who interact with one another on a regular basis. The members of a women's basketball team, of a hospital's business office, or of a symphony orchestra constitute a group. However, the residents of a suburb would not be considered a group, since they rarely interact with one another at one time.

Every society comprises many groups in which daily social interaction takes place. We seek out groups to establish friendships, to accomplish certain goals, and to fulfil social roles that we have acquired. We'll explore the various types of groups in which people interact in detail in Chapter 6, where sociological investigations of group behaviour will also be examined.

Groups play a vital part in a society's social structure. Much of our social interaction takes place within groups and is influenced by their norms and sanctions. Being a teenager or a retired person takes on special meanings when you interact within groups designed for people with that particular status. The expectations associated with many social roles, including those accompanying the statuses of brother, sister, and student, become more clearly defined in the context of a group.

New technology has broadened the definition of groups to include those who interact electronically. Not all the "people" with whom we converse online are real. At some Web sites, *chatterbots*—fictitious correspondents created by artificial intelligence programs—respond to questions as if a human were replying. While answering product or service-related questions, the chatterbot may begin "chatting" with an online consumer about family or the weather. Ultimately, such conversations may develop into a chat group that includes other online correspondents, both real and artificial. New groups organized around old interests, such as antique collection or bowling, have already arisen from this type of virtual reality (Van Slambrouck 1999).

For the human participant, such online exchanges offer a new opportunity to alter one's image—what Goffman (1959) refers to as impression management. How might you present yourself to an online discussion group?

p. 76

Social Networks and Technology

Groups do not merely serve to define other elements of the social structure, such as roles and statuses; they also are an intermediate link between the individual and the larger society. We are all members of a number of different groups and through our acquaintances make connections with people in different social circles. This connection is known as a ***social network,*** that is, a series of social relationships that links a person directly to others and through them indirectly to still more people. Social networks may constrain people by limiting the range of their interactions, yet these networks may also

Research in Action 5-2 Immigrant Women's Social Networks

Although sociologists have rightly given a good deal of attention to men's networks, there has been growing interest in the social networks created by women.

In her study of Hong Kong Chinese immigrant female entrepreneurs in Richmond, British Columbia, Frances Chiang (2001) used semistructured interviews to document the experiences of 58 immigrant women. Chiang found that "co-ethnic informal networks," which she defined as personalized relationships established informally through friends, family, kin, and clients who share the same ethnic background, were used to attract, maintain, and increase clientele. According to Chiang, these networks were even more significant when gender was taken into account, in relation to female business owners and their female co-ethnic clientele, leading her to observe that "the unique femaleness of women-to-women relationships facilitated by co-ethnic gendered resources plays a key role in these women-run businesses" (2001:341). Among these immigrant female entrepreneurs, said Chiang, socializing with clients became a way of building trust and establishing good client relations.

Sociologist Pierrette Hondagneu-Sotelo (2001) conducted observation research and interviews among Hispanic women (primarily Mexican immigrants) who live in San Francisco and are employed as domestic workers in middle- and upper-class homes. These women engage in what sociologist Mary Romero has called "job work." That is, the domestic worker has several employers and cleans each home on a weekly or biweekly basis for a flat rate of pay for the work completed (in Spanish, *por el trabajo*) as opposed to being paid an hourly rate (*por la hora*). Job work typically involves low pay, no reimbursement for transportation costs, and no health care benefits.

At first glance, we might expect that women engaged in such job work would be isolated from each other since they work alone. However, Hondagneu-Sotelo found that these Hispanic women have created strong social networks. Through interactions in various social settings—such as picnics, baby showers, church events, and informal gatherings at women's homes—they share such valuable information as cleaning tips, remedies for work-related physical ailments, tactics for negotiating better pay and gratuities, and advice on how to leave undesirable jobs.

Applying Theory

1. Have you ever participated in a job- or school-related network? If so, did you benefit from the opportunities it offered? In what way?
2. Suppose you want to land a professional job in the field of your choice. What people or organizations might help you to reach your goal? How would you get started?

Sources: Chiang 2001; Gabor 1995: Hondagneu-Sotelo 2001.

empower people by making available vast resources (Lin 1999).

Involvement in social networks—commonly known as *networking*—is especially valuable in finding employment. Albert Einstein was successful in finding a job only when a classmate's father put him in touch with his future employer. These kinds of contacts, even those that are weak and distant, can be crucial in establishing social networks and facilitating transmission of information.

In the workplace, networking pays off more for men than for women because of the traditional presence of men in leadership positions. A 1997 survey of executives found that 63 percent of men use networking to find new jobs compared with 41 percent of women. Thirty-one percent of the women use classified advertisements to find jobs, compared with only 13 percent of the men. A study of women who were leaving the welfare rolls to enter the paid workforce found that networking was an effective tool in their search for employment. Informal networking also helped them to locate child care and better housing—keys to successful employment (Carey and McLean 1997; Henly 1999). See Box 5-2 for a discussion of immigrant women's social networks.

With advances in technology, we can now maintain social networks electronically. We don't need face-to-face contacts for knowledge sharing any more. It is not uncommon for those looking for employment or for a means of identifying someone with common interests to first turn to the Internet. First impressions now begin on the Web. Many high school students get a first look at their future university via a Web page. A survey of post-secondary students found that 79 percent consider the quality of an employer's Web site important in deciding whether to apply for a job there (Jobtrak.com 2000).

Sociologist Manuel Castells (1997, 1998, 2000) views the emerging electronic social networks as fundamental to new organizations and the growth of existing businesses and associations. One emerging electronic network, in particular, is changing the way people interact. "Texting" began first in Asia in 2000 and has now taken off in North America and Europe. It refers to wireless e-mails exchanged over cell phones and other wireless devices. Initially, texting was popular among young users, who sent shorthand messages such as "WRU" (where are you?) and CU2NYT" (see you tonight). But now the business world has seen the advantages of transmitting updated business or financial emails via cell phones or handheld personal digital assistants (PDAs). Sociologists, however, caution that such devices create a workday that never ends and that increasingly people are busy checking their digital devices rather than actually conversing with those around them (Rosen 2001).

Use Your Sociological Imagination

If you were deaf, what impact might instant messaging on the Internet have for you?

Social Institutions

The mass media, the government, the economy, the family, and the health care system are all examples of social institutions found in our society. ***Social institutions*** can be viewed as organized patterns of beliefs and behaviour centred on the provision of basic social needs as well as the production and reproduction of social relations.

A close look at social institutions gives sociologists insight into the structure of a society. Consider religion, for example. The institution of religion adapts to the segment of society that it serves. Church work has very different meanings for ministers who serve a skid row area or a suburban middle-class community. Religious leaders assigned to a skid row mission will focus on tending to the ill and providing food and shelter. By contrast, clergy in affluent suburbs will be occupied with counselling those considering marriage and divorce, arranging youth activities, and overseeing cultural events. The church also serves to produce and reproduce patterns of social inequality, such as the inequality between women and men as it relates to who holds power in the church.

Functionalist View

One way to understand social institutions is to see how they fulfil essential functions. Anthropologist David F. Aberle and his colleagues (1950) and sociologists Raymond Mack and Calvin Bradford (1979) have identified five major tasks, or functional prerequisites, that a society or relatively permanent group must accomplish if it is to survive (see Table 5-1):

Table 5-1 Functions and Institutions

Functional Prerequisite	Social Institutions
Replacing personnel	Family Government (immigration)
Teaching new recruits	Family (basic skills) Economy (occupations) Education (schools) Religion (sacred teachings)
Producing and distributing goods and services	Family (food preparation) Economy Government (regulations regarding commerce) Health care system
Preserving order	Family (child rearing, regulation of sexuality) Government Religion (morals)
Providing and maintaining a sense of purpose	Government (patriotism) Religion

1. *Replacing personnel.* Any group or society must replace personnel when they die, leave, or become incapacitated. This is accomplished through such means as immigration, annexation of neighbouring groups of people, acquisition of slaves, or sexual reproduction of members. The Shakers, a religious sect that came to North America in 1774, are a conspicuous example of a group that has *failed* to replace personnel. Their religious beliefs commit the Shakers to celibacy; to survive, the group must recruit new members. At first, the Shakers proved successful in attracting members and reached a peak of about six thousand members during the 1840s. However, as of 2001, the only Shaker community left was a farm in Maine with six members (Associated Press 2001).
2. *Teaching new recruits.* No group or society can survive if many of its members reject the established behaviour and responsibilities. Thus, finding or producing new members is not sufficient. The

group or society must encourage recruits to learn and accept its values and customs. This learning can take place formally within schools (where learning is a manifest function) or informally through interaction and negotiation in peer groups (where instruction is a latent function).

3. *Producing and distributing goods and services.* Any relatively permanent group or society must provide and distribute desired goods and services for its members. Each society establishes a set of rules for the allocation of financial and other resources. The group must satisfy the needs of most members to some extent, or it will risk the possibility of discontent and, ultimately, disorder.
4. *Preserving order.* The native people of Tasmania, a large island just south of Australia, are now extinct. During the 1800s, they were destroyed by the hunting parties of European conquerors, who looked upon the Tasmanians as half-human. This annihilation underscores a critical function of every group or society—preserving order and protecting itself from attack. Because the Tasmanians were unable to defend themselves against the more developed European technology of warfare, an entire people was wiped out.
5. *Providing and maintaining a sense of purpose.* People must feel motivated to continue as members of a group or society in order to fulfil the previous four requirements. After the September 11, 2001, attacks on New York City and Washington, D.C., memorial services and community gatherings across the United States allowed people to affirm their allegiance to their country and bind up the psychic wounds inflicted by the terrorists. Patriotism, then, assists some people in developing and maintaining a sense of purpose. For others, tribal identities, religious values, or personal moral codes are especially meaningful. Whatever the motivator, in any society there remains one common and critical reality: If an individual does not have a sense of purpose, he or she has little reason to contribute to a society's survival.

This list of functional prerequisites does not specify *how* a society and its corresponding social institutions will perform each task. For example, one society may protect itself from external attack by amassing a frightening arsenal of weaponry, while another may make determined efforts to remain neutral in world politics and to promote cooperative relationships with its neighbours. No matter what its particular strategy, any society or relatively permanent group must attempt to satisfy all these functional prerequisites for survival. If it fails on even one condition, as the Tasmanians did, the society runs the risk of extinction.

Conflict View

Conflict theorists do not concur with the functionalist approach to social institutions. Although both perspectives agree that institutions are organized to meet basic social needs, conflict theorists object to the implication that the outcome is necessarily efficient and desirable.

From a conflict perspective, the present organization of social institutions is no accident. Major institutions, such as education, help to maintain the privileges of the most powerful individuals and groups within a society, while contributing to the powerlessness of others. As one example, public schools in Canada are financed largely through property taxes. This allows more affluent areas to provide their children with better-equipped schools and better-paid teachers than low-income areas can

Celebrating Canada Day helps to encourage patriotism and create a sense of purpose among Canadians.

afford. As a result, children from prosperous communities are better prepared to compete academically than children from impoverished communities. The structure of the nation's educational system permits and even promotes such unequal treatment of school children.

Conflict theorists argue that social institutions, such as education, have an inherently conservative nature. Without question, it has been difficult to implement educational reforms that promote equal opportunity—whether in the area of English as a second language (ESL) or the inclusion of students with disabilities. From a functionalist perspective, social change can be dysfunctional, since it often leads to instability. However, from a conflict view, why should we preserve the existing social structure if it is unfair and discriminatory?

Feminist Perspectives

Feminist thinkers, such as Patricia Hill Collins (1998), argue that social institutions operate in gendered and racist environments. In schools, offices, and governmental institutions, assumptions about what people can do reflect the sexism and racism of the larger society. For instance, some people may assume that women cannot make tough decisions—even women in the top echelons of corporate management. Others might assume that all Aboriginal students at top universities represent equity policy admissions. Inequality based on gender, class, race, and ethnicity thrives in such an environment—to which we might add discrimination based on age, physical disability, and sexual orientation. The truth of this assertion can be seen in routine decisions by employers on how to advertise jobs as well as whether to provide fringe benefits, such as child care and parental leave.

Liberal feminists, or equality feminists as they are sometimes called, stress these types of benefits as a means of strengthening employment opportunities for women, thus promoting gender equality. Radical feminists, however, believe that a much more fundamental change must occur throughout the various social institutions in order to achieve gender equality—the elimination of patriarchy.

Use Your Sociological Imagination

Do you think that social networks might be more important for a migrant worker in southern Ontario than for someone with political and social clout? Why or why not?

Interactionist View

Social institutions affect our everyday behaviour, whether we are driving down the street or waiting in a long shopping line. Sociologist Mitchell Duneier (1994a, 1994b) studied the social behaviour of the word

Social institutions affect the way we behave. How might the worshippers at this mosque in Egypt interact differently in school or in the workplace?

processors, all women, who work in the service centre of a large law firm. Duneier was interested in the informal social norms that emerged in this work environment and the rich social network that these female employees had created.

The Network Center, as it is called, is merely a single, windowless room in a large office building where the law firm occupies seven floors. This centre is staffed by two shifts of word processors, who work either from 4:00 p.m. to midnight or from midnight to 8:00 a.m. Each word processor works in a cubicle with just enough room for her keyboard, terminal, printer, and telephone. Work assignments for the word processors are placed in a central basket and then completed according to precise procedures.

At first glance, we might think that these women labour with little social contact, apart from limited work breaks and occasional conversations with their supervisor. However, drawing on the interactionist perspective,

Duneier learned that despite working in a large office, these women find private moments to talk (often in the halls or outside the washroom) and share a critical view of the law firm's lawyers and day-shift secretaries. Indeed, the word processors routinely suggest that their assignments represent work that the "lazy" secretaries should have completed during the normal workday. Duneier (1994b) tells of one word processor who resented the lawyers' superior attitude and pointedly refused to recognize or speak with any lawyer who would not address her by name.

Interactionist theorists emphasize that our social behaviour is conditioned by the roles and statuses that we accept, the groups to which we belong, and the institutions within which we function. For example, the social roles associated with being a judge occur within the larger context of the criminal justice system. The status of "judge" stands in relation to other statuses, such as lawyer, plaintiff, defendant, and witness, as well as to the social institution of government. Although courts and jails have great symbolic importance, the judicial system derives its continued significance from the roles people carry out in social interactions (Berger and Luckmann 1966).

SOCIAL STRUCTURE IN GLOBAL PERSPECTIVE

Modern societies are complex, especially when compared with earlier social arrangements. Sociologists Ferdinand Tönnies and Gerhard Lenski have offered ways to contrast modern societies with simpler forms of social structure.

Tönnies's *Gemeinschaft* and *Gesellschaft*

Ferdinand Tönnies (1855–1936) was appalled by the rise of an industrial city in his native Germany during the late nineteenth century. In his view, this city marked a dramatic change from the ideal type of a close-knit community, which Tönnies termed *Gemeinschaft,* to that of an impersonal mass society known as *Gesellschaft* (Tönnies [1887] 1988).

The ***Gemeinschaft*** (pronounced guh-MINE-shoft) community is typical of rural life. It is a small community in which people have similar backgrounds and life experiences. Virtually everyone knows one another, and social interactions are intimate and familiar, almost as might be found among kinfolk. There is a commitment to the larger social group and a sense of togetherness among community members. People relate to others in a personal way, not just as "clerk" or "manager." With this more personal interaction comes less privacy: we know more about everyone.

Social control in the *Gemeinschaft* community is maintained through informal means, such as moral persuasion, gossip, and even gestures. These techniques work effectively because people genuinely care about how others feel toward them. Social change is relatively limited in the *Gemeinschaft;* the lives of members of one generation may be quite similar to those of their grandparents.

By contrast, the ***Gesellschaft*** (pronounced guh-ZELL-shoft) is an ideal type characteristic of modern urban life. Most people are strangers and feel little in common with other community residents. Relationships are governed by social roles that grow out of immediate tasks, such as purchasing a product or arranging a business meeting. Self-interests dominate, and there is generally little consensus concerning values or commitment to the group. As a result, social control must rely on more formal techniques, such as laws and legally defined punishments. Social change is an important aspect of life in the *Gesellschaft;* it can be strikingly evident even within a single generation.

Table 5-2 summarizes the differences between the *Gemeinschaft* and the *Gesellschaft* as described by Tönnies. Sociologists have used these terms to compare social structures stressing close relationships with those that emphasize less personal ties. It is easy to view *Gemeinschaft* with nostalgia as a far better way of life than the "rat race" of contemporary existence. However, the more intimate relationships of the *Gemeinschaft* come with a price. The prejudice and discrimination found there can be quite confining; ascribed statuses, such as family

"I'd like to think of you as a person, David, but it's my job to think of you as personnel."

In a *Gesellschaft,* people are likely to relate to one another in terms of their roles rather than their individual backgrounds.

Table 5-2 Comparison of *Gemeinschaft* and *Gesellschaft*

Gemeinschaft	*Gesellschaft*
Rural life typifies this form.	Urban life typifies this form.
People share a feeling of community that results from their similar backgrounds and life experiences.	People perceive little sense of commonality. Their differences in background appear more striking than their similarities.
Social interactions, including negotiations, are intimate and familiar.	Social interactions, including negotiations, are more likely to be task-specific.
There is a spirit of cooperation and unity of will.	Self-interests dominate.
Tasks and personal relationships cannot be separated.	The task being performed is paramount; relationships are subordinate.
There is little emphasis on individual privacy.	Privacy is valued.
Informal social control predominates.	Formal social control is evident.
There is less tolerance of deviance.	There is greater tolerance of deviance.
Emphasis is on ascribed statuses.	There is more emphasis on achieved statuses.
Social change is relatively limited.	Social change is very evident—even within a generation.

Think about It
How would you classify the communities with which you are familiar? Are they more *Gemeinschaft* or *Gesellschaft?*

background, often outweigh a person's unique talents and achievements. In addition, *Gemeinschaft* tends to be distrustful of the individual who seeks to be creative or just to be different.

Lenski's Sociocultural Evolution Approach

Sociologist Gerhard Lenski takes a very different view of society and social structure. Rather than distinguishing between two opposite types of societies, as Tönnies had, Lenski sees human societies as undergoing change according to a dominant pattern, known as ***sociocultural evolution.*** This term refers to the "process of change and development in human societies that results from cumulative growth in their stores of cultural information" (Lenski et al. 1995:75).

In Lenski's view, a society's level of technology is critical to the way it is organized. He defines technology as "information about the ways in which the material resources of the environment may be used to satisfy human needs and desires" (Nolan and Lenski 1999:414). The available technology does not completely define the form that a particular society and its social structure take. Nevertheless, a low level of technology may limit the degree to which it can depend on such things as irrigation or complex machinery. As technology advances, Lenski sees society as evolving from preindustrial to industrial to postindustrial.

Preindustrial Societies

How does a preindustrial society organize its economy? If we know that, it is possible to categorize the society. The first type of preindustrial society to emerge in human history was the ***hunting-and-gathering society,*** in which people simply rely on whatever foods and fibres are readily available. Technology in such societies is minimal. Organized in groups, people move constantly in search of food. There is little division of labour into specialized tasks.

Hunting-and-gathering societies comprise small, widely dispersed groups. Each group consists almost entirely of people related to one another. As a result, kinship ties are the source of authority and influence, and the social institution of the family takes on a particularly important role. Tönnies would certainly view such societies as examples of *Gemeinschaft.*

Since resources are scarce, there is relatively little inequality in terms of material goods. Social differentiation within the hunting-and-gathering society is based on such ascribed statuses as gender, age, and family background. The last hunting-and-gathering societies had virtually disappeared by the close of the twentieth century (Nolan and Lenski 1999).

Horticultural societies, in which people plant seeds and crops rather than subsist merely on available foods, emerged about 10 000 to 12 000 years ago. Members of horticultural societies are much less nomadic than hunters and gatherers. They place greater emphasis on the production of tools and household objects. Yet technology within horticultural societies remains rather limited. They cultivate crops with the aid of digging sticks or hoes (Wilford 1997).

The last stage of preindustrial development is the ***agrarian society,*** which emerged about five thousand years ago. As in horticultural societies, members of agrarian societies are primarily engaged in the production of food. However, the introduction of new technological innovations, such as the plow, allows farmers to dramatically increase their crop yield. They can cultivate the same fields over generations, thereby allowing for the emergence of still larger settlements.

The social structure of the agrarian society continues to rely on the physical power of humans and animals (as opposed to mechanical power). Nevertheless, the social structure has more carefully defined roles than in horticultural societies. Individuals focus on specialized tasks, such as repair of fishing nets or work as a blacksmith. As human settlements become more established and stable, social institutions become more elaborate, and property rights take on greater importance. The comparative permanence and greater surpluses of agrarian society make it more feasible to create artifacts, such as statues, public monuments, and art objects, and to pass them on from one generation to the next.

Industrial Societies

Although the Industrial Revolution did not topple monarchs, it produced changes every bit as significant as those resulting from political revolutions. The Industrial Revolution, which took place largely in England during the period 1760 to 1830, was a scientific revolution focused on the application of nonanimal (mechanical) sources of power to labour tasks. An ***industrial society*** is a society that depends on mechanization to produce its goods and services. Industrial societies rely on new inventions that facilitate agricultural and industrial production and on new sources of energy, such as steam.

As the industrial revolution proceeded, a new form of social structure emerged. Many societies underwent an irrevocable shift from an agrarian-oriented economy to an industrial base. No longer did an individual or a family typically make an entire product. Instead, specialization of tasks and manufacturing of goods became increasingly common. Workers, generally men but also women and even children, left family homesteads to work in central locations, such as factories.

The process of industrialization had distinctive social consequences. Families and communities could not continue to function as self-sufficient units. Individuals, villages, and regions began to exchange goods and services and become interdependent. As people came to rely on the labour of members of other communities, the family lost its unique position as the source of power and authority. The need for specialized knowledge led to more formalized education, and education emerged as a social institution distinct from the family.

Postindustrial Societies

When the sociocultural evolutionary approach first appeared in the 1960s, it paid relatively little attention to how maturing industrialized societies changed with the emergence of even more advanced forms of technology.

More recently, Lenski and other sociologists have studied the significant changes in the occupational structure of industrial societies as they shift from manufacturing to service economies. Social scientists call these technologically advanced nations *postindustrial societies.* Sociologist Daniel Bell (1999) defines ***postindustrial society*** as a society whose economic system is engaged primarily in the processing and control of information. The main output of a postindustrial society is services rather than manufactured goods. Large numbers of people become involved in occupations devoted to the teaching, generation, or dissemination of ideas.

Bell views this transition from industrial to postindustrial society as a positive development. He sees a general decline in organized working-class groups and a rise in interest groups concerned with such national issues as health, education, and the environment. Bell's outlook is functionalist because he portrays postindustrial society as basically consensual. Organizations and interest groups will engage in an open and competitive process of decision making. The level of conflict between diverse groups will diminish, leading to much greater social stability.

Conflict theorists take issue with Bell's functionalist analysis of postindustrial society. For example, Michael Harrington (1980), who alerted the nation to the problems of the poor in his book *The Other America,* was critical of the significance that Bell attached to the growing class of white-collar workers. Harrington conceded that scientists, engineers, and economists are involved in important political and economic decisions, but he disagreed with Bell's claim that they have a free hand in decision making, independent of the interests of the rich. Harrington followed in the tradition of Marx by arguing that conflict between social classes will continue in postindustrial society.

Ferdinand Tönnies and Gerhard Lenski present two visions of society's social structure. Although different, both approaches are useful, and this textbook will draw on both. The sociocultural evolutionary approach emphasizes a historical perspective. It does not picture different types of social structures coexisting within the same society. Consequently, according to this approach, we would not expect a single society to include hunters and gatherers along with a postindustrial culture. By contrast, sociologists frequently observe that a *Gemeinschaft* and a *Gesellschaft* can be found in the same society. For example, a rural Quebec community less than 100 kilometres from Montreal is linked to the metropolitan area by the technology of the modern information age.

The work of Tönnies and Lenski reminds us that a major focus of sociology has been to identify changes in social structure and the consequences for human behaviour. At the macrolevel, we see society shifting to more advanced forms of technology. The social structure becomes increasingly complex, and new social institutions emerge to assume some functions previously performed by the family. On the microlevel, these changes affect the nature of social interactions between people. Each individual takes on multiple social roles, and people come to rely more on social networks rather than solely on kinship ties. As the social structure becomes more complex, people's relationships tend to become more impersonal, transient, and fragmented.

In the social policy section we will examine the impact of the AIDS crisis on the social structure and social interaction around the globe.

SOCIAL POLICY AND SOCIAL STRUCTURE: The AIDS Crisis

The Issue

In his novel *The Plague,* Albert Camus (1948:34) wrote, "There have been as many plagues as wars in history, yet always plagues and wars take people equally by surprise." Regarded by many as the distinctive plague of the modern era, AIDS certainly caught major social institutions—particularly the government, the health care system, and the economy—by surprise when it initially became noticed by medical practitioners in the 1970s. It has since spread around the world. Although there are encouraging new therapies to treat people, there is currently no way to eradicate AIDS by medical means. Therefore, it is essential to protect people by reducing the transmission of the fatal virus. But how is this to be done? And whose responsibility is it? What role do social institutions have?

The Setting

AIDS is the acronym for *acquired immune deficiency syndrome.* Rather than being a distinct disease, AIDS is actually a predisposition to disease caused by a virus, the human immunodeficiency virus (HIV). This virus gradually destroys the body's immune system, leaving the carrier vulnerable to infections, such as pneumonia, that those with healthy immune systems can generally resist. Transmission of the virus from one person to another appears to require either intimate sexual contact or exchange of blood or bodily fluids (whether from contaminated hypodermic needles or syringes, transfusions of infected blood, or transmission from an infected mother to her child before or during birth). Health practitioners pay particular attention to methods of transmitting HIV because there is no cure or vaccine for AIDS at this time.

The first cases of HIV in Canada were reported in 1985. Although the numbers of new cases and deaths have recently shown some evidence of decline, approximately 56 000 people in Canada were living with AIDS or HIV by the end of 2002. Women account for a growing proportion of new cases. Aboriginal people accounted for approximately 13 percent of all cases. Worldwide, AIDS is on the increase, with an estimated 39 million people infected and 3 million dying annually (see Figure 5-2). AIDS is not evenly distributed, and those areas least equipped to deal with it—the developing nations of sub-Saharan Africa—face the greatest challenge (Centers for Disease Control and Prevention 2002; UNAIDS 2004).

FIGURE 5-2

The Geography of People Living with HIV/AIDS, 2004

Mapping Life WORLDWIDE

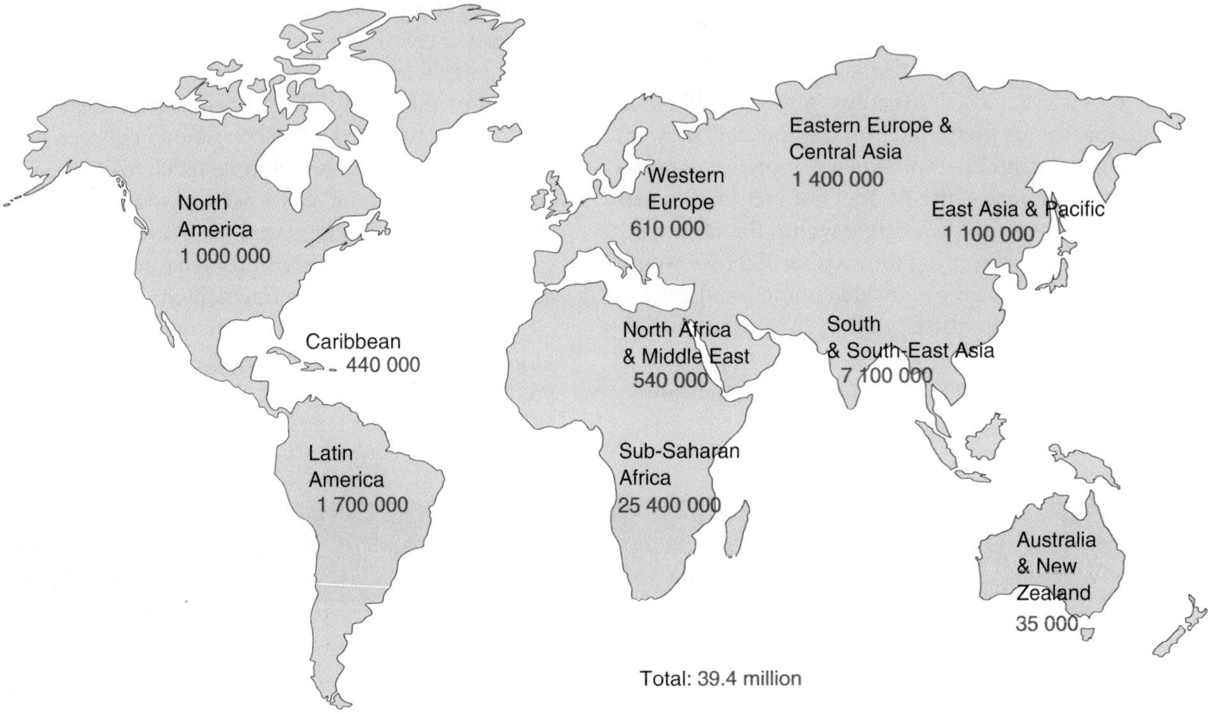

Source: UNAIDS 2004.

UNAIDS's 2004 report on the global AIDS epidemic shows tremendous global inequality in the spread of the disease. The report highlighted some examples of this inequality:

- Sharp increases have occurred in Asia, particularly in China, Indonesia, and Vietnam. With 60 percent of the world's population in Asia, the increase of the disease in the region has profound global implications.
- India is home to one in seven HIV-positive people worldwide—an estimated 5.1 million people in that country live with the disease.
- Although Brazil has a national HIV rate of less than 1 percent, infection rates were reported to be more than 60 percent among injection drug users.
- In Russia, an increasing number of women have contracted the disease—up from one in four in 2001 to one in three in 2002. Eighty percent of the infected people in that country are under age 30, compared with 30 percent in North America and Western Europe.
- Approximately 25 million people are living with the disease in sub-Saharan Africa. Although rates have stabilized in that region, the rates are misleading. This seeming stabilization is due to a rise in the rates of AIDS deaths, offset by new infections, which have also continued to increase.

Sociological Insights

Dramatic crises, like the AIDS epidemic, are likely to bring about certain transformations in a society's social structure. From a functionalist perspective, if established social institutions cannot meet a crucial need, new social networks are likely to emerge to fill that function. In the case of AIDS, self-help groups—especially in the gay communities of major cities—have organized to care for the sick, educate the healthy, and lobby for more responsive public policies.

The label of "person with AIDS" or "HIV-positive" often functions as a master status. People with AIDS or infected with the virus actually face a powerful dual stigma. Not only are they associated with a lethal and contagious disease, but they have a disease that disproportionately afflicts already stigmatized groups, such as gay males and intravenous drug users. This linkage with stigmatized groups delayed recognition of the severity of the AIDS epidemic; the media took little interest in the disease until it seemed to be spreading beyond the gay community.

Viewed from a conflict perspective, policymakers were slow to respond to the AIDS crisis because those in high-risk groups—gay men and IV drug users—were comparatively powerless. Furthermore, a study in 2002 documented that female and minority groups are less likely to receive experimental treatments for the HIV infection (Gifford et al. 2002).

On the microlevel of social interaction, observers widely forecast that AIDS would lead to a more conservative sexual climate—among both homosexuals and heterosexuals—in which people would be much more cautious about involvement with new partners. Yet it appears that many sexually active people have not heeded precautions about "safe sex." Data from studies conducted in the early 1990s indicated a growing complacency about AIDS, even among those most vulnerable (*AIDS Alert* 1999).

Another interactionist concern is the tremendous impact that taking the appropriate medication has on a person's daily routine. Tens of thousands of AIDS patients are having to reorder their lives around their medical regimens. Even infected patients without the symptoms of AIDS find the concentrated effort that is needed to fight the disease—taking 95 doses of 16 different medications every 24 hours—extremely taxing. Think for a moment about the effect such a regimen would have on your own life, from eating and sleeping to work, study, child care, and recreation.

Policy Initiatives

AIDS has struck all societies, but not all nations can respond in the same manner. Studies in North America show that people with the virus and with AIDS who receive appropriate medical treatment are living longer than before. This may put additional pressure on policymakers to address the issues raised by the spread of AIDS (Steinhauer 2000).

In some nations, cultural practices may prevent people from dealing with the AIDS epidemic, making them less likely to take the necessary preventive measures, including more open discussion of sexuality, homosexuality, and drug use. Prevention has shown signs of working among target groups, such as drug users, pregnant women, and gay men and lesbians, but these initiatives are few and far between in developing nations. The prescribed treatment for a pregnant woman to reduce mother-to-baby transmission of AIDS costs about $1000—many times the average annual income in much of the world where the risk of AIDS is greatest. Africa, for example, accounts for 80 percent of the world's AIDS deaths. Even more costly is the medication for adult patients with HIV, which costs $71 000 a year (Pear 1997a; Sawyer 2000; Specter 1998; Sternberg 1999).

The high cost of drug treatment programs has generated intensive worldwide pressure on the major pharmaceutical companies to lower their prices to patients in developing nations of the world, especially sub-Saharan Africa. In 2001, bowing to this pressure, several of the companies agreed to make the combination therapies available at cost (about $600 per person per year). Even this much lower cost will not be easily met by developing countries so devastated by AIDS. Moreover, the prospect of cheaper medicine is sure to stimulate the demand for care, which, in turn, will create the need for more resources (Brundtland 2001).

Applying Theory

1. What perspective might feminist sociologists bring to the discussion on the global crisis of HIV/AIDS?
2. From a conflict perspective, what groups would be less likely to receive experimental treatments for HIV/AIDS? Why?
3. If you were an interactionist sociologist who wanted to understand why some people knowingly ignore the dangers of AIDS, how would you go about studying the problem?

CHAPTER RESOURCES

Summary

Social interaction refers to the ways in which people respond to one another. ***Social structure*** refers to the way in which a society is organized into predictable relationships. This chapter examined the basic elements of social structure: statuses, social roles, groups, networks, and institutions.

1. We shape our social reality based on what we learn through our social interactions. Social change comes from redefining or reconstructing social reality. Sometimes change results from ***negotiation***.
2. An ***ascribed status*** is generally assigned to a person at birth, whereas an ***achieved status*** is attained largely through one's own effort.
3. Ascribed statuses, such as age and sex, can function as ***master statuses*** that have an important impact on a person's potential to achieve a desired professional and social status.
4. With each distinctive status—whether ascribed or achieved—come particular ***social roles,*** the set of expectations for people who occupy that status.
5. Much of our patterned behaviour takes place within ***groups*** and is influenced by the norms and sanctions established by groups. Groups serve as links to ***social networks*** and their vast resources.
6. The mass media, the government, the economy, the family, and the health care system are all examples of ***social institutions***.
7. One way to understand social institutions is to see how they fulfil essential functions, such as replacing personnel, training new recruits, and preserving order.
8. The conflict perspective argues that social institutions help to maintain the privileges of the powerful while contributing to the powerlessness of others.
9. Interactionist theorists emphasize that our social behaviour is conditioned by the roles and ***statuses*** that we accept, the groups to which we belong, and the institutions within which we function.
10. Ferdinand Tönnies distinguished the close-knit community of ***Gemeinschaft*** from the impersonal mass society known as ***Gesellschaft***.
11. Gerhard Lenski views human societies as changing historically as technology advances, which he calls ***sociocultural evolution***.
12. The AIDS crisis affects every social institution, including the family, the schools, the health care system, the economy, and the government, as well as the social interactions of people touched by the epidemic.

Critical Thinking Questions

1. People in certain professions seem particularly susceptible to role conflict. For example, journalists commonly experience role conflict during disasters, crimes, and other distressing situations. Should they offer assistance to the needy or cover breaking news as reporters? Select two other professions and discuss the types of role conflict people in them might experience.
2. The functionalist, conflict, interactionist, and feminist perspectives can all be used in analyzing social institutions. What are the strengths or weaknesses in each perspective's analysis of social institutions?
3. In what ways does HIV serve to underscore issues of race, class, and gender in the world today?
4. Do you think your sense of self could be altered in a fundamental way if your place in the social structure were radically changed, such as what happened to the students in Zimbardo's prison experiment?

Key Terms

Achieved status A social position attained by a person largely through his or her own efforts. (page 97)

Agrarian society The most technologically advanced form of preindustrial society. Members are primarily engaged in the production of food but increase their crop yield through such innovations as the plow. (108)

Ascribed status A social position "assigned" to a person by society without regard for the person's unique talents or characteristics. (96)

Gemeinschaft Close-knit communities, often found in rural areas, in which strong personal bonds unite members. (106)

Gesellschaft Communities, often urban, that are large and impersonal, with little commitment to the group or consensus on values. (106)

Group Any number of people with similar norms, values, and expectations who interact with one another on a regular basis. (101)

Horticultural societies Preindustrial societies in which people plant seeds and crops rather than subsist merely on available foods. (108)

Hunting-and-gathering society A preindustrial society in which people rely on whatever foods and fibres are readily available in order to live. (107)

Industrial society A society that depends on mechanization to produce its goods and services. (108)

Master status A status that dominates others and thereby determines a person's general position within society. (97)

Negotiated order A social structure that derives its existence from the social interactions through which people define and redefine its character. (96)

Negotiation The attempt to reach agreement with others concerning some objective. (96)

Postindustrial society A society whose economic system is primarily engaged in the processing and control of information. (108)

Role conflict The situation that occurs when incompatible expectations arise from two or more social positions held by the same person. (99)

Role exit The process of disengagement from a role that is central to self-identity and reestablishment of an identity in a new role. (100)

Role strain The situation that occurs when the same social position imposes conflicting demands and expectations. (99)

Social institutions Organized patterns of beliefs and behaviour centred on basic social needs. (103)

Social interaction The ways in which people respond to one another. (94)

Social network A series of social relationships that links a person directly to others and through them indirectly to still more people. (101)

Social role A set of expectations for people who occupy a given social position or status. (97)

Social structure The way in which a society is organized into predictable relationships. (94)

Sociocultural evolution The process of change and development in human societies that results from cumulative growth in their stores of cultural information. (107)

Status A term used by sociologists to refer to any of the full range of socially defined positions within a large group or society. (96)

Additional Readings

Altman, Dennis. 2002. *Global Sex.* Chicago: University of Chicago Press. A look at how mass media, transportation, new technologies, and multinational corporations are reshaping our sexual practices and views in an increasingly globalized world.

Danesi, Marcel. 2003. *Forever Young: The "Teen-Aging" of Modern Culture.* Toronto: University of Toronto Press. An examination of the glorification of youth and the structures—primarily economic—that underpin its prevalence.

Gurstein, Penny. 2001. *Wired to the World, Chained to the Home.* Vancouver: UBC Press. Gurstein analyzes a diverse group of teleworkers, examining how working at home may change people's activity patterns, social networks, and working spaces.

Online Learning Centre

Visit the *Sociology: A Brief Introduction* Online Learning Centre at www.mcgrawhill.ca/college/schaefer to access quizzes, interactive exercises, video clips, and other research and study tools related to this chapter.

Reel Society Interactive Movie CD-ROM 2.0

Reel Society 2.0 can be used to spark discussion about the following topics from this chapter:

- Social roles
- Social roles and expectations of others

chapter

6

GROUPS AND ORGANIZATIONS

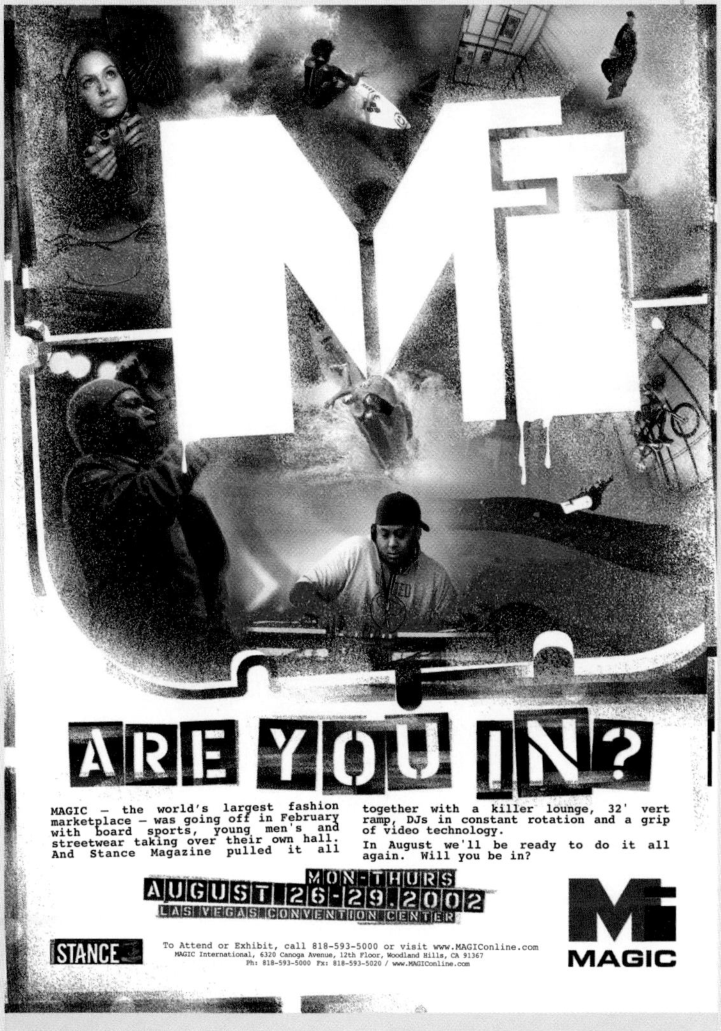

ARE YOU IN?
MAGIC — the world's largest fashion marketplace — was going off in February with board sports, young men's and streetwear taking over their own hall. And Stance Magazine pulled it all together with a killer lounge, 32' vert ramp, DJs in constant rotation and a grip of video technology.
In August we'll be ready to do it all again. Will you be in?
MON-THURS
AUGUST 26-29.2002
LAS VEGAS CONVENTION CENTER
STANCE
To Attend or Exhibit, call 818-593-5000 or visit www.MAGIConline.com
MAGIC International, 6320 Canoga Avenue, 12th Floor, Woodland Hills, CA 91367
Ph: 818-593-5000 Fx: 818-593-5020 / www.MAGIConline.com
MAGIC

Groups come in all sizes and cover a broad array of interests. This poster is directed to a group of people interested in a marketplace featuring fashions for young men. It asks: "Are you in?"

Ray Kroc, the genius behind the franchising of McDonald's restaurants, was a man with big ideas and grand ambitions. But even Kroc could not have anticipated the astounding impact of his creation. McDonald's is the basis of one of the most influential developments in contemporary society. Its reverberations extend far beyond its point of origin in the United States and in the fast-food business. It has influenced a wide range of undertakings, indeed the way of life, of a significant portion of the world. And that impact is likely to expand at an accelerating rate.

However, this is not a book about McDonald's, or even about the fast-food business. . . . Rather, McDonald's serves here as the major example, the paradigm, of a wide-ranging process I call *McDonaldization*. . . . As you will see, McDonaldization affects not only the restaurant business but also education, work, health care, travel, leisure, dieting, politics, the family, and virtually every other aspect of society. McDonaldization has shown every sign of being an inexorable process, sweeping through seemingly impervious institutions and regions of the world. . . .

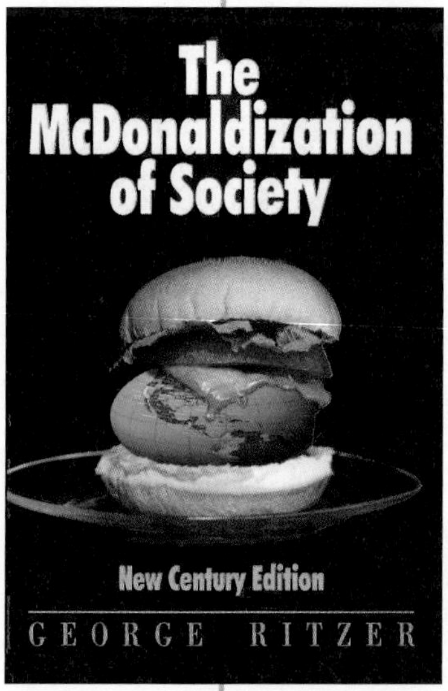

Other types of businesses are increasingly adapting the principles of the fast-food industry to their needs. Said the vice chairman of Toys 'R' Us, "We want to be thought of as a sort of McDonald's of toys." . . . Other chains with similar ambitions include Jiffy Lube, AAMCO Transmissions, Midas Muffler & Brake Shops, Hair Plus, H&R Block, Pearle Vision Centers. . . .

Other nations have developed their own variants of this American institution. . . . Paris, a city whose love for fine cuisine might lead you to think it would prove immune to fast food, has a large number of fast-food croissanteries; the revered French bread has also been McDonaldized. India has a chain of fast-food restaurants, Nirula's, that sells mutton burgers (about 80% of Indians are Hindus, who eat no beef) as well as local Indian cuisine. Mos Burgers is a Japanese chain with over fifteen hundred restaurants that, in addition to the usual fare, sell Teriyaki chicken burgers, rice burgers, and "Oshiruko with brown rice cake." Russkoye Bistro, a Russian chain, sells traditional Russian fare such as pirogi (meat and vegetable pies), blini (thin pancakes), Cossack apricot curd tart, and, of course, vodka. . . .

McDonald's is such a powerful model that many businesses have acquired nicknames beginning with Mc. Examples include "McDentists" and "McDoctors," meaning drive-in clinics designed to deal quickly and efficiently with minor dental and medical problems; "McChild" care centers, meaning child care centers such as Kinder-Care; "McStables," designating the nationwide race horse–training operation of Wayne Lucas; and "McPaper," designating the newspaper *USA TODAY*. *(Ritzer 2000:1–4, 10)* ■

In this excerpt from *The McDonaldization of Society,* sociologist George Ritzer contemplates the enormous influence of a well-known fast-food organization on modern-day culture and social life. Ritzer defines ***McDonaldization*** as "the process by which the principles of the fast-food restaurant are coming to dominate more and more sectors of American society as well as the rest of the world" (Ritzer 2000:1). Drawing on the work of Max Weber, he shows how the business principles on which the fast-food industry is founded—efficiency, calculability, predictability, and control—have changed not only the way North Americans do business but also the way they live their lives.

Despite the runaway success of McDonald's and its imitators, and the advantages these enterprises bring to millions of people around the world, Ritzer is critical of their effect on society. The waste and environmental degradation created by billions of disposable containers and the dehumanized work routines of fast-food crews are two of the disadvantages he cites in his critique. Would the modern world be a better one, Ritzer asks, if it were less McDonaldized?

This chapter considers the impact of groups and organizations on social interaction. Do you think that you behave differently in large groups than in small ones? What effect do you think social change today is having on the structure of groups? The chapter begins by noting the distinctions between various types of groups, with particular attention given to the dynamics of small groups. We will examine how and why formal organizations came into existence and describe Max Weber's model of the modern bureaucracy. We'll also look at technology's impact on the organization of the workplace. The social policy section will focus on the status of organized labour unions today. ■

Use Your Sociological Imagination www.mcgrawhill.ca/college/schaefer

Have you ever worked in a fast-food restaurant? If so, what were your experiences like?

UNDERSTANDING GROUPS

Most of us use the term *group* loosely to describe any collection of individuals, whether three strangers sharing an elevator or hundreds attending a rock concert. However, in sociological terms a group is any number of people with similar norms, values, and expectations who interact with one another on a regular basis. University clubs, dance companies, tenants' associations, and chess clubs are all examples of groups. The important point is that members of a group share some sense of belonging. This characteristic distinguishes groups from mere *aggregates* of people, such as passengers who happen to be together on an airplane flight, and from *categories* of people, those who share a common feature (such as being retired) but otherwise do not act together.

Consider the case of an *a cappella* singing group. It has agreed-on values and social norms. All members want to improve their singing skills and schedule lots of performances. In addition, like many groups, the singing ensemble has both a formal and an informal structure. The members meet regularly to rehearse; they choose leaders to run the rehearsals and manage their affairs. At the same time, some group members may take on unofficial leadership roles by coaching new members in singing techniques and performing skills.

The study of groups has become an important part of sociological investigation because they play such a key role in the transmission of culture. As we interact with others, we pass on our ways of thinking and acting—from language and values to ways of dressing and leisure activities. Studying groups may involve employing sociological concepts used by multiple theoretical perspectives—perspectives that are set out below.

Interactionist Perspective on Groups

Sociologists have made a number of useful distinctions between types of groups—primary and secondary groups, in-groups and out-groups, and reference groups to name a few. Charles Horton Cooley (1902:2357) coined the term ***primary group*** to refer to a small group characterized by intimate, face-to-face association and cooperation. The members of a street gang constitute a primary group; so do members of a family living in the same household, as well as a group of "sisters" in a sorority.

Primary groups play a pivotal role both in the socialization process (see Chapter 4) and in the development of roles and statuses (see Chapter 5). Indeed, primary groups can be instrumental in a person's day-to-day existence. When we find ourselves identifying closely with a group, it is probably a primary group.

We also participate in many groups that are not characterized by close bonds of friendship, such as large university classes and business associations. The term ***secondary group*** refers to a formal, impersonal group in which there is little social intimacy or mutual understanding (see Table 6-1). According to interactionists, the distinction between primary and secondary groups is not always clear-cut. Some social clubs may become so large and impersonal that they no longer function as primary groups.

Secondary groups often emerge in the workplace among those who share special understandings about their occupation. Almost all of us have come in contact with people who deliver food, but, using observation research, two sociologists have given us new understanding of the secondary group ties that emerge in this occupation (see Box 6-1).

Table 6-1 Comparison of Primary and Secondary Groups

Primary Group	Secondary Group
Generally small	Usually large
Relatively long period of interaction	Relatively short duration, often temporary
Intimate, face-to-face association	Little social intimacy or mutual understanding
Some emotional depth in relationships	Relationships generally superficial
Cooperative, friendly	More formal and impersonal

Studying Small Groups

Sociological research on the microlevel and research from the interactionist perspective usually focus on the study of small groups. The term ***small group*** refers to a group small enough for all members to interact simultaneously, that is, to talk with one another or at least be well acquainted. Certain primary groups, such as families, may also be classified as small groups. However, many small groups differ from primary groups in that they do not necessarily offer the intimate personal relationships characteristic of primary groups. For example, a manufacturer may bring together its seven-member regional sales staff twice a year for an intensive sales conference. The salespeople, who live in different cities and rarely see one another, constitute a small secondary group, not a primary group.

We may think of small groups as being informal and unpatterned; yet, as interactionist researchers have revealed, there are distinct and predictable processes at work in the functioning of small groups. A long-term ethnographic study of street gangs in Chicago revealed an elaborate structure resembling that of a family business. A street gang there comprises several geographically based units called *sets*, each of which possesses a leader, lower-ranking officers, and a rank-and-file membership. Besides staffing the economic network of the drug trade, gang members develop relationships with tenant leaders in public housing projects and participate in nondelinquent social activities important to the maintenance of their authority in the neighbourhood (Venkatesh 2000).

The Raging Grannies, shown here, like many groups, have both a formal and an informal structure.

Research in Action 6-1 Pizza Delivery Employees as a Secondary Group

We all tend to take pizza delivery for granted. We may not even take note of the person who brings the pizza to our door. But sociologists Patrick Kinkade and Michael Katovich did (1997). Using an interactionist perspective, they explored the social relationships that developed among urban pizza delivery drivers as they socialized during work while waiting for orders and after work in bars. In fact, one of the researchers spent 18 months as a pizza delivery person at three locales in Ft. Worth, Texas. What they found was that pizza deliverers form a tight network based on the ordinary transactions and the occasional dangerous interactions of their profession.

Within their culture, the pizza delivery drivers take risks and receive minimal rewards. Although attacks on them are usually publicized, they are not documented statistically. But the drivers themselves are well aware of the possible dangers and talk to one another a great deal about them. During the observation period, two drivers were robbed and eight others were "tailed," resulting in four automobile accidents.

The researchers found that the world of this secondary group is "hypermasculine," with racist and sexist overtones. The drivers uniformly characterized the dangers to their safety as coming from members of racial and ethnic communities, even when there was no evidence of this. The drivers also regularly boasted of their sexual prowess and told and retold accounts of sexual favours they received from customers.

Among the 106 drivers studied by the researchers, five types emerged:

- *The comedian.* This individual uses humour to neutralize or trivialize the anxiety of making runs into neighbourhoods perceived as high-risk.
- *The adventurer.* The adventurer claims to invite problems and actually looks forward to testing himself in dangerous situations.
- *The denier.* This individual attempts to neutralize anxiety by suggesting a problem does not exist or is exaggerated.
- *The fatalist.* This person recognizes and admits the risk of danger but simply accepts it without making any effort to neutralize it.
- *The pro.* The pro generally has had a long history in the delivery business, having worked for several pizza services, often serving as an assistant manager, if not a manager, at one of the other stores.

In general, the researchers found through observation and interview that urban pizza deliverers derive more satisfaction from their secondary group membership than from monetary rewards. Group membership and identity, therefore, are very important. The study shows how people, especially in urban environments, make use of secondary groups to "carve out a niche" in the larger social world. They accept their identity as a delivery person and assume a particular type that they feel comfortable with.

Applying Theory

1. What insights might feminist sociologists bring to the study of pizza delivery employees as a secondary group?
2. Why is the dangerous person usually described by drivers as a member of a visible minority? How does this contribute to racism?
3. Are there any other "types" of drivers that you have come across or know to exist?

Source: Kinkade and Katovich 1997.

Size of a Group

At what point does a collection of people become too large to be called a small group? That is not clear. If there are more than 20 members, it is difficult for individuals to interact regularly in a direct and intimate manner. But even within a range of 2 to 20 people, group size can substantially alter the quality of social relationships. For example, as the number of group participants increases, the most active communicators become even more active relative to others. Therefore, a person who dominates a group of 3 or 4 members will be relatively more dominant in a 15-person group.

Group size also has noticeable social implications for members who do not assume leadership roles. In a larger group, each member has less time to speak, more points of view to absorb, and a more elaborate structure to function in. At the same time, an individual has greater freedom to ignore certain members or viewpoints than he or she would in a smaller group. It is harder to disregard someone in a 4-person workforce than in an office with 30 employees or someone in a string quartet than in an orchestra with 50 members.

German sociologist Georg Simmel (1858–1918) is credited as being the first sociologist to emphasize the importance of interaction processes within groups and note how they change as group size changes. The simplest of all social groups or relationships is the ***dyad,*** or two-member group. A wife and a husband constitute a dyad, as does a business partnership or a singing duo. In a dyad, people are able to achieve a special level of intimacy that cannot be duplicated in larger groups. However, as Simmel ([1917] 1950) noted, a dyad, unlike any other group, can be destroyed by the loss of a single member. Therefore, the threat of termination hangs over a dyadic relationship perhaps more than over any other type.

Obviously, the introduction of one additional person to a dyad dramatically transforms the character of the small group. The dyad now becomes a three-member group, or ***triad.*** The new member has many ways of interacting with and influencing the dynamics of the group. The new person may play a *unifying* role within a triad. When a married couple has its first child, the baby may serve to bind the group closer together. A newcomer may also play a *mediating* role within a three-person group. If two roommates in an apartment are perpetually sniping at each other, the third roommate may attempt to remain on good terms with both and arrange compromise solutions to problems. Finally, a member of a triad can choose to employ a *divide-and-rule* strategy. This is the case, for example, with a coach who hopes to gain greater control over two assistants by making them rivals (Nixon 1979).

Coalitions

As groups grow to the size of triads or larger, we can expect coalitions to develop. A ***coalition*** is a temporary or permanent alliance geared toward a common goal. Coalitions can be broad-based or narrow, and can take on many different objectives. Sociologist William Julius Wilson (1999) has described community-based organizations in Texas that include whites and Latinos, working class and affluent, who have banded together to work for improved sidewalks, better drainage systems, and comprehensive street paving. Out of this type of coalition building, Wilson hopes, will emerge better interracial understanding.

Some coalitions are intentionally short lived. Short-term coalition building is a key to success in the popular TV program *Survivor.* In *Survivor I,* broadcast in 2000, the four members of the Tagi alliance banded together to vote fellow castaways off the island. The political world is also the scene of many temporary coalitions. For example, in 1997 big U.S. tobacco companies joined with anti-smoking groups to draw up a settlement for reimbursing states for tobacco-related medical costs. Soon after the settlement was announced, the coalition members returned to their decades-long fight against each other (Pear 1997b).

The effects of group size and coalitions on group dynamics are but two of the many aspects of the small group that interactionist sociologists have studied. Another

Survivor I's coalition, the Tagi alliance: Kelly, Rudy, Susan, and Richard (left to right).

area, conformity and deviance, is examined in Chapter 7. Although it is clear that small-group encounters have a considerable influence on our lives, we are also deeply affected by much larger groupings of people, as we'll see in a later section.

Functionalist Perspective on Groups

A group can hold special meaning for members because of its relationship to other groups. People in one group sometimes feel antagonistic toward or threatened by another group, especially if that group is perceived as being different culturally or racially. Sociologists identify these "we" and "they" feelings by using two terms first employed by functionalist William Graham Sumner (1906): *in-group* and *out-group.*

An ***in-group*** can be defined as any group or category to which people feel they belong. Simply put, it comprises everyone who is regarded as "we" or "us." The in-group may be as narrow as a teenage clique or as broad as an entire society. The very existence of an in-group implies that there is an ***out-group*** viewed as "they" or "them." An out-group is a group or category to which people feel they do *not* belong.

In-group members typically feel distinct and superior, and see themselves as better than people in the out-group. Proper behaviour for the in-group is simultaneously viewed as unacceptable behaviour for the out-group. This double standard enhances the sense of superiority. Functionalist sociologist Robert Merton (1968) describes this process as the conversion of "in-group virtues" into "out-group vices." We can see this differential standard operating in worldwide discussions of terrorism. When a group or a nation takes aggressive actions, it usually justifies them as necessary, even if civilians are hurt and killed. Opponents are quick to label such actions with the emotion-laden term of *terrorist* and appeal to the world community for condemnation. Yet these same people may themselves retaliate with actions that hurt civilians, which the first group will then condemn.

Conflict between in-groups and out-groups can turn violent on a personal as well as a political level. In 1999 two disaffected students at Columbine High School in Littleton, Colorado, launched an attack on the school that left 15 students and teachers dead, including themselves. The gunmen, members of an out-group that other students referred to as the Trenchcoat Mafia, apparently resented taunting by an in-group referred to as the Jocks. Similar episodes have occurred in schools across North America, where rejected adolescents, overwhelmed by personal and family problems, peer group pressure, academic responsibilities, or media images of violence, have struck out against more popular classmates.

Adolescent in-group members who actively provoke out-group members may have their own problems, including limited time and attention from working parents. Sociologists David Stevenson and Barbara Schneider (1999), who studied seven thousand teenagers, found that despite many opportunities for group membership, young people spend an average of 3.5 hours alone every day. Although youths may claim they want privacy, they also crave attention, and striking out at members of an in-group or out-group, be they the wrong gender, race, or friendship group, seems to be one way to get it.

Use Your Sociological Imagination

Try putting yourself in the shoes of an out-group member. What does your in-group look like from that perspective?

Functionalist sociologists call any group that individuals use as a standard for evaluating themselves and their own behaviour a ***reference group.*** For example, a high school student who aspires to join a social circle of hip-hop music devotees will pattern his or her behaviour after that of the group. The student will begin dressing like these peers, listening to the same tapes and CDs, and hanging out at the same stores and clubs.

Reference groups have two basic purposes. They serve a normative function by setting and enforcing standards of conduct and belief. The high school student who wants the approval of the hip-hop crowd will have to follow the group's dictates to at least some extent. Reference groups also perform a comparison function by serving as a standard against which people can measure themselves and others. An actor will evaluate himself or herself against a reference group comprising others in the acting profession (Merton and Kitt 1950).

Reference groups may help the process of anticipatory socialization. For example, a business student majoring in finance may read the *Financial Post,* study the annual reports of corporations, and listen to midday stock market news on the radio. The student is using financial experts as a reference group to which he or she aspires.

Often, two or more reference groups influence us at the same time. Our family members, neighbours, and co-workers all shape different aspects of our self-evaluation. In addition, reference group attachments change during the life cycle. A corporate executive who quits the rat race at age 45 to become a social worker will find new reference groups to use as standards for evaluation. We shift reference groups as we take on different statuses during our lives.

UNDERSTANDING ORGANIZATIONS

Formal Organizations and Bureaucracies

As contemporary societies have shifted to more advanced forms of technology and their social structures have become more complex, our lives have become increasingly dominated by large secondary groups referred to as *formal organizations.* A ***formal organization*** is a group

"So long, Bill. This is my club. You can't come in."

An exclusive social club is an in-group whose members consider themselves superior to others.

designed for a special purpose and structured for maximum efficiency. Canada Post, the McDonald's fast-food industry, the Regina Symphony, and the university you attend are all examples of formal organizations. Organizations vary in their size, specificity of goals, and degree of efficiency, but they all are structured to facilitate the management of large-scale operations. They also have a bureaucratic form of organization (described in the next section).

In our society, formal organizations fulfil an enormous variety of personal and societal needs and shape the lives of every one of us. In fact, formal organizations have become such a dominant force that we must create organizations to supervise other organizations, such as the Ontario Securities Commission (OSC) to regulate the brokerage companies. It sounds much more exciting to say that we live in the "computer age" than in the "age of formal organization"; however, the latter is probably a more accurate description of our times (Azumi and Hage 1972; Etzioni 1964).

Could the terrorist attacks of September 11, 2001, have been prevented? Some critics put blame on the division of labour among government spy agencies, which prevented intelligence on Osama bin Laden's network from being gathered and analyzed in a central place.

Ascribed statuses, such as gender, race, and ethnicity, influence how we see ourselves within formal organizations. For example, a study of female lawyers in America's largest law firms found significant differences in these women's self-images. In firms in which fewer than 15 percent of partners were women, the female lawyers were likely to believe that "feminine" traits were strongly devalued and that masculinity was equated with success. As one female lawyer put it, "Let's face it: this is a man's environment, and it's sort of Jock City, especially at my firm." Women in firms where female lawyers were better represented in positions of power had a stronger desire for and higher expectations of promotion (Ely 1995:619).

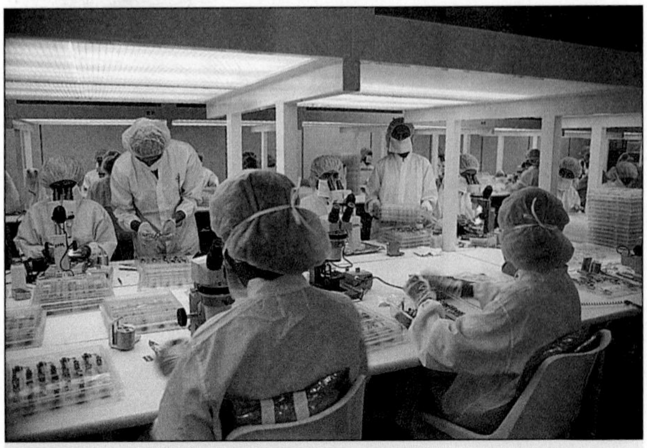

These workers in an electronics factory in India perform specialized tasks, a characteristic of division of labour in an organization.

Characteristics of a Bureaucracy

A ***bureaucracy*** is a component of formal organization that uses rules and hierarchical ranking to achieve efficiency. Rows of desks staffed by seemingly faceless people, endless lines and forms, impossibly complex language, and frustrating encounters with red tape—all these unpleasant images have combined to make *bureaucracy* a dirty word and an easy target in political campaigns. As a result, few people want to identify their occupation as "bureaucrat" despite the fact that all of us perform various bureaucratic tasks. Elements of bureaucracy enter into almost every occupation in an industrial society.

Complaints about bureaucracy are not limited to the business world. During the 1990s, the bureaucratic nature of the United Nations' humanitarian efforts in Somalia came under attack. The five international agencies designated to run relief efforts in Somalia had more than 12 000 employees, of whom only 116 were serving in the impoverished, war-torn African nation. Moreover, like many bureaucracies, the relief apparatus was slow in dealing with a drastic problem. In the words of a former United Nations worker in Somalia, "The average U.N. person takes 15 days to reply to a fax. . . . 3,000 people can die in 15 days" (Longworth 1993:9).

Max Weber ([1922] 1947) first directed researchers to the significance of bureaucratic structure. In an important sociological advance, Weber emphasized the basic similarity of structure and process found in the otherwise dissimilar enterprises of religion, government, education, and business. Weber saw bureaucracy as a form of organization quite different from the family-run business. For analytical purposes, he developed an *ideal type* of bureaucracy that would reflect the most characteristic aspects of all human organizations. By ideal type Weber meant a construct or model that could serve as a standard for evaluating specific cases. In actuality, perfect bureaucracies do not exist; no real-world organization corresponds exactly to Weber's ideal type.

Weber proposed that whether the purpose is to run a church, a corporation, or an army, the ideal bureaucracy displays five basic characteristics. A discussion of those characteristics, as well as the dysfunctions (or potential negative consequences) of a bureaucracy, follows. (Table 6-2 summarizes the discussion.)

1. **Division of labour.** Specialized experts perform specific tasks. By working at a specific task, people are more likely to become highly skilled and carry out a job with maximum efficiency. This emphasis on specialization is so basic a part of our lives that we may not realize that it is a fairly recent development in Western culture.

   The downside of division of labour is that the fragmentation of work into smaller and smaller tasks can divide workers and remove any connection they might feel to the overall objective of the bureaucracy. In *The Communist Manifesto* (written in 1848), Karl Marx and Friedrich Engels charged that the capitalist system reduces workers to a mere "appendage of the machine" (Feuer 1959). Such a work arrangement, they wrote, produces extreme ***alienation***—a condition of estrangement or dissociation from the surrounding society. According to both Marx and conflict theorists, restricting workers to very small tasks also weakens their job security, since new employees can be easily trained to replace them.

   Although division of labour has certainly enhanced the performance of many complex bureaucracies, in some cases it can lead to ***trained incapacity;*** that is, workers become so specialized that they develop blind spots and fail to notice obvious problems. Even worse, they may not care about what is happening in the next department. Some observers believe that such developments have caused workers to become less productive on the job.
2. **Hierarchy of authority.** Bureaucracies follow the principle of hierarchy; that is, each position is under the supervision of a higher authority.

Table 6-2 Characteristics of a Bureaucracy

Characteristic	Positive Consequence	Negative Consequence: For the Individual	Negative Consequence: For the Organization
Division of labour	Produces efficiency in large-scale corporation	Produces trained incapacity	Produces a narrow perspective
Hierarchy of authority	Clarifies who is in command	Deprives employees of a voice in decision making	Permits concealment of mistakes
Written rules and regulations	Let workers know what is expected of them	Stifle initiative and imagination	Lead to goal displacement
Impersonality	Reduces bias	Contributes to feelings of alienation	Discourages loyalty to company
Employment based on technical qualifications	Discourages favouritism and reduces petty rivalries	Discourages ambition to improve oneself elsewhere	Allows Peter principle to operate

3. **Written rules and regulations.** Rules and regulations are an important characteristic of bureaucracies. Ideally, through such procedures, a bureaucracy ensures uniform performance of every task.

   Through written rules and regulations, bureaucracies generally offer employees clear standards for an adequate (or exceptional) performance. In addition, procedures provide a valuable sense of continuity in a bureaucracy. Individual workers will come and go, but the structure and past records give the organization a life of its own that outlives the services of any one bureaucrat.

   Of course, rules and regulations can overshadow the larger goals of an organization and become dysfunctional. If blindly applied, rules no longer serve as a means of achieving an objective but instead become important (and perhaps too important) in their own right. Robert Merton (1968) has used the term ***goal displacement*** to refer to overzealous conformity to official regulations.
4. **Impersonality.** Max Weber wrote that in a bureaucracy, work is carried out *sine ira et studio,* "without hatred or passion." Bureaucratic norms dictate that officials perform their duties without the personal consideration of people as individuals. Although this is intended to guarantee equal treatment for each person, it also contributes to the often cold and uncaring feeling associated with modern organizations.
5. **Employment based on technical qualifications.** Within the ideal bureaucracy, hiring is based on technical qualifications rather than on favouritism, and performance is measured against specific standards. Written personnel policies dictate who gets promoted, and people often have a right to appeal if they believe that particular rules have been violated. Such procedures protect bureaucrats against arbitrary dismissal, provide a measure of security, and encourage loyalty to the organization.

   In this sense, the "impersonal" bureaucracy can be considered an improvement over nonbureaucratic organizations.

   Although any bureaucracy ideally will value technical and professional competence, personnel decisions do not always follow this ideal pattern. Dysfunctions within bureaucracy have become well publicized, particularly because of the work of Laurence J. Peter. According to the ***Peter principle,*** every employee within a hierarchy tends to rise to his or her level of incompetence (Peter and Hull 1969). This hypothesis, which has not been directly or systematically tested, reflects a possible dysfunctional outcome of structuring advancement on the basis of merit. Talented people receive promotion after promotion until, sadly, some of them finally achieve positions that they cannot handle with their usual competence (Blau and Meyer 1987).

These members of the Toronto Symphony Orchestra must be technically proficient and professionally trained, or they will never make beautiful music together. Technical qualification is one of the characteristics of a well-structured bureaucracy.

The five characteristics of bureaucracy, developed by Max Weber more than 80 years ago, describe an ideal type rather than offer a precise definition of an actual bureaucracy. Not every formal organization will possess all of Weber's characteristics. In fact, there can be wide variation among actual bureaucratic organizations. In Box 6-2, we consider how some bureaucracies function today in Russia and how they differ from those in Western countries.

Bureaucratization as a Process

In a typical citizen's nightmare, you have to speak to 10 or 12 individuals in a corporation or government agency to

Sociology in the Global Community

6-2 Management, Russian Style

Are organizational structures "culture free"? That is, would similar organizations in different cultures exhibit similar characteristics in how they are structured and controlled? That is a popular hypothesis among many social scientists. But a study of organizations in Russia suggests otherwise. Sociologists George Miller and Olga Gubin (2000) conducted in-depth interviews with the CEOs of 35 organizations in the greater Moscow area, including banks, hospitals, hotels, trading companies, and manufacturing concerns. On their evidence, organizations in Russia are to some extent "culture bound."

The Russian organizations differ in very basic ways from comparable Western organizations. In industrial societies, studies have generally found that, with increasing size and specialization of tasks, organizations tend to formalize rules and procedures and to *decentralize* control. Not only do lower-level executives have more decision-making power, but the formalized rules also provide an impersonal means of ensuring that various organizational tasks get done. In Russia, however, Miller and Gubin found that increased organizational size, specialization, and formalization were all associated with *greater,* not less, centralization of control and decision making.

Why this difference? Miller and Gubin propose several cultural factors. First, Russia has a long history of authoritarian government, from the tsars through the communist revolution. Second, the former Soviet system gave a few people tremendous authority. Most of the executives today were trained in that system and felt that "the leader is responsible for everything" (p. 83). They have brought their centralized communist managerial techniques and attitudes to the new market economy. Finally, Miller and Gubin point to the turbulent economic environment in Russia today, which makes falling back on old practices easier than learning new managerial skills. Added to this turbulence is the pervasive influence of the Russian mafia. To protect their organizations from criminal infiltration, many chief executives say they have to rule with a heavy hand.

As new organizational leaders emerge and as Russians gain more experience with capitalist practices, it will be interesting to see whether the centralization of authority persists. For now, as one bank president put it, "My organization is extremely centralized it is true. If my employees don't like it or disagree with me, I fire them."

Applying Theory

1. Miller and Gubin's research showed that, to some extent, Russian organizations are "culture bound." What elements or observations might feminist sociologists add to this conclusion?
2. What theoretical perspective do you think would be the most useful for studying the culture of Russian organizations? Why?

Source: Miller and Gubin 2000:83–84.

find out which official has jurisdiction over a particular problem. You get transferred from one department to another until you finally hang up in disgust. Sociologists have used the term ***bureaucratization*** to refer to the process by which a group, an organization, or a social movement becomes increasingly bureaucratic.

Normally, we think of bureaucratization in terms of large organizations. But bureaucratization also takes place within small-group settings. Sociologist Jennifer Bickhan Mendez (1998) studied domestic houseworkers employed in central California by a nationwide franchise. She found that housekeeping tasks were minutely defined, to the point that employees had to follow 22 written steps for cleaning a bathroom. Complaints and special requests went not to the workers, but to an office-based manager. The impersonality and efficiency of this bureaucratic system is yet another example of the McDonaldization of the workplace.

Conflict Perspective on Groups and Organizations

Conflict theorists have examined the bureaucratizing influence on groups and organizations. German sociologist Robert Michels (1915) studied socialist parties and labour unions in Europe before World War I and found that such organizations were becoming increasingly bureaucratic. The emerging leaders of these organizations—even some of the most radical—had a vested interest in clinging to power. If they lost their leadership posts, they would have to return to full-time work as manual labourers.

Through his research, Michels originated the idea of the ***iron law of oligarchy,*** which describes how even a democratic organization will develop into a bureaucracy ruled by a few (the oligarchy). Why do oligarchies emerge? People who achieve leadership roles usually have the skills, knowledge, or charismatic appeal (as Weber noted) to direct, if not control, others. Michels argues that the rank and file of a movement or an organization look to leaders for direction and thereby reinforce the process of rule by a few. In addition, members of an oligarchy are strongly motivated to maintain their leadership roles, privileges, and power.

Michels's insights continue to be relevant today. Contemporary labour unions in Canada and Western Europe bear little resemblance to those organized spontaneously by exploited workers. Conflict theorists have pointed to the longevity of union leaders, who are not always responsive to the needs and demands of the membership and seem more concerned with maintaining their own positions and power. (The policy section at the end of this chapter focuses on the status of labour unions today.)

Although the "iron law" may sometimes help us to understand the concentration of formal authority within organizations, sociologists recognize that there are a number of checks on leadership. Groups often compete for power within a formal organization. For example, in an automotive corporation, divisions manufacturing heavy machinery and passenger cars compete against each other for limited research and development funds. Moreover, informal channels of communication and control can undercut the power of top officials of an organization, as we will now see.

Sometimes informal understandings within a corporation can lead to illegal activities, as revelations about several large companies in 2002 made clear. Executives at Enron Corporation (headquarters shown here) engaged in highly risky accounting practices, undisclosed transactions, conflicts of interest, and excessive compensation plans, which ultimately brought the huge corporation to bankruptcy and caused enormous shareholder losses.

Feminist Perspectives on Groups and Organizations

The diversity of feminist perspectives found in sociology contributes to the rich and diverse ways we can study groups and organizations. Many feminist perspectives point to the ways in which a group's or an organization's culture—including its values, norms, goals, practices, policies, and procedures—are "gendered." The work of Gillian Creese (1999) on the role that unions play in constructing and negotiating class, race, and gender relations demonstrates how power relations are embedded in the workplace of B.C. Hydro. Creese documents how the union organization of B.C. Hydro spent great time and effort in negotiating separate technical and clerical streams of white-collar work. Men's office work became defined as "technical," while women's work was defined as "clerical" and constructed as marginal and less skilled than the technical office work done by men. As a result of this construction of a division between technical and clerical office workers, gendered occupational segregation became embedded in the workplace, ensuring women's subordination and lower pay.

Other studies have examined organizational characteristics and their impact on the quality of women's experiences in the paid labour force. Organizational characteristics, such as job classification and the sexual composition of the work group, for example, have been found to be associated with varying incidence rates of sexual harassment (Ehrlich Martin 1984).

Marxist feminist perspectives tend to focus on work and economic inequality, thus shedding light on groups and organizations; these perspectives recognize that "class and gender relations are constituted through practices in at least two primary spheres of activity, paid workplaces and households" (Livingstone and Luxton 1989:270).

Bureaucracy and Organizational Culture

How does bureaucratization affect the average individual who works in an organization? The early theorists of formal organizations tended to neglect this question. Max Weber, for example, focused on management personnel within bureaucracies, but he had little to say about workers in industry or clerks in government agencies.

According to the ***classical theory*** of formal organizations, also known as the ***scientific management approach,*** workers are motivated almost entirely by economic rewards. This theory stresses that only the physical constraints of workers limit productivity. Therefore, workers are treated as a resource, much like the machines that began to replace them in the twentieth century.

Management attempts to achieve maximum work efficiency through scientific planning, established performance standards, and careful supervision of workers and production. Planning under the scientific management approach involves efficiency studies but not studies of workers' attitudes or feelings of job satisfaction.

It was not until workers organized unions—and forced management to recognize that they were not objects—that theorists of formal organizations began to revise the classical approach. Along with management and administrators, social scientists became aware that informal groups of workers have an important impact on organizations (Perrow 1986). An alternative way of considering bureaucratic dynamics, the ***human relations approach,*** emphasizes the role of people, communication, and participation within a bureaucracy. This type of analysis reflects the interest of interactionist theorists in small-group behaviour. Unlike planning under the scientific management approach, planning based on the human relations perspective focuses on workers' feelings, frustrations, and emotional need for job satisfaction.

The gradual move away from a sole focus on the physical aspects of getting the job done—and toward the concerns and needs of workers—led advocates of the human relations approach to stress the less formal aspects of bureaucratic structure. Informal groups and social networks within organizations develop partly as a result of people's ability to create more direct forms of communication than under the formal structure. Charles Page (1946) has used the term *bureaucracy's other face* to refer to the unofficial activities and interactions that are such a basic part of daily organizational life.

A series of classic studies illustrates the value of the human relations approach. The Hawthorne studies alerted sociologists to the fact that research subjects may alter their behaviour to match the experimenter's expectations. The major focus of the Hawthorne studies, however, was the role of social factors in workers' productivity. One aspect of the research investigated the switchboard-bank wiring room, where 14 men were making parts of switches for telephone equipment. The researchers discovered that these men were producing far below their physical capabilities. This was especially surprising because they would earn more money if they produced more parts.

pp. 35–36

Why was there such an unexpected restriction of output? The men feared that if they produced switch parts at a faster rate, their pay rate might be reduced or some might lose their jobs. As a result, this group of workers established their own (unofficial) norm for a proper day's work. They created informal rules and sanctions to enforce it. Yet management was unaware of such practices and actually believed that the men were working as hard as they could (Roethlisberger and Dickson 1939; for a different perspective, see Vallas 1999).

Voluntary Associations

In the mid-nineteenth century, the French writer Alexis de Tocqueville noted that people in North America are "forever forming associations." In 2003, there were an estimated 161 000 nonprofit and national voluntary associations in Canada. ***Voluntary associations*** are organizations established on the basis of common interest, whose members volunteer or even pay to participate. The Girl Guides of Canada, the Canadian Jewish Congress, the Kiwanis Club, and Rotary clubs are all considered voluntary associations; so, too, are the American Association of Aardvark Aficionados, the Cats on Stamps Study Group, the Red Hat Society, the Raging Grannies, and the William Shatner Fellowship (Gale Research Group 2002).

The categories of "formal organization" and "voluntary association" are not mutually exclusive. Large voluntary associations, such as the Lions Club and the Masons, have structures similar to those of profit-making corporations. At the same time, certain formal organizations, such as the Young Men's Christian Association (YMCA), have philanthropic and educational goals usually found in voluntary associations. The New Democratic Party and the United Farm Workers of America (Canadian office) union are considered examples of voluntary associations. Even though membership in a political party or union can be a condition of employment and therefore not genuinely voluntary, political parties and labour unions are usually included in discussions of voluntary associations.

An analysis of 15 industrial nations showed that active memberships in voluntary associations typically increased during the 1980s and 1990s. Only relatively inactive memberships in religious organizations and labour unions have showed a decline. On the whole, then, voluntary associations are fairly healthy (Baer et al. 2000).

Voluntary associations can provide support to people in preindustrial societies. During the post–World War II period, migration from rural areas of Africa to the cities was accompanied by a growth in voluntary associations, including trade unions, occupational societies, and mutual aid organizations developed along old tribal ties. As people moved from the *Gemeinschaft* of the countryside to the *Gesellschaft* of the city, these voluntary associations provided immigrants with substitutes for the extended groups of kinfolk that they had had in their villages (Little 1988).

p. 106

The importance of voluntary associations—and especially of their unpaid workers (or volunteers)—is increasingly being recognized. Traditionally, we have devalued unpaid work, even though the skill levels, experience, and training demands are often comparable with those of wage labour. Viewed from a conflict perspective, the critical difference has been that women perform a substantial amount of volunteer work. Feminists and conflict theorists agree that, like the unpaid child care and household labour of homemakers, the effort of volunteers has been too often ignored by scholars—and awarded too little respect by the larger society—because it is viewed as "women's work." Failure to recognize women's volunteerism obscures a critical contribution women make to a society's social structure (Daniels 1987, 1988).

TECHNOLOGY'S IMPACT ON THE WORKPLACE

Telecommuting

Computers have affected the way we work in dramatic ways (Liker, Hoddard, and Karlin 1999). Increasingly, the workforce is turning into *telecommuters* in many industrial countries. ***Telecommuters*** are employees who work full-time or part-time at home rather than in an outside office and who are linked to their supervisors and colleagues through computer terminals, phones, and fax machines (see Chapter 13). A 2001 study by Ottawa-based Ekos Research Associates found that the idea of working from home was either "appealing" or "very appealing" to 52 percent of the Canadian population. According to Statistics Canada, 15 percent of working Canadians now telecommute at least part of the time (Galt 2003).

What are the social implications of this shift toward the virtual office? From an interactionist perspective, the workplace is a major source of friendships; restricting face-to-face social opportunities could destroy the trust that is created by face-to-face "handshake agreements." Thus, telecommuting may move society further along the continuum from *Gemeinschaft* to *Gesellschaft*. On a more positive note, telecommuting may be the first social change that pulls fathers and mothers back into the home rather than pushing them out. The trend, if it continues, should also increase autonomy and job satisfaction for many employees (Castells 2001; Nie 1999).

Use Your Sociological Imagination

If your first full-time job after university involved telecommuting, what do you think would be the advantages and disadvantages of working out of a home office? Do you think you would be satisfied as a telecommuter? Why or why not?

Electronic Communication

Electronic communication in the workplace has generated some heat lately. On the one hand, emailing is a convenient way to push messages around, especially with the CC (carbon copy) button. It's democratic too: lower-status employees are more likely to participate in email discussions than in face-to-face communications, which gives organizations the benefit of the experiences and views of more of their workforce. But emailing is almost too easy to use. At Computer Associates, a software company, people were emailing colleagues in the next cubicle. To deal with the electronic chaos, the company's CEO took the unusual step of banning all emails from 9:30 to 12 and 1:30 to 4. Other companies have limited the number of CCs that can be sent and banned systemwide messages (Gwynne and Dickerson 1997).

There are other problems with email. It doesn't convey body language, which in face-to-face communication can soften insensitive phrasing and make unpleasant messages (such as a reprimand) easier to take. It also leaves a permanent record, and that can be a problem if messages are written thoughtlessly. In an

Telecommuters are linked to their supervisors and colleagues through computer terminals, phones, and fax machines.

antitrust case that the federal government brought against Microsoft in 1998, the prosecutors used as evidence email sent to and from Microsoft's CEO Bill Gates. Finally, as will be discussed in detail in Chapter 16, companies can monitor email as a means of "watching" their employees. Dartmouth professor Paul Argenti advises those who use email, "Think before you write. The most important thing to know is what not to write" (Gwynne and Dickerson 1997:90).

SOCIAL POLICY AND ORGANIZATIONS: The State of the Unions

The Issue

How many people do you know who belong to a labour union? Chances are you can name fewer people than someone could 25 years ago. In 1977, unions represented 33 percent of workers in the Canadian economy; in 2001, they represented 30.5 percent (Statistics Canada 2004a). What has happened to diminish the representation for organized labour today? Have unions perhaps outlived their usefulness in a rapidly changing global economy dominated by the service industry? Are there differences between Canada and the United States in terms of legal impediments to union organization? Is Canada more labour friendly than the United States?

The Setting

Labour unions consist of organized workers sharing either the same skill (as in electronics) or the same employer (as in the case of postal employees). Unions began to emerge during the Industrial Revolution in England in the eighteenth century. Groups of workers banded together to extract concessions from employers, as well as to protect their positions. They frequently tried to protect their jobs by limiting entry to their occupation based on gender, race, ethnicity, citizenship, age, and sometimes rather arbitrary measures of skill levels. Today we see less of this protection of special interests, but individual labour unions are still often the target of charges of discrimination (as are employers) (Form 1992).

The experience of labour unions varies widely in different countries. In some, such as Britain and Mexico, unions play a key role in the foundation of governments. In others, such as Japan and Korea, their role in politics is very limited and even their ability to influence the private sector is relatively weak. Stark differences exist between Canada and the United States in terms of union experiences. As Figure 6-1 illustrates, Canada's overall rate of unionization is more than double that of the United States. Although both countries have much lower rates of unionization in the private sector than in the public sector, Canada's percentages of union membership in both sectors far exceed those in the United States. The United States also exhibits greater disparities between rates of unionization for men and women and between rates for full-time and part-time employees (U.S. Bureau of Labor Statistics 2004). The increase in rates of unionization for women in Canada, which Statistics Canada (2004a) has referred to as a profound transformation in Canadian union membership, has not been duplicated in the United States. Unions in Canada sometimes can have a significant influence on employers and elected officials, but their effect may vary dramatically by type of industry and even region of the country.

Few people today would dispute the fact that the Canadian union movement is in transition. What accounts for this transition? Among the reasons offered are the following:

1. **The feminization of the movement.** In 1977, approximately 10 percent of female workers were unionized; by 2003 the number had risen to 30 percent. According to Statistics Canada (2004a), this growth can be attributed to such factors as the growing proportion of women in the paid labour force, their increased representation in the heavily unionized public sector, the rising unionization rate of part-time and temporary workers, and the expansion of unions into female-dominated and nonunionized or less-unionized workplaces, such as the service sector.
2. **The rising rate of unionization of the public sector and the falling rate of unionization of the private sector.** The rate of unionization of the public sector has remained stable for the last 30 years, while the rate for the private sector has fallen from 26 percent to 18 percent.

FIGURE 6-1

Comparison of Canadian and American Unionization Rates, 2004

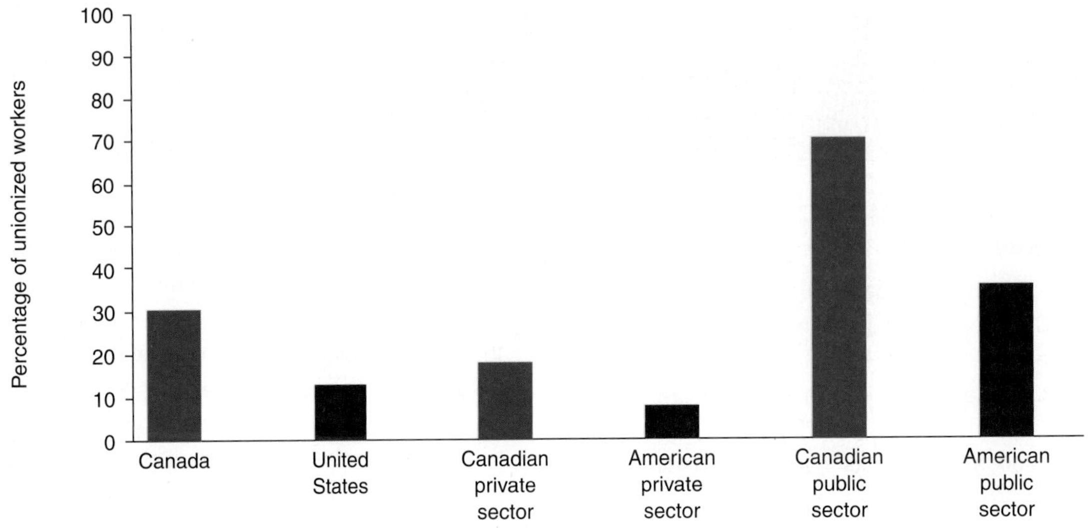

Sources: Statistics Canada 2004a; U.S. Bureau of Labor Statistics 2004.

Think about It

What is the relationship between union membership and public or private sector employment in both Canada and the United States?

3. **The waning influence of international unions headquartered outside Canada.** In 1962, unions with headquarters outside the country accounted for two-thirds of union membership in Canada; in 2003, the proportion had fallen to just more than one-fourth.
4. **The changing scope of union membership.** The largest inroads in union membership have occurred among women, youth, public administration workers, and child care and home support workers, while losses have been experienced among technical health workers (Statistics Canada 2004a).

Sociological Insights

Both Marxists and functionalists would view unions as a logical response to the emergence of impersonal, large-scale, formal, and often alienating organizations. This view certainly characterized the growth of unions in major manufacturing industries with a sharp division of labour. However, as manufacturing has declined, unions have had to look elsewhere for growth (Statistics Canada 2004a).

Today labour unions in the United States and Europe bear little resemblance to those early unions organized spontaneously by exploited workers. In line with the oligarchic model developed by Robert Michels (see p. 125), unions have become increasingly bureaucratized under a self-serving leadership. Conflict theorists would point out that the longer union leaders are in office the less responsive they are to the needs and demands of the rank and file and the more concerned they are with maintaining their own positions and power.

Yet research shows that under certain circumstances union leadership can change significantly. Smaller unions are vulnerable to changes in leaders, as are unions whose members shift in composition, such as going from being predominantly male to female.

Many union employees encounter role conflict. For example, they agree to provide a needed service and then organize a "strike" to withhold it. This role conflict is especially apparent in the so-called helping occupations: teaching, social work, nursing, law enforcement, and paramedics. These workers may feel torn between carrying out their professional

p. 99

responsibilities and enduring working conditions they find unacceptable (Aronowitz and Di Fazio 1994).

Sociologists have observed another role conflict: employees who suddenly become "owners" of a business. Take the case of United Airlines (UAL). Since 1994, the employees have owned the majority of shares of the company. They may have changed the slogan from "fly the friendly skies" to "fly our friendly skies," but tensions still prevail. Union after union within UAL has threatened to strike or has enacted slowdowns, even though the members constitute the major shareholders of the company. Obviously, although everybody agreed to call the workers "owners," the pilots, mechanics, airline attendants, and others did not act like owners, and UAL management did not treat them like owners (L. Zuckerman 2001).

Policy Initiatives

United States law grants workers the right to organize via unions. But that country is unique among industrial democracies in allowing employers to actively oppose their employees' decision to organize (Comstock and Fox 1994).

A major barrier to union growth exists in the 20 states that have so-called right to work laws. In these states, workers cannot be *required* to join or pay dues or fees to a union. The very term *right to work* reflects the anti-union view that a worker should not be forced to join a union, even if that union may negotiate on his or her behalf and achieve results that benefit that worker. In contrast to the United States, Canada has fewer legal impediments to union organization. Labour laws are under the control of the provinces and territories, and some jurisdictions are considered more labour friendly than others. For example, Quebec, Saskatchewan, and British Columbia will certify a bargaining unit without a vote as soon as the majority of workers in that particular unit have signed a union card (McKenna 2004). In the United States, where union activity is covered by federal law, employers can stall or block a vote on union organization for a significant period; by the time the vote takes place, disgruntled workers may have left the company and the drive to unionize may have waned (McKenna 2004).

Applying Theory

1. If conflict thinker Karl Marx were alive today, how do you think he would view the role of unions in contemporary Canadian society?
2. How do you view the relevance of unions as a means of promoting gender equality?

CHAPTER RESOURCES

Summary

Social interaction among human beings is necessary to the transmission of culture and the survival of every society. This chapter examined the social behaviour of groups, formal organizations, and voluntary associations.

1. When we find ourselves identifying closely with a group, it is probably a ***primary group***. A ***secondary group*** is more formal and impersonal.
2. People tend to see the world in terms of ***in-groups*** and ***out-groups***, a perception often fostered by the very groups to which they belong.
3. ***Reference groups*** set and enforce standards of conduct and perform a comparison function for people's evaluations of themselves and others.
4. Interactionist researchers have revealed that there are distinct and predictable processes at work in the functioning of ***small groups***. The simplest group is a ***dyad***, composed of two members. ***Triads*** and larger groups increase ways of interacting and allow for ***coalitions*** to form.
5. As societies have become more complex, large ***formal organizations*** have become more powerful and pervasive.
6. Max Weber argued that, in its ideal form, every ***bureaucracy*** shares five basic characteristics: division of labour, hierarchical authority, written rules and regulations, impersonality, and employment based on technical qualifications.
7. Bureaucracy can be understood as a process and as a matter of degree; thus, an organization is more or less bureaucratic than other organizations.
8. When leaders of an organization build up their power, it can lead to oligarchy (rule by a few).

9. The informal structure of an organization can undermine and redefine official bureaucratic policies.
10. People belong to ***voluntary associations*** for a variety of purposes—for example, to share in joint activities or to get help with personal problems.
11. Technology has transformed workplace organizations through telecommuting and electronic communication.
12. ***Labour unions*** are more common in the public sector than in the private sector.

Critical Thinking Questions

1. Think about how behaviour is shaped by reference groups. What different reference groups at different periods in your life have shaped your outlook and your goals? In what ways have they done so?
2. Within a formal organization, are you likely to find primary groups, secondary groups, in-groups, out-groups, and reference groups? From a functionalist perspective, what roles do these groups serve for the formal organization? What dysfunctions might occur as a result of their presence?
3. Max Weber identified five basic characteristics of bureaucracy. Select an actual organization familiar to you (for example, your university, a workplace, a religious institution, or civic association you belong to) and apply Weber's analysis to that organization. To what degree does it correspond to Weber's ideal type of bureaucracy?
4. When you visit a country outside North America and see McDonald's golden arches, what is your reaction?

Key Terms

Alienation A condition of estrangement or dissociation from the surrounding society. (page 123)

Bureaucracy A component of formal organization that uses rules and hierarchical ranking to achieve efficiency. (122)

Bureaucratization The process by which a group, organization, or social movement becomes increasingly bureaucratic. (125)

Classical theory An approach to the study of formal organizations that views workers as being motivated almost entirely by economic rewards. (126)

Coalition A temporary or permanent alliance geared toward a common goal. (120)

Dyad A two-member group. (119)

Formal organization A group designed for a special purpose and structured for maximum efficiency. (121)

Goal displacement Overzealous conformity to official regulations within a bureaucracy. (124)

Human relations approach An approach to the study of formal organizations that emphasizes the role of people, communication, and participation within a bureaucracy and tends to focus on the informal structure of the organization. (127)

In-group Any group or category to which people feel they belong. (120)

Iron law of oligarchy A principle of organizational life under which even democratic organizations will become bureaucracies ruled by a few individuals. (125)

Labour unions Organized workers who share either the same skill or the same employer. (129)

McDonaldization The process by which the principles of the fast-food restaurant industry have come to dominate certain sectors of society, both in Canada and throughout the world. (117)

Out-group A group or category to which people feel they do not belong. (120)

Peter principle A principle of organizational life according to which each individual within a hierarchy tends to rise to his or her level of incompetence. (124)

Primary group A small group characterized by intimate, face-to-face association and cooperation. (117)

Reference group Any group that individuals use as a standard in evaluating themselves and their own behaviour. (121)

Scientific management approach Another name for the *classical theory* of formal organizations. (126)

Secondary group A formal, impersonal group in which there is little social intimacy or mutual understanding. (118)

Small group A group small enough for all members to interact simultaneously, that is, to talk with one another or at least be acquainted. (118)

Telecommuters Employees who work full-time or part-time at home rather than in an outside office and who are linked to their supervisors and colleagues through computer terminals, phone lines, and fax machines. (128)

Trained incapacity The tendency of workers in a bureaucracy to become so specialized that they develop blind spots and fail to notice obvious problems. (123)

Triad A three-member group. (120)

Voluntary associations Organizations established on the basis of common interest, whose members volunteer or even pay to participate. (127)

Additional Readings

Balkan, Joel. 2004. *The Corporation: The Pathological Pursuit of Profit and Power.* Toronto: Penguin Canada. This book examines the modern business corporation—its history, its power, and its relationships to government, society, and the environment—likening it to a psychopathic personality.

Clement, Wallace, and Leah V. Vosko, eds. 2003. *Changing Canada: Political Economy as Transformation.* Montreal: McGill-Queen's University Press. The book examines how capitalism is producing new political transformations in Canada, including welfare state restructuring and new forms of resistance.

Krahn, Harvey, and Graham S. Lowe. 2002. *Work, Industry, and Canadian Society,* 4th ed. Toronto: ITP Nelson. A comprehensive examination of work in the Canadian context, covering such topics as paid work and education, "nonstandard" work, and unionization.

Online Learning Centre

Visit the *Sociology: A Brief Introduction* Online Learning Centre at www.mcgrawhill.ca/college/schaefer to access quizzes, interactive exercises, video clips, and other research and study tools related to this chapter.

Reel Society Interactive Movie CD-ROM 2.0

Reel Society 2.0 can be used to spark discussion about the following topics from this chapter:

- Understanding groups

chapter 7

DEVIANCE AND SOCIAL CONTROL

Health Canada's **NEW HEALTH WARNING** messages on cigarette packages...
WARNING
TOBACCO USE CAN MAKE YOU IMPOTENT
Cigarettes may cause sexual impotence due to decreased blood flow to the penis. This can prevent you from having an erection.
Health Canada
It's time to see how sexy smoking really is.
www.infotobacco.com
1 800 O-Canada (1 800 622-6232)
Canada

Cigarette smoking has become stigmatized in Canada. This newspaper advertisement, sponsored by Health Canada, reverses the typical advertising strategy of equating smoking with sexiness.

There comes a magical gambler's moment when simple thrills magnify to become 3-D fantasies—a moment when greed chews up ethics and the casino system is just another mountain waiting to be conquered. In that single moment the idea of a foolproof way to beat the tables or the machines not only kicks in but kicks one's breath away.

Alex Mayfield and three of his friends did more than daydream. Like many other hacks, this one started as an intellectual exercise just to see if it looked possible. In the end, the four actually beat the system, taking the casinos for "about a million dollars," Alex says. In the early 1990s, the four were working as consultants in high-tech and playing life loose and casual. "You know—you'd work, make some money, and then not work until you were broke."

Las Vegas was far away, a setting for movies and television shows. So when a technology firm offered the guys an assignment to develop some software and then accompany it to a trade show at a high-tech convention there, they jumped at the opportunity. It would be the first time in Vegas for each of them, a chance to see the flashing lights for themselves, all expenses paid; who would turn that down? . . . Alex says they didn't know much about gambling and didn't know what to expect. "You get off the plane and you see all the old ladies playing the slots. It seems funny and ironic, and you soak that in."

After the four had finished doing the trade show, they and the two ladies were sitting around in the casino of their hotel playing slot machines and enjoying free beers when Alex's wife offered a challenge: *"Aren't these machines based on computers? You guys are into computers, can't you do something so we win more?"*

The guys adjourned to Mike's suite and sat around tossing out questions and offering up theories on how the machines might work. That was the trigger. The four "got kinda curious about all that, and we started looking into it when we got back home," Alex says, warming up to the vivid memories of that creative phase. It took only a little while for the research to support what they already suspected. "Yeah, they're computer programs basically. So then we were interested in, was there some way that you could crack these machines?"

There were people who had beaten the slot machines by "replacing the firmware"—getting to the computer chip inside a machine and substituting the programming for a version that would provide much more attractive payoffs than the casino intended. Other teams had done that, but it seemed to require conspiring with a casino employee, and not just any employee but one of the slot machine techies. To Alex and his buddies, "swapping ROMs would have been like hitting an old lady over the head and taking her purse." They figured if they were going to try this, it would be as a challenge to their programming skills and their intellects. And besides, they had no advanced talents in social engineering; they were computer guys, lacking any knowledge of how you sidle up to a casino employee and propose that he join you in a little scheme to take some money that doesn't belong to you. ***(Mitnick and Simon 2005)*** ■

In this excerpt from their book *The Art of Intrusion: The Real Stories Behind the Exploits of Hackers, Intruders, and Deceivers*, Kevin D. Mitnick and William L. Simon explore the role of law and social control in an area considered by some to be a "victimless crime." In the case of computer hacking for the purposes of winning using casino video poker machines discussed by Mitnick and Simon, are there victims of this type of activity?

As Mitnick and Simon's book on computer hacking points out, what behaviours should be considered deviant may not always be obvious. Take the issue of binge drinking on campus. On the one hand, we can view it as *deviant,* violating a school's standards of conduct, but on the other hand it can be seen as *conforming,* complying with a peer culture. In Canada, people are socialized to have mixed feelings about both conforming and nonconforming behaviour. The term *conformity* can conjure up images of mindless imitation of a peer group—whether a group of teenagers with pierced tongues or a group of business executives dressed in similar grey suits. Yet the same term can also suggest that an individual is cooperative or a "team player." What about those who do not conform? They may be respected as individualists, leaders, or creative thinkers who break new ground. Or they may be labelled as "troublemakers" and "weirdos" (Aronson 1999).

This chapter examines the relationship between conformity, deviance, and social control. It begins by distinguishing between conformity and obedience and then looks at two experiments regarding conforming behaviour and obedience to authority. The informal and formal mechanisms used by societies to encourage conformity and discourage deviance are analyzed. We give particular attention to the legal order and how it reflects underlying social values.

The second part of the chapter focuses on theoretical explanations for deviance, including the functionalist approach employed by Émile Durkheim and Robert Merton; the interactionist-based theories; labelling theory, which draws on both the interactionist and the conflict perspectives; conflict theory; and feminist theories.

The third part of the chapter focuses on crime, a specific type of deviant behaviour. As a form of deviance subject to official, written norms, crime has been a special concern of policymakers and the public in general. We will look at various types of crime found in Canada, the ways crime is measured, and international crime rates. Finally, the social policy section considers the use of illicit drugs in Canada. ■

Use Your Sociological Imagination www.mcgrawhill.ca/college/schaefer

How do you think society views a computer hacker as opposed to, for example, someone who engages in the break and enter of a home? Are you concerned about the security of your online activities at home or at work? What kinds of questions would be raised by interactionist sociologists in their study of computer hacking?

SOCIAL CONTROL

As we saw in Chapter 3, each culture, subculture, and group has distinctive norms governing what it deems appropriate behaviour. Laws, dress codes, bylaws of organizations, course requirements, and rules of sports and games all express social norms.

How does a society bring about acceptance of basic norms? The term ***social control*** refers to the techniques and strategies for preventing deviant human behaviour in any society. Social control occurs on all levels of society. In the family, we are socialized to obey our parents simply because they are our parents. Peer groups introduce us to informal norms, such as dress codes, that govern the behaviour of members. Universities establish standards they expect of their students. In bureaucratic organizations, workers encounter a formal system of rules and regulations. Finally, the government of every society legislates and enforces social norms.

Most of us respect and accept basic social norms and assume that others will do the same. Even without thinking, we obey the instructions of police officers, follow the day-to-day rules at our jobs, and move to the rear of elevators when people enter. Such behaviour reflects an effective process of socialization to the dominant standards of a culture. At the same time, we are well aware

Research in Action 7-1 Street Kids

Fiona was a fairly typical 16-year-old, living in Barrie, Ontario. She was struggling to complete high school and to learning how to get along with her mother's new common-law partner. Often she and her mother's partner would argue over Fiona's contribution to the running of their household or whether she should be able to stay overnight at her boyfriend's apartment. He often would resort to verbal and physical abuse in attempting to make Fiona comply with his wishes. Although Fiona felt her mother loved her, she felt betrayed by her mother's silence when it came to protecting her from the abuse.

Fiona decided she couldn't endure the strain and sense of betrayal at home and convinced her boyfriend, Michael, to leave Ontario. They drove across Canada, ending up on the west coast—in Vancouver. Shortly after Fiona and Michael arrived in Vancouver, Michael's money supply ran out and he decided to return to Ontario. Fiona, also facing a shortage of cash, resorted to panhandling on Robson Street in downtown Vancouver and began "living on the streets."

Fiona's case is reflective of a general pattern of street kids in British Columbia. That is, nearly 61 percent of street kids in Vancouver are from provinces other than British Columbia. A major report released in 2001 by the McCreary Centre Society, entitled "No Place to Call Home," noted that most street youth have experienced sexual or physical abuse and most have either run away or been kicked out of home. Many engage in behaviours that are considered high risk, such as involvement in the sex trade and addiction to drugs. The study revealed that most street youth in the cities are not literally homeless but live in shelters or abandoned buildings or "squats."

Although it is common to view the phenomenon of youth living on the street as a big city problem, the study revealed that, although many troubled young people migrate to the larger cities, smaller communities, such as Prince Rupert, also experience the phenomenon.

Other major findings of the study revealed the following:

- More than one-fourth of street youth have attempted suicide in the past year.
- More than half of all street youth have been in government care, including foster care or group homes.
- Street youth reported that they began risky behaviour when they were young, many by age 13. Some of these risky behaviours include involvement in the sex trade, unprotected sex, and addiction to alcohol and drugs.
- Street kids had an average age of 16 in the smaller centres, while the average age was 18 for those in Vancouver.
- More than one-third planned to attend some form of postsecondary education.

When the researchers asked the more than five hundred youth, aged 12 to 19, why they were living on the street, the responses included

- Friends hang out on street (34 percent)
- Don't get along with parents (37 percent)
- Feel accepted there, kicked out of home (38 percent)
- Travelling (35 percent)
- Ran away from home (30 percent)
- Can't find a job (24 percent)
- Addiction problems (22 percent)
- Violence or abuse at home (20 percent)
- Can't find affordable housing (18 percent)
- Conflict at home because of sexual orientation (4 percent)

Applying Theory

1. Why do you think street kids might be likely to engage in so-called high-risk behaviours? What sociological perspective(s) would be useful in studying this phenomenon?
2. Have you ever known someone who lived on the street? If so, what were his or her reasons for doing so?

Source: McCreary Centre Society 2001; Steffenhagen 2001.

that individuals, groups, and institutions *expect* us to act "properly." If we fail to do so, we may face punishment through informal *sanctions*, such as fear and ridicule, or formal sanctions, such as jail sentences or fines. The challenge to effective social control is that people often receive competing messages about how to behave. Although the state or government may clearly define acceptable behaviour, friends or fellow employees may encourage quite different behaviour patterns. Box 7-1 presents the latest research on a behaviour that is officially frowned on but nevertheless engaged in by many young people—living on the streets.

pp. 57–58

Functionalists contend that people must respect social norms if any group or society is to survive. In their view, societies literally could not function if massive numbers of people defied standards of appropriate conduct. By contrast, conflict theorists maintain that "successful functioning" of a society will consistently benefit the powerful and work to the disadvantage of other groups. They point out, for example, that widespread resistance to social norms was necessary to overturn the institution of slavery.

Conformity and Obedience

Techniques for social control operate on both the group level and the societal level. People whom we regard as our peers or as our equals influence us to act in particular ways; the same is true of people who hold authority over us or occupy awe-inspiring positions. Stanley Milgram (1975) made a useful distinction between these two important levels of social control.

Milgram defined ***conformity*** as going along with peers—individuals of our own status, who have no special right to direct our behaviour. By contrast, ***obedience*** is defined as compliance with higher authorities in a hierarchical structure. Thus, a recruit entering military service will typically *conform* to the habits and language of other recruits and will *obey* the orders of superior officers. Students will *conform* to the drinking behaviour of their peers and will *obey* the requests of campus security officers.

Conformity to Prejudice

We often think of conformity in terms of rather harmless situations, such as members of an expensive health club who all work out in elaborate and costly sportswear. But researchers have found that people may conform to the attitudes and behaviour of their peers even when such conformity means expressing intolerance toward others.

Fletcher Blanchard, Teri Lilly, and Leigh Ann Vaughn (1991) conducted an experiment at an American university and found that statements people overhear others make influence their own expressions of opinion on the issue of racism. A student employed by the researchers approached 72 white students as each was walking across the campus to get responses for an opinion poll she said she was conducting for a class. At the same time, a second white student—actually another working with the researchers—was stopped and asked to participate in the survey. Both students were then asked how their university should respond to anonymous racist notes actually sent to four black students in 1989. The student employed by the researchers always answered first. In some cases, she condemned the notes; in others, she justified them.

Blanchard and his colleagues (1991:102–103) conclude that "hearing at least one other person express strongly antiracist opinions produced dramatically more strongly antiracist public reactions to racism than hearing others express equivocal opinions or opinions more accepting of racism." A second experiment demonstrated that when the student working on behalf of the researchers expressed sentiments justifying racism, subjects were much *less* likely to express antiracist opinions than were those who heard no one else offer opinions. In these experiments, social control (through the process of conformity) influenced people's attitudes, or at least the expression of those attitudes. In the next section, we will see that social control (through the process of obedience) can alter people's behaviour.

Obedience to Authority

If ordered to do so, would you comply with an experimenter's instruction to give people increasingly painful electric shocks? Most people would say no; yet, the research of social psychologist Stanley Milgram (1963, 1975) suggests that most of us *will* obey such orders. In Milgram's words (1975:xi), "Behaviour that is unthinkable in an individual . . . acting on his own may be executed without hesitation when carried out under orders."

Milgram placed advertisements in New Haven, Connecticut, newspapers to recruit subjects for what was announced as a learning experiment at Yale University. Participants included postal clerks, engineers, high school teachers, and labourers. They were told that the purpose of the research was to investigate the effects of punishment on learning. The experimenter, dressed in a grey technician's coat, explained that in each testing, one subject would be randomly selected as the "learner" while another would function as the "teacher." However, this lottery was rigged so that the "real" subject would always be the teacher while an associate of Milgram's served as the learner.

At this point, the learner's hand was strapped to an electric apparatus. The teacher was taken to an electronic "shock generator" with 30 lever switches. Each switch was labelled with graduated voltage designations from 15 to 450 volts. Before beginning the experiment, subjects were given sample shocks of 45 volts to convince them of the authenticity of the experiment.

The experimenter instructed the teacher to apply shocks of increasing voltage each time the learner gave an incorrect answer on a memory test. Teachers were told that "although the shocks can be extremely painful, they cause no permanent tissue damage." In reality, the learner did not receive any shocks.

The learner deliberately gave incorrect answers and acted out a prearranged script. For example, at 150 volts, the learner would cry out, "Experimenter, get me out of here! I won't be in the experiment any more!" At 270 volts, the learner would scream in agony. When the shock reached 350 volts, the learner would fall silent. If the teacher wanted to stop the experiment, the experimenter would insist that the teacher continue, using such statements as "The experiment requires that you continue"

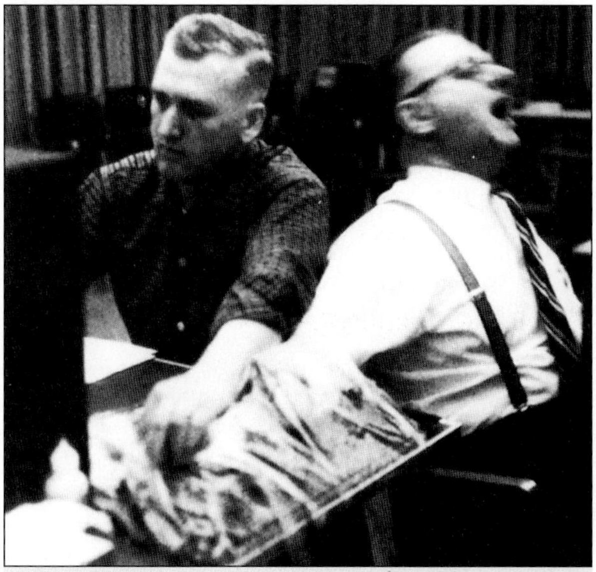

In one of Stanley Milgram's experiments, a supposed victim received an electric shock when his hand rested on a shock plate. At the 150-volt level, the victim would demand to be released, and would refuse to place his hand on the shock plate. The experimenter would then order the actual subject to force the victim's hand onto the plate, as shown in the photo. Though 40 percent of the true subjects stopped complying with Milgram at this point, 60 percent did force the victim's hand onto the shock plate, despite his pretended agony.

and "You have no other choice; you *must* go on" (Milgram 1975:19–23).

The results of this unusual experiment stunned and dismayed Milgram and other social scientists. A sample of psychiatrists had predicted that virtually all subjects would refuse to shock innocent victims. In their view, only a "pathological fringe" of less than 2 percent would continue administering shocks up to the maximum level. Yet almost *two-thirds* of participants fell into the category of "obedient subjects."

Why did these subjects obey? Why were they willing to inflict seemingly painful shocks on innocent victims who had never done them any harm? There is no evidence that these subjects were unusually sadistic; few seemed to enjoy administering the shocks. Instead, in Milgram's view, the key to obedience was the experimenter's social role as a "scientist" and "seeker of knowledge."

Milgram pointed out that in the modern industrial world, we are accustomed to submitting to impersonal authority figures whose status is indicated by a title (professor, lieutenant, doctor) or by a uniform (the technician's coat). The authority is viewed as larger and more important than the individual; consequently, the obedient individual shifts responsibility for his or her behaviour to the authority figure. Milgram's subjects frequently stated, "If it were up to me, I would not have administered shocks." They saw themselves as merely doing their duty (Milgram 1975).

From an interactionist perspective, one important aspect of Milgram's findings is the fact that subjects in follow-up studies were less likely to inflict the supposed shocks as they were moved physically closer to their victims. Moreover, interactionists emphasize the effect of *incrementally* administering additional dosages of 15 volts. In effect, the experimenter negotiated with the teacher and convinced the teacher to continue inflicting higher levels of punishment. It is doubtful that anywhere near the two-thirds rate of obedience would have been reached had the experimenter told the teachers to administer 450 volts immediately to the learners (B. Allen 1978; Katovich 1987).

Milgram launched his experimental study of obedience to better understand the involvement of Germans in the annihilation of six million Jews and millions of other people during World War II. In an interview conducted long after the publication of his study, he suggested that "if a system of death camps were set up in the United States of the sort we had seen in Nazi Germany, one would be able to find sufficient personnel for those camps in any medium-sized American town" (CBS News 1979:7–8).

Use Your Sociological Imagination

If you were a participant in Milgram's research on conformity, how far do you think you would go in carrying out orders? Do you see any ethical problem with the experimenter's manipulation of the control subjects?

Informal and Formal Social Control

The sanctions used to encourage conformity and obedience—and to discourage violation of social norms—are carried out through informal and formal social control. As the term implies, people use ***informal social control*** casually to enforce norms. Examples of informal social control include smiles, laughter, a raised eyebrow, and ridicule.

In Canada, the United States, and many other cultures, one common and yet controversial example of informal social control is parental use of corporal punishment. Adults often view spanking, slapping, or kicking children as a proper and necessary means of maintaining authority. Child development specialists counter that

Sociology in the Global Community

7-2 Singapore: A Nation of Campaigns

"Males with Long Hair Will Be Attended to Last!" "Throwing Litter from Apartments Can Kill!" "No Spitting!" These are some of the posters sponsored by the Singapore government in its effort to enforce social norms in this small nation of some four million people living in a totally urbanized area in southeast Asia.

Although Singapore is governed by a democratically elected Parliament, one party has dominated the government since the country's independence in 1965. And it has not hesitated to use its authority to launch a number of campaigns to shape the social behaviour of its citizens. In most cases these campaigns are directed against "disagreeable" behaviour—littering, spitting, chewing gum, failing to flush public toilets, teenage smoking, and the like. Courtesy is a major concern, with elaborate "Courtesy Month" celebrations scheduled to both entertain and educate the populace.

Some campaigns take on serious issues and are backed by legislation. For example, in the 1970s the government asked its citizens to "Please Stop at Two" in family planning; tax and schooling benefits rewarded those who complied. However, this campaign was so successful that in the 1980s the government began a "Have Three or More If You Can Afford To" campaign. In this case it provided school benefits for larger families. In another attempt at social control, the government has launched a "Speak Mandarin" campaign to encourage the multiethnic, multilingual population to accept Mandarin as the dialect of choice.

For the most part, Singaporeans cheerfully accept their government's admonitions and encouragement. They see the results of being clean and courteous: Singapore is a better place to live. Corporations also go along with the government and even help to sponsor some of the campaigns. As one corporate sponsor noted: "If (people) see Singapore as a clean country, they will view companies here as clean." Political scientist Michael Haas refers to this compliance as "the Singapore puzzle": citizens of Singapore accept strict social control dictates in exchange for continuing prosperity and technological leadership in the world.

Applying Theory

1. How would a functionalist thinker view an administration-sponsored campaign at your educational institution against drinking? What would be some latent functions of such a campaign?
2. According to conflict thinkers, why would these social control campaigns work in Singapore?

Sources: Dorai 1998; Haas 1999; Haub and Cornelius 2000; Instituto del Tercer Mundo 1999.

corporal punishment is inappropriate because it teaches children to solve problems through violence. They warn that slapping and spanking can escalate into more serious forms of abuse. Yet, despite the fact that pediatric experts now believe that physical forms of discipline are undesirable and encourage their patients to use nonphysical means of discipline (Tidmarsh 2000), approximately 70 percent of Canadian parents have used physical punishment (Durrant and Rose-Krasnor 1995). In 1999, the Canadian Foundation for Youth and the Law challenged the constitutionality of section 43 of the Criminal Code of Canada, which allows parents to use reasonable force in disciplining their children. The section was upheld.

Sometimes informal methods of social control are not adequate to enforce conforming or obedient behaviour. In those cases, ***formal social control*** is carried out by authorized agents, such as police officers, physicians, school administrators, employers, military officers, and managers of movie theatres. It can serve as a last resort when socialization and informal sanctions do not bring about desired behaviour. In Canada, for every 43 offences that occur, one person is sentenced to a penitentiary or prison. Of those who end up in a penitentiary or prison, a disproportionately high number are Aboriginal people, who account for between 8 percent and 10 percent of federal correctional institutions' populations, and even a greater percentage of the population in provincial and territorial institutions (A. Nelson and Fleras 1995).

Societies vary in deciding which behaviours will be subjected to formal social control and how severe the sanctions will be. In Singapore, chewing gum is prohibited, feeding birds can lead to fines of up to U.S.$640, and there is even a U.S.$95 fine for failing to flush the toilet (see Box 7-2). Singapore deals with serious crimes especially severely. The death penalty is mandatory for murder, drug trafficking, and crimes committed with firearms. Japan has created a special prison for reckless drivers. While some are imprisoned for vehicular homicide, others serve prison time for drunken driving and fleeing the scene of an accident (M. Elliott 1994).

Another controversial example of formal social control is the use of surveillance techniques. In 1992, police in Great Britain began to install closed-circuit television systems on "high streets" (the primary shopping and business areas of local communities) in an effort to reduce street crime. Within two years, three hundred British towns had installed or made plans to install such surveillance cameras, and the use of public surveillance had spread to North America. Supporters of surveillance believe that it will make the public feel more secure. Moreover, it can be cheaper to install and maintain cameras than to put more police officers on street patrol. For critics, however, the use of surveillance cameras brings to mind the grim, futuristic world presented by Britain's own George Orwell (1949) in his famous novel *1984*. In the world of *1984,* an all-seeing "Big Brother" represented an authoritarian government that watched people's every move and took immediate action against anyone who questioned the oppressive regime (Halbfinger 1998; Uttley 1993).

Law and Society

Some norms are so important to a society they are formalized into laws controlling people's behaviour. *Law* may be defined as governmental social control (D. Black 1995). Some laws, such as the prohibition against murder, are directed at all members of society. Others, such as fishing and hunting regulations, primarily affect particular categories of people. Still others govern the behaviour of social institutions (corporate law and laws regarding the taxing of nonprofit enterprises).

Sociologists have become increasingly interested in the creation of laws as a social process. Laws are created in response to perceived needs for formal social control. Sociologists have sought to explain how and why such perceptions arise. In their view, law is not merely a static body of rules handed down from generation to generation. Rather, it reflects continually changing standards of what is right and wrong, of how violations are to be determined, and of what sanctions are to be applied (Schur 1968).

Sociologists representing varying theoretical perspectives agree that the legal order reflects underlying social values. Therefore, the creation of criminal law can be a most controversial matter. Should it be against the law to employ illegal immigrants in a factory (see Chapter 9), to have an abortion (see Chapter 10), or to smoke on an airplane? Such issues have been bitterly debated because they require a choice among competing values. Not surprisingly, laws that are unpopular—such as the Canadian law requiring the registration of firearms—become difficult to enforce owing to lack of consensus supporting the norms.

Socialization is actually the primary source of conforming and obedient behaviour, including obedience to law. Generally, it is not external pressure from a peer group or authority figure that makes us go along with social norms. Rather, we have internalized such norms as valid and desirable and are committed to observing them. In a profound sense, we want to see ourselves (and to be seen) as loyal, cooperative, responsible, and respectful of others. In Canada and other societies around the world, people are socialized both to want to belong and to fear being viewed as different or deviant.

Control theory suggests that our connection to members of society leads us to systematically conform to society's norms. According to sociologist Travis Hirschi (1969) and other control theorists, we are bonded to our family members, friends, and peers in a way that leads us to follow the mores and folkways of our society while giving little conscious thought to whether we will be sanctioned if we fail to conform. Socialization develops our self-control so well that we don't need further pressure to obey social norms. Although control theory does not effectively explain the rationale for every conforming act, it nevertheless reminds us that although the media may focus on crime and disorder, most members of most

In an attempt to reduce crime, many businesses have installed video surveillance cameras. Some cities are using them on the streets as well. Although some people are comforted by a camera's presence, others see it as a violation of the right to privacy.

societies conform to and obey basic norms (Gottfredson and Hirschi 1990; Hirschi 1969).

DEVIANCE

What Is Deviance?

For sociologists, the term *deviance* does not mean perversion or depravity. ***Deviance*** is behaviour that violates the standards of conduct or expectations of a group or society (Wickman 1991:85). In Canada, alcoholics, compulsive gamblers, and people with mental illnesses would all be classified as deviants. Being late for class is categorized as a deviant act; the same is true of dressing too casually for a formal wedding. On the basis of the sociological definition, we are all deviant from time to time. Each of us violates common social norms in certain situations.

Is being overweight an example of deviance? In North America and many other cultures, unrealistic standards of appearance and body image place a huge strain on people—especially on women and girls—based on how they look. Journalist Naomi Wolf (1992) has used the term *the beauty myth* to refer to an exaggerated ideal of beauty, beyond the reach of all but a few females, which has unfortunate consequences. In order to shed their "deviant" image and conform to (unrealistic) societal norms, many women and girls become consumed with adjusting their appearances. For example, in a *People* magazine "health" feature, a young actress stated that she knows it is time to eat when she passes out on the set. When females carry adherence to "the beauty myth" to an extreme, they may develop eating disorders or undertake costly and unnecessary cosmetic surgery procedures. Yet what is deviant in our culture may be celebrated in another. In Nigeria, for example, being fat is a mark of beauty. Part of the coming-of-age ritual calls for young girls to spend months in a "fattening room." Among the Nigerians, being thin at this point in the life course is deviant (Simmons 1998).

Deviance involves the violation of group norms, which may or may not be formalized into law. It is a comprehensive concept that includes not only criminal behaviour but also many actions not subject to prosecution. The public official who takes a bribe has defied social norms, but so has the high school student who refuses to sit in an assigned seat or cuts class. Of course, deviation from norms is not always negative, let alone criminal. A member of an exclusive social club who speaks out against its traditional policy of excluding women and Jews from admittance is deviating from the club's norms. So is a police officer who "blows the whistle" on corruption or brutality within the department.

Standards of deviance vary from one group (or subculture) to another. In Canada, it is generally considered acceptable to sing along at a folk or rock concert, but not at the opera. Just as deviance is defined by place, so too is it relative to time. For instance, drinking alcohol at 6:00 p.m. is a common practice in our society, but engaging in the same behaviour at breakfast is viewed as a deviant act and as symptomatic of a drinking problem. Table 7-1 offers additional examples of untimely acts that we regard as deviant in North America.

From a sociological perspective, deviance is viewed according to normative standards. It is subject to social definitions within a particular society; in most instances, those individuals and groups with the greatest status and power define what is acceptable and what is deviant. For example, despite serious medical warnings about the dangers of tobacco as far back as 30 years ago, cigarette smoking continued to be accepted—in good part

The North American ideal of feminine beauty is often typified by celebrities. To avoid being labelled deviant, many girls and women become consumed with changing their appearance.

Table 7-1 Untimely Acts

Ringing a doorbell at 2 a.m.
Working on New Year's Eve
Having sex on a first date
Playing a stereo loudly in early morning hours
Having an alcoholic drink with breakfast
Ending a university class after 15 minutes
Getting married after having been engaged for only a few days

Source: Reese and Katovich 1989.

because of the power of tobacco farmers and cigarette manufacturers. It was only after a long campaign led by public health and anti-cancer activists that cigarette smoking became more of a deviant activity. Today many local laws limit where people can smoke.

Although deviance can include relatively minor day-to-day decisions about our personal behaviour, in some cases it can become part of a person's identity. This process is called *stigmatization,* as we will now see.

Deviance and Social Stigma

There are many ways a person can acquire a deviant identity. Because of physical or behavioural characteristics, some people are unwillingly cast in negative social roles. Once they have been assigned a deviant role, they have trouble presenting a positive image to others and may even experience lowered self-esteem. Whole groups of people—for instance, "short people" or "redheads"—may be labelled in this way (Heckert and Best 1997). The interactionist Erving Goffman (see Chapters 1 and 4) coined the term ***stigma*** to describe the labels society uses to devalue members of certain social groups (Goffman 1963a).

Prevailing expectations about beauty and body shape may prevent people who are regarded as ugly or obese from advancing as rapidly as their abilities permit. Both obese and anorexic people are assumed to be weak in character, slaves to their appetites or to media images. Because they do not conform to the beauty myth, they may be viewed as "disfigured" or "strange" in appearance, bearers of what Goffman calls a "spoiled identity." However, what constitutes disfigurement is a matter of interpretation. Of the more than one million cosmetic procedures done every year in Canada and the United States, many are performed on women who would be objectively defined as having a normal appearance. And although feminist sociologists have accurately noted that the beauty myth makes many women feel uncomfortable with themselves, men too lack confidence in their appearance. The number of males who choose to undergo cosmetic procedures has risen sharply in recent years; men now account for 14.5 percent of such surgeries, including liposuction (C. Kalb 1999; P. Saukko 1999; Schmidt 2004).

The American Board of Plastic Surgery, made up of doctors from Canada and the United States, track the statistics on the number of cosmetic surgeries performed in both countries. Since 1998, the number has increased dramatically (from 1 045 000 in 1998 to 9 210 627 in 2004), as Table 7-2 illustrates.

Often people are stigmatized for deviant behaviours they may no longer engage in. The labels "compulsive gambler," "ex-convict," "recovering alcoholic," and "ex-mental patient" can stick to a person for life. Goffman (1963a) draws a useful distinction between a prestige symbol that draws attention to a positive aspect of a person's identity, such as a wedding band or a badge, and a stigma symbol that discredits or debases a person's identity, such as a conviction for child molestation. Although stigma symbols may not always be obvious, they can

Table 7-2 Selected Cosmetic Procedures in Canada and the United States

	1998	2004
Liposuction	172 079	324 891
Breast augmentation	132 378	264 041
Facelift	70 947	114 279
Nose reshaping	55 953	305 475
Tummy tuck	46 597	107 019
Breast lift	31 525	75 805
Male breast reduction	9 023	13 963
Buttock lift	1 246	3 496

Sources: Adapted from American Society of Plastic Surgeons 2002, 2005.

become a matter of public knowledge. Some communities, for instance, publish the names and addresses, and in some instances even the pictures, of convicted sex offenders on the Web.

A person need not be guilty of a crime to be stigmatized. Homeless people often have trouble getting a job, because employers are wary of applicants who cannot give a home address. Moreover, hiding homelessness is difficult, since agencies generally use the telephone to contact applicants about job openings. If a homeless person has access to a telephone at a shelter, the staff generally answer the phone by announcing the name of the institution—a sure way to discourage prospective employers. Even if a homeless person surmounts these obstacles and manages to get a job, she or he is often fired when the employer learns of the situation.

> Kim had been working as a receptionist in a doctor's office for several weeks when the doctor learned she was living in a shelter and fired her. "If I had known you lived in a shelter," Kim said the doctor told her, "I would never have hired you. Shelters are places of disease." "No," said Kim. "Doctors' offices are places of disease." (Liebow 1993:64–54)

Regardless of a person's positive attributes, employers regard the spoiled identity of homelessness as sufficient reason to dismiss an employee.

Although some types of deviance will stigmatize a person, other types do not carry a significant penalty. Some good examples of socially tolerated forms of deviance can be found in the world of high technology.

Deviance and Technology

Technological innovations, like pagers and voice mail, can redefine social interactions and the standards of behaviour related to them. When the Internet was first made available to the general public, no norms or regulations governed its use. Because online communication offers a high degree of anonymity, uncivil behaviour—speaking harshly of others or monopolizing chat rooms—quickly became common. Today, online bulletin boards designed to carry items of community interest must be policed to prevent users from posting commercial advertisements. Such deviant acts are beginning to provoke calls for the establishment of formal rules for online behaviour. For example, policymakers have debated the wisdom of regulating the content of Web sites featuring hate speech and pornography.

The sheer length of time people spend using the Internet may soon be an indication of deviance. Some psychiatrists and psychologists are now deciding whether or not Internet "addiction" may eventually be labelled a new disorder and, thus, a new form of deviant behaviour. Dr. Kimberly Young, of the University of Pittsburgh, has studied Internet addiction in the United States, placing it in the same category as pathological gambling and compulsive shopping. She found "addicted" users spent an average of 38 hours per week online, compared with 8 hours per week for "non-addicts" (Dalfen 2000). Canadians, according to a January 2000 Media Matrix study, use the Internet 27 percent more than Americans do (Dalfen 2000).

Some deviant uses of technology are criminal, though not all participants see it that way. The pirating of software, motion pictures, and CDs has become a big business. At conventions and swap meets, pirated copies of movies and CDs are sold openly. Some of the products are obviously counterfeit, but many come in sophisticated packaging, complete with warranty cards. When vendors are willing to talk, they say they merely want to be compensated for their time and the cost of materials, or that the software they have copied is in the public domain.

Though most of these black market activities are clearly illegal, many consumers and small-time pirates are proud of their behaviour. They may even think themselves smart for figuring out a way to avoid the "unfair" prices charged by "big corporations." Few people see the pirating of a new software program or a first-run movie as a threat to the public good, as they would embezzling from a bank. Similarly, most businesspeople who "borrow" software from another department, even though they lack a site licence, do not think they are doing anything wrong. No social stigma attaches to their illegal behaviour.

Deviance, then, is a complex concept. Sometimes it is trivial, sometimes profoundly harmful. Sometimes it is accepted by society and sometimes soundly rejected. What accounts for deviant behaviour and people's reaction to it? In the next section we will examine four theoretical explanations for deviance.

Explaining Deviance

Why do people violate social norms? We have seen that deviant acts are subject to both informal and formal sanctions of social control. The nonconforming or disobedient person may face disapproval, loss of friends, fines, or even imprisonment. Why, then, does deviance occur?

Early explanations for deviance identified supernatural causes or genetic factors (such as "bad blood" or evolutionary throwbacks to primitive ancestors). By the 1800s, there were substantial research efforts to identify biological factors that lead to deviance and especially to criminal activity. Although such research was discredited in the twentieth century, contemporary studies, primarily by biochemists, have sought to isolate genetic factors leading to a likelihood of certain personality traits. Although criminality (much less deviance) is hardly a personality characteristic, researchers have focused on traits that might lead to crime, such as aggression. Of course, aggression can also lead to success in the corporate world, professional sports, or other areas of life.

The contemporary study of possible biological roots of criminality is but one aspect of the larger sociobiology debate. In general, sociologists reject any emphasis on genetic roots of crime and deviance. The limitations of current knowledge, the possibility of reinforcing racist and sexist assumptions, and the disturbing implications for rehabilitation of criminals have led sociologists to largely draw on other approaches to explain deviance (Sagarin and Sanchez 1988).

Functionalist Perspective

According to functionalists, deviance is a common part of human existence, with positive (as well as negative) consequences for social stability. Deviance helps to define the limits of proper behaviour. Children who see one parent scold the other for belching at the dinner table learn about approved conduct. The same is true of the driver who receives a speeding ticket, the department store cashier who is fired for yelling at a customer, and the university student who is penalized for handing in papers weeks overdue.

Durkheim's Legacy

Émile Durkheim (1964, original edition 1895) investigated a range of social tacts that illuminated different forms of social solidarity within societies. In Durkheim's view, the punishments established within a culture (including both formal and informal mechanisms of social control) help to define acceptable behaviour and thus contribute to stability. If improper acts were not committed and then sanctioned, people might stretch their standards of what constitutes appropriate conduct.

Kai Erikson (1966) illustrated this boundary-maintenance function of deviance in his study of the Puritans of seventeenth-century New England. By today's standards, the Puritans placed tremendous emphasis on conventional morals. Their persecution of Quakers and execution of women as witches represented continuing attempts to define and redefine the boundaries of their community. In effect, their changing social norms created "crime waves," as people whose behaviour was previously acceptable suddenly faced punishment for being deviant (Abrahamson 1978; N. Davis 1975).

Durkheim (1951, original edition 1897) also introduced the term *anomie* into sociological literature. Anomie is a state of normlessness that typically occurs during a period of profound social change and disorder, such as a time of economic collapse. People may become more aggressive or depressed, and this may result in higher rates of violent crime and suicide. Since there is much less agreement on what constitutes proper behaviour during times of revolution, sudden prosperity, or economic depression, conformity and obedience become less significant as social forces. It also becomes much more difficult to state exactly what constitutes deviance.

p. 8

Merton's Theory of Deviance

What do a mugger and a teacher have in common? Each is "working" to obtain money that can then be exchanged for desired goods. As this example illustrates, behaviour that violates accepted norms (such as mugging) may be performed with the same basic objectives in mind as those of people who pursue more conventional lifestyles.

Using the above analysis, sociologist Robert Merton (1968) adapted Durkheim's notion of anomie to explain why people accept or reject the goals of a society, the socially approved means of fulfilling their aspirations, or both. Merton maintained that one important cultural goal in capitalist societies is success, measured largely in terms of money. In addition to providing this goal for people, our society offers specific instructions on how to pursue success—go to school, work hard, do not quit, take advantage of opportunities, and so forth.

What happens to individuals in a society with a heavy emphasis on wealth as a basic symbol of success? Merton reasoned that people adapt in certain ways, either by conforming to or by deviating from such cultural expectations. Consequently, he developed the ***anomie theory of deviance,*** which posits five basic forms of adaptation (see Table 7-3).

Conformity to social norms, the most common adaptation in Merton's typology, is the opposite of deviance. It involves acceptance of both the overall societal goal ("become affluent") and the approved means ("work hard"). In Merton's view, there must be some consensus regarding accepted cultural goals and legitimate means for attaining them. Without such consensus, societies could exist only as collectives of people—rather than as unified cultures—and might function in continual chaos.

Of course, in a society such as ours, conformity is not universal. For example, the means for realizing objectives are not equally distributed. People in the lower social classes often identify with the same goals as those of more powerful and affluent citizens yet lack equal access to high-quality education and training for skilled work. Even within a society, institutionalized means for realizing objectives vary. For example, a Statistics Canada report found that in 1997 access to legalized gambling varied across provinces and territories. Lotteries were legal in all provinces and territories, government casinos

Table 7-3 Modes of Individual Adaptation

Mode	Institutionalized Means (Hard Work)	Societal Goal (Acquisition of Wealth)
NONDEVIANT		
Conformity	+	+
DEVIANT		
Innovation	−	+
Ritualism	+	−
Retreatism	−	−
Rebellion	±	±

Source: Merton 1968:1940.

Note: + indicates acceptance; − indicates rejection; ± indicates replacement with new means and goals.

were legal in approximately half of the provinces, and VLTs (video lottery terminals) were legal in most provinces (Marshall 1999).

The other four types of behaviour represented in Table 7-3 all involve some departure from conformity. The "innovator" accepts the goals of a society but pursues them through means regarded as improper. For example, Harry King—a professional thief who specialized in safe-cracking for 40 years—gave a lecture to a sociology class and was asked if he had minded spending time in prison. King responded,

> I didn't exactly like it. But it was one of the necessary things about the life I had chosen. Do you like to come here and teach this class? I bet if the students had their wishes they'd be somewhere else, maybe out stealing, instead of sitting in this dumpy room. But they do it because it gets them something they want. The same with me. If I had to go to prison from time to time, well, that was the price you pay. (Chambliss 1972:x)

Harry King saw his criminal lifestyle as an adaptation to the goal of material success or "getting something you want." Denied the chance to achieve success through socially approved means, some individuals (like King) turn to illegitimate paths of upward mobility.

In Merton's typology, the "ritualist" has abandoned the goal of material success and become compulsively committed to the institutional means. Work becomes simply a way of life rather than a means to the goal of success, as in the case of bureaucratic officials who blindly apply rules and regulations without remembering the larger goals of an organization. Certainly this would be true of a welfare caseworker who refuses to assist a homeless family because their last apartment was in another district.

The "retreatist," as described by Merton, has basically withdrawn (or "retreated") from both the goals *and* the means of a society. In Canada, drug addicts and residents of skid row are typically portrayed as retreatists. There is also growing concern that adolescents addicted to alcohol will become retreatists at an early age.

The final adaptation identified by Merton reflects people's attempts to create a *new* social structure. The "rebel" feels alienated from dominant means and goals and may seek a dramatically different social order. Members of revolutionary political organizations, such as the Irish Republican Army (IRA) or right-wing militia groups, can be categorized as rebels according to Merton's model.

Merton has stressed that he was not attempting to describe five types of individuals. Rather, he offered a typology to explain the actions that people *usually* take. Thus, leaders of organized crime syndicates will be categorized as innovators, since they do not pursue success through socially approved means. Yet they may also attend church and send their children to medical school. Conversely, "respectable" people may occasionally cheat on their taxes or violate traffic laws. According to Merton, the same person will move back and forth from one mode of adaptation to another, depending on the demands of a particular situation.

Merton's theory, though popular, has had relatively few applications. Little effort has been made to determine to what extent all acts of deviance can be accounted for by his five modes. Moreover, although Merton's theory is useful in examining certain types of behaviour, such as illegal gambling by disadvantaged people functioning as innovators, his formulation fails to explain key differences in rates. Why, for example, do some disadvantaged groups have lower rates of reported crime than others? Why is criminal activity not viewed as a viable alternative by many people in adverse circumstances? Merton's theory of deviance does not answer such questions easily (Cloward 1959; Hartjen 1978).

Still, Merton has made a key contribution to the sociological understanding of deviance by pointing out that deviants (such as innovators and ritualists) share a great deal with conforming people. The convicted felon may hold many of the same aspirations as people with no criminal background have. Therefore, we can understand deviance as socially created behaviour, rather than as the result of momentary pathological impulses.

Interactionist Perspective

The functionalist approach to deviance explains why rule violation continues to exist in societies despite pressures to conform and obey. However, functionalists do not indicate how a given person comes to commit a deviant act or why on some occasions crimes do or do not occur. The emphasis on everyday behaviour that is the focus of the interactionist perspective is reflected in two explanations of crime—cultural transmission and routine activities theory.

Cultural Transmission

White teenagers in the suburbs and cities attempt to achieve fame within a subculture of "taggers." These young people "tag" (spray graffiti on) poles, utility boxes, bridges, and freeway signs. Although law enforcement officials prefer to view them as "visual terrorists," the taggers gain respect from their peers by being "up the most" on prominent walls and billboards and by displaying the flashiest styles. Even parents may tolerate or endorse such deviant behaviour by declaring, "At least my kid's not shooting people. He's still alive" (Wooden 1995:124).

The graffiti of teenagers can be seen on walls in most urban settings. According to the interactionist Edwin Sutherland, teenagers are socialized into engaging in such deviant acts.

These teenagers demonstrate that humans *learn* how to behave in social situations—whether properly or improperly. There is no natural, innate manner in which people interact with one another. These simple ideas are not disputed today, but this was not the case when sociologist Edwin Sutherland (1883–1950) first advanced the argument that an individual undergoes the same basic socialization process whether learning conforming or deviant acts.

Sutherland's ideas have been the dominating force in criminology. He drew on the ***cultural transmission*** school, which emphasizes that a person learns criminal behaviour through interactions with others. Such learning includes not only techniques of lawbreaking (for example, how to break into a car quickly and quietly) but also the motives, drives, and rationalizations of criminals. We can also use the cultural transmission approach to explain the behaviour of people who engage in habitual—and ultimately life-threatening—use of alcohol or drugs.

Sutherland maintained that through interactions with a primary group and significant others, people acquire definitions of proper and improper behaviour. He used the term ***differential association*** to describe the process through which exposure to attitudes *favourable* to criminal acts leads to violation of rules. Research suggests that this view of differential association also applies to such noncriminal deviant acts as sitting down during the singing of the national anthem or lying to a friend (E. Jackson, Tittle, and Burke 1986).

To what extent will a given person engage in activity regarded as proper or improper? For each individual, it will depend on the frequency, duration, and importance of two types of social interaction experiences—those that endorse deviant behaviour and those that promote acceptance of social norms. People are more likely to engage in norm-defying behaviour if they are part of a group or subculture that stresses deviant values, such as a street gang.

Sutherland offers the example of a boy who is sociable, outgoing, and athletic and who lives in an area with a high rate of delinquency. The youth is very likely to come into contact with peers who commit acts of vandalism, fail to attend school, and so forth, and may come to adopt such behaviour. However, an introverted boy living in the same neighbourhood may stay away from his peers and avoid delinquency. In another community, an outgoing and athletic boy may join a baseball team or a Scout troup because of his interactions with peers. Thus, Sutherland views learning improper behaviour as the result of the types of groups to which a person belongs and the kinds of friendships that person has with others (Sutherland and Cressey 1978).

According to its critics, however, the cultural transmission approach may explain the deviant behaviour of juvenile delinquents or graffiti artists, but it fails to explain the conduct of the first-time impulsive shoplifter or the impoverished person who steals out of necessity. Although not a precise statement of the process through which someone becomes a criminal, differential association theory does direct our attention to the paramount role of social interaction in increasing a person's motivation to engage in deviant behaviour (Cressey 1960; E. Jackson, Tittle, and Burke 1986; Sutherland and Cressey 1978).

Routine Activities Theory

Another, more recent interactionist explanation considers the requisite conditions for a crime or deviant act to occur: there must be at the same time and in the same place a perpetrator, a victim, and/or an object of property. ***Routine activities theory*** contends that criminal victimization is increased when motivated offenders and suitable targets converge. It goes without saying that you cannot have car theft without automobiles, but the greater availability of more valuable automobiles to potential thieves *heightens* the likelihood that such a crime will occur. Campus and airport parking lots, where vehicles may be left in isolated locations for long periods, represent a new target for crime unknown just a generation ago. Routine activity of this nature can occur even in the home. For example, adults may save money by buying 24-packs of beer, but buying in bulk also allows juveniles to siphon off contents without attracting attention to their "crime." The theory derives its name of "routine" from the fact that the elements of a criminal or deviant act come together in normal, legal, and routine activities.

Advocates of this theory see it as a powerful explanation for the rise in crime during the past 50 years. Routine activity has changed to make crime more likely. Homes left vacant during the day or during long vacations are more accessible as targets of crime. The greater presence of consumer goods that are highly portable, such as video equipment and computers, also makes crime more likely (Cohen and Felson 1979; Felson 1998).

Some significant research supports the routine activities explanation. Studies of urban crime have documented the existence of "hot spots" where people are more likely to be victimized because of their routine comings and goings (Cromwell, Olson, and Avarey 1995; Sherman, Gartin, and Buerger 1989).

Perhaps what is most compelling about this theory is that it broadens our effort to understand crime and deviance. Rather than focus just on the criminal, routine activities theory also brings into the picture the behaviour of the victim. However, we need to resist the temptation to *expect* the higher victimization of some groups, such as racial and ethnic minorities, much less to consider it their own fault (Akers 1997).

Labelling Theory

The Saints and Roughnecks were two groups of high school males who were continually engaged in excessive drinking, reckless driving, truancy, petty theft, and vandalism. There the similarity ended. None of the Saints was ever arrested, but every Roughneck was frequently in trouble with police and townspeople. Why the disparity in their treatment? On the basis of his observation research in their high school, sociologist William Chambliss (1973) concluded that social class played an important role in the varying fortunes of the two groups.

The Saints effectively produced a facade of respectability. They came from "good families," were active in

ATMs invite trouble: they provide an ideal setting for the convergence of a perpetrator, a victim, and an article of property (cash). According to routine activities theory, crimes are more likely to occur wherever motivated offenders meet suitable targets.

school organizations, expressed the intention of attending university, and received good grades. People generally viewed their delinquent acts as a few isolated cases of "sowing wild oats." By contrast, the Roughnecks had no such aura of respectability. They drove around town in beat-up cars, were generally unsuccessful in school, and were viewed with suspicion no matter what they did.

We can understand such discrepancies by using an approach to deviance known as ***labelling theory.*** Unlike Sutherland's work, labelling theory does not focus on why some individuals come to commit deviant acts. Instead, it attempts to explain why certain people (such as the Roughnecks) are *viewed* as deviants, delinquents, "bad kids," "losers," and criminals, while others whose behaviour is similar (such as the Saints) are not seen in such harsh terms. Reflecting the contribution of interactionist theorists, labelling theory emphasizes how a person comes to be labelled as deviant or to accept that label. Sociologist Howard Becker (1963:9; 1964), who popularized this approach, summed it up with this statement: "Deviant behavior is behavior that people so label."

Labelling theory is also called the ***societal-reaction approach,*** reminding us that it is the *response* to an act and not the behaviour itself that determines deviance. For example, studies have shown that some school personnel and therapists expand educational programs designed for students who have learning disabilities to include those with behavioural problems. Consequently, a "troublemaker" can be improperly labelled as having a learning disability and vice versa.

A recent study by three British psychologists underscores the implications of using different labels to describe people with learning difficulties or disabilities. A total of 111 subjects completed a questionnaire designed to assess attitudes toward three labelled groups: "mentally subnormal adults," "mentally handicapped adults," and "people with learning difficulties." The researchers found that subjects reacted more positively to the label "people with learning difficulties" than to the other labels. Subjects view "people with learning difficulties" as more competent and as deserving of more rights than "mentally handicapped" or "mentally subnormal" individuals (Eayrs, Ellis, and Jones 1993).

Traditionally, research on deviance has focused on people who violate social norms. In contrast, labelling theory focuses on police, probation officers, psychiatrists, judges, teachers, employers, school officials, and other regulators of social control. These agents, it is argued, play a significant role in creating the deviant identity by designating certain people (and not others) as "deviant." An important aspect of labelling theory is the recognition that some individuals or groups have the power to *define* labels and apply them to others. This view recalls the conflict perspective's emphasis on the social significance of power.

In recent years the practice of *racial or ethnic profiling,* in which people are identified as criminal suspects purely on the basis of their race or ethnicity, has come under public scrutiny. American studies confirm the public's suspicions that in some jurisdictions, police officers are much more likely to stop black males than white males for routine traffic violations. In Canada, the United States, and many European countries, the events of September 11, 2001, have caused civil rights activists to raise concerns about the use of racial profiling in safety and security policies and practices.

The labelling approach does not fully explain why certain people accept a label and others are able to reject it. In fact, this perspective may exaggerate the ease with which societal judgments can alter our self-images. Labelling theorists do suggest, however, that how much power a person has relative to others is important in determining that person's ability to resist an undesirable label. Competing approaches (including that of Sutherland) fail to explain why some deviants continue to be viewed as conformists rather than as violators of rules. According to Howard Becker (1973), labelling theory was not conceived as the *sole* explanation for deviance; its proponents merely hoped to focus more attention on the undeniably important actions of those people officially in charge of defining deviance (N. Davis 1975; compare with Cullen and Cullen 1978).

The popularity of labelling theory is reflected in the emergence of a related perspective, called social constructionism. According to the ***social constructionist perspective,*** deviance is the product of the culture we live in. Social constructionists focus specifically on the decision-making process that creates the deviant identity. They point out that "missing children," "deadbeat dads," "spree killers," and "date rapists" have always been with us but at times have become *the* major social concern of the moment because of intensive media coverage (Liska and Messner 1999; Wright, Gronfein, and Owens 2000).

Use Your Sociological Imagination

You are a teacher. What kinds of labels freely used in educational circles might be attached to your students?

Conflict Perspective

For many years a husband who forced his wife to have sexual intercourse—without her consent and against her will—was not legally considered to have committed rape.

The laws defined rape as pertaining only to sexual relations between people not married to each other. These laws reflected the overwhelmingly male composition of government and legal decision makers. Conflict theorists would not be surprised by this. They point out that people with power protect their own interests and define deviance to suit their own needs. It wasn't until 1983 in Canada that rape laws were broadened to sexual assault laws and it became a criminal act for a man to rape his wife.

Feminist legal scholar Catherine MacKinnon (1987) argues that male sexual behaviour represents "dominance eroticized," in that male sexuality is linked to dominance and power. Edwin Schur (1983:148) expands on this view of male sexuality, stating that "forced sex is the ultimate indicator and preserver of male dominance." Canadian laws have historically sanctioned the abuse of women within marriage, based on the assumption of male control and ownership of his family (H. Johnson 1996). According to Status of Women Canada (2000), female victims of spousal abuse are more likely to be subjected to sexual assault and more severe forms of violence, such as beating and choking, than are male victims.

Sociologist Richard Quinney (1974, 1979, 1980) is a leading exponent of the view that the criminal justice system serves the interests of the powerful. Crime, according to Quinney (1970), is a definition of conduct created by authorized agents of social control—such as legislators and law enforcement officers—in a politically organized society. He and other conflict theorists argue that lawmaking is often an attempt by the powerful to coerce others into their own morality (see also S. Spitzer 1975).

This helps to explain why our society has laws against gambling, drug usage, and prostitution, many of which are violated on a massive scale (we will examine these "victimless crimes" later in the chapter). According to the conflict school, criminal law does not represent a consistent application of societal values but instead reflects competing values and interests. Thus, cocaine is outlawed in Canada because it is alleged to be harmful to users, yet cigarettes and alcohol are sold legally almost everywhere.

Conflict theorists contend that the entire criminal justice system of Canada treats suspects differently on the basis of their racial, ethnic, or social class background. The case of Donald Marshall, an Aboriginal man from Nova Scotia who was wrongfully convicted of murder, and who served years in prison for a crime he did not commit, is one of the most illustrative examples of the bias against Aboriginal persons in Canadian legal history.

Today, Aboriginal men have the highest rate of overrepresentation in prisons of any group in Canada. Quinney (1974) argues that, through such differential applications of social control, the criminal justice system helps to keep the poor and oppressed in their deprived position. In his view, disadvantaged individuals and groups who represent a threat to those with power become the primary targets of criminal law. He maintains the real criminals in poor neighbourhoods are not the people arrested for vandalism and theft but rather absentee landlords and exploitative store owners. Even if we do not accept this challenging argument, we cannot ignore the role of the powerful in creating a social structure that perpetuates suffering.

The perspective advanced by labelling and conflict theorists forms quite a contrast to the functionalist approach to deviance. Functionalists view standards of deviant behaviour as merely reflecting cultural norms, whereas conflict and labelling theorists point out that the most powerful groups in a society can shape laws and standards and determine who is (or is not) prosecuted as a criminal. Thus, the label "deviant" is rarely applied to the corporate executive whose decisions lead to large-scale environmental pollution. In the opinion of conflict theorists, agents of social control and powerful groups

Demonstrators in Vancouver show their support for safe injection sites in that city.

can generally impose their own self-serving definitions of deviance on the general public.

Feminist Perspectives

Although feminist theories of deviance are varied and diverse, most tend to challenge other mainstream theories on the grounds that women's experiences have not been included and that gender-based perspectives have not been employed. Feminist theories of deviance are generally eager to understand the gendered nature of institutions, such as the criminal justice system, and the inequities in the system that lead to differential treatment of men and women.

Many feminist perspectives contend that courts, prisons, law enforcement agencies, welfare agencies, and families alike are organized on the basis of gender as well as power, class, race, and sexuality (Elliot and Mandell 1998). Of concern are ways in which such factors as gender, sexuality, class, and race intersect to produce patterns of and responses to deviant behaviour. As well, these perspectives in general hold the view that since gender relations are not "natural," but rather produced by social, cultural, and historical conditions, gendered patterns of deviance will reflect these conditions. For example, the social acceptability of smoking for women (and the labelling of some women smokers as deviants) has been shaped by history, class, and sexuality. From the 1800s to the 1920s in North America, smoking by women was associated with prostitution and lesbianism. Women who smoked were labelled "sluts," "whores," and "sinners" and were considered "fallen women" (Greaves 1996:18).

As previously mentioned, feminist perspectives are diverse and varied. For example, liberal feminist perspectives tend to view women's rates of crime and deviance as a reflection of the degree to which they participate in all areas of social life—sports, politics, business, education, and so on. Because women are confronted with obstacles in their climb to top corporate positions, they are limited in their opportunities to engage in particular deviant acts, such as corporate crime.

In contrast, radical feminist perspectives see patriarchy (the set of social relations that maintains male control) as the key to understanding female crime and deviance. Patriarchy, according to radical feminist analysis, puts men in control of women's bodies and minds and sets in place oppressive social institutions, such as the family and the law, in order to maintain control. Sexual offences for women, therefore, are more common, since men control the institutions that regulate activities such as prostitution. This imbalance of power results in a higher rate of arrest and conviction for the female prostitute than for the male customer.

CRIME

Crime is a violation of criminal law for which some governmental authority applies formal penalties. It represents a deviation from formal social norms administered by the state. Laws divide crimes into various categories, depending on the severity of the offence, the age of the offender, the potential punishment that can be levied, and the court that holds jurisdiction over the case.

Crimes tend to affect some groups more than others; for example, their impact can be gender-specific and age-specific. In Canada, of all the victims of crimes against the person, women and girls make up the majority of victims of sexual assault (82 percent), criminal harassment (78 percent), kidnapping or abduction (62 percent), and common assault (52 percent) (Status of Women Canada 2000).

Types of Crime

Rather than relying solely on legal categories, sociologists classify crimes in terms of how they are committed and how society views the offences. In this section, we will examine four types of crime as differentiated by sociologists: professional crime, organized crime, white-collar crime, and "victimless crimes."

Professional Crime

Although the adage "crime doesn't pay" is familiar, many people do make a career of illegal activities. A ***professional criminal*** is a person who pursues crime as a day-to-day occupation, developing skilled techniques and enjoying a certain degree of status among other criminals. Some professional criminals specialize in burglary, safecracking, hijacking of cargo, pickpocketing, and shoplifting. Such people have acquired skills that reduce the likelihood of arrest, conviction, and imprisonment. As a result, they may have long careers in their chosen "professions."

Edwin Sutherland (1937) offered pioneering insights into the behaviour of professional criminals by publishing an annotated account written by a professional thief. Unlike the person who engages in crime only once or twice, professional thieves make a business of stealing. They devote their entire working time to planning and executing crimes and sometimes travel across the nation to pursue their "professional duties." Like people in regular occupations, professional thieves consult with their colleagues concerning the demands of work, thus becoming part of a subculture of similarly occupied individuals. They exchange information on possible places to burglarize, on outlets for unloading stolen goods, and on ways of securing bail bonds if arrested.

Organized Crime

For our purposes, we will consider ***organized crime*** to be the work of a group that regulates relations among various criminal enterprises involved in the smuggling and sale of drugs, prostitution, gambling, and other illegal activities. Organized crime dominates the world of illegal business just as large corporations dominate the conventional business world. It allocates territory, sets prices for goods and services, and acts as an arbitrator in internal disputes.

Organized crime is a secret, conspiratorial activity that generally evades law enforcement. Organized crime takes over legitimate businesses, gains influence over labour unions, corrupts public officials, intimidates witnesses in criminal trials, and even "taxes" merchants in exchange for "protection" (National Advisory Commission on Criminal Justice 1976). An example of the intimidation tactics used by organized crime is the gunning down of the Montreal crime reporter Michel Auger in 2000. Auger specialized in stories on organized crime and biker gangs in Quebec. Auger was shot five times, but recovered. Although it has not yet been proven that biker gangs were responsible for the execution-style attack, the attack came a day after his paper, *Le Journal*, printed one of his articles on biker-related murders.

There has always been a global element in organized crime. But recently law enforcement officials and policymakers have acknowledged the emergence of a new form of organized crime that takes advantage of advances in electronic communications. *Transnational* organized crime includes drug and arms smuggling, money laundering, and trafficking in illegal immigrants and stolen goods, such as automobiles (Office of Justice Programs 1999).

White-Collar and Technology-Based Crime

Income tax evasion, stock manipulation, consumer fraud, bribery and extraction of "kickbacks," embezzlement, and misrepresentation in advertising—these are all examples of ***white-collar crime,*** illegal acts committed in the course of business activities, often by affluent, "respectable" people. Edwin Sutherland (1949, 1983) likened these crimes to organized crime because they are often perpetrated through occupational roles (Friedrichs 1998).

A new type of white-collar crime has emerged in recent decades: computer crime. The use of such high technology allows people to carry out embezzlement or electronic fraud without leaving a trace, or to gain access to a company's inventory without leaving home. An adept programmer can gain access to a firm's computer by telephone and then copy valuable files. It is virtually impossible to track such people unless they are foolish enough to call from the same phone each time. According to a 2000 study by the FBI and the Computer Security Institute, 70 percent of companies in the United States relying on computer systems reported theft of electronic information for an estimated loss of U.S.$265 million in 1999 alone (Zuckerman 2000).

Sutherland (1940) coined the term *white-collar crime* in 1939 to refer to acts by individuals, but the term has been broadened more recently to include offences by businesses and corporations as well. *Corporate crime,* or any act by a corporation that is punishable by the government, takes many forms and includes individuals, organizations, and institutions among its victims. Corporations may engage in anticompetitive behaviour, acts that lead to environmental pollution, tax fraud, stock fraud and manipulation, the production of unsafe goods, bribery and corruption, and worker health and safety violations (Simpson 1993).

Given the economic and social costs of white-collar crime, you might expect the criminal justice system to take this problem quite seriously. Yet research done in the United States shows that white-collar offenders are more likely to receive fines than prison sentences. In federal courts—where most white-collar cases end up—probation is granted to 40 percent of those who have violated antitrust laws, 61 percent of those convicted of fraud, and

"BUT IF WE GO BACK TO SCHOOL AND GET A GOOD EDUCATION, THINK OF ALL THE DOORS IT'LL OPEN TO WHITE-COLLAR CRIME."

70 percent of convicted embezzlers (Gest 1985). Amitai Etzioni's study (1985, 1990) found that in 43 percent of the incidents, either no penalty was imposed or the company was required merely to cease engaging in the illegal practice and to return any funds gained through illegal means (for a different view, see Manson 1986).

Moreover, conviction for such illegal acts does not generally harm a person's reputation and career aspirations nearly as much as conviction for street crime would. Apparently, the label "white-collar criminal" does not carry the stigma of the label "felon convicted of a violent crime." Conflict theorists don't find such differential labelling and treatment surprising. They argue that the criminal justice system largely disregards the white-collar crimes of the affluent, while focusing on crimes often committed by the poor. If an offender holds a position of status and influence, his or her crime is treated as less serious, and the sanction is much more lenient (Maguire 1988).

Use Your Sociological Imagination

As a newspaper editor, how might you treat stories on corporate crime differently from those on violent crimes?

Victimless Crimes

White-collar or street crimes endanger people's economic or personal well-being against their will (or without their direct knowledge). By contrast, sociologists use the term ***victimless crimes*** to describe the willing exchange among adults of widely desired, but illegal, goods and services (Schur 1965, 1985).

Although the term *victimless crime* is widely used, many people object to the notion that there is no victim other than the offender in such crimes. Excessive drinking, compulsive gambling, and illegal drug use contribute to an enormous amount of personal and property damage. And feminist sociologists contend that the so-called victimless crime of prostitution, as well as the more disturbing aspects of pornography, reinforce the misconception that women are "toys" who can be treated as objects rather than as people (Flavin 1998; Jolin 1994).

Nonetheless, some activists are working to decriminalize many of these illegal practices. Supporters of decriminalization are troubled by the attempt to legislate a moral code of behaviour for adults. In their view, it is impossible to prevent prostitution, gambling, and other victimless crimes. The already overburdened criminal justice system should instead devote its resources to "street crimes" and other offences with obvious victims. However, opponents of decriminalization insist that such offences do indeed have victims, in the sense that they can bring harm to innocent people. For example, a person with a drinking problem can become abusive to a spouse or children; a compulsive gambler or drug user may steal to pursue the obsession. According to critics of decriminalization, society must not give tacit approval to conduct that has such harmful consequences (National Advisory Commission on Criminal Justice 1976; Schur 1968, 1985).

The controversy over decriminalization reminds us of the important insights of labelling and conflict theories presented earlier. Underlying this debate are two interesting questions: Who has the power to define gambling, prostitution, and public drunkenness as "crimes"? And who has the power to label such behaviours as "victimless"? It is generally the government and, in some cases, the police and the courts.

Again, we can see that criminal law is not simply a universal standard of behaviour agreed on by all members of society. Rather, it reflects the struggle among competing individuals and groups to gain governmental support for their particular moral and social values. For example, such organizations as Mothers Against Drunk Driving (MADD) and Students Against Drunk Driving (SADD) have had success in recent years in modifying public attitudes toward drunkenness. Rather than being viewed as a victimless crime, drunkenness is increasingly being associated with the potential dangers of driving while under the influence of alcohol. As a result, the mass media are giving greater (and more critical) attention to people who are guilty of drunk driving, and many provincial and territorial governments have instituted more severe fines and jail terms for a wide variety of alcohol-related offences.

Crime Statistics

Crime statistics are not as accurate as social scientists would like. However, since they deal with an issue of grave concern to people in many countries, they are frequently cited as if they were completely reliable. Such data do serve as an indicator of police activity, as well as an approximate indication of the level of certain crimes. Yet it would be a mistake to interpret these data as an exact representation of the incidence of crime.

Public opinion polls reveal that Canadians believe the rate of crime is increasing in this country, despite the release of statistics that indicate the national crime rate has been on a downward trend since 1991 (Statistics Canada 2003b). In 2002, the rate of violent crime in Canada dropped 2 percent; the rate of attempted murder fell 6 percent over the previous year, while homicides rose 4 percent after remaining stable the previous two years (Statistics Canada 2003b).

Within Canada, vast regional differences exist in rates of crime. As Figure 7-1 illustrates, in 2003, the territories' crime rates were the highest, followed by Saskatchewan, Manitoba and British Columbia, Ontario, Newfoundland and Labrador, and Quebec had the lowest rates of crime in the country. In 2002, rates of violent crimes decreased, driven by a 3 percent decline in the rate of robberies and a 2 percent decline in the rate of assaults (Statistics Canada 2003b). Before 1993, the violent crime rate had increased each year since 1977. In 2000, the rates of violent crime were approximately the same as they were in 1990; however, they are 54 percent higher than in 1970 (Statistics Canada 2001b).

Canada's crime rates are significantly lower than those of our American neighbours, particularly for violent crimes, such as homicide, for which the American rate is more than three times greater than that for Canada (A. Nelson and Fleras 1995). Research has shown, however, that Canadian and American rates converge in the area of spousal assault, showing that "Canadian men are just as, if not more, likely to beat their spouses as American men" (DeKeseredy and Schwartz 1998:vii).

International comparisons aside, results from the Canadian National Survey on woman abuse on campus reveal that it is not only women in marital or cohabiting relationships who are in danger of abuse, but also those at postsecondary institutions who are in dating relationships (DeKeseredy and Schwartz 1998). Despite the fact that women attending postsecondary institutions in Canada are most likely to be sexually assaulted not only by men they know but also by men who might actually like them, and that the assault is most likely to take place in a private location, they fear "stranger danger" (DeKeseredy and Schwartz 1998). Table 7-4 illustrates the perception of safety of 1835 Canadian female students on campuses across the country.

Sociologists have several ways of measuring crime. Historically, they have relied on official statistics, but underreporting has always been a problem with such measures. Because members of racial and ethnic minority groups have not always trusted law enforcement agencies, they have often refrained from contacting the police. Feminist sociologists and others have noted that many women do not report sexual assault or spousal abuse out of fear that officials will regard the crime as the women's fault. Partly because of the deficiencies of official statistics, ***victimization surveys*** question ordinary people, not police officers, to learn how much crime occurs.

Unfortunately, like other crime data, victimization surveys have particular limitations. They require first that victims understand what has happened to them and then that victims disclose such information to interviewers. Fraud, income tax evasion, and blackmail are examples of crimes that are unlikely to be reported in victimization studies. Even though victimization surveys have their limitations, they can be helpful in augmenting police statistics. For example, both police statistics and victimization surveys report that, although the majority of offenders of violent crimes tend to be males, victims are equally likely to be male and female (H. Johnson 1996).

International Crime Rates

If it is difficult to develop reliable crime data in Canada, it is even more difficult to make useful cross-national comparisons. Nevertheless, with some care, we can offer preliminary conclusions about how crime rates differ around the world.

During the 1980s and 1990s, violent crimes were much more common in the United States than in Canada

FIGURE 7-1

Crime Rates by Province and Territory, 2003

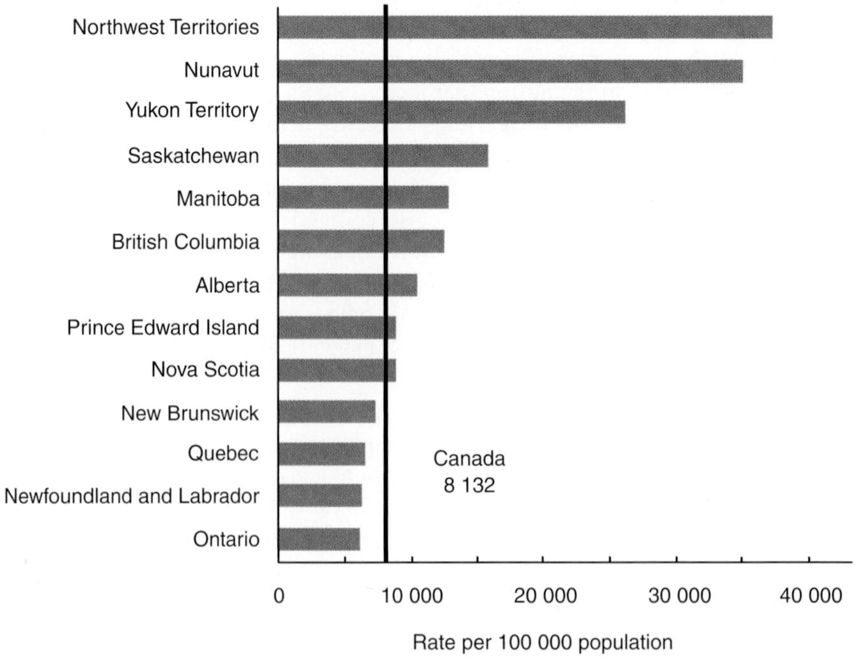

Source: Statistics Canada 2004c.

Table 7-4 Reported Feelings of Safety on Campus and Surrounding Areas of 1835 Canadian Women Postsecondary Students

Activity	% Reporting Feeling Unsafe	% Reporting Feeling Very Unsafe
Walking alone after dark	36.1	25.9
Riding a bus or streetcar alone after dark	35.7	12.9
Riding a subway alone after dark	34.8	38.7
Walking alone to a car in a parking lot after dark	42.5	25.7
Waiting for public transportation alone after dark	41.0	31.2
Walking past men they don't know while alone after dark	36.3	38.9

Source: DeKeseredy and Schwartz 1998:3; Kelly and DeKeseredy 1994.

Think about It

Do you think that women's feelings of safety on campus contribute to their overall assessment of the quality of their university?

and Western Europe. Murders, rapes, and robberies were reported to the police at much higher rates in the United States. Yet the incidence of certain other types of crime appears to be higher elsewhere. For example, England, Italy, Australia, and New Zealand all have higher rates of car theft than in the United States (Rotella 1999; Russell 1995).

Why are rates of violent crime so much higher in the United States? Although there is no simple answer to this question, sociologist Elliot Currie (1985, 1998) has suggested that American society places greater emphasis on individual economic achievement than do other societies. At the same time, many observers have noted that the culture of the United States has long tolerated, if not condoned, many forms of violence. When coupled with sharp disparities between poor and affluent citizens, significant unemployment, and substantial alcohol and drug abuse, all these factors combine to produce a climate conducive to crime.

There are, however, disturbing increases in violent crime evident in other Western societies. For example, crime in Russia has skyrocketed since the overthrow of communist party rule (with its strict controls on guns and criminals) in 1991. Whereas there were fewer than 260 homicides in Moscow in 1978 and again in 1988, there are now more than 1000 homicides per year. Organized crime has filled a power vacuum in Moscow since the end of communism; one result is that gangland shootouts and premeditated "contract hits" have become more common. Some prominent reformist politicians have been targeted as well. Russia is the only nation in the world that incarcerates a higher proportion of its citizens than the United States. Russia imprisons 580 per 100 000 of its adults on a typical day compared with 550 in the United States, 150 in Canada, fewer than 100 in Mexico or Britain, and only 16 in Greece (Currie 1998; Shinkai and Zvekic 1999).

SOCIAL POLICY AND SOCIAL CONTROL: Illicit Drug Use in Canada

The Issue

Vancouver spends more money per capita in dealing with illicit drugs than any other city in Canada (Bula 2000). In 2000, then mayor of Vancouver Philip Owen claimed that although Vancouver's drug problem is so well-known and has been highlighted in many media reports, it does not mean that other big cities are not struggling with the same concerns. Owen stated: "Everyone has a drug problem, all the big-city mayors have talked about this. Every single one is looking for solutions. But nobody is prepared to stand up to the plate" (Bula 2000). In response to this problem, Vancouver authorities devised a drug strategy and harm-reduction plan. According to the former mayor, this is an "international crisis," and cities such as Yokohama, Japan, and Seattle, Washington, have asked for a copy of Vancouver's drug strategy (Bula 2000).

The Setting

National surveys have shown that in Canada, people living in British Columbia were most likely to report the personal use of illicit substances (A. Nelson and Fleras 1995). The drug "problem" is particularly apparent in Vancouver's Downtown Eastside, an area that is the poorest in all of Canada and that houses some of the most severe social, economic, and health problems in the country. The death rate in the area is high because of the growing incidence of hepatitis C and HIV, acquired through intravenous-injection drug use. Activities, such as youth prostitution and panhandling, become the means through which addicts can sustain their addiction.

Sociological Insights

Functionalists view alienation and anomie to be the cause of many forms of addiction, including alcohol and drug addiction (A. Nelson and Fleras 1995). The activities of addicts, according to functionalist theorists, have functional consequences for society. For example, they demonstrate the boundaries of so-called "rule-breaking behaviour" and they create social agreement and cohesion regarding unacceptable behaviours.

Conflict theorists, in contrast, ask the questions "Who benefits?" and "Why is it that some drug users receive the label 'addict,' while other users do not?" Conflict thinkers argue that the state and its various agencies, such as prisons, police, and rehabilitation programs, serve to benefit from such labels because they create employment for correction officers, police officers, social workers, and counsellors. They also address the reasons why society does not label those addicted to prescription drugs and "legal" drugs, such as tobacco, in the same manner as it labels and scapegoats those addicted to such drugs as cocaine and heroin.

Feminist approaches to addiction are as diverse as feminist theories themselves. Some argue that for women, addiction grows out of their overall status of subordination in society; that is, that women's powerlessness leads to various forms of self-destructive escapes, such as drug use (Lundy 1991). Other feminist theories argue that the concept of gender and the various related roles and behaviours deny both men and women full expression of their own humanity; addiction becomes a metaphor for the gender stereotypes in our society (A. Nelson and Fleras 1995).

Interactionist approaches frame drug addiction in the context of continual action on the part of the drug addict and reaction on the part of those around her or him. They stress the process through which the person is identified as an "addict" and the impact that this label has on her or his sense of self. Goffman's dramaturgical approach is an example of this process of individual action and social reaction, in which the individual plays many roles, as would an actor. The drug addict, for example, may play one role in dealing with the police (for example, presenting himself or herself as someone trying to get "clean") while presenting a different image to peers.

Policy Initiatives

Vancouver's drug strategy and harm-reduction plan is the first of its kind in North America. It shifts the focus away from drug use as a criminal activity and toward drug use as a health and safety issue; under the plan, users would receive treatment rather than jail terms and special treatment beds would be allocated to young users.

The drug strategy and harm-reduction plan, similar to those implemented in many European cities, is based on a four-pillar approach:

1. **Enforcement.** This pillar includes a pilot drug-treatment court that would weigh various options of treatment, an increase in the police drug and organized-crime squads to target larger dealers, and the creation of a "drug action team" that would respond to neighbourhood drug issues.
2. **Harm reduction.** This notion encompasses the creation of an overdose-death prevention campaign, the provision of short-term shelter and housing for drug users on the street, and the establishment of street-drug testing.
3. **Treatment.** The treatment element of the plan would provide treatment beds for young people outside the Downtown Eastside; special treatment for women who are pregnant and/or have children; needle exchanges in primary health care clinics, hospitals, and pharmacies; pilot day centres for addicts; and different kinds of housing for users and those trying to go clean.

4. **Prevention.** This pillar of the plan would give communities and neighbourhoods more power to combat drug abuse and to develop a pilot citywide school curriculum on drugs and drug abuse.

As part of its harm-reduction strategy, in 2003 Vancouver opened its first safe injection site—a facility where people with addictions can safely inject drugs in a clean, sterile environment rather than on the streets with needles that may be dirty. This site is the first of its kind in North America and, as a consequence, the whole world has been watching. In 2004, the International Narcotics Board—an independent U.N. organization—criticized the Vancouver safe injection site, claiming that it violated international drug treatises. The current mayor of Vancouver, Larry Campbell, dismissed the Board's criticisms, stating that, because of its overwhelming U.S. funding, the Board simply reflects the American policy on the "war on drugs," which does not embrace the principle or practice of harm reduction.

Applying Theory

1. How might conflict sociologists explain why certain drugs, and the individuals who use them, have been treated so differently?
2. According to functionalist perspectives, what functions might drug or alcohol addiction have in society?

CHAPTER RESOURCES

Summary

Conformity and *deviance* are two ways in which people respond to real or imagined pressures from others. In this chapter, we examined the relationship among conformity, deviance, and mechanisms of social control.

1. A society uses ***social control*** to bring about acceptance of basic norms.
2. Stanley Milgram defined ***conformity*** as going along with our peers; ***obedience*** is defined as compliance with higher authorities in a hierarchical structure.
3. Some norms are so important to a society they are formalized into laws. Socialization is a primary source of conforming and obedient behaviour, including obedience to law.
4. Deviant behaviour violates social norms. Some forms of deviance carry a negative social ***stigma,*** while other forms are more or less accepted.
5. From a functionalist point of view, ***deviance*** and its consequences help to define the limits of proper behaviour.
6. Interactionists maintain that we *learn* criminal behaviour from interactions with others (***cultural transmission***). They also stress that for crime to occur, there has to be a convergence of motivated offenders and suitable targets of crime (***routine activities theory***).
7. The theory of ***differential association*** holds that deviance results from exposure to attitudes favourable to criminal acts.
8. An important aspect of ***labelling theory*** is the recognition that some people are *viewed* as deviant while others engaged in the same behaviour are not.
9. The conflict perspective views laws and punishments as reflecting the interests of the powerful.
10. ***Crime*** represents a deviation from formal social norms administered by the state.
11. Sociologists differentiate among ***professional crime, organized crime, white-collar crime,*** and ***victimless crimes*** (such as drug use and prostitution).
12. Crime statistics are among the least reliable social data, partly because so many crimes are not reported to law enforcement agencies.
13. Harm-reduction plans shift the focus away from drug use as a criminal activity toward drug use as a health and safety issue.

Critical Thinking Questions

1. What mechanisms of formal and informal social control are evident in your university or college classes and in day-to-day life and social interactions at your school?
2. What approach to deviance do you find most persuasive: that of functionalists, conflict theorists, interactionists, labelling theorists, or feminist theorists? Why is this approach more convincing than the others? What are the main weaknesses of each approach?
3. Rates of violent crime are lower than in Canada, Western Europe, Australia, and New Zealand than in the United States. Draw on as many of the theories discussed in the chapter as possible to explain why Canada is such a comparably less violent society.
4. Why do you think a computer hacker might be viewed differently from a person who commits a break and enter or steals something from Wal-Mart?

Key Terms

Anomie theory of deviance Robert Merton's theory that explains deviance as an adaptation either of socially prescribed goals or of the norms governing their attainment, or both. (page 145)

Conformity Going along with peers, individuals of a person's own status who have no special right to direct that person's behaviour. (138)

Control theory A view of conformity and deviance that suggests that our connection to members of society leads us to systematically conform to society's norms. (141)

Crime A violation of criminal law for which some governmental authority applies formal penalties. (151)

Cultural transmission A school of criminology that argues that criminal behaviour is learned through social interactions. (147)

Deviance Behaviour that violates the standards of conduct or expectations of a group or society. (142)

Differential association A theory of deviance proposed by Edwin Sutherland that holds that violation of rules results from exposure to attitudes favourable to criminal acts. (147)

Formal social control Social control carried out by authorized agents, such as police officers, judges, school administrators, and employers. (140)

Informal social control Social control carried out casually by ordinary people through such means as laughter, smiles, and ridicule. (139)

Labelling theory An approach to deviance that attempts to explain why certain people are viewed as deviants while others engaging in the same behaviour are not. (149)

Obedience Compliance with higher authorities in a hierarchical structure. (138)

Organized crime The work of a group that regulates relations among various criminal enterprises involved in the smuggling and sale of drugs, prostitution, gambling, and other illegal activities. (152)

Professional criminal A person who pursues crime as a day-to-day occupation, developing skilled techniques and enjoying a certain degree of status among other criminals. (151)

Routine activities theory The notion that criminal victimization increases when there is a convergence of motivated offenders and suitable targets. (148)

Social constructionist perspective An approach to deviance that emphasizes the role of culture in the creation of the deviant identity. (149)

Social control The techniques and strategies for preventing deviant human behaviour in any society. (136)

Societal-reaction approach Another name for *labelling theory*. (149)

Stigma A label used to devalue members of deviant social groups. (143)

Victimization surveys Questionnaires or interviews used to determine whether people have been victims of crime. (154)

Victimless crime A term used by sociologists to describe the willing exchange among adults of widely desired, but illegal, goods and services. (153)

White-collar crime Crimes committed by affluent individuals or corporations in the course of their daily business activities. (152)

Additional Readings

Boritch, Helen. 1997. *Fallen Woman: Female Crime and Criminal Justice in Canada.* Toronto: ITP Nelson. A comprehensive account and interpretation of rates of female crime in Canada and the treatment of female crime in the criminal justice system.

DeKeseredy, Walter S., and Martin D. Schwartz. 1998. *Women Abuse on Campus: Results from the Canadian Nationl Survey.* Thousand Oaks, CA: Sage Publications. This volume provides the results of a national survey on the abuse of women on Canadian postsecondary campuses. The authors expose a "hidden campus curriculum" that contributes to the perpetuation of gender inequality.

Finkenauer, James O., and Patricia W. Gavin. 1999. *Scared Straight: The Panacea Phenomenon Revisited.* Prospect Heights, IL: Waveland Press. A critical look at programs in which prisoners speak to juveniles in an effort to scare them away from crime. Drawing on data from both the United States and Norway, the authors find such programs have had little success but remain immensely popular with the general public.

Gamson, Joshua. 1998. *Freaks Talk Back: Tabloid Talk Shows and Sexual Nonconformity.* Chicago: University of Chicago Press. A sociologist looks at the presentation of socially dysfunctional or stigmatized behaviours on television talk shows.

Online Learning Centre

Visit the *Sociology: A Brief Introduction* Online Learning Centre at www.mcgrawhill.ca/college/schaefer to access quizzes, interactive exercises, video clips, and other research and study tools related to this chapter.

Reel Society Interactive Movie CD-ROM 2.0

Reel Society 2.0 can be used to spark discussion about the following topics from this chapter:

- Conformity and obedience
- Informal and formal social control
- Deviance
- Discretionary justice

chapter 8

STRATIFICATION IN CANADA AND WORLDWIDE

"Life is beautiful—if you don't look too closely" is the message in UNICEF's poster, which calls attention to the 250 million victims of forced child labour throughout the world. A highly stratified society, widespread poverty, unequal life chances, and a global economy all contribute to the use of child labour.

Instantly recognized throughout the world, the *Nike swoosh* sometimes seems to be everywhere—on shirts and caps and pants. The icon is no longer confined to shoes as sponsorship deals have plastered the *swoosh* across jerseys and sporting arenas of all manner, from basketball to football to volleyball to track to soccer to tennis to hockey. *Nike*'s growth strategy is based on penetrating new markets in apparel while making acquisitions in sporting goods. The value of the *swoosh* now runs so deep that visitors to remote, rural, and impoverished regions of the Third World report finding peasants sewing crude *swoosh* imitations onto shirts and caps, not for the world market but for local consumption. . . . As the *Nike* symbol has grown ascendant in the marketplace of images, *Nike* has become the sign some people love to love and the sign others love to hate. . . .

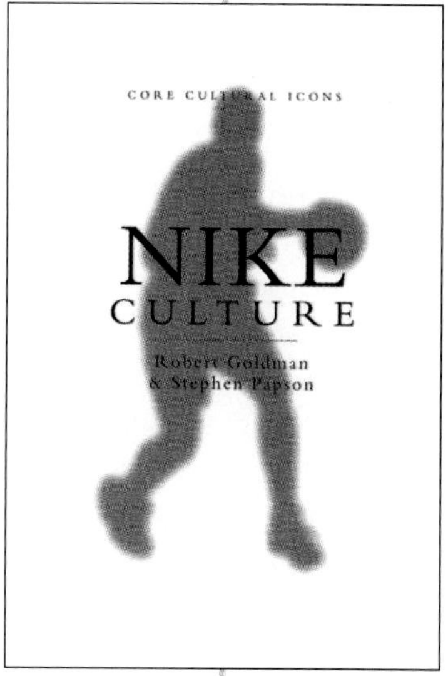

Nike is a transnational corporation that links national economies into a complex web of global production arrangement. . . . Almost all production of shoes, apparel and accessories is outsourced to contract suppliers in developing nations while the home office in Beaverton, Oregon, designs, develops, and markets the branded goods. . . .

It is very difficult to compete in today's athletic footwear industry without engaging in the outsourcing of labour to relatively unskilled labourers in impoverished nations. Companies in the athletic footwear industry depend on the existence of poor Asian nations where there is a ready surplus of labour force in need of work and wages, even if those wages are below the poverty line. . . .

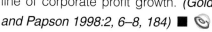

Nike speaks the language of universal rights, concern for children, transcendence over the categories of age, race, gender, disability or any social stereotype. As moral philosophy, its images speak out against racism, sexism, and ageism. *Nike*'s imagery celebrates sport, athletic activity, and play as universally rewarding categories. Playing makes for healthier, more productive citizens, and better self-actualized human beings. However, no matter what its imagery suggests, *Nike,* like any other capitalist firm, must operate within the relationships and constraints of competitive capitalist marketplaces. No matter how many P.L.A.Y. commercials *Nike* runs on TV, there will still be haunting images of production practices in Pakistan, Indonesia, and Vietnam. As the world grows more unified, it becomes increasingly difficult to suppress entirely those gaps between image and practice, between humanism and capitalism, between moral philosophy and the bottom line of corporate profit growth. ***(Goldman and Papson 1998:2, 6–8, 184)*** ■

As sociologists Robert Goldman and Stephen Papson note in their book *Nike Culture,* the Nike symbol (the swoosh) and philosophy ("Just do it") have swept the world. People in all parts of the globe pay up to hundreds of dollars for a pair of Air Jordan shoes, and teams in all kinds of sporting arenas wear the Nike logo. Unfortunately, there is another side to Nike's global dominance. Its products are made in harsh sweatshop conditions for very little compensation, mostly in the developing nations. One group critical of Nike's practices claimed in 1996 that the 45 Indonesian workers who participated in making a $70 pair of Air Pegasus shoes shared a total of $1.60. Other stories of Vietnamese and Chinese women who are subject to health and safety hazards, pitifully underpaid, and physically harassed by shop floor managers have also helped to fuel concern about human rights violations.

This concern has recently given rise to such organizations as Students Against Sweatshops—Canada, based on university campuses across the country. Because this is an issue that combines women's rights, immigrant rights, environmental concerns, and human rights, it has linked disparate groups on campus. Nike is not their only target. Many apparel manufacturers contract out their production to take advantage of cheap labour and overhead costs. The student movement—ranging from sit-ins and "knit-ins" to demonstrations and building occupations—has been aimed at ridding campus stores of all products made in sweatshops, both at home and abroad. Pressed by their students, many colleges and universities have agreed to adopt anti-sweatshop codes governing the products they make and stock on campus. And Nike and Reebok, partly in response to student protests, have raised the wages of some 100 000 workers in their Indonesian factories (to about 20 cents an hour—still far below what is needed to raise a family) (Appelbaum and Dreier 1999; Global Alliance for Workers and Communities 2001).

The global corporate culture of the apparel industry focuses our attention on worldwide social stratification—on the enormous gap between wealthy nations and poorer nations. In many respects, the wealth of rich nations depends on the poverty of poor nations. As Figure 8-1 shows, people in industrialized societies benefit when they buy consumer goods made by low-wage workers in developing countries. And yet the low wages workers earn in multinational factories are comparatively high for those countries.

Ever since people first began to speculate about the nature of human society, their attention has been drawn to the differences between individuals and groups within any society. The term ***social inequality*** describes a condition in which members of a society have different amounts of wealth, prestige, or power. Some degree of social inequality characterizes every society.

When a system of social inequality is based on a hierarchy of groups, sociologists refer to it as ***stratification:*** a structured ranking of entire groups of people that perpetuates unequal economic rewards and power in a society. These unequal rewards are evident not only in the distribution of wealth and income but also in the distressing mortality rates of impoverished communities. Stratification involves the ways in which one generation passes on social inequalities to the next, thereby producing groups of people arranged in rank order from low to high.

Stratification is a crucial subject of sociological investigation because of its pervasive influence on human interactions and institutions. It inevitably results in social inequality because certain groups of people stand higher in social rankings, control scarce resources, wield power, and receive special treatment. As we will see in this chapter, the consequences of stratification are evident in the unequal distribution of wealth and income within industrial societies. The term ***income*** refers to salaries and wages. By contrast, ***wealth*** is an inclusive term encompassing all of a person's material assets, including land, stocks, and other types of property.

Do you think that social inequality is an inevitable part of any society? How do you think government policy affects the life chances of the working poor? How are wealth and income distributed, and how much opportunity does the average worker have to move up the social ladder? What economic and political conditions explain the divide between rich nations and poor? This chapter focuses on the unequal distribution of socially valued rewards and its consequences. We will examine three general systems of stratification, paying particular attention to the theories of Karl Marx and

FIGURE 8-1

The Sweat behind the Shirt

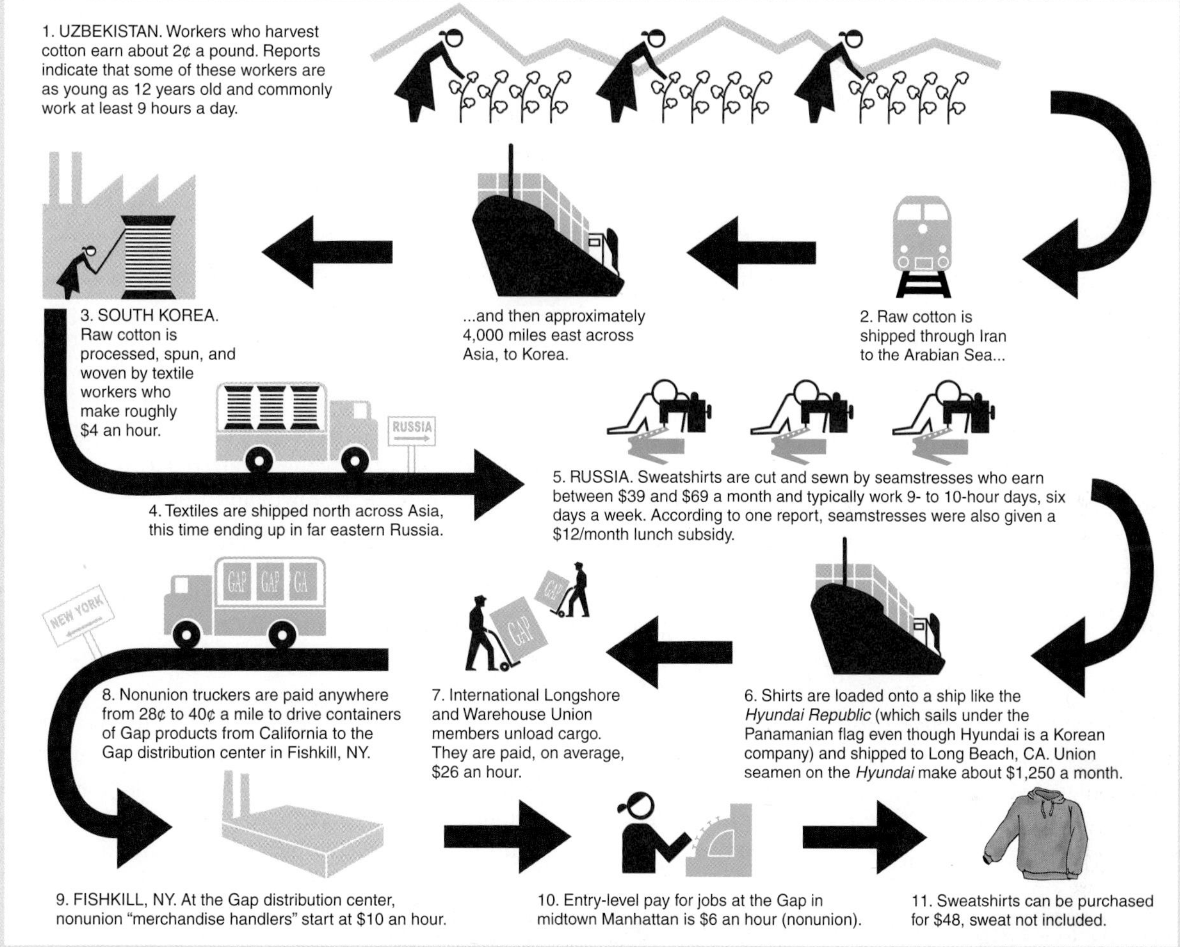
1. UZBEKISTAN. Workers who harvest cotton earn about 2¢ a pound. Reports indicate that some of these workers are as young as 12 years old and commonly work at least 9 hours a day.
2. Raw cotton is shipped through Iran to the Arabian Sea...
...and then approximately 4,000 miles east across Asia, to Korea.
3. SOUTH KOREA. Raw cotton is processed, spun, and woven by textile workers who make roughly $4 an hour.
RUSSIA
4. Textiles are shipped north across Asia, this time ending up in far eastern Russia.
5. RUSSIA. Sweatshirts are cut and sewn by seamstresses who earn between $39 and $69 a month and typically work 9- to 10-hour days, six days a week. According to one report, seamstresses were also given a $12/month lunch subsidy.
6. Shirts are loaded onto a ship like the *Hyundai Republic* (which sails under the Panamanian flag even though Hyundai is a Korean company) and shipped to Long Beach, CA. Union seamen on the *Hyundai* make about $1,250 a month.
GAP
7. International Longshore and Warehouse Union members unload cargo. They are paid, on average, $26 an hour.
NEW YORK
GAP GAP GA
8. Nonunion truckers are paid anywhere from 28¢ to 40¢ a mile to drive containers of Gap products from California to the Gap distribution center in Fishkill, NY.
9. FISHKILL, NY. At the Gap distribution center, nonunion "merchandise handlers" start at $10 an hour.
10. Entry-level pay for jobs at the Gap in midtown Manhattan is $6 an hour (nonunion).
11. Sweatshirts can be purchased for $48, sweat not included.

Source: Gordon, Jesse, and Knickerbocker 2001.

Think about It

To what extent does the affluence people in Canada enjoy depend on the labour of workers in less-developed countries?

Max Weber, as well as to functionalist, interactionist, conflict, and feminists theories. We will see how sociologists define social class and examine the consequences of stratification for people's wealth and income, health, and educational opportunities. And we will confront the question of social mobility, both upward and downward. We will consider who controls the world marketplace and examine the trend toward modernization. Then we will focus on stratification *within* nations. Finally, in the social policy section, we will address the issue of welfare reform in both North America and Europe. ■

Use Your Sociological Imagination www.mcgrawhill.ca/college/schaefer

What might some feminist theorists contribute to a discussion on the ways in which Nike operates in the global marketplace? How might conflict thinkers conceptualize the practices of Nike in this so-called "complex web of global production"? How might a functionalist sociologist interpret the practices of Nike, and other transnational corporations, in terms of the economic conditions workers face in such countries as Pakistan, Indonesia, and Vietnam?

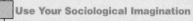

UNDERSTANDING STRATIFICATION

Systems of Stratification

Look at the three general systems of stratification examined here—slavery, castes, and social classes—as ideal types useful for purposes of analysis. Any stratification system may include elements of more than one type.

To understand these systems better, it may be helpful to review the distinction between *achieved status* and *ascribed status,* described in Chapter 5. pp. 96–97 Ascribed status is a social position "assigned" to a person without regard for that person's unique characteristics or talents. By contrast, achieved status is a social position attained by a person largely through his or her own effort. The two are closely linked. The nation's most affluent families generally inherit wealth and status, while many members of racial and ethnic minorities inherit disadvantaged status. Age and gender, as well, are ascribed statuses that influence a person's wealth and social position.

Slavery

The most extreme form of legalized social inequality for individuals or groups is ***slavery.*** What distinguishes this oppressive system of stratification is that enslaved individuals are *owned* by other people. They treat these human beings as property, just as if they were household pets or appliances.

Slavery has varied in the way it has been practised. In ancient Greece, the main sources of slaves were captives of war and piracy. Although succeeding generations could inherit slave status, it was not necessarily permanent. A person's status might change depending on which city-state happened to triumph in a military conflict. In effect, all citizens had the potential of becoming slaves or of being granted freedom, depending on the circumstances of history. By contrast, in the United States and Latin America, where slavery was an ascribed status, racial and legal barriers prevented the freeing of slaves. As Box 8-1 shows, millions of people still live as slaves around the world.

Castes

Castes are hereditary systems of rank, usually religiously dictated, that tend to be fixed and immobile. The caste system is generally associated with Hinduism in India and other countries. In India there are four major castes, called *varnas.* A fifth category, referred to as *untouchables,* is considered to be so lowly and unclean as to have no place within this system of stratification. There are also many minor castes. Caste membership is an ascribed status (at birth, children automatically assume the same position as their parents). Each caste is quite sharply defined, and members are expected to marry within that caste.

Caste membership generally determines a person's occupation or role as a religious functionary. An example of a lower caste in India is the *Dons,* whose main work is the undesirable job of cremating bodies. The caste system promotes a remarkable degree of differentiation. Thus, the single caste of chauffeurs has been split into two separate subcastes: drivers of luxury cars have a higher status than drivers of economy cars.

In recent decades, industrialization and urbanization have taken their toll on India's rigid caste system. Many villagers have moved to urban areas where their low-caste status is unknown. Schools, hospitals, factories, and public transportation facilitate contacts between different castes that were previously avoided at all costs. In addition, the government has tried to reform the caste system. India's constitution, adopted in 1950, includes a provision abolishing discrimination against untouchables, who had traditionally been excluded from temples, schools, and most forms of employment. Yet the

Jacob Lawrence's painting, *Harriet Tubman* Series No. 9, graphically illustrates the torment of slavery. Slavery is the most extreme form of legalized social inequality.

Sociology in the Global Community 8-1 Slavery in the Twenty-First Century

Around the world, at least 27 million people were still enslaved at the beginning of the twenty-first century. And yet the 1948 Universal Declaration of Human Rights, which is supposedly binding on all members of the United Nations, holds that "No one shall be held in slavery or servitude; slavery and the slave trade shall be prohibited in all their forms" (Masland 1992:30, 32).

Canada considers any person a slave who is unable to withdraw his or her labour voluntarily from an employer. In many parts of the world, bonded labourers are imprisoned in virtual lifetime employment as they struggle to repay small debts. In other places human beings are owned outright.

The Swiss-based human rights group Christian Solidarity International has focused worldwide attention on the plight of slaves in the African nation of Sudan. The organization solicits funds and uses them to buy slaves their freedom—at about $50 a slave.

Although contemporary slavery may be most obvious in developing countries, it also afflicts the industrialized nations of the West. Throughout Europe, guest workers and maids are employed by masters who hold their passports, subject them to degrading working conditions, and threaten them with deportation if they protest. Similar tactics are used to essentially imprison young women from Eastern Europe and Asia who have been brought (through deceptive promises) to work in the sex industries of Canada, Belgium, France, Germany, Greece, the Netherlands, and Switzerland.

Within Canada and other developed countries, illegal immigrants are forced to labour for years under terrible conditions, either to pay off debts or to avoid being turned over to immigration authorities. Estimates of the number of women brought into Canada as forced sex workers in 2000 vary from 8000 to 16 000.

Applying Theory

1. According to conflict theorists, why are many bonded labourers around the world in the position of slaves?
2. What explanations might some feminist sociologists have for the varying incidence rates of forced sex work from one country to another?

Sources: Fisher 1999; France 2000; Jacobs 2001; Masland 1992; Richard 2000.

caste system prevails, and its impact is now evident in electoral politics, as various political parties compete for the support of frustrated untouchable voters who constitute one-third of India's electorate. For the first time, India has someone from an untouchable background serving in the symbolic but high-status position of president. Meanwhile, however, dozens of low-caste people continue to be killed for overstepping their lowly status in life (Dugger 1999; Schmetzer 1999).

Social Classes

A ***class system*** is a social ranking based primarily on economic position in which achieved characteristics can influence social mobility. In contrast to slavery and caste systems, the boundaries between classes are imprecisely defined, and people can move from one stratum, or level, of society to another. Even so, class systems maintain stable stratification hierarchies and patterns of class divisions, and they, too, are marked by unequal distribution of wealth and power.

Income inequality is a basic characteristic of a class system. In 2000, the median household income in Canada was $55 000. In other words, half of all households had higher incomes in that year and half had lower incomes. Yet this fact may not fully convey the income disparities in our society. In 2000, Canadian families in the top 10 percent of income accounted for 28 percent of total family income, while families in the bottom 10 percent earned less than 2 percent of total family income (Statistics Canada 2003c). Canada's rich are getting richer, with their collective net worth reaching an all-time high of $130 billion in 2004 (Horsey 2004). These one hundred individuals include Michael Lazaridis and James Balsillie, co-founders of Research and Motion; Jeff Skoll of eBay; and Galen Weston of George Weston Ltd., which controls the Loblaw supermarket chain. In stark contrast to this increase in wealth among the wealthy, the rate of child poverty in Canada increased in 2002, bringing the number of children who live in poverty to 1 065 000 or nearly one in six (Campaign 2000 2004).

The people with the highest incomes, generally those heading private companies, earn well above even affluent wage earners. Figure 8-2 shows the average annual pay package for CEOs (chief executive officers) in many industrial countries. The compensation CEOs receive is not necessarily linked to conventional measures of success. For example, the U.S. economy worsened in 2002, an analysis showed that the CEOs who received the

FIGURE 8-2

Around the World: What's a CEO Worth?

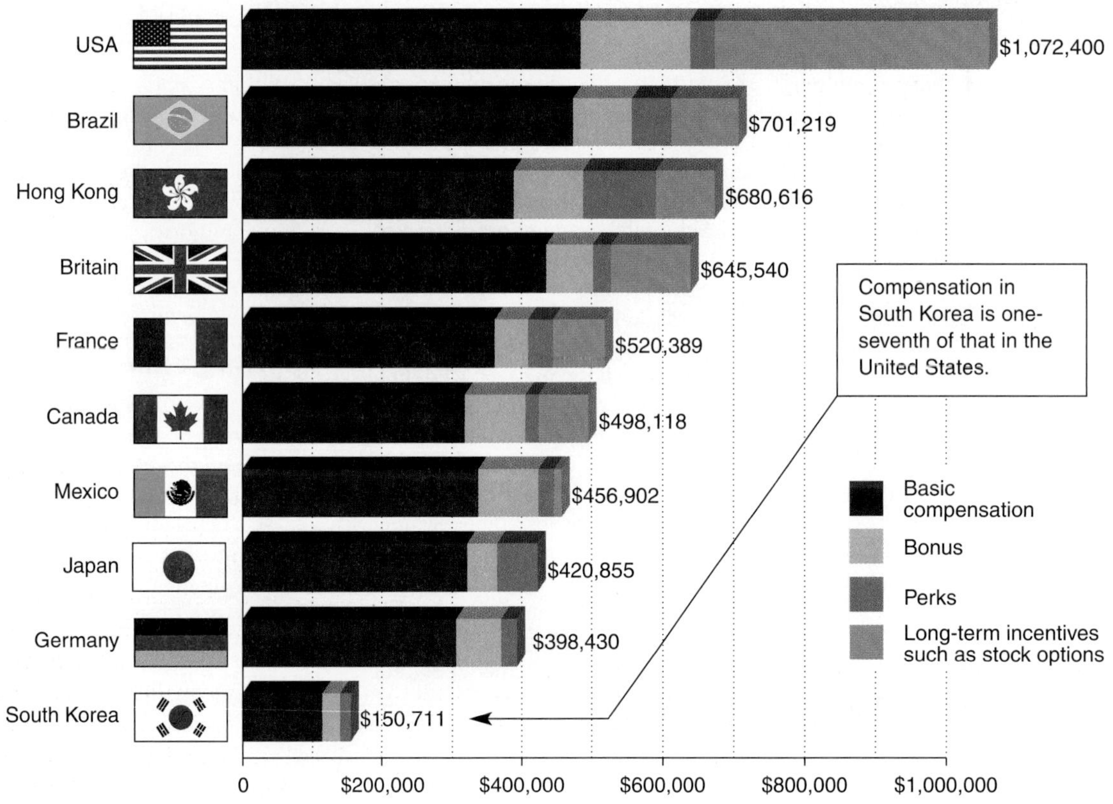

Source: Towers Perrin in Bryant 1999: Section 4, p. 1.

Note: The average annual pay package of the chief executive officer (CEO) of an industrial company with annual revenues of $250 million to $500 million in 10 countries. Figures are from April 1998 and are not weighted to compensate for different costs of living or levels of taxation.

Think about It

Why are CEOs in the United States "worth" more than those in other countries?

highest compensation were generally those who authorized the largest layoffs (Klinger et al. 2002).

A 2004 study conducted by Leger Marketing, on behalf of Amex Canada, revealed some characteristics of wealthy or affluent Canadians, defined as those with annual household incomes or investable assets of $200 000 or more (*The Globe and Mail* 2004a):

- Affluent Canadians take, on average, three vacations a year, expecting to pay $2000 per person.
- Affluent Canadians dine out, on average, seven times per month.
- Thirty-nine percent of affluent Canadians own two properties.
- Twenty-five percent of affluent Canadians send their children to private schools.
- Twenty-five percent of affluent Canadians belong to private clubs (e.g., golf, tennis).
- Forty percent of affluent Canadians have home theatres.

Statistics reflecting personal wealth or *net worth* (assets minus debts) demonstrate an enormous gap between the richest 10 percent and the poorest 10 percent of Canadian families. In 1999, for example, the poorest 10 percent of Canadian families had an average net worth of –$7110 (meaning that they owed more than they owned), while the richest 10 percent had an average net worth of $1 059 423 (Statistics Canada 2001c). What is most distressing about this disparity is that the poorest 10 percent control –0.6 percent of the total wealth of Canadian families, while the richest 10 percent control 55.7 percent of the total wealth.

Studies show that wealthy Canadians take, on average, three vacations a year. Their expensive lifestyle underscores the unequal distribution of wealth and power in Canada.

Both of these groups, at opposite ends of the nation's economic hierarchy, reflect the importance of ascribed status and achieved status. Ascribed statuses, such as race, gender, and class, clearly influence a person's wealth and social position. And sociologist Richard Jenkins (1991) has researched how the ascribed status of having a disability marginalizes people in society. People with disabilities are particularly vulnerable to unemployment, are often poorly paid, and in many cases are on the lower rung of occupational ladders. Regardless of their actual performance on the job, people with disabilities are stigmatized as not "earning their keep." Such are the effects of ascribed status.

Social class is one of the independent or explanatory variables most frequently used by social scientists to shed light on social issues. In later chapters, we will analyze the relationships between social class and divorce patterns (Chapter 11), religious behaviour (Chapter 12), and formal schooling (Chapter 12), as well as other relationships in which social class is a variable.

Theoretical Perspectives on Social Stratification

Must some members of society receive greater rewards than others? Do people need to feel socially and economically superior to others? Can social life be organized without structured inequality? These questions have been debated for centuries, especially among political activists. Utopian socialists, religious minorities, and members of recent countercultures have all attempted to establish communities that, to some extent or other, would abolish inequality in social relationships.

Social science research has found that inequality exists in all societies—even the simplest. For example, when anthropologist Gunnar Landtman ([1938] 1968) studied the Kiwai Papuans of New Guinea, he initially noticed little differentiation among them. Every man in the village did the same work and lived in similar housing. However, on closer inspection, Landtman observed that certain Papuans—the men who were warriors, harpooners, and sorcerers—were described as "a little more high" than others. By contrast, villagers who were female, unemployed, or unmarried were considered "down a little bit" and were barred from owning land.

Stratification is universal in that all societies maintain some form of social inequality among members. Depending on its values, a society may assign people to distinctive ranks based on their religious knowledge, skill in hunting, beauty, trading expertise, or ability to provide health care. But why has such inequality developed in human societies? And how much differentiation among people, if any, is actually essential?

Functionalist and conflict sociologists offer contrasting explanations for the existence and necessity of social stratification. Functionalists maintain that a differential system of rewards and punishments is necessary for the efficient operation of society. Conflict theorists argue that competition for scarce resources results in significant political, economic, and social inequality. Some feminist sociologists argue that gender and its interconnections with race, age, class, and disability come together to produce various levels of inequality in society. Interactionist sociologists focus their attention on the interactions among individuals that serve to create and maintain social inequality.

Functionalist View

Would people go to school for many years to become physicians if they could make as much money and gain as much respect working as street cleaners? Functionalists say no, which is partly why they believe that a stratified society is universal.

In the view of Kingsley Davis and Wilbert Moore (1945), society must distribute its members among a variety of social positions. It must not only make sure that these positions are filled but also see that they are staffed by people with the appropriate talents and abilities. Rewards, including money and prestige, are based on the importance of a position and the relative scarcity of qualified personnel. Yet this assessment often devalues work performed by certain segments of society, such as women's work as homemakers or in occupations traditionally filled by women, or low-status work in fast-food outlets.

Davis and Moore (1945) argue that stratification is universal and that social inequality is necessary so that people will be motivated to fill functionally important positions. But, critics say, unequal rewards are not the only means of encouraging people to fill critical positions and occupations. Personal pleasure, intrinsic satisfaction, and value orientations also motivate people to enter particular careers. Functionalists agree but note that society must use some type of reward to motivate people to enter unpleasant or dangerous jobs and jobs that require a long training period. This response does not justify stratification systems in which status is largely inherited, such as slave or caste societies. Similarly, it is difficult to explain the high salaries our society offers to professional athletes or entertainers on the basis of how critical these jobs are to the survival of society (R. Collins 1975; Kerbo 2000; Tumin 1953, 1985).

Even if stratification is inevitable, the functionalist explanation for differential rewards does not explain the wide disparity between the rich and the poor. Critics of the functionalist approach point out that the richest 10 percent of households account for 20 percent of the nation's income in Sweden, 25 percent in France, 28 percent in Canada, and 31 percent in the United States. In their view, the level of income inequality found in contemporary industrial societies cannot be defended—even though these societies have a legitimate need to fill certain key occupations (World Bank 2002:74–76).

Conflict View

Karl Marx's View of Stratification

Sociologist Leonard Beeghley (1978:1) aptly noted that "Karl Marx was both a revolutionary and a social scientist." Marx was concerned with stratification in all types of human societies, beginning with primitive agricultural tribes and continuing into feudalism. But his main focus was on the effects of economic inequality on all aspects of nineteenth-century Europe. The plight of the working class made him feel that it was imperative to strive for changes in the class structure of society.

In Marx's view, social relations during any period of history depend on who controls the primary mode of economic production, such as land or factories. Differential access to scarce resources shapes the relationship between groups. Thus, under the feudal estate system, most production was agricultural, and the land was owned by the nobility. Peasants had little choice but to work according to terms dictated by those who owned the land.

Using this type of analysis, Marx examined social relations within ***capitalism***—an economic system in which the means of production are largely in private hands and the main incentive for economic activity is the accumulation of profits (Rosenberg 1991). Marx focused on the two classes that began to emerge as the feudal estate system declined—the bourgeoisie and the proletariat. The ***bourgeoisie,*** or capitalist class, owns the means of production, such as factories and machinery, whereas the ***proletariat*** is the working class. In capitalist societies, the members of the bourgeoisie maximize profit in competition with other firms. In the process,

As popular songs and movies suggest, long-haul truck drivers take pride in their low-prestige job. According to the conflict perspective, the cultural beliefs that form a society's dominant ideology, such as the popular image of the truck driver as hero, help the wealthy to maintain their power and control at the expense of the lower classes.

they exploit workers, who must exchange their labour for subsistence wages. In Marx's view, members of each class share a distinctive culture. He was most interested in the culture of the proletariat, but he also examined the ideology of the bourgeoisie, through which it justifies its dominance over workers.

According to Marx, exploitation of the proletariat will inevitably lead to the destruction of the capitalist system because the workers will revolt. But, first, the working class must develop ***class consciousness***—a subjective awareness of common vested interests and the need for collective political action to bring about social change. Workers must often overcome what Marx termed ***false consciousness,*** or an attitude held by members of a class that does not accurately reflect its objective position. A worker with false consciousness may adopt an individualistic viewpoint toward capitalist exploitation ("*I* am being exploited by *my* boss"). By contrast, the class-conscious worker realizes that *all* workers are being exploited by the bourgeoisie and have a common stake in revolution (Vanneman and Cannon 1987).

For Karl Marx, class consciousness is part of a collective process whereby the proletariat comes to identify the bourgeoisie as the source of its oppression. Revolutionary leaders will guide the working class in its class struggle. Ultimately, the proletariat will overthrow the rule of the bourgeoisie and the government (which Marx saw as representing the interests of capitalists) and will eliminate private ownership of the means of production. In his rather utopian view, classes and oppression will cease to exist in the postrevolutionary workers' state.

How accurate were Marx's predictions? He failed to anticipate the emergence of labour unions, whose power in collective bargaining weakens the stranglehold that capitalists maintain over workers. Moreover, as contemporary conflict theorists note, he did not foresee the extent to which political liberties and relative prosperity could contribute to "false consciousness." Many people have come to view themselves as individuals striving for improvement within "free" societies with substantial mobility—rather than as downtrodden members of social classes facing a collective fate. Finally, Marx did not predict that communist party rule would be established and later overthrown in the Commonwealth of Independent States (the former Soviet Union) and throughout Eastern Europe. Still, the Marxist approach to the study of class is useful in stressing the importance of stratification as a determinant of social behaviour and the fundamental separation in many societies between two distinct groups, the rich and the poor.

The writings of Karl Marx are at the heart of conflict theory. Marx viewed history as a continuous struggle between the oppressors and the oppressed that would ultimately culminate in an egalitarian, classless society. In terms of stratification, he argued that the dominant class under capitalism manipulated the economic and political systems in order to maintain control over the exploited proletariat. Marx did not believe that stratification was inevitable, but he did see inequality and oppression as inherent in capitalism (Wright et al. 1982).

The Views of Ralf Dahrendorf

Like Marx, contemporary conflict theorists believe that human beings are prone to conflict over such scarce resources as wealth, status, and power. However, where Marx focused primarily on class conflict, more recent theorists have extended this analysis to include conflicts based on gender, race, age, and other dimensions. British sociologist Ralf Dahrendorf is one of the most influential contributors to the conflict approach.

Dahrendorf (1959) modified Marx's analysis of capitalist society to apply to *modern* capitalist societies. For Dahrendorf, social classes are groups of people who share common interests resulting from their authority relationships. In identifying the most powerful groups in society, he includes not only the bourgeoisie—the owners of the means of production—but also the managers of industry, legislators, the judiciary, heads of the government bureaucracy, and others. In that respect, Dahrendorf has merged Marx's emphasis on class conflict with Weber's recognition that power is an important element of stratification (Cuff et al. 1990).

Conflict theorists, including Dahrendorf, contend that the powerful of today, like the bourgeoisie of Marx's time, want society to run smoothly so that they can enjoy their privileged positions. Because the status quo suits those with wealth, status, and power, they have a clear interest in preventing, minimizing, or controlling societal conflict.

Max Weber's View of Stratification

Unlike Karl Marx, Max Weber insisted that no single characteristic (such as class) totally defines a person's position within the stratification system. Instead, writing in 1916, he identified three distinct components of stratification: class, status, and power (Gerth and Mills 1958).

Weber used the term ***class*** to refer to people who have a similar level of wealth and income. For example, certain workers in Canada try to support their families through minimum-wage jobs. According to Weber's definition, these wage earners constitute a class because they share the same economic position and fate. Although Weber agreed with Marx on the importance of this economic dimension of stratification, he argued that the actions of individuals and groups could not be understood *solely* in economic terms.

How does it feel to sit in the chairperson's seat? A more important question, however, is *who* gets to sit in this seat?

Weber used the term ***status group*** to refer to people who rank the same in prestige or lifestyle. An individual gains status through membership in a desirable group, such as the medical profession. But status is not the same as economic class standing. In our culture, a successful pickpocket may be in the same income class as a university professor. Yet the thief is widely regarded as a member of a low-status group, whereas the professor holds high status.

For Weber, the third major component of stratification reflects a political dimension. ***Power*** is the ability to exercise our will over others. In Canada, power stems from membership in particularly influential groups, such as corporate boards of directors, government bodies, and interest groups. Conflict theorists generally agree that two major sources of power—big business and government—are closely interrelated (see Chapter 13).

In Weber's view, then, each of us has not one rank in society but three. Our position in a stratification system reflects some combination of class, status, and power. Each factor influences the other two, and in fact the rankings on these three dimensions often tend to coincide. Pierre Trudeau came from a wealthy family, attended exclusive schools, graduated from elite universities, such as Harvard and Sorbonne, and went on to become prime minister of Canada. Like Trudeau, many people from affluent backgrounds achieve impressive status and power.

At the same time, these dimensions of stratification may operate somewhat independently in determining a person's position. Jean Chrétien had a small legal practice in Shawinigan, Quebec, but he used a political power base to work his way up into federal politics to eventually become prime minister. A widely published poet may achieve high status while earning a relatively modest income. Successful professional athletes have little power but enjoy a relatively high position in terms of class and status. To understand the workings of a culture more fully, sociologists must carefully evaluate the ways in which it distributes its most valued rewards, including wealth and income, status, and power (Duberman 1976; Gerth and Mills 1958).

One way for the powerful to maintain the status quo is to define and disseminate the society's dominant ideology. The term dominant ideology describes a set of cultural beliefs and practices that helps to maintain powerful social, economic, and political interests. For Karl Marx, the dominant ideology in a capitalist society serves the interests of the ruling class. From a conflict perspective, the social significance of the dominant ideology is that not only do a society's most powerful groups and institutions control wealth and property, but, even more important, they also control the means of producing beliefs about reality through religion, education, and the media (Abercrombie, Hill, and Turner 1980, 1990; Robertson 1988).

pp. 59–60

The powerful, such as leaders of government, also use limited social reforms to buy off the oppressed and reduce the danger of challenges to their dominance. For example, minimum wage laws and unemployment compensation unquestionably give some valuable assistance to needy men and women. Yet these reforms also serve to pacify those who might otherwise rebel. Of course, in the view of conflict theorists, such manoeuvres can never entirely eliminate conflict, since workers will continue to demand equality, and the powerful will not give up their control of society.

Conflict theorists see stratification as a major source of societal tension and conflict. They do not agree with Davis and Moore (1945) that stratification is functional for a society or that it serves as a source of stability. Rather, conflict sociologists argue that stratification will inevitably lead to instability and to social change (R. Collins 1975; Coser 1977).

Feminist Views

As described earlier, feminist sociological perspectives comprise a diverse group of viewpoints. A central belief, however, unites the various feminist perspectives: gender inequality is pervasive and women are the subordinated and dominated sex. Feminist thinkers, however, differ greatly in their views on the root causes of gender inequality; on how gender inequality manifests itself in homes, workplaces, and political arenas; and on how to address this inequality. Radical feminists, for example, place great emphasis on patriarchy—as a form of social organization and ideology. In 1971 radical feminist Kate Millet (1971:25) wrote:

pp. 14–15

> Our society . . . is a patriarchy. The fact is evident at once if one recalls that the military, industry, technology, universities, science, political offices, finances—in short, every avenue of power within our society, including the coercive force of the police, is entirely in male hands.

In effect, radical feminists maintain that gender stratification is systemic, permeating society and creating a culture in which male values and priorities prevail. Since women are excluded from this culture, they stand to be controlled and oppressed by it.

Liberal feminists, in contrast, recognize the inequality that women face but believe that it could be addressed by providing women with greater access to the public sphere and by making that sphere (i.e., workplaces) more "female friendly."

Liberal feminists, then, believe less in a systemic pattern of gender inequality and more in the necessity of approaches that would provide women with greater access to employment opportunities, upward mobility, and, eventually, economic equality.

Interactionist View

Although functionalist, conflict, and some feminist perspectives tend to use a macrosociological approach to examine social inequality, interactionist thinkers tend to be more micro in their orientation. They are interested in the "person-to-person" (Naiman 2004:19) ways in which social stratification is maintained, perhaps in the forms of interpersonal and nonverbal communication. Erving Goffman (1967) theorized on the activity of *deference*, a symbolic act that conveys appreciation from one person to another. The pattern of showing deference, in which one person is the giver and the other is the recipient, often is symbolic of the unequal power relations between the two and, thus, serves to maintain and perpetuate social inequality. For example, would an employee be more likely than an employer to open a door for the other? to call the other "Ms." or "Mr." rather than by a first name? to let the other lead in the conversation and not be prone to interrupt? Judith Rollins's study (1985) of the person-to person interactions between domestic workers and their employers, based on interviews and participant observation, showed the patterns of deference displayed between white female employers and primarily women who were members of a visible minority.

Rollins found that touching (or the absence thereof), calling the domestic workers "girls" regardless of their age, and keeping certain spatial distances were all rituals of deference that served to maintain the social class inequality between the two women.

Lenski's Viewpoint

Let's return to a question posed earlier—Is stratification universal?—and consider the sociological response. Some form of differentiation is found in every culture, from the most primitive to the most advanced industrial societies of our time. Sociologist Gerhard Lenski, in his sociocultural evolution approach, described how economic systems change as their level of technology becomes more complex, beginning with hunting and gathering and culminating eventually with industrial society. In subsistence-based, hunting-and-gathering societies, people focus on survival. Although some inequality and differentiation are evident, a stratification system based on social class does not emerge because there is no real wealth to be claimed.

p. 52

As a society advances in technology, it becomes capable of producing a considerable surplus of goods. The emergence of surplus resources greatly expands the possibilities for inequality in status, influence, and power and allows a well-defined, rigid social class system to develop. To minimize strikes, slowdowns, and industrial sabotage, the elites may share a portion of the economic surplus with the lower classes, but not enough to reduce their own power and privilege.

As Lenski argued, the allocation of surplus goods and services controlled by those with wealth, status, and power reinforces the social inequality that accompanies stratification systems. Although this reward system may once have served the overall purposes of society, as functionalists contend, the same cannot be said for the large disparities separating the haves from the have-nots in current societies. In contemporary industrial society, the degree of social and economic inequality far exceeds what is needed to provide for goods and services (Lenski 1966; Nolan and Lenski 1999).

STRATIFICATION BY SOCIAL CLASS

Measuring Social Class

We continually assess how wealthy people are by looking at the cars they drive, the houses they live in, the clothes they wear, and so on. Yet it is not so easy to locate an individual within our social hierarchies as it would be in slavery or caste systems of stratification. To determine someone's class position, sociologists generally rely on the objective method.

Objective Method

The ***objective method*** of measuring social class views class largely as a statistical category. Researchers assign individuals to social classes on the basis of criteria such as occupation, education, income, and residence. The key to the objective method is that the *researcher*, rather than the person being classified, identifies an individual's class position.

The first step in using this method is to decide what indicators or causal factors will be measured objectively, whether wealth, income, education, or occupation. The prestige ranking of occupations has proved to be a useful indicator of a person's class position. For one thing, it is much easier to determine accurately than income or wealth. The term ***prestige*** refers to the respect and admiration that an occupation holds in a society. "My daughter, the physicist" connotes something very different from "my daughter, the waitress." Prestige is independent of the particular individual who occupies a job, a characteristic that distinguishes it from esteem. ***Esteem*** refers to the reputation that a specific person has earned within an occupation. Therefore, one can say that the position of prime minister of Canada has high prestige, even though it has been occupied by people with varying degrees of esteem. A hairdresser may have the esteem of his clients, but he lacks the prestige of a corporation president.

Table 8-1 ranks the prestige of a number of well-known occupations. In a series of national surveys, sociologists assigned prestige rankings to about 500 occupations, ranging from physician to newspaper vendor. The highest possible prestige score was 100, and the lowest was 0. Physician, lawyer, dentist, and professor were the most highly regarded occupations. Sociologists have used such data to assign prestige rankings to virtually all jobs and have found a stability in rankings from 1925 to 1991. Similar studies in other countries have also developed useful prestige rankings of occupations (Hodge and Rossi 1964; Lin and Xie 1988; Treiman 1977).

Table 8-1 Prestige Rankings of Occupations

Occupation	Score	Occupation	Score
Physician	86	Secretary	46
Lawyer	75	Insurance agent	45
Dentist	74	Bank teller	43
Professor	74	Nurse's aide	42
Architect	73	Farmer	40
Clergy	69	Correctional officer	40
Pharmacist	68	Receptionist	39
Registered nurse	66	Barber	36
High school teacher	66	Child care worker	35
Accountant	65	Hotel clerk	32
Airline pilot	60	Bus driver	32
Police officer and detective	60	Truck driver	30
Preschool teacher	55	Retail clerk (shoes)	28
Librarian	54	Garbage collector	28
Firefighter	53	Waiter and waitress	28
Social worker	52	Bartender	25
Electrician	51	Farm worker	23
Funeral director	49	Janitor	22
Mail carrier	47	Newspaper vendor	19

Sources: J. Davis and Smith 2001; Nakao and Treas 1990, 1994; National Opinion Research Center 1994.

Gender and Occupational Prestige

For many years, studies of social class tended to neglect the occupations and incomes of *women* as determinants of social rank. In an exhaustive study of 589 occupations, sociologists Mary Powers and Joan Holmberg (1978) examined the impact of women's participation in the paid labour force on occupational status. Since women tend to dominate the relatively low-paying occupations, such as bookkeepers and child care workers, their participation in the workforce leads to a general upgrading of the status of most male-dominated occupations. More recent research conducted in both the United States and Europe has assessed the occupations of husbands *and* wives in determining the class positions of families (Sørensen 1994). With more than half of all married women now working outside the home (see Chapter 10), this approach seems long overdue, but it also raises some questions. For example, how is class or status to be judged in dual-career families—by the occupation regarded as having greater prestige, the average, or some other combination of the two occupations?

Sociologists—and, in particular, feminist sociologists in Great Britain—are drawing on new approaches in assessing women's social class standing. One approach is to focus on the individual (rather than the family or household) as the basis of categorizing a woman's class position. Thus, a woman would be classified based on her own occupational status rather than that of her spouse (O'Donnell 1992).

Another feminist effort to measure the contribution of women to the economy reflects a more clearly political agenda. International Women Count Network, a global grassroots feminist organization, has sought to give a monetary value to women's unpaid work. Besides providing symbolic recognition of women's role in labour, this value would also be used to calculate pension programs and benefits that are based on wages received. In 1995 the United Nations placed an $11 trillion price tag on unpaid labour by women, largely in child care, housework, and agriculture. Whatever the figure today, the continued undercounting of many workers' contribution to a family and to an entire economy means virtually all measures of stratification are in need of reform (United Nations Development Programme 1995; Wages for Housework Campaign 1999).

Multiple Measures

Another complication in measuring social class is that advances in statistical methods and computer technology have multiplied the factors used to define class under the objective method. No longer are sociologists limited to annual income and education in evaluating a person's class position. Today, studies use as criteria the value of homes, sources of income, assets, years in present occupations, neighbourhoods, and considerations regarding dual careers. Adding these variables will not necessarily paint a different picture of class differentiation in Canada, but it does allow sociologists to measure class in a more complex and multidimensional way.

Whatever the technique used to measure class, the sociologist is interested in real and often dramatic differences in power, privilege, and opportunity in a society. The study of stratification is a study of inequality. Nowhere is this more evident than in the distribution of wealth and income (see Figure 8-3).

Wealth and Income

Wealth in Canada is much more unevenly distributed than is income. As Figure 8-3 shows, in 1999, the richest fifth of the population held 70 percent of the nation's wealth. Researchers have also found dramatic disparities in wealth between families headed by a single parent (particularly a mother) and those headed by two parents, between those headed by Aboriginal parents and by non-Aboriginal parents, and between those headed by parents

FIGURE 8-3

Comparison of Distribution of Family Income and Wealth in Canada

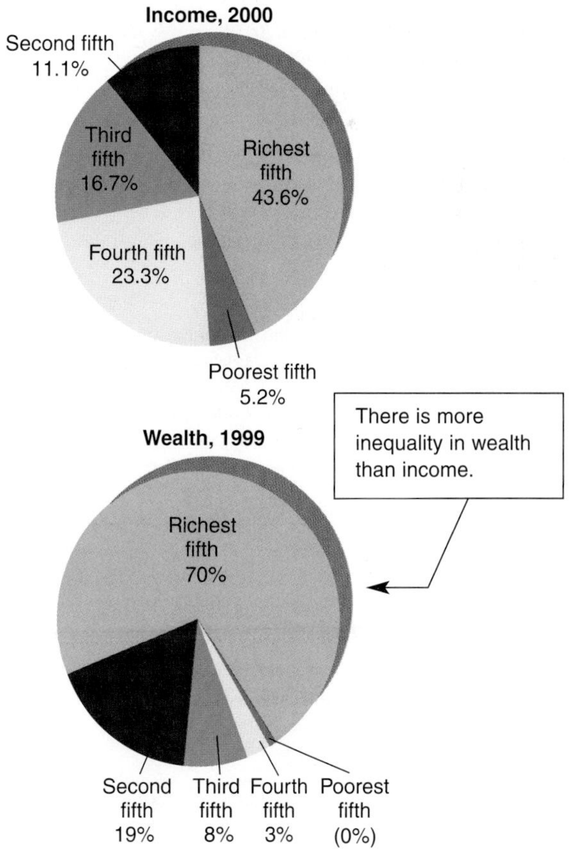

Sources: Statistics Canada 2004d; Statistics Canada 2003c.

Note: Data do not add to 100 percent due to rounding.

who have a mental or physical disability and by those who do not (Wolff 2002).

By all measures, income in Canada is distributed unevenly. Nobel Prize–winning economist Paul Samuelson has described the situation in the following words: "If we made an income pyramid out of building blocks, with each layer portraying $500 of income, the peak would be far higher than Mount Everest, but most people would be within a few feet of the ground" (Samuelson and Nordhaus 2001:386).

Recent data support Samuelson's analogy. In 2000, members of the richest tenth (or top 10 percent) of Canada's population earned $185 070 on average, accounting for 28 percent of the nation's total income. In contrast, members of the bottom tenth of the nation's population earned just $10 341, on average, accounting for less than 2 percent of the nation's total income (see Figure 8-4).

Survey data show that more than 50 percent of Canadians (as opposed to 38 percent of Americans) believe that government should take steps to reduce the income disparity between the rich and the poor. By contrast, 80 percent of people in Italy, 66 percent in Germany, and 65 percent in Great Britain support governmental efforts to reduce income inequality. It is not surprising, then, that many European countries, particularly in Scandinavia, provide more extensive "safety nets" to assist and protect the disadvantaged. By contrast, the strong cultural value placed on individualism in the United States leads to greater possibilities for both economic success and failure (Lipset 1996).

FIGURE 8-4

The Growing Income Gap in Canada, 1990–2000

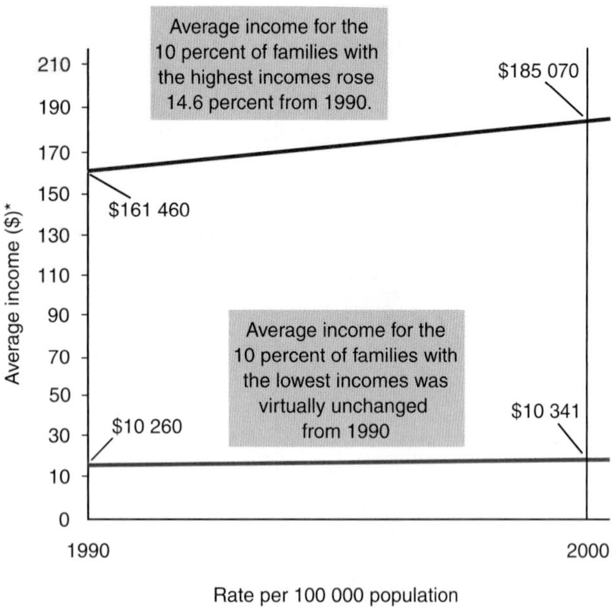

Source: Statistics Canada 2004d.

**Note:* Average income is in thousands of dollars, adjusted for inflation and expressed in constant 2000 dollars.

Think about It

In addition to generous raises and favourable government policies, what else might have accounted for the sharp rise in income for the richest 10 percent of Canadians?

Poverty

Approximately one out of every six children in this country lives below the low-income cutoff established by the federal government. The 2004 Report Card on Child and Family Poverty in Canada (Campaign 2000 2004) reported that 1 065 000 children are living in low-income households and that one-third of all Canadian children have experienced poverty for at least one year since 1996. The economic boom of the 1990s passed these people by. Despite the Government of Canada's goal of eradicating child poverty by 2000, a UNICEF report showed that, in 2005, 15 percent of Canadian children lived below the low-income cutoff. The same report indicated that Canada's ranking among other countries, in respect to child poverty, had not changed from 2000 (UNICEF 2005). In this section, we'll consider just how we define "poverty" and who is included in that category (Bauman 1999; Proctor and Dalaker 2002).

Studying Poverty

The efforts of sociologists and other social scientists to better understand poverty are complicated by the difficulty of defining it. This problem is evident even in government programs that conceive of poverty in either absolute or relative terms. ***Absolute poverty*** refers to a minimum level of subsistence that no family should be expected to live below. Policies concerning minimum wages, labour market barriers for excluded groups, housing standards, or school lunch programs for the poor imply a need to bring citizens up to some predetermined level of existence.

Although Canada does not have an official poverty line, it does have what is called a LICO (low-income cutoff), which is calculated for families of different sizes, and for individuals, living in different communities of varying size, from rural to urban. If a family spends more than 20 percent more than the average family does on the essentials (e.g., clothing, food, shelter), it falls below the LICO. Figure 8-5 shows poverty rates in Canada and in other countries. Canada's poverty rate, although higher than those in Norway, Finland, and Sweden, is significantly lower than that of the United States.

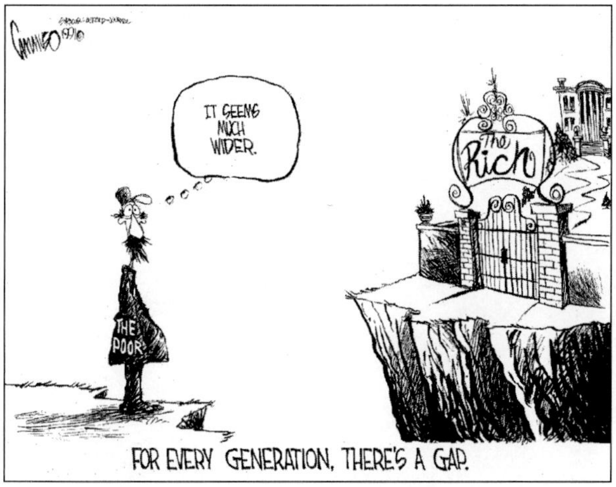

If anything, this cross-national comparison understates the extent of poverty in the United States, since U.S. residents are likely to pay more for housing, health care, child care, and education than residents of other countries, where such expenses are often subsidized.

By contrast, ***relative poverty*** is a floating standard of deprivation by which people at the bottom of a society, whatever their lifestyles, are judged to be disadvantaged *in comparison with the nation as a whole.* Therefore, even if the poor of the 2000s are better off in absolute terms than the poor of the 1930s or 1960s, they are still seen as deserving special assistance.

Campaign 2000 is an organization made up of more than 90 national, provincial or territorial, and community groups focused on the goal of eliminating child and family poverty in Canada. In its 2004 report (Campaign 2000 2004), it stated that, despite continued economic growth and rising employment, child and family poverty remain a "social deficit" in Canada. The organization made the following recommendations to help alleviate poverty in Canada:

- Establish a multiyear social investment plan, which would include a maximum child benefit of $4900 a year.
- Establish a high-quality, universally accessible, publicly funded system of early learning and child care.
- Expand affordable housing programs.
- Create more good jobs that provide living wages.
- Renew the social safety net.

FIGURE 8-5

Absolute Poverty in Selected Industrial Countries

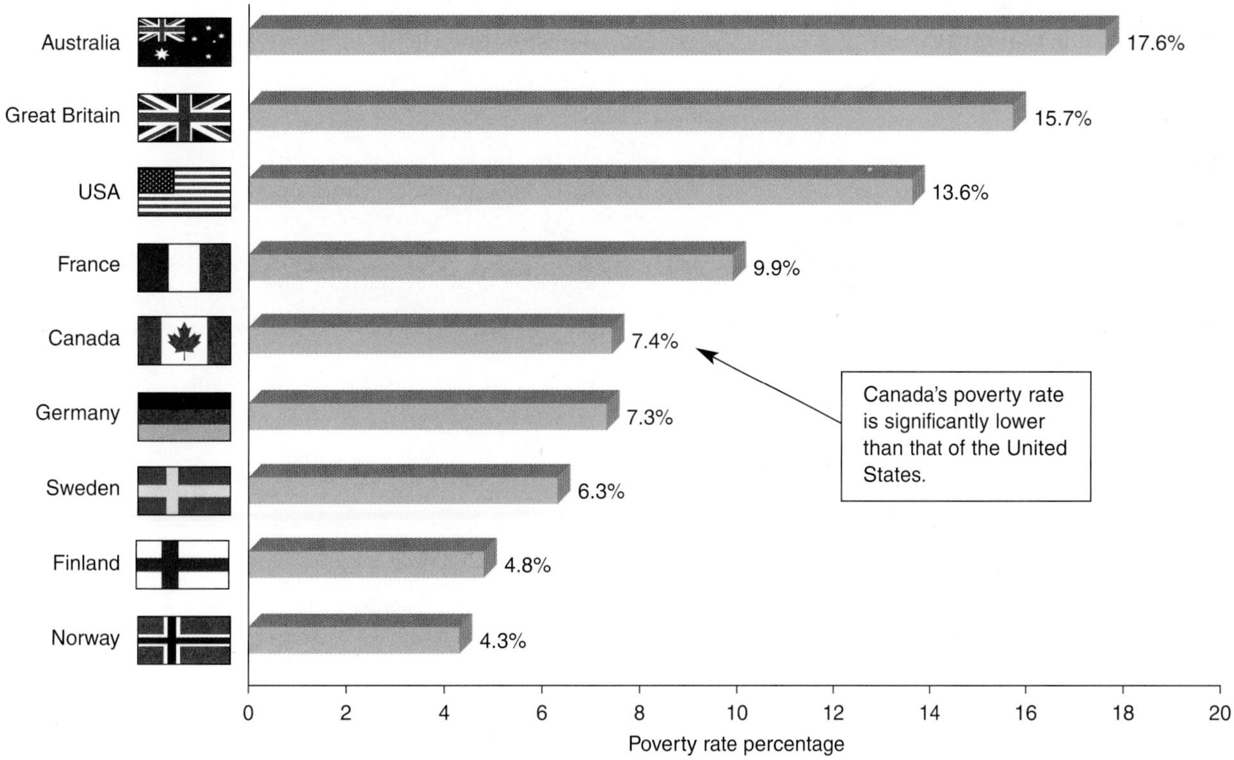

Source: Smeeding et al. 2001:51.

Who Are the Poor?

Not only does the category of the poor defy any simple definition, but it also counters the common stereotypes about "poor people" that Barbara Ehrenreich addressed in her book *Nickel and Dimed* (2001). For example, many people in Canada believe that the vast majority of the poor are able to work but will not. Yet many poor adults do work outside the home. Sociological researchers call this group the *working poor*. A working poor individual is one who works a minimum number of hours a year and whose family income falls below the LICO (low-income cutoff). In 2001 in Canada, 460 000 individuals were in this category. The working poor accounted for 33 percent of all poor, unattached individuals and 45 percent of all poor families in 2001 (Fortin and Fleury 2004).

Poverty hits women particularly hard throughout the world, a situation known as the "feminization of poverty." Shown here are women and children in India.

A sizable number of the poor live in urban areas, however. Poverty is no stranger in rural areas, ranging from Saskatchewan's hard-hit farming regions to fishing communities in Newfoundland and Labrador. Table 8-2 provides additional statistical information regarding these low-income people in Canada.

An increasing proportion of the low-income people in Canada are women, many of whom are single parents. Approximately 46 percent of Canadians with low incomes in 2000 were in lone-parent families that had at least one child under age 18; the vast majority of these families were headed by women. Canadian women's

Table 8-2 Percentage of Individuals and Census Families Living in Low Income,[1] Canada, 2001

Individuals and Selected Family Types[2]	Percentage in Low Income[1] 2001
Individuals	16.2
Couple families with no children	8.2
Couple families with at least one child under 18 years	11.2
Couple families whose children are all 18 years and over	5.8
Lone-parent families with at least one child under 18 years	45.8
Lone-parent families whose children are all 18 years and over	16.5

Source: Adapted by the authour, Statistics Canada 2003c.

1. Those living below the low-income cutoffs.
2. Families living in single-family households with no aditional persons (e.g., grandparents, uncles, aunts); all individuals except those living in Yukon, Northwest Territories, Nunavut, or on reserves, or in institutions.

wages remain unequal to those of Canadian men, and many women in Canadian workplaces still hold jobs in female-dominated job ghettos. This alarming reality, known as the *feminization of poverty*, is evident not just in Canada but also around the world.

A major factor in the feminization of poverty has been the increase in the number of families with women as single heads of the household (see Chapter 11). In 2001, 11.7 percent of all people in the United States lived in poverty, compared to 26.4 percent of households headed by single mothers. Some feminist thinkers trace the higher rates of poverty among women to such factors as the difficulty in finding affordable child care, sexual harassment, and sex discrimination in the labour market, while others attribute it to more deep-rooted systemic factors (see Chapter 10).

p. 87

Sociologist William Julius Wilson (1980, 1987, 1989, 1996) and other social scientists have used the term ***underclass*** to describe the long-term poor who lack training and skills. In Canada, this class is often associated with such factors as race, ethnicity, age, disability, geographic region, and age. For example, persistently and disproportionately represented in the so-called underclass of Canadian society are those of Aboriginal heritage. The social condition of Canada's Aboriginal people will be explored in greater detail in Chapter 9.

Conflict theorists, among others, have expressed alarm at the portion of Canada's population living on this lower rung of the stratification hierarchy and at society's reluctance to address the lack of economic opportunities for these people. Often, portraits of the underclass seem to "blame the victims" for their own plight while ignoring other factors that push people into poverty.

Analyses of the poor in general reveal that they are not a static social class. The overall composition of the poor changes continually, because some individuals and families near the top edge of poverty move above the poverty level after a year or two while others slip below it. Still, hundreds of thousands of people remain in poverty for many years at a time.

Explaining Poverty

Why is it that pervasive poverty continues within a nation of such vast wealth? Sociologist Herbert Gans (1995) has applied functionalist analysis to the existence of poverty and argues that various segments of society actually *benefit* from the existence of the poor. Gans has identified a number of social, economic, and political functions that the poor perform for society:

- The presence of poor people means that society's dirty work—physically dirty or dangerous, dead-end and underpaid, undignified and menial jobs—will be performed at low cost.
- Poverty creates jobs for occupations and professions that service the poor. It creates both legal employment (public health experts, welfare caseworkers) and illegal jobs (drug dealers, numbers runners).
- The identification and punishment of the poor as deviants upholds the legitimacy of conventional social norms and mainstream values regarding hard work, thrift, and honesty.
- Within a relatively hierarchical society, the existence of poor people guarantees the higher status of the more affluent. As psychologist William Ryan (1976) has noted, affluent people may justify inequality (and gain a measure of satisfaction) by "blaming the victims" of poverty for their disadvantaged condition.
- Because of their lack of political power, the poor often absorb the costs of social change. Under the policy of deinstitutionalization, people with mental illnesses released from long-term hospitals have been "dumped" primarily into low-income communities and neighbourhoods. Similarly, halfway houses for rehabilitated drug abusers are often rejected by more affluent communities and end up in poorer neighbourhoods.

p. 145

In Gans's view, then, poverty and the poor actually satisfy positive functions for many nonpoor groups in society.

Life Chances

Max Weber saw class as closely related to people's ***life chances***—that is, their opportunities to provide themselves with material goods, positive living conditions, and favourable life experiences (Gerth and Mills 1958). Life chances are reflected in such measures as housing, education, and health. Occupying a higher position in a society improves your life chances and brings greater access to social rewards. By contrast, people in the lower social classes are forced to devote a larger proportion of their limited resources to the necessities of life.

In times of danger, the affluent and powerful have a better chance of surviving than people of ordinary means. When the supposedly unsinkable British ocean-liner *Titanic* hit an iceberg in 1912, it was not carrying enough lifeboats to accommodate all its passengers. Plans had been made to evacuate only first- and second-class passengers. About 62 percent of the first-class passengers survived the disaster. Despite a rule that women and children would go first, about a third of those passengers were male. In contrast, only 25 percent of the passengers in third class survived. The first attempt to alert them to the need to abandon ship came at least 45 minutes after other passengers had been notified (D. Butler 1998; Crouse 1999; Riding 1998).

Class position also affects health in important ways. In fact, class is increasingly being viewed as an important predictor of health. The affluent avail themselves of

In the movie *Titanic,* the romantic fantasy of a love affair that crossed class lines obscured the real and deadly effects of the social class divide.

improved health services while such advances bypass poor people. The chances of a child's dying during the first year of life are much higher in poor families than among the middle class. This higher infant mortality rate results in part from the inadequate nutrition received by low-income expectant mothers. Even when they survive infancy, the poor are more likely than the affluent to suffer from serious, chronic illnesses, such as arthritis, bronchitis, diabetes, and heart disease.

All these factors contribute to differences in the death rates of the poor and the affluent. Studies drawing on health data in Canada document the impact of class (as well as race) on mortality. Ill health among the poor only serves to increase the likelihood that the poor will remain impoverished (Link and Phelan 1995).

Like disease, crime can be particularly devastating when it attacks the poor. People in low-income families were more likely to be assaulted, raped, or robbed than were the most affluent people. Furthermore, if accused of a crime, a person with low income and status is likely to be represented by an overworked publicly funded lawyer. Whether innocent or guilty, the accused may sit in jail for months, unable to raise bail (Rennison 2002).

Some people have hoped that the Internet revolution would help level the playing field by making information and markets uniformly available. Unfortunately, however, not everyone is able to get onto the "information highway," and so yet another aspect of social inequality has emerged—the *digital divide.* People who are poor, who have less education, who are members of minority groups, or who live in rural communities are not getting connected at home or at work. For example, in 2003, 64 percent of all households had access to the Internet. However, about 88 percent of households whose head had a university degree had access to the Internet, while only 32 percent of those families whose head had less than a high school education did. As more-educated people continue to buy high-speed Internet connections, they will be able to take advantage of even more sophisticated interactive services and the digital divide will grow larger (Statistics Canada 2004e).

Wealth, status, and power may not ensure happiness, but they certainly provide additional ways of coping with problems and disappointments. For this reason, the opportunity for advancement—for social mobility—is of special significance to those who are at the bottom of society looking up. These people want the rewards and privileges that are granted to high-ranking members of a culture.

Use Your Sociological Imagination

Imagine a society in which there are no social classes—no differences in people's wealth, income, and life chances. What would such a society be like? Would it be stable, or would its social structure change over time?

SOCIAL MOBILITY

Jimmy Pattison, a self-made billionaire and international businessman, grew up in impoverished circumstances in Luseland, Saskatchewan. He began his business career by selling used cars. Today, he is one of the wealthiest individuals in Canada and sole owner of one of the largest companies in Canada. The rise of a child from a poor background to a position of great prestige, power, and financial reward is an example of social mobility. The term ***social mobility*** refers to movement of individuals or groups from one position of a society's stratification system to another. But how significant—how frequent, how dramatic—is mobility in such a class society as Canada?

Open versus Closed Stratification Systems

Sociologists use the terms *open stratification system* and *closed stratification system* to indicate the amount of social mobility in a society. An ***open system*** implies that the position of each individual is influenced by the person's *achieved* status. At the other extreme of social mobility is the ***closed system,*** which allows little or no possibility of moving up. The slavery and caste systems of stratification are examples of closed systems. In such societies, social placement is based on *ascribed* statuses, such as race or family background, which cannot be changed.

Types of Social Mobility

An airline pilot who becomes a police officer moves from one social position to another of the same rank. Each occupation has the same prestige ranking: 60 on a scale ranging from a low of 0 to a high of 100 (see Table 8-1 on page 172). Sociologists call this kind of movement ***horizontal mobility.*** However, if the pilot were to become a lawyer (prestige ranking of 75), he or she would experience ***vertical mobility,*** the movement from one social position to another of a different rank. Vertical mobility can also involve moving *downward* in a society's stratification system, as would be the case if the airline pilot became a bank teller (ranking of 43). Pitirim Sorokin ([1927] 1959) was the first sociologist to distinguish between horizontal and vertical mobility. Most sociological analysis, however, focuses on vertical rather than horizontal mobility.

One way of examining vertical social mobility is to contrast intergenerational and intragenerational mobility. ***Intergenerational mobility*** involves changes in the social position of children relative to their parents. Thus, a plumber whose father was a physician provides an example of downward intergenerational mobility. A film star whose parents were both factory workers illustrates upward intergenerational mobility.

Intragenerational mobility involves changes in social position within a person's adult life. A woman who enters the paid labour force as a teacher's aide and eventually becomes superintendent of the school district experiences upward intragenerational mobility. A man who becomes a taxicab driver after his accounting firm goes bankrupt undergoes downward intragenerational mobility.

Social Mobility in Canada

The belief in upward mobility is an important value in our society. Does this mean that Canada is indeed the land of opportunity? Are rags to riches stories the exception or are they the rule? Only if such ascriptive characteristics as race, gender, and family background have ceased to be significant in determining someone's future prospects. We can see the impact of these factors in the occupational structure.

Occupational Mobility

"You are three times more likely as a young man to move from rags to rags than rags to riches. And moving from riches to riches is the most likely of all." These are the words of the authors of a major Canadian study on the occupational mobility of 400 000 men between the ages of 16 and 19 (Corak and Heisz 1996). The authors concluded that although there is limited upward mobility in the middle ranges of the Canadian occupational hierarchy, the richest and poorest individuals tend to reproduce the income level of their fathers. This study is consistent with studies of intragenerational mobility in Canada, which found that the majority of Canadians experienced no occupational mobility in their working lives (Creese, Guppy, and Meissner 1991). In Canada, achievement is not simply based on hard work and merit; ascribed characteristics, such as race, gender, and ethnicity, are significant in their influence on a person's chances for both intergenerational and intragenerational occupational mobility.

The Impact of Education

Education plays a critical role in social mobility. The impact of advanced education on adult status is clearly evident in Canada, as documented in statistics showing the relationship between the highest level of educational achievement and income and wealth in adulthood. Generally, the higher a person's level of educational achievement, the higher his or her level of income and wealth (expressed as net worth). For example, according to the 2001 census, people with master's degrees in commerce made, on average, $88 396 per year, while those holding bachelor's degrees made, on average, $63 117 per year. The same pattern exists in the field of education: those with master's degrees had an average income of $50 379, while those with bachelor's degrees had an average income of $40 408. For other fields, such as history and agricultural science, the differences in earnings between those holding master's degrees and those holding bachelor's degrees were insignificant (*Vancouver Sun* 2004a).

Although educational achievement is linked to social mobility, the stark reality is that the chance of achieving an education continues to be associated with family background. In 1999, 34 percent of students from the lowest socioeconomic quartile did not complete high school, compared with 23 percent of students from the highest quartile; 20 percent of students from the lowest quartile attended university, compared with 40 percent of those from the highest quartile (Canadian Education Statistics Council 2000). With the increased costs of tuition and other expenses associated with a postsecondary education, students who attend university are increasingly likely to have parents from the higher socioeconomic groups.

The Impact of Race

The variables of race, class, and gender are intertwined in such a way as to produce diverse chances for both intergenerational mobility and intragenerational mobility. Earnings data of recent immigrants to Canada show that after one year, a male immigrant earned 63.1 percent of what his Canadian-born counterpart earned. After 10 years, that figure increased to 79.8 percent (Statistics Canada 2003d). A female immigrant earned 60.5 percent after one year and 87.3 percent after 10 years of what her Canadian-born counterpart earned. Canadian women who are members of visible minorities earn less than other Canadian women. They also earn less than men, whether the men are members of visible minorities or not. The glaring absence of members of visible minorities from corporate boardrooms, political office, and other positions of power and influence reflects a systemic pattern of inequality. As Joseph Mensah (2002:129) states in his book on black people in Canada, "the unabashed racial discrimination in the job market impacts Blacks more than any other form of bigotry."

Rita Tsang, president and CEO of Tour East Holidays (Canada) Inc., is one of the few women in Canada who have risen to the top of the corporate hierarchy. Despite the implementation of employment equity policies, occupational barriers still limit women's social mobility.

The Impact of Gender

Studies of mobility, even more than those of class, have traditionally ignored the significance of gender, but some research findings are now available that explore the relationship between gender and mobility.

Women's employment opportunities are much more limited than men's (as Chapter 10 will show). Moreover, according to recent research, women whose skills far exceed the jobs offered them are more likely than men to withdraw entirely from the paid labour force. This withdrawal violates an assumption common to traditional mobility studies: that most people will aspire to upward mobility and seek to make the most of their opportunities.

In contrast to men, women's jobs are heavily concentrated in the sales and service areas. But the modest salary ranges and few prospects for advancement in many of these positions limit the possibility of upward mobility. Self-employment as shopkeepers, entrepreneurs, independent professionals, and the like—an important road to upward mobility for men—is difficult for women, who find it harder to secure the necessary financing. Although sons often follow in the footsteps of their fathers, women are less likely to move into their fathers' positions. Consequently, gender remains an important factor in shaping social mobility within Canada. Women in Canada (and in other parts of the world) are especially likely to be trapped in poverty and unable to rise out of their low-income status (Heilman 2001).

So far we have focused on stratification and social mobility within Canada. In the next part of the chapter, we broaden our focus to consider stratification from a global perspective.

STRATIFICATION IN THE WORLD SYSTEM

Kwabena Afari is a pineapple exporter in Ghana. But for years his customers had to show a great deal of ingenuity to get in touch with him. First a call had to be placed to Accra, the capital city. Someone there would call the post office in Afari's hometown. Then the post office would send a messenger to his home. Afari has recently solved his problem by getting a cellular phone, but his long-time dilemma symbolizes the problems of the roughly 600 million people who live in sub-Saharan Africa and are being left behind by the trade and foreign investment transforming the global economy. One African entrepreneur notes, "It's not that we have been left behind. It's that we haven't even started" (Buckley 1997:8).

It is true that technology, the information highway, and innovations in telecommunications have all made the world a smaller and more unified place. Yet although the world marketplace is gradually shrinking in space and tastes, business profits are not being shared equally. There remains a substantial disparity between the world's "have" and "have-not" nations. For example, in 2002, the average value of goods and services produced per citizen (per capita gross national income) in the industrialized countries of the United States, Japan, Switzerland, Belgium, and Norway was more than \$27 000. In seven poorer countries, the value was below \$700. In fact, the richest 1 percent of the world's population received as much income as the poorest 57 percent. Figure 8-6 illustrates these stark contrasts. Three forces discussed below are particularly responsible for the domination of the world marketplace by a few nations: the legacy of colonialism, the advent of multinational corporations, and modernization (Haub 2002; United Nations Development Programme 2001).

The Legacy of Colonialism

Colonialism occurs when a foreign power maintains political, social, economic, and cultural domination over a people for an extended time. In simple terms, it is rule by outsiders. The long reign of the British Empire over much of North America, parts of Africa, and India is an example of colonial domination. The same can be said of French rule over Algeria, Tunisia, and other parts of North Africa. Relations between the colonial nation and colonized people are similar to those between the dominant capitalist class and the proletariat as described by Karl Marx.

By the 1980s, colonialism had largely disappeared. Most of the world's nations that were colonies before World War I had achieved political independence and established their own governments. However, for many of these countries, the transition to genuine self-rule was not yet complete. Colonial domination had established patterns of economic exploitation that continued even after nationhood was achieved—in part because former colonies were unable to develop their own industry and technology. Their dependence on more industrialized nations, including their former colonial masters, for managerial and technical expertise, investment capital, and manufactured goods kept former colonies in a subservient position. Such continuing dependence and foreign domination constitute ***neocolonialism.***

The economic and political consequences of colonialism and neocolonialism are readily apparent. Drawing on the conflict perspective, sociologist Immanuel Wallerstein (1974, 1979a, 2000) views the global economic system as divided between nations that control wealth and those from which resources are taken. Neocolonialism allows industrialized societies to accumulate even more capital.

Wallerstein has advanced a ***world systems analysis*** to describe the unequal economic and political relationships in which certain industrialized nations (among them Canada, the United States, Japan, and Germany) and their global corporations dominate the *core* of the system. At the *semiperiphery* of the system are countries with marginal economic status, such as Israel, Ireland, and South Korea. Wallerstein suggests that the poor developing countries of Asia, Africa, and Latin America are on the *periphery* of the world economic system. Core nations and their corporations control and exploit the developing nations' economies, much as the old colonial empires ruled their colonies (Chase-Dunn and Grimes 1995).

The division between core and periphery nations is significant and remarkably stable. A study by the International Monetary Fund (2000) found little change over the course of the *past one hundred years* for the 42 economies that were studied. The only changes were Japan's movement up into the group of core nations and China's movement down toward the margins of the semiperiphery nations. Yet Wallerstein (2000) speculates that the world system as we currently understand it may soon undergo unpredictable changes. The world is becoming increasingly urbanized, a trend that is gradually eliminating the large pools of low-cost workers in rural areas. In the future, core nations will have to find other ways to reduce their labour costs. The exhaustion of land and water resources through clear-cutting and other forms of pollution is also driving up the costs of production.

Wallerstein's world systems analysis is the most widely used version of ***dependency theory.*** According to this theory, even as developing countries make economic advances, they remain weak and subservient to core nations and corporations within an increasingly intertwined global economy. This allows industrialized nations to continue to exploit developing countries for their own gain. In a sense, dependency theory applies the conflict perspective on a global scale.

In the view of world systems analysis and dependency theory, a growing share of the human and natural

FIGURE 8-6

Gross National Income per Capita, 2001

Mapping Life WORLDWIDE

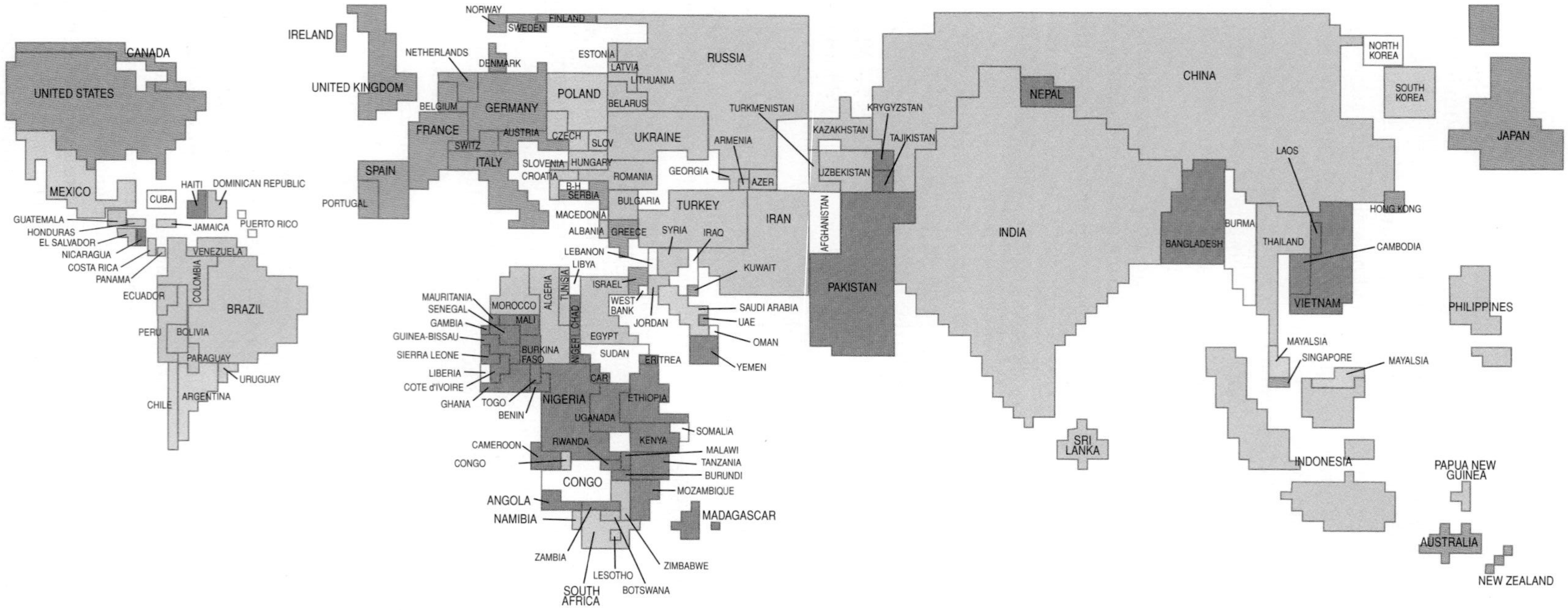

Key:
GNI per capita

- $2200 and less
- $2205–$6995
- No available data
- $7000–$14 995
- More than $15 000

Sources: Haub 2002; Weeks 2002:22–23.

Note: Size based on 2000 population estimates.

This stylized map reflects the different sizes in population of the world's nations. The colour for each country shows the 2001 estimated *gross national income* (the total value of goods and services produced by the nation in a given year) per capita. As the map shows, some of the world's most populous countries—such as Nigeria, Bangladesh, and Pakistan—are among the nations with the lowest standard of living, as measured by per capita GNI.

Sociology in the Global Community

8-2 Poverty and Global Inequality

Rustica Banda is a midwife who delivers 10 to 13 babies a day at a community hospital near Lilongwe in Malawi, in sub-Saharan Africa. In 2004, sub-Saharan Africa had 25 million people living with human immunodeficiency virus/acquired immune deficiency syndrome (HIV/AIDS), more than half of whom were women. The percentage of women in the region living with HIV/AIDS is increasing, contributing to what has been called the "feminization of HIV/AIDS" (UNAIDS 2004). Because of a lack of state funding to local hospitals for wages and basic medical supplies, such as plastic gloves, Rustica Banda, and others like her, work for low wages in unsafe and dangerous conditions to care for patients, some of whom have HIV/AIDS. Banda attributes the poverty in her country to global economic interconnectedness, more specifically, to debts with other countries. Owing more than 1.5 times its annual income, Malawi is one of the most heavily indebted countries in the world. In 2003, the country spent more than twice its funding for health care in servicing its debt. In this context, Rustica Banda (*Guardian Unlimited* 2005) describes the conditions in her life:

> I have five children to support, as well as five orphaned grandchildren. There is a great staff shortage here in Mitunda. At any one time, there are only two nurses on duty. . . . The pregnant woman must buy her own things for labour; a plastic sheet to put on the bed to protect her from the blood of other patients. . . . I have to use my bare hands when collecting blood, even when I don't know the HIV status of the patient. . . . The government says it does not have money for salaries or to buy enough equipment to run the hospital. It has too many debts with other countries. I call on the state of Malawi to consider its nurses and our salaries; we should not be running away from the government hospitals. I also ask the G8 to cancel Malawi's debt.

Make Poverty History, an alliance of charities, religious organizations, trade unions, antipoverty groups, rock stars, and celebrities, mobilized to promote global awareness (e.g., Live 8) and to apply pressure on the G8 leaders (that is, leaders of the richest countries: Canada, the United States, Great Britain, Italy, Germany, France, Russia, and Japan) when they met in Scotland in 2005 for the G8 Summit. Make Poverty History called for governments and international decision makers to change policies regarding three inextricably connected areas—trade, debt, and aid—as they relate to the dealings between the world's richest and poorest countries. Falling short of some antipoverty and AIDS activist groups' expectations (Clark 2005), the G8 leaders did, however, agree to the following:

- to increase aid by U.S.$25 billion annually to Africa by 2010
- to provide universal access to AIDS treatment by 2010
- to establish efforts to save 600 000 lives lost to malaria by 2015
- to train 20 000 additional peacekeepers for an African union peace force
- to call for trade talks to eliminate agricultural subsidies, which would help African products find markets

Applying Theory

1. Have you ever been involved in a fundraising or awareness-raising campaign in your community or university to fight poverty in Africa?
2. Do you think that Canada is doing enough in its efforts to close the gap between the rich and the poor countries of the world?

Sources: Clark 2005; *Guardian Unlimited* 2005; UNAIDS 2004.

resources of developing countries is being redistributed to the core industrialized nations. In part, this is because developing countries owe huge sums of money to industrialized nations as a result of foreign aid, loans, and trade deficits. This global debt crisis has intensified the dependency begun under colonialism, neocolonialism, and multinational investment. International financial institutions are pressuring indebted countries to take severe measures to meet their interest payments. The result is that developing nations may be forced to devalue their currencies, freeze workers' wages, increase privatization of industry, and reduce government services and employment (see Box 8-2).

Closely related to these problems is ***globalization,*** or the worldwide integration of government policies, cultures, social movements, and financial markets through trade and the exchange of ideas. Because world financial markets transcend governance by conventional nation states, international organizations such as the World Bank and the International Monetary Fund have emerged as major players in the global economy. The function of these institutions, heavily funded and influenced by core nations, is to encourage economic trade and development and to ensure the smooth operation of international financial markets. As such they are seen as promoters of globalization and defenders primarily of the interests of core nations. Critics call attention to a variety of issues, including violations of workers' rights, the destruction of the environment, the loss of cultural identity, and discrimination against minority groups in periphery nations.

Some observers see globalization and its effects as the natural result of advances in communications technology, particularly the Internet and satellite transmission of the mass media. Others view it more critically, as a process that allows multinational corporations to expand unchecked, as we will see in the next section (Chase-Dunn, Kawano, and Brewer 2000; Feketekuty 2001; Feuer 1959; Pearlstein 2001; Third World Institute 2001).

Use Your Sociological Imagination

You are travelling through a developing country. What evidence do you see of neocolonialism and globalization?

Multinational Corporations

A key role in neocolonialism today is played by worldwide corporate giants. The term ***multinational corporations*** refers to commercial organizations that are headquartered in one country but do business throughout the world. Such private trade and lending relationships are not new; merchants have conducted business abroad for hundreds of years, trading gems, spices, garments, and other goods. However, today's multinational giants are not merely buying and selling overseas; they are also *producing goods* all over the world, as we saw in the case of Nike (Wallerstein 1974).

Moreover, today's "global factories" (the factories throughout the developing world run by multinational corporations) now have the "global office" alongside them. Multinationals based in core countries are beginning to establish reservations services, centres to process insurance claims, and data-processing centres in the periphery nations. As service industries become a more important part of the international marketplace, many companies are concluding that the low costs of overseas operations more than offset the expense of transmitting information around the world.

Do not underestimate the size of these global corporations. Table 8-3 on the next page shows that the total revenues of multinational businesses are on a par with the total value of goods and services exchanged in *entire nations.* Foreign sales represent an important source of profit for multinational corporations, a fact that encourages them to expand into other countries (in many cases, the developing nations).

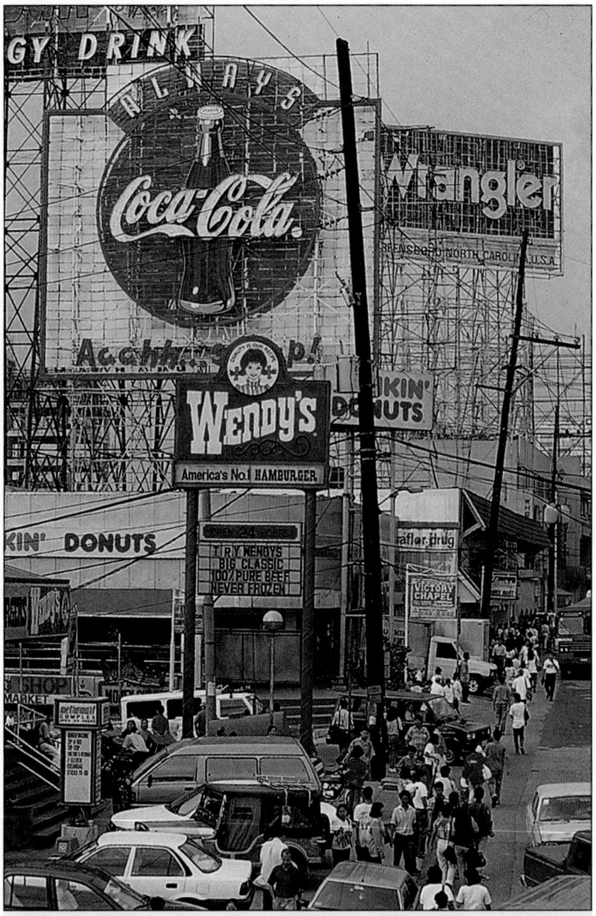

The influence of multinational corporations abroad can be seen in this street scene from Manila, capital of the Philippines.

Functionalist View

Multinational corporations can actually help the developing nations of the world. They bring jobs and industry to areas where subsistence agriculture previously served as the only means of survival. Multinationals promote rapid development through diffusion of inventions and innovations from industrial nations. Viewed from a functionalist perspective, the combination of skilled technology and management provided by multinationals and the relatively cheap labour available in developing nations is ideal for a global enterprise. Multinationals can take maximum advantage of technology while reducing costs and boosting profits.

The international ties of multinational corporations also facilitate the exchange of ideas and technology around the world. They make the nations of the world

Table 8-3 Multinational Corporations Compared to Nations

Corporation	Revenues ($ millions)	Comparable Nation(s)	Gross Domestic Product ($ millions)
1. Wal-Mart (USA)	$219 812	Turkey	$199 900
2. Exxon Mobil (USA)	191 581	Austria	189 000
3. General Motors (USA)	177 260	Egypt plus Philippines	173 400
4. BP–British Petroleum (Britain)	174 218	Saudi Arabia	173 300
5. Ford Motor (USA)	164 412	Norway	161 800
7. DaimlerChrysler (Germany)	136 897	Colombia plus Peru	134 800
9. General Electric (USA)	125 913	South Africa	125 900
10. Toyota Motor (Japan)	120 814	Finland	121 500
11. Citigroup (USA)	112 022	Greece	112 600
16. Nippon Telephone and Telegraph (Japan)	93 425	Ireland	93 900

Sources: For corporate data, *Fortune* 2002; for GDP data, United Nations Development Programme 2002:190–193.

Notes: Revenues are for 2001. GDP data are for 2000, based on local currencies converted to prevailing U.S. dollar equivalents. Corporations are ranked by their placement on the Fortune 500 list of global corporations.

Think about It
What happens to society when corporations grow economically bigger than countries and spill across international borders?

more interdependent. And these ties may prevent certain disputes from reaching the point of serious conflict. A country cannot afford to sever diplomatic relations, or engage in warfare, with a nation that is the headquarters for its main business suppliers or is a key outlet for exports.

Conflict View

Conflict theorists challenge this favourable evaluation of the impact of multinational corporations. They emphasize that multinationals exploit local workers to maximize profits. Starbucks—the international coffee retailer based in Seattle—gets some of its coffee from farms in Guatemala. But to earn enough money to buy a pound (half a kilogram) of Starbucks coffee, a Guatemalan farmworker would have to pick 500 pounds (225 kilograms) of beans, representing five days of work (Entine and Nichols 1996).

The pool of cheap labour in the developing world prompts multinationals to move factories out of core countries. An added bonus for the multinationals is that the developing world discourages strong trade unions. Organized labour in industrialized countries insists on decent wages and humane working conditions, but governments seeking to attract or keep multinationals may develop a "climate for investment" that includes repressive antilabour laws restricting union activity and collective bargaining. If labour's demands become threatening, the multinational firm will simply move its plant elsewhere, leaving a trail of unemployment behind. Nike, for example, moved its factories from the United States to Korea to Indonesia to Vietnam, seeking the lowest labour costs. Conflict theorists conclude that, on the whole, multinational corporations have a negative social impact on workers in *both* industrialized and developing nations.

Workers in developed countries are beginning to recognize that their own interests are served by helping to organize workers in developing nations. As long as multinationals can exploit cheap labour abroad, they will be in a strong position to reduce wages and benefits in industrialized countries. With this in mind, in the 1990s, labour unions, religious organizations, campus groups, and other activists mounted public campaigns to pressure companies, such as Nike, Starbucks, Reebok, the Gap, and Wal-Mart, to improve the wages and working conditions in their overseas operations (Appelbaum and Dreier, 1999).

Several sociologists who have surveyed the effects of foreign investment conclude that, although it may initially contribute to a host nation's wealth, it eventually increases economic inequality within developing nations. This is true in both income and ownership of land. The upper and middle classes benefit most from economic expansion, whereas the lower classes are less likely to benefit. Multinationals invest in limited areas of an economy and in restricted regions of a nation. Although certain sectors of the host nation's economy expand, such as hotels and expensive restaurants, this very expansion appears to retard growth in agriculture and other economic sectors. Moreover, multinational corporations often buy out or force out local entrepreneurs and companies, thereby increasing economic and cultural dependence (Bornschier, Chase-Dunn, and Rubinson 1978; Chase-Dunn and Grimes 1995; Evans 1979; Wallerstein 1979b).

Modernization

Millions of people around the world are witnessing a revolutionary transformation of their day-to-day life. Contemporary social scientists use the term ***modernization*** to describe the far-reaching process by which peripheral nations move from traditional or less developed institutions to those characteristic of more developed societies.

Wendell Bell (1981), whose definition of modernization we are using, notes that modern societies tend to be urban, literate, and industrial. They have sophisticated transportation and media systems. Families tend to be organized within the nuclear family unit rather than the extended-family model (see Chapter 11). Members of societies that have undergone modernization shift allegiance from such traditional sources of authority as parents and priests to newer authorities, such as government officials.

Many sociologists are quick to note that terms such as *modernization* and even *development* contain an ethnocentric bias. The unstated assumptions behind these terms are that "they" (people living in developing countries) are struggling to become more like "us" (in the core industrialized nations). Viewed from a conflict perspective, these terms perpetuate the dominant ideology of capitalist societies.

There is similar criticism of ***modernization theory,*** a functionalist approach proposing that modernization and development will gradually improve the lives of people in developing nations. According to this theory, even though countries develop at uneven rates, development in peripheral countries will be assisted by the innovations transferred from the industrialized world. Critics of modernization theory, including dependency theorists, counter that any such technology transfer only increases the dominance of core nations over developing countries and facilitates further exploitation.

When we see all the Coca-Cola and IBM signs going up in developing countries, it is easy to assume that globalization and economic change are effecting cultural change. But that is not always the case, researchers note. Distinctive cultural traditions, such as a particular religious orientation or a nationalistic identity, often persist in a developing nation and can soften the impact of modernization. Some contemporary sociologists emphasize that both developed and developing countries are "modern." Current researchers are increasingly viewing modernization as movement along a series of social indicators—among them degree of urbanization, energy use, literacy, political democracy, and use of birth control. Clearly, these are often subjective indicators; even in industrialized nations, not everyone would agree that wider use of birth control represents an example of "progress" (Armer and Katsillis 1992; Hedley 1992; Inglehart and Baker 2000).

Current modernization studies generally take a convergence perspective. Using the indicators noted above, researchers focus on how societies are moving closer together, despite traditional differences. From a conflict perspective, modernization in developing countries often perpetuates their dependence on and continued exploitation by more industrialized nations. Conflict theorists view such a continuing dependence on foreign powers as an example of contemporary neocolonialism.

STRATIFICATION WITHIN NATIONS: A COMPARATIVE PERSPECTIVE

At the same time as the gap between rich and poor nations is widening, so too is the gap between rich and poor citizens *within* nations. As discussed earlier, stratification in developing nations is closely related to their relatively weak and dependent position in the global economy. Local elites work hand in hand with multinational corporations and prosper from such alliances. Simultaneously, the economic system creates and perpetuates the exploitation of industrial and agricultural workers. That's why foreign investment in developing countries tends to increase economic inequality (Bornschier et al. 1978; Kerbo 2000).

In at least 20 nations around the world, the most affluent 10 percent of the population receives at least

40 percent of all income: Swaziland (the leader at 50 percent of all income), Brazil, Burkina Faso, Central African Republic, Chile, Colombia, Guatemala, Guinea-Bissau, Honduras, Lesotho, Mali, Mexico, Nicaragua, Nigeria, Papua New Guinea, Paraguay, Sierra Leone, South Africa, Zambia, and Zimbabwe. Figure 8-7 compares the distribution of income in selected industrialized and developing nations (World Bank 2002).

Women in developing countries find life especially difficult. Karuna Chanana Ahmed, an anthropologist from India who has studied women in developing nations, calls women the most exploited among oppressed people. Women face sex discrimination beginning at birth. They are commonly fed less than male children, are denied educational opportunities, and are often hospitalized only when critically ill. Whether inside or outside the home, women's work is devalued. When economies fail, as they did in Asian countries in the late 1990s, women are the first to be laid off from work (Anderson and Moore 1993; Kristof 1998).

The social policy section that closes this chapter focuses on the Canadian welfare system, a government program that serves many women (and men) who are trapped in poverty. The aim of welfare reform has been to encourage these people to find jobs and become self-supporting. We'll also see how other governments have approached welfare reform, and what the results have been.

FIGURE 8-7

Distribution of Income in Nine Nations

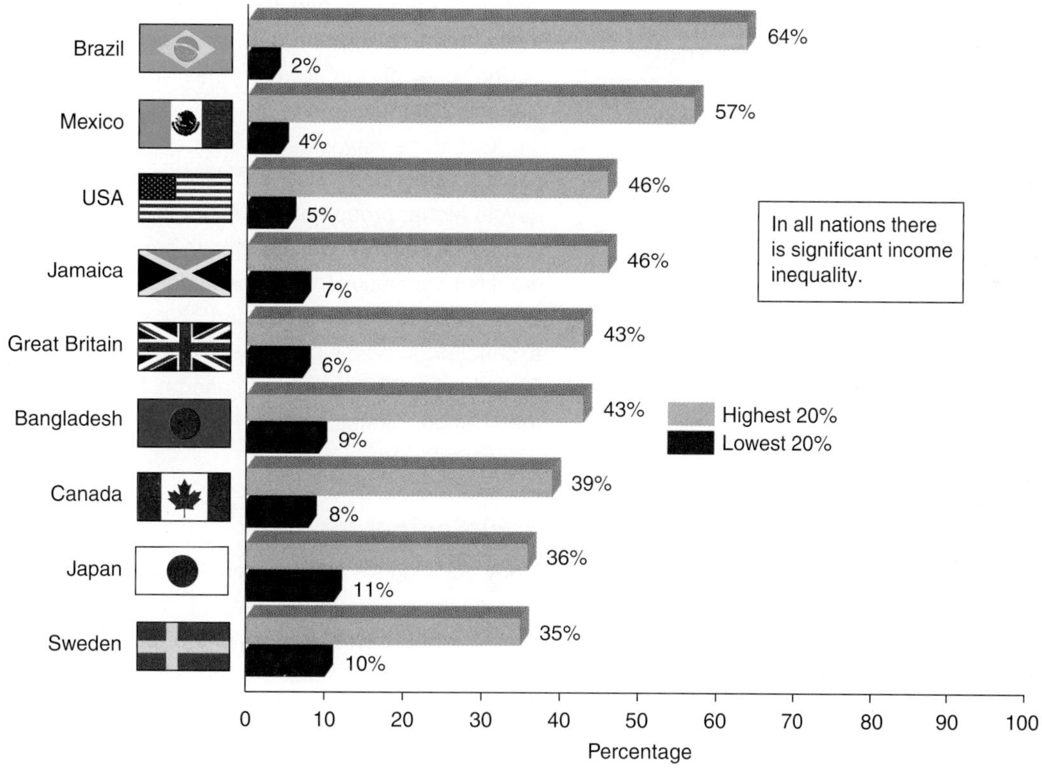

Source: Based on data from World Bank 2002:74–76.

Note: Data are considered comparable although based on statistics covering 1992 to 1997.

Think about It

Why is income inequality higher in the United States than in Canada, Japan, and Sweden?

SOCIAL POLICY AND STRATIFICATION

Rethinking Welfare in North America and Europe

The Issue

- After five years on Saskatchewan's welfare rolls, a single mother of three is a success story. The 28-year-old has landed a job at a storage company and moved up to a $12-an-hour customer service position. However, another single mother employed in a nearby hotel for $8.00 per hour worries about being edged back into unemployment by the stiff competition for low-wage jobs.
- Hélène Desegrais, a single mother in Paris, France, waited for four months to obtain a place in government-subsidized day care for her daughter. Now she can seek a full-time job, but she is concerned about government threats to curtail such services to keep taxes down (Simons 1997).
- Marcia Missouri of Worcester, Massachusetts, tacks up a handwritten advertisement in the public housing project in which she lives to say that she is available to clean yards and braid hair for a few extra dollars. The sign lists a friend's phone number; she doesn't have a phone of her own (Vobejda and Havenmann 1997).

These are the faces of people living on the edge—often women with children seeking to make a go of it amid changing social policies. Governments in all parts of the world are searching for the right solution to welfare: How much subsidy should they provide? How much responsibility should fall on the shoulders of the poor?

The Setting

By the 1990s, there was intense debate in Canada over the issue of welfare. Welfare programs were costly, and there was widespread concern (however unfounded) that welfare payments discouraged recipients from seeking jobs. On the one hand, there were declarations to "end poverty as we know it" (Pear 1996:20), but on the other, neoconservative forces in Canada voiced concern about government spending.

A study released by Statistics Canada in 2004 showed that the number of people on Canada's welfare rolls has decreased by more than one million since 1994. The study attributed the decline to new rules that make it tougher to qualify for social assistance and to improvements in the economies of various provinces (Statistics Canada 2004d). The greatest change in terms of family type of those collecting social assistance occurred among single mothers. In 1995, almost one-half of Canada's single mothers received social assistance; by 2000 that rate had declined to almost one-third.

During the 1990s, the governments of Ontario and Alberta led the way in making social assistance more difficult for people to receive. As of 2000, Alberta had the lowest rate of welfare recipients, Quebec and Newfoundland and Labrador had the highest, and Ontario had moved from having one of the highest rates in 1992 to having one of the lowest rates in 2000 (Statistics Canada 2004d).

Countries vary widely in their commitment to social service programs. But some industrialized nations devote higher proportions of their expenditures to housing, social security, welfare, health care, and unemployment compensation than Canada does. Data available in 2002 indicated that in Ireland, 76 percent of health expenditures were paid for by the government; in Switzerland, 73 percent; in Canada, 71 percent; but in the United States, only 44 percent (World Bank 2002:102–104d).

Sociological Insights

Many sociologists tend to view the debate over welfare throughout industrialized nations from a conflict perspective: the "haves" in positions of policymaking listen to the interests of other "haves," while the cries of the "have-nots" are drowned out. Critics of so-called welfare reform believe that Canada's economic problems are unfairly being blamed on welfare spending and the poor. From a conflict perspective, this backlash against welfare recipients reflects deep fears and hostility toward the country's poor and dispossessed.

Those critical of the backlash note that "welfare scapegoating" conveniently ignores the lucrative government handouts that go to *affluent* individuals and families. British Columbia, for example, has reduced income taxes for all residents, including the wealthy, while at the some time reducing or eliminating government services and programs that most benefit the poor.

Those who take a conflict perspective also urge policymakers and the general public to look closely at *corporate welfare*—the tax breaks, direct payments, and grants that the government makes to corporations—rather than to focus on the comparatively small allowances being given to mothers on social assistance and their children. Any suggestion to curtail such "corporate welfare" brings a strong response from special-interest groups that are much more powerful than any coalition on behalf of the poor. One example of corporate welfare is the airline bailout bill that was passed in the wake of the terrorist attacks in September 2001. Within 11 days the U.S. government had approved the bailout, whose positive impact was felt largely by airline executives and shareholders. Relatively low-paid airline employees were still laid off, and hundreds of thousands of low-wage workers in airports, hotels, and related industries received little or no assistance. Efforts to broaden unemployment assistance to help these marginally employed workers failed (Hartman and Miller 2001).

Policy Initiatives

The government likes to highlight success stories. It is true that many people who previously depended on tax dollars are now working and paying taxes themselves. But it is much too soon to see whether welfare reform will be successful. The new jobs that were generated by the booming economy of the late 1990s may be an unrealistic test of the system. Prospects for the hard-core jobless—those people who are hard to train or who have drug or alcohol dependency, physical disabilities, or child care needs—remain a challenge.

In the United States, fewer people are on welfare since enactment of the welfare reform law in August 1996. By January 2002, nearly 7 million people had left the system, reducing the rolls to 5.4 million people. Yet research showed that most adults who had gone off welfare had taken low-wage jobs that did not offer benefits. As they moved off welfare, their Medicaid coverage ended, leaving them without health insurance. Support has also been lacking for working parents who need high-quality child care. And assistance to immigrants, even those who are legal residents, continues to be limited (Department of Health and Human Services 2002, 2000; Ehrenreich and Piven 2002).

European governments have encountered some of the same citizen demands as those found in North America: Keep our taxes low, even if it means reducing services to the poor. However, nations in Eastern and Central Europe have faced a special challenge since the end of communism. The governments in those nations had traditionally provided an impressive array of social services, but they differed from capitalist systems in several important respects. First, the communist system was premised on full employment, so there was no need to provide employment insurance or social services focused on older people and those with disabilities. Second, subsidies, such as for housing and even utilities, played an important role. With new competition from the West and tight budgets, some of these countries are beginning to realize that universal coverage is no longer affordable and must be replaced with targeted programs. Even Sweden, despite its long history of social welfare programs, is feeling the pinch. Still, only modest cutbacks have been made in European social service programs, leaving them much more generous than those in Canada and the United States (Gornick 2001).

Both in North America and Europe, people are beginning to turn to private means to support themselves. For instance, they are investing money for their later years rather than depending on government social security programs. But that solution only works if you have a job and can save money. Increasing proportions of people are seeing the gap growing between themselves and the affluent with fewer government programs aimed at assisting them. Solutions are frequently left to the private sector, while government policy initiatives at the national level all but disappear.

Applying Theory

1. What might be the focus of some feminist sociologists as they studied the changes in welfare reform in Canada and elsewhere?
2. How would you explain the trend of the decreasing number of Canadians receiving social assistance?
3. Have you or has anyone you know applied for social assistance? If so, what caused you or them to do so?

CHAPTER RESOURCES

Summary

Stratification is the structured ranking of entire groups of people that perpetuates unequal economic rewards and power in a society. In this chapter, we examined three general systems of stratification, social inequality as reflected in social class and social mobility, stratification within the world economic system, and the welfare system in North America and Europe.

1. Some degree of ***social inequality*** characterizes all cultures.
2. Systems of ***stratification*** include ***slavery, castes,*** and social ***class.***
3. Karl Marx saw that differences in access to the means of production created social, economic, and political inequality and distinct classes of owners and labourers.
4. Max Weber identified three analytically distinct components of stratification: ***class, status group,*** and ***power.***
5. Functionalists argue that stratification is necessary to motivate people to fill society's important positions; conflict theorists see stratification as a major source of societal tension and conflict.
6. One measure of social class is occupational ***prestige.*** A consequence of social class in Canada is that both ***wealth*** and ***income*** are distributed unevenly.
7. The category of the "poor" defies any simple definition, and counters common stereotypes about "poor people." The long-term poor, who lack training and skills, form an ***underclass.***
8. Functionalists find that the poor satisfy positive functions for many of the nonpoor in capitalist societies.
9. A person's ***life chances***—opportunities for obtaining material goods, positive living conditions, and favourable life experiences—are related to social class. Occupying a high social position improves a person's life chances.
10. ***Social mobility*** is more likely to be found in an ***open system*** that emphasizes achieved status than in a ***closed system*** that focuses on ascribed characteristics. Race, gender, and class intersect to produce compounded chances for social mobility.
11. Former colonized nations are kept in subservient positions, subject to foreign domination, through the process of ***neocolonialism.***
12. Drawing on the conflict perspective, the ***world systems analysis*** of sociologist Immanuel Wallerstein views the global economic system as divided between nations that control wealth *(core nations)* and those from which capital is taken *(periphery nations).*
13. According to ***dependency theory,*** even as developing countries make economic advances, they remain weak and subservient to core nations and corporations within an increasingly intertwined global economy.
14. ***Multinational corporations*** bring jobs and industry to developing nations, but they also tend to exploit the workers there in order to maximize profits.
15. According to ***modernization theory,*** development in peripheral countries will be assisted by the innovations transferred from the industrialized world.
16. Many governments are struggling with how much tax revenue to spend on welfare programs.
17. Welfare rolls in Canada have shrunk by more than one million people since 1994.

Critical Thinking Questions

1. How would functional thinkers explain the growing gap between the rich and the poor in Canada? What about among nations?
2. Sociological study of stratification generally is conducted at the macrolevel and draws most heavily on the functionalist and conflict perspectives. How might sociologists use the *interactionist* perspective to examine social class inequalities within a university?
3. Imagine you have the opportunity to do research on changing patterns of social mobility in a developing nation from a feminist perspective. What specific question would you want to investigate, and how would you go about it?
4. Why do you think companies like Nike do not produce their products in their own country?

Key Terms

Absolute poverty A standard of poverty based on a minimum level of subsistence below which families should not be expected to live. (page 174)

Bourgeoisie Karl Marx's term for the capitalist class, comprising the owners of the means of production. (168)

Capitalism An economic system in which the means of production are largely in private hands and the main incentive for economic activity is the accumulation of profits. (168)

Castes Hereditary systems of rank, usually religiously dictated, that tend to be fixed and immobile. (164)

Class A group of people who have a similar level of wealth and income. (169)

Class consciousness In Karl Marx's view, a subjective awareness held by members of a class regarding their common vested interests and need for collective political action to bring about social change. (169)

Class system A social ranking based primarily on economic position in which achieved characteristics can influence social mobility. (165)

Closed system A social system in which there is little or no possibility of individual mobility. (179)

Colonialism The maintenance of political, social, economic, and cultural dominance over a people by a foreign power for an extended period of time. (181)

Dependency theory An approach that contends that industrialized nations continue to exploit developing countries for their own gain. (181)

Esteem The reputation that a particular individual has earned within an occupation. (172)

False consciousness A term used by Karl Marx to describe an attitude held by members of a class that does not accurately reflect their objective position. (169)

Globalization The worldwide integration of government policies, cultures, social movements, and financial markets through trade and the exchange of ideas. (183)

Horizontal mobility The movement of an individual from one social position to another of the same rank. (179)

Income Salaries and wages. (162)

Intergenerational mobility Changes in the social position of children relative to their parents. (179)

Intragenerational mobility Changes in a person's social position within his or her adult life. (179)

Life chances People's opportunities to provide themselves with material goods, positive living conditions, and favourable life experiences. (177)

Modernization The far-reaching process by which peripheral nations move from traditional or less developed institutions to those characteristic of more developed societies. (186)

Modernization theory A functionalist approach that proposes that modernization and development will gradually improve the lives of people in peripheral nations. (186)

Multinational corporations Commercial organizations that, although headquartered in one country, own or control other corporations and subsidiaries throughout the world. (184)

Neocolonialism Continuing dependence of former colonies on foreign countries. (181)

Objective method A technique for measuring social class that assigns individuals to classes on the basis of such criteria as occupation, education, income, and place of residence. (172)

Open system A social system in which the position of each individual is influenced by his or her achieved status. (179)

Power The ability of people to exercise their will over others. (170)

Prestige The respect and admiration that an occupation holds in a society. (172)

Proletariat Karl Marx's term for the working class in a capitalist society. (168)

Relative poverty A floating standard of deprivation by which people at the bottom of a society, whatever their lifestyles, are judged to be disadvantaged in comparison with the nation as a whole. (175)

Slavery A system of enforced servitude in which people are legally owned by others and in which enslaved status is transferred from parents to children. (164)

Social inequality A condition in which members of a society have different amounts of wealth, prestige, or power. (162)

Social mobility Movement of individuals or groups from one position of a society's stratification system to another. (178)

Status group People who have the same prestige or lifestyle, independent of their class positions. (170)

Stratification A structured ranking of entire groups of people that perpetuates unequal economic rewards and power in a society. (162)

Underclass People who are poor for the long term and who lack training and skills. (177)

Vertical mobility The movement of a person from one social position to another of a different rank. (179)

Wealth An inclusive term encompassing all of a person's material assets, including land and other types of property. (162)

World systems analysis A view of the global economic system as divided between certain industrialized nations that control wealth and developing countries that are controlled and exploited. (181)

Additional Readings

Carroll, William. 2003. *Corporate Power in a Globalizing World.* Toronto: Oxford University Press. This book offers a systematic analysis of the Canadian corporate network in the global context, arguing that it constitutes the leading edge of the ruling class.

Grabb, Edward G. 2002. *Theories of Social Inequality,* 4th ed. Toronto: Harcourt. This book provides a comprehensive overview and analysis of both classical and contemporary theories of social inequality.

Van der Gaag, Nikki. 2004. *The No-Nonsense Guide to Women's Rights.* Toronto: New Internationalist Publications. This book places poverty in a global context, focusing on those who suffer the most—women and children.

Online Learning Centre

Visit the *Sociology: A Brief Introduction* Online Learning Centre at www.mcgrawhill.ca/college/schaefer to access quizzes, interactive exercises, video clips, and other research and study tools related to this chapter.

Reel Society Interactive Movie CD-ROM 2.0

Reel Society 2.0 can be used to spark discussion about the following topics from this chapter:

- Understanding stratification
- Stratification by social class
- Social mobility

chapter 9

RACIAL AND ETHNIC INEQUALITY

The Canadian Race Relations Foundation advocates to end racism and discrimination through its Program for Initiatives Against Racism. The program works to increase the understanding of racism and racial discrimination in Canada, reveal the causes of racism, and dispel misconceptions about groups affected by racism and racial discrimination.

Let's be clear: There is also a New Canada out there. If Canadians can't see it themselves, they certainly pay attention when others see it on our behalf. Thus, *The Economist* magazine captured our attention in the fall of 2003 when it put on its cover a moose in sunglasses under the headline "Canada's new spirit" and went on to laud our tolerance and cultural diversity and describe our major cities as vibrant, cosmopolitan places. . . .

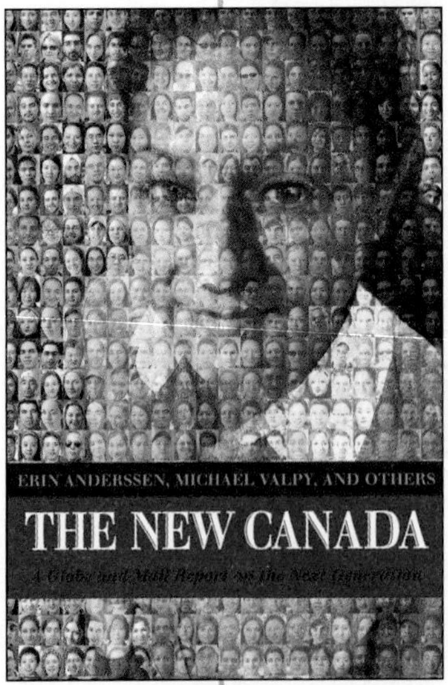

Our embrace of multiculturalism presents the most obvious manifestation of the New Canada. But it goes well beyond the mere fact of scores of different ethnic groups co-existing peacefully in our global cities, however notable an achievement that may represent in international terms.

Our schools ring out with the sound of different tongues, giving our children an early and ever-lasting lesson in the very Canadian balance of individual expression and social peace. The New Canada of which we speak flows from the long cherished frontier value of freedom. The New Canada is about the freedom to be who you are and still belong to the larger group. . . .

Virtually nobody under the age of 30 thinks that a similar ethnic or racial background is an important consideration in choosing a spouse—even if that means holding two separate weddings to unite the couple. . . .

Immigration died down during the Depression and the Second World War. Then, starting in the post-war period, Canada attracted a wave of skilled and semi-skilled blue-collar workers from southern Europe. Many of the children of this second wave sit proudly today in our legislatures and Parliament.

And then the third wave—the one that has so demonstrably changed the look of our cities over the past generation. Chinese, Sri Lankans, Filipinos, Sikhs, Ismailis, West Indians, North and sub-Saharan Africans—an influx that has changed our capacities but strengthened our fabric. Thanks to the education system and the media, integration occurs far faster than ever before—usually within the same generation for younger Canadians. As Queen's University professor Matthew Mendelsohn, a consultant on the New Canada series, points out, in France, Britain, Italy, the United States and elsewhere, anywhere from 30 to 50 per cent of people say that relations between ethnic groups are a problem. In Canada, just 12 per cent think so.

This process of ethnic diversification is inevitably changing our world outlook—making us less parochial in all our dealings. When you see a *pure laine* Québécois boy strolling down Rue St. Denis with his Haitian-Canadian girlfriend and their Moroccan-Canadian schoolmates, it is hard to imagine them being overly agitated about the hanging of Louis Riel. They are connected to a vibrant world, not stuck in an historical rant. *(Anderssen, Valpy, et al. 2004)* ■

This excerpt from the book by Erin Anderssen, Michael Valpy, and others depicts a "New Canada" characterized as tolerant, peaceful, and culturally diverse, with vibrant cosmopolitan cities. It is a Canada, according to the authors, where people, particularly those under the age of 30, do not consider similar ethnocultural background an important consideration in choosing a mate. It is a Canada, as the authors point out, where just 12 percent of Canadians say that relations between ethnic groups are a problem, in sharp contrast to such countries as France, Britain, Italy, and the United States, where 30 percent to 50 percent of the people say that relations between ethnic groups are a problem. Despite this seemingly glowing view of ethnic diversity in Canada, patterns of inequality exist and persist, whereby some groups are systematically subjugated by the dominant groups, restricting their access to opportunity and upward mobility.

Today, thousands of people who are members of racial and ethnic minorities continue to experience the often bitter contrast between the Canadian ideal of multiculturalism and the grim realities of poverty, prejudice, and discrimination. Class, gender, and the social definitions of race and ethnicity intersect to produce systems of inequality, not only in this country but throughout the world. High incomes, a good command of French or English, and hard-earned professional credentials do not always override racial and ethnic stereotypes or protect those who fit them from the sting of racism.

What is prejudice, and how is it institutionalized in the form of discrimination? In what ways have race and ethnicity affected the experience of immigrants from other countries? What are the fastest-growing minority groups in Canada today? In this chapter we will focus on the meaning of race and ethnicity. We will begin by identifying the basic characteristics of a minority group and distinguishing between racial groups and ethnic groups. Then we will examine the dynamics of prejudice and discrimination. After considering the functionalist, conflict, feminist, and interactionist perspectives on race and ethnicity, we'll look at patterns of intergroup relations, particularly in Canada. Finally, in the social policy section, we will explore issues related to immigration worldwide. ■

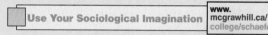

Use Your Sociological Imagination www.mcgrawhill.ca/college/schaefer

Does Anderssen and Valpy's view of Canada match your own experiences or situation? Do you think the statistic that only 12 percent of Canadians say that relations between ethnic groups are a problem masks the everyday experiences of many Canadians who face discrimination because of their skin colour or ethnocultural identity?

MINORITY, RACIAL, AND ETHNIC GROUPS

Categories of people can often be thought of as "racial" and ethnic groups. The term ***racial group*** describes a category that is set apart and treated differently from others because of real or perceived physical differences. White, black, and Asian Canadians are all considered racial groups in Canada. It is the culture of a particular society, however, that constructs and attaches social significance to these differences, as we will see later. Unlike racialized groups, an ***ethnic group*** is set apart from others primarily because of its national origin or distinctive cultural patterns. In Canada, Italian Canadians, Jewish people, and Polish Canadians are all categorized as ethnic groups. Both types of groups are considered to be *minority groups* by sociologists, as the next section shows.

Minority Groups

A numerical minority is any group that makes up less than half of some larger population. The population of Canada includes thousands of numerical minorities, including television actors, green-eyed people, tax lawyers, and snow boarders. However, these numerical minorities are not considered to be minorities in the sociological sense; in fact, the number of people in a group does not necessarily determine its status as a social minority (or a dominant group). When sociologists define a minority group, they are primarily concerned with the economic and political power, or powerlessness, of that group. A ***minority group*** is a subordinate group whose members have significantly less control or power over their own lives than the members of a dominant or majority group have over their own.

In Canada, the term ***visible minority*** is used to refer to those Canadians who are non-white or are identified as being physically different from white Canadians of European descent, who compose the dominant group. Visible minorities, according to the official government definition, include such groups as South Asians, Japanese, Arabs, Latin Americans, and Chinese. Aboriginal people form a distinct and unique minority group in Canada, and for government and statistical purposes, they are not categorized as a minority group. Aboriginal people, however, have been and continue to be treated as a visible minority group, experiencing generations of systemic brutalization by white Europeans—most notably via the residential school system. The cruel treatment that Aboriginal people have received from the dominant ethnic groups will be explained more fully later in this chapter.

Sociologists have identified five basic properties of a minority group: unequal treatment, physical or cultural traits, ascribed status, solidarity, and in-group marriage (Wagley and Harris 1958):

1. Members of a minority group experience unequal treatment as compared with members of a dominant group. For example, the management of an apartment complex may refuse to rent to blacks, Hispanics, or Jews. Social inequality may be created or maintained by prejudice, discrimination, segregation, or even extermination.
2. Members of a minority group share physical or cultural characteristics that distinguish them from the dominant group. Each society arbitrarily decides which characteristics are most important in defining the groups.
3. Membership in a minority (or dominant) group is not voluntary; people are born into the group. Thus, race and ethnicity are considered *ascribed* statuses. p. 96
4. Minority group members have a strong sense of group solidarity. William Graham Sumner, writing in 1906, noted that people make distinctions between members of their own group (the *in-group*) and everyone else (the *out-group*). When a group is the object of long-term prejudice and discrimination, the feeling of "us versus them" can and often does become extremely intense. p. 120
5. Members of a minority generally marry others from the same group. A member of a dominant group is often unwilling to marry into a supposedly inferior minority. In addition, the minority group's sense of solidarity encourages marriages within the group and discourages marriages to outsiders.

Race

As explained, the term *racial group* refers to those minorities (and the corresponding dominant groups) set apart from others by what are perceived to be obvious physical differences. But what is an "obvious" physical difference? Each society determines which differences are important while ignoring other characteristics that could serve as a basis for social differentiation. In Canada, we see differences in both skin colour and hair colour. Yet people learn informally that differences in skin colour have a dramatic social and political meaning, while differences in hair colour do not.

When observing skin colour, people in Canada tend to lump others rather casually into such categories as "black," "brown," "white," and "Asian." More subtle differences in skin colour often go unnoticed. However, this is not the case in other societies. Many nations of Central America and South America have colour gradients distinguishing people on a continuum from light to dark skin colour. Brazil has approximately 40 colour groupings, while in other countries people may be described as "Mestizo Hondurans," "Mulatto Colombians," or "African Panamanians." What people see as "obvious" differences, then, are subject to each society's social definitions.

Three groups make up the largest visible minorities in Canada: Chinese, blacks, and South Asians. Figure 9-1 provides information about where the vast majority of immigrants settle—Montreal, Vancouver, and Toronto. A disproportionately high and growing number of immigrants to those cities are members of visible minority groups.

Biological Significance of Race

Viewed from a biological perspective, the term *race* would refer to a genetically isolated group with distinctive gene frequencies. But it is impossible to scientifically define or identify such a group. Contrary to popular belief, there are no "pure races." Nor are there physical traits—whether skin colour or baldness—that can be used to describe one group to the exclusion of all others. If scientists examine a smear of human blood under a microscope, they cannot tell whether it came from a Chinese or Aboriginal person or black Canadian. There is, in fact, more genetic variation *within* races than across them.

Migration, exploration, and invasion have led to intermingling of races. Research indicates that the

FIGURE 9-1

Share of Immigrants 10 Years or Less in Canada: Montreal, Toronto, and Vancouver, 1981, 1991, 2001

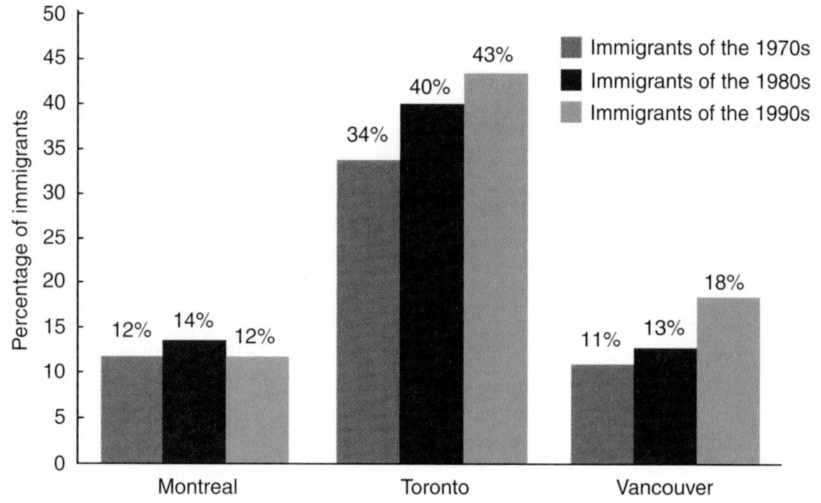

Source: Statistics Canada 2003d.

percentage of North American blacks with white ancestry ranges from 20 percent to as much as 75 percent. Such statistics challenge the view that we can accurately categorize, for example, "black" and "white." Therefore, the belief that we are able to neatly categorize individuals according to race is a myth.

Some people would like to find biological explanations to help social scientists understand why certain peoples of the world have come to dominate others (see the discussion of sociobiology in Chapter 4). p. 74 Given the absence of pure racial groups, there can be no satisfactory biological answers for such social and political questions.

Social Construction of Race

In the southern part of the United States, it was known as the "one-drop rule." If a person had even a single drop of "black blood," that person was defined and viewed as black, even if he or she *appeared* to be white. Clearly, race had social significance in that region, enough so that white legislators established official standards about who was "black" and "white."

The one-drop rule was a vivid example of the *social construction of race*—the process by which people come to define a group as a "race" based in part on physical characteristics, but also on historical, cultural, and economic factors.

According to the 2001 census, approximately 11 million or 38 percent of Canadians reported having multiple ethnic origins. With rates of intermarriage increasing in Canada, so too is the multiplicity of backgrounds. In 2001, almost four million Canadians—more than 13 percent—defined themselves as members of a visible minority group.

A dominant or majority group has the power not only to define itself legally but to define a society's values. Sociologist William I. Thomas (1923), an early critic of theories of racial and gender differences, saw that the "definition of the situation" could mould the personality of the individual. To put it another way, Thomas, writing from the interactionist perspective, observed that people respond not only to the objective features of a situation or person but also to the *meaning* that situation or person has for them. Thus, we can create false images or stereotypes that become real in their

Children who have one black parent are categorized as "black," even though they may appear to be "white." This is an example of how race is socially constructed.

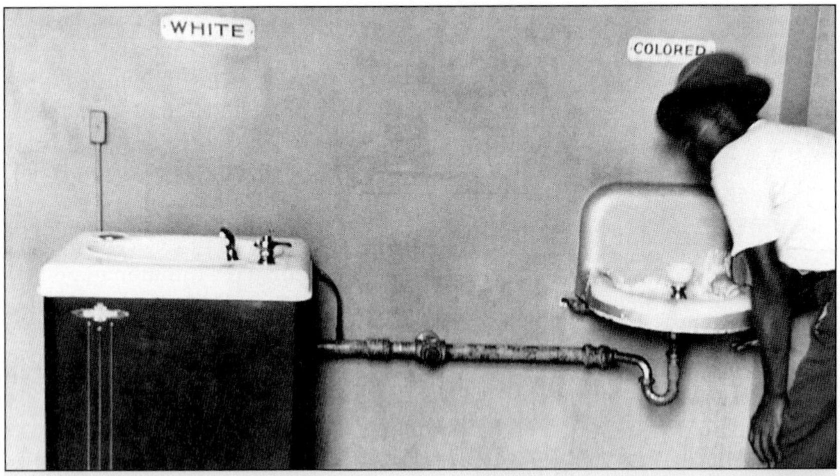

"Whites only" was a common sign in the southern states when "Jim Crow" laws enforced official segregation of the races. In this blatant example of institutional discrimination, blacks were not allowed to use a new water fountain reserved for whites and had to drink from an older fixture nearby.

consequences. ***Stereotypes*** are unreliable generalizations about all members of a group that do not recognize individual differences within the group.

In the last 30 years, critics have pointed out the power of the mass media to perpetuate false racial and ethnic stereotypes. Television is a prime example: Almost all the leading dramatic roles are cast as whites, even in urban-based programs. Blacks tend to be featured mainly in crime-based dramas.

Use Your Sociological Imagination

Using a TV remote control, how quickly do you think you could find a television show in which all the characters share your own racial or ethnic background? What about a show in which all the characters share a different background from your own—how quickly could you find one?

Ethnicity

An ethnic group, unlike a racial group, is set apart from others because of its national origin or distinctive cultural patterns. Among the ethnic groups in Canada are people with a French-speaking background, which includes people from Tracadie, New Brunswick; Paris, France; Coderre, Saskatchewan; and Quebec City. Other ethnic groups in this country include Jewish, Irish, Italian, and Norwegian Canadians. Although these groupings are convenient, they serve to obscure differences *within* these ethnic categories as well as to overlook the mixed ancestry of so many ethnic people in Canada.

The Canadian census, however, does address this problem, to some extent, by providing Canadians with the option of giving single or multiple responses to the question of ethnic origin (see Table 9-1). For example, the 2001 census reported that 211 725 Canadians identified themselves as being of Jamaican origin, with 138 180 declaring this as their sole response and 73 545 declaring this as one of multiple responses.

The distinction between racial and ethnic minorities is not always clear-cut. Some members of racial minorities, such as Asian Canadians, may have significant cultural differences from other groups. At the same time, certain ethnic minorities, such as Indo-Canadians, may have obvious physical differences that set them apart from other residents of Canada.

Despite categorization problems, sociologists continue to feel that the distinction between racial groups and ethnic groups is socially significant. In most societies, including Canada, physical differences tend to be more visible than ethnic differences. Partly as a result of this fact, racialized stratification is more resistant to change than is stratification along ethnic lines. Members of an ethnic minority sometimes can become, over time, indistinguishable from the majority—although this process may take generations and may never include all members of the group. By contrast, members of a racialized minority find it much more difficult to blend in with the larger society and to gain acceptance from the majority.

PREJUDICE AND DISCRIMINATION

In recent years, university campuses across the United States have been the scene of bias-related incidents. Student-run newspapers and radio stations have ridiculed racial and ethnic minorities; threatening literature has been stuffed under the doors of minority students; graffiti endorsing the views of white supremacist organizations, such as the Ku Klux Klan, have been scrawled on university walls. In some cases, there have even been violent clashes between groups of white and black students (Bunzel 1992; R. Schaefer 2004).

In April 2004, the United Talmud Torahs elementary school—a Jewish school in Montreal—was firebombed, destroying the school's library and adjoining offices and classrooms. The attack on the school was accompanied

Table 9-1 Population by Selected Ethnic Origins, Canada, 2001 Census

	Total Responses	Single Responses	Multiple Responses
Total Population	**29 639 035**	**18 307 545**	**11 331 490**
Ethnic Origin			
Canadian	11 682 680	6 748 135	4 934 545
English	5 978 875	1 479 525	4 499 355
French	4 668 410	1 060 760	3 607 655
Scottish	4 157 210	607 235	3 549 975
Irish	3 822 660	496 864	3 325 795
German	2 742 765	705 600	2 037 170
Italian	1 270 370	726 275	544 090
Chinese	1 094 700	936 210	158 490
Ukrainian	1 071 060	326 195	744 860
North American Indian	1 000 890	455 805	545 085
Dutch (Netherlands)	923 310	316 220	607 090
Polish	817 085	260 415	556 665
East Indian	713 330	581 665	131 665
Norwegian	363 760	47 230	316 530
Portuguese	357 690	252 835	104 855
Welsh	350 365	28 445	321 920
Jewish	348 605	186 475	162 130
Russian	337 960	70 895	267 070
Filipino	327 550	266 140	61 405
Métis	307 845	72 210	235 635
Swedish	282 760	30 440	252 325
Hungarian (Magyar)	267 255	91 800	175 455
American (USA)	250 005	25 205	224 805
Greek	215 105	143 785	71 325
Spanish	213 105	66 545	146 555
Jamaican	211 725	138 180	73 545
Danish	170 780	33 795	136 985
Vietnamese	151 410	119 120	32 290

Source: Statistics Canada 2005b.

by a rash of anti-Semitic actions around the world. Since then, Jewish schools in Canada have spent millions of dollars implementing tighter security measures in an attempt to ensure the safety of their students and staff.

Prejudice

Prejudice is a negative attitude toward an entire category of people, often an ethnic or a racial minority. If you resent your roommate because he or she is sloppy, you are not necessarily guilty of prejudice. However, if you immediately stereotype your roommate on the basis of such characteristics as race, ethnicity, or religion, that is a form of prejudice. Prejudice tends to perpetuate false definitions of individuals and groups.

Sometimes prejudice results from ethnocentrism—the tendency to assume that your own culture and way of life represent the norm or are superior to all others.

Research in Action

9-1 Prejudice against Arabs and Muslims in Post–September 11 America

As marginal groups with little political power, Arabs and Muslims living in America are vulnerable to prejudice and discrimination. In the first five days after the terrorist attack on the World Trade Center in September 2001, these groups filed more than three hundred reports of harassment and abuse, including one death. Six years earlier, when the bombing of a federal office building in Oklahoma City was mistakenly attributed to Middle East terrorism, many Arabic and Islamic schoolchildren in the United States felt the repercussions. One boy in Grade 5 was told, "Go back where you came from!" His mother, an attorney and a second-generation Syrian American, asked where her children were supposed to go. One was born in Texas, the other in Oklahoma.

Sociologists have observed two trends in the United States over the past 20 years. First, the numbers of people in the United States who are Arab or who practise the Muslim faith have increased dramatically. Second, the open expression of hostility toward Arab and Muslim people has also increased. Obviously, the coinciding of these two trends has made life unpleasant for many people.

Following the attack on the World Trade Center, media representatives recognized how little insight Americans have into Arab cultures and Islamic religious practices. Content analysis of the media has shown that Arabs and Muslims are repeatedly presented as almost cartoonlike figures, whether camel drivers, outrageously wealthy sheiks, or deranged terrorists. Even Disney's 1993 animated film *Aladdin* referred to Arabs as "barbaric." The movie depicted an Arabic guard threatening to cut off a young girl's hand for stealing food but did not point out that such punishment would violate Islamic law.

Racial profiling at airports has put some citizens under special surveillance. Fearing terrorist attacks, a number of airlines and law enforcement authorities use appearance and ethnic-sounding names to identify and take aside Arab Americans (or those who match the profile) and search their belongings. After the terrorist attacks of September 11, 2001, two Canadian Muslim men in Nova Scotia sued the RCMP for violating their Charter rights by wrongfully arresting them based on ethnic profiling.

Muslim women who wear head scarves or *hijab* in keeping with their tradition to dress modestly encounter harassment from strangers in the street. Many employers insist that the women shed the covering if they want to get a job or expect to be promoted. These women find it difficult to understand such attitudes in a nation founded on religious freedom.

Many people in the United States inaccurately lump together Arab Americans and Muslims. Although these groups overlap, many Arab Americans are Christians (as is true of many Arabs living in the Middle East) and many Muslims (such as blacks, Iranians, and Pakistanis) are non-Arabs. Currently, there are an estimated 870 000 Arab Americans, and their numbers are rising. Many cling to the culture of their nation of origin, which can vary considerably. For example, Arabs constitute an ethnic group in 22 nations of North Africa and the Middle East, including Morocco, Syria, Iraq, Saudi Arabia, and Somalia.

At present, perhaps as many as three million Muslims live in the United States, of whom about 42 percent are black, 24 percent are South Asian, 12 percent are Arab, and 22 percent are "other." Muslims are followers of Islam, the world's second-largest faith after Christianity. Islam is based on the teachings found in the Koran (or Al-Qur'an) of the seventh-century prophet Mohammed. Islamic believers are divided into a variety of faiths and sects, such as Sunnis and Shiites, which are sometimes antagonistic toward one another (just as there are religious rivalries among Christians and among Jews).

The first known mosque in the United States was founded in 1929. Today, there are more than 1200 mosques in the United States, of which 80 percent have been established in the last 25 years. The largest group of Muslims in the United States, blacks, is divided between those who follow mainstream Islamic doctrine and those who follow the teachings of the controversial Nation of Islam (headed by Minister Louis Farrakhan). The Muslim population of the United States is growing significantly, owing to high birthrates, substantial immigration of Muslims, and conversion of non-Muslims.

Applying Theory

1. Do you know an Arab or a Muslim person who has been the subject of ethnic profiling in Canada or the United States? If so, explain the circumstances. What was the person's reaction to the experience?
2. How would interactionist sociologists study the problems of prejudice and discrimination against Arab and Muslim people?

Sources: El-Badry 1994; Henneberger 1995; Lindner 1998; Power 1998; Shaheen 1999; T. Smith 2001; Weinstein et al. 2001.

p. 64

Ethnocentric people judge other cultures by the standards of their own group, which leads quite easily to prejudice against cultures viewed as inferior.

One important and widespread form of prejudice is ***racism,*** the belief that one race is supreme and all others are innately inferior. When racism prevails in a society, members of subordinate groups generally experience prejudice, discrimination, and exploitation.

In the wake of the terrorist attacks of September 11, 2001, hate crimes against Asian Americans and Muslim Americans escalated rapidly. Box 9-1 examines prejudice against Arabs and Muslims who live in the United States.

The activity level of organized hate groups appears to be increasing, both in reality and in virtual reality. Although only a few hundred such groups may exist, there were at least two thousand Web sites advocating racial hatred on the Internet in 1999. The technology of the Internet has allowed race-hate groups to expand far beyond their regional bases to reach millions (Sandberg 1999).

Discriminatory Behaviour

John and Glenn are alike in almost every way—about the same age, they are both university graduates with good jobs. But they find they have different experiences in everyday routines, such as walking into a store. John gets instant attention from the same sales staff that ignores Glenn, even though he has been waiting five minutes. When Glenn is locked out of his car, passersby ignore him, while John receives many offers of help. At an employment agency, Glenn is lectured on laziness and told he will be monitored closely; John is encouraged.

What accounts for these differences in the everyday life experiences of two men? Very simply, John is white and Glenn is black. The two were part of an experiment, conducted by the television newsmagazine *Primetime Live* to assess the impact of race on the day-to-day lives of residents in a typical U.S. city. Over a three-week period reporters closely monitored the two men, who had been trained to present themselves in an identical manner. Not once or twice, but "every single day," said program host Diane Sawyer, John and Glenn were treated differently (ABC News 1992).

Prejudice often leads to ***discrimination,*** the denial of opportunities and equal rights to individuals and groups based on some type of arbitrary bias. Say that a white corporate president with a prejudice against Indo-Canadians has to fill an executive position. The most qualified candidate for the job is of Indian descent. If the president refuses to hire this candidate and instead selects an inferior white candidate, he or she is engaging in an act of racial discrimination.

Prejudiced *attitudes* should not be equated with discriminatory *behaviour.* Although the two are generally related, they are not identical, and either condition can be present without the other. A prejudiced person does not always act on his or her biases. The white president, for example, might choose—despite his or her attitude—to hire the Indo-Canadian. This would be prejudice without discrimination. However, a white corporate president with a completely respectful view of Indo-Canadians might refuse to hire them for executive posts out of fear that biased clients would take their business elsewhere. In this case, the president's action would constitute discrimination without prejudice.

Discrimination persists even for the most educated and qualified minority group members from the best family backgrounds. Despite their talents and experiences, they sometimes encounter attitudinal or organizational bias that prevents them from reaching their full potential. The term ***glass ceiling*** refers to an invisible barrier that blocks the promotion of a qualified individual in a work environment because of the individual's gender, race, or ethnicity (R. Schaefer 2004; Yamagata et al. 1997).

Glass ceilings continue to block women and minority group men from top management positions in government, education, politics, and business. Even in *Fortune* magazine's 2002 listing of the most diversified corporations, white men held more than 80 percent both of the board of directors seats and of the top 50 paid positions in the firms. The existence of this glass ceiling results principally from the fears and prejudices of many middle- and upper-level white male managers, who believe that the inclusion of women and minority group men in management circles will threaten their own prospects for advancement (Hickman 2002).

The other side of discrimination is the privilege enjoyed by dominant groups. Though most white people rarely think about their "whiteness," taking their status for granted, sociologists and other social scientists are interested in what it means to be "white." Feminist scholar Peggy McIntosh (1988) has compiled a list of advantages that come with being white, including (1) avoiding having to spend time with people she was trained to mistrust, or who have learned to mistrust her kind; (2) being considered financially reliable when using cheques, credit cards, or cash; (3) never having to speak for all the people in her racial group; (4) taking a job without having her co-workers suspect she got it because of her race; and (5) being able to worry about racism without being regarded as self-serving. And white people can turn on the television or open up the newspaper and see members of their own race widely represented. Whiteness *does* carry privileges.

Institutional Discrimination

Discrimination is practised not only by individuals in one-to-one encounters but also by institutions in their daily operations. Social scientists are particularly concerned with the ways in which structural factors, such as employment, housing, health care, and government operations, maintain the social significance of race and ethnicity. ***Institutional discrimination*** refers to the denial of opportunities and equal rights to individuals and groups that results from the normal operations of a society. This kind of discrimination consistently affects certain racial and ethnic groups more than others.

People from white ethnic groups tend to underestimate the value of racial privilege. Employers generally hire those with backgrounds similar to their own, as this all-white committee meeting suggests.

The following are examples of institutional discrimination:

- Rules requiring that only English be spoken at a place of work, even when it is not a business necessity to restrict the use of other languages
- Preferences shown by law and medical schools in the admission of children of wealthy and influential alumni, nearly all of whom are not members of minorities
- Restrictive employment-leave policies, coupled with prohibitions on part-time work, that make it difficult for the heads of single-parent families (most of whom are women) to obtain and keep jobs

Racial or ethnic profiling, which is the use of the social construct of race as a consideration in suspect profiling in law enforcement and national security practices, is a form of institutional discrimination. A study released in 2005 and conducted by University of Toronto criminologist Scott Wortley using Kingston, Ontario, police statistics found that young black men and Aboriginal men had a greater chance of being stopped by the police than did members of other groups. More specifically, the study showed that a black man was 3.7 times more likely to be stopped by police than was a white man (CBC 2005).

Computer technology represents another area of institutional discrimination. As technology increases globally, access to this technology will be crucial in determining who moves ahead and who stays behind. In Canada, a disproportionate number of those with postsecondary education and higher income are from white ethnic and non-Aboriginal groups. Similarly, a disproportionately high number of Aboriginal people are from lower income and lower education groups. As of 2003, Canadians with postsecondary education and higher income levels have been at the forefront of Internet use in the home (Statistics Canada 2004f).

The significance of differential access may only increase as better-paying jobs, and even information itself, become increasingly tied to computer technology (Rainie and Pakel 2001).

Use Your Sociological Imagination

Suddenly, you don't have access to a desktop computer—not at home, at school, or even at work. How will your life change?

For more than 20 years, employment equity programs have been instituted in an attempt to make the workforce more diverse and to overcome discrimination. ***Employment equity*** refers to positive efforts to recruit historically disadvantaged groups for jobs, promotions, and educational opportunities. Some people, however, resent these programs, arguing that advancing one group's cause merely shifts the discrimination to another group. Critics argue that by giving priority to visible minorities in school admissions, for example, more qualified white ethnic group candidates may be overlooked.

Discriminatory practices continue to pervade nearly all areas of life in Canada today. In part, this is because various individuals and groups actually *benefit* from racial and ethnic discrimination in terms of money, status, and influence. Discrimination permits members of the majority to enhance their wealth, power, and prestige at the expense of others. Less-qualified people get jobs and promotions simply because they are members of the dominant group. Such individuals and groups will not surrender these advantages easily. We'll take a closer look at this functionalist analysis, as well as the conflict, feminist, and interactionist perspectives.

Women wearing head scarves or *hijabs* participate in a worldwide protest outside the French consulate in Montreal in January 2004. The women were protesting France's ban on *hijabs* in public schools.

STUDYING RACE AND ETHNICITY

Relations among dominant and ethnic minority groups lend themselves to analysis from the four major perspectives of sociology. From the macrolevel, functionalists observe that racism toward ethnic minorities serves positive functions for dominant groups, whereas conflict theorists see the economic structure as a central factor in the exploitation of minorities. The feminist perspective looks at both microlevel and macrolevel issues. The microlevel analysis of interactionist researchers stresses the manner in which everyday contact between people from different ethnic minorities contributes to tolerance or leads to hostility.

Functionalist Perspective

What possible use could racism have for society? Functionalist theorists, while agreeing that racism is hardly to be admired, point out that it indeed serves positive functions for those practising discrimination.

Anthropologist Manning Nash (1962) has identified three functions of racist beliefs for the dominant group:

1. Racist views provide a moral justification for maintaining an unequal society that routinely deprives a minority of its rights and privileges. Slavery has been justified, for example, by believing that Africans were physically and spiritually subhuman and devoid of souls (Hoebel 1949).
2. Racist beliefs discourage the subordinate minority from attempting to question its lowly status, which would be to question the very foundations of society.
3. Racial myths suggest that any major societal change (such as an end to discrimination) would only bring greater poverty to the minority and lower the majority's standard of living. As a result, Nash suggests, racial prejudice grows when a society's value system (for example, one underlying a colonial empire or a regime perpetuating slavery) is being threatened.

Although racism may serve the interests of the powerful, such unequal treatment can also be dysfunctional to a society and even to its dominant group. Sociologist Arnold Rose (1951) outlines four dysfunctions associated with racism:

1. A society that practises discrimination fails to use the resources of all individuals. Discrimination limits the search for talent and leadership to the dominant group.
2. Discrimination aggravates social problems, such as poverty, delinquency, and crime, and places the financial burden to alleviate these problems on the dominant group.
3. Society must invest a good deal of time and money to defend its barriers to full participation of all members.
4. Racial prejudice and discrimination often undercut goodwill and friendly diplomatic relations between nations.

Conflict Perspective

Conflict theorists would certainly agree with Arnold Rose that racial prejudice and discrimination have many harmful consequences for society. Sociologists such as Oliver Cox (1948), Robert Blauner (1972), and Herbert M. Hunter (2000) have used the ***exploitation theory*** (or *Marxist class theory*) to explain the basis of racial subordination. pp. 168–169 As we saw in Chapter 8, Karl Marx viewed the exploitation of the lower class as a basic part of the capitalist economic system. From a Marxist point of view, racism keeps minority group members in low-paying jobs, thereby supplying the capitalist ruling class with a pool of cheap labour. Moreover, by forcing racial minorities to accept low wages, capitalists can restrict the wages of *all* members of the proletariat. Workers from the dominant group who demand higher wages can always be replaced by minorities who have no choice but to accept low-paying jobs.

The conflict view of race relations seems persuasive in a number of instances. In the late nineteenth century, the Canadian government encouraged thousands of Chinese workers to come to Canada, without their families, to build the Canadian Pacific Railway. These men faced dangerous working and living conditions and many died before the railway was completed in 1885. After the railway's completion, when their labour was no longer needed, the government attempted to force the workers to return to China. To discourage future immigration from China, the Canadian government imposed what was called a head tax on every Chinese immigrant.

However, the exploitation theory is too limited to explain prejudice in its many forms. Not all minority groups have been economically exploited to the same extent. In addition, some groups, such as the Jews, have been victimized by prejudice for other than economic reasons. Still, as Gordon Allport (1979:210) concludes, the exploitation theory correctly "points a sure finger at one of the factors involved in prejudice, . . . rationalized self-interest of the upper classes."

Feminist Perspectives

Given the great diversity of feminist perspectives, it is, perhaps, not surprising to discover differences among these theories in their treatment of race. Some feminist perspectives have taken white, middle-class, heterosexual women's experiences to be the norm, while ignoring "the specificity of black, native, and other ethnic and cultural experiences" (Elliot and Mandell 1998:14). Although such perspectives as radical feminism treat women as a uniform, undifferentiated group whose major source of oppression is sexism, other perspectives have strenuously challenged this point of view (Grant 1993; Brand 1993). Such perspectives as anti-racist and critical race feminism point out that gender is not the sole source of oppression; gender, race, and other sources of oppression intersect to produce multiple degrees of inequality. Anti-racist feminists argue that all people are racialized, gendered, and differently constructed—they do not participate on an equal footing in social interactions, and unequal power relations permeate all social institutions. According to Enakshi Dua, anti-racist feminism "attempts to integrate the way race and gender function together in structuring inequality" (1999:9). Like anti-racist feminism, critical race feminism examines the interconnection of race or racism and other forms of oppression with gender, emphasizing the social difference and multiplicity within feminism (Hua 2003). Unlike white, middle-class women, immigrant women, visible minority women, and Aboriginal women, for example, experience the compounded effects of inequality associated with their race and class as well as their gender.

Patricia Hill Collins (1998) uses the term "outsiders-within" to describe the condition of black women situated in academic, legal, business, and other communities. As "outsiders-within," Hill Collins argues, these women are members of a given community but at the same time are dually marginalized in that community as women and as blacks; they find themselves unable to access the knowledge and possess the full power granted to others in the community.

Interactionist Perspective

An Aboriginal woman is transferred from a job on an assembly line to a similar position working next to a

Ethnic Albanian women mourn the death of a man killed by Serbs in the province of Kosovo. Such "ethnic cleansings" have met with worldwide condemnation.

white man. At first, the white man is patronizing, assuming that she must be incompetent. She is cold and resentful; even when she needs assistance, she refuses to admit it. After a week, the growing tension between the two leads to a bitter quarrel. Yet, over time, each slowly comes to appreciate the other's strengths and talents. A year after they begin working together, these two workers become respectful friends. This is an example of what interactionists call the *contact hypothesis* in action.

The ***contact hypothesis*** states that interracial contact between people of equal status in cooperative circumstances will cause them to become less prejudiced and to abandon previous stereotypes. People begin to see one another as individuals and discard the broad generalizations characteristic of stereotyping. Note the factors of *equal status* and *cooperative circumstances.* In the example above, if the two workers had been competing for one vacancy as a supervisor, the racial hostility between them might have worsened (Allport 1979; R. Schaefer 2004; Sigelman et al. 1996).

As visible minorities slowly gain access to better-paying and more responsible jobs in Canada, the contact hypothesis may take on even greater significance. The trend in our society is toward increasing contact between individuals from dominant and subordinate groups. This may be one way of eliminating—or at least reducing—racial and ethnic stereotyping and prejudice. Another may be the establishment of interracial coalitions, an idea suggested by sociologist William Julius Wilson (1999b). To work, such coalitions would obviously need to be built on an equal role for all members.

Contact between individuals occurs on the microlevel. We turn now to a consideration of intergroup relations on a macrolevel.

PATTERNS OF INTERGROUP RELATIONS

Racial and ethnic groups can relate to one another in a wide variety of ways, ranging from friendships and intermarriages to the killing of those from particular minority groups, from behaviours that require mutual approval to behaviours imposed by the dominant group.

Conflict sociologists emphasize the ways in which dominant groups exercise their political, social, economic, and cultural domination over other groups. Historically, dominant groups—primarily white—have subjugated less powerful groups whom they perceived to be different and constructed these groups as the "other." This subjugation, as discussed in the previous chapter on stratification, can take the form of colonialism, and, more recently, neocolonialism. Thus, as conflict and some feminist sociologists have pointed out, "otherized" groups have historically been exploited, oppressed, and controlled by dominant groups through such systems as colonialism, globalized labour exploitation, slavery, and genocide (Hua 2003).

Genocide is the deliberate, systematic killing of an entire people or nation. This term describes the killing of one million Armenians by Turkey beginning in 1915. It is most commonly applied to Nazi Germany's extermination of six million European Jews, as well as gays, lesbians, and the Romani people, during World War II. The term *genocide* is also appropriate in describing the United States' policies toward Native Americans in the nineteenth century. During the Seven Years' War (1756–1763), germ warfare decimated the North American Aboriginal population. Blankets contaminated with smallpox were distributed to Aboriginal groups that were allied with France (Harrison and Friesen 2004). In a recent example of genocide, in Rwanda in 1994, an estimated 800 000 Tutsis were slaughtered by Hutus in one hundred days.

The *expulsion* of a people is another extreme means of acting out racial or ethnic prejudice. In 1979, Vietnam expelled nearly one million ethnic Chinese, partly as a result of centuries of hostility between Vietnam and neighbouring China. In a more recent example of expulsion (which had aspects of genocide), Serbian forces began a program of "ethnic cleansing" in 1991 in the newly independent states of Bosnia and Herzegovina. Throughout the former nation of Yugoslavia, the Serbs drove more than one million Croats and Muslims from their homes. Some were tortured and killed, others abused and terrorized, in an attempt to "purify" the land for the remaining ethnic Serbs. In 1999, Serbs were again the focus of worldwide condemnation as they sought to "cleanse" the province of Kosovo of ethnic Albanians.

Genocide and expulsion are arguably the most extreme examples of intergroup relations. Other patterns of intergroup relations that are explored by sociologists are assimilation, segregation, and multiculturalism. Each pattern defines the dominant group's actions and the minority group's responses. Intergroup relations are rarely restricted to only one of the three patterns, although invariably one does tend to dominate. Therefore, think of these patterns primarily as ideal types.

"Ho, ho, ho" apparently works in any language. As Japanese Americans assimilated the norms and values of mainstream U.S. culture, they created their own "Shogun Santa." This one can be found in the Little Tokyo neighbourhood of Los Angeles.

Assimilation

Many Hindus in India complain about Indian citizens who copy the traditions and customs of the British. In Australia, Aborigines who have become part of the dominant society refuse to acknowledge their darker-skinned grandparents on the street. In Canada, some Poles, Ukrainians, and Jews have changed their ethnic-sounding family names to names that are typically found among British and Northern European families.

Assimilation is the process by which a person forsakes his or her own cultural tradition to become part of a different culture. Generally, it is practised by a minority group member who wants to conform to the standards of the dominant group. Assimilation can be described as an ideology in which $A + B + C \rightarrow A$. The majority A dominates in such a way that members of minorities B and C imitate A and attempt to become indistinguishable from the dominant group (Newman 1973).

Assimilation can strike at the very roots of a person's identity. Alphonso D'Abuzzo, for example, changed his name to Alan Alda. The British actress Joyce Frankenberg changed her name to Jane Seymour. Name changes, switches in religious affiliation, and dropping of native languages can obscure a person's roots and heritage. However, assimilation does not necessarily bring acceptance for the minority group individual. A Chinese Canadian may speak English fluently, achieve high educational standards, and become a well-respected professional or businessperson and *still* be seen as different. Some Canadians may reject him or her as a business associate, neighbour, or marriage partner, simply because she or he is seen as different.

Use Your Sociological Imagination

You have immigrated to another country with a very different culture. How are you treated?

Segregation

Separate schools, separate seating sections on buses and in restaurants, separate washrooms, even separate drinking fountains—these were all part of the lives of African Americans in the American South when segregation ruled early in the twentieth century. ***Segregation*** refers to the physical separation of two groups of people in terms of residence, workplace, and social events. Generally, a dominant group imposes it on a minority group. Segregation is rarely complete, however. Intergroup contact inevitably occurs, even in the most segregated societies.

From 1948 (when it received its independence) to 1990, the Republic of South Africa severely restricted the movement of blacks and other non-whites by means of a wide-ranging system of segregation known as ***apartheid.*** Apartheid even included the creation of homelands where blacks were expected to live. However, decades of local resistance to apartheid, combined with international pressure, led to marked political changes in the 1990s. In 1994, a prominent black activist, Nelson Mandela, was elected as South Africa's president, the first election in which blacks (the majority of the nation's population) were allowed to vote. Mandela had spent almost 28 years in South African prisons for his anti-apartheid activities. His election was widely viewed as the final blow to South Africa's oppressive policy of apartheid.

Perhaps the most blatant form of segregation in Canada is that of the reserve system established by the federal government for Aboriginal peoples. Although Aboriginal people do have a choice as to where they live, they do not receive the same privileges off the reserve as they would on the reserve. Effectively, reserves segregate Aboriginal people by placing their schools, housing, recreational facilities, and medical services in remote areas, separate from the larger community. This segregation creates centres of "shiftlessness and inertia," where Aboriginal people are transformed into a "great family of wards, dependent on government for direction and assistance" (Harrison and Friesen 2004:187).

Some forms of segregation can be voluntary and thus may be referred to as ***self-segregation.*** An example of self-segregation is the residential segregation found in Canada's major cities, such as Toronto, Vancouver, and Montreal, where residents in Chinese-, Jewish-, and Indo-Canadian neighbourhoods remain residentially separated from other ethnic groups.

Multiculturalism

In 1969, the Government of Canada adopted an official policy of bilingualism in response to the rise of nationalism in Quebec (Harrison and Friesen 2004). But in 1971, the government adopted a policy of multiculturalism in recognition of the growing number of Canadians who are from ethnic backgrounds other than British or French. The multiculturalism policy, therefore, was an attempt to establish a larger framework within which to respond to Canadian ethnic and racial diversity.

The meaning of multiculturalism in Canada goes beyond simply describing what is (or the obvious)—that Canada is a country comprising people from many diverse ethnic and racial origins. Multiculturalism, officially, is a policy that attempts to promote ethnic and racial diversity in all aspects of Canadian life and establish diversity as a fundamental characteristic of a Canadian identity. The policy of multiculturalism, however, is not without its critics, who assert that it is simply window-dressing that diverts attention from the economic and political inequalities that persist among various ethnic groups (e.g., between members of visible minorities and members of other minorities).

Whether this policy of multiculturalism is reflected in today's mainstream media is discussed in Box 9-2.

RACE AND ETHNICITY IN CANADA

Few societies have a more diverse population than Canada; the nation is truly a multiracial, multi-ethnic society. Of course, this has not always been the case. The population of what is now Canada has changed dramatically since the arrival of French settlers in the 1600s. Immigration has largely been responsible for shaping the racial and ethnic makeup of our present-day society.

Canada's diversity is evident from the statistical profile presented in Table 9-1 (p. 199). That diversity, particularly with regard to visible minority status, has been increasing dramatically in recent years. Between the early 1960s and the last census of 2001, there was a marked shift away from Europe and toward Asia as the source of the majority of immigrants to Canada (Statistics Canada 2003d).

Ethnic Groups

The 2001 Canadian census revealed the 10 top ethnic origins to be, in descending order, Canadian, English, French, Scottish, Irish, German, Italian, Chinese, Ukrainian, and North American Indian. Below we will explore some of the groups that make up Canada's multiethnic character.

Aboriginal People

The history of Aboriginal groups in Canada is one, first and foremost, of colonialism, the effects of which continue to be felt by Aboriginal people today. The historical legacy of oppression is one many Aboriginals still cope with daily, as they continue to be marginalized and struggle against various forms of racism. They have endured years of overt attempts on the part of the dominant culture to eradicate their Aboriginal identities.

The Indian Act of 1876 granted the federal government the power to control most aspects of Aboriginal life, denying Aboriginal people the right to vote or to buy land. This pivotal piece of legislation transformed Aboriginals from self-governing, autonomous peoples to externally regulated, controlled, and, thus, dependent

Eye on the Media

9-2 Racism and the Mainstream Media

Augie Fleras and Jean Lock Kunz, in their book *Media and Minorities* (2001), observe that Canada's mainstream media is frequently accused of being racist. Fleras and Lock Kunz provide some vignettes that illustrate the complexity of racism as it relates to media representations of male and female members of minority groups (pp. 30–31):

- After watching 114 hours of TV, the *Toronto Star* television critic concluded that members of minority groups are still underrepresented on air, both in television shows and in advertisements, in relation to their populations and relative to whites. Advertisers justify this practice, stating that using members of minority groups could offend their customers.
- A study of five major Canadian papers over a month confirmed that Muslims are typically cast as barbaric fanatics by the media. Muslims are portrayed as violent people or terrorists whose fundamentalist religion condones their brutal acts.
- "When people of colour commit a crime . . . collective responsibility is imposed on an entire race . . . [while] white criminal violence is a matter of individual responsibility" (p. 31). For example, Paul Bernardo's killing of two women was seen as the fault of the individual, not of his entire race. "No one in the media asked, 'What's wrong with blue-eyed, blond-haired men of Italian descent?' " (p. 31).

Before the 2002 fall television season, executives of the major U.S. TV networks once again renewed their commitment to diversify both who is on television and who is responsible for the content. It proved to be a tough commitment to keep. Only 2 of the 26 new fall series had even one minority person in a leading role. Furthermore, a Directors Guild of America report indicated that of all 826 episodes of the 40 most popular series in 2001, 80 percent were directed by white males and 11 percent by white females. That left only 9 percent directed by blacks, Latinos, or Asian Americans, who collectively account for more than 25 percent of U.S. television viewers.

In the 1999–2000 season, the leading characters in all 26 new prime-time series were white; network gatekeepers seemed surprised by the news. Producers, writers, executives, and advertisers blamed one another for the oversight. Television programming was dictated by advertisers, a former executive claimed; if advertisers said they wanted blatantly biased programming, the networks would provide it. Jery Isenberg, chairman of the Caucus for Producers, Writers & Directors, blamed the networks, saying that writers would produce a series about three-headed Martians if the networks told them to.

Beyond these excuses, real reasons can be found for the departure from the diversity exhibited in past shows and seasons. In recent years, the rise of more networks, cable TV, and the Internet has fragmented the broadcast entertainment market, siphoning viewers away from the general-audience sitcoms and dramas of the past.

Meanwhile, the mainstream network executives, producers, and writers remain overwhelmingly white and tend to write and produce stories about people like themselves. Marc Hirshfeld, an NBC executive, claims some white producers have told him they don't know how to write for black characters. Stephen Bochco, producer of *NYPD Blue*, is a rare exception. His series *City of Angels* featured a mostly non-white cast, like the people Bochco grew up with in an inner-city neighbourhood. The series ran for 23 episodes before being cancelled in 2000.

In the long run, media observers believe, the major networks will need to integrate the ranks of gatekeepers before they achieve true diversity in programming. Adonis Hoffman, director of the Corporate Policy Institute, has urged network executives to throw open their studios and boardrooms to minorities. There are some signs of agreement from the networks. According to Doug Herzog, president of Fox Entertainment, real progress means incorporating diversity from within.

Why should it matter that minority groups aren't visible on major network television, if they are well represented on other channels, such as Aboriginal Peoples Television Network (APTV)? The problem is that whites as well as visible minorities see a distorted picture of their society every time they turn on network TV. In the case of American television, Hoffman states, "African Americans, Latinos and Asians, while portrayed as such, are not merely walk-ons in our society—they are woven into the fabric of what has made this country great" (A. Hoffman 1997:M6).

Applying Theory

1. Do you watch network TV? If so, how well do you think it represents the diversity of Canadian society?
2. Have you seen a movie or TV show recently that portrayed members of a visible minority group in a sensitive and realistic way—as real people rather than as stereotypes or token walk-ons? If so, describe the show.

Sources: Bielby and Bielby 2002; Braxton and Calvo 2001; Children Now 2002; Directors Guild of America 2002; Fleras and Kunz 2001; A. Hoffman 1997; Navarro 2002; Poniewozik 2001; Soriano 2001; Wood 2000.

ones. Ten years before, after breaking treaty after treaty to make way for European settlement, the government decided that particular parcels of land would be used for reserves. Yet, as Lee Maracle argues in her 1996 book *I Am Woman: A Native Perspective on Sociology and Feminism* (p. 92), Native people in Canada, despite decades of colonization, have not had their culture "stolen":

> We have not "lost our culture" or had it "stolen." Much of the information that was available to us through our education process has been expropriated and consigned to deadwood leaves in libraries. The essence of Native culture still lives on in the hearts, minds, and spirits of our folk. Some of us have forsaken our culture in the interests of becoming integrated. This is not the same thing a losing something. The expropriation of the accumulated knowledge of Native peoples is one legacy of colonization. Decolonization will require the repatriation and rematriation of the knowledge by Native people's themselves.

The ethnic mosaic of the Canadian community has marginalized First Nations peoples. In recent years, the Assembly of First Nations and local native groups have had great success in focusing attention on the ongoing discrimination to which they are subjected.

Almost 160 years ago, Egerton Ryerson, chief superintendent of education for Upper Canada, set out to "civilize" Aboriginal children through, as a federal government report published in 1847 described it, a "weaning from the habits and feelings of their ancestors and the acquirement of the language, arts and customs of civilized life." Residential schools established in the mid-nineteenth century, with mandatory attendance beginning in 1920, were run as a partnership between the federal government and the major churches. Thousands of Aboriginal children were excised from their families and communities to be "whitened" and "educated" in the ways of European culture.

Many of these children endured conditions of neglect; isolation; and emotional, physical, and sexual abuse. As many have argued, they were also the victims of a cultural genocide. The final report of the Royal Commission on Aboriginal Peoples, issued in 1996, stated "the schools were . . . part of the contagion of colonialization. In their direct attack of language, beliefs and spirituality, the schools had been a particularly virulent strain of that epidemic of empire, sapping children's bodies and beings" (D. Wilson 2000). The last residential schools closed in the mid-1980s; however, the now-adult survivors continue to struggle with the traumatic effects of their experiences as children in these schools.

British Columbia psychiatrist and professor Charles Brasfield (2001:80), who runs a practice focusing on the needs of Aboriginal people, suggests that "residential school syndrome" might be a diagnostic term appropriately applied to survivors of the residential school system. In his practice, Brasfield treats Aboriginal people who are trying to overcome nightmares, flashbacks, relationships problems, sleeping difficulties, and anger-management issues, all of which are rooted in their experiences in the residential schools. Not having good parenting role models while in the schools, many now lack parenting skills. Often, Brasfield sees his Aboriginal clients struggling to deal with alcohol or drug abuse.

In November 2005, the federal announced plans to distribute a $2 billion compensation package to survivors of Aboriginal residential schools. Approximately 86 000 former students are eligible to receive a $10 000 basic payment and $3000 for every year spent in a residential school. In addition, compensation will be offered for claims of sexual and physical abuse, and loss of language and culture. The Aboriginal Healing Foundation will receive five years of funding ($125 million), $60 million will be available for a truth and reconciliation process, and $10 million will be spent to commemorate what happened in the schools. In return, the recipients give up the right to sue the federal government and the churches that ran the schools, except in cases of sexual and serious physical abuse. An official apology was not part of the federal government's package. Because of the number of outstanding lawsuits over the issue, the compensation deal must be approved by the courts.

In addition to, and interrelated with, the effects of the legacy of residential schools, Aboriginal people have higher rates of poverty, suicide, tuberculosis, infant mortality, and incarceration than the non-Aboriginal population (Statistics Canada 2003h). Aboriginal people also have lower rates of education and employment than non-Aboriginals, and have shorter life expectancies.

In 2001, Canada's Aboriginal population (those claiming to be Aboriginal as either a single or a multiple response on the census) totalled 1.3 million or 4.4 percent of the population (Statistics Canada 2003h). Between 1951 and 2001, the Aboriginal population grew sevenfold, while the overall Canadian population doubled.

Despite more than a century of colonial oppression, Aboriginal people have made strides toward regaining self-determination and autonomy. For example, the 1999 conclusion and ratification of treaty negotiations with the Nisga'a of northern British Columbia established a precedent for Aboriginal land claims and political autonomy. Figure 9-2 shows the First Nations People of British Columbia.

Asian Canadians

Peter Li, author of *Chinese in Canada* (1988), argues that Asian, and Chinese in particular, is a racial distinctiveness and cultural inferiority articulated in the ideology

FIGURE 9-2

First Nations People of British Columbia

Mapping Life WORLDWIDE

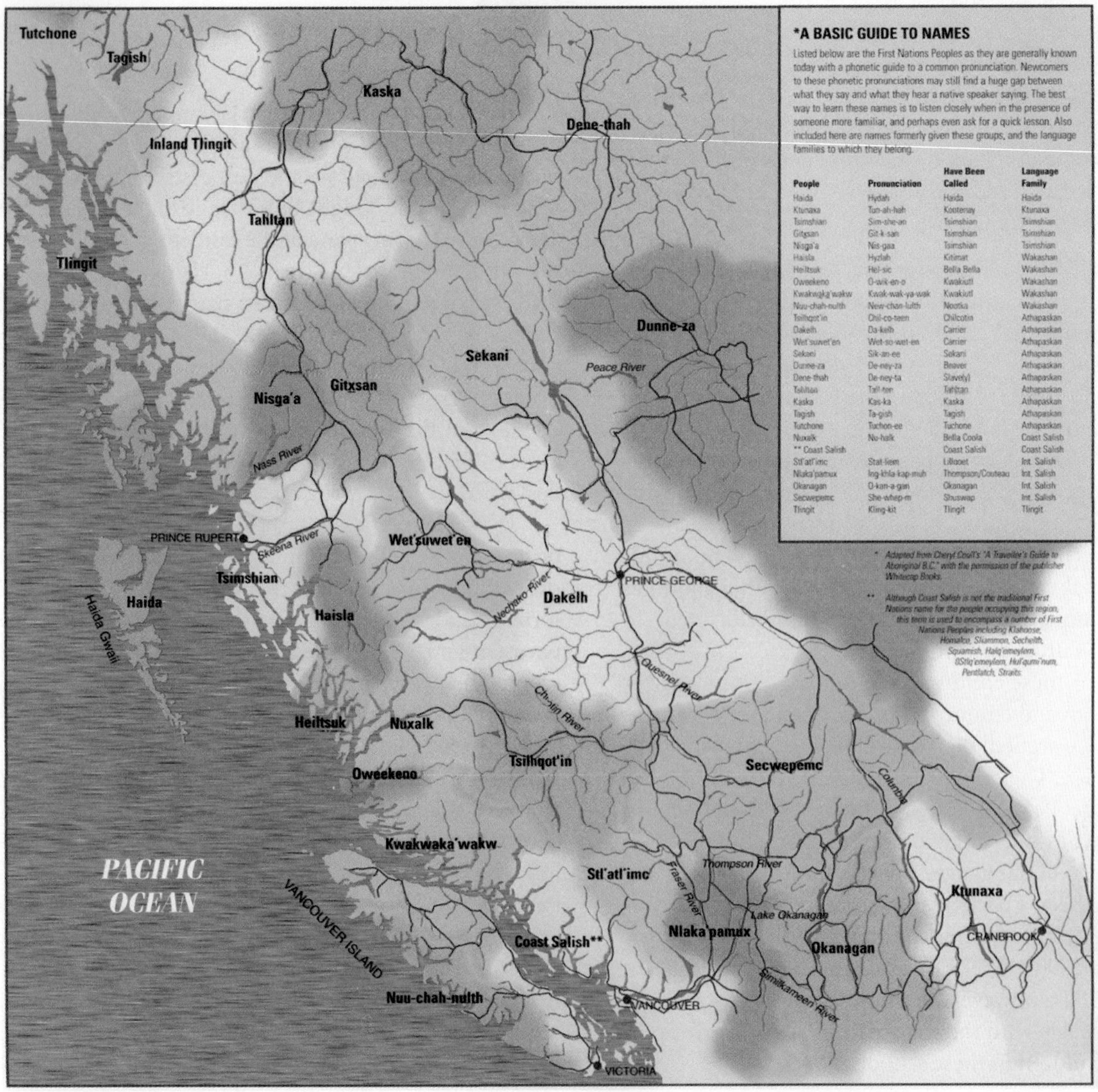

Source: Sovereign Indigenous Nations Territorial Boundaries in British Columbia.

and practice of Canada, while the normative order upholding Europeans as the desirable race is well entrenched (P. Li 2003). The social significance of race is also evident in public discourse, economic relations, and the arts and media (Fleras and Kunz 2001; P. Li 2003). Canadians are fed a steady diet of mainstream media images in which Asians are portrayed as a homogeneous group, defined on the basis of a single racialized identity:

> We make up more than one half of the world's population, yet in spite of our numbers and contributions to the world, our images and perspectives are seldom seen. Our histories and our cultures are obscured, overlooked, buried or tokenized in a world dominated by Western classism. Our voices are seldom heard, our stories are left untold and our realities are seldom represented by those who control the means and resources to name and shape a picture of reality. (S. Park 1997)

Immigrants from China, initially denied membership in the communities within which they settled, ultimately established their own neighbourhoods. Chinatowns, like this one in Vancouver, have subsequently become cultural havens for their populations.

These images are translated through the mainstream media into "us and them" scenarios (Fleras and Kunz 2001:131–132). For example, Asian Canadians are often portrayed in films as

- being foreigners who cannot be assimilated
- having no power or influence when playing leading roles
- having restricted features or mannerisms that are comical or sinister
- playing supporting roles even in the contexts that are unmistakably Asian
- having a negative or nonexistent sexuality (for men)
- having regressive speech patterns that compound low intellectual capabilities
- having suicidal impulses in defence of honour, name, or country
- being overachievers but emotionally bankrupt

Given a normative social order in which Europeans were seen as desirable, the histories of Asian Canadians are ones in which institutional racism was entrenched in the social, political, and economic life of Canada. Chinese immigrants, who, for example, first came to Canada in the late 1850s to work in the mines, establish small businesses, and provide necessary labour for the building of the national railway, were viewed as a threatening and potentially dangerous "other" and treated accordingly. The Canadian government actively recruited Chinese labourers to complete the most dangerous phases of work on the Canadian Pacific Railway, paying them a fraction of the wages paid to white workers (Creese et al. 1991; Lampkin 1985). Institutional racism, as carried out by the Government of Canada, became more pronounced in 1885 with an Act to restrict and regulate Chinese immigration to Canada. With this Act began the imposition of a head tax of $50 in 1885, $100 in 1901, and $500 in 1904—a year's wages (A. Finkel et al. 1993)—to be paid by every Chinese immigrant entering Canada.

Institutional racism toward Chinese immigrants became even more wide-ranging in 1923, with the passing of the Chinese Exclusion Act, which, among other restrictions, barred the families of men working in Canada from joining them, resulting in years of separation of family members. Despite a history of institutional racism and current self-reported experiences of discrimination, Chinese Canadians are now among the best-educated groups in Canada, many having attained middle-class status, frequently as professionals (Derouin 2004; Nguyen 1982; Reitz 1980).

Other Asian groups have also endured various forms of racism, including institutional racism. In 1907, a Vancouver-bound ship carrying more than one thousand Japanese immigrants and some Sikh immigrants was met by a racist mob of workers protesting their arrival on the grounds that they were a threat to the job security of white workers. This anti-Asian riot, organized by the

NUMBER 85605

DOMINION OF CANADA

NEW C.I. 5 SERIES

IMMIGRATION BRANCH — DEPARTMENT OF THE INTERIOR

RECEIVED FROM

Lee Don whose photograph is attached hereto, on the date and at the place hereunder mentioned, the sum of Five Hundred Dollars being the head tax due under the provisions of the Chinese Immigration Act. The above mentioned party who claims to be a native of Hai Kok in the District of Hoi Ping of the age of 22 years arrived or landed at Victoria, B.C. on the 23rd day of July 1918 ex Kashima Maru. The declaration in this case is C.I.L. No. 31726

Dated at Vancouver on 2nd August 1918

CONTROLLER OF CHINESE IMMIGRATION.

A Chinese head tax receipt, issued by the Canadian Immigration Branch, Vancouver, August 2, 1918.

Asiatic Exclusion League, also targeted Asian-run businesses in downtown Vancouver. Vandals smashed windows and destroyed signs. Two decades later, in 1941, Japanese Canadians faced a major attack of institutional racism by the Canadian government. The government rounded up Japanese Canadians who lived within one hundred miles (160 kilometres) of the Pacific coast for reasons of "national security," regardless of whether or not they supported Japan's involvement in World War II. Japanese Canadians were placed in internment camps in the interior of British Columbia and on sugar beet farms in Alberta and Manitoba (David Suzuki, the Canadian environmentalist and television producer, spent part of his childhood with his family in an internment camp in British Columbia). Between 1943 and 1946, the federal government sold all the property and possessions of the internees, and new Japanese immigrants were barred from entering Canada until 1967, when of a new immigration policy was introduced based on a point system. In 1988, the Government of Canada offered an apology and compensation to Japanese Canadians for the racist treatment they had received during the internment. No similar apology or financial compensation has ever been given to Chinese Canadians.

Institutional racism is also entrenched in the history of Indo-Canadians, with the case of the *Komagata Maru*—a ship carrying four hundred passengers from India to Canada in 1914—being perhaps the most notable example. The ship remained anchored just off the Vancouver coast for three months, while debates based on racist ideologies on the part of the government and the public ensued. During this time, passengers and crew were left without adequate supplies of food and water and without proper medical care. Conditions on board deteriorated rapidly. Eventually, based on the view that the Indian passengers constituted the category of "other," and thus warranted racist treatment, the Canadian government did not allow the ship to dock, forcing it to return to India.

In 1939, the Supreme Court of Canada ruled that discrimination based on race was legally enforceable (F. Henry et al. 1995). This ruling that remained in place until the multiculturalism policy of 1971 was enacted, which brought about the modification of rules of engagement and entitlement for the "containment" of ethnicity (Fleras and Kunz 2001). Today, Asian Canadians, who tend to settle in Toronto, Vancouver, and Montreal, are the fastest-growing segment of new immigrants to Canada. The diverse groups found within this category are often are stereotyped as "model" or ideal minority groups, as many members tend to succeed, educationally and economically, even while enduring various forms of racism.

pp. 196–197

The success of many of the members of these visible minorities, particularly the Chinese, may be used to bolster the position of those who argue that all it takes to get ahead in Canada is hard work and effort (as discussed when examining the functionalist view in the previous chapter). The implication of this view is that if some members of visible minorities do succeed, those who do not must suffer from personal inadequacies. However, in their review of the vertical mosaic thesis, Lian and Matthews (1998:475–476) concluded that "similar educational qualifications carried different economic values in the Canadian labour market for individuals of different 'racial' origins and that a 'coloured mosaic' now exists, in which educational achievement at any level fails to protect persons of visible minority background from being disadvantaged in terms of income they receive."

The disadvantage of having a visible minority background affects those born outside Canada, as well as those born in Canada (Pendakur and Pendakur 2002). A 2004 study showed that one-third of members of visible minorities in Canada—more than one million people—reported having been discriminated against or treated unfairly because of their ethnicity, culture, race, skin colour, language, accent, or religion (Derouin 2004). Asian Canadians reported lower levels of discrimination than members of the visible minority category did overall, with Chinese Canadians reporting marginally lower rates of discrimination than members of the Asian category did overall (see Figure 9-3). It is imperative to keep in mind the ways in which categories, such as gender and age, intersect with a visible minority background, diversifying and compounding the degrees of discrimination experienced by many Canadians.

White Ethnic Groups

Unlike minority groups whose identities have been racialized, those of both dominant and minority white ethnic groups have not. As a result of their "invisibility," they experience a greater chance of social inclusion and, in the case of white minorities, a lesser chance of social exclusion through racism, discrimination, and exploitation after the initial adaptation period (Fleras and Elliott 1992). As Peter Li argues, "social inclusion of 'racial' groups that have been historically marginalized implies the use of 'race' as grounds to signify the value of people. In contrast, racial exclusion involves constructing social boundaries based on phenotypic features [physical appearance], by which individuals or groups are denied social opportunities, economic rewards and other privileges as a result of their 'racial" designation'" (2003:1).

Given that *race* is a value-laden term, racial markers have provided the basis on which to distinguish the "desirable" from the "undesirable," "us" from "them" (Li 2003). The normative social order of Canada has favoured Europeans, positioning them as "us," institutionalizing their interests and cultural values and thus providing them greater power to set the norms of society. Initial immigrant policies were racist in orientation, intending to encourage assimilation, and had an exclusionary result (Fleras and Elliott 2003). "Preferred" groups were from Northern and Western Europe and, later, in response to the settlement needs of Western Canada, groups from Eastern and Southern Europe that, although lower in preferred ranking, were also deemed acceptable. These groups faced limited or no entry restrictions, while other groups, such as Jews and Mediterranean populations, "otherized" on the basis of perceived racial differences, required special permits for entry.

John Porter's landmark study *The Vertical Mosaic* (1965) used the concept of *charter groups* to represent the French and English, the so-called founding groups of Canadian society. Porter's work documented the imbalances in the distribution of power, wealth, and resources, showing that the British and French were more positively rewarded and evaluated than were newly arrived immigrants (Fleras and Elliott 1992; Kazemipur 2002). Porter's thesis study, as discussed in earlier chapters, in which various ethnic groups were hierarchically arranged such that European groups held higher socioeconomic positions than non-European groups, has been reexamined in more contemporary contexts. These studies show that whites are advantaged over non-whites in relation to occupational status and earnings (Geschwender 1994; Lautard and Loree 1984; Lautard and Guppy 1999; P. Li 1988). Even when such factors as demographic features are controlled for, substantial income disparities persist between Canadians of European origin and those of visible minority groups (Beach and Worswick 2003; Boyd 1984, 1992; P. Li 1992, 2000; Pendakur and Pendakur 1998). Studies conducted

p. 11

FIGURE 9-3

Percentage Reporting Discrimination or Unfair Treatment "Sometimes" or "Often" in the Past Five Years, by Visible Minority Status, 2002

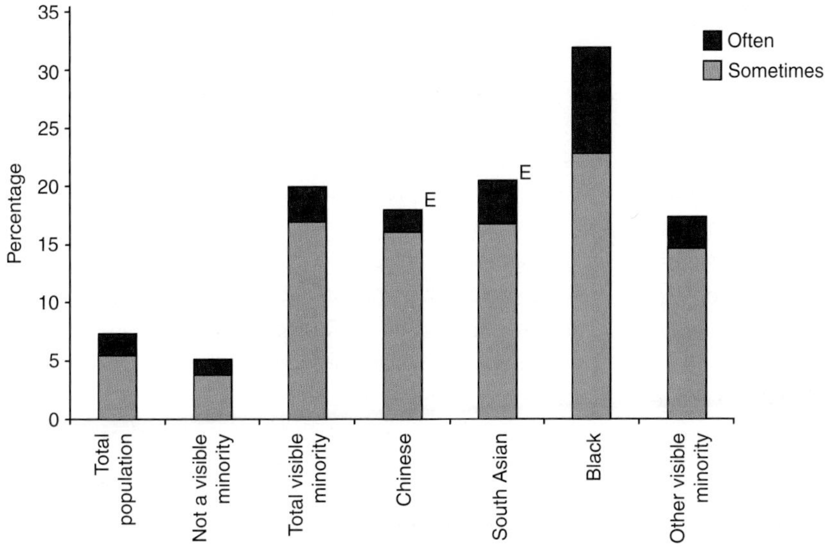

Source: Statistics Canada 2003e.

E Use with caution

Note: Refers to Canada's non-Aboriginal population aged 15 and older reporting discrimination or unfair treatment in Canada because of ethnocultural characteristics.

since the release of *The Vertical Mosaic,* which included the impact of the major influx of immigrants from non-European countries, have "resulted in an increase in the salience of race at the expense of ethnicity . . . as the 1960's reforms in Canadian immigration policy have raised the number of visible minority immigrants, and along with it the potential to racial discrimination" (Kazemipur 2002).

Members of white ethnic groups, who continue to hold the bulk of economic and political power in Canada (federal and provincial or territorial), have co-opted Canada's ethnic and racial diversity for trade, investment, and commercial purposes. For example, in her article "Multiculturalism, or the United Colors of Capitalism?" Katharyne Mitchell argues that Canada's multicultural character has been used by Canadian powerholders to attract transnational elites to Canada, by selling an ideology of racial harmony that may provide reassurance for nervous investors (Fleras and Kunz 2001).

SOCIAL POLICY AND RACE AND ETHNICITY: Global Immigration

The Issue

Worldwide immigration is at an all-time high. Each year, two million to four million people move from one country to another. As of the mid-1990s, immigrants totalled about 125 million, representing 2 percent of the global population (Martin and Widgren 1996). Their constantly increasing numbers and the pressure they put on job opportunities and welfare capabilities in the countries they enter raise troubling questions for some of the world's economic powers. Who should be allowed in? At what point should immigration be curtailed? At what point should it be expanded?

The Setting

The migration of people is not uniform across time or space. At certain times, wars or famines may precipitate large movements of people either temporarily or permanently. Temporary dislocations occur when people wait until it is safe to return to their home areas. However, more and more migrants who cannot make adequate livings in their home nations are making permanent moves to developed nations. The major migration streams flow into North America, the oil-rich areas of the Middle East, and the industrial economies of Western Europe and Asia. Currently, seven of the world's wealthiest nations (including Canada, Germany, France, the United Kingdom, and the United States) shelter about one-third of the world's migrant population, but less than one-fifth of the total world population. As long as there are disparities in job opportunities among countries, there is little reason to expect this international migration trend to end.

Countries, such as Canada, that have long been a destination for immigrants have a history of policies to determine who has preference to enter. Often, clear racial and ethnic biases are built into these policies. Until recently, Canadian immigration policy has favoured immigrants from northern Europe and Britain. Immigrants who were members of visible minority groups were explicitly excluded and discriminated against, as Canadian politicians and policymakers believed that they were not a "good fit" for Canadian society. The first hundred years of post-Confederation immigration were essentially about European migration to Canada. Not all Europeans, however, were treated equally or looked on favourably by Canadian immigration policy. The British and Northern Europeans were preferred over Eastern and Southern Europeans, the latter only being recruited if there were not sufficient numbers of eligible British and Northern Europeans.

Since the late 1960s, policies in Canada have encouraged immigration of people from non-European nations. This change has significantly altered the pattern of immigrants' country of birth. Previously, Europeans dominated, but for the last 20 years, immigrants have come primarily from Asia (see Figure 9-4).

People from China, India, Pakistan, the Philippines, and Korea made up 42 percent of immigrants in 2001. The impact that immigration has on Canada, however, is not experienced by all Canadians; it is experienced, for the most part, by those living in particular urban centres. More specifically, 73 percent of immigrants arriving in Canada between 1991 and 2001 settled in Toronto, Montreal, or Vancouver (see Figure 9-5).

Sociological Insights

Immigration can provide many valuable functions. For the receiving society, it alleviates labour shortages, such as in the areas of health care business and technology in Canada. For the sending nation, migration can relieve

FIGURE 9-4

Immigrants to Canada, by Country of Last Permanent Residence, 2003

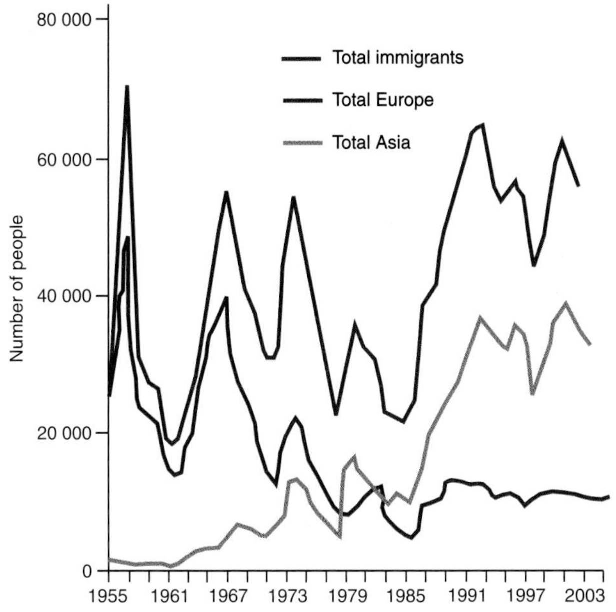

Source: Adapted by the author from Statistics Canada (CANSIM) 2004b.

economies unable to support large numbers of people. Often overlooked is the large amount of money that immigrants send *back* to their home nations. For example, worldwide immigrants from Portugal alone send more than $4 billion annually *back* to their home country (World Bank 1995).

Immigration can be dysfunctional as well. Although studies generally show that immigration has a positive impact on the receiving nation's economy, areas experiencing high concentrations of immigrants may find it difficult to meet short-term social service needs. Critics of the way in which the federal government is handling immigration say that although we may be creating a few vibrantly multicultural urban centres, we are also creating cities that lack the services to deal with this growth and diversity. When migrants with skills or educational potential leave developing countries, it can be dysfunctional for those nations. No amount of payments sent back home can make up for the loss of valuable human resources from poor nations (Martin and Midgley 1999).

Conflict theorists note how much of the debate over immigration is phrased in economic terms. But this debate is intensified when the arrivals are of different racial and ethnic background from the host population. For example, Europeans often refer to "foreigners," but the term does not necessarily mean one of foreign birth. In Germany, "foreigners" refers to people of non-German ancestry, even if they were *born* in Germany; it does not refer to people of German ancestry born in another country who may choose to come to their "mother country." Fear and dislike of "new" ethnic groups may divide countries throughout the world (Martin and Widgren 1996). In Canada, fear or dislike of high levels of immi-

FIGURE 9-5

Cities of Choice

The chart below shows a comparison of the percentage of all immigrants in the total population of selected Canadian cities.

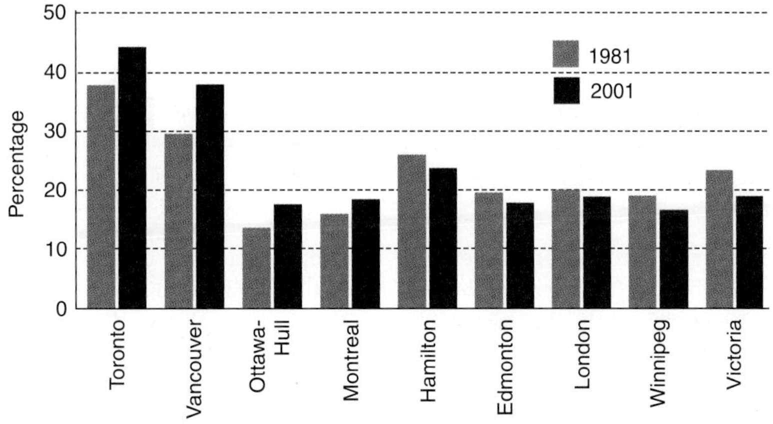

Source: Jimenez and Lunman 2004:A5; Statistics Canada 2004g.

gration is not as evident as that experienced in other countries.

Policy Initiatives

The long border with Mexico provides ample opportunity for illegal immigration into the United States. Throughout the 1980s, there was a perception, among some, that the United States had lost control of its borders. Feeling public pressure for immigration control, the U.S. Congress ended a decade of debate by approving the Immigration Reform and Control Act of 1986. The Act marked a historic change in immigration policy. For the first time, hiring of illegal aliens was outlawed, and employers caught violating the law became subject to fines and even prison sentences. Just as significant a change was the extension of amnesty and legal status to many illegal immigrants already living in the United States. Almost two decades later, however, the 1986 immigration law appears to have had mixed results. Substantial numbers of illegal immigrants continue to enter the country each year, with an estimated 8 million to 10 million present at any given time (Deardorff and Blumerman 2001).

Of particular concern for Canadian policymakers is the distribution or dispersion of immigrants. Since the vast majority of newcomers to Canada, arriving between 1991 and 2001, settled in large metropolitan regions, this creates a problem of "two solitudes—overtaxed megalopolises and waning small towns" (Jimenez and Lunman 2004:A5). In the large centres, pressure is placed on public housing, English-language courses, support services for immigrants, public transportation, and the cities' infrastructures in general. Policymakers and politicians at all levels of government are currently devising strategies to deal with these challenges.

The entire world feels the overwhelming impact of economic globalization on immigration patterns. Europe is also wrestling with policy initiatives. The European Union agreement of 1997 gave the governing commission authority to propose Europe-wide legislation on immigration beginning in 2002. However, the policies must be accepted unanimously, which seems unlikely. An EU policy that would allow immigrants to live and work in one EU country would allow them to work anywhere. The immigration issue is expected to complicate efforts by the sending nations (such as Turkey) to become members of the EU (Light 1999; Sassen 1999).

The intense debate over immigration reflects deep value conflicts in the culture of many nations. One strand of our culture, for example, has traditionally emphasized egalitarian principles and a desire to help people in their time of need. At the same time, however, hostility to potential immigrants and refugees reflects not only racial, ethnic, and religious prejudice but also a desire to maintain the dominant culture of the in-group by keeping out those viewed as outsiders.

Applying Theory

1. Did you or your parents or grandparents immigrate to Canada? If so, when and where did your family come from, and why? Did they face discrimination?
2. Do you live, work, or study with recent immigrants to Canada? If so, are they well accepted in your community, or do they face prejudice and discrimination?
3. In your opinion, is there a backlash against immigrants in Canada?
4. In your view, does the functionalist perspective on race and ethnicity provide a realistic interpretation of unequal access to opportunity in Canada?

CHAPTER RESOURCES

Summary

The social dimensions of race and ethnicity are important factors in shaping people's lives in Canada and other countries. In this chapter, we examined the meaning of race and ethnicity and studied the major racial and ethnic minorities of Canada.

1. A ***racial group*** is set apart from others by obvious physical differences, whereas an ***ethnic group*** is set apart primarily because of national origin or distinctive cultural patterns.
2. When sociologists define a ***minority group***, they are primarily concerned with the economic and political power, or powerlessness, of the group.
3. There is no biological basis for the concept of race, and there are no physical traits that can be used to describe one ***racial group*** to the exclusion of all others.

4. The meaning that people give to the physical differences between races gives social significance to race, leading to ***stereotypes***.
5. ***Prejudice*** often leads to ***discrimination***, but the two are not identical, and each can be present without the other.
6. ***Institutional discrimination*** results when the structural components of a society create or foster differential treatment of groups.
7. Functionalists point out that discrimination is both functional and dysfunctional in society. Conflict theorists explain racial subordination by ***exploitation theory***. Standpoint or anti-racist feminists point out that gender is not the sole source of oppression, and that gender, race, and class intersect to produce multiple degrees of inequality. Interactionists focus on the microlevel of race relations, posing ***contact hypotheses*** as a means of reducing prejudice and discrimination.
8. Three patterns describe typical intergroup relations in North America and elsewhere: ***assimilation, segregation***, and ***multiculturalism***.
9. In Canada, the ideal pattern of intergroup relations is ***multiculturalism***. In our country, there is an ongoing debate over whether the ideal is in fact the reality of life for most minority Canadians.
10. After a century and half of degradation, Canada's Aboriginal people are poised to reclaim their status as an independent, self-determining people.
11. In Canadian society, the socially constructed category of "Asian" obscures the differences among various groups that are placed in this broad category.
12. Non-white immigrants commonly find themselves stereotyped, portrayed as the "other," and marginalized by mainstream Canadian society.
13. Porter's "vertical mosaic" is as accurate a portrayal of Canadian multiculturalism today as it was in 1965; however, "race" is now more salient than ethnicity.
14. The increase in immigration worldwide has raised questions in individual nations about how to control the process.

Critical Thinking Questions

1. How is institutional discrimination even more powerful than individual discrimination? How would functionalists, conflict theorists, feminists, and interactionists examine institutional discrimination?
2. Do you think that multiculturalism in Canada is real or an ideal? Can you think of ways in which it might serve to mask the disparities between various ethnic and racial groups?
3. What place do you see Canada's Aboriginal peoples occupying in the twenty-first century? Do you think Aboriginal people will become more integrated into mainstream culture or distance themselves from it by reestablishing their traditional communities?

Key Terms

Apartheid The policy of the South African government designed to maintain the separation of blacks and other non-whites from the dominant whites. (page 207)

Assimilation The process by which a person forsakes his or her own cultural tradition to become part of a different culture. (206)

Contact hypothesis An interactionist perspective that states that interracial contact between people of equal status in cooperative circumstances will reduce prejudice. (205)

Discrimination The process of denying opportunities and equal rights to individuals and groups because of prejudice or for other arbitrary reasons. (201)

Employment equity A federal act that attempts to eliminate barriers faced in the area of employment. (203)

Ethnic group A group that is set apart from others because of its national origin or distinctive cultural patterns. (195)

Exploitation theory A Marxist theory that views racial subordination, such as that in Canada, as a manifestation of the class system inherent in capitalism. (204)

Genocide The deliberate, systematic killing of or blatant disregard for the well-being of an entire people or nation. (205)

Glass ceiling An invisible barrier that blocks the promotion of a qualified individual in a work environment because of the individual's gender, race, or ethnicity. (201)

Institutional discrimination The denial of opportunities and equal rights to individuals and groups that results from the normal operations of a society. (202)

Minority group A subordinate group whose members have significantly less control or power over their own lives than the members of a dominant or majority group have over theirs. (196)

Prejudice A negative attitude toward an entire category of people, such as a racial or an ethnic minority. (199)

Racial group A group that is set apart from others because of perceived physical attributes and treated differently. (195)

Racial or ethnic profiling The use of a social construct of race as a consideration in suspect profiling in law enforcement and national security practices. (202)

Racism The belief that one race is supreme and all others are innately inferior. (201)

Segregation The act of physically separating two groups; often imposed on a minority group by a dominant group. (206)

Self-segregation The situation that arises when members of a minority deliberately develop residential, economic, or social network structures that are separate from those of the majority population. (207)

Stereotypes Unreliable generalizations about all members of a group that do not recognize individual differences within the group. (198)

Visible minority Canadians who are non-white or are identified as being physically different from white Canadians of European descent. (196)

Additional Readings

Day, Richard J. F. 2000. *Multiculturalism and the History of Canadian Diversity.* Toronto: U of T Press. The author contends that formal legislation cannot resolve culture-based issues. Day criticizes the federal policy as fantasy, arguing that equality is a myth in a society as diverse as Canada's.

Fleras, Augie and Jean Lock Kunz. 2001. *Media and Minorities.* Toronto: Thompson. The book examines how race, ethnicity, and Aboriginality are interpreted by mainstream media and the public discourses produced and consumed as a result of these interpretations.

O'Hearn, Claudine Chiawei, ed. 1998. *Half and Half: Writers on Growing Up Biracial and Bicultural.* New York: Parthenon Books. Eighteen essayists address the difficulties of fitting into, and the benefits of being part of, two worlds.

Schaefer, Richard T. 2002. *Racial and Ethnic Groups*, 9th ed. Upper Saddle River, NJ: Prentice Hall. Comprehensive in its coverage of race and ethnicity, this text also discusses women as a subordinate minority and examines dominant–subordinate relations in Canada, Northern Ireland, Israel and the Palestinian territory, Mexico, and South Africa.

Online Learning Centre

Visit the *Sociology: A Brief Introduction* Online Learning Centre at www.mcgrawhill.ca/college/schaefer to access quizzes, interactive exercises, video clips, and other research and study tools related to this chapter.

Reel Society Interactive Movie CD-ROM 2.0

Reel Society 2.0 can be used to spark discussion about the following topics from this chapter:

- Race
- Ethnicity
- Prejudice and discrimination

chapter

10

GENDER RELATIONS

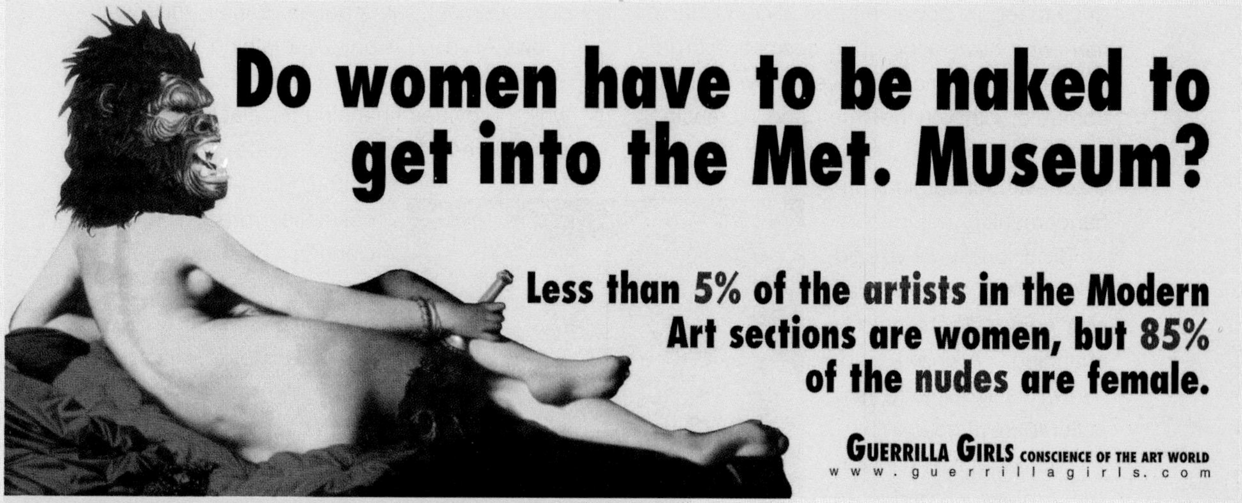

Do women have to be naked to get into the Met. Museum?
Less than 5% of the artists in the Modern Art sections are women, but 85% of the nudes are female.
GUERRILLA GIRLS CONSCIENCE OF THE ART WORLD
www.guerrillagirls.com

In 1989 a group called the Guerrilla Girls called attention to sexism in the art world with this poster, which protests the under-representation of female artists at the world-famous Metropolitan Museum of Art in New York City. This poster and others dealing with sexism in the arts can be viewed at www.guerrillagirls.com.

The lost status of the distinguished older man and the emerging clout of the power woman are driving men to cosmetic surgeons at a record rate, new research suggests.

Sociologist Michael Atkinson tracks this drive to regain power in his study of Canadian men who have undergone cosmetic surgery. He said many men believed they could not compete with younger men and increasingly couldn't compete with women in the workplace without surgical enhancement.

"Traditionally, we've said to men, 'You can get away with aging.' That's quickly changing," Atkinson said. "Now, the older form isn't culturally revered at all."

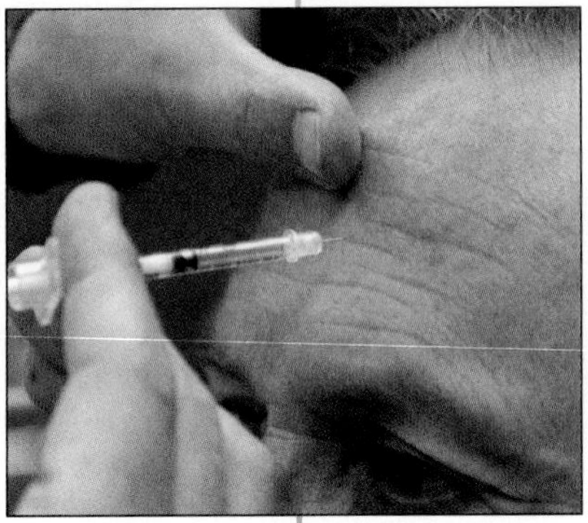

The McMaster University professor conducted interviews with 44 men who have undergone cosmetic surgery procedures once considered the exclusive domain of women, including Botox injections and eye lifts. Atkinson also interviewed 12 surgeons and found a clear fault line in the motivating factors for men and women.

"Men are doing it more to maintain a position rather than attain a position, to hold on to a sense of power or masculinity. For some women, it's about staying pretty. That's a disempowering image. That's not the same as a guy trying to keep their job," said Atkinson, who will present the results of the study . . . at the Technology and Body conference in Ottawa.

. . . The Social Sciences and Humanities Research Council (SSHRC), a federal government agency that funds university-based research, awarded Atkinson its Aurora Prize for his groundbreaking research on the emerging cosmetic surgery phenomenon.

The prize, valued at $25,000, honours an outstanding new researcher who has demonstrated particular originality and insight in social science and humanities research. Atkinson has also studied tattooing, extreme exercising and ticket scalping.

The first survey of Canadian cosmetic surgeons and dermatologists about cosmetic enhancement, undertaken earlier this year, shows Atkinson is on to something.

Toronto-based Medicard Finance Inc., which provides financing for elective medical procedures, found that male clients now account for 14.5 per cent of cosmetic procedures in Canada. The top services requested by men are liposuction, rhinoplasty, eye lifts and Botox injections, according to the survey of 2,650 cosmetic surgeons.

Over all, the number of cosmetic surgeries increased 16 per cent from 2002 to 2003, the survey showed. The number of Botox injections jumped an estimated 19 per cent and the number of Canadians who used injectable wrinkle fillers increased by 23 per cent.

Medicard CEO Ann Kaplan says men's acceptance of eye laser surgery in recent years has opened up the possibility of other cosmetic procedures to preserve or enhance their looks.

"You could almost chart it. I believe the eventual acceptance of laser eye surgery allowed men to say, 'This surgery worked for me. These procedures do work.' It has helped them accept other procedures," says Kaplan.

Today, men represent 21 per cent of Medicard's business.

Atkinson said the male cosmetic surgery phenomenon speaks to a fundamental shift in how men see themselves. "Men's roles and responsibilities have already shifted, and we've been slow to notice," he said. ***(Schmidt 2004)*** ■

This article by Sarah Schmidt discusses the research of McMaster University sociologist Michael Atkinson, documenting the growing number of Canadian men currently undergoing cosmetic procedures, such as rhinoplasty, eye lifts, and Botox injections—an increase of 16 percent from 2002 to 2003. After interviewing 44 men and 12 surgeons, Atkinson studied the motivating factors that propelled men to undergo cosmetic surgery procedures.

Much has been written about the "beauty myth" as a societal control mechanism that is meant to keep women in their place—as subordinates to men at home and on the job. But some men are now captive to unrealistic expectations regarding their physical appearance. In hopes of regaining a younger look and maintaining their power in the workplace, more and more men, as Michael Atkinson documents, are now having Botox injections or electing to undergo cosmetic surgery.

Expectations related to physical appearance are one example of how cultural norms may lead to differentiation based on gender. Such differentiation is evident in virtually every human society about which we have information. We saw in Chapters 8 and 9 that most societies establish hierarchies based on social class, race, and ethnicity. This chapter will examine the ways in which societies stratify their members on the basis of gender, in relation to social class, race, and ethnicity.

We begin by looking at how various cultures, including our own, assign women and men to particular social roles. Then we will consider sociological explanations for gender stratification. Next, the chapter will focus on the diverse experiences of women as an oppressed majority, analyzing the social, economic, and political aspects of women's subordinate position. The chapter also examines the emergence of the feminist movement, its goals, and its contradictions. Finally, the social policy section will analyze links among abortion, new reproductive technology, and women's reproductive choices. ■

Use Your Sociological Imagination www.mcgrawhill.ca/college/schaefer

Do you think you would ever elect to have cosmetic surgery? If so, what would be your motivating factor?

SOCIAL CONSTRUCTION OF GENDER

How many air passengers do you think feel a start when the captain's voice from the cockpit belongs to a woman? Consciously or unconsciously, many assume that flying a commercial plane is a *man's* job. Gendered practices and organization are an integral part of our social world, so much so that we may take them for granted and only take notice when they deviate from conventional behaviour and expectations.

Although a few people begin life with an unclear sexual identity, the overwhelming majority begin with a definite sex and quickly receive societal messages about how to behave. Thus, the term *sex* is a biological category. Many societies have established distinctions between "female" and "male" that are not "natural" but are cultural and social. This is what is meant by *gender*. When we use the term gender, we are "using a shorthand term which encodes a crucial point: that our basic social identities as men and women are socially constructed rather than based on fixed biological characteristics" (Young 1988:98).

In studying gender, sociologists are interested in the gender-role socialization that leads women and men to behave differently. In Chapter 4, *gender roles* were defined as expectations regarding the proper behaviour, attitudes, and activities of men and women. The application of traditional gender roles leads to many forms of differentiation between women and men. Both sexes are physically capable of learning to cook and sew, yet most Western societies determine that women should perform these tasks. Both men and women are capable of learning to weld and fly airplanes, but these functions are generally assigned to men.

p. 82

Gender roles are evident not only in our work and behaviour but also in how we react to others. We are constantly "doing gender" without realizing it. If a father sits in the doctor's office with his son in the middle of a workday, he will probably receive approving glances from the receptionist and from other patients. "Isn't he a wonderful father?" runs through their minds. But if the boy's mother leaves *her* job and sits with the son in the doctor's office, she will not receive such silent applause.

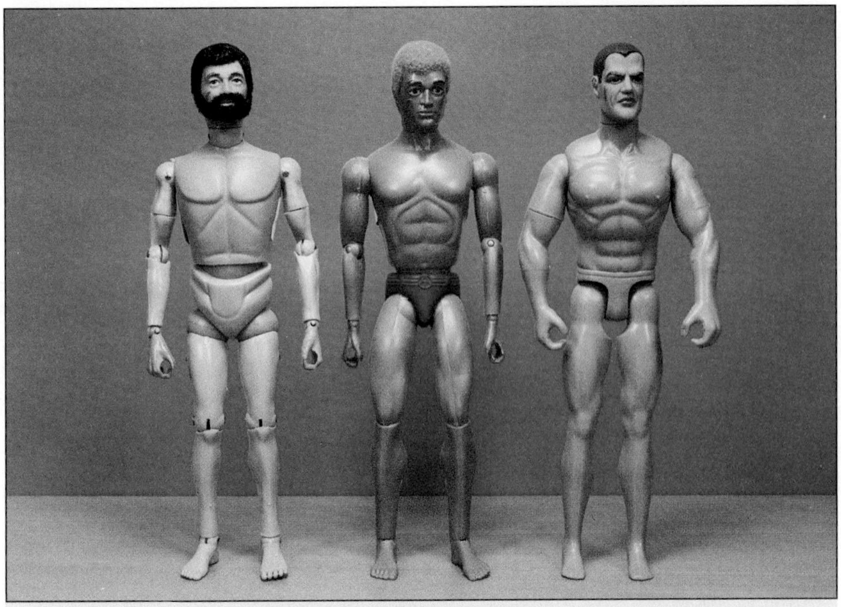

Society often exaggerates male–female differences in appearance and behaviour. In 1964, the G.I. Joe doll (left) had a realistic appearance, but by 1992 (middle) it had begun to acquire the exaggerated muscularity characteristic of professional wrestlers (right). The change intensified the contrast with ultra-thin female figures, like the Barbie doll (Angier 1998).

We socially construct our behaviour so that male–female differences are either created or exaggerated. For example, men and women come in a variety of heights, sizes, and ages. Yet traditional norms regarding marriage and even casual dating tell us that in heterosexual couples, the man should be older, taller, and wiser than the woman. As we will see throughout this chapter, such social norms help to reinforce and legitimize patterns of male dominance.

In recent decades, women have increasingly entered occupations and professions previously dominated by men. Yet our society still focuses on "masculine" and "feminine" qualities as if men and women must be evaluated in these terms. Clearly, we continue to "do gender," and this social construction of gender continues to define significantly different expectations for females and males in North America (Lorber 1994; L. Rosenbaum 1996; C. West and Zimmerman 1987).

Gender Roles in North America

Gender-Role Socialization

Male babies get blue blankets, while female babies get pink ones. Boys are expected to play with trucks, blocks, and toy soldiers; girls are given dolls and kitchen goods. Boys must be masculine—active, aggressive, tough, daring, and dominant—whereas girls must be feminine—soft, emotional, sweet, and submissive. These traditional gender-role patterns have been influential in the socialization of children in North America.

An important element in traditional views of proper "masculine" and "feminine" behaviour is fear of homosexuality. *Homophobia* is a fear of and prejudice against homosexuality. Homophobia contributes significantly to rigid gender-role socialization, since many people stereotypically associate male homosexuality with femininity and lesbianism with masculinity. Consequently, men and women who deviate from traditional expectations about gender roles are often presumed to be gay. Despite the advances made by the gay liberation movement, the continuing stigma attached to homosexuality in our culture places pressure on all males (whether gay or not) to exhibit only narrow masculine behaviour and on all females (whether lesbian or not) to exhibit only narrow feminine behaviour (Seidman 1994; see also Lehne 1995).

It is *adults,* of course, who play a critical role in guiding children into those gender roles deemed appropriate in a society. Parents are normally the first and most crucial agents of socialization. But other adults, older siblings, the mass media, and religious and educational institutions also exert an important influence on gender role socialization in Canada and elsewhere.

It is not hard to test how rigid gender-role socialization can be. Just try transgressing some gender norms—say, by smoking a cigar in public if you are female or carrying a purse if you are male. That was exactly the assignment given to a group of sociology students. Professors asked the students to behave in ways that they thought violated norms of how a man or woman should act. The students had no trouble coming up with gender norm "transgressions" (see Table 10-1), and they kept careful notes on how others reacted to their behaviour, ranging from amusement to disgust (Nielsen, Walden, and Kunkel 2000).

Gender-Role Socialization and Social Class

The 2000 movie *Billy Elliott* portrays the life of a young boy growing up in a British mining town and the gender socialization he undergoes. His father and older brother,

Table 10-1 An Experiment of Gender Norm Violations by University Students

Norm Violations by Women	Norm Violations by Men
Send men flowers	Wear fingernail polish
Spit in public	Needlepoint in public
Use men's bathroom	Throw Tupperware party
Buy jock strap	Cry in public
Buy/chew tobacco	Have pedicure
Talk knowledgeably about cars	Apply to babysit
Open doors for men	Shave body hair

Source: Nielsen et al. 2000:287.

Sociology students were asked to behave in ways that might be regarded as violating gender norms. This is a sample of their actual choices over a seven-year period.

Think about It

Do you agree that the actions taken by the students in Table 10-1 test the boundaries of conventional gender behaviour?

both striking coal miners, discover that Billy is secretly attending ballet classes rather than the boxing lessons he pretended to be taking. Billy's behaviour causes his father great concern and displeasure. He sees his son's dancing as a lack of conformity to gender-role expectations. Billy's father actively discourages him from pursuing his love of dance, until he comes to the realization that Billy possesses great talent. At that point, even though his son is defying cultural norms and community standards of appropriate male behaviour, the father begins to support and encourage Billy in his dream to become a professional dancer.

Research shows that patterns of gender socialization are not homogeneous, but rather vary according to the social class to which a person belongs. Working-class parents tend to be more concerned with their children's outward conformity to society's norms and roles (M. Kohn, Kazimierz, and Schoenbach 1986). Middle-class parents, in contrast, tend to be more concerned with their children's motivation for certain behaviours and focus on developing such qualities as self-expression and self-control (Langman 1987). Moreover, upper-middle-class families are most likely to support more egalitarian gender relations and thus socialize their children accordingly (Langman 1987; Lips 1993). Children who are raised by middle-class, career-oriented mothers tend to hold more egalitarian attitudes relating to men's and women's roles (Tuck, Rolfe, and Adair 1994).

Women's Gender Roles

How does a girl come to develop a feminine self-image whereas a boy develops one that is masculine? In part, they do so by identifying with females and males in their families and neighbourhoods and in the media. If a young girl regularly sees female characters on television working as defence lawyers and judges, she may believe that she herself can become a lawyer. And it will not hurt if women that she knows—her mother, sister, parents' friends, or neighbours—are lawyers. By contrast, if this young girl sees women portrayed in the media only as models, nurses, and secretaries, her identification and self-image will be quite different. Even if she does become a professional, she may secretly regret falling short of the media stereotype—a shapely, sexy young woman in a bathing suit (N. Wolf 1992).

Television is far from being alone in stereotyping women. Studies of children's books published in North America in the 1940s, 1950s, and 1960s found that females were significantly underrepresented in central roles and illustrations. Virtually all female characters were portrayed as helpless, passive, incompetent, and in need of a strong male caretaker. By the 1980s, there was somewhat less stereotyping in children's books, with some female characters shown to be active. Nevertheless, boys were still shown engaged in active play three times as often as girls (Kortenhaus and Demarest 1993).

Social research on gender roles reveals some persistent differences between men and women in North America and Europe. Women experience a mandate to both marry and be a mother. Often, marriage is viewed as the true entry into adulthood. And women are expected not only to become mothers but to *want* to be mothers. Obviously, men play a role in these events, but the events do not appear to be as critical in identifying the life course for a man. Society defines men's roles by economic success. Although women may achieve recognition in the labour force, it is not as important to their identity as it is for men (Doyle and Paludi 1998; Russo 1976).

Traditional gender roles have most severely restricted females. Throughout this chapter, we will see how women have been confined to subordinate roles within the political and economic institutions of Canada and elsewhere. Yet it is also true that gender roles have restricted males.

Men's Gender Roles

> During the game I always played the outfield. Right field. Far right field. And there I would stand in the hot sun wishing I was anyplace else in the world. (Fager et al. 1971)

This is the childhood recollection of a man who, as a boy, disliked sports, dreaded gym classes, and had particular problems with baseball. Obviously, he did not conform to the socially constructed male gender role and no doubt paid the price for it.

Men's roles are socially constructed in much the same way as women's roles are. Family, peers, and the media all influence how a boy or a man comes to view his appropriate role in society. Robert Brannon (1976) and James Doyle (1995) have identified five aspects of the male gender role:

- Antifeminine element—show no "sissy stuff," including any expression of openness or vulnerability.
- Success element—prove their masculinity at work and sports.
- Aggressive element—use force in dealing with others.
- Sexual element—initiate and control all sexual relations.
- Self-reliant element—stay cool and unflappable.

No systematic research has established all these elements as common aspects among boys and men, but specific studies have confirmed individual elements.

Being antifeminine is basic to men's gender roles. Males who do not conform to the socially constructed gender role face constant criticism and even humiliation both from children when they are boys and from adults as men. It can be agonizing to be treated as a "chicken" or a "sissy"—particularly if such remarks come from his father or brothers. At the same time, boys who successfully adapt to cultural standards of masculinity may grow up to be inexpressive men who cannot share their feelings with others. They remain forceful and tough—but as a result they are also closed and isolated (Faludi 1999; McCreary 1994; Sheehy 1999).

In the past 35 years, inspired in good part by the contemporary feminist movement (examined later in the chapter), increasing numbers of men in North America have criticized the restrictive aspects of the traditional male gender role. Some men have taken strong public positions in support of women's struggle for full equality and have even organized voluntary associations, such as the White Ribbon Campaign (WRC), founded in Canada in 1991 to end men's violence against women. Nevertheless, the traditional male gender role remains well entrenched as an influential element of our culture (Messner 1997).

Cross-Cultural Perspective

To what extent do actual biological differences between the sexes contribute to the cultural differences associated with gender? This question brings us back to the debate over "nature versus nurture." In assessing the alleged and real differences between men and women, it is useful to examine cross-cultural data.

p. 71

The research of anthropologist Margaret Mead points to the importance of cultural conditioning—as opposed to biology—in defining the social roles of males

Cultural conditioning is important in the development of gender role differences. This sister and brother from Sudest Island in Papua New Guinea expect women to be the honorary heads of the family.

and females. In *Sex and Temperament,* Mead (1963, original edition 1935; 1973) describes typical behaviours of each sex in three different cultures in New Guinea:

> In one [the Arapesh], both men and women act as we expect women to act—in a mild parental responsive way; in the second [the Mundugumor], both act as we expect men to act—in a fierce initiating fashion; and in the third [the Tchambuli], the men act according to our stereotypes for women—are catty, wear curls, and go shopping—while the women are energetic, managerial, unadorned partners. (Preface to 1950 ed.)

If biology determined all differences between the sexes, then cross-cultural differences, such as those described by Mead, would not exist. Her findings confirm the influential role of culture and socialization in gender-role differentiation. There appears to be no innate or biological reason to designate completely different gender roles for men and women.

In any society, gender stratification requires not only individual socialization into traditional gender roles within the family, but also the promotion and support of these traditional roles by other social institutions, such as religion and education. Moreover, even with all major institutions socializing the young into conventional gender roles, every society has women and men who resist and successfully oppose these stereotypes: strong women who become leaders or professionals, gentle men who care for children, and so forth. It seems clear that differences between the sexes are not dictated by biology. Indeed, the maintenance of traditional gender roles requires constant social controls—and these controls are not always effective.

Use Your Sociological Imagination

How would your life and the lives of your family and friends be different if you lived in a society that was not gendered?

EXPLAINING GENDER RELATIONS

Cross-cultural studies indicate that societies dominated by men are much more common than those in which women play the decisive role. Sociologists have turned to all the major theoretical perspectives to understand how and why these social distinctions are established. Each approach focuses on culture, rather than biology, as the primary determinant of gender differences. Yet, in other respects, there are wide disagreements among advocates of these sociological perspectives. Box 10-1 discusses the role of education in the empowerment of women.

The Functionalist View

Functionalists maintain that gender differentiation has contributed to overall social stability. Sociologists Talcott Parsons and Robert Bales (1955) argued that to function most effectively, the family requires adults who will specialize in particular roles. They viewed the traditional arrangement of gender roles as arising out of this need to establish a division of labour between marital partners.

Parsons and Bales contended that women take the expressive, emotionally supportive role and men the instrumental, practical role, with the two complementing each other. ***Instrumentality*** refers to emphasis on tasks, focus on more distant goals, and a concern for the external relationship between the family and other social institutions. ***Expressiveness*** denotes concern for maintenance of harmony and the internal emotional affairs of the family. According to this theory, women's interest in expressive goals frees men for instrumental tasks, and vice versa. Women become "anchored" in the family as wives, mothers, and household managers; men are anchored in the occupational world outside the home. Of course, Parsons and Bales offered this framework in the 1950s, when many more women were full-time homemakers than is true today. These theorists did not explicitly endorse traditional gender roles, but they implied that dividing tasks between spouses was functional for the family unit.

Given the typical socialization of women and men in North America, the functionalist view is initially persuasive. However, it would lead us to expect girls and women with no interest in children to become baby-sitters and mothers. Similarly, males who love spending time with children might be "programmed" into careers in the business world. Such differentiation might harm the individual who does not fit into prescribed roles while also depriving society of the contributions of many talented people who are confined by gender stereotyping. Moreover, the functionalist approach does not convincingly explain why men should be categorically assigned to the instrumental role and women to the expressive role.

The Conflict Response

Viewed from a conflict perspective, this functionalist approach masks underlying power relations between men and women. Parsons and Bales never explicitly presented the expressive and instrumental tasks as unequally valued by society, yet this inequality is quite evident. Although social institutions may pay lip service to women's expressive skills, it is men's instrumental skills that are most highly rewarded—whether in terms of money or prestige. Consequently, according to feminists

Sociology in the Global Community

10-1 The Empowerment of Women through Education

International declarations and targets to achieve certain rights for women include the education of girls and women as a key priority. For example, the U.N. Women's Conference in Cairo in 1990, the U.N. Social Summit in Copenhagen in 1995, the U.N. Conference in Beijing in 1995, and the U.N. Millennium Summit in 2000 all made declarations to close the gender gap in primary and secondary education by the year 2005. All four international conferences set a target date of 2015 for the provision of universal primary education in all countries. Many of these declarations may not be achieved by the stated target date; however, they are often used as benchmarks for the overall social and economic development of a country. As well, the declarations may be used by women's groups of various countries to lobby for the achievement of these goals locally (van der Gaag 2004).

Globally, great disparities exist among the young women of the world: in 2002, 95 percent or more of young women in the North were literate, while in the rest of the world, 11 countries had literacy rates of less than 10 percent for young women (van der Gaag 2004). Although sociocultural, gender-based barriers to education and literacy are factors that have been associated with the disempowerment of girls and women, educating girls and women has profound empowering benefits for them as individuals:

- It decreases their fertility.
- It improves their health as well as that of their children.
- It increases their productivity.
- It enhances their ability to make informed decisions.
- It increases their status and power within the family.
- It increases their opportunity to take on leadership roles in the community.
- It decreases their chances, and their children's chances, of living in poverty.

These benefits are inextricably connected to those of the community as a whole. Many countries, recognizing its key role in countries' social and economic development, are addressing the issue of girls' and women's education through integrated socioeconomic, cultural, and institutional approaches to improve the educational participation of girls and women (UNESCO 2002). In Benin, for example, school fees for girls are being eliminated in public primary schools in the rural areas, and a media campaign to sensitize parents on issues related to gender and education has been implemented (van der Gaag 2004).

Applying Theory

1. Why is the education of girls and women such a powerful force in changing the social and economic conditions of a community as a whole?
2. In what way does the empowerment of women through education relate to class and race?
3. How might conflict sociologists explain the global disparities in girls' and women's access to education?

Sources: UNESCO 2002; van der Gaag 2004.

and conflict theorists, any division of labour by gender into instrumental and expressive tasks is far from neutral in its impact on women.

Conflict theorists contend that the relationship between females and males has traditionally been one of unequal power and ownership of resources, with men in a dominant position over women. Men may originally have become powerful in preindustrial times because their size, physical strength, and freedom from childbearing duties allowed them to dominate women physically. In contemporary societies, such considerations are not as important, yet cultural beliefs about the sexes are long established, as anthropologist Margaret Mead and feminist sociologist Helen Mayer Hacker (1951, 1974) both stressed. Such beliefs support a social structure that places males in controlling positions.

Thus, conflict theorists see gender inequality as the systematic subjugation of women. If we use an analogy to Marx's analysis of class conflict in capitalist societies, we can say that males are like the bourgeoisie, or capitalists; they control most of the society's wealth, prestige, and power. Females are like the proletarians, or workers; they can acquire valuable resources only by following the dictates of their "bosses." Men's work is uniformly valued, while women's work (whether unpaid labour in the home or wage labour) is devalued.

pp. 168–169

Both functionalist and conflict theorists acknowledge that it is not possible to change gender roles drastically without dramatic revisions in a culture's social structure. Functionalists perceive potential for social disorder, or at least unknown social consequences, if all aspects of traditional gender stratification are disturbed. Yet, for conflict theorists, no social structure is ultimately desirable if it is maintained by oppressing a majority of its citizens. These theorists argue that gender stratification may be functional for men—who hold power and privilege—but it is hardly in the interests of women (R. Collins 1975; Schmid 1980).

Feminist Perspectives

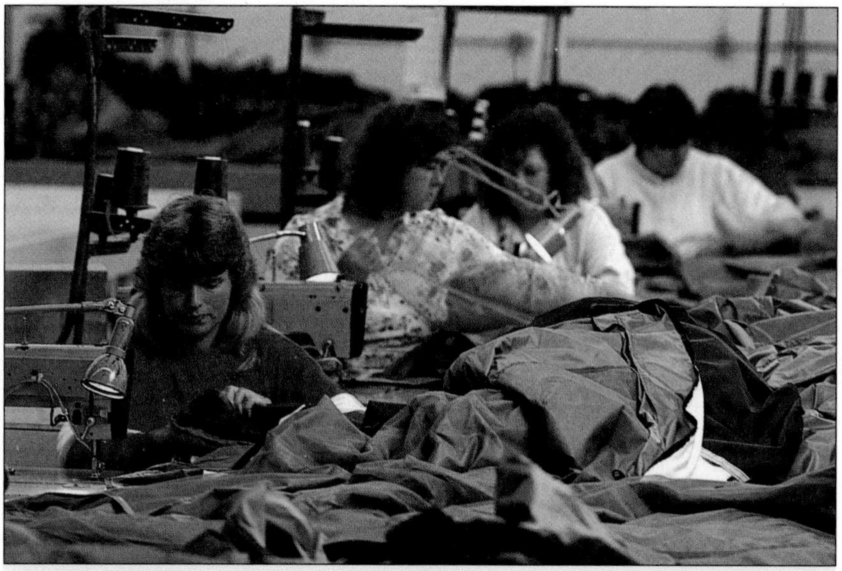

Conflict theorists emphasize that men's work is uniformly valued, while women's work (whether unpaid labour in the home or wage labour) is devalued. These women are making tents in a factory.

As we have noted in earlier chapters, feminist perspectives encompass a wide-ranging and diverse group of theories focusing on gender inequality, its causes, and its remedies. Feminist perspectives, however, despite their diversity, share the belief that women have been subordinated, undervalued, underrepresented, and excluded in male-dominated societies, which in practical terms means most of the world. As varied as political philosophies, feminist perspectives include postmodern feminism, global feminism, liberal feminism, Marxist feminism, socialist feminism, standpoint feminism, cultural feminism, eco-feminism, and radical feminism, to name a few. Some of these streams have been discussed in the first chapter. To briefly recap these theories, liberal feminism advocates that women's equality can be attained through minor adjustments to key institutions, creating greater opportunities for women's advancement in the public sphere. Marxist feminism places capitalism, with its private ownership of resources and unequal class relations, at fault for the oppression of women. Socialist feminism, in contrast, is based on the belief that the inextricably connected systems of capitalism and patriarchy are responsible for women's subjugation. Radical feminists see the root of women's oppression as being embedded in the patriarchy that exists in all societies, whether they are capitalist, communist, or socialist.

Ongoing developments and debates in feminist theory are producing theories of global feminism, which acknowledge and pay attention to differences in power, material resources, and histories (i.e., colonialism) and reject the use of the Western world as the normative standard (Weedon 1999).

Although it might appear that there has been an explosion in the growth of feminist perspectives since the mid-1960s, the critique of women's position in society and culture goes back to some of the earliest works that have influenced sociology. Among the most important are Mary Wollstonecraft's *A Vindication of the Rights of Women* (originally published in 1792), John Stuart Mill's *The Subjection of Women* (originally published in 1869), and Friedrich Engels's *The Origin of Private Property, the Family, and the State* (originally published in 1884).

Engels, a close associate of Karl Marx's, argued that women's subjugation coincided with the rise of private property during industrialization. Only when people moved beyond an agrarian economy could males "enjoy" the luxury of leisure and withhold rewards and privileges from women. Drawing on the work of Marx and Engels, some contemporary feminist theorists view women's subordination as part of the overall exploitation and injustice that they see as inherent in capitalist societies. Some radical feminist theorists, however, view the oppression of women as inevitable in *all* male-dominated societies, whether they be labelled "capitalist," "socialist," or "communist" (Feuer 1959; Tuchman 1992).

Feminist sociologists are more likely to embrace a political action agenda. Also, some feminist perspectives argue that the very discussion of women and society has been distorted by the exclusion of women from academic thought, including sociology. Perhaps one of the best examples of this exclusion of women from academic sociology is that of the American sociologist Jane Addams (1860–1935). Although Addams made significant contributions to sociology through her work on women and the family, urban settlements, and working-class immigrants, she was viewed by mainstream sociology as an outsider and not as a legitimate member of academia. At the time, her efforts, while valued as humanitarian, were seen as unrelated to the research and conclusions being reached in academic circles, which, of course, were male academic circles (M. Andersen 1997; J. Howard 1999).

For most of the history of sociology, studies were conducted on male subjects or about male-led groups and organizations, and the findings were generalized to all people. For example, for many decades studies of urban life focused on street corners, neighbourhood taverns, and bowling alleys—places where men typically congregated. Although the insights were valuable, they did not give a true impression of city life because they overlooked the areas where women were likely to gather (L. Lofland 1975).

Since men and women have had different life experiences, the issues they approach are different, and even when they have similar concerns, they approach them from different perspectives. For example, women who enter politics today typically do so for different reasons than men do. Men often embark on a political career to make business contacts or build on them, a natural extension of their livelihood; women generally become involved because they want to help. This difference in interests is relevant to the likelihood of their future success. The areas in which women achieve political recognition revolve around such social issues as day care, the environment, education, and child protection—areas that do not attract a lot of big donors. Men focus on tax policies, business regulation, and trade agreements—issues that excite big donors. Sometimes women do become concerned with these issues but then they must constantly reassure voters they still are concerned about "family issues." Male politicians who occasionally focus on family issues, however, are seen as enlightened and ready to govern (G. Collins 1998).

Feminist theorists emphasize that male dominance in Canada and the world goes far beyond the economic sphere. In fact, although on the surface economic inequality may appear to be separate from gender inequality, it is actually inextricably related to spousal abuse, sexual harassment, and sexual assault—issues we have been discussing throughout this text. Violence toward women by men is a major component of many interrelated experiences that contribute to women's inequality in Canada and elsewhere.

Gender inequality is embedded in the various institutions of Canadian society—the family, the workplace, the state, the mass media, the religious organizations—and thus produces a systemic pattern of discrimination. This systemic pattern of discrimination on the basis of gender does not work alone but rather is interconnected with race, class, sexual orientation, and disability to produce multiple layers of inequality and discrimination. Standpoint feminists, in particular, point to the diversity of women's lives and situations, maintaining that gender alone cannot fully explain how Canadian women experience inequality.

The Interactionist Approach

Although functionalists and conflict theorists studying gender stratification typically focus on macrolevel social forces and institutions, interactionist researchers often examine gender stratification on the microlevel of everyday behaviour. As an example, studies show that men initiate up to 96 percent of all interruptions in cross-sex (male–female) conversations. Men are more likely than women to change topics of conversation, to ignore topics chosen by members of the opposite sex, to minimize the contributions and ideas of members of the opposite sex, and to validate their own contributions. These patterns reflect the conversational (and, in a sense, political) dominance of males. Moreover, even when women occupy a prestigious position, such as that of physician, they are more likely to be interrupted than their male counterparts are (A. Kohn 1988; Tannen 1990; C. West and Zimmerman 1983).

In certain studies, all participants are advised in advance of the overall finding that males are more likely than females to interrupt during a cross-sex conversation. After learning this information, men reduce the frequency of their interruptions, yet they continue to verbally dominate conversations with women. At the same time, women reduce their already low frequency of interruption and other conversationally dominant behaviours.

These findings regarding cross-sex conversations have been frequently replicated. They have striking implications when we consider the power dynamics underlying likely cross-sex interactions—employer and job seeker, professor and student, husband and wife, to name only a few. From an interactionist perspective, these simple, day-to-day exchanges are one more battleground in the struggle for sexual equality—as women try to "get a word in edgewise" in the midst of men's interruptions and verbal dominance (Tannen 1994a, 1994b).

WOMEN: THE OPPRESSED MAJORITY

Many people—both male and female—find it difficult to conceive of women as a subordinate and oppressed group. Yet take a look at the political structure of Canada: Women remain noticeably underrepresented. For example, in October 2005, none of the provincial or territorial premiers in Canada was female. Although the past decades have brought many firsts for women in Canadian public life—Beverly McLachlin as the first woman to serve as Chief Justice of the Supreme Court of Canada (2000), Catherine Callbeck of P.E.I. as the first female to be elected premier (1993), Kim Campbell as first woman to serve as Canada's prime minister (1993)—women remain underrepresented in both federal and provincial or territorial politics. As of October 2005, women made up approximately 21 percent of those elected to the federal House of Commons, while women, as a group, made up approximately 51 percent of the Canadian population.

This lack of women in decision-making positions is evidence of women's powerlessness in Canada. In Chapter 9, we identified five basic properties that define a minority or subordinate group. If we apply this model to the situation of women in this country, we find that a numerical majority group fits our definition of a subordinate minority (Dworkin 1982; Hochschild 1973f).

A photo of the provincial and territorial premiers taken in 2004 illustrates the obvious: that power and privilege in Canada are inextricably related to gender and race.

1. Women experience unequal treatment. In 2000, the mean income for male workers 15 years and over was $38 853; for comparable female workers, it was $24 912 (Statistics Canada 2003f).

   Visible minority women in Canada not only earned less than both visible and non-visible minority men but also earned less than other women. In 2000, female visible minority workers 15 years and over earned an average of approximately $3000 less than non-visible minority women. As Table 10-2 illustrates, these women, in turn, earned less than both visible minority men and non-visible minority men (Statistics Canada 2003f).

   The majority of women employed continue to work in occupations in which women have traditionally been concentrated—nursing and other health-related occupations; sales and service; clerical and administrative positions; and teaching (Statistics Canada 1999a).

   Moreover, women are increasingly dominating the ranks of the impoverished, leading to what has been called the *feminization of poverty.* pp. 177–178

   Globally, women and girls make up a disproportionate number of the world's poor. The United Nations Population Fund's *State of World Population Report 2000* stated that women and girls the world over are still being denied access to health care and education. In Canada, women make up a disproportionate number of those with low incomes. In 1997, 2.8 million women (19 percent of the total female population) were living with low incomes, compared with 16 percent of the male population (Statistics Canada 2000a).
2. Women, despite their diversity, share physical and cultural characteristics that distinguish them from the dominant group (men).
3. Membership in this subordinate group is involuntary.

Table 10-2 Average Employment Earnings for Visible Minority Women Compared with Non-visible Minority Women, Visible Minority Men, and Non-visible Minority Men

Category	Earnings ($)
Women from Visible Minorities	22 621
Women from Non-visible Minorities	25 247
Men from Visible Minorities	31 743
Men from Non-visible Minorities	39 861

Source: Statistics Canada 2003f.

Note: Figures are for paid workers, 15 years and over, 2000.

4. Through the rise of contemporary feminism, women are developing a greater sense of group solidarity, as we will see later in the chapter.
5. Many women feel that their subordinate status is most irrevocably defined within the institution of marriage. Even when women are employed outside the home, they are still largely responsible for the care of their homes and families. As a result, they experience higher levels of time stress and have less time for leisure activities then do their male counterparts (Statistics Canada 2000a).

Sexism and Sex Discrimination

Just as visible minorities in Canada are victimized by racism, women suffer from the sexism of our society. ***Sexism*** is the ideology that one sex is superior to the other. The term is generally used to refer to male prejudice and discrimination against women. In Chapter 9, we noted that visible minorities can suffer from both individual acts of racism and institutional discrimination. *Institutional discrimination* was defined as the denial of opportunities and equal rights to individuals or groups that results from the normal operations of a society. In the same sense, women suffer both from individual acts of sexism (such as sexist remarks and acts of violence) and from institutional sexism.

p. 202

It is not simply that particular men in Canada and elsewhere are biased in their treatment of women. All the major institutions of our society—including the government, armed forces, large corporations, the media, universities, and the medical establishment—are controlled by men. These institutions, in their "normal," day-to-day operations, often discriminate against women and perpetuate sexism. For example, if the central office of a nationwide bank sets a policy that single women are a bad risk for loans—regardless of their income and investments—the institution will discriminate against women as a group. It will do so even at bank branches in which loan officers hold no personal biases concerning women but are merely "following orders." We will examine institutional discrimination against women within the educational system in Chapter 12.

Our society is run by male-dominated institutions, yet with the power that flows to men comes responsibility and stress. Men have higher reported rates of certain types of mental illness, shorter life spans, and greater likelihood of death from heart attack or strokes (see Chapter 14). The pressure on men to succeed—and then to remain on top in a competitive world of work—can be especially intense. This is not to suggest that gender stratification is as damaging to men as it is to women. But it is clear that the power and privilege men enjoy are no guarantee of well-being.

The Status of Women Worldwide

Inequality is a theme that figures large when we examine the status of the world's women.

It is estimated that women grow half the world's food, but they rarely own land. They constitute one-third of the world's paid labour force but are generally found in the lowest-paying jobs. Single-parent households headed by women—which appear to be on the increase in many nations—are typically found in the poorest sections of the population. The feminization of poverty has become a global phenomenon. As in Canada, women worldwide are underrepresented politically.

A detailed overview of the status of the world's women, issued by the United Nations in 1995, noted that "too often, women and men live in different worlds—worlds that differ in access to education and work opportunities, and in health, personal security, and leisure time." While acknowledging that much has been done in the past 20 years to sharpen people's awareness of gender inequities, the report identified a number of areas of continuing concern:

- Despite advances in higher education for women, women still face major barriers when they attempt to use their educational achievements to advance in the workplace. For example, women rarely hold more than 1 percent to 2 percent of top executive positions.
- Women almost always work in occupations with lower status and pay than men do. In both developing and developed countries, many women work as unpaid family labourers. (Figure 10-1 shows the paid labour force participation of women in seven industrialized countries.)
- Despite social norms regarding support and protection, many widows around the world find that they have little concrete support from extended family networks.
- In many African and a few Asian nations, traditions mandate the cutting of female genitals, typically by practitioners who fail to use sterilized instruments. This can lead to immediate and serious complications from infection and to long-term health problems.
- Although males outnumber females as refugees, refugee women have unique needs, such as protection against physical and sexual abuse (United Nations 1995:xvi, xvii, xxii, 11, 46, 70).

Moreover, according to a *World Development Report* issued by the World Bank (2000b), there are twice as many illiterate women in developing countries as illiterate men. Some societies do not allow women to attend school. Of 1.2 billion people living on less than a dollar a

FIGURE 10-1

Percentage of Adult Women in the Paid Labour Force by Country

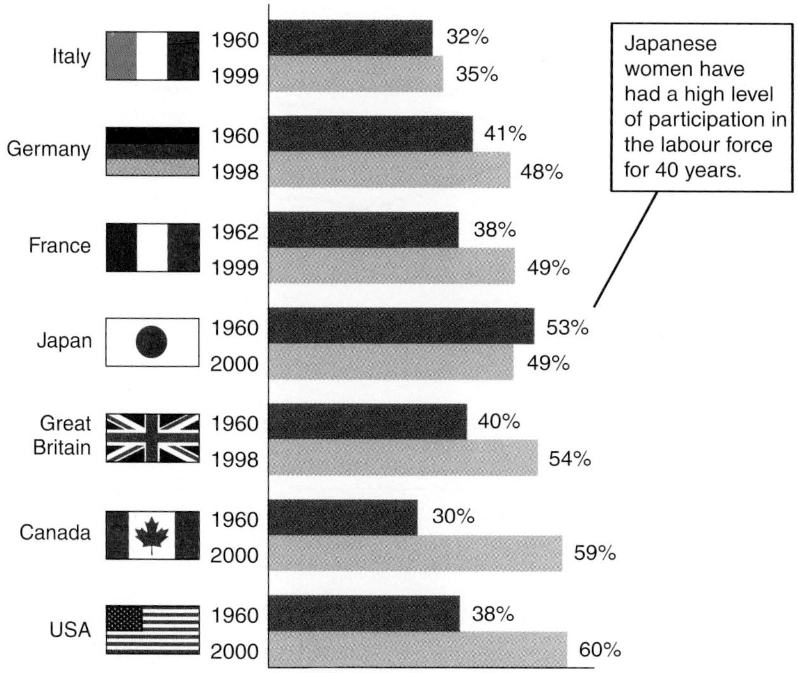

Source: Bureau of Labour Statistics 2001.

> **Think about It**
> In industrialized nations, what appears to be the trend in women's labour force participation?

day around the world, 70 percent are female (World Bank 2000b; 23, 277).

The United Nations' report *State of World Population 2000* reiterated that, globally, women and girls bare a disproportionate brunt of the world's burdens. The report stated that discrimination, abuse, and violence remain "firmly rooted" in cultures around the world where women and girls are denied access to education, health care, and safety. The report pointed out that governments around the world had pledged to halve the 1990 rate of global illiteracy for women and girls by 2005 (United Nations Population Fund 2000).

What conclusions can we make about women's equality worldwide? First, as anthropologist Laura Nader (1986:383) has observed, even in the relatively more egalitarian nations of the West, women's subordination is "institutionally structured and culturally rationalized, exposing them to conditions of deference, dependency, powerlessness, and poverty." Although the situation for women in Sweden and Canada is significantly better than in Saudi Arabia and Bangladesh, women nevertheless remain in a second-class position in the world's most affluent and developed countries.

Second, there is a link between the wealth of industrialized nations and the poverty of the developing countries. Viewed from a conflict perspective, the economies of developing nations are controlled and exploited by industrialized countries and multinational corporations based in those countries. Much of the exploited labour in developing nations, especially in the nonindustrial sector, is performed by women. Female workers typically toil long hours for low pay but contribute significantly to their families' incomes. The affluence of Western industrialized nations has come, in part, at the expense of women in developing countries (Jacobson 1993).

Women in the Paid Workforce in Canada

One of the most significant social changes witnessed in Canada over the past half-century has been the movement of women into the paid workforce. Even though the majority of Canadian women now work for pay outside the home, most continue to experience gendered patterns of inequality relating to pay, working conditions, and opportunities for advancement.

A Statistical Overview

No longer is the adult woman associated solely with the role of caregiver. Instead, millions of women—married and single, with and without children—are working in the labour force (see Figure 10-2). In 2002, 56 percent of all women in Canada aged 15 and over had jobs in the paid labour force, up from 42 percent in 1976. A majority of women are now members of the paid labour force, not full-time caregivers. The vast majority of employed women in Canada return to the paid labour force after giving birth. Of those who gave birth in 1993 or 1994, 21 percent returned to work one month after giving birth. Within one year of giving birth, 86 percent of Canadian mothers returned to paid work; within two years, 93 percent had returned (Statistics Canada 2000a).

FIGURE 10-2

Employment of Women with Children under Age 16, by Family Status, 1976–2002

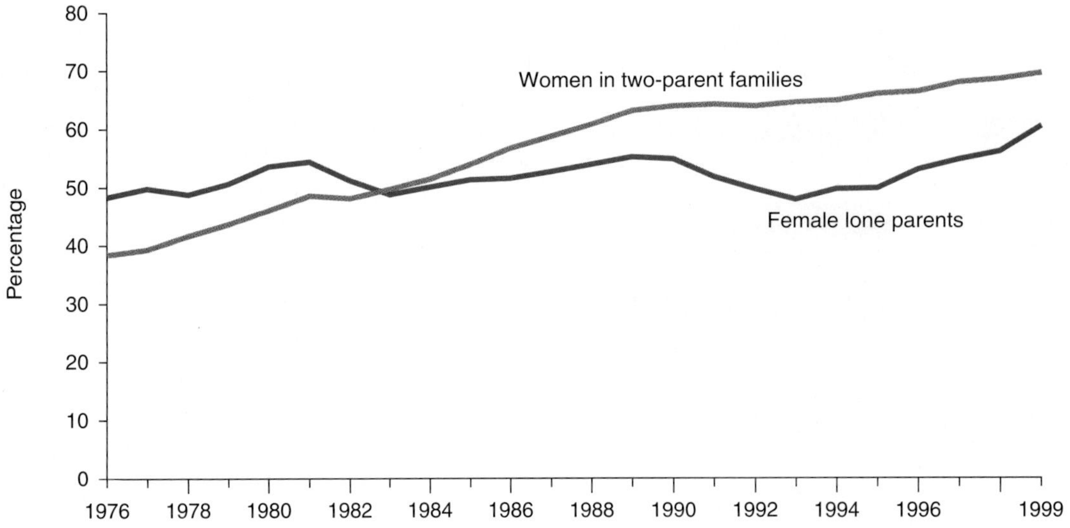

Source: Statistics Canada 2003g.

Yet women entering the job market find their options restricted in important ways. Particularly damaging is occupational segregation, or confinement to sex-typed "women's jobs." For example, in 2002, women accounted for 87.3 percent of all nursing, therapy, and other health-related jobs; 75 percent of all clerical, administrative jobs; and 58.6 percent of all sales and service jobs. Entering such sex-typed occupations places women in "service" roles that parallel the traditional gender-role standard under which housewives "serve" their husbands.

Women are *underrepresented* in occupations historically defined as "men's jobs," which often carry much greater financial rewards and prestige than women's jobs. For example, in 2002, women accounted for approximately 46 percent of the paid labour force of Canada. Yet they constituted only 25.1 percent of senior managers; 21.3 percent of those employed in natural science, engineering, and mathematics fields; and 6.5 percent in trades, transport, and construction. Canadian women have, however, made gains in the areas of business and finance, medicine, and dentistry, where they now account for almost half of all professionals in these previously male-dominated fields (see Table 10-3). In Box 10-2, we consider unique situations that run *against* sex-typing: male nurses and female hockey players.

Women from all groups, particularly those from visible minorities or those from older age groups, are at increased risk of encountering attitudinal or organizational bias that prevents them from reaching their full potential. As we saw in Chapter 9, the term *glass ceiling* refers to an invisible barrier that

p. 201

Table 10-3 Canadian Women in Selected Occupations, 2002

	Women as Percentage of Total Employed in Occupation
Underrepresented	
Trades, transport, and construction	6.5%
Natural sciences, engineering, mathematics	21.3%
Senior management	25.1%
Overrepresented	
Nursing, therapy, other health-related	87.3%
Clerical and administrative	75.0%
Teaching	64.4%
Sales and service	58.6%
Roughly Equally Represented	
Business and finance	48.2%
Doctors, dentists, other health occupation	54.4%
Artistic, literary, recreational	53.5%

Source: Statistics Canada 2003g.

Research in Action 10-2 Female Hockey Players and Male Nurses

When you sit down to watch ice hockey, you expect to watch men playing. When you are being assisted by a nurse, you expect it to be a woman. And in almost every case you would be correct, but not always.

In Canada, about 5 percent of all registered nurses are male (Canadian Institute for Health Information 1999). Sociologist E. Joel Heikes (1991) wondered what characteristics male nurses exhibit when entering a traditionally female occupation, so he conducted in-depth interviews with male registered nurses employed in hospital settings. Heikes reports that male nurses felt more visible than female nurses and typically responded by overachieving. Although they did not feel polarized from the female nurses, they did feel socially isolated as "tokens" in the workplace. Typically, they were excluded from traditionally female gatherings, such as female nurses' baby and bridal showers. Such social isolation did not reduce the male nurses' skills training, but it excluded them from informal interactions in which they could have "networked" with female nurses and learned more about the day-to-day workings of the hospital.

Stereotyping was also evident. Male nurses were commonly mistaken for physicians. Even though being mistaken for someone of higher status may appear to be advantageous, it can often have a negative impact on the male nurse. It is a constant reminder of his deviant position in a traditionally female occupation. The implicit message is that men should be doctors rather than nurses. When correctly identified as nurses, men face a much more serious form of stereotyping. Because of the persistence of traditional gender roles, it is assumed that all male nurses must be gay. Many male nurses told Heikes that they felt a need to deny this stigmatized identity.

Sociologist Christine Williams (1992, 1995) examined the underrepresentation of men in four predominantly female professions: nursing, elementary school teaching, librarianship, and social work. Drawing on in-depth interviews with 99 men and women in these professions, Williams found that the experience of tokenism is very different for women and men. Although men in these traditionally female professions commonly experience negative stereotyping, they nevertheless benefit from hidden *advantages* stemming from their status as men, such as receiving early and disproportionate encouragement to become administrators. By contrast, women in traditionally male professions often find that their advancement is limited and their token status is hardly an asset.

Like male nurses, female hockey players are rare specimens, although they have actually been around almost as long as male players. A photograph of the daughter of Lord Stanley, donor of the coveted Stanley Cup given to the champions in professional hockey, shows her playing the sport in 1890. A rivalry between the American and Canadian women's teams goes back to 1916. But women were never taken very seriously as hockey players—until quite recently. In 1998, women made their first appearance on the rink in the Olympics.

Although increasing numbers of women have come into their own in hockey, they still are put down for not being as "tough and strong" as male hockey players. Hockey rules do not allow women to body check, which calls for shoving an opponent hard into the boards on the side of the rink. Their game relies more on finesse than on strength.

Using both observation and interviews, sociologist Nancy Theberge (1997) studied a female Canadian league. She found that although the players generally acknowledge that the game is more skill-oriented without body checking, they favour including body checking in women's hockey to make the sport more professional. They reason that if they can make a living at the sport, then they should accept the risk of injury that comes with "hard checks." Ironically, their willingness to accept a more intense level of the game comes at a time when many people feel that men's professional hockey has become too physical and too violent; hard body checking leads to the fights that accompany many games.

Theberge found that even without body checking, injury and pain were routine features of the lives of female hockey players. She notes, "For these athletes, overcoming injury and pain is a measure of both ability and commitment." Some observers, however, find it troubling that as women's involvement in hockey grows, the pressure increases to develop a system that normalizes injury and pain in the sport.

Applying Theory

1. On what basis might functionalist sociologists argue that it is "functional" to maintain nursing as a female-dominated profession?
2. According to conflict thinkers, why has female hockey been treated differently from male hockey in terms of visibility, popularity, and financial support?

Sources: Canadian Institute for Health Information 1999; DeSimone 2000; Elliott 1997; Heikes 1991; Lillard 1998; Theberge 1997; Williams 1992, 1995; Zimmer 1988.

blocks the promotion of a qualified individual in a work environment because of the individual's gender, race, or ethnicity. A study of Boards of Directors in Canada found that only 6.2 percent of the seats on these boards were held by women (Catalyst 1998).

One response to the "glass ceiling" and other gender bias in the workplace is to start your own business and work for yourself. This route to success, traditionally taken by men from immigrant and racial minority groups, has become more common among women as they have increasingly sought paid employment outside the home. Female entrepreneurs constitute a rapidly growing employment category in Canada. As of 2002, women represented 35 percent of the self-employed, up from 31 percent in 1985. According to an international report on the status of women in 140 countries, Canadian women have started businesses at a rate three times the rate for men, while their success rate is twice the rate for men (Neft and Levine 1997).

The workplace patterns described here have one crucial result: Women earn much less money than men in the paid labour force of Canada. In 2001, the average earnings of full-time female workers were about 72 percent of those for full-time male workers. Given these data, it is hardly surprising to learn that many women are living in poverty, particularly when they must function as heads of households. In the discussion of poverty in Chapter 8, we noted that female heads of households and their children accounted for most of the nation's poor people living in families. Yet not all women are in equal danger of experiencing poverty. Aboriginal women as well as women who are members of visible minorities suffer from "double jeopardy" or "multiple jeopardies." *Double jeopardy* refers to the discrimination that women experience as a result of the compounded effects of gender and race and ethnicity, while *multiple jeopardies* refers to the compounded effects of gender, race and ethnicity, class, age, or physical disability. Aboriginal women are more likely to live in poverty, to experience family violence, to be unemployed, to experience poor health, to be paid lower wages, to possess lower levels of education, and even to live shorter lives than non-Aboriginal women. Aboriginal women hold multiple memberships in disadvantaged categories and experience multiple forms of discrimination, all at the same time. As Nelson and Robinson (1999:261) explain:

> Women possessing multiple memberships in disadvantaged categories are in jeopardy of experiencing double, triple, or more forms of discrimination simultaneously. Since multiple jeopardies are difficult to disentangle, it is almost impossible to isolate which disadvantaged status has been accorded primary discrimination.

Social Consequences of Women's Employment

"What a circus we women perform every day of our lives. It puts a trapeze artist to shame." These words by the writer Anne Morrow Lindbergh (1955) attest to the lives of women today who try to juggle their work and family lives.

The consequence of this "role complexity" for women is higher levels of severe time stress (Statistics Canada 2000a). In 1998, 38 percent of employed, married women between the ages of 25 and 44 who had children reported they were time-stressed, compared with 26 percent of employed, married men of the same age who had children. The variety of roles that married women with children must play, coupled with the greater responsibility for unpaid work in the home (e.g., cooking, laundry, caring for a sick child, grocery shopping), contributes to their time stress. Figure 10-3 shows the differences in severe time stress, according to gender and the presence of children. Although married men's time stress was the same, regardless of whether or not they had children, married women with children experienced almost twice the time stress of their married counterparts without children.

This situation has many social consequences. For one thing, it puts pressure on child care facilities and on public financing of day care and even on the fast-food

FIGURE 10-3

Percentage of People Aged 25–44 Employed Full-Time Who Are Severely Time Stressed, 1998

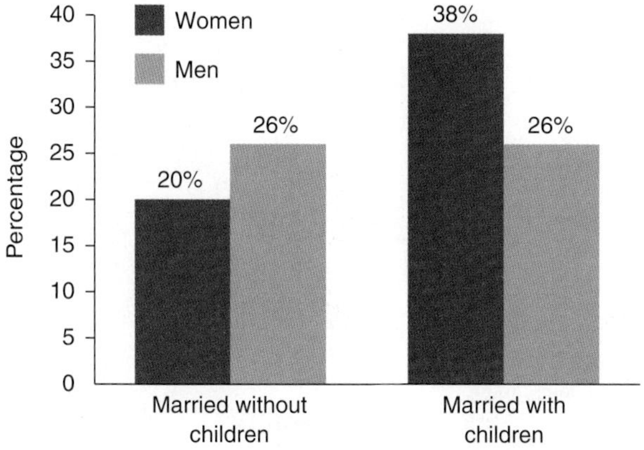

Source: Statistics Canada 2000a, p. 115.

> **Think about It**
> How might these figures be related to growing rates of depression and anxiety among working women?

industry, which provides many of the meals that women used to prepare during the day. For another, it raises questions about what responsibility male wage earners have in the household.

Who does do the housework when women become productive wage earners? Studies indicate that there continues to be a clear gender gap in the performance of housework, although the differences are narrowing. Still, the most recent study finds women doing more housework and spending more time on child care than men, whether it be on a workday or when off work. Taken together, then, a woman's workday on and off the job is much longer than a man's.

Canadian women in 1998 worked approximately 80 hours more per year than did Canadian men, calculating their total hours of paid and unpaid work (Statistics Canada 1999b). In addition, women are financially compensated for less of their work. Joanna Hemm, a 34-year-old banquet server from Ottawa, expressed the reality of women's unpaid labour as follows:

> Men have their jobs. . . . When they come home they feel the need to unwind. They don't regard housework or cooking or cleaning as something that needs to be stuck to. (Freeze 2001)

Sociologist Arlie Hochschild (1989, 1990) has used the phrase "second shift" to describe the double burden—work outside the home followed by child care and housework—that many women face and few men share equitably. On the basis of interviews with and observations of 52 couples over an eight-year period, Hochschild reports that the wives (and not their husbands) drive home from the office while planning domestic schedules and play dates for children—and then begin their second shift. Drawing on national studies, she concludes that women spend 15 fewer hours in leisure activities each week than their husbands do. In a year, these women work an extra month of 24-hour days because of the "second shift"; over a dozen years, they work an extra year of 24-hour days. Hochschild found that the married couples she studied were fraying at the edges, and so were their careers and their marriages. Juggling so many roles means that more things can go wrong for women, which contributes to stress. A study by a Harvard sociologist found that married women are 50 percent more likely than married men to complain of being in a bad mood (Kessler 1998).

With such reports in mind, many feminists have advocated greater governmental and corporate support pp. 87–89 for child care, more flexible family leave policies, and other reforms designed to ease the burden on the nation's families.

For some women the workday seems to never end. Women who undertake most of the child care and housework in addition to working outside the home have a double burden, known as a "second shift."

Most studies of gender, child care, and housework focus on the time actually spent by women and men performing these duties. However, sociologist Susan Walzer (1996) was interested in whether there are gender differences in the amount of time that parents spend *thinking* about the care of their children. Drawing on interviews with 25 couples, Walzer found that mothers are much more involved than fathers in the invisible, mental labour associated with taking care of a baby. For example, while involved in work outside the home, mothers are more likely to think about their babies and to feel guilty if they become so consumed with the demands of their jobs that they *fail* to think about their babies.

The very idea of what constitutes "work" in our society, whether it is done by men or women, at home or in the public sphere, is shaped by a "male work-role model" (Pleck and Corfman 1979). This model assumes that work will be full-time, continuous from graduation to retirement, that all other roles will be subordinate, and that a man's self-actualization will be based on this role. Implicit to this model is the assumption of paid work and stereotypical masculinity (A. Nelson and Robinson 2002). Since Canadian women, on average, engage in greater amounts of mental and physical labour in the care of their families and households, they run a greater risk of not having their labour considered as "work."

Women: The Emergence of Feminism in Canada

Social movements involve the organized attempts of masses of people to bring about social change through their collective action. The women's movement, or feminist movement, is one such movement by which women and men have attempted to change their society—not only for the betterment of women but also for the betterment of society as a whole. Often, however, those in the movement have been white, middle-class women who fought for their own vision of social or moral reform—a vision that might improve the welfare of some women (depending on their race, ethnicity, and class) but not necessarily all. From the mid-nineteenth century to the mid-twentieth century women's movements emerged in 32 countries worldwide (A. Nelson and Robinson 1999).

In Canada, the first wave of feminism beginning in the mid-nineteenth century had three faces—moral reform (or maternal feminism), liberalism, and socialism (Banks 1981). It concentrated largely on female suffrage and efforts to expand educational and employment opportunities for girls and women. Nellie McClung, perhaps Canada's foremost "maternal feminist," believed women were the "guardians of the race" and that it was therefore their responsibility to "lift high the standard of morality" (Adamson, Briskin, and McPhail 1998:31).

Nellie McClung was one of a group of Canadian women's rights activists who later became known as the "Famous Five." Although the "Famous Five" were concerned about the social injustice encountered by some Canadian women, their concerns excluded injustices because of ethnicity, race, and class.

During the 1920s, McClung and four fellow suffragettes—Irene Parlby, Henrietta Muir Edwards, Louise McKinney, and Emily Murphy—petitioned the Supreme Court of Canada to declare that women could become members of the Senate. The "Famous Five," as they were later known, appealed the negative decision of the Supreme Court of Canada to the British Privy Council. In 1929, the British Privy Council declared that women were "persons" in the eyes of law, making them eligible for appointment to the Senate. The "Persons case" marked a significant achievement for Canadian women.

The Famous Five were willing to fight for equality of some women; however, they were also willing to exclude others from their cause. Emily Murphy, Nellie McClung, and Louise McKinney were supporters of the eugenics movement, a movement that espoused the desirability of certain races, ethnic groups, and classes. Emily Murphy, for example, spoke out against "aliens of colour," targeting the "black and yellow" races and advocating "whites-only" immigration and citizenship policies. The progress of the women's movement has affected Canadian women unevenly, depending on their race, ethnicity, and class.

Although women in Canada were granted the right to vote in federal elections in 1918 (Manitoba, Saskatchewan, Alberta, British Columbia, and Ontario had granted the provincial vote to women shortly before 1918), until 1960, Aboriginal women and men were entitled to vote only if they gave up their Indian status (Mossman 1994). It is worth noting that although Clare Brett Martin, in 1897, was the first woman to become a lawyer in the Commonwealth, "it was not until 1946 that the first Asian Canadian woman graduated from law school in Ontario" (A. Nelson and Robinson 1999: 493).

The second wave of feminism emerged in Canada in the 1960s, coinciding with the rise of feminist consciousness in the United States. The second wave of the movement in Canada focused on two areas of concern: (1) that women were treated differently and discriminated against (at home as well as in the paid workplace) and (2) that women's unique qualities were undervalued (arguing for the recognition of these qualities) (Black 1993). This wave saw the huge growth of feminist perspectives in the social sciences, where feminists scholars challenged mainstream or "malestream" sociology's treatment of gender as it relates to studying crime, deviance, morality, aging, politics, and so on.

During this period, feminism began to become entrenched in institutions. Although essentially a grassroots movement, governments and international agencies around the world began to address some of the movement's concerns. In 1967, the Canadian government established the Royal Commission on the Status of Women, and the United Nations declared 1975–1985 the decade for women. Today, there are movements on behalf of women in most countries of the world; however, the disparities of advantage and disadvantage remain great among the world's girls and women, not only between them and their male counterparts but also between females in developing and developed countries.

SOCIAL POLICY AND GENDER RELATIONS

Abortion and Sex Selection: The "New Eugenics"

The Issue

Today in Canada, a woman's decision to have an abortion is usually made in consultation with her doctor based on factors related to her overall health and well-being. However, as new reproductive and genetic technologies, referred to collectively as "reprogenetics" (McTeer 1999), emerge in our society and around the world, the twinning of abortion and reprogenetics presents new ethical and moral considerations. The most controversial of these is what some sociologists are calling "the new eugenics"—a new movement to promote the reproduction of those with particular characteristics, while attempting to limit or control the reproduction of those with other, less desirable traits. Thus, with new reproductive and genetic technologies, abortion has the potential to become no longer a choice a woman makes simply on the basis of her health and well-being, but an instrument of social control as to what "type" (e.g., sex) of person is to be reproduced.

The Setting

Canada's first Criminal Code, established in 1892, made "procuring or performing an abortion a crime punishable by life imprisonment" (McTeer 1999:32). In 1968, amendments to the Criminal Code made abortion legal under certain conditions. The conditions included the approval of a special committee and that the abortion take place in an accredited hospital. However, hospitals and provincial or territorial governments were not required to establish the committee and many did not, thus making abortion inaccessible to many women in Canada, particularly those in non-urban areas. In 1988, the law on abortion was changed again; today, it is a decision "left to the pregnant woman alone, and usually made in consultation with her doctor" (McTeer 1999:33).

In 1993, approximately 105 000 abortions were performed in Canada—27 abortions for every 100 live births. Race, class, and age differences are apparent as they relate to the incidence of abortion in Canada (Calliste 2001). For example, Aboriginal women in Canada were subjected to forced sterilization as a tactic of genocide, thus a policy of abortion on demand did not reflect their needs. In 1995, more than 42 percent of therapeutic abortions were performed on women between the ages of 18 and 24 (Statistics Canada 2000a). In the late 1980s, the Canadian government called for the establishment of a Royal Commission investigating new reproductive technologies. These technologies and procedures included assisted reproduction, for example, artificial insemination (AI), in vitro fertilization (IVF), and direct ovum and sperm transfer (DOST); surrogacy (one woman carrying a pregnancy to term for another); and prenatal diagnosis (PND), which can include identification of the sex of the fetus. With the emergence of those technologies, the question becomes "How can we as a society protect those who might be exploited or mistreated (e.g., surrogates, IVF-created human embryos, female fetuses) while still safeguarding women's reproductive rights relating to abortion and contraception?" (McTeer 1999).

In 1996, the Canadian government introduced Bill C-47, a legislative attempt to ban practices, such as commercial surrogacy and sex selection, for reasons other than those related to the health of the fetus (i.e., sex-linked hereditary diseases). Bill C-47, which set out to ban 13 different reproductive technological practices, died "on the order paper" when the 1997 federal election was called.

Sociological Insights

Sociologists see gender and social class as largely defining the issues surrounding abortion. The intense conflict over reproductive rights reflects broad differences over women's position in society. Sociologist Kristin Luker (1984) has offered a detailed study of activists in the pro-choice and pro-life movements. Luker interviewed 212 activists, overwhelmingly women, who spent at least five hours a week working for one of these movements. According to Luker, each group has a consistent, coherent view of the world. Feminists involved in defending abortion rights typically believe that men and women are essentially similar; they support women's full participation in work outside the home and oppose all forms of sex discrimination. By contrast, most pro-life activists believe that men and women are fundamentally different. In their view, men are best suited for the public world of work, whereas women are best suited for the demanding and crucial task of rearing children. These activists are troubled by women's growing participation in work outside the home, which they view as destructive to the family and ultimately to society as a whole. The pro-life, or antiabortion, activists see abortion as an act that denies nurturance and therefore diminishes the family since the family is viewed as the major source of nurturance in society. Thus, these activists hold a view similar to that of functionalism, which connects the family to particular functions (Collier, Rosaldo, and Yanagisako 2001).

Feminist perspectives on abortion and reproductive technology have been led by the radical feminist vanguard, later to be joined by liberal and socialist perspectives (A. Nelson and Robinson 1999). The hope that technology would offer women escape from the "tyranny of their reproduction biology" (Firestone 1970) is now being tempered by the possible negative impact that technology could have on women's lives. Thus, radical feminist perspectives are now joined by many other forms of feminism in defining abortion, reproductive rights, and reproductive technologies as feminist issues (A. Nelson and Robinson 1999).

Policy Initiatives

The policies of the United States and the developing nations are intertwined. Throughout the 1980s, antiabortion members of Congress often successfully blocked foreign aid to countries that might use the funds to encourage abortion. And yet these developing nations generally have the most restrictive abortion laws. As shown in Figure 10-4, it is primarily in Africa, Latin America, and parts of Asia that women are not able to terminate a pregnancy on request. As might be expected, illegal abortions are most common in these nations. In general, the more restrictive a nation's legislation on abortion, the higher its rate of unsafe abortions, for pregnancies may typically be terminated by unskilled health providers or by the pregnant women themselves.

Globally, countries' responses to new reproductive and genetic technologies vary in terms of the guidelines and legislation set in place to regulate their use. For example, Australia, Austria, Brazil, Czech Republic, Denmark, Egypt, France, Germany, Hungary, Israel, Mexico, The Netherlands, Norway, Saudi Arabia, Singapore, South Africa, Spain, Sweden, Taiwan, Turkey, and the United Kingdom have some form of legislation to deal with how these technologies can be used. Other countries, such as Argentina, Egypt, Finland, Italy, Poland, Japan, South Korea, Switzerland, and the United States, have guidelines rather than legislation for the use of assisted reproductive technologies. Since the failure of Bill C-47 to become law, Canada has established a voluntary moratorium on certain reproductive and genetic practices.

Such countries as Greece, India, Jordan, and Portugal, however, have neither legislation nor guidelines. In such countries as India, where cultural preferences for

FIGURE 10-4

The Global Divide on Abortion

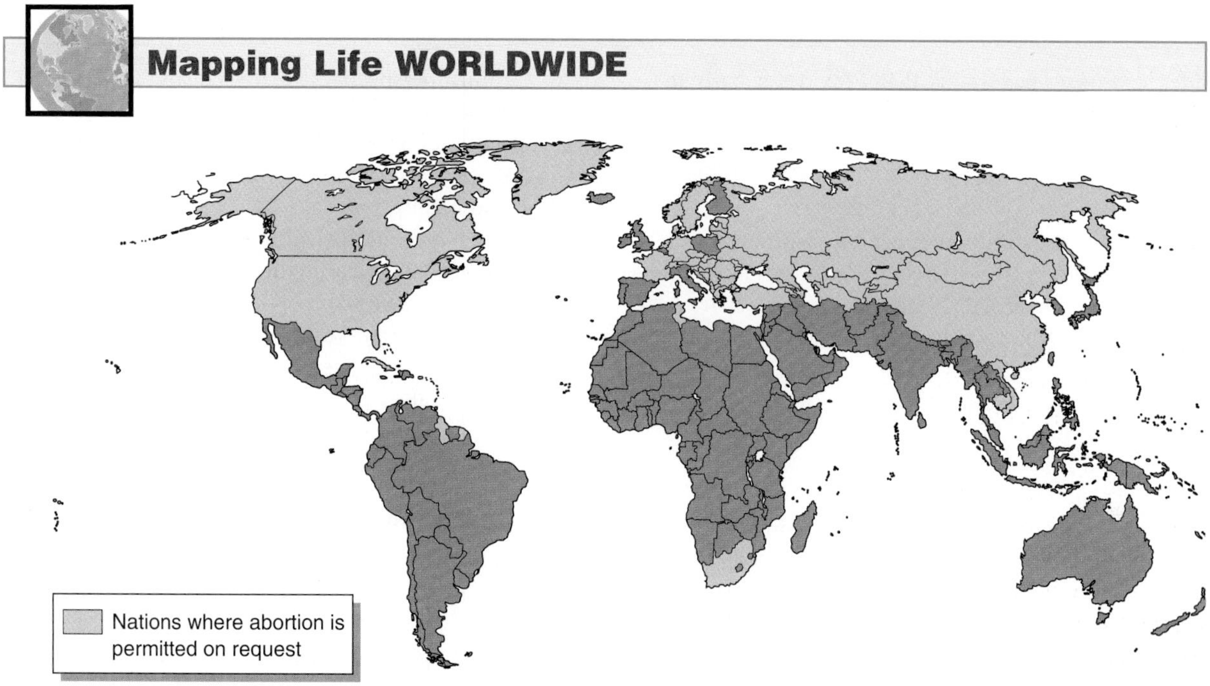

Sources: Developed by the author based on United Nations Population Division 1998 and Gonnut 2001.
Note: Data current as of June 2001.

male offspring remain strong, the coupling of prenatal diagnosis techniques, such as ultrasound and amniocentesis, which identify the sex of the fetus, and the use of abortion can result in the birth of fewer female children. Although these Western-based prenatal diagnosis technologies can be used to identify and abort fetuses with genetic abnormalities, they also open the door to sex selection for cultural or social reasons. Saraswati Raju, a professor of gender and demography at Jawaharlal Nehra University in New Delhi, states that the fate of the female infant in India has been getting worse in recent decades (Lakshimi 2001). The most recent Indian census showed that the percentage of girls under age 6 has dropped since the previous census. Although the government has banned the use of sex selection tests and doctors' associations have discouraged their use, the tests persist and the government is unable to stop the practice. Despite widespread societal efforts to improve the status of girls and women in Indian society, a baby girl is viewed as a liability and a strong cultural preference for male children persists.

Although it is rarer, sex selection can be used to produce female offspring as well. In 2000, a Scottish couple attempted to use a human rights bill in their country to force the British government to allow them to use sex selection technology to produce a daughter. The couple already had four boys and recently had lost their three-year old daughter in a tragic accident.

According to Maureen McTeer (1999), a former member of the Royal Commission on New Reproductive Technologies, sex selection violates our notions of equality as enshrined in the Canadian Charter of Rights and Freedoms and in our human rights laws. In addition, she argues, sex selection denies Canada's international commitment to eliminate discrimination against women.

Applying Theory

1. According to conflict thinkers, who is most vulnerable to exploitation through the use of new reproductive and genetic technologies?
2. How might some feminist perspectives weigh the individual's right to reproduce against the society's need to regulate the use of these new technologies?
3. How might interactionist sociologists approach the study of reproductive or genetic technology for the

CHAPTER RESOURCES

Summary

Gender is an ascribed status that provides a basis for social differentiation. This chapter examined the social construction of gender, theories of stratification by gender, and women as an oppressed majority group.

1. The social construction of gender continues to define significantly different expectations for females and males in Canada.
2. Gender roles show up in our work and behaviour and in how we react to others.
3. Females have been more severely restricted by traditional gender roles, but these roles have also restricted males.
4. The research of anthropologist Margaret Mead points to the importance of cultural conditioning in defining the social roles of males and females.
5. Functionalists maintain that sex differentiation contributes to overall social stability, whereas conflict theorists contend that the relationship between females and males has been one of unequal power, with men in a dominant position over women. This dominance also shows up in everyday interactions.
6. Feminist perspectives are diverse and vary in their explanation of the sources of women's inequality.
7. Although numerically a majority, in many respects women fit the definition of a subordinate minority group within Canada.
8. Women around the world experience ***sexism*** and institutional discrimination.
9. As women have taken on more and more hours of paid employment outside the home, they have been only partially successful in getting their husbands to take a greater role in homemaking duties, including child care.
10. The first wave of feminism in Canada began in the mid-nineteenth century and concentrated largely on female suffrage and expanding educational and employment opportunities for women. The second wave emerged in the 1960s. It focused on differential and discriminatory treatment of women and the need to recognize and value women's differences while at the same time treat them equally.

Critical Thinking Questions

1. Sociologist Barbara Bovee Polk (1974) suggests that women are oppressed because they constitute an alternative subculture that deviates from the prevailing masculine value system. Does it seem valid to view women as an "alternative subculture"? In what ways do women support and deviate from the prevailing masculine value system evident in Canada?
2. In what ways is the social position of white women in Canada similar to that of Asian Canadian women, black women, or Aboriginal women? In what ways is a woman's social position markedly different, given her racial and ethnic status?
3. In what ways do you think your behaviour, values, educational choices, or career plans have been influenced by gender socialization? Can you think of ways in which the social class of your family has influenced your gender socialization?
4. How might interactionist sociologists approach the emerging trend of more men engaging in cosmetic surgery?

Key Terms

Expressiveness A term used to refer to concern for maintenance of harmony and the internal emotional affairs of the family. (page 225)

Instrumentality A term used to refer to emphasis on tasks, focus on more distant goals, and a concern for the external relationship between family and other social institutions. (225)

Sexism The ideology that one sex is superior to the other. (230)

Additional Readings

Epstein, Cynthia Fuchs, Carroll Seron, Bonnie Oglensky, and Robert Saute. 1999. *The Part-Time Paradox: Time Norms, Professional Life, Family and Gender.* New York: Routledge. The authors explore the conflict and tension between the time demands of career and family life; they also examine the choice of part-time work as a solution.

Mandell, Nancy, ed. 1998. *Feminist Issues: Race, Class, and Sexuality*, 2nd ed. Scarborough: Prentice Hall Allyn and Bacon Canada. This book covers a broad and diverse range of topics, including beauty, status and aging, violence, men in feminism, women and religion, and lesbianism.

Nelson, Adie. 2006. *Gender in Canada*, 3rd ed. Toronto: Pearson Prentice Hall. A comprehensive review of gender in Canada, covering such topics as intimate relations, gender and aging, marriage and parenting, work, and symbolic representations of gender.

Pollack, William. 1998. *Real Boys: Rescuing Our Sons from the Myths of Boyhood.* New York: Henry Holt. A researcher at Harvard Medical School explores why boys are confused by conventional expectations of masculinity.

Online Learning Centre

Visit the *Sociology: A Brief Introduction* Online Learning Centre at www.mcgrawhill.ca/college/schaefer to access quizzes, interactive exercises, video clips, and other research and study tools related to this chapter.

Reel Society Interactive Movie CD-ROM 2.0

Reel Society 2.0 can be used to spark discussion about the following topics from this chapter:

- Gender roles in North America
- Cross-cultural perspectives on gender
- Sexism and sex discrimination
- The status of women worldwide

chapter 11

THE FAMILY AND INTIMATE RELATIONSHIPS

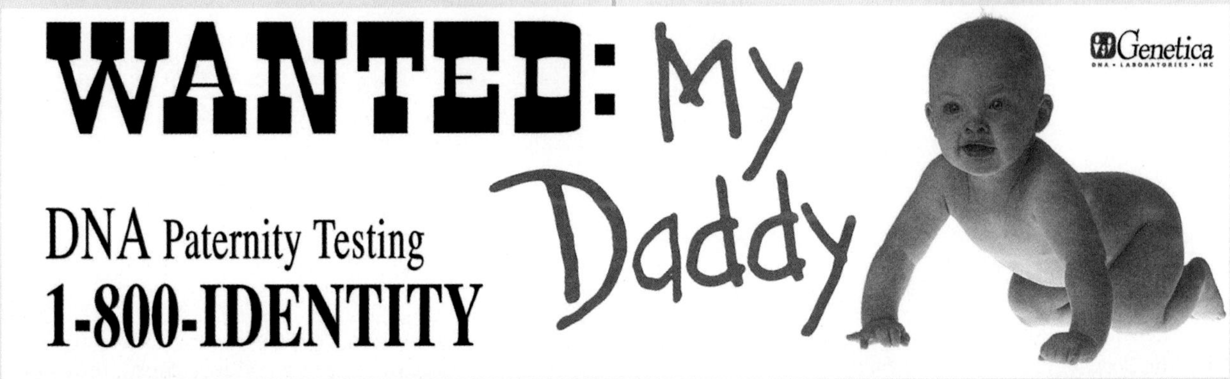

New technology has sparked a demand for testing services to determine who is and who is not the father of a child. When billboards advertising these services appeared in 1997, some people found them amusing while others perceived them as further evidence of the problems confronting the family.

He says that when his one-time girlfriend phoned him to let him know she was pregnant, she excitedly greeted him with the words: "Hello Papa."

The man had donated his sperm so that the ex-girlfriend and her lesbian partner could have a child.

Today, in a quarrel for the age in which we live, the man is in court to have himself recognized as the child's father so that, he says, he can develop "a loving and stable relationship" with the little child.

To the usual bitterness of any family-law dispute, this feud also features novel dimensions, from the ethical complexities of modern reproductive technologies to the new legal dynamics of same-sex marriages.

The litigation is "deciding the fate of this child in very arduous circumstances," Anne-France Goldwater, the lawyer of the biological mother, told a Quebec Superior Court hearing yesterday.

The case has raised concerns among lesbian couples who have had to turn to donors to become parents, said Laurie Arron, director of advocacy of the gay-rights group Egale Canada. "Families come in all forms and the law should match the facts of a family," he said.

Details that can lead to the identification of the parties cannot be published. This story will refer to the biological mother as Jane.

The man says he and Jane used to date and remained friends even after they broke up and she soon began a relationship with a woman.

Jane eventually married her girlfriend.

Then, after they broke up, the man says in his court petition, he and Jane started talking about having a child.

"Much soul-searching went on by both parties and serious in-depth discussions took place," the man's motion says.

The man says that he has played an active role in the endeavour, that he was even at the hospital at birth and that "it was always agreed between [him] and [Jane] that they would both be actively involved in the child's life as mother and father of the child."

The two women say he wasn't the only man they approached and that the candidates were told the donor would not have legal status.

The women's lawyers cite an article of the Quebec Civil Code that states that there can be no bond of filiation if there hasn't been sexual intercourse. On the birth certificate, the two women are listed as the little child's parents.

The man says in his court filings that when he advised the couple that he would launch court proceedings, he was told all contact with the child would be ended and he "was advised not even to bother phoning."

"This attitude is totally destructive . . . depriving [the child's] rights to her father, preventing her from further developing a loving and stable relationship with [the father]," his motion says.

Last spring, the man obtained a ruling granting him access to the child.

The women went to curtail that, fearing that any attachment between the toddler and the man could be cited eventually as a way for him to be the "psychological parent" of the child.

Mr. Justice Jean-Pierre Sénécal was to begin hearing the case yesterday. However, both sides wanted the case to unfold behind closed doors.

After a day-long debate, Judge Sénécal rejected the request, saying that, as long as they did not identify the parties, the media should be present because the proceedings were in the public interest.

The case has been suspended while the issue of media access is taken to the Quebec Court of Appeal. *(Ha 2004)* ■

In *The Globe and Mail* article that opened the chapter, Tu Thanh Ha illustrates the diverse forms of families, underscored by social factors, such as the ethical complexities of modern reproductive technologies and new legal dynamics of same-sex marriage. New laws, new technologies, new child-rearing patterns have all combined to create new forms of family life. Today, for example, more women are essential contributors to their families through their paid work, whether married or as a single parent. Blended families—the result of divorces and remarriages—are almost the norm. Many Canadians are seeking intimate relationships outside marriage, particularly in Quebec, whether it be in same-sex or opposite-sex cohabiting arrangements. And, of course, same-sex civil marriage became legal in Canada in 2005.

This chapter addresses family and intimate relationships in Canada as well as in other parts of the world. As we will see, family patterns differ from one culture to another and within the same culture. A ***family*** can be defined as a set of people related by blood, marriage (or some other agreed-on relationship), or adoption who share the primary responsibility for reproduction and caring for members of society. A census family, as defined by Statistics Canada, is "a now-married couple, a common-law couple or a lone-parent with a child or youth who is under the age of 25 and who does not have his or her spouse living in the household. Now-married couples may or may not have such children and youth living with them" (Statistics Canada 2005c). According to the last census, conducted in 2001, married couples and common-law couples were classified as husband-and-wife families and the partners in the couple were classified as spouses (Statistics Canada 2005c). With the 2005 passage of Bill C-38, the Civil Marriage Act, gays and lesbians will now be afforded the same status as "spouses," as their civil unions became legal in all Canadian jurisdictions.

In this chapter, we will see that the family is universal—found in every culture—however varied in its organization. We will look at the family and intimate relationships from the functionalist, conflict, interactionist, and feminist points of view and at the variations in marital patterns and family life, including different family forms of child rearing. We'll pay particular attention to the increasing number of people in dual-income or single-parent families and the legalization of same-sex marriage in Canada. We will examine divorce in Canada and consider diversity patterns, including cohabitation, remaining single, lesbian and gay relationships, and marriage without children. The social policy section will look at controversial issues surrounding the use of reproductive technology. ■

Use Your Sociological Imagination www.mcgrawhill.ca/college/schaefer

What was your view of Bill C-38? What do you think the major reasons were for those who opposed the passage of the bill?

GLOBAL VIEW OF THE FAMILY

Among Tibetans, a woman may be simultaneously married to more than one man, usually brothers. This system allows sons to share the limited amount of good land. A Hopi woman may divorce her husband by placing her belongings outside the door. A Trobriand Island couple signals marriage by sitting in public on a porch eating yams provided by the bride's mother. She may continue to provide cooked yams for a year while the groom's family offers in exchange such valuables as stone axes and clay pots (Haviland 1999).

As these examples illustrate, there are many variations in "the family" from culture to culture. Yet the family as a social institution is present in all cultures. Moreover, certain general principles concerning its composition, kinship patterns, and authority patterns are universal.

Composition: What Is the Family?

If we were to take our information on what a family is from what we see on television, we might come up with some very strange scenarios (see Box 11-1). The media

Eye on the Media 11-1 The Family in TV Land

Put an alien creature from outer space in front of a television, and it would have no idea of what family life is like in North America. It would conclude that most adults are men, most adults are not married, few are gay or lesbian, almost no one is over age 50, very few adults have children, most mothers don't work for pay, and child care is simply not an issue. When parents are depicted, they are either not around for the most part or they are clueless. On *The O.C.* parents and children are depicted as living lives disconnected from one another—parents with secret lives hidden from their children and children with secret lives hidden from their parents. Even the cartoon show *Rugrats,* aimed at young children, portrays talking babies as making their way in the world on their own.

Television Reality versus Social Reality

	Adult TV Characters	Adult Population
Women	38%	51%
Over age 50	14%	38%
Parents of minor children	15%	32%

These shows are beamed into the living rooms of Canadians each week. In fact, American programs, particularly dramas and comedies, are viewed substantially more often by Canadians than most Canadian programming. Many American television actors are household names in our country (Meisel 2001).

Whether the audience is Canadian or American, however, the fact is that *The Simpsons, The O.C., Will and Grace, The Sopranos,* and similar programs present lives that most households find fascinating but not exactly true to their own lives. Eight out of 10 adults in the United States think that almost no TV family is like their own; nearly half find no TV family like theirs.

These conclusions come out of a content analysis of prime-time TV programming conducted by Katharine Heintz-Knowles, a communications professor at the University of Washington and the mother of three children, who knows first-hand what a work–family conflict looks like. She has had to deal with finding sitters on short notice, taking children to work with her when a sitter was unavailable, and missing meetings to tend to a sick child. In fact, she acknowledges that her "life today is one big work–family conflict" (Gardner 1998:13). But when she watched television, she didn't see much of her life reflected on the screen.

Her study, called "Balancing Acts: Work/Family Issues on Prime-Time TV," carried out content analysis of 150 episodes of 92 different programs on commercial networks over a two-week period. She found that of the 820 TV characters studied, only 38 percent were women, only 15 percent could be identified as parents of minor children, and only 14 percent were over age 50 (see the table for how these percentages compare with the adult population of the United States). Only 3 percent of the TV characters faced recognizable conflicts between work and family, and no TV family made use of a child care centre. Canadians are presented with images of work–family roles that are strikingly similar to those of our American neighbours, since 80 percent of the characters on Canadian television, both in French and English shows, appear in American productions (Graydon 2001).

Television is the major storyteller in our lives today, and we may interpret its meanings in diverse ways. Unfortunately, television gives a distorted view of family life in North America, not only to our hypothetical alien but also to viewers at home and in other societies around the world. Canadian research has revealed that women with young families are critical of television's portrayal of poor role models; they expressed a desire to have their children exposed to positive portrayals of women successfully coping with a variety of situations and lifestyles (ComQuest Research Group 1993).

If very few shows depict real-life challenges in family life and possible solutions, then viewers may well go away thinking their own problems are unique and unsolvable. By confronting these issues, television could call attention to what needs to be changed—both on an individual level and on a societal level—and offer hope for solutions. It appears, however, that most TV programmers offer up a fantasy world in order to satisfy people who seek entertainment and escape from their everyday lives.

Applying Theory

1. If you were a conflict sociologist hired to help produce a television show on families, what perspective might you take or what advice might you give?
2. Based on your own family life, what meanings do you give to the portrayal of families on current television comedies?

Sources: Blanco 1998; ComQuest Research Group 1993; M. Gardner 1998; Graydon 2001; Meisel 2001; National Partnership for Women and Families 1998.

In wedding ceremonies in Sumatra, Indonesia, the bride's headdress indicates her village and her social status—the more elaborate the headdress, the higher her status. After she is married, the bride and her husband live with her maternal family, and all property passes from mother to daughter.

don't always help us get a realistic view of the family. Moreover, many people still think of the family in very narrow terms—as a heterosexual married couple and their unmarried children living together, like the family in the old *Cosby Show* or *Family Ties* or *Growing Pains.* However, this is but one type of family, what sociologists refer to as a ***nuclear family.*** The term *nuclear family* is well chosen, since this type of family serves as the nucleus, or core, upon which larger family groups are built. Some people in Canada may see the nuclear family as the preferred family arrangement. Yet, as Figure 11-1 shows, by 2001 only about 42 percent of the nation's family households fit this model.

The proportion of households in Canada comprising married heterosexual couples with children at home has decreased steadily over the past 30 years, and this trend is expected to continue. At the same time, there have been increases in the number of single-parent households (see Figure 11-1). Similar trends are evident in other industrialized nations, including the United States, Great Britain, and Japan.

A family in which relatives—such as grandparents, aunts, or uncles—live in the same home as parents and their children is known as an ***extended family.*** Although not common, such living arrangements do exist in Canada. The structure of the extended family offers certain advantages over that of the nuclear family. Crises, such as death, divorce, and illness, put less strain on family members, since there are more people who can provide assistance and emotional support. In addition, the extended family constitutes a larger economic unit than the nuclear family. If the family is engaged in a common enterprise—a farm or a small business—the additional family members may represent the difference between prosperity and failure.

FIGURE 11-1

Types of Family Households in Canada, 1981 and 2001

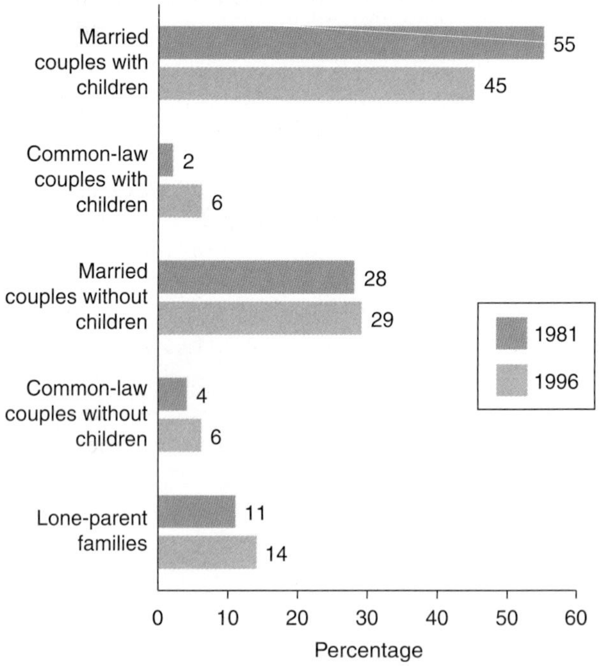

Source: Adapted from Statistics Canada 2002a.

Think about It
What changes would you expect to see in these percentages by 2011?

In considering these differing family types, we have limited ourselves to the form of marriage that is characteristic of Canada—monogamy. The term ***monogamy*** describes a form of marriage in which two people are married only to each other. Some observers, noting the rate of divorce in Canada, have suggested that "serial monogamy" is a more accurate description of the form that monogamy takes in Canada. Under ***serial monogamy,*** a person may have several spouses in his or her life but only one spouse at a time.

Some cultures allow an individual to have several spouses simultaneously. This form of marriage is known as ***polygamy.*** In fact, most societies throughout the world, past and present, have preferred polygamy to monogamy. Anthropologist George Murdock (1949, 1957) sampled 565 societies and found that more than 80 percent had some type of polygamy as their preferred form. Although polygamy steadily declined through most of the twentieth century, in at least five countries in Africa 20 percent of men are still in polygamous marriages (Population Reference Bureau 1996).

There are two basic types of polygamy. According to Murdock, the most common—endorsed by the majority of cultures he sampled—was ***polygyny.*** Polygyny refers to the marriage of a man to more than one woman at the same time. The various wives are often sisters, who are expected to hold similar values and who have already had experience sharing a household. In polygynous societies, relatively few men actually have multiple spouses. Most individuals live in typical monogamous families; having multiple wives is viewed as a mark of status.

The other principal variation of polygamy is ***polyandry,*** under which a woman can have more than one husband at the same time. This is the case in the culture of the Todas of southern India. Polyandry, however, tends to be exceedingly rare in the world today. It has been accepted by some extremely poor societies that practise female infanticide (the killing of baby girls) and thus have a relatively small number of women. Like many other societies, polyandrous cultures devalue the social worth of women.

Kinship Patterns: To Whom Are We Related?

Many of us can trace our roots by looking at a family tree or listening to elderly family members tell us about their lives—and about the lives of ancestors who died long before we were even born. Yet a person's lineage is more than simply a personal history; it also reflects societal patterns that govern descent. In every culture, children encounter relatives to whom they are expected to show an emotional attachment. The state of being related to others is called ***kinship.*** Kinship is culturally learned and is not totally determined by biological or marital ties. For example, adoption creates a kinship tie that is legally acknowledged and socially accepted.

The family and the kin group are not necessarily the same. Although the family is a household unit, kin do not always live together or function as a collective body on a daily basis. Kin groups include aunts, uncles, cousins, in-laws, and so forth. In such a society as Canada, the kinship group may come together only rarely, as for a wedding or funeral. However, kinship ties frequently create obligations and responsibilities. We may feel compelled to assist our kin and feel free to call on relatives for many types of aid, including loans and baby-sitting.

How do we identify kinship groups? The principle of descent assigns people to kinship groups according to their relationship to an individual's mother or father. There are three primary ways of determining descent. Generally, Canada follows the system of ***bilateral descent,*** which means that both sides of a person's family are regarded as equally important. For example, no higher value is given to the brothers of a father than to the brothers of a mother.

Most societies—according to George Murdock, 64 percent—give preference to one side of the family or the other in tracing descent. ***Patrilineal*** (from Latin *pater,* "father") ***descent*** indicates that only the father's relatives are important in terms of property, inheritance, and emotional ties. Conversely, in societies that favour ***matrilineal*** (from Latin *mater,* "mother") ***descent,*** only the mother's relatives are significant.

New forms of reproductive technology (discussed in the policy section) will force a new way of looking at kinship. Today a combination of biological and social processes can "create" a family member, requiring that more distinctions be made about who is related to whom (C. Cussins 1998).

Authority Patterns: Who Rules?

Imagine that you have recently married and must begin to make decisions about the future of your new family. You and your spouse face many questions. Where will you live? How will you furnish your home? Who will do the cooking, the shopping, the cleaning? Whose friends will be invited to dinner? Each time a decision must be made, an issue is raised: Who has the power to make the decision? In simple terms, who rules the family? The conflict perspective examines these questions in the context of gender stratification, in which men hold dominant positions over women in capitalist societies in general and in opposite-sex families in particular.

pp. 13–14

Societies vary in the way that power within the family is distributed. If a society expects males to dominate in all family decision making, it is termed a ***patriarchy***. Frequently, in patriarchal societies, such as Iran, the eldest male wields the greatest power, although wives are expected to be treated with respect and kindness. A woman's status in Iran is typically defined by her relationship to a male relative, usually as a wife or daughter. In many patriarchal societies women find it more difficult to obtain a divorce than a man does (G. Farr 1999). By contrast, in a ***matriarchy,*** women have greater authority than men. Matriarchies, which are very uncommon, emerged among Aboriginal tribal societies and in nations in which men were absent for long periods of time for warfare or food gathering.

Smile—it's family reunion time! The state of being related to others is called *kinship*. Kin groups include aunts, uncles, cousins, and so forth, as shown in this family from Slovakia.

A third type of authority pattern, the ***egalitarian family,*** is one in which spouses are regarded as equals. This does not mean, however, that each decision is shared in such families. Wives may hold authority in some spheres, husbands in others. Many sociologists believe the egalitarian family has begun to replace the patriarchal family as the social norm in Canada.

STUDYING THE FAMILY

Do we really need the family? A century ago, Friedrich Engels (1884), a colleague of Karl Marx's, described the family as the ultimate source of social inequality because of its role in the transfer of power, property, and privilege. More recently, conflict theorists have argued that the family contributes to societal injustice, denies opportunities to women that are extended to men, and limits freedom in sexual expression and selection of a mate. By contrast, the functionalist perspective focuses on the ways in which the family gratifies the needs of its members and contributes to the stability of society. The interactionist view considers more intimate, face-to-face relationships.

Functionalist View

There are six paramount functions performed by the family, first outlined more than 65 years ago by sociologist William F. Ogburn (Ogburn and Tibbits 1934):

1. **Reproduction.** For a society to maintain itself, it must replace dying members. In this sense, the family contributes to human survival through its function of reproduction.
2. **Protection.** Unlike the young of other animal species, human infants need constant care and economic security. The extremely long period of dependency for children places special demands on older family members. In all cultures, it is the family that assumes ultimate responsibility for the protection and upbringing of children.
3. **Socialization.** Parents and other kin monitor a child's behaviour and transmit the norms, values, and language of a culture to the child (see Chapters 3 and 4).

pp. 81–83

4. **Regulation of sexual behaviour.** Sexual norms are subject to change over time (for instance, changes in customs for dating) and across cultures (Islamic Saudi Arabia compared with more permissive Denmark). However, whatever the time period or cultural values in a society, standards of sexual behaviour are most clearly defined within the family circle. The structure of society influences these standards. In male-dominated societies, for example, formal and informal norms generally permit men to express and enjoy their sexual desires more freely than women may.
5. **Affection and companionship.** Ideally, the family provides members with warm and intimate relationships and helps them feel satisfied and secure. Of course, a family member may find such rewards outside the family—from peers, in school,

at work—and may perceive the home as an unpleasant place. Nevertheless, unlike other institutions, the family is obligated to serve the emotional needs of its members. We *expect* our relatives to understand us, to care for us, and to be there for us when we need them.

6. **Provision of social status.** We inherit a social position because of the "family background" and reputation of our parents and siblings. The family unit presents the newborn child with an ascribed status of race and ethnicity that helps to determine his or her place within a society's stratification system. Moreover, family resources affect children's ability to pursue certain opportunities, such as higher education and specialized lessons.

The family has traditionally fulfilled a number of other functions, such as providing religious training, education, and recreational outlets. Ogburn argued that other social institutions have gradually assumed many of these functions. Although the family once played a major role in religious life, this function has largely shifted to churches, synagogues, and other religious organizations. Similarly, education once took place at the family fireside; now it is the responsibility of professionals working in schools and universities. Even the family's traditional recreational function has been transferred to outside groups, such as Little Leagues, athletic clubs, and Internet chat rooms.

Conflict View

Conflict theorists view the family not as a contributor to social stability, but as a reflection of the inequality in wealth and power found within the larger society. Feminist theorists and conflict theorists note that the family has traditionally legitimized and perpetuated male dominance. Throughout most of human history—and in a very wide range of societies—husbands have exercised overwhelming power and authority within the family. pp. 236–237 Not until the first wave of contemporary feminism in North America in the mid-nineteenth century was there a substantial challenge to the historic status of wives and children as the legal property of husbands.

Although the egalitarian family has become a more common pattern in North America in recent decades—owing in good part to the activism of feminists beginning in the late 1960s and early 1970s—male dominance within the family has hardly disappeared. Sociologists have found that women are significantly more likely to leave their jobs when their husbands find better employment opportunities than men are when their wives receive desirable job offers (Bielby and Bielby 1992). And unfortunately, many husbands reinforce their power and control over wives and children through acts of domestic violence. (Box 11-2 considers cross-cultural findings about violence within the home.)

Conflict theorists also view the family as an economic unit that contributes to societal injustice. The family is the basis for transferring power, property, and privilege from one generation to the next. North America pp. 13–14 is widely viewed as a "land of opportunity," yet social mobility is restricted in important ways. Children "inherit" the privileged or less-than-privileged social and economic status of their parents (and, in some cases, of earlier generations as well). As conflict theorists point out, the social class of their parents significantly influences children's socialization experiences and the protection they receive. This means that the socioeconomic status of a child's family will have a marked influence on his or her nutrition, health care, housing, educational opportunities, and, in many respects, life chances as an adult. For that reason, conflict theorists argue that the family helps to maintain inequality.

Interactionist View

Interactionists focus on the microlevel of family and other intimate relationships. They are interested in how individuals interact with one another, whether they are gay, lesbian, or heterosexual couples, and so on. For example, interactionists have looked at the nature of family interactions and relationship quality (e.g., interparental conflict, parenting stress, love between parents and for their children), and have found that those factors, rather than the parents' sexual orientation, strongly predict children's behavioural adjustment (Chan, Rayboy, and Patterson 1998).

Another interactionist study might examine the role of the step-parent. The increased number of single parents who remarry has sparked an interest in those who are helping to raise other people's children. Although children likely do not dream about one day becoming a stepmom or stepdad, this is hardly an unusual occurrence today. Studies have found that stepmothers are more likely to accept the blame for bad relations with their stepchildren, whereas stepfathers are less likely to accept responsibility. Interactionists theorize that stepfathers (like most fathers) may simply be unaccustomed to interacting directly with children when the mother isn't there (Bray and Kelly 1999; Furstenberg and Cherlin 1991).

Feminist Views

No single theory represents how feminist theories conceptualize the family. Feminist perspectives do, however, share certain assumptions in their study of family. Some

Sociology in the Global Community 11-2 Domestic Violence

The phone rings two or three dozen times a day at the Friend of the Family Hotline in San Salvador, the capital city of El Salvador. Each time the staff receives a report of family violence, a crisis team is immediately dispatched to the caller's home. Caseworkers provide comfort to victims, as well as accumulate evidence for use in the attacker's prosecution. In the first three years of its existence, Friend of the Family handled more than 28 000 cases of domestic violence.

Wife battering and other forms of domestic violence are not confined to El Salvador. Drawing on studies conducted throughout the world, we can make the following generalizations:

- Women are most at risk of violence from the men they know.
- Violence against women occurs in all socioeconomic groups.
- Family violence is at least as dangerous as assaults committed by strangers.
- Though women sometimes exhibit violent behaviour toward men, the majority of violent acts that cause injury are perpetrated by men against women.
- Violence within intimate relationships tends to escalate over time.
- Emotional and psychological abuse can be at least as debilitating as physical abuse.
- Use of alcohol exacerbates family violence but does not cause it.

Using the conflict and feminist models, researchers have found that in relationships in which the inequality between men and women is great, the likelihood of assault on wives increases dramatically. This discovery suggests that much of the violence between intimates, even when sexual in nature, is about power rather than sex.

The family can be a dangerous place not only for women but also for children and the elderly. In 2002, 3287 women and 2999 children were living in shelters in Canada: 84 percent of the women and 73 percent of the children were there to escape family violence (Statistics Canada 2003i). In 2001, 344 violent incidents were reported to the police for every 100 000 women in Canada aged 15 and over (Statistics Canada 2003i).

Applying Theory

1. Do you know of a family that has experienced domestic violence? Did the victim(s) seek outside help, and if so, was it effective?
2. Why might the degree of equality in a relationship correlate to the likelihood of domestic violence? How might conflict theorists explain this finding?

Sources: American Bar Association 1999; Gelles and Cornell 1990; Heise, Ellseberg, and Gottemuelle 1999; Rennison and Welchans 2000; Spindel, Levy, and Connor 2000; Statistics Canada 2003i; Valdez 1999; J. Wilson 2000.

of these assumptions include a rejection of the belief in the family's "naturalness" (Luxton 2001). Feminist theorists argue that the family is a socially constructed institution and, thus, varies according to time and place. Families are not seen as "monolithic" or the same, but rather as diverse, flexible, and changeable. Although feminists' views on the family agree that women have a position of inequality and discrimination in the family, they argue that these too vary according to class, race, and ethnicity. The functional view of family is challenged by feminist theorists, who raise the question "For whom and for whose interests is the family functional?"

Canadian feminist theorist Margrit Eichler (2001) argues that the ways in which sociologists study the family often contain biases. These include a *monolithic bias*, which is a tendency to assume "the family" is uniform rather than diverse; a *conservative bias*, which treats recent changes in the family as fleeting and ignores or treats as rare some of the uglier aspects of family life (e.g., family violence); an *ageist bias*, which regards children and the aged only as passive members of families; a *sexist bias*, which is exhibited in such patterns as double standards and gender insensitivity; a *microstructural bias*, which overemphasizes microlevel variables and neglects macrolevel variables; a *racist bias*, which explicitly or implicitly assumes the superiority of the family form of the dominant group and ignores race and racism when relevant; and a *heterosexist bias*, which either ignores same-sex families or treats them as problematic and deviant.

MARRIAGE AND FAMILY: DIVERSITY OF PATTERNS

Historically, the most consistent aspect of family life in this country has been the high rate of heterosexual marriage. In fact, despite the increase in divorce rates in Canada in the 1970s and 1980s, Canada's rate of divorce is much lower than that of the United States. Of those

When fathers interact regularly with their children, it's a win/win situation. The fathers get close to their offspring, and studies show that the children end up with fewer behaviour problems.

who do divorce, most heterosexuals will go on to remarry (M. Baker 2001).

In this part of the chapter, we will examine various aspects of love, marriage, and parenthood in Canada and contrast them with cross-cultural examples. In Western societies romance and mate selection are often viewed as strictly a matter of individual preference. Yet, sociological analysis tells us that social institutions and distinctive cultural norms and values also play an important role.

Courtship and Mate Selection

"My rugby mates would roll over in their graves," says Tom Buckley of his online courtship and subsequent marriage to Terri Muir. But Tom and Terri are hardly alone these days in turning to the Internet for matchmaking services. By the end of 1999 more than 2500 Web sites were helping people find mates. You could choose from oneandonly.com or 2ofakind.com or cupidnet.com, among others. One service alone claimed two million subscribers. Tom and Terri carried on their romance via email for a year before they met. According to Tom, "E-mail made it easier to communicate because neither one of us was the type to walk up to someone in the gym or a bar and say, 'You're the fuel to my fire' " (B. Morris 1999:D1).

Internet romance is only the latest courtship practice. In the central Asian nation of Uzbekistan and many other traditional cultures, courtship is defined largely through the interaction of two sets of parents. They arrange spouses for their children. Typically, a young Uzbekistani woman will be socialized to eagerly anticipate her marriage to a man whom she has met only once, when he is presented to her family at the time of the final inspection of her dowry. In Canada, by contrast, courtship is conducted primarily by individuals who may have a romantic interest in each other. In our culture, courtship often requires these individuals to rely heavily on intricate games, gestures, and signals. Despite such differences, courtship—whether in Canada, Uzbekistan, or elsewhere—is influenced by the norms and values of the larger society (C. J. Williams 1995).

One unmistakable pattern in mate selection is that the process appears to be taking longer today than in the past. A variety of factors, including concerns about financial security and personal independence, has contributed to this delay in marriage. Most people are now well into their 20s before they marry, both in Canada and in other countries (see Figure 11-2).

Take our choice of a mate. Why are we drawn to a particular person in the first place? To what extent are these judgments shaped by the society around us?

Aspects of Mate Selection

Many societies have explicit or unstated rules that define potential mates as acceptable or unacceptable. These norms can be distinguished in terms of endogamy and exogamy. ***Endogamy*** (from the Greek *endon,* "within") specifies the groups within which a spouse must be found and prohibits marriage with others. For example, in Canada, many people are expected to marry within their own racial, ethnic, or religious group and are strongly discouraged or even prohibited from marrying outside the group. Endogamy is intended to reinforce the cohesiveness of the group by suggesting to the young that they should marry someone "of our own kind."

By contrast, ***exogamy*** (from the Greek *exo,* "outside") requires mate selection outside certain groups, usually outside the family or certain kinfolk. The ***incest taboo,*** a social norm common to virtually all societies, prohibits sexual relationships between certain culturally

FIGURE 11-2

Percentage of People Aged 20 to 24 Ever Married, Selected Countries

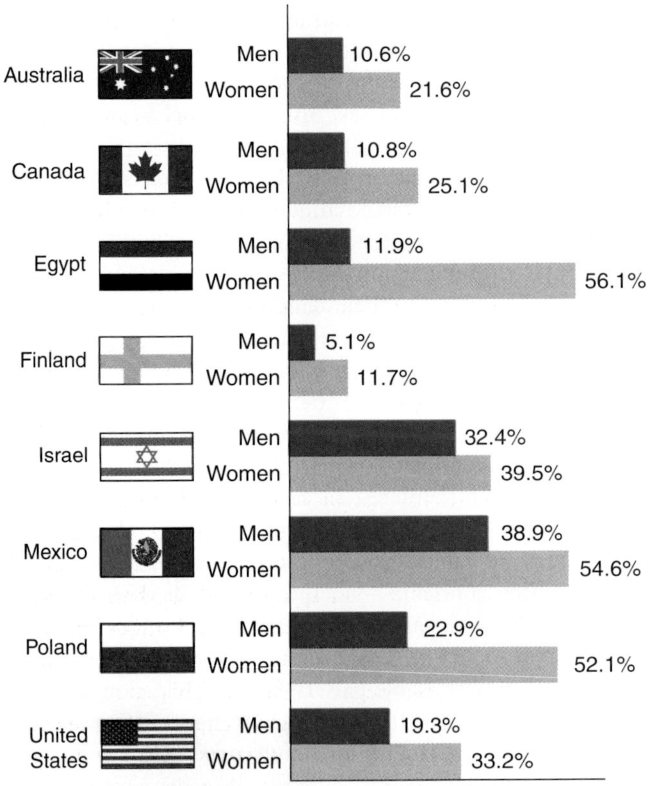

Source: United Nations Population Division 2001.

> **Think about It**
> Why is the percentage of young women who are married particularly high in Egypt, Mexico, and Poland, and particularly low in Finland?

specified relatives. For people in Canada, this taboo means that we must marry outside the nuclear family. We cannot marry our siblings; however, we are able to marry our first cousins.

Endogamous restrictions may be seen as preferences for one group over another. In the United States, such preferences are most obvious in racial barriers. Until the 1960s, some states outlawed interracial marriages. This practice was challenged by Richard Loving (a white man) and Mildred Jeter Loving (a part-black, part-Aboriginal woman), who married in 1958. Eventually, in 1967, the Supreme Court ruled that it was unconstitutional to prohibit marriage solely on the basis of race. The decision struck down statutes in Virginia and 16 other U.S. states.

In Canada, there is evidence to suggest that people are more likely to marry someone outside of their own ethnic group the longer they reside in Canada. Northern, Western, and Eastern European ethnic groups are the most likely to marry outside their own ethnic group, while Asians, Africans, and Latin Americans are the least likely. Despite the effort the Canadian government expends promoting the ideology and policies of multiculturalism, Canadian families are coming to resemble one another more and more through increased intermarriage among various ethnic groups. Although 11 percent of immigrants to this country report more than one ethnic background, approximately one-third of those born in Canada had a mixed ethnic background (Howell, Albanese, and Obusu-Mensah 2001).

Increasing numbers of exogamous unions force a society to reconsider its definitions of race and ethnicity. In Chapter 9, we noted that race is socially constructed in Canada and around the world. As increasing proportions of children in Canada come from backgrounds of more than one race or ethnicity, single ethnic and racial identifiers become less relevant. The Canadian census allows individuals to report two or more ethnic choices as well as to respond to an "Other" category for race, for those whose racial background does not fall neatly into one category (Howell et at. 2001).

pp. 197–198

The Love Relationship

Whatever the social construction of "love," most people would agree it is a complicated one. Listen to what a university student has to say on the subject:

> Love isn't in the air these days, at least not in New Haven . . . my peers and I find ourselves in a new world of romance, and we're feeling a little out of our league. We are children of the Age of Divorce, born into the AIDS crisis, reared on Madonna, *Friends,* and *Beverly Hills 90210.* No wonder we're confused. We know we want this thing called love. More than previous generations, though, we're unsure of what love is and how to get it—and we're not so sure that finding it will be worth the trouble. (Rodberg 1999:1–2)

Another student claims that "love, like everything else, must be pondered, and we have too many other things to ponder—no matter how much we profess to want love" (quoted in Rodberg 1999:4).

For a variety of reasons, hinted at in these quotations, some members of this generation of postsecondary students seem more likely to "hook up" or cruise in large packs than to engage in the romantic dating relationships of their parents and grandparents. Still, at some point in their adult lives the great majority of today's students will meet someone they "love" and enter into a long-term relationship that focuses on creating a family.

In North America, love is socially constructed as important in the courtship process. Living in their own

Interracial unions are becoming increasingly common among the under-30 age group, especially in such centres as Vancouver and Toronto.

home may make the affectional bond between an opposite-sex couple especially important. The couple may be expected to develop its own emotional ties, free of the demands of other household members for affection. Sociologist William Goode (1959) observed that opposite-sex spouses in a nuclear family have to rely heavily on each other for the companionship and support that might be provided by other relatives in an extended-family situation.

Given this social construction of love, parents in North America tend to value it highly as a rationale for marriage, and they encourage their children to develop intimate relationships based on heterosexual love and affection. In addition, songs, films, books, magazines, television shows, and even cartoons and comic books reinforce the theme of heterosexual love. At the same time, our society may expect parents and peers to help a person confine his or her search for a mate to "socially acceptable" members of the opposite sex.

The social construction of love-and-marriage, as witnessed in North America, is by no means a cultural universal. In fact, in many cultures (both today and in the past) love and marriage are unconnected and are sometimes at odds with each other. For example, feelings of love are not a prerequisite for marriage among the Yaruros of inland Venezuela or in other cultures where there is little freedom for mate selection. The Yaruro male of marriageable age doesn't engage in the kind of dating behaviour so typical of young people in Canada. Rather, he knows that, under the traditions of his culture, he must marry one of his mother's brothers' daughters or one of his father's sisters' daughters. The young man's choice is further limited because one of his uncles selects the eligible cousin that he must marry (Freeman 1958; Lindholm 1999).

Many of the world's cultures give priority in mate selection to factors other than romantic feelings. In societies with *arranged marriages,* often engineered by parents or religious authorities, economic considerations play a significant role. The newly married couple is expected to develop a feeling of love *after* the legal union is formalized, if at all.

Within Canada, some subcultures carry on the arranged marriage practices of their native cultures (Nanda 1991). Young people among the Sikhs and Hindus who have immigrated from India and among Islamic Muslims and Hasidic Jews allow their parents or designated matchmakers to find spouses within their ethnic community. As one young Sikh declared, "I will definitely marry who my parents wish. They know me better than I know myself" (R. Segall 1998:48). This practice of arranged marriage may be gradually changing, however, because of the influence of the larger society's cultural practices. Young people who have emigrated without their families often turn to the Internet to find partners who share their background and goals. Matrimonial ads for the Indian community run on such Web sites as SuitableMatch.com and INDOLINK.com. One Hasidic Jewish woman noted that the system of arranged marriages "isn't perfect, and it doesn't work for everyone, but this is the system we know and trust, the way we couple, and the way we learn to love. So it works for most of us" (p. 53).

Use Your Sociological Imagination

Your parents or a matchmaker are going to arrange a marriage for you. What kind of mate will they select? Will your chances of having a successful marriage be better or worse than if you had selected your own mate?

Social Class Differences

Various studies have documented the differences in family organization among social classes in North America. The upper-class emphasis is on lineage and maintenance of family position. If you are in the upper class, you are not simply a member of a nuclear family but rather a member of a larger family tradition. As a result, upper-class families are quite concerned about what they see as "proper training" for children.

Lower-class families do not often have the luxury of worrying about the "family name"; they must first struggle to pay their bills and survive the crises often associated with life in poverty. Such families are more likely to have only one parent in the home, creating special challenges in child care and financial needs. Children in lower-class families typically assume adult responsibilities—including marriage and parenthood—at an earlier age than children of affluent homes. In part, this is because they may lack the money needed to remain in school.

Social class differences in family life are less striking than they once were. In the past, family specialists agreed that there were pronounced contrasts in child-rearing practices. Lower-class families were found to be more authoritarian in rearing children and more inclined to use physical punishment. Middle-class families were more permissive and more restrained in punishing their children. However, these differences may have narrowed as more and more families from all social classes have turned to the same books, magazines, and even television talk shows for advice on rearing children (M. Kohn 1970; Luster, Rhoades, and Haas 1989).

Among the poor, women often play a significant role in the economic support of the family. The National Council of Welfare (1999) reported that in 1997, 57.1 percent of lone-parent mothers in Canada were living below the poverty line, compared with 11.1 percent of couples with children.

Many racial and ethnic groups appear to have distinctive family characteristics. However, racial and class factors are often closely related. In examining family life among racial and ethnic minorities, keep in mind that certain patterns may result from class as well as cultural factors.

Racial and Ethnic Differences

The ways in which race, ethnicity, gender, and class intersect contributes to the diversity of Canadian families. The subordinate status of racial and ethnic minorities and Canada's Aboriginal people has profound effects on the family life of these groups.

Aboriginal people are a heterogeneous group with different histories, geographies, languages, economies, and cultures. Their families, which often include those who are kin as well as those who come together in a common community purpose, have been fundamentally disrupted by hundreds of years of European domination. For example, the First Nations peoples of the Montagnais-Naskapi of the eastern Labrador Peninsula underwent major changes in family structure and gender relations as they moved to trapping, introduced by Europeans, and away from traditional hunting and fishing. The sexual division of labour became more specialized and families began to become smaller, approaching the size of a nuclear family (Leacock 2001).

Aboriginal families have been devalued and undermined by the Canadian government and religious institutions. In the past, children were sent away from their homes to residential schools, where they were punished for speaking their own language and expressing their own culture. There, they were often subjected to sexual and physical abuse by the hands of those who ran the schools—those who were assigned to be their guardians.

p. 209

In the 1960s, Aboriginal children were put up for adoption and adopted by, most often, white families in Canada and the United States, rather than by those from within their own band (Eichler 1997). Today, after years of cultural oppression under government control, problems of domestic abuse, youth suicide, and substance abuse plague Aboriginal families.

Research carried out in Nova Scotia and Toronto on black families of opposite-sex couples demonstrates the

The ways in which race, ethnicity, gender, and class intersect contribute to the diversity of Canadian families. Above, Korean immigrant spouses work together in a family business.

links among the effects of race, class, and gender and their impact on black families (Calliste 2001). Significantly more black families were headed by women than non-black families; these women-headed black families earn approximately half of the income of their married counterparts, who in turn earn less than non-black families headed by married couples. The study concludes that the high rate of teenage pregnancy and the feminization of poverty need to be addressed by black community groups and government in the form of education, employment equity, sex education, and parenting sessions (Calliste 2001:417). Some similarities exist between Canadian black families and American black families, because the effects of race, class, and gender intersect to produce inequality for families in both countries.

Child-Rearing Patterns in Family Life

The Nayars of southern India acknowledge the biological role of fathers, but the mother's eldest brother is responsible for her children (Gough 1974). By contrast, uncles play only a peripheral role in child care in North America. Caring for children is a universal function of the family, yet the ways in which different societies assign this function to family members can vary significantly. Within Canada, child-rearing patterns are varied. We'll look here at parenthood and grandparenthood, adoption, dual-income families, single-parent families, and stepfamilies. (See Figure 11-3 for an idea of the types of families in Canada in which children live today.)

Parenthood and Grandparenthood

The socialization of children is essential to the maintenance of any culture. Consequently, parenthood is one of the most important (and most demanding) social roles in North America. Sociologist Alice Rossi (1968, 1984) has identified four factors that complicate the transition to parenthood and the role of socialization. First, there is little anticipatory socialization for the social role of caregiver. The normal school curriculum gives scant attention to the subjects most relevant to successful family life—such as child care and home maintenance. Second, only limited learning occurs during the period of pregnancy itself. Third, the transition to parenthood is quite abrupt. Unlike adolescence, it is not prolonged; unlike socialization for work, you cannot gradually take on the duties of caregiving. Finally, in Rossi's view, our society lacks clear and helpful guidelines for successful parenthood. There is little consensus on how parents can produce happy and well-adjusted offspring—or even on what it means to be "well adjusted." For these reasons, socialization for parenthood involves difficult challenges for most men and women in North America.

p. 81

FIGURE 11-3

Distribution of Children Aged 0 to 14 by Family Structure, 2001

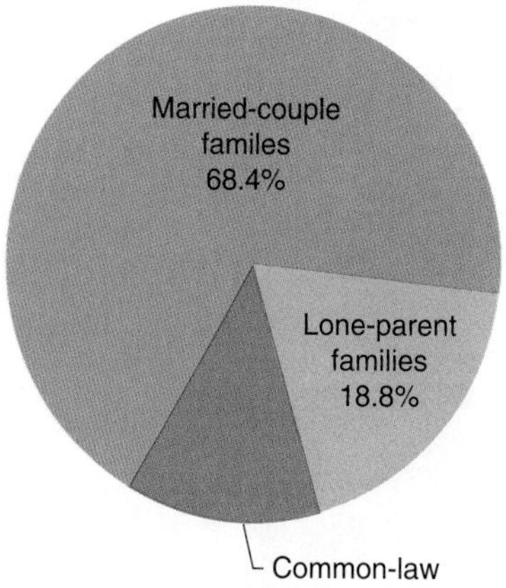

Source: Statistics Canada 2002a.

One recent development in family life in Canada has been the extension of parenthood, as adult children continue to (or return to) live at home. In 1990, more children over the age of 18 lived with their parents while completing postsecondary education than in the early 1980s (Boyd and Pryor 1990). In other instances, financial difficulties are at the heart of these living arrangements. Although rents and real estate prices skyrocketed in the 1990s, salaries for younger workers did not keep pace, and many found themselves unable to afford their own homes. Moreover, with many marriages now ending in divorce—most commonly in the first seven years of marriage—divorced sons and daughters are returning to live with their parents, sometimes with their own children.

Is this living arrangement a positive development for family members? Social scientists have just begun to examine this phenomenon, sometimes called the "boomerang generation" or the "full-nest syndrome" in the popular press. One survey in the United States seemed to show that neither the parents nor their adult children were happy about continuing to live together. The children often felt resentful and isolated, but the parents also suffered: Learning to live without children in the home is an essential stage of adult life and may even be a significant turning point for a marriage (*Berkeley Wellness Letter* 1990; Mogelonsky 1996).

As life expectancy increases in North America, more and more parents are becoming grandparents and even great-grandparents. After interviewing many grandparents, sociologists Andrew Cherlin and Frank Furstenberg, Jr. (1992) identified three principal styles of grandparenting:

The love expressed by this father to his child testifies to successful parenting. Even though parenthood is a crucial social role, society generally provides few clear guidelines.

1. More than half (55 percent) of grandparents surveyed functioned as "specialists in recreational care-giving." They enriched their grandchildren's lives through recreational outings and other special activities.
2. More than one-fourth (29 percent) carried on a "ritualistic" (primarily symbolic) relationship with their grandchildren. In some instances, this was because the grandparents lived far away from their grandchildren and could see them only occasionally.
3. About one-sixth (16 percent) of grandparents surveyed were actively involved in everyday routine care of their grandchildren and exercised substantial authority over them.

Adoption

In a legal sense, ***adoption*** is a "process that allows for the transfer of the legal rights, responsibilities, and privileges of parenthood" to a new legal parent or parents (E. Cole 1985:638). In many cases, these rights are transferred from a biological parent or parents (often called birth parents) to an adoptive parent or parents.

Viewed from a functionalist perspective, government has a strong interest in encouraging adoption. Policymakers, in fact, have both a humanitarian and a financial stake in the process. In theory, adoption offers a stable family environment for children who otherwise might not receive satisfactory care. Moreover, government data show that unwed mothers who keep their babies tend to be of lower socioeconomic status and often require public assistance to support their children. Government can lower its social welfare expenses if children are transferred to economically self-sufficient families. From a conflict perspective, however, such financial considerations raise the ugly spectre of adoption as a means whereby affluent (often infertile) couples "buy" the children of the poor (C. Bachrach 1986). For decades during the last century in Canada, many Aboriginal children were adopted to white families in this country and the United States; this practice has since been identified as a form of cultural genocide (P. Johnson 1983).

With greater access to contraception and legal abortion, the rate of unplanned births to young women has declined since the 1950s, and the availability of Canadian infants has decreased. As well, more and more single mothers have been keeping their babies and supporting them through earnings or social assistance. In addition, the goals of family preservation in the Canadian child welfare system, and Canadians' current preference to adopt infants and younger children, will make the case for international adoption (most likely from developing countries) more compelling (M. Baker 2001). This supports the conflict view that the wealthier, more powerful countries have control over the poorer, less powerful countries. In this case, it involves the "purchase" of children.

Dual-Income Families

The idea of a family consisting of a wage-earning husband and a wife who stays at home has largely given way to the *dual-income household.* In Canadian two-parent families, 70 percent of women with children under 16 were employed in the paid labour force in 1999 (Statistics Canada 2001c). Why has there been such a rise in the number of dual-income heterosexual couples? A major factor is economic need. The Vanier Institute of the Family (1999) estimated the costs of raising a child from birth to age 18 to be approximately $160 000. Raising children in urban centres, where the bulk of the Canadian population resides, is expensive. An Ontario study found two-child families in that province spent 18 percent of their gross income on child-related expenses (Douthitt and Fedyk 1990). Other factors contributing to the rise of the dual-income model include the nation's declining birthrate (see Chapter 14), the increase in the proportion of women with postsecondary educations, the shift in

In Canadian two-parent families, 70 percent of women with children under 16 are in the paid workforce. Mothers and fathers are increasingly sharing child care responibilities.

the economy of North America from manufacturing to service industries, and the impact of the feminist movement in changing women's consciousness.

Single-Parent Families

In recent decades, the stigma attached to "unwed mothers" and other single parents has significantly diminished. ***Single-parent families,*** in which there is only one parent present to care for the children, can hardly be viewed as a rarity in Canada. In 2001, approximately 16 percent of families were headed by a lone parent (up from approximately 11 percent in 1981), the overwhelming majority of which were female-headed. Variation and diversity exists among lone-parent families. For example, in 1991, the percentage of female-headed black families was more than three times the percentage of female-headed non-black families. The interaction of race, class, and gender is evident in patterns of black family structure (Calliste 2001).

Although marital dissolution is the major cause of the increase in lone-parent families, never-married lone parents are growing in number. The children of these unions tend to divide their time between both parents (Marcil-Gratton 1999). This growing trend of nonlegal relationships is evident in Canada as well as in most industrialized countries. In Quebec, for example, 38 percent of all children and 48 percent of first births were categorized as "out-of-wedlock," but 90 percent of these children were born to parents living together in nonlegal relationships (Le Bourdais and Marcil-Gratton 1994).

The lives of single parents and their children are not inevitably more difficult than life in a traditional nuclear family. It is as inaccurate to assume that a single-parent family is necessarily "deprived" as it is to assume that a two-parent family is always secure and happy. Nevertheless, life in a single-parent family can be extremely stressful, in both economic and emotional terms. Economic inequality and poverty are striking characteristics of lone-parent families. When compared with two-parent families, female-led, lone-parent families are the most vulnerable to poverty, a fact that contributes to the phenomenon known as the "feminization of poverty."

A family headed by a single mother faces especially difficult problems if the mother is a teenager. Drawing on two decades of social science research, sociologist Kristin Luker (1996:11) observes:

> The short answer to why teenagers get pregnant and especially to why they continue those pregnancies is that a fairly substantial number of them just don't believe what adults tell them, be it about sex, contraception, marriage, or babies. They don't believe in adult conventional wisdom.

Why might low-income teenage women want to have children and face the obvious financial difficulties of motherhood? Viewed from an interactionist perspective, these women tend to have low self-esteem and limited options; a child may provide a sense of motivation and purpose for a teenager whose economic worth in our society is limited at best. Given the barriers that many young women face because of their gender, race, ethnicity, and class, many teenagers may believe that they have little to lose and much to gain by having a child.

Countries belonging to the Organisation for Economic Co-operation and Development (OECD) (i.e., developed nations) have experienced an increase in lone-parent families since the early 1970s, with the greatest increase occurring in the United States (M. Baker 2001). However, poverty rates for these families vary among industrialized countries, depending on the availability of social welfare programs, the rates of male and female unemployment, government disincentives to work while receiving social assistance, the availability of social welfare programs, and the availability of special employment training programs and child care.

Despite the current concern over the increase in the number of lone-parent families, this family type has existed for more than a hundred years in Canada. In 1901, the ratio of lone-parent to two-parent families was only slightly lower than today's ratio. A major interdisciplinary study carried out at the University of Victoria, based on 1901 census data, concluded that the family has always been a variable and flexible institution. With unsanctioned or non-formalized divorce being more common in the past than is generally known, "there was much more volatility and shifting of marital status than anyone was prepared to admit at the state level" (Gram 2001).

Blended Families

Approximately 20 percent of heterosexual Canadians have married, divorced, and remarried. The rising rates of divorce and remarriage have led to a noticeable increase in stepfamily relationships. In 1967, 12.3 percent of marriages involved one spouse who had been previously married, but by 1998 the rate had more than doubled to 33 percent (Dumas 1994).

Stepfamilies are an exceedingly complex form of family organization. Here is how one 13-year-old boy described his family.

> Tim and Janet are my stepbrother and sister. Josh is my stepdad. Carin and Don are my real parents, who are divorced. And Don married Anna and together they had Ethan and Ellen, my half-sister and brother. And Carin married Josh and had little Alice, my half-sister.
> (A. Bernstein 1988)

The exact nature of these blended families has social significance for adults and children alike. Certainly resocialization is required when an adult becomes a step-parent or a child becomes a stepchild and stepsibling. Moreover, an important distinction must be made between first-time stepfamilies and households where there have been repeated divorces, breakups, or changes in custodial arrangements.

In evaluating the rise of stepfamilies, some observers have assumed that children would benefit from remarriage because they would be gaining a second custodial parent and potentially would enjoy greater economic security. However, after reviewing many studies on stepfamilies, sociologist Andrew Cherlin (1999:421) concluded that "the well-being of children in stepfamily households is no better, on average, than the well-being of children in divorced, single-parent households." Step-parents can play valuable and unique roles in their stepchildren's lives, but their involvement does not guarantee an improvement. In fact, standards may decline. Some studies conducted by an economist in the United States found that children raised in families with stepmothers are likely to have less health care, education, and money spent on their food than are children raised by biological mothers. The measures are also negative for children raised by a stepfather but only half as negative as in the case of stepmothers. This doesn't mean that stepmothers are "evil"—it may be that the stepmother steps back out of concern of seeming too intrusive or relies mistakenly on the biological father to carry out these parental duties (Lewin 2000).

Family Violence in Canada

The family is often portrayed through the mass media and other institutions as a source of comfort, security, and safety; as a place to which its members retreat to escape the rough and tumble of the public world of work and school. This social construction of the family as a "haven in a heartless world"(Lasch 1977) often obscures the reality that many members of families face; that is, the family is a source of conflict and, possibly, danger. Sociologists Gelles and Straus (1988:18) point out that "You are more likely to be physically assaulted, beaten, and killed in your own home at the hands of a loved one than anyplace else, or by anyone else in society." There are various types of family violence, including violence against women, violence against children, sibling violence, and violence against elders (DeKeseredy 2001).

In 1999, Statistics Canada reported the rate of wife assault in Canada to be 3 percent, while the rate of those reporting wife assault over a five-year period was 8 percent, down from 12 percent in 1993 (Statistics Canada 2001d). Statistics Canada's definition of spousal "violence" or "assault" includes being beaten, slapped, choked, pushed, threatened with a gun, knife, or other object, or being forced to have unwanted sexual activity. Between 1993 and 1999, the overall decline in spousal assault against women in Canada may have been due to such factors as increased availability of shelters for abused women, increased reporting to police by victims of abuse, mandatory arrest policies for men who assault their wives, growth in the number of treatment programs for violent men, changes in the economic and social status of women that allow them to more easily leave violent relationships, and changes in society's attitudes recognizing assault of female spouses as a crime (Statistics Canada 2001d).

Contrary to a commonly held assumption that spousal violence ends after the breakdown of a marriage, violence continues and often occurs for the first time after the couple separates. In 1999 in Canada, approximately 63 000 women and 35 000 men were assaulted for the first time after their marriages had broken down (Statistics Canada 2001d). Male "proprietariness" or male sexual jealousy has often been used to explain patterns of male violence toward female ex-partners, particularly in acts of killing (Gartner, Dawson, and Crawford 2001).

Although spousal violence against women occurs in all cultures, Aboriginal women run a greater risk of being harmed in episodes of family violence. From 1993 to 1999, 25 percent of Aboriginal women were assaulted by a current or former spouse, which was twice the rate of Aboriginal men and three times the rate of non-Aboriginal women (Statistics Canada 2001d).

Canadian children and youth who die from homicide are most likely to be killed by family members (Statistics

Canada 2001d). Family members were responsible for 63 percent of solved homicides of children and youth recorded by police in Canada between 1974 and 1999. In 1998, the majority of cases of violence toward children where abuse had been substantiated involved inappropriate punishment, while the most common form of child sexual abuse was touching and fondling of genitals. Children's exposure to family violence (e.g., hearing or seeing one parent assault the other) was the most common form of emotional maltreatment (Statistics Canada 2001d).

Divorce

"Do you promise to love, honour, and cherish . . . until death do you part?" Every year, people of all social classes, racial and ethnic groups, and now sexual orientations make this legally binding agreement. Yet an increasing number of these promises shatter in divorce. Although divorce rates among opposite-sex partners may vary among regions (Alberta and B.C. have rates higher than the national average, while the Atlantic provinces have rates that are lower), divorce is a nationwide phenomenon.

Statistical Trends in Divorce

Just how common is divorce? Surprisingly, this is not a simple question; divorce statistics are difficult to interpret.

The media frequently report that one out of every three opposite-sex marriages ends in divorce. And in 2004, the first same-sex legal divorce occurred in Canada. Figures can be misleading, since many marriages last for decades. They are based on a comparison of all divorces that occur in a single year (regardless of when the couples were married) against the number of new marriages in the same year.

Heterosexual divorce in Canada, and many other countries, began to increase in the late 1960s but then started to level off and even decline since the late 1980s (Bélanger 1999) (see Figure 11-4). This is partly due to the aging of the baby boomer population and the corresponding decline in the proportion of people of marriageable age.

Getting divorced obviously has not soured heterosexual people on marriage. The majority of divorced people remarry, while lone parents have higher rates of remarriage than those without children (M. Baker 2001). Women are less likely than men to remarry because many retain custody of children after a divorce, which complicates establishing a new adult relationship (Bianchi and Spain 1996).

Some people regard the nation's high rate of remarriage among opposite-sex couples as an endorsement of the institution of marriage, but it does lead to the new challenges of a remarriage kin network comprising current and prior marital relationships. This network can be

FIGURE 11-4

Marriage and Divorce Rates in Canada, 1967–2002

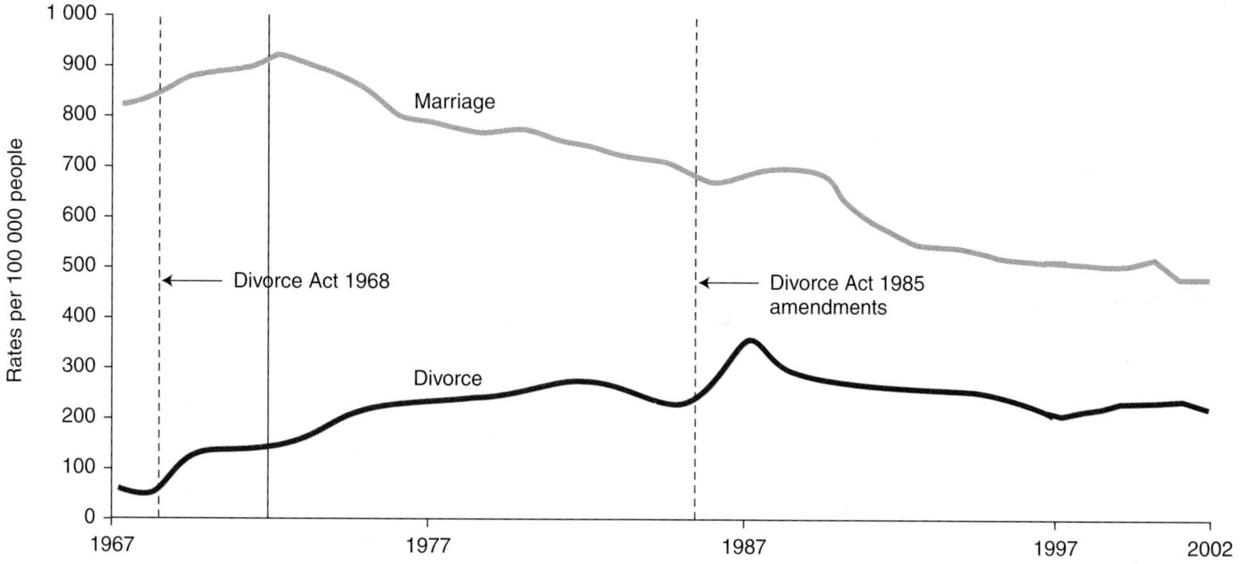

Source: M. Baker 2001a:218; Statistics Canada. *Divorces*, 1987–1988, 1990, 1991, 1992, 1993, 1994, 1995, 1996, 1997b, 2002b, 2003j, 2004h, 2004i.

particularly complex if children are involved or if an ex-spouse remarries.

Factors Associated with Divorce

Perhaps the most important factor in the increase in heterosexual divorce throughout the twentieth century has been the greater social *acceptance* of divorce. It's no longer considered necessary to endure an unhappy marriage. Most importantly, various religious denominations have relaxed negative attitudes toward divorce, and most religious leaders no longer treat it as a sin. The growing acceptance of divorce is a worldwide phenomenon. In 1998, a few months after a highly publicized divorce by pop superstar Seiko Matsuda, the prime minister of Japan released a survey showing that 54 percent of those polled supported uncontested divorce, compared with 20 percent in 1979 (Kyodo News International 1998a).

A few other factors deserve mention:

- No-fault divorce provisions, allowing a couple to end their marriage without fault on either side (such as specifying adultery), accounted for an initial surge in the divorce rate after they were introduced in 1985, although they appear to have had little effect beyond that.
- Divorce has become a more practical option in newly formed families, since they now tend to have fewer children than in the past.
- A general increase in family incomes, coupled with the availability of free legal aid for some poor people, has meant that more couples can afford costly divorce proceedings.
- As society provides greater opportunities for women, more and more wives are becoming less dependent on their husbands—both economically and emotionally. They may then feel more able to leave if the marriage seems hopeless.

Impact of Divorce on Children

Divorce can be traumatic for all involved. But it has special meaning for children involved in custody disputes. There were more than 75 000 such children in Canada in 2000 (Statistics Canada 2002b). For some of these children, divorce signals the welcome end to being witness to a very dysfunctional relationship. An American study conducted by sociologists Paul Amato and Alan Booth (1997) found that in about one-third of divorces, the children benefit from parental separation because it lessens their exposure to conflict. But in about 70 percent of all divorces, they found that the parents engaged in a low level of conflict; in these cases, the realities of divorce appear to be harder for the children to bear than living with the marital unhappiness. Other researchers, using differing definitions of conflict, have found greater unhappiness for children living in homes with marital differences. Still, it would be simplistic to assume that children are automatically better off following the breakup of their parents' marriage. The interests of the parents do not necessarily serve children well. A study based on a representative sample of heterosexual Canadians showed that although men experience moderate increases in their level of economic well-being after divorce, women experience a dramatic economic decline (Finnie 1993). Since women's wages are lower than men's, and since women are more likely to be awarded child custody, children of divorce often encounter serious economic consequences.

Divorce can obviously be a painful experience for children, but we should avoid labelling young people as "children of divorce," as if this *parental* experience is the singular event defining the life of a girl or boy. Large-scale studies in the United States and Great Britain have shown that some of the alleged negative effects of heterosexual divorce actually resulted from conditions (such as poverty) that existed *before* the parental separation. Moreover, if divorce does not lower children's access to resources and does not increase stress, its impact on children may be neutral or even positive. Divorce does not ruin the life of every child it touches, though its effect on a child is not always benign (Cherlin 1999; Wallerstein, Lewis, and Blakeslee 2000).

Use Your Sociological Imagination

In a society that maximizes the welfare of all family members, how easy should it be for couples to divorce? How easy should it be to get married?

Cohabitation

One of the most dramatic trends of recent years in Canada has been the tremendous increase in the number of opposite-sex couples who choose to live together without marrying, engaging in what is commonly called ***cohabitation.***

In 2001, one in seven Canadian couples were cohabiting. Younger Canadians are choosing cohabitation over marriage at increasing rates (S. Wilson 2001). According to the 2001 census, a total of 34 200 same-sex common-law couples were counted, representing 0.5 percent of all couples (Statistics Canada 2002c).

We can also find increases in cohabitation in the United States, France, Sweden, Denmark, and Australia. Data released in Great Britain indicate that more than 12 percent of people ages 18 to 24 are cohabiting. One report notes that in Sweden it is almost universal for couples to live together before marriage. Demographers in Denmark call the practice of living together *marriage*

Many young couples, like this one in England, are cohabitating. For some, it's an alternative to marriage; for others it's a precursor.

without papers. In Australia, these couples are known as *de factos* (Blanc 1984; Levinson 1984; O'Donnell 1992; Thomson and Colella 1992).

Some countries have governmental policies that do not encourage marriage. For example, Sweden offers no married-couple allowance for tax purposes, no tax deduction for raising children, and no way for couples to jointly file their income taxes. Not surprisingly, many Swedish couples choose to cohabit rather than to marry. About half of the babies in Sweden are born to unmarried mothers—although there are proportionately many fewer unmarried *teenage* mothers in Sweden than in the United States (*The Economist* 1995).

In Canada, Quebec stands out from the rest of the country in its rates of marriage and cohabitation. It has the lowest marriage rate among the provinces and territories and one of the lowest rates of marriage in the world (S. Wilson 2001). Quebec residents are increasingly turning away from traditional institutions, such as church and state, in the establishment of their families. More people in this province than any other jurisdiction live in common-law relationships; in 2001, the ratio was approximately one in every three couples. Moreover, Quebecers are more inclined than other Canadians to have children in common-law relationships. Cohabitation, then, is increasingly common for older Quebecers who have children and not just the younger, childless groups that represent the major trend in the rest of the country. Although common-law unions enjoy a longer duration in Quebec, nationally, cohabiting couples experience more than twice the rate of breakdown as that of married couples (Beaujot et al. 1995). Research has shown that cohabiters generally have less commitment to their particular relationship and to the institution of marriage in general. As well, heterosexual couples who choose cohabitation may share characteristics and values that have a negative impact on the stability of the relationship (Wu 1999).

Census figures have documented increases in cohabitation among older people in Canada (Wu and Pollard 2000). Older couples may choose cohabitation rather than marriage for many reasons: because of religious differences, to preserve the full pension benefits they receive as single people, out of fear of commitment, to avoid upsetting children from previous marriages, because one partner or both are not legally divorced, or because one or both have lived through a spouse's illness and death and do not want to experience that again. But some older couples simply see no need for marriage and report being happy living together as they are.

Remaining Single

Looking at TV programs today, as Box 11-1 pointed out, you would be justified in thinking most households are composed of singles. Although this is not the case, it is true that more and more people in Canada are *postponing* entry into first marriages. In 1996, 59 percent of all people between 25 and 29 years of age had never married, compared with 50 percent in 1991 (Statistics Canada 1997a). As well as the postponement of marriage and the increase in common-law relationships, Canadians are experiencing a decline in any form of heterosexual union (Fox 2001).

The trend toward maintaining a single lifestyle for a longer period of time is related to the growing economic independence of young people. This is especially significant for women. Freed from financial needs, women don't necessarily have to marry to enjoy a satisfying life.

pp. 231–232

There are many reasons why a person may choose not to marry. Singleness is an attractive option for those who do not want to limit their sexual intimacy to one lifetime partner. Also, some men and women do not want to become highly dependent on any one person—and do not want anyone depending heavily on them. In a society that values individuality and self-fulfilment, the single lifestyle can offer certain freedoms that married couples may not enjoy.

Remaining single represents a clear departure from societal expectations; indeed, it has been likened to "being single on Noah's Ark." A single adult must confront the inaccurate view that he or she is always lonely, is a workaholic, and is immature. These stereotypes help support the traditional assumption in North America and most other societies that to be truly happy and fulfilled, a person must get married and raise a family. To help counter these societal expectations, singles have formed numerous support groups, such as Alternatives to Marriage Project (www.unmarried.org).

Lesbian and Gay Relationships

> We were both raised in middle-class families, where the expectation was we would go to college, we would become educated, we'd get a nice white-collar job, we'd move up and own a nice house in the suburbs. And that's exactly what we've done. (*New York Times* 1998:B2)

Sound like a heterosexual couple? In this case the "we" described here is a gay couple.

The lives of lesbians and gay men vary greatly. Some live in long-term, monogamous relationships, legal or common law. Some couples live with adopted children or children from former heterosexual marriages. Some live alone, others with roommates. Some remain married to an opposite-sex partner and do not publicly acknowledge their homosexuality.

In the past, recognition of same-sex partnerships was not uncommon in Europe, including Denmark, Holland, Switzerland, France, Belgium, and parts of Germany, Italy, and Spain. In 2001 the Netherlands converted their "registered same-sex partnerships" into full-fledged marriages, with divorce provisions (S. Daley 2000).

Gay activist organizations emphasize that despite the passage of laws protecting the civil rights of lesbians and gay men, lesbian couples and gay male couples are prohibited from marrying in some countries—and therefore from gaining traditional partnership benefits. Some jurisdictions have passed legislation allowing for registration of domestic partnerships. A ***domestic partnership*** may be defined as two unrelated adults who reside together; agree to be jointly responsible for their dependants, basic living expenses, and other common necessities; and share a mutually caring relationship. Domestic partnership benefits can apply to such areas as inheritance, parenting, pensions, taxation, housing, immigration, workplace fringe benefits, and health care. Although the most passionate support for domestic partnership legislation has come from lesbian and gay male activists, the majority of those eligible for such benefits would be cohabiting heterosexual couples.

Domestic partnership legislation, however, faces strong opposition from conservative religious and political groups. In the view of opponents, support for domestic partnership undermines the historic societal preference for the nuclear family. Advocates of domestic partnership counter that such relationships fulfil the same functions for the individuals involved and for society as the traditional family and should enjoy the same legal protections and benefits. The gay couple quoted at the beginning of this section consider themselves a family unit, just like the nuclear family that lives down the street in their suburb. They cannot understand why they have been denied a family membership at their municipal swimming pool and why they have to pay more than a married couple (*New York Times* 1998).

In 2001, after a decade of court challenges and demonstrations over the rights of same-sex couples, Nova Scotia became the first jurisdiction in Canada to register same-sex and common law relationships as legal domestic partnerships. This change allowed same-sex couples many of the same rights accorded married couples in that province—equal division of property and spousal support if the relationship dissolves, and full

In 2005, Bill C-38 was passed by the Canadian government, making same-sex civil marriage legal in all jurisdictions. Here, a wedding witness signs the register following a same-sex marriage.

spousal benefits and pensions to partners. The registration of domestic partnerships, however, is not considered "marriage." In November 2004, Saskatchewan became the seventh Canadian jurisdiction (following Ontario, British Columbia, Manitoba, Yukon, Quebec, and Nova Scotia) to allow same-sex marriage. The courts in the respective regions ruled that it was a violation of the Charter of Rights and Freedoms to discriminate against same-sex marriage. On December 21, 2004, same-sex marriage became legal in Newfoundland and Labrador. In September 2004, Canada's first same-sex divorce was granted in Ontario.

In 2005, Bill C-38 was passed by the Canadian government, making same-sex civil marriage legal in *all* jurisdictions in Canada. Canada became the third country in the world to legalize same-sex marriage, following Belgium and the Netherlands. Shortly after Canada's passage of Bill C-38, Spain's government announced the legalization of same-sex marriage.

Marriage is an emotionally charged issue among the gay and lesbian communities. Some believe that it represents a sign of legitimacy and normalization to their already established relationships. Others believe that marriage, given its history of patriarchy and oppression, is not an institution to be emulated by gay and lesbian couples. Nova Scotian Ross Boutilier, who, along with his partner, was among the first to register for domestic partnership, stated, "It does make a difference because it's a formalization of the understanding we have that we're in this together and this is an equal partnership" (K. Cox 2001).

The debate over the legalization of same-sex marriage played out over such concerns as rights (e.g., in the Federal Department of Justice), human dignity and concern over the perpetuation of prejudicial attitudes (e.g., in the United Church of Canada), consequences for freedom of religion and conscience (e.g., in the Canadian Conference of Bishops), and the concern of being "over-inclusive" (e.g., by the Attorney General of Alberta).

Marriage without Children

There has been a modest increase in childlessness in Canada. According to data from the General Social Survey, 12 percent of women between the ages of 20 and 39 state that they do not intend to have children. Rates of childlessness began to increase for women born after 1941. These women entered young adulthood at a time when options were expanding for women in the form of advanced education and job opportunities. As well, this time in history witnessed the second wave of feminism, when ideas such as those expressed by Betty Friedan in *The Feminine Mystique* (1963) challenged conventional views about full-time motherhood and caregiving. Despite changing attitudes and the expansion of educational and employment options for women born after this date, women today continue to "pay a price in the labour market for marriage and motherhood, and shoulder more responsibility for housework and childcare at home than men" (Fox 2001:164). This reality contributes to the trend of women postponing marriage or never marrying, and postponing child bearing or remaining childfree.

Childlessness within opposite-sex marriage has generally been viewed as a problem that can be solved through such means as adoption and artificial insemination. More and more couples today, however, choose not to have children and regard themselves as childfree, not childless. They do not believe that having children automatically follows from marriage, nor do they feel that reproduction is the duty of all married couples. Childfree opposite-sex couples have formed support groups (with names like "No Kidding") and set up Web sites on the Internet (Terry 2000).

Economic considerations have contributed to this shift in attitudes; having children has become quite expensive. Aware of the financial pressures, some couples are having fewer children than they otherwise might, and others are weighing the advantages of a childfree marriage.

Meanwhile, some childless couples, both same-sex and opposite-sex, who desperately want children may be willing to try any means necessary to get pregnant. The social policy section that follows explores the controversy surrounding recent advances in reproductive technology.

Use Your Sociological Imagination

What would happen to our society if more married couples decided not to have children? How would society change if cohabitation or singlehood became the norm?

SOCIAL POLICY AND THE FAMILY — Reproductive Technology

The Issue

The 1997 feature film *Gattaca* told the story of a future in which genetic engineering enhanced people's genes. Those who were not "enhanced" in the womb—principally those whose parents could not afford the treatments—suffer discrimination and social hurdles throughout their lives. To borrow a line from the movie, "Your genes are your résumé."

Far-fetched? Perhaps, but today we are witnessing quite commonly aspects of reproductive technology that were regarded as so much science fiction just a generation ago. "Test tube" babies, frozen embryos, surrogate mothers, sperm and egg donation, and cloning of human cells are raising questions about the ethics of creating and shaping human life. How will these technologies change the nature of families and the definitions we have of motherhood and fatherhood? To what extent should social policy encourage or discourage innovative reproductive technology?

The Setting

In an effort to overcome infertility, many couples turn to a recent reproductive advance known as *in vitro fertilization* (IVF). In this technique, an egg and a sperm are combined in a laboratory dish. If the egg is fertilized, the resulting embryo (the so-called test tube baby) is transferred into a woman's uterus. The fertilized egg could be transferred into the uterus of the woman from whom it was harvested or of a woman who has not donated the egg but who plays the role of surrogate (i.e., substitute). A surrogate mother carries the pregnancy to term and then transfers the child to the social mother. After this occurs, depending on the agreement between the social mother and the surrogate mother, the child may or may not be a part of the surrogate mother's life.

These possibilities, and many more, make the definition and attending responsibilities of motherhood complicated and somewhat murky. How should motherhood be defined—as providing gestation, as providing care for the child, as providing the egg, or all or some combination of these?

Sociological Insights

Replacing personnel is a functional prerequisite that the family as a social institution performs. Obviously, p. 103 advances in reproductive technology allow childless couples to fulfil their personal and societal goals. The new technology also presents opportunities not previously considered. A small but growing number of same-sex couples are using donated sperm or eggs to have genetically related children and fulfil their desire to have children and a family (Bruni 1998).

As mentioned earlier, sometimes it is difficult to define relationships. For example, in 1995, an American couple, John and Luanne Buzzanca, hired a married woman to carry a child to term for them—a child conceived of the sperm and egg of anonymous, unrelated donors. One month before birth, John filed for divorce and claimed he had no parental responsibilities, including child support. Eventually the court ruled that the baby girl had no legal parents; she is temporarily living with Luanne, who may seek to adopt the baby. Although this is an unusual case, it suggests the type of functional confusion that can arise in trying to establish kinship ties (Weiss 1998).

Feminist sociologist Margrit Eichler has developed a typology of motherhood in this age of new reproductive technology. She states that there can be up to 25 types of mothers, considering that mothers can now be "partial biological mothers—genetic but not gestational, or gestational but not genetic" (Eichler 1997:80). Her list of possible types of mothers include (1) genetic and gestational but not social mothers (mothers who have given up their child); (2) genetic, nongestational, and nonsocial mothers (those who provide an egg); (3) nongenetic, but gestational, social, exclusive, full mothers (those who receive an egg); (4) dead mother whose egg has been fertilized (mother #1), implanted in a carrier (mother #2), and transferred to a third woman (mother #3).

Eichler adds that new reproductive technologies have had a far less dramatic impact on fatherhood, the most noticeable change coming in the form of what she calls "post-mortem biological fathers" (Eichler 1997:72). This term refers to fatherhood that occurs after a man's death, when his sperm is harvested and used to impregnate a woman.

In the future depicted in *Gattaca,* the poor were at a disadvantage because they were not able to genetically control their lives. The conflict perspective would note that in the world today, the technologies available are

The possibility of cloning humans in the future, eerily foreshadowed in Andy Warhol's *The Twenty Marilyns*, poses major ethical dilemmas.

often accessible only to the most affluent. In addition, a report by the Royal Commission on New Reproductive Technologies issued in 1993 warned these technologies could potentially be used for commercial purposes (e.g., surrogacy), making women of lower classes vulnerable to exploitation. Thus, today in Canada, there is a voluntary ban on the use of many technologies that could be used commercially and that would enable those with resources to "buy" a reproductive service and those with perhaps few resources to "sell" the services in demand.

Interactionists observe that the quest for information and social support connected with reproductive technology has created new social networks. Like other special-interest groups, couples with infertility problems band together to share information, offer support to one another, and demand better treatment. They develop social networks—sometimes through voluntary associations or Internet support groups—where they share information about new medical techniques, insurance plans, and the merits of particular physicians and hospitals. One Internet self-help group, Mothers of Supertwins, offers supportive services for mothers but also lobbies for improved counselling at infertility clinics to better prepare couples for the demands of many babies at one time (MOST 1999).

Policy Initiatives

In Japan, some infertile couples have caused a controversy by using eggs or sperm donated by siblings for in vitro fertilization. This violates an ethical (though not legal) ban on "extramarital fertilization," the use of genetic material from anyone other than a spouse for conception. Although opinion is divided on this issue, most Japanese agree that there should be government guidelines on reproductive technology. Many nations, including England and Australia, bar payments to egg donors, resulting in very few donors in these countries. Even more countries limit how many times a man can donate sperm. Because the United States has no such restrictions, infertile foreigners who can afford the costs view that country as a land of opportunity (Efron 1998; Kolata 1998).

The legal and ethical issues connected with reproductive technology are immense. Many people feel we should be preparing for the possibility of a human clone. At this time, however, industrial societies are hard-pressed to deal with present advances in reproductive technology, much less future ones. Already, reputable hospitals are mixing donated sperm and eggs to create embryos that are frozen for future use. This raises the possibility of genetic screening as couples choose what they regard as the most "desirable" embryo—a "designer baby" in effect. Couples can select (some would say adopt) a frozen embryo that matches their requests in terms of race, sex, height, body type, eye colour, intelligence, ethnic and religious background, and even national origin (Begley 1999; Rifkin 1998).

Applying Theory

1. How might functional thinkers view the changing definitions of motherhood and fatherhood?
2. What concerns might some feminist thinkers raise over recent innovations in the area of reproductive technology?

CHAPTER RESOURCES

Summary

The ***family***, in its many varying forms, is present in all human cultures. This chapter examined the state of marriage, the family, and other intimate relationships in Canada and illustrated the diversity in family formation.

1. There are many variations in the family from culture to culture and even within the same culture.
2. The structure of the ***extended family*** can offer certain advantages over that of the ***nuclear family***.
3. We determine kinship by descent from both parents ***(bilateral descent)***, from the father ***(patrilineal)***, or from the mother ***(matrilineal)***.
4. Sociologists do not agree on whether the ***egalitarian family*** has replaced the ***patriarchal family*** as the social norm in Canada.
5. Sociologists have identified six basic functions of the family: reproduction, protection, socialization, regulation of sexual behaviour, companionship, and the provision of social status.
6. Conflict theorists argue that the family contributes to societal injustice and denies opportunities to women that are extended to men.
7. Interactionists focus on the microlevel—on how individuals interact in the family and other intimate relationships.
8. Feminist views on the family are diverse yet hold the common assumption that families are socially constructed.
9. Mates are selected in a variety of ways. Some marriages are arranged. Some people are able to choose their mates. Some societies require choosing a mate within a certain group ***(endogamy)*** or outside certain groups ***(exogamy)***.
10. In Canada, there is considerable variation in family life associated with sexual orientation, social class, race, and ethnic differences.
11. Currently, the majority of all married couples in Canada have both partners active in the paid labour force.
12. Among the factors that contribute to the current divorce rate among opposite-sex couples in Canada are the greater social acceptance of divorce and the liberalization of divorce laws.
13. More and more people are living together without marrying, thereby engaging in what is called ***cohabitation***. People are also staying single longer in general or deciding not to have children within marriage.
14. Nova Scotia has passed ***domestic partnership*** legislation. Such proposals continue to face strong opposition from conservative religious and political groups.
15. Canada passed Bill C-38, the Civil Marriage Act, in 2005, which legalized same-sex civil marriages.
16. Reproductive technology has advanced to such an extent that ethical questions have arisen about the creation and shaping of human life.

Critical Thinking Questions

1. Recent political discussions have focused on the definition of "family." Should some governments promote the model of family that includes both same-sex and opposite-sex couples? Are there ways in which "family" might be defined other than on the basis of sexual orientation? If so, name them.
2. In an increasing proportion of couples in Canada, both partners work outside the home. What are the advantages and disadvantages of the dual-income model for women, for men, for children, and for society as a whole?
3. Given the current rate of divorce in Canada, is it more appropriate to view divorce as dysfunctional or as a normal part of our marriage system? What are the implications of viewing divorce as normal rather than as dysfunctional?
4. What might be the focus of interactionist sociologists in their study of biological and nonbiological parents' relationship with their children?

Key Terms

Adoption In a legal sense, a process that allows for the transfer of the legal rights, responsibilities, and privileges of parenthood to a new legal parent or parents. (page 256)

Bilateral descent A kinship system in which both sides of a person's family are regarded as equally important. (247)

Cohabitation The practice of living together as a couple without marrying. (260)

Domestic partnership Two unrelated adults who have chosen to share each other's lives in a relationship of mutual caring, who reside together, and who agree to be jointly responsible for their dependants, basic living expenses, and other common necessities. (262)

Egalitarian family An authority pattern in which the adult members of the family are regarded as equals. (248)

Endogamy The restriction of mate selection to people within the same group. (251)

Exogamy The requirement that people select mates outside certain groups. (251)

Extended family A family in which relatives—such as grandparents, aunts, or uncles—live in the same home as parents and their children. (246)

Family A set of people related by blood, marriage (or some other agreed-on relationship), or adoption who share the responsibility for reproducing and caring for members of society. (244)

Incest taboo The prohibition of sexual relationships between certain culturally specified relatives. (251)

Kinship The state of being related to others. (247)

Matriarchy A society in which women dominate in family decision making. (248)

Matrilineal descent A kinship system that favours the relatives of the mother. (247)

Monogamy A form of marriage in which one woman and one man are married only to each other. (247)

Nuclear family A married couple and their unmarried children living together. (246)

Patriarchy A society in which men dominate family decision making. (248)

Patrilineal descent A kinship system that favours the relatives of the father. (247)

Polyandry A form of polygamy in which a woman can have more than one husband at the same time. (247)

Polygamy A form of marriage in which an individual can have several husbands or wives simultaneously. (247)

Polygyny A form of polygamy in which a husband can have several wives at the same time. (247)

Serial monogamy A form of marriage in which a person can have several spouses in his or her lifetime but only one spouse at a time. (247)

Single-parent families Families in which there is only one parent present to care for children. (257)

Additional Readings

Baker, Maureen, ed. 2001. *Families: Changing Trends in Canada*, 4th ed. Toronto: McGraw-Hill Ryerson. An edited collection by sociologists examining such areas as family violence, ethnic families, biases in family literature, and divorce and remarriage.

Eichler, Margrit. 1997. *Family Shifts: Families, Policies, and Gender Equality*. Toronto: Oxford University Press. A sociologist outlines the ways in which our conception of family has not kept pace with recent developments in reproductive technologies.

Milan, Anne. 2000. "One Hundred Years of Families." *Canadian Social Trends*. Statistics Canada, Catalogue No. 11-008 (Spring):2–13. This article provides a demographic overview of the changing Canadian family.

Weeks, Jeffrey, Brian Heaphy, and Catherine Donovan. 2001. *Same Sex Intimacies: Families of Choice and Other Life Experiments*. London: Routledge.

Online Learning Centre

Visit the *Sociology: A Brief Introduction* Online Learning Centre at www.mcgrawhill.ca/college/schaefer to access quizzes, interactive exercises, video clips, and other research and study tools related to this chapter.

Reel Society Interactive Movie CD-ROM 2.0

Reel Society 2.0 can be used to spark discussion about the following topics from this chapter:

- Studying the family
- Marriage and family
- Diversity in families

chapter 12

RELIGION AND EDUCATION

In this billboard distributed by Volkswagen of France, the figure of Jesus at the Last Supper says to his apostles, "Rejoice, my friends, for a new Golf is born." Although an image of Jesus is sacred for Christians, it is used here in a secular manner—to advertise cars.

I am the grandson of the late Joseph Michael Augustine.

My father was a devout Catholic. He was baptized Catholic, raised by strong Christian beliefs and ascended into heaven shortly after our parish priest stood over his bedside to read him his last rites.

I record this religious aspect of his life in the home of one of his daughter's—Aunt Madeline to me—where today I write from within a small, antiquated room in her basement. On each surrounding wall hang large, life-like portraits of religious figures with names like Pontifex Pius X and Leo XIII and His Holiness Pope John XXIII. As was my grandfather, my aunt is a member of the Catholic Church.

With such strong ties to the Catholic religion, should I not feel ashamed of the fact that I do not even understand why each of these figures looming above me is holding the same pose, with right hand raised in the air and two fingers pointing upwards, obviously communicating to the observer something of righteous significance?

Or should I be ashamed that I choose not to understand the righteous significance of these men with all their symbolic gestures, and how they seemingly stare right though me, from every direction of this room, as if God might strike me down for recording such thoughts on religion.

I do not wish to be disrespectful, for my grandfather did not raise us in this way. I respect the Catholic religion, and my family for practising its teachings. However, I was raised in the generation where aboriginal culture and spiritual traditions have since been reawakened, and despite being born into a strong Catholic family, I choose to honour our Great Spirit—God—through the practises and ceremonies originally given to the First Peoples of this land.

Rather than going to church, I attend a sweat lodge; rather than accepting bread and toast from the Holy Priest, I smoke a ceremonial pipe to come into Communion with the Great Spirit; and rather than kneeling with my hands placed together in prayer, I let sweetgrass be feathered over my entire being for spiritual cleansing and allow the smoke to carry my prayers into the heavens. I am a Mi'kmaq, and this is how we pray. *(Augustine 2000)* ■

This excerpt from Noah Augustine's article "Grandfather was a Knowing Christian," which appeared in the *Toronto Star*, contrasts the religious beliefs of his grandfather to his own. Augustine, a Mi'kmaq, came to practise Aboriginal spiritual traditions—attending a sweat lodge and smoking a ceremonial pipe—even though he had been born into what he calls a "strong Catholic family." His grandfather, however, who was also a Mi'kmaq, practised Catholicism and was never "reawakened" by the spiritual traditions of his Aboriginal heritage. Noah Augustine's reawakening represents part of a growing trend among Aboriginal people in Canada in which Aboriginal spirituality is again being expressed after years of suppression by the dominant culture.

Religion plays a major role in people's lives, and religious practices of some sort are evident in every society. That makes religion a cultural universal, along with other general practices found in every culture, such as dancing, food preparation, the family, and personal names. At present, an estimated four billion people belong to the world's many religious faiths (see Figure 12-1).

When religion's influence on other social institutions in a society diminishes, the process of ***secularization*** is said to be underway. During this process, religion will survive in the private sphere of individual and family life; it may even thrive on a personal level. But, at the same time, other social institutions—such as the economy, politics, and education—maintain their own sets of norms independent of religious guidance (Stark and Iannaccone 1992).

Education, like religion, is a cultural universal. As such it is an important aspect of socialization—the lifelong process of learning the attitudes, values, and behaviour considered appropriate to members of a particular culture, as we saw in Chapter 4. When learning is explicit and formalized—when some people consciously teach, while others adopt the role of learner—the process of socialization is called ***education.***

This chapter first looks at religion as it has emerged in modern industrial societies. It begins with a brief overview of the approaches that Émile Durkheim first introduced and those that later sociologists have used in studying religion. We will explore religion's role in societal integration, social support, social change, and social control. We'll examine three important dimensions of religious behaviour—belief, ritual, and experience—as well as the basic forms of religious organization. We will pay particular attention to the emergence of new religious movements.

The second part of this chapter focuses on the formal systems of education that characterize modern industrial societies, beginning with a discussion of four theoretical perspectives on education: functionalist, conflict, interactionist, and feminist. As we will see, education can both perpetuate the status quo and foster social change. An examination of schools as formal organizations—as bureaucracies and subcultures of teachers and students—follows. Two types of education that are becoming more common in North America today, adult education and home schooling, merit special mention. The chapter closes with a social policy discussion of the controversy over religion in public schools. ■

Use Your Sociological Imagination www.mcgrawhill.ca/college/schaefer

Why have Aboriginal people had their expressions of spirituality denied for generations? Have you ever attended a sweat lodge to observe or to receive spiritual cleansing? If so, what was the experience like for you?

DURKHEIM AND THE SOCIOLOGICAL APPROACH TO RELIGION

If a group believes that it is being directed by a "vision from God," sociologists will not attempt to prove or disprove this revelation. Instead, they will assess the effects of the religious experience on the group. What sociologists are interested in is the social impact of religion on individuals and institutions (McGuire 1981:12).

Émile Durkheim was perhaps the first sociologist to recognize the critical importance of religion in human societies. He saw its appeal for the individual, but—more importantly—he stressed the *social* impact of religion. In Durkheim's view, religion is a

p. 6

FIGURE 12-1

Religions of the World

Mapping Life WORLDWIDE

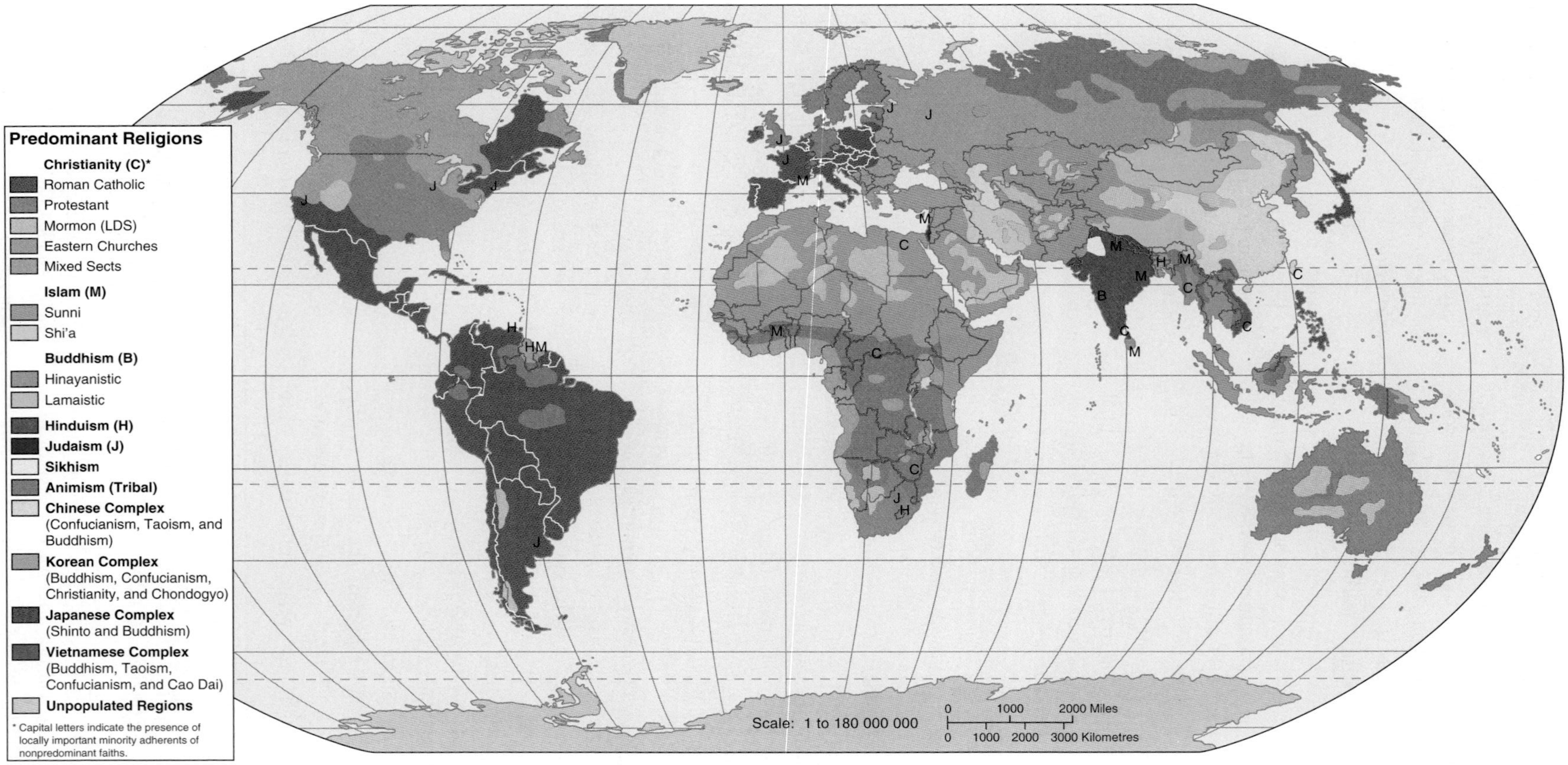

Source: J. Allen 2003:28.

collective act and includes many forms of behaviour in which people interact with others. As in his work on suicide, Durkheim was not as interested in the personalities of religious believers as he was in understanding religious behaviour within a social context.

Durkheim defined ***religion*** as a "unified system of beliefs and practices relative to sacred things." In his view, religion involves a set of beliefs and practices that are uniquely the property of religion—as opposed to other social institutions and ways of thinking. Durkheim (1947, original edition 1912) argued that religious faiths distinguish between certain events that transcend the ordinary and the everyday world. He referred to these realms as the *sacred* and the *profane.*

The ***sacred*** encompasses elements beyond everyday life that inspire awe, respect, and even fear. People become a part of the sacred realm only by completing some ritual, such as prayer or sacrifice. Believers have faith in the sacred; this faith allows them to accept what they cannot understand. By contrast, the ***profane*** includes the ordinary and commonplace. It can get confusing, however, because the same object can be either sacred or profane depending on how it is viewed. A normal dining room table is profane, but it becomes sacred to Christians if it bears the elements of a communion. A candelabra becomes sacred for Jews when it is a menorah. For Confucians and Taoists, incense sticks are not mere decorative items; they are highly valued offerings to the gods in religious ceremonies marking new and full moons.

At a Jain temple in the United States, a monk sweeps the walk carefully to avoid stepping on insects. Adherents of Jainism revere all forms of life.

Following the direction established by Durkheim almost a century ago, contemporary sociologists view religions in two different ways. They study the norms and values of religious faiths through examination of their substantive religious beliefs. For example, it is possible to compare the degree to which Christian faiths literally interpret the Bible, or Muslim groups follow the Qur'an (or Koran), the sacred book of Islam. At the same time, sociologists examine religions in terms of the social functions they fulfil, such as providing social support or reinforcing the social norms. By exploring both the beliefs and the functions of religion, we can better understand its impact on the individual, on groups, and on society as a whole.

THE ROLE OF RELIGION

Since religion is a cultural universal, it is not surprising that it plays a basic role in human societies. In sociological terms, these include both manifest and latent functions. p. 13 Among its *manifest* (open and stated) functions, religion defines the spiritual world and gives meaning to the divine. Religion provides an explanation for events that seem difficult to understand, such as what happens after death.

The *latent* functions of religion are unintended, covert, or hidden. Even though the manifest function of church services is to offer a forum for religious worship, they might at the same time fulfil a latent function as a meeting ground for unmarried members.

Functionalists and conflict theorists both evaluate religion's impact as a social institution on human societies. We'll consider a functionalist view of religion's role in integrating society, in social support, and in promoting social change, and then look at religion as a means of social control from the conflict perspective. Note that, for the most part, religion's impact is best understood from a macrolevel viewpoint, oriented toward the larger society. The social support function is an exception: it is best viewed on the microlevel, directed toward the individual.

The Integrative Function of Religion

Émile Durkheim viewed religion as an integrative power in human society—a perspective reflected in functionalist thought today. Durkheim sought to answer a perplexing question: "How can human societies be held together when they are generally composed of individuals and social groups with diverse interests and aspirations?" In his view, religious bonds often transcend these personal and divisive forces. Durkheim acknowledged that religion is not the only integrative force—nationalism or patriotism may serve the same end.

How does religion provide this "societal glue"? Religion, whether it be Buddhism, Islam, Christianity, or Judaism, offers people meaning and purpose for their lives. It gives them certain ultimate values and ends to hold in common. Although subjective and not always fully accepted, these values and ends help a society to function as an integrated social system. For example, funerals, weddings, bar and bat mitzvahs, and confirmations serve to integrate people into larger communities by providing shared beliefs and values about the ultimate questions of life.

The integrative power of religion can be seen in the role that churches, synagogues, temples, and mosques have traditionally played and continue to play for immigrant groups in Canada. For example, Roman Catholic immigrants may settle near a parish church that offers services in their native language, such as Polish or Portuguese. Similarly, Korean immigrants may join a Presbyterian church with many Korean Canadian members and with religious practices like those of churches in Korea. Like other religious organizations, these Roman Catholic and Presbyterian churches help to integrate immigrants into their new homeland.

Yet another example of the integrative impact of religion is provided by the Universal Fellowship of Metropolitan Community Churches. It was established in the United States in 1968 to offer a welcoming place of worship for lesbians and gays. This spiritual community is especially important today, given the many organized religions openly hostile to homosexuality. The Metropolitan Community Church has 42 000 members in its local churches in 15 countries, including Canada, where there are three such churches in Toronto alone. As part of its effort to support lesbian and gay rights, the Metropolitan Community Church for years has performed same-sex marriages, which it calls "holy union ceremonies" (Stammer 1999). In 2005, Canada became the fourth county in the world to legally recognize same-sex marriage, a move that was considered progressive by some and that outraged others. Many religious leaders argue that the government does not have the right to redefine marriage. The research of Canadian sociologist Reginald Bibby (2004) shows that religious affiliation and participation are linked to opposition of same-sex marriage. This relationship exists in both Canada and the United States; however, Americans were more likely to be against same-sex marriage.

In some instances, religious loyalties are *dysfunctional;* they contribute to tension and even to conflict between groups or nations. During the Second World War, the German Nazis attempted to exterminate the Jewish people; approximately six million European Jews were killed. In modern times, nations, such as Lebanon (Muslims versus Christians), Israel (Jews versus Muslims as well as Orthodox versus secular Jews), Northern Ireland (Roman Catholics versus Protestants), and India (Hindus versus Muslims and, more recently, Sikhs), have been torn by clashes that are in large part based on religion.

Religious conflict (though on a less violent level) is evident in Canada as well. Christian fundamentalists in many communities battle against their liberal counterparts for control of the secular culture. The battlefield is

Some churches, such as the Metropolitan Community Church in Toronto, perform marriage ceremonies joining same-sex couples.

an array of familiar social issues, among them multiculturalism, abortion, sex education in schools, and gay and lesbian rights.

Religion and Social Support

Most of us find it difficult to accept the stressful events of life—death of a loved one, serious injury, bankruptcy, divorce, and so forth. This is especially true when something "senseless" happens. How can family and friends come to terms with the death of a talented university student, not even 20 years old, from a terminal disease?

Through its emphasis on the divine and the supernatural, religion allows us to "do something" about the calamities we face. In some faiths, adherents can offer sacrifices or pray to a deity in the belief that such acts will change their earthly condition. At a more basic level, religion encourages us to view our personal misfortunes as relatively unimportant in the broader perspective of human history—or even as part of an undisclosed divine purpose. Friends and relatives of the deceased university student may see this death as being "God's will" and as having some ultimate benefit that we cannot understand now. This perspective may be much more comforting than the terrifying feeling that any of us can die senselessly at any moment—and that there is no divine "answer" as to why one person lives a long and full life, while another dies tragically at a relatively early age.

Faith-based community organizations have taken on more and more responsibilities in the area of social assistance. In fact, as part of an effort to cut back on government-funded welfare programs, government leaders have advocated shifting the social "safety net" to private organizations in general and to churches and religious charities in particular. These organizations identify experienced leaders and assemble them into nonsectarian coalitions devoted to community development (K. Starr 1999).

Religion and Social Change

The Weberian Thesis

When someone seems driven to work and succeed, we often attribute the "Protestant work ethic" to that person. The term comes from the writings of Max Weber, who carefully examined the connection between religious allegiance and capitalist development. His findings appeared in his pioneering work *The Protestant Ethic and the Spirit of Capitalism* (1958a, original edition 1904).

Weber noted that in European nations with both Protestant and Catholic citizens, an overwhelming number of business leaders, owners of capital, and skilled workers were Protestant. In his view, this was no mere coincidence. Weber pointed out that the followers of John Calvin (1509–1564), a leader of the Protestant Reformation, emphasized the disciplined work ethic, this-worldly concerns, and rational orientation to life that have become known as the ***Protestant ethic.*** One by-product of the Protestant ethic was a drive to accumulate savings that could be used for future investment. This "spirit of capitalism," to use Weber's phrase, contrasted with the moderate work hours, leisurely work habits, and lack of ambition that he saw as typical of the times (Winter 1977; Yinger 1974).

Few books on the sociology of religion have aroused as much commentary and criticism as Weber's work. It has been hailed as one of the most important theoretical works in the field and as an excellent example of macro-level analysis. Like Durkheim, Weber demonstrated that religion is not solely a matter of intimate personal beliefs. He stressed that the collective nature of religion has social consequences for society as a whole.

Weber provides a convincing description of the origins of European capitalism. But this economic system has subsequently been adopted by non-Calvinists in many parts of the world. Apparently, the "spirit of capitalism" has become a generalized cultural trait rather than a specific religious tenet (Greeley 1989).

Conflict theorists caution that Weber's theory—even if it is accepted—should not be regarded as an analysis of mature capitalism as reflected in the rise of multinational corporations that cross national boundaries. Marxists would disagree with Max Weber not on the origins of capitalism but on its future. Unlike Marx, Weber believed that capitalism could endure indefinitely as an economic system. He added, however, that the decline of religion as an overriding force in society opened the way for workers to express their discontent more vocally (R. Collins 1980).

p. 184

Liberation Theology

Sometimes the clergy can be found in the forefront of social change. Many religious activists, especially in the Roman Catholic church in Latin America, support ***liberation theology***—the use of a church in a political effort to eliminate poverty, discrimination, and other forms of injustice evident in a secular society. Advocates of this religious movement sometimes sympathize with Marxism. Many believe that radical change, rather than economic development in itself, is the only acceptable solution to the desperation of the masses in impoverished developing countries. Activists associated with liberation theology believe that organized religion has a moral responsibility to take a strong public stand against the oppression of the poor, members of racial and ethnic minorities, and women (C. Smith 1991).

The term *liberation theology* dates back to the 1973 publication of the English translation of *A Theology of Liberation*. This book was written by a Peruvian priest, Gustavo Gutierrez, who lived in a slum area of Lima during the early 1960s. After years of exposure to the vast poverty around him, Gutierrez concluded that "in order to serve the poor, one had to move into political action" (Brown 1980:23; Gutierrez 1990).

Politically committed Latin American theologians came under the influence of social scientists who viewed the domination of capitalism and multinational corporations as central to the hemisphere's problems. One result was a new approach to theology that rejected the models developed in Europe and the United States and instead built on the cultural and religious traditions of Latin America.

Although many worshippers support liberation theology, religious leaders in the Roman Catholic church are not happy with the radical movement. The official position of many in the church hierarchy is that clergy should adhere to traditional pastoral duties and keep a distance from radical politics (Pagani 1999).

Liberation theology may possibly be dysfunctional, however. Some Roman Catholics have come to believe that by focusing on political and governmental injustice, the clergy are no longer addressing their personal and spiritual needs. Partly as a result of such disenchantment, some Catholics in Latin America are converting to mainstream Protestant faiths or to Mormonism.

Use Your Sociological Imagination

The social support that religious groups provide is suddenly withdrawn from your community. How will your life or the lives of others change? What will happen if religious groups stop pushing for social change?

Religion and Social Control: A Conflict View

Liberation theology is a relatively recent phenomenon and marks a break with the traditional role of churches. It was this traditional role that Karl Marx opposed. In his view, religion *impeded* social change by encouraging oppressed people to focus on other-worldly concerns rather than on their immediate poverty or exploitation. Marx described religion as an "opiate" particularly harmful to oppressed peoples. He felt that religion often drugged the masses into submission by offering a consolation for their harsh lives on Earth: the hope of salvation in an ideal afterlife. For example, Aboriginal children housed in residential schools in Canada were forbidden to practise their own forms of spirituality and were forced to adopt the Christian religion. Christianity taught them that obedience would lead to salvation and eternal happiness in the hereafter. Viewed from a conflict perspective, Christianity may have pacified certain oppressed groups and blunted the rage that often fuels rebellion (McGuire 1992; Yinger 1970).

Marx acknowledged that religion plays an important role in propping up the existing social structure. The values of religion, as already noted, reinforce other social institutions and the social order as a whole. From Marx's perspective, however, religion's promotion of stability within society only helps to perpetuate patterns of social inequality. According to Marx, the dominant religion reinforces the interests of those in power (Harap 1982).

Consider, for example, India's traditional caste system. It defined the social structure of that society, at least among the Hindu majority. The caste system was almost certainly the creation of the priesthood, but it also served the interests of India's political rulers by granting a certain religious legitimacy to social inequality.

pp. 164–165

Contemporary Christianity, like the Hindu faith, reinforces traditional patterns of behaviour that call for the subordination of the less powerful. Like Marx, conflict theorists argue that to whatever extent religion actually does influence social behaviour, it reinforces existing patterns of dominance and inequality.

From a Marxist perspective, religion functions as an "agent of de-politicization" (J. Wilson 1973). In simpler terms, religion keeps people from seeing their lives and societal conditions in political terms—for example, by obscuring the overriding significance of conflicting economic interests. Marxists suggest that by inducing a "false consciousness" among the disadvantaged, religion lessens the possibility of collective political action that can end capitalist oppression and transform society.

p. 14

The positions of women in religious organizations tend to be ones of subjugation. Assumptions about gender often place women in subservient positions, both within many religious faiths and in the private sphere. In fact, women find it as difficult to achieve leadership positions in many religious organizations as they do in large corporations. For example, only 20 percent of Anglican priests are female and approximately 40 percent of ordained ministers in the United Church of Canada are female (Harvey 2004). Among Canadian Aboriginals, however, women have traditionally been granted roles of spiritual leadership.

Female spiritual leaders are more likely to serve in subsidiary roles and to wait longer for desirable assignments.

Although women may play a significant role as volunteers in religious communities, men are more likely to make the major theological and financial judgments for nationwide spiritual organizations.

Feminist perspectives on religion and female spirituality recognize the diversity of women's spiritual expression and reveal the ways in which religious systems are "gendered," reflecting dominant political and cultural assumptions (Stuckey 1998). These perspectives run the gamut from those that suggest that religions revise their messages and interpretations, to those that unequivocally reject religious traditions as "irremediably sexist" (Stuckey 1998:269).

RELIGIOUS BEHAVIOUR

All religions have certain elements in common, yet these elements are expressed in the distinctive manner of each faith. The patterns of religious behaviour, like other patterns of social behaviour, are of great interest to sociologists, since they underscore the relationship between religion and society.

Religious beliefs, religious rituals, and religious experience all help to define what is sacred and to differentiate the sacred from the profane. Let us now examine these three dimensions of religious behaviour.

Belief

Some people believe in life after death, in supreme beings with unlimited powers, or in supernatural forces. ***Religious beliefs*** are statements to which members of a particular religion adhere. These views can vary dramatically from religion to religion.

The Adam and Eve account of creation found in Genesis, the first book of the Old Testament, is an example of a religious belief. Some people in Canada strongly adhere to this biblical explanation of creation. These people, known as *creationists,* are worried by the secularization of society and oppose teaching that directly or indirectly questions biblical scripture. As Figure 12-2 shows, the strength of belief in God varies dramatically worldwide.

FIGURE 12-2

Belief in God Worldwide

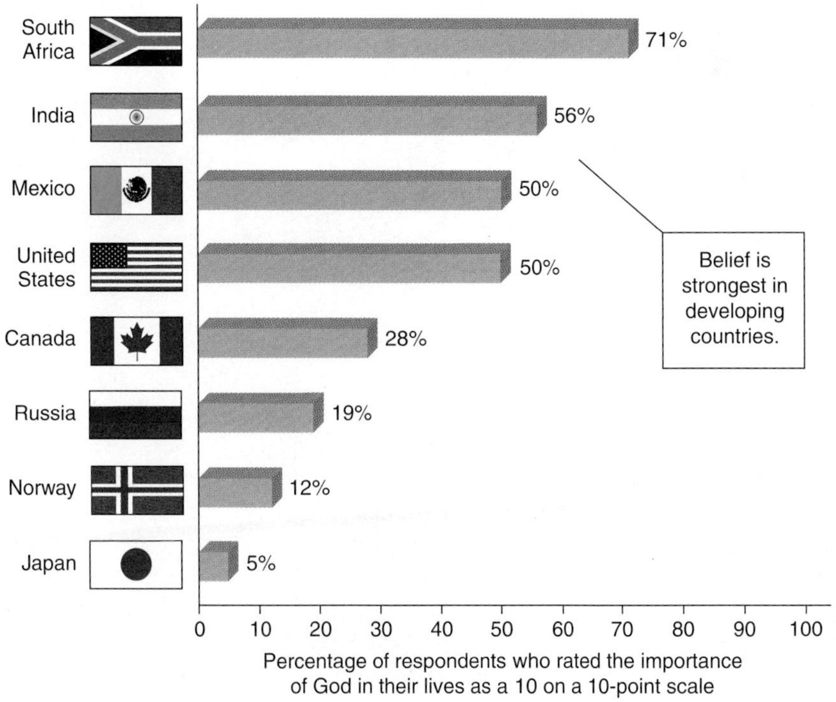

Source: Inglehart and Baker 2000:47.

Note: Data are from World Values surveys for 1995–1998, except for Canada, 1990–1991.

Use Your Sociological Imagination

Canada and the United States are similar in many ways. Why would faith in God be less important to Canadians than to U.S. citizens?

Ritual

Religious rituals are practices required or expected of members of a faith. Rituals usually honour the divine power (or powers) worshipped by believers; they also remind adherents of their religious duties and responsibilities. Rituals and beliefs can be interdependent; rituals generally involve the affirmation of beliefs, as in a public or private statement confessing a sin (Roberts 1995). Like any social institution, religion develops distinctive normative patterns to structure people's behaviour. Moreover, there are sanctions attached to religious rituals, whether rewards (bar mitzvah gifts) or penalties (expulsion from a religious institution for violation of norms).

In North America, rituals may be very simple, such as saying grace at a meal or observing a moment of silence to commemorate someone's death. Yet certain rituals, such as the process of canonizing a saint, are quite elaborate. Most religious rituals in our culture focus on services conducted at houses of worship. Attendance at a service, silent and spoken prayers, and singing of spiritual hymns and chants are common forms of ritual behaviour that generally take place in group settings. From an interactionist perspective, these rituals serve as important face-to-face encounters in which people reinforce their religious beliefs and their commitment to their faith.

For Muslims, a very important ritual is the *hajj,* a pilgrimage to the Grand Mosque in Mecca, Saudi Arabia. Every Muslim who is physically and financially able is expected to make this trip at least once. Each year, two million pilgrims go to Mecca during the one-week period indicated by the Islamic lunar calendar. Muslims from all over the world make the *hajj,* including those in Canada, where many tours are arranged to facilitate this ritual.

Some rituals induce an almost trancelike state. The First Nations of the American Plains eat or drink peyote, a cactus containing the powerful hallucinogenic drug mescaline. Similarly, the ancient Greek followers of the god Pan chewed intoxicating leaves of ivy in order to become more ecstatic during their celebrations. Of course, artificial stimulants are not necessary to achieve a religious "high." Devout believers, such as those who practise the pentecostal Christian ritual of "speaking in tongues," can reach a state of ecstasy simply through spiritual passion.

Experience

In the sociological study of religion, the term ***religious experience*** refers to the feeling or perception of being in direct contact with the ultimate reality, such as a divine being, or of being overcome with religious emotion. A religious experience may be rather slight, such as the feeling of exaltation a person receives from hearing a choir sing Handel's "Hallelujah Chorus." But many religious experiences are more profound, such as a Muslim's experience on a *hajj.* In his autobiography, the late American black activist Malcolm X (1964:338) wrote of his *hajj* and how deeply moved he was by the way that Muslims in Mecca came together across lines of race and colour. For Malcolm X, the colour blindness of the Muslim world "proved to me the power of the One God."

Still another profound religious experience is being "born again"—that is, at a turning point in one's life, making a personal commitment to Jesus. According to a 1999 national survey, 46 percent of people in the United States claimed that they had a born-again Christian experience at some time in their lives. An earlier survey found that Baptists (61 percent) were the most likely to report such experiences; by contrast, only 18 percent of Catholics and 11 percent of Episcopalians stated that they had been born again. In Canada, 10 percent of Canadians stated they are "born again" (CBC 2000). The collective nature of religion, as emphasized by Durkheim, is evident in these statistics. The beliefs and rituals of a particular faith can create an atmosphere either friendly or hostile to this type of religious experience. Thus, a Baptist would be encouraged to come forward and share such experiences with others, whereas an Episcopalian who claimed to have been born again would receive much less support (Princeton Religions Research Center 2000).

Use Your Sociological Imagination

Choose a religious tradition other than your own. How would your religious beliefs, rituals, and experience differ if you had been raised in that tradition?

The representation of religion can take many forms. This motorcycle club organizes itself as a strong Christian group, even though its attire and lifestyle may be objectionable to many Christians.

RELIGIOUS ORGANIZATION

The collective nature of religion has led to many forms of religious association. In modern societies, religion has become increasingly formalized. Specific structures, such as churches and synagogues, are constructed for religious worship; individuals are trained for occupational roles within various fields. These developments make it possible to distinguish clearly between the sacred and secular parts of life—a distinction that could not be made in earlier societies in which religion was largely a family activity carried out in the home.

Sociologists find it useful to distinguish among four basic forms of organization: the ecclesia, the denomination, the sect, and the new religious movement or cult. We can see differences among these types of organizations in such factors as size, power, degree of commitment expected from members, and historical ties to other faiths.

Ecclesiae

An ***ecclesia*** (plural, *ecclesiae*) is a religious organization that claims to include most or all of the members of a society and is recognized as the national or official religion. Since virtually everyone belongs to the faith, membership is by birth rather than conscious decision. Examples of ecclesiae include the Lutheran church in Sweden, the Catholic church in Spain, Islam in Saudi Arabia, and Buddhism in Thailand. However, there can be significant differences even within the category of ecclesia. In Saudi Arabia's Islamic regime, leaders of the ecclesia hold vast power over actions of the state. By contrast, the Lutheran church in contemporary Sweden has no such power over the Riksdag (Parliament) or the prime minister.

Generally, ecclesiae are conservative in that they do not challenge the leaders of a secular government. In a society with an ecclesia, the political and religious institutions often act in harmony and mutually reinforce each other's power over their relative spheres of influence. Within the modern world, ecclesiae tend to be declining in power.

Denominations

A ***denomination*** is a large, organized religion not officially linked with the state or government. Like an ecclesia, it tends to have an explicit set of beliefs, a defined system of authority, and a generally respected position in society. Denominations claim as members large segments of a population. Generally, children accept the denomination of their parents and give little thought to membership in other faiths. Denominations also resemble ecclesiae in that generally few demands are made on members. However, there is a critical difference between these two forms of religious organization. Although the denomination is considered respectable and is not viewed as a challenge to the secular government, it lacks the official recognition and power held by an ecclesia (Doress and Porter 1977).

Although approximately 43 percent of all Canadians were Roman Catholic in 2001, this country is marked by great religious diversity. With the exception of Aboriginals, we are a country of immigrants and Canadian religious diversity reflects patterns of immigration and population change.

Protestantism follows Catholicism in popularity and is practised by 29 percent of the population in Canada; 9.6 percent of people belonging to a Protestant denomination are members of the United Church. From 1991 to 2001, the percentage of Muslims in Canada more than doubled, increasing to almost 600 000. The percentage of Jews increased by approximately 4 percent from one census period to the next, increasing to almost 330 000. The percentage of people declaring no religious affiliation rose from 12.3 percent in 1991 to 16.2 percent in 2001; at the same time, the percentage of those belonging to Protestant denominations dropped by approximately 8 percent. A significant increase in affiliation was reported in the category "Christian, not included elsewhere" (see Table 12-1), which includes Christian fundamentalist denominations. That category rose 121 percent from 1991 to 2001.

These overall trends do not reveal the great diversity that exists regionally in relation to religious membership. In 2001, people in Yukon were the Canadians most likely to declare no religious affiliation (37 percent). By contrast, in Newfoundland and Labrador, less than 2 percent declared no religious affiliation (Statistics Canada 2003j).

Attendance at religious services tends to vary according to age, rural/urban setting, immigrant status, and family status. In 1998, married couples aged 25 to 44 with young children were more likely to worship regularly than those who were of the same age but childfree (Statistics Canada 2000b). Seniors aged 75 and over had the highest rates of attendance. Those born in Canada were less likely to be regular attendees of religious services than were immigrants. Approximately 50 percent of Asian immigrants who entered Canada between 1994 and 1998 attended worship services regularly, compared with approximately one in five European immigrants who entered the country during the same period. According to the 2001 General Social Survey by Statistics Canada, Canadians' attendance at religious services has fallen dramatically over the last 15 years. In 2001, 20 percent of Canadians aged 15 and over attended religious services

Table 12-1 **Major Religious Denominations, Canada, 1991[1] and 2001**

	2001		1991		Percentage Change
	number	%	number	%	1991–2001
Roman Catholic	12 793 125	43.2	12 203 625	45.2	4.8
Protestant	8 654 854	29.2	9 427 675	34.9	–8.2
Christian Orthodox	479 620	1.6	387 395	1.4	23.8
Christian, not included elsewhere[2]	780 450	2.6	353 040	1.3	121.1
Muslim	579 640	2.0	253 265	0.9	128.9
Jewish	329 995	1.1	318 185	1.2	3.7
Buddhist	300 345	1.0	163 415	0.6	83.8
Hindu	297 200	1.0	157 015	0.6	89.3
Sikh	278 415	0.9	147 440	0.5	88.8
No religion	4 796 352	16.2	3 333 245	12.3	43.9

Source: Statistics Canada 2003j.

1. For comparability purposes, 1991 data are presented according to 2001 boundaries.

2. Includes persons who report "Christian," as well as those who report "Apostolic," "Born-again Christian," and "Evangelical."

on a weekly basis, compared with 28 percent in 1986 (Statistics Canada 2003j).

In the past 20 years, some distinctions among denominations have started to blur. Certain faiths have even allowed members of other faiths to participate in some of their most sacred rituals, such as communion. Even more dramatic has been the appearance of ***megachurches***—large congregations that often lack direct ties to a worldwide denomination, as described in Box 12-1.

Sects

A ***sect*** can be defined as a relatively small religious group that has broken away from some other religious organization to renew what it considers the original vision of the faith. Many sects, such as that led by Martin Luther during the Reformation, claim to be the "true church" because they seek to cleanse the established faith of what they regard as extraneous beliefs and rituals (Stark and Bainbridge 1985). Max Weber (1958b:114, original edition 1916) termed the sect a "believer's church," because affiliation is based on conscious acceptance of a specific religious dogma.

Sects are fundamentally at odds with society and do not seek to become established national religions. Unlike ecclesiae and denominations, sects require intensive commitments and demonstrations of belief by members. Partly owing to their "outsider" status in society, sects frequently exhibit a higher degree of religious fervour and loyalty than more established religious groups do. Recruitment focuses mainly on adults, and acceptance comes through conversion. One current-day sect is called the People of the Church, a movement within the Roman Catholic Church that began in Vienna, Austria. This sect has called for reforms of Catholicism, such as the ordination of women, local election of bishops, and optional celibacy for priests (*Religion Watch* 1995).

New Religious Movements or Cults

The Branch Davidians began as a sect of the Seventh-Day Adventists church, basing their beliefs largely on the biblical book of Revelation and its doomsday prophecies. In 1984, the Davidians' sect split, with one group emerging as a cult under the leadership of David Koresh. In 1993, violence erupted at their compound near Waco, Texas. After a 51-day standoff against federal authorities, Koresh and 85 of his followers died when the Federal Bureau of Investigation (FBI) attempted to seize control of the compound and its arsenal of weapons. In 1997,

Sociology in the Global Community

12-1 The Emergence of the Megachurch

The Yoido Full Gospel Church in Seoul, South Korea, has six daily services in a facility with 13 000 seats. Unable to serve all of its 700 000 members, the church reaches 30 000 other worshippers via closed-circuit television, and 50 000 tune in from 20 satellite congregations across the metropolitan area. Worshippers listen to the sermons of Pastor David Cho and join in singing with 11 choirs, accompanied by a pipe organ or a 24-piece orchestra.

This is just an example of the growing emergence worldwide of megachurches, large worship centres only loosely affiliated, if at all, with existing denominations.

Megachurches that begin with denominational ties frequently break them when they become financially self-sufficient. They often break away not so much on the basis of doctrinal issues as from a desire to be viewed as unique and to be free of church hierarchy.

Sociologists have observed the significant impact on religious organizations of these megachurches, whose growth is sometimes defined by the size of the parking lot. Their size often provokes hostility from more traditional churches that fear being overwhelmed or, in some cases, from the preexisting dominant faith (such as Buddhism in South Korea). Some people view the megachurch as the latest intrusion of European/North American culture into the local landscape, especially in Latin America and Africa.

Megachurches appeal particularly to younger people, who seem prepared to shop around for religious faith just as they would for a postsecondary institution or an automobile. The very size of the megachurch facility may attract someone used to working in large bureaucracies or dealing with huge supermarkets, large medical clinics, or shopping malls. People comfortable in these settings may find the anonymity of a huge religious place of worship preferable to the intimacy of a small church with 50 to 100 members genuinely interested in getting to know them as individuals. Perhaps most importantly, the megachurch is willing to use the latest marketing tools, multimedia presentations, and motivational techniques to reach out to those who feel disenchanted with traditional denominations.

Applying Theory

1. Are there ways in which the megachurch can be viewed as "functional"? If so, what are they?
2. Do you think the meaning or significance of religious attendance would change if you were to attend a megachurch?

Sources: Carey and Mosemak 1999; Luo 1999; Ostling 1993; Schaller 1990.

38 members of the Heaven's Gate cult were found dead in Southern California after a mass suicide timed to occur with the appearance of the Hale-Bopp comet. They believed the comet hid a spaceship on which they could ride once they had broken free of their "bodily containers." In Canada, news of the Order of the Solar Temple cult suicides in 1994 shocked the nation.

Partly as a result of the notoriety generated by such groups, the popular media have stigmatized the word *cult* by associating cults with the occult and the use of intense and forceful conversion techniques. The stereotyping of cults as uniformly bizarre and unethical has led sociologists to abandon the term and refer to a cult instead as a *new religious movement (NRM).* Although some NRMs, like the Branch Davidians, exhibit strange behaviour, many do not. They attract new members just like any other religion and often follow teachings similar to established Christian denominations but with less ritual.

It is difficult to distinguish sects from cults. A ***new religious movement (NRM)*** or ***cult*** is a generally small, secretive religious group that represents either a new religion or a major innovation of an existing faith. NRMs are similar to sects in that they tend to be small and are often viewed as less respectable than more established faiths.

However, unlike sects, NRMs normally do not result from schisms or breaks with established ecclesiae or denominations. Some cults, such as those focused on UFO sightings, may be totally unrelated to the existing faiths in a culture. Even when a cult does accept certain fundamental tenets of a dominant faith—such as belief in Jesus as divine or Muhammad as a messenger of God—it will offer new revelations or new insights to justify its claim to be a more advanced religion (Stark and Bainbridge 1979, 1985).

Like sects, NRMs may undergo transformation over time into other types of religious organizations. An example is the Christian Science church, which began as a new religious movement under the leadership of Mary Baker Eddy. Today, this church exhibits the characteristics of a denomination. NRMs tend to be in the early stages of what may develop into a denomination, or they may just as easily fade away through loss of members or weak leadership (J. Richardson and van Driel 1997).

Comparing Forms of Religious Organization

How can we determine whether a particular religious group falls into the sociological category of ecclesia, denomination, sect, or NRM? As we have seen, these types of religious organizations have somewhat different relationships to society. Ecclesiae are recognized as national churches; denominations, although not officially approved by the state, are generally widely respected. By contrast, sects as well as NRMs are much more likely to be at odds with the larger culture.

Still, ecclesiae, denominations, and sects are best viewed as ideal types along a continuum rather than as mutually exclusive categories. Table 12-2 summarizes some of the primary characteristics of these ideal types. Since Canada has no ecclesia, sociologists studying this country's religions have naturally focused on the denomination and the sect. These religious forms have been pictured on either end of a continuum, with denominations accommodating to the secular world and sects making a protest against established religions. NRMs have also been included in Table 12-2 but are outside the continuum because they generally define themselves as a new view of life rather than in terms of existing religious faiths (Chalfant, Beckley, and Palmer 1994).

Advances in electronic communications have led to still another form of religious organization: the electronic church. Facilitated by cable television and satellite transmissions, *televangelists* direct their messages to more people—especially in the United States—than are served by all but the largest denominations. The Internet has given the electronic church another dimension. In one study, researchers estimated that on a typical day in 2000, as many as two million people used the Internet for religious purposes (Larsen 2000). Much of the spiritual content on the Internet is tied to organized denominations. People use cyberspace to learn more about their faith or the activities of their own place of worship.

But as increasing numbers of people are discovering, the church they locate on the World Wide Web exists only in virtual reality. For some purposes, virtual religious experiences simply will not do. For example, a *minyan*, a set quorum for Jewish prayers, requires 10 Jews to gather in one space; cyberspace does not count. And although Muslims can view the Kabbah, or the Holy Shrine, in Mecca on the Internet, they cannot fulfil their religious obligations except by the actual pilgrimage there. The

Table 12-2 Characteristics of Ecclesiae, Denominations, Sects, and New Religious Movements

Characteristic	Ecclesia	Denomination	Sect	New Religious Movement (or Cult)
Size	Very large	Large	Small	Small
Wealth	Extensive	Extensive	Limited	Variable
Religious Services	Formal, little participation	Formal, little participation	Informal, emotional	Variable
Doctrines	Specific, but interpretation may be tolerated	Specific, but interpretation may be tolerated	Specific, purity of doctrine emphasized	Innovative, pathbreaking
Clergy	Well-trained, full-time	Well-trained, full-time	Trained to some degree	Unspecialized
Membership	By virtue of being a member of society	By acceptance of doctrine	By acceptance of doctrine	By an emotional commitment
Relationship to the State	Recognized, closely aligned	Tolerated	Not encouraged	Ignored or challenged

Source: Adapted from G. Vernon 1962; see also Chalfant et al. 1994.

Internet, then, isn't suitable for some forms of religious and spiritual expression, but it certainly has added a new dimension to religious behaviour (G. Zelizer 1999).

We turn now to another major social institution in every society—education. It prepares citizens for the various roles demanded by other institutions, including religion. Education and religion sometimes get intertwined, as we will see in the social policy section about the role of religion in the schools.

SOCIOLOGICAL PERSPECTIVES ON EDUCATION

Education is a major industry in Canada. In the last few decades, increasing numbers of people have obtained a high school diploma and at least some postsecondary education (Figure 12-3 shows where Canada ranks among other developed nations). Nine percent of females and 15 percent of males at age 20 had not completed high school in 1999, compared with 14 percent and 22 percent, respectively, in 1991 (Statistics Canada 2002d).

Globally, enrolments in educational institutions have been increasing; however, vast regional and national differences exist in this overall trend. For example, in less developed regions, although progress has been made, only 79 percent of boys and 66 percent of girls finished primary education in 2002 (Unicef 2004). These numbers mask the fact that most girls in less developed countries receive less education than boys do, and in some of the world's poorest countries, fewer than half of young women receive the basic seven years of schooling (Unicef 2004). According to the United Nations Population Fund *State of World Population Report 2000*, girls and women throughout the world are still routinely denied access to education. As a result, the United Nations Children's Fund reported in 2004, only 42 percent of women in the least-developed countries can read, compared with 62 percent of men (Unicef 2004).

The functionalist, conflict, interactionist, and feminist perspectives offer distinctive ways of examining education as a social institution.

Functionalist View

Like other social institutions, education has both manifest (open, stated) and latent (hidden) functions. The most basic *manifest* function of education is the

FIGURE 12-3

Percentage of Population Aged 25 to 54 Who Have Completed Postsecondary Education, 2001

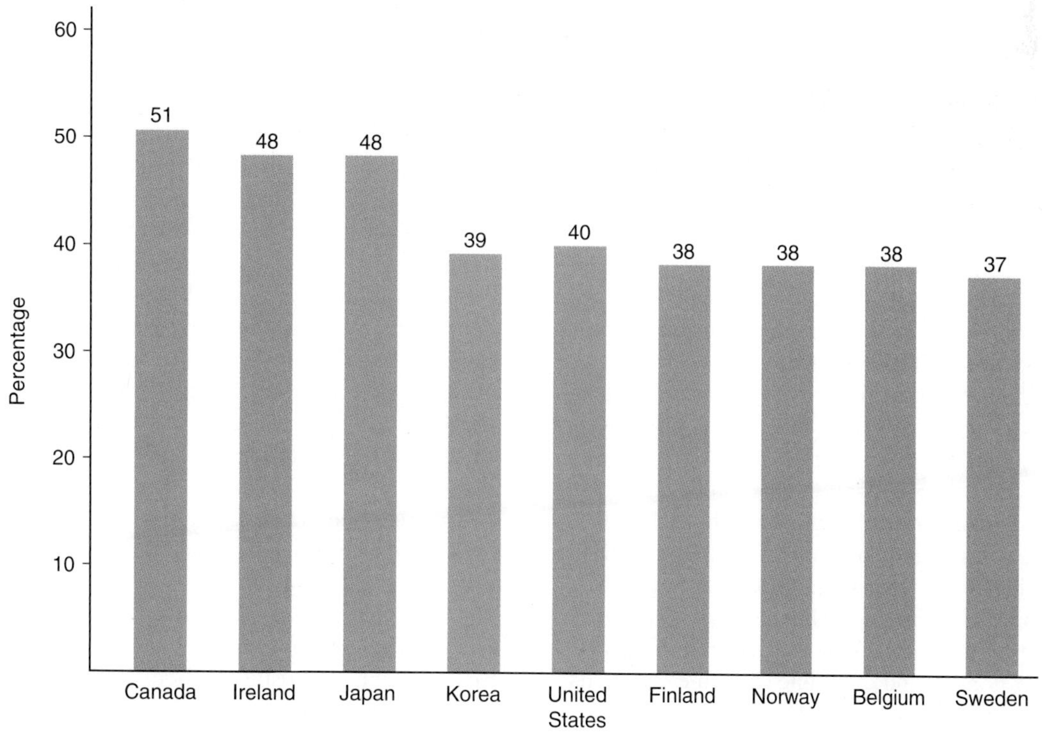

Source: OECD 2003, Table A2.3. Modified by author.

transmission of knowledge. Schools teach students such things as how to read, speak foreign languages, and repair automobiles. Education has another important manifest function: bestowing status. Because many believe this function is performed inequitably, it will be considered later, in the section on the conflict view of education.

In addition to these manifest functions, schools perform a number of *latent* functions: transmitting culture, promoting social and political integration, maintaining social control, and serving as agents of change.

Transmitting Culture

As a social institution, education performs a conservative function—transmitting the dominant culture. Schooling exposes each generation of young people to the existing beliefs, norms, and values of their culture. In our society, we learn respect for social control and reverence for established institutions, such as religion, the family, and government. Of course, this is true in many other cultures as well.

In Great Britain, the transmission of the dominant culture in schools goes far beyond learning about monarchs and prime ministers. In 1996, the government's chief curriculum adviser—noting the need to fill a void left by the diminishing authority of the Church of England—proposed that British schools socialize students into a set of core values. These include honesty, respect for others, politeness, a sense of fair play, forgiveness, punctuality, nonviolent behaviour, patience, faithfulness, and self-discipline (Charter and Sherman 1996).

Sometimes nations need to reassess their ways of transmitting culture. When an economic crisis hit Asian countries in 1997 and 1998, many Asian students who had been studying abroad could no longer afford to do so. Now their home countries had to figure out how to accommodate thousands more students pursuing higher education at home. In South Korea, people also began to question the content of the curriculum. Their schools traditionally teach Confucian values with a focus on rote memorization. This leads to an emphasis on accumulating facts as opposed to using reasoning. Entrance to university turns on a highly competitive exam that tests knowledge of facts. Once in university, a student has virtually no opportunity to change his or her program, and the classes continue to rely on memorization. The combination of an economic crisis and growing complaints about the educational process has caused government officials to reevaluate the educational structure. Moreover, growth in juvenile crime, although low by our standards, has led the government to introduce a new civic education program emphasizing honesty and discipline (Institute of International Education 1998; Woodard 1998).

At all levels of the education system in Canada, controversy surrounds the exclusion from the curriculum of authors and historical figures who do not represent the dominant culture. Critics charge that standard academic curricula have failed to represent the important contributions of immigrants and Aboriginals, women and people of colour to history, literature, and other fields of study. Several underlying questions are raised by this debate and are still to be resolved: Which ideas and values are essential for instruction? Which cultures should be transmitted by the schools and postsecondary institutions of Canada?

Promoting Social and Political Integration

Many prestigious American universities require their first- and second-year students to live together on campus in order to foster a sense of community among diverse groups. Education serves the latent function of promoting social and political integration by transforming a population comprising diverse racial, ethnic, and religious groups into a society whose members share—to some extent—a common identity. Schools have historically played an important role in socializing the children of immigrants into the norms, values, and beliefs of the dominant culture. From a functionalist perspective, the common identity and social integration fostered by education contribute to societal stability and consensus (Touraine 1974).

In Canada, perhaps the most egregious example of an attempt to promote social integration through education is that of residential schools. Residential schools were established by the Canadian government and operated by the Roman Catholic, Anglican, United, and Presbyterian churches for the purpose of assimilating Aboriginal children into the dominant culture. Operating until the middle decades of the twentieth century, these schools had as their express purpose the goal of cultural assimilation. Aboriginal children were taken from their homes and forced to speak languages other than their own. In residential schools, they learned the values and norms of the dominant European groups and at the same time learned that their own culture was inferior and thus needed to be replaced. In this process of promoting conformity to the dominant culture, many Aboriginal children were emotionally, physically, and sexually abused by those operating the residential schools. Today, many First Nations adults are enduring difficult lives because of their traumatizing experiences as children in these schools.

pp. 207–210

The attempt on the part of schools to promote social and political integration has resulted in Innu children today being taught using methods that are inappropriate to their culture (*The Globe and Mail* 2004b). A report by the federal Government of Canada in 2004 stated that the education system was failing Innu children miserably by, among other things, not properly training teachers to deal with language and cultural differences.

Maintaining Social Control

In performing the manifest function of transmitting knowledge, schools go far beyond teaching such skills as reading, writing, and mathematics. Like other social institutions, such as the family and religion, education prepares young people to lead productive and orderly lives as adults by introducing them to the norms, values, and sanctions of the larger society.

Through the exercise of social control, schools teach students various skills and values essential to their future positions within the labour force. They learn punctuality, discipline, scheduling, and responsible work habits, as well as how to negotiate their way through the complexities of a bureaucratic organization. As a social institution, education reflects the interests of the family and in turn prepares young people for their participation in yet another social institution—the economy. Students are being trained for what is ahead, whether it be the assembly line or a physician's office. In effect, then, schools serve as a transitional agent of social control—between parents and employers in the life cycle of most individuals (Bowles and Gintis 1976; M. Cole 1988).

Schools direct and even restrict students' aspirations in a manner that reflects societal values and prejudices. School administrators may allocate funds for athletic programs while giving much less support to music, art, and dance. Teachers and guidance counsellors may encourage male students to pursue careers in the sciences but steer equally talented female students into careers as early childhood teachers. Such socialization into traditional gender roles can be viewed as a form of social control.

pp. 83–84

Serving as an Agent of Change

So far, we have focused on conservative functions of education—on its role in transmitting the existing culture, promoting social and political integration, and maintaining social control. Yet education can also stimulate or bring about desired social change. Sex education classes were introduced in public schools in response to higher rates of sexual activity among teens. Special "girls only" science and mathematics class were created in response to girls' low participation rates in such fields as science, technology, and engineering. Anti-racism programs in schools have responded to the prevalence of racism in schools themselves and in society in general.

Education also promotes social change by serving as a meeting ground where distinctive beliefs and traditions can be shared. In 1998, there were approximately 36 000 international students in Canada, enrolled in undergraduate and graduate programs, either on a part-time or full-time basis. Students from France represented the largest group of international students, followed by those from the United States and then China (Association of Universities and Colleges of Canada 2001). Cross-cultural exchanges between these visitors and citizens of Canada ultimately broaden the perspective of both the hosts and their guests. The same is certainly true when students from Canada attend schools in Europe, Latin America, Africa, or the Far East.

Numerous sociological studies have revealed that increased numbers of years of formal schooling are associated with openness to new ideas and more liberal social and political viewpoints. Sociologist Robin Williams points out that better educated people tend to have greater access to factual information, more diverse opinions, and the ability to make subtle distinctions in analysis. Formal education stresses both the importance of qualifying statements (in place of broad generalizations) and the need at least to question (rather than simply accept) established truths and practices. As we saw in

In response to teen pregnancy rates, many schools have begun to offer sex education courses that promote abstinence. When schools attempt to remedy negative social trends, they are serving as agents of social change.

Chapter 2, the scientific method relies on *testing* hypotheses and reflects the questioning spirit that characterizes modern education (R. Williams et al. 1964).

Conflict View

Sociologist Christopher Hurn (1985) has compared the functionalist and conflict views of schooling. According to Hurn, the functionalist perspective portrays contemporary education as basically benign. For example, it argues that schools rationally sort and select students for future high-status positions, thereby meeting society's need for talented and expert personnel. By contrast, the conflict perspective views education as an instrument of elite domination. Schools convince subordinate groups of their inferiority, reinforce existing social class inequality, and discourage alternative and more democratic visions of society.

Criticizing the functionalist view, conflict theorists argue that the educational system socializes students into values dictated by the powerful, that schools stifle individualism and creativity in the name of maintaining order, and that the level of change promoted by education is relatively insignificant. From a conflict perspective, the inhibiting effects of education are particularly apparent in the "hidden curriculum" as well as in the differential way in which status is bestowed.

The Hidden Curriculum

Schools are highly bureaucratic organizations. Many teachers rely on the rules and regulations of schools to maintain order. Unfortunately, the need for control and discipline can take precedence over the learning process. Teachers may focus on obedience to the rules as an end in itself. If this occurs, students and teachers alike become victims of what Philip Jackson (1968) has called the *hidden curriculum* (see also P. Freire 1970).

The term ***hidden curriculum*** refers to standards of behaviour that are deemed proper by society and are taught subtly in schools. According to this curriculum, children must not speak until the teacher calls on them and must regulate their activities according to the clock or bells. In addition, they are expected to concentrate on their own work rather than assist other students who learn more slowly. A hidden curriculum is evident in schools around the world. For example, Japanese schools offer guidance sessions during lunch that seek to improve the classroom experience but also to develop healthy living skills. In effect, these sessions instil values and encourage behaviour useful for the Japanese business world, such as self-discipline and openness to group problem solving and decision making (Okano and Tsuchiya 1999).

In a classroom overly focused on obedience, value is placed on pleasing the teacher and remaining quiet—rather than on creative thought and academic learning (Leacock 1969). Habitual obedience to authority may result in the type of distressing behaviour documented by Stanley Milgram in his classic obedience studies.

p. 84

Bestowal of Status

Both functionalist and conflict theorists agree that education performs the important function of bestowing status. As noted earlier, an increasing proportion of people in Canada are obtaining high school diplomas; postsecondary certificates, diplomas, and degrees; and advanced professional degrees. From a functionalist perspective, this widening bestowal of status is beneficial not only to particular recipients but also to society as a whole. In the view of Kingsley Davis and Wilbert Moore (1945), society must distribute its members among a variety of social positions. Education can contribute to this process by sorting people into appropriate levels and courses of study that will prepare them for appropriate positions within the labour force.

pp. 167–168

Conflict sociologists are far more critical of the *differential* way education bestows status. They stress that schools sort pupils according to social class background. Although the educational system helps certain poor children to move into middle-class professional positions, it denies most disadvantaged children the same educational opportunities afforded children of the affluent. In this way, schools tend to preserve social class inequalities in each new generation (Giroux 1988; Labaree 1986; Mingle 1987).

Statistics Canada's Pan-Canadian Education Indicators Program reports on the many facets of education in Canada. One finding of the research has to do with educational attainment and family socioeconomic status, as measured by quartiles. When assessing the background of those who completed high school, the data indicate that 34 percent of those in the lowest quartile had not completed high school, compared with 23 percent of those in the upper quartile. At the same time, a gap exists in university participation rates between persons from the lowest and the highest quartile. Fewer than 20 percent of young people from the lowest quartile attend university, compared with 40 percent of those from the highest quartile (CESC 2000).

Even a single school can reinforce class differences by putting students in tracks. The term ***tracking*** refers to the practice of placing students in specific curriculum groups on the basis of test scores and other criteria. Tracking begins very early in the classroom, often in reading groups during Grade 1. These tracks can reinforce the disadvantages that children from less affluent families may face if they haven't been exposed to reading materials and

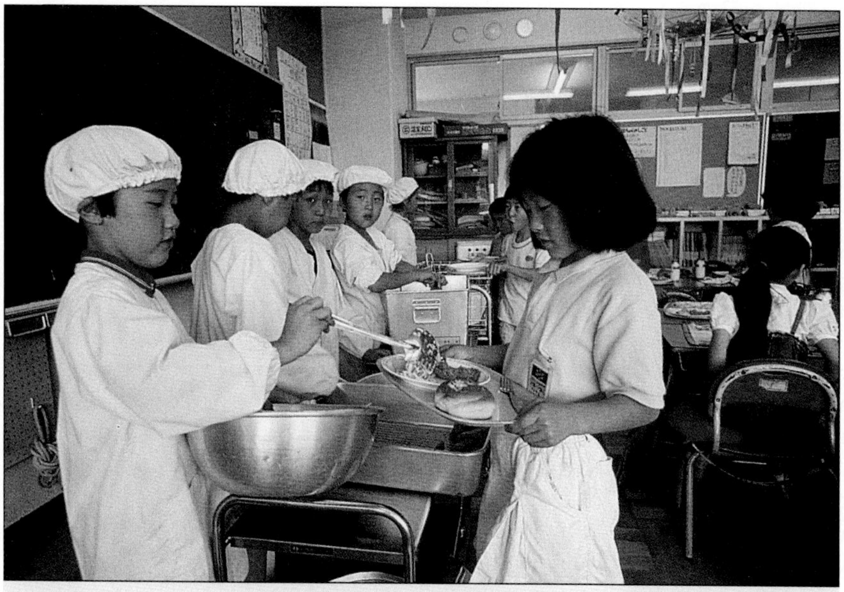

In Tokyo's public schools, students learn adult responsibilities early on. In this classroom, classmates take turns serving the lunch.

computers and other forms of educational stimulation in their homes during their early childhood years.

Tracking and differential access to higher education are evident in many nations around the world. Japan's educational system mandates equality in school funding and insists that all schools use the same textbooks. Nevertheless, only the more affluent Japanese families can afford to send their children to *juku*, or cram schools. These afternoon schools prepare high school students for examinations that determine admission into prestigious colleges (Efron 1997).

According to a study of teachers' attitudes toward students in the "outback" in rural Australia—an area where sheep vastly outnumber people—students are being prepared to stay in the "bush." Only a small minority seek out electives geared toward preparation for university. However, beginning in the 1980s, parents questioned this agriculture-oriented curriculum in view of rural Australia's declining employment base (M. Henry 1989).

Conflict theorists hold that the educational inequalities resulting from tracking are designed to meet the needs of modern capitalist societies. Samuel Bowles and Herbert Gintis (1976) argue that capitalism requires a skilled, disciplined labour force and that the educational system of the United States is structured with this objective in mind. Citing numerous studies, they offer support for what they call the ***correspondence principle.***

According to this approach, schools with students from different social classes promote the values expected of individuals in each class and perpetuate social class divisions from one generation to the next. Thus, working-class children, assumed to be destined for subordinate positions, are more likely to be placed in high school vocational and general tracks, which emphasize close supervision and compliance with authority. By contrast, young people from more affluent families are largely directed to university preparatory tracks, which stress leadership and decision-making skills—corresponding to their likely futures. Although the correspondence principle continues to be persuasive, researchers have noted that the impact of race and gender on students' educational experiences may even overshadow that of class (M. Cole 1988).

Conflict views of the development of the Canadian school system have included the idea that urban-based priorities were imposed on rural schools because of the power of the industrial and mercantile elites located nearby, in local towns (H. Johnson 1960).

Interactionist View

In George Bernard Shaw's play *Pygmalion*, later adapted into the hit Broadway musical *My Fair Lady*, flower girl Eliza Doolittle is transformed into a "lady" by Professor Henry Higgins. He changes her manner of speech and teaches her the etiquette of "high society." When she is introduced into society as an aristocrat, she is readily accepted. People treat her as a "lady" and she responds as one.

The labelling approach suggests that if we treat people in particular ways, they may fulfil our expectations. Children labelled as "troublemakers" come to view themselves as delinquents. A dominant group's stereotyping of racial minorities may limit their opportunities to break away from expected roles.

pp. 148–149

Can this labelling process operate in the classroom? Because of their focus on microlevel classroom dynamics, interactionist researchers have been particularly interested in this question. Howard Becker (1952) studied public schools in low-income and more affluent areas of Chicago. He noticed that administrators expected less of students from poor neighbourhoods, and he wondered if teachers were accepting this view. Subsequently, in *Pygmalion in the Classroom*, psychologist Robert Rosenthal and school principal Lenore Jacobson and Elisha Babad

(1968) documented what they referred to as a ***teacher-expectancy effect***—the impact that a teacher's expectations about a student's performance may have on the student's actual achievements. This appears to be especially true in lower grades (through Grade 3) (Brint 1998).

Between 1965 and 1966, children in a San Francisco elementary school were administered a verbal and reasoning pretest. Rosenthal and Jacobson then *randomly* selected 20 percent of the sample and designated them as "spurters"—children of whom teachers could expect superior performance. On a later verbal and reasoning test, the spurters were found to score significantly higher than before. Moreover, teachers evaluated them as more interesting, more curious, and better adjusted than their classmates. These results were striking. Apparently, teachers' perceptions that these students were exceptional led to noticeable improvements in performance.

Studies have revealed that teachers wait longer for an answer from a student believed to be a high achiever and are more likely to give such children a second chance. In one experiment, teachers' expectations were even shown to have an impact on students' athletic achievements. Teachers obtained better athletic performance—as measured in the number of sit-ups or push-ups performed—from those students of whom they *expected* higher numbers (R. Rosenthal, Babad, and Jacobson 1985).

Despite these findings, some researchers continue to question the accuracy of this self-fulfilling prophecy because of the difficulties in defining and measuring teacher expectancy. Further studies are needed to clarify the relationship between teacher expectations and actual student performance. Nevertheless, interactionists emphasize that ability alone may be less predictive of academic success than one might think (Brint 1998).

Feminist Views

In 1928, in her book *A Room of One's Own*, Virginia Woolf advocated the value of educational reform so that the female student could "live and write her poetry"(Woolf 1977:123). She contended that even if someone had to struggle in "poverty and obscurity" to bring about educational reform on behalf of girls and women, it was worthwhile. Although feminist perspectives on education are diverse, today many share the view that educational institutions must attempt to prevent gendered patterns of inequality found in the larger society from being perpetuated in the classroom.

Feminist perspectives on education raise a wide range of concerns stemming from the historical exclusion of girls and women in education and the persistent "chilly climate" that many females experience in educational institutions that treat them as outsiders. Some perspectives have articulated the need to understand how gender plays a role in the educational experiences of girls and women from elementary school to university, and how these experiences are connected to such factors as race, class, and age (Mandell 1998). The "hidden curriculum" of the school system contributes to gender socialization through classroom interaction patterns that give greater "air time" and praise to male students (D. Richardson and Robinson 1993). The hidden curriculum also uses language that is not gender-inclusive, curricula that are androcentric, and role models of male principals and female elementary school teachers that reinforce traditional patterns of male dominance and authority (Rees 1990).

Since the 1970s, Canadian universities and colleges have been developing women's studies programs that provide feminist frameworks for research, teaching, and educational reform.

SCHOOLS AS FORMAL ORGANIZATIONS

In many respects, today's schools, when viewed as an example of a formal organization, are similar to factories, hospitals, and business firms. Like these organizations, schools do not operate autonomously; they are influenced by the market of potential students. This is especially true of private schools. Currently, approximately 5 percent of students in Canada attend private schools (Mackie 2001). The parallels between schools and other types of formal organizations will become more apparent as we examine teaching as an occupational role and the student subculture (Dougherty and Hammack 1992).

Teachers: Employees and Instructors

Whether they serve as instructors of preschoolers or graduate students, teachers are employees of formal organizations with bureaucratic structures. There is an inherent conflict in serving as a professional within a bureaucracy. The organization follows the principles of hierarchy and expects adherence to its rules, but professionalism demands the individual responsibility of the practitioner. This conflict is very real for teachers, who experience all the positive and negative consequences of working in bureaucracies.

A teacher undergoes many perplexing stresses every day. Although teachers' academic assignments have become more specialized, the demands on their time remain diverse and contradictory. There are conflicts inherent in serving as an instructor, a disciplinarian, and an employee of a school district at the same time. For university professors, different types of role strain arise. Although formally employed as teachers, they are also expected to work on committees and are encouraged to conduct scholarly research. In many universities, security of position (tenure) is based primarily on the publication of original scholarship. As a result, instructors must fulfil goals that compete for time.

University professors rarely have to take on the role of disciplinarian, but this task has become a major focus of schoolteachers' work in such countries as the United States. Order is needed to establish an environment in which students can actually learn. Some observers believe that schools have been the scene of increasingly violent misbehaviour in recent years, although these concerns may be overblown (see Box 12-2).

Canada is becoming an increasingly "schooled society" (Guppy and Davies 1998), which will contribute to the employment prospects of students wanting to become teachers. The increasing proportion of our population between the ages of 5 and 19, the resultant increase in the number of schools, and overall increases in enrolments in postsecondary education, contributes to this trend (McVey and Kalbach 1995). As well, the demographic composition of teachers is changing, reflecting the aging population; a greater number of retiring teachers will need to be replaced in the near future. This trend is also occurring in the United States where, because of teacher shortages in some regions, school boards are advertising for and recruiting teachers from Canada.

The status of any job reflects several factors, including the level of education required, the financial compensation, and the respect given the occupation within society. The teaching profession (see Table 8-1, page 172) is feeling pressure in all three of these areas. First, the amount of formal schooling required for teaching remains high, and now the public has begun to call for new competency examinations for teachers. Second, statistics demonstrate that teachers' salaries are significantly lower than those of many professionals and skilled workers. Wages differ by field of study; graduates of education and social science, who are disproportionately female, earn less, for example, than graduates of commerce and engineering, who are disproportionately male (Statistics Canada 1999c). Finally, as we have seen, the overall prestige of the teaching profession has declined in the last decade. Many teachers have become disappointed and frustrated and have left the educational world for careers in other professions. Many are simply "burned out" by the severe demands, limited rewards, and general sense of alienation that they experience on the job.

p. 172

The Student Subculture

An important latent function of education relates directly to student life: Schools provide for students' social and recreational needs. Education helps toddlers and young children develop interpersonal skills that are essential during adolescence and adulthood. During high school and the years of postsecondary education, students may meet future partners and may establish lifelong friendships.

When people observe high schools and postsecondary institutions from the outside, students appear to constitute a cohesive, uniform group. However, the student subculture is actually much more complex and diverse. High school cliques and social groups may crop up based on race, social class, physical attractiveness, placement in courses, athletic ability, and leadership roles in the school and community. In his classic community study of "Elmtown," August Hollingshead (1975) found some 259 distinct cliques in a single high school. These cliques, whose average size was five, were centred on the school itself, on recreational activities, and on religious and community groups.

We can find a similar diversity at the postsecondary level. Burton Clark and Martin Trow (1966) and, more recently, Helen Lefkowitz Horowitz (1987) have identified distinctive subcultures among postsecondary students. Here are four ideal types of subcultures that come out of their analyses:

1. The *collegiate* subculture focuses on having fun and socializing. These students define what constitutes a "reasonable" amount of academic work (and what amount of work is "excessive" and leads to being labelled as a "grind"). Members of the collegiate subculture have little commitment to academic pursuits.
2. By contrast, the *academic* subculture identifies with the intellectual concerns of the faculty and values knowledge for its own sake.
3. The *vocational* subculture is primarily interested in career prospects and views college or university as means of obtaining degrees that are essential for advancement.
4. Finally, the *nonconformist* subculture is hostile to the university or college environment and seeks out ideas that may or may not relate to studies. It may find outlets through campus publications or issue-oriented groups.

Each student is eventually exposed to these competing subcultures and must determine which (if any) seems most in line with his or her feelings and interests.

The typology used by these researchers reminds us that school is a complex social organization—almost like a community with different neighbourhoods. Of course, these four subcultures are not the only ones evident on postsecondary campuses. For example, one might find subcultures of mature students and part-time students.

Research in Action 12-2 Violence in the Schools

Littleton Colorado, and Taber, Alberta, were two relatively unexceptional locations before they became associated with school killings. In both communities, students died after being shot by fellow students. Now, the schools resonate with the sound of gunshots, of kids killing kids on school grounds. In addition to killings like these, school-based violence can take the form of minor discipline problems (e.g., disobedience, taunting, and teasing), obscene gesturing, verbal and physical threats, aggression, bullying, assault (with or without a weapon), vandalism, extortion, and gang-related activities (Day et al. 1995). As a result, people no longer perceive schools as safe havens. But how accurate is that impression?

In Canada, there is growing concern on the part of school officials surrounding the problem of violence in schools. Many researchers, however, disagree with school officials about its prevalence. There are those who suggest that violence in our schools is relatively low key and that we should not assume that what is happening in American schools is happening here (W. West 1993). Some studies actually suggest that school-based violence is decreasing (Fitzpatrick 1994; W. West 1993). Others point to an increase in certain forms of school-based violence. One study surveying 881 schools, conducted by the Ontario Teachers' Federation, reported a 150 percent increase in such incidents as biting, kicking, punching, and using weapons over the period from 1987 to 1990 (Roher 1993). This study's findings, however, must be viewed with caution as the number of schools supplying data for the 1987–1990 period varied and a significant number of schools reported that there were no assaults (Day et al. 1995).

Research on the problem of school-based violence indicates great regional variation. For example, students in the Niagara region of Ontario and in Nova Scotia did not consider violence a particular problem (Robb 1993; Rodgers 1993). Though there are obviously many opinions on the prevalence of school-based violence in Canada, one observation does not seem to be disputed: there is a greater scope and severity of youth violence spilling over into the schools in the United States than in this country.

Even in the United States, however, studies of school violence put the recent spate of school killings in perspective:

- A child has less than a one-in-a-million chance of being killed at school.
- The number of people shot and killed in school in the 1997–1998 school year was 40 (including adults), about average over the last six years.
- According to the Center for Disease Control in Atlanta, 99 percent of violent deaths of school-aged children in 1992–1994 occurred *outside* school grounds.
- Fewer students are now being found with guns in school.
- Data from the National School Safety Center at Pepperdine University in the United States suggest there was a 27 percent decline in school-associated violent deaths from 1992 through the 1997–1998 school year.
- Twenty-three times more children are killed in gun *accidents* than in school killings.

Sociologist Joe Feagin has studied a distinctive collegiate subculture: black students at predominantly white American universities. These students must function academically and socially within universities where there are few black faculty members or black administrators, where harassment of blacks by campus police is common, and where the curricula place little emphasis on black contributions. Feagin (1989:11) suggests that "for minority students life at a predominantly white college or university means long-term encounters with *pervasive whiteness.*" In Feagin's view, black students at such institutions experience both blatant and subtle racial discrimination, which has a cumulative impact that can seriously damage the students' confidence (see also Feagin, Vera, and Imani 1996).

Adult Education

Picture a college, university-college, or university student. Most likely, you will imagine someone under 25 years of age. This reflects the belief that education is something experienced and completed during the first two or three decades of life and rarely supplemented after that. However, many postsecondary institutions have witnessed a dramatic increase in the number of older students pursuing higher education. These older students are more likely to be female than is the typical 19- or 20-year-old postsecondary student. Viewed from a conflict perspective, it is not surprising that women are overrepresented among older students; they are the most likely to miss out on higher education the first time around (Best and Eberhard 1990).

Schools, then, are safer than neighbourhoods, but people still are unnerved by the perception of an alarming rise in schoolyard violence that has been generated by heavy media coverage of the recent incidents. Some conflict theorists object to the huge outcry about recent violence in schools. After all, they note, violence in and around city schools has a long history. It seems that only when middle-class, white children are the victims does school violence become a plank on the national policy agenda. When violence hits the middle class, the problem is viewed not as an extension of delinquency but as a structural issue in need of remedies.

Meanwhile, feminists observe that the offenders are male and, in some instances, the victims are disproportionately female. The precipitating factor for violence is often a broken-off dating relationship—yet another example of violence of men against women (or, in this case, boys against girls).

Increasingly, efforts to prevent school violence are focusing on the ways in which the socialization of young people contributes to violence. For example, the *Journal of the American Medical Association* published a study of Second Step, a violence prevention curriculum for elementary school students that teaches social skills related to anger management, impulse control, and empathy. The study evaluated the impact of the program on urban and suburban elementary school students and found that it appeared to lead to a moderate decrease in physically aggressive behaviour and an increase in neutral and prosocial behaviour in school.

A national study done in Canada, providing a snapshot of violence prevention programs in Canadian schools (Day et. al. 1995), concluded that the school boards' response to school violence must be one in which students themselves are involved in the development of policies. School boards, the study concluded, must not take the view that certain youth are "out of hand" and need to be controlled; rather, they must make a strong effort to promote a prosocial environment, develop comprehensive policies, establish developmentally appropriate consequences for certain behaviours, and institute a multifaceted violence-prevention program (on both the macro- and the microlevels).

In one province, at least, violence in schools has received attention from politicians. In 2004, the Ontario government announced the formation of a committee—the Safe Schools Action Groups—and $9 million for school safety audits, security access equipment, and antibullying programs and hotlines (Moore 2004).

Applying Theory

1. Has a violent episode ever occurred at your school? If so, how did students react? Do you feel safer at school than at home, as experts say you are?
2. What steps have administrators at your school taken to prevent violence? Have they been effective, or should other steps be taken?
3. How might some feminist sociologists study the issue of school violence?

Sources: Bowles 1999; Chaddock 1998; Day et al. 1995; Department of Education 1999; Donohue, Schiraldi, and Ziedenberg 1998; Fitzpatrick 1994; Grossman et al. 1997; O. Moore 2004; National Center for Education Statistics 1998; Robb 1993; Rodgers 1993; Roher 1993; S. Schaefer 1996; W. West 1993.

The 1998 General Social Survey by Statistics Canada found that 15 percent of Canadians aged 25 and over reported that they had taken a course or training session in the last month. As well, in 2000–2001 approximately 29 percent of undergraduates were 25 years of age or older (Statistics Canada 2003k). Obviously, sociological models of the postsecondary subculture will have to be revised significantly in light of such changes. Moreover, as the age of the "typical" university student increases, there will be a growing need for on-campus child care.

pp. 87–89

One explanation for the adult education boom is that society is changing rapidly in an age of technological innovation and a growing knowledge-based economy. Business firms have come to accept the view of education as lifelong and may encourage (or require) employees to learn job-related skills. Thus, secretaries are sent to special schools to be trained to use the latest computer software. Realtors attend classes to learn about alternative forms of financing for home buyers. In occupation after occupation, longtime workers and professionals are going back to school to adapt to the new demands of their jobs. Taking a conflict perspective, Canadian sociologist David Livingstone (1999) argues that despite Canadians' growing technological proficiency and growing levels of training and education, employers are failing to fully utilize their skills, thus contributing to "underemployment."

Not all adult education happens at the formal level. According to the 1998 General Social Survey, more than

Today, many classrooms in Canada integrate students with disabilities and those without, contributing to greater diversity of the student population.

six million Canadians aged 25 and over reported that they engaged in "informal" learning during the previous month. This type of learning involves self-directed activity done at the learner's own time and pace that aim to "enrich their ability to function within their communities and homes, to deal with family issues and enjoy their leisure time. Increasingly, people are also encouraged to view lifelong learning as a means of combating the mental deterioration associated with aging" (Silver, Williams, and McOrmond 2001:19). Although gender had little effect on whether or not a person was likely to study informally, gendered patterns of subject interest were found to exist. Women were more likely to study health and child care than were men, while men were more likely to study trade-related subjects (C. Silver et al. 2001).

Home Schooling

When most people think of school, they think of bricks and mortar and the teachers, administrators, and other employees who staff school buildings. But for an increasing number of students in Canada and the United States, home is the classroom and the teacher is a parent. Estimates of the number of children being home schooled in Canada vary. The Home-School Legal Defense Association (HSLDA) estimates the number to be as high as 80 000, while Statistics Canada reported 19 114 registered home-schooled students in 1997 (Wake 2000). Statistics Canada warned, however, that those figures underestimate the total number, since many home schools are not registered.

In the past, families that taught their children at home lived in isolated environments or held strict religious views at odds with the secular environment of public schools. But today, home schooling is attracting a broader range of families not necessarily tied to organized religion. Poor academic quality, threat of school strikes, peer pressure, and school violence are motivating many parents to teach their children at home. In addition, the growing presence of computers in the home and the availability of educational resources online have motivated some parents to educate their children at home. Rates of home schooling in Canada have increased every year since 1980. The greatest increases have been in Western Canada, where the number of registered home-schoolers grew by 10 percent between 1995–1996 and 1996–1997 (Wake 2000).

Although supporters of home schooling feel that children can do just as well or better in home schools as in public schools, critics counter that because home-schooled children are isolated from the larger community, they lose an important chance to improve their socialization skills. But proponents of home schooling claim their children benefit from contact with others besides their own age group. They also see home schools as a good alternative for children who suffer from attention deficit disorder (ADD) and learning disorders (LDs). Such children often do better in smaller classes, which present fewer distractions to disturb their concentration (National Homeschool Association 1999).

Quality control is an issue in home schooling. Although home schooling is legal in Canada, the provincial and territorial governments require that parents register their children. In Alberta, where home schooling is particularly popular, estimates point to a high number of unregistered children—children the government cannot monitor in terms of curricular and academic achievement. Many of these children are from families where the motivating factor to home school is religion; these families believe that the secular school system does not reflect their values, particularly those concerning abortion, homosexuality, and evolution. In 1988, Canada's Supreme Court ruled that the province of Alberta had a "compelling interest" in ensuring that the children of that province were properly educated (Mitchell 1999). This would mean making sure that home-schooled children followed a government-approved curriculum and were tested annually according to provincial standards. Despite the court ruling, many Christian parents continue to believe that the government should not be in the business of monitoring their children's education and that the values of secular education are not those to which they want their children exposed. Home schooling works, particularly for those who have made a commitment to it (D. Calhoun 2000; Matthews 1999; Paulson 2000).

Who are the people who are running home schools? In general, they tend to have higher-than-average incomes and educational levels. Most are two-parent families, and their children watch less television than average—both factors that are likely to support superior educational performance. The same students, with the same types of family and the same support from their parents, would probably do just as well in the public schools. As research has repeatedly shown, small classes are better than big classes, and strong parental and community involvement is key (L. Schnaiberg 1999).

Home schooling allows parents to integrate religion into their children's studies if they choose, but controversy brews when public schools do so, as the social policy section shows.

SOCIAL POLICY AND RELIGION

Religion in the Schools

The Issue

Should public schools be allowed to sponsor organized prayers in the classroom? Should the Lord's Prayer be part of the agenda at weekly school assemblies? How about reading Bible verses? Or just a collective moment of silence? Can public school athletes offer up a group prayer in a team huddle? Should students be able to initiate voluntary prayers at school events? Should a school be allowed to post the Ten Commandments in a hallway? Each of these situations has been an object of great dissension among those who see a role for prayer in public schools and those who want to maintain a strict separation of church and state.

Another area of controversy centres on the teaching of theories about the origin of humans and of the universe. Mainstream scientific thinking theorizes that humans evolved over billions of years from one-celled organisms and that the universe came into being 15 billion years ago as a result of a "big bang." But these theories are challenged by people who hold to the biblical account of the creation of humans and the universe some 10 000 years ago—a viewpoint known as ***creationism.*** Creationists want their theory taught in the schools as the only one or, at the very least, as an alternative to the theory of evolution.

Who has the right to decide these issues? And what is considered the "right" decision? Religion in the public schools constitutes one of the thorniest issues in Canadian public policy today.

The Setting

In Canada, the Charter of Rights and Freedoms provides for freedom of religion. The Charter, along with the Canadian Constitution, protects the rights and privileges held by denominational schools at the time of Confederation in 1867. This has meant that in addition to the public school system, some provinces and territories fund Catholic school education, while Quebec, where the majority of schools are Catholic, funds Protestant education. In 1999, a government-mandated task force in Quebec recommended that the Catholic and Protestant status for public schools be abolished and replaced with "secular" public schools. In the case of nondenominational or so-called secular schools, where explicit religious affiliation is not established, the issue of religious content in the form of prayers and Bible readings has become a contentious one.

Quebec is not the only province to experience these tensions in the secular schools. In 1999, Saskatchewan became the fourth province in Canada to oppose prayer in public schools. In 1993, a complaint by nine Saskatoon parents launched a challenge against the 100-year-old tradition of encouraging public school teachers to say the Lord's Prayer in classrooms and at assemblies. The Saskatchewan Act, part of the provincial constitution, permitted prayer and Bible readings in the public schools. The group of nine Saskatoon parents, which included Muslims, Jews, Unitarians, and atheists, complained that this practice violated the Saskatchewan

Human Rights Code. More specifically, they argued, it violated their children's (and other children's) right to freedom of conscience and that students were being denied the right to enjoy an education without discrimination because of creed or religion. As a result, in 1999, a board of inquiry ruled that it was discriminatory to require recitation of the Lord's Prayer in Saskatoon classrooms and assemblies.

Sociological Insights

Supporters of school prayer and of creationism feel that strict court rulings force too great a separation between what Émile Durkheim called the *sacred* and the *profane.* They insist that use of nondenominational prayer can in no way lead to the establishment of an ecclesia in Canada. Moreover, they believe that school prayer—and the teaching of creationism—can provide the spiritual guidance and socialization that many children today do not receive from parents or regular church attendance. Many communities also believe that schools should transmit the dominant culture of Canada by encouraging prayer.

According to a 1998 General Social Survey, 55 percent of adults in the United States disapprove of a Supreme Court ruling against the required reading of the Lord's Prayer or Bible verses in public schools. A national survey in 1999 showed that 68 percent of the public favours teaching creationism along with evolution in public schools, and 40 percent favours teaching *only* creationism. No other Western society has such a large body of opinion supporting views that depart so much from contemporary scientific understanding. Perhaps this is a reflection of a deep-rooted and enduring strain of religious fundamentalism in the United States and the fact that religious belief in general is stronger in the United States than in Canada and other Western societies (Davis and Smith 1999; G. Johnson 1999; Lewis 1999).

Opponents of school prayer argue that a religious majority in a community might impose religious viewpoints specific to its faith, at the expense of religious minorities. Viewed from a conflict perspective, organized school prayer could reinforce the religious beliefs, rituals, and interests of the powerful; violate the rights of the powerless; increase religious dissension; and threaten the multiculturalism of Canada. These critics question whether school prayer can remain truly voluntary. Drawing on the interactionist perspective and small-group research, they suggest that children will face enormous social pressure to conform to the beliefs and practices of a religious majority.

Policy Initiatives

The latest case involving the Saskatoon Board of Education provides a good example of how in some communities policymakers are trying to find a compromise between those who want prayer in schools and those who do not. In 2001, two years after the Lord's Prayer was removed from the daily routine of public schools, the Saskatoon public school board is considering a Christian education program for children of religious parents. Modelled after the Logos Christian Education program already in place in Edmonton public schools, Christian students would receive instruction in a separate classroom with a religious environment. Opposition to the proposal has been raised by those who feel that the Logos program would divide students along religious lines and undermine the basis of the public school system.

The activism of religious fundamentalists in the nation's public school system raises a more general question: Whose ideas and values deserve a hearing in classrooms? Critics see this campaign as one step toward sectarian religious control of public education. They worry that, at some point in the future, teachers may not be able to use books, or make statements, that conflict with fundamentalist interpretations of the Bible. For advocates of a liberal education who are deeply committed to intellectual (and religious) diversity, this is a genuinely frightening prospect.

Applying Theory

1. Do you think promoting religious observance is a legitimate function of the social institution of education?
2. Do you agree with a conflict view on the issue of organized school prayer?
3. Are there functions served by Christian fundamentalists and their allies attempting to reshape public education in Canada?

CHAPTER RESOURCES

Summary

Religion and ***education*** are cultural universals, found throughout the world, although in varied forms. This chapter examined the dimensions and functions of religion, types of religious organizations, sociological views of education, and schools as examples of formal organizations.

1. Émile Durkheim stressed the social impact of religion and attempted to understand individual religious behaviour within the context of the larger society.
2. Religion serves the functions of integrating people in a diverse society and providing social support in time of need.
3. Max Weber saw a connection between religious allegiance and capitalistic behaviour through a religious orientation known as the ***Protestant ethic.***
4. ***Liberation theology*** uses the church in a political effort to alleviate poverty and social injustice.
5. From a Marxist point of view, religion serves to reinforce the social control of those in power. It lessens the possibility of collective political action that can end capitalist oppression and transform society.
6. Religious behaviour is expressed through ***beliefs, rituals,*** and ***religious experience.***
7. Sociologists have identified four basic types of religious organization: the ***ecclesia,*** the ***denomination,*** the ***sect,*** and the ***new religious movement (NRM)*** or ***cult.*** Advances in communication have led to a new type of church organization—the electronic church.
8. Transmission of knowledge and bestowal of status are manifest functions of ***education.*** Among its latent functions are transmitting culture, promoting social and political integration, maintaining social control, and serving as an agent of social change.
9. In the view of conflict theorists, education serves as an instrument of elite domination through the ***hidden curriculum*** and by bestowing status unequally.
10. The ***teacher-expectancy effect*** can sometimes have an impact on a student's actual achievements.
11. For more than three decades, the proportion of older adults enrolled in Canadian postsecondary institutions has been rising steadily, in part because of sweeping changes in business, industry, and technology. For many Canadians, education has become a lifelong pursuit.
12. Home schooling has become a viable alternative to traditional public and private schools. More than 19 000 children in Canada are now educated at home.
13. How much religion—if any—should be permitted in the schools is a matter of debate in Canadian society today.

Critical Thinking Questions

1. From a conflict point of view, explain how religion could be used to bring about social change.
2. Why is it so difficult for women to become leaders of religious organizations?
3. What are the functions and dysfunctions of tracking in schools? Viewed from an interactionist perspective, how would tracking of high school students influence the interactions between students and teachers? In what ways might tracking have positive and negative impacts on the self-concepts of various students?
4. Why are some religions granted greater social approval or higher status than are others?

Key Terms

Correspondence principle The tendency of schools to promote the values expected of individuals in each social class and to prepare students for the types of jobs typically held by members of their class. (page 287)

Creationism A literal interpretation of the Bible regarding the creation of humanity and the universe used to argue that evolution should not be presented as established scientific fact. (293)

Denomination A large, organized religion not officially linked with the state or government. (279)

Ecclesia A religious organization that claims to include most or all of the members of a society and is recognized as the national or official religion. (279)

Education A formal process of learning in which some people consciously teach while others adopt the social role of learner. (271)

Hidden curriculum Standards of behaviour that are deemed proper by society and are taught subtly in schools. (286)

Liberation theology Use of a church, primarily Roman Catholicism, in a political effort to eliminate poverty, discrimination, and other forms of injustice evident in a secular society. (275)

Megachurches Large worship centres affiliated only loosely, if at all, with existing denominations. (280)

New religious movement (NRM) or **cult** A generally small, secretive religious group that represents either a new religion or a major innovation of an existing faith. (281)

Profane The ordinary and commonplace elements of life, as distinguished from the sacred. (273)

Protestant ethic Max Weber's term for the disciplined work ethic, this-worldly concerns, and rational orientation to life emphasized by John Calvin and his followers. (275)

Religion A unified system of beliefs and practices relative to sacred things. (273)

Religious beliefs Statements to which members of a particular religion adhere. (277)

Religious experience The feeling or perception of being in direct contact with the ultimate reality, such as a divine being, or of being overcome with religious emotion. (278)

Religious rituals Practices required or expected of members of a faith. (277)

Sacred Elements beyond everyday life that inspire awe, respect, and even fear. (273)

Sect A relatively small religious group that has broken away from some other religious organization to renew what it views as the original vision of the faith. (280)

Secularization The process through which religion's influence on other social institutions diminishes. (271)

Teacher-expectancy effect The impact that a teacher's expectations about a student's performance may have on the student's actual achievements. (288)

Tracking The practice of placing students in specific curriculum groups on the basis of test scores and other criteria. (286)

Additional Readings

Adams, Michael. 2003. *Fire and Ice: The United States and Canada and the Myth of Converging Values.* Toronto: Penguin Press. A comparison of Canadian and American values, including those related to religion. Adam's book reveals that Canadians and Americans have different beliefs about the role religion plays in their daily lives.

Bibby, Reginald. 1996. *Fragmented Gods: The Poverty and Potential of Religion in Canada.* Toronto: Irwin. A comprehensive picture of religion in Canada and its potential in the future.

Guppy, Neil, and Scott Davies. 1998. *Education in Canada: Recent Trends and Future Challenges.* Ottawa: Statistics Canada. An in-depth statistical analysis of the state of education in Canada based on 1991 census data. Particular attention is paid to gender, race, ethnicity, and social class.

Online Learning Centre

Visit the *Sociology: A Brief Introduction* Online Learning Centre at www.mcgrawhill.ca/college/schaefer to access quizzes, interactive exercises, video clips, and other research and study tools related to this chapter.

Reel Society Interactive Movie CD-ROM 2.0

Reel Society 2.0 can be used to spark discussion about the following topics from this chapter:

- Durkheim and the sociological approach to religion
- The role of religion
- World religions
- Religious belief, ritual, and experience
- Sociological perspectives on education
- Trends in contemporary education

chapter 13

GOVERNMENT AND THE ECONOMY

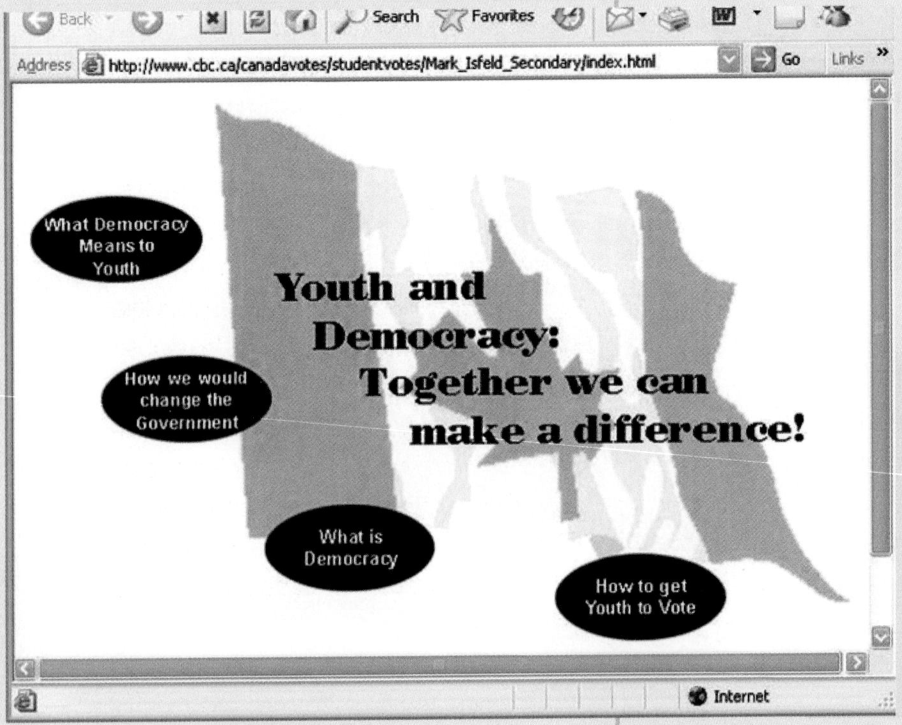

Voter turnout has been on the decline in Canada, especially among young people. In a contest held by the Canadian Broadcasting Corporation, this school in Courtenay, B.C., took third place. The contest asked students to think about what democracy means to them and how to encourage youth to vote.

Current numbers have led some observers to conclude that the problem of women's underrepresentation in electoral spaces is well on its way to being solved. We disagree, for four reasons. First, while Canada's record with respect to electing women stacks up well against several other countries, including the United States, the United Kingdom, and France, we continue to lag behind the Nordic countries, Australia, New Zealand, and Germany. Indeed, Canada ranks only thirty-fourth in the world when it comes to electing women to its national Parliament (lower house), below many similarly industrialized nations. Secondly, the percentage of elected women in Canada continues to fall far short of 50 per cent. In contrast, some countries are approaching gender parity. Denmark, Iceland, Finland, Netherlands, and Norway feature more than 35 per cent women in their national assemblies, and 43 per cent of Sweden's parliamentarians are women. Yet over 80 per cent—four out of five—of the elected representatives in Canada's legislatures are men. Nowhere in Canada do women comprise more than one-quarter of the legislators.

Thirdly, electoral progress for women in Canada appears to have stalled. A relatively steady increase in the numbers of elected women since the 1980s obscured the fact that most recently, in several jurisdictions, the percentage of female legislators has either stayed the same or actually dropped slightly. . . . Women's representation in Canada's federal Parliament has reached a plateau at about 21 per cent.

Finally, not all women are equally well represented as women. Who, exactly, is making progress? Female politicians are certainly no more representative of the general public than are male politicians; in general, they are overwhelmingly white, middle to upper class, able-bodied, relatively privileged in their amount of education, and publicly heterosexual. So, when we take account of the fact that, on average, close to one-fifth of our elected representatives are women, we must remember that many Canadian women and some men do not see themselves (or people like them in important respects) in public office. At present only the already privileged women are likely to be selected. Women's diversity in its entirety is not currently represented in our legislative institutions, and . . . this lack of diversity has clear implications for effective public policy-making.

Despite a recent modest increase in the overall percentage of elected women, the political environment is still a difficult one for female political aspirants, activists, legislators, and party leaders. Significant barriers remain to women's substantive representation in formal arenas of political deliberation and decision-making. . . . We maintain that, as in the business world and other areas traditionally dominated by men, electoral politics features its own version of the glass ceiling: the invisible barriers that effectively keep women from rising beyond a certain level in hierarchical organizations. Moreover, it is this electoral glass ceiling on which female political aspirants are now bumping their heads. *(Trimble and Arscott 2004)* ■

In *Still Counting: Women in Politics Across Canada,* Linda Trimble and Jane Arscott examine the elected political representation of women in Canada, comparing it with that of other industrialized nations. According to Trimble and Arscott, politics, like most areas of public life, is one in which women encounter invisible barriers—glass ceilings—when it comes to rising beyond certain levels.

Half a century ago C. Wright Mills (1956), the originator of the phrase *the sociological imagination,* articulated the concept of the power elite—a select male group of decision makers who in effect rule a country. Today, a few privileged women occupy positions in the power elite, but the majority of the nation's decision makers are still, for the most part, white men.

The power elite operates within the framework of the existing political system, be it local, state, national, or international. By ***political system,*** sociologists mean the social institution that is founded on a recognized set of procedures for implementing and achieving society's goals, such as the allocation of valued resources. Like religion and the family, the political system is a cultural universal: It is found in every society. In Canada, the political system holds the ultimate responsibility for addressing the social policy issues examined in this textbook: child care, the AIDS crisis, welfare reform, and so forth.

The term ***economic system*** refers to the social institution through which goods and services are produced, distributed, and consumed. As with social institutions, such as the family, religion, and government, the economic system shapes other aspects of the social order and is, in turn, influenced by them. Throughout this textbook, you have been reminded of the economy's impact on social behaviour—for example, individual and group behaviour in factories and offices. You have studied the work of Karl Marx and Friedrich Engels, who emphasized that the economic system can promote social inequality. And you have learned that foreign investment in developing countries can intensify inequality among residents.

pp. 8–9

p. 184

It is hard to imagine two social institutions more intertwined than government and the economy. In addition to being the largest employer in the nation, government at all levels regulates commerce and entry into many occupations. At the same time, the economy generates the revenue to support government services. This close relationship raises serious concerns about the state of the environment. On one hand, the government must oversee the quality of the air and water for the public well-being; on the other hand, business leaders claim that strict environmental standards hamstring an expanding economy. Another complicating factor for maintaining a clean and healthy environment is the sheer pressure of population growth throughout the world.

How does the power elite maintain its power? What is the face of the workforce in a technological, service-oriented economy? What effect do government decisions and human behaviour have on the environment? This chapter begins with a macrolevel analysis of two *ideal types* of economic systems: capitalism and socialism. Then we will look at the sources of power in a political system and the three major types of authority. We will see how politics works in Canada and consider two models of power: the elite and the pluralist models. Finally, we'll examine the ways in which the economy is changing at the beginning of the twenty-first century. ■

Use Your Sociological Imagination www.mcgrawhill.ca/college/schaefer

What other barriers do women face when running for elected positions? Do you think that the women who currently sit in the federal Parliament are representative of all women?

ECONOMIC SYSTEMS

The sociocultural evolution approach developed by Gerhard Lenski categorizes preindustrial societies according to the way in which the economy is organized. The principal types of preindustrial societies, as you recall, are hunting-and-gathering societies, horticultural societies, and agrarian societies (Lenski et al. 1995).

p. 171

As noted in Chapter 5, the *industrial revolution*—which took place largely in England from 1760 to 1830—brought about changes in the social organization of the workplace. People left their homesteads and began working in central locations, such as factories. As the industrial revolution proceeded, a new form of social structure emerged: the industrial society, a society that depends on mechanization to produce its goods and services.

Two basic types of economic systems distinguish contemporary industrial societies: capitalism and socialism. As described in the following sections, capitalism and socialism serve as ideal types of economic systems. No nation precisely fits either model. Instead, the economy of each individual state represents a mixture of capitalism and socialism, although one type or the other is generally predominant. China's economy, for example, has been primarily socialist, whereas Canada's economy is much more capitalistic.

Capitalism

In preindustrial societies, land functioned as the source of virtually all wealth. The industrial revolution changed all that. It required that certain individuals and institutions be willing to take substantial risks in order to finance new inventions, machinery, and business enterprises. Eventually, bankers, industrialists, and other holders of large sums of money replaced landowners as the most powerful economic force. These people invested their funds in the hope of realizing even greater profits and thereby became owners of property and business firms.

The transition to private ownership of business was accompanied by the emergence of the capitalist economic system. Capitalism is an economic system in which the means of production are largely in private hands and the main incentive for economic activity is the accumulation of profits. In practice, capitalist systems vary in the degree to which the government regulates private ownership and economic activity (Rosenberg 1991).

Immediately following the industrial revolution, the prevailing form of capitalism was what is termed ***laissez-faire*** ("let them do"). Under the principle of laissez-faire, as expounded and endorsed by British economist Adam Smith (1723–1790), people could compete freely with minimal government intervention in the economy. Business retained the right to regulate itself and essentially operated without fear of government regulation (Smelser 1963).

Two centuries later, capitalism has taken on a somewhat different form. Private ownership and maximization of profits still remain the most significant characteristics of capitalist economic systems. However, in contrast to the era of laissez-faire, capitalism today features extensive government regulation of economic relations. Without restrictions, business firms can mislead consumers, endanger the safety of their workers, and even defraud the companies' investors—all in the pursuit of greater profits. That is why the government of a capitalist nation often monitors prices, sets safety and environmental standards for industries, protects the rights of consumers, and regulates collective bargaining between labour unions and management. Yet, under capitalism as an ideal type, government rarely takes over ownership of an entire industry.

Contemporary capitalism also differs from laissez-faire in another important respect. Capitalism tolerates monopolistic practices. A ***monopoly*** exists when a single business firm controls the market. Domination of an industry allows the firm to effectively control a commodity

In the movie *Wall Street* (1987), actors Charlie Sheen and Michael Douglas played greedy speculators engaged in insider trading and stock price manipulation. Popular culture often presents capitalists as selfish people who profit unfairly from the labour of others. Recent corporate scandals have reinforced this negative image of capitalists.

by dictating pricing, standards of quality, and availability. Buyers have little choice but to yield to the firm's decisions; there is no other place to purchase the product or service. Monopolistic practices violate the ideal of free competition cherished by Adam Smith and other supporters of laissez-faire capitalism.

Some capitalistic nations, such as Canada, outlaw monopolies through competition legislation. Such laws prevent any business from taking over so much of the competition in an industry that it controls the market. The federal government allows monopolies to exist only in certain exceptional cases, such as the utility and transportation industries. Even then, regulatory agencies scrutinize these officially approved monopolies and protect the public. In the United States, the protracted legal battle between the Justice Department and Microsoft, owner of the dominant operating system for personal computers, illustrates the uneasy relationship between government and private monopolies in capitalistic countries.

Conflict theorists point out that although *pure* monopolies are not a basic element of the economy of capitalist societies, competition is much more restricted than we might expect in what is called a *free enterprise system.* In numerous industries, a few companies largely dominate the field and keep new enterprises from entering the marketplace.

Soon after the U.S. government lifted its trade embargo against Vietnam in 1994, Coca-Cola and Pepsi rushed in to corner the market. Coca-Cola made its "biggest" statement on the steps of the Opera House in Hanoi.

Socialism

pp. 8–9

Socialist theory was refined in the writings of Karl Marx and Friedrich Engels. These European "radicals" were disturbed by the exploitation of the working class as it emerged during the industrial revolution. In their view, capitalism forced large numbers of people to exchange their labour for low wages. The owners of an industry profit from the labour of their workers, primarily because they pay workers less than the value of the goods produced.

pp. 168–169

As an ideal type, a socialist economic system attempts to eliminate such economic exploitation. Under ***socialism,*** the means of production and distribution in a society are collectively rather than privately owned. The basic objective of the economic system is to meet people's needs rather than to maximize profits. Socialists reject the laissez-faire philosophy that free competition benefits the general public. Instead, they believe that the central government, acting as the representative of the people, should make basic economic decisions. Therefore, government ownership of all major industries—including steel production, automobile manufacturing, and agriculture—is a primary feature of socialism as an ideal type.

In practice, socialist economic systems vary in the extent to which they tolerate private ownership. For example, in Great Britain, a nation with some aspects of both a socialist and a capitalist economy, passenger airline service is concentrated in the government-owned corporation British Airways. Yet private airline companies are allowed to compete with it.

Socialist societies differ from capitalist nations in their commitment to social service programs. For example, the U.S. government provides health care and health insurance for the elderly and poor through the Medicare and Medicaid programs. But socialist countries typically offer government-financed medical care for *all* citizens. In theory, the wealth of the people as a collective is used to provide health care, housing, education, and other key services for each individual and family.

Marx believed that each socialist state would eventually "wither away" and evolve into a *communist* society. As an ideal type, ***communism*** refers to an economic system under which all property is communally owned and no social distinctions are made on the basis of people's ability to produce. In recent decades, the Soviet Union, the People's Republic of China, Vietnam, Cuba, and nations in Eastern Europe were popularly thought of as examples of communist economic systems. However, this represents an incorrect usage of a term with sensitive political connotations. All nations known as communist in the twentieth century fell far short of the ideal type.

By the early 1990s, communist parties were no longer ruling the nations of Eastern Europe. The first major challenge to communist rule came in 1980 when Poland's Solidarity movement—led by Lech Walesa and backed by many workers—questioned the injustices of that society. Although martial law initially forced Solidarity underground, it eventually negotiated the end of communist party rule in 1989. Over the next two years, dominant communist parties were overthrown after popular uprisings in the Soviet Union and throughout Eastern Europe. The former Soviet Union, Czechoslovakia, and Yugoslavia were then subdivided to accommodate the ethnic, linguistic, and religious differences within these areas.

As of 2003, China, Cuba, and Vietnam remained socialist societies ruled by communist parties. Even in these countries, however, capitalism was making inroads. Fully 25 percent of China's production originated in the private business sector. At the Chinese communist party's eightieth anniversary celebration in 2001, President Jiang Zemin asked the party to formally welcome private business owners as members (C. Wolf 2001).

Cuba, in particular, is adjusting to a dual economy. Although the communist government leader Fidel Castro remains firmly committed to Marxism, the centrally controlled economy was in ruins following the end of Soviet aid and the continued trade embargo by the United States. Reluctantly, Castro has allowed small-scale family-managed businesses, such as restaurants and craft shops, to operate and accept dollars rather than the heavily devalued Cuban peso. This leads to an ironic situation in which government-employed teachers and doctors earn less than the small business operators, taxi drivers, and hotel workers who have access to foreign currency. This situation underscores how difficult it is to understand any nation's economy without considering its position in the global economy (McKinley 1999).

In many countries, there is an aspect of the economy that defies description as either capitalist or socialist. It is known as the ***informal economy,*** in which transfers of money, goods, or services take place but are not reported to the government. Examples of an informal economy would be trading services with someone—say, a haircut for a computer lesson—selling goods on the street, not reporting tips, and even making illegal transactions, such as gambling or drug deals. Participants in this type of economy avoid taxes and government regulations. In developing nations, the informal economy represents a significant and often unmeasured part of total economic activity. Yet because this sector of the economy depends to a large extent on the labour of women, work in the informal economy is undervalued or even unrecognized the world over (see Box 13-1).

As we have seen, capitalism and socialism serve as ideal types of economic systems. In reality, the economy of each industrial society—including Canada, the European Union, and Japan—includes certain elements of both capitalism and socialism. Whatever the differences, whether they more closely fit the ideal type of capitalism or socialism, all industrial societies rely chiefly on mechanization in the production of goods and services.

Use Your Sociological Imagination

In a Canadian economy that becomes predominantly socialist rather than capitalist, what would you as a worker have that you did not have before? What would you lack?

POWER AND AUTHORITY

An economic system does not exist in a vacuum. Someone or some group makes important decisions about how to use resources and how to allocate goods, whether it be a tribal chief or a Parliament or a dictator. A cultural universal common to all societies, then, is the exercise of power and authority. The struggle for power and authority inevitably involves ***politics,*** which political scientist Harold Lasswell (1936) tersely defined as "who gets what, when, and how." In their study of politics and government, sociologists are concerned with social interactions among individuals and groups and their impact on the larger political and economic order.

Power

p. 170

Power is at the heart of a political system. According to Max Weber, power is the ability to exercise will over others. To put it another way, whoever can control the behaviour of others is exercising power. Power relations can involve large organizations, small groups, or even people in an intimate association.

There are three basic sources of power within any political system: force, influence, and authority. ***Force*** is the actual or threatened use of coercion by people to impose their will on others. When leaders imprison or even execute political dissidents, they are applying force; so, too, are terrorists when they seize or bomb an embassy or assassinate a political leader. ***Influence,*** conversely, refers to the exercise of power through a process

Research in Action 13-1 Working Women in Nepal

Nepal, a small and mountainous Asian country of about 24 million people, has a per capita gross domestic product (GDP) of just $1280 per year. (The comparable figure in Canada is $22 390.) But gross domestic product seriously understates the true production level in Nepal, for several reasons. Among the most important is that many Nepalese women work in the informal economy, whose activities are not included in the GDP.

Because women's work is undervalued in this traditional society, it is also underreported and underestimated. Official figures state that women account for 27 percent of GDP and form 40 percent of the labour force. But Nepalese women are responsible for 60 percent of additional nonmarket production, that is, work done in the informal economy, and 93 percent of the housework (see figure).

Most female workers cultivate corn, rice, and wheat on the family farm, where they spend hours on time-intensive tasks, such as fetching water and feeding livestock. Because much of the food they raise is consumed at home, however, it is considered to be nonmarket production. At home, women concentrate on food processing and preparation, caregiving, and other household tasks, such as clothes making. Childbearing, childrearing, and elder care are particularly crucial activities. Yet these chores are considered part of GDP; instead, they are dismissed as "women's work," both by economists and by the women themselves.

Gender Contributions to GDP and Household Maintenance in Nepal

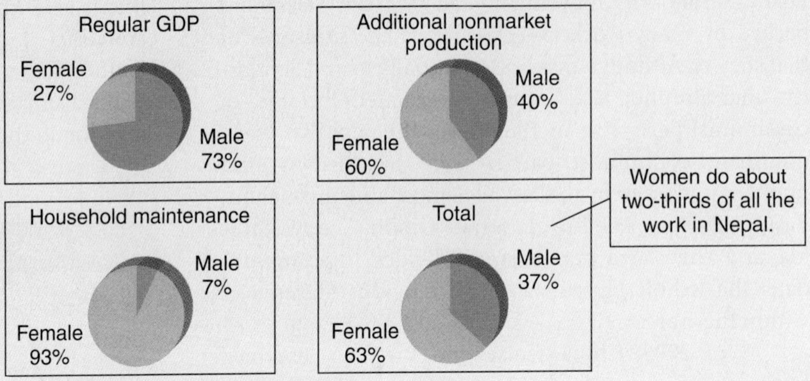

Source: Survey by S. Acharya as cited in Mahbub ul Haq Human Development Centre 2000:54.

The figures on housework and nonmarket production in Nepal come from an independent economic study. To compile them, researchers had to adapt the conventional accounting system by adding a special account dedicated to household maintenance activities. When they did so, women's "invisible work" suddenly became visible and valuable. Not just in Nepal but in every country, economists need to expand their definitions of work and the labour force to account for the tremendous contributions women make to the world economy.

Applying Theory

1. In your own family, is "women's work" taken for granted? Have you ever tried to figure out what it would cost your family to pay for all the unpaid work women do?
2. According to some feminist sociologists, recognizing women's work is important. How might life for both men and women change if the true economic value of women's work were recognized?

Sources: Acharya 2000; Haub and Cornelius 2001; Mahbub ul Haq Human Development Centre 2000:54–57.

of persuasion. A citizen may change his or her view of a Supreme Court appointment because of a newspaper editorial, the expert testimony of a law school dean at a Senate Committee hearing, or a stirring speech at a rally by a political activist. In each case, sociologists would view such efforts to persuade people as examples of influence. Now let's take a look at the third source of power, *authority.*

Types of Authority

The term ***authority*** refers to institutionalized power that is recognized by the people over whom it is exercised. Sociologists commonly use the term in connection with those who hold legitimate power through elected or publicly acknowledged positions. A person's authority is often limited. Thus, a referee has the authority to decide whether a penalty should be called during a football game but has no authority over the price of tickets to the game.

Max Weber ([1922] 1947) developed a classification system regarding authority that has become one of the most useful and frequently cited contributions of early sociology. He identified three ideal types of authority: traditional, legal-rational, and charismatic. Weber did not insist that only one type applies to a given society or organization. All can be present, but their relative importance will vary. Sociologists have found Weber's typology valuable in understanding different manifestations of legitimate power within a society.

The emotional appeal that former prime minister Pierre Trudeau had to many Canadians was an example of charismatic authority.

Traditional Authority

Until the late twentieth century, Japan was ruled by a revered emperor, whose power was absolute and passed down from generation to generation. In a political system based on ***traditional authority,*** legitimate power is conferred by custom and accepted practice. A king or queen is accepted as ruler of a nation simply by virtue of inheriting the crown; a tribal chief rules because that is the accepted practice. The ruler may be loved or hated, competent or destructive; in terms of legitimacy, that does not matter. For the traditional leader, authority rests in custom, not in personal characteristics, technical competence, or even written law. People accept this authority because "this is how things have always been done." Traditional authority is absolute when the ruler has the ability to determine laws and policies.

Legal-Rational Authority

The Constitution Acts, 1867–1982 give our government the authority to make and enforce laws and policies. Power made legitimate by law is known as ***legal-rational authority.*** Leaders derive their legal-rational authority from the written rules and regulations of political systems, such as a constitution. Generally, in societies based on legal-rational authority, leaders are thought to have specific areas of competence and authority but are not thought to be endowed with divine inspiration, as in certain societies with traditional forms of authority.

Charismatic Authority

Joan of Arc was a simple peasant girl in medieval France, yet she was able to rally the French people and lead them in major battles against English invaders. How was this possible? As Weber observed, power can be legitimized by the *charisma* of an individual. The term ***charismatic authority*** refers to power made legitimate by a leader's exceptional personal or emotional appeal to his or her followers.

Charisma lets a person lead or inspire without relying on set rules or traditions. In fact, charismatic authority is derived more from the beliefs of followers than from the actual qualities of leaders. As long as people *perceive* a leader as having qualities that set him or her apart from ordinary citizens, that leader's authority will remain secure and often unquestioned.

Unlike traditional rulers, charismatic leaders often become well known by breaking with established institutions and advocating dramatic changes in the social structure and the economic system. Their strong hold over their followers makes it easier to build protest movements that challenge the dominant norms and values of a society. Thus, such charismatic leaders as Joan of Arc, Mahatma Gandhi, Malcolm X, and Martin Luther King all used their power to press for changes in accepted social behaviour. But so did Adolf Hitler, whose charismatic appeal turned people toward violent and destructive ends in Nazi Germany.

Observing from an interactionist perspective, sociologist Carl Couch (1996) points out that the growth of the electronic media has facilitated the development of charismatic authority. During the 1930s and 1940s, the heads of state in the United States, Great Britain, and Germany all used radio to issue direct appeals to citizens. In recent decades, television has allowed leaders to "visit" people's homes and communicate with them. Time and again, Saddam Hussein rallied the Iraqi people through shrewd use of television appearances. In both Taiwan and South Korea in 1996, troubled political leaders facing reelection campaigns spoke frequently to national audiences and exaggerated military threats from neighbouring China and North Korea, respectively.

As was noted earlier, Weber used traditional, legal-rational, and charismatic authority as ideal types. In reality, particular leaders and political systems combine elements of two or more of these forms. Pierre Trudeau, arguably one of the most remarkable prime ministers in Canadian history, wielded power through both legal-rational and charismatic forms of authority. The excitement generated by Trudeau's charismatic style of leadership, dubbed "Trudeaumania," prompted many Canadians—especially younger Canadians—to become engaged in and excited by politics in Canada.

Use Your Sociological Imagination

What would our government be like if it were founded on traditional rather than legal-rational authority? What difference would it make to the average citizen?

POLITICAL BEHAVIOUR IN CANADA

Citizens of Canada may take for granted many aspects of their political system. They are accustomed to living in a nation with a Charter of Rights and Freedoms, an elected prime minister, provincial or territorial and local governments distinct from the federal government, and so forth. Yet each society has its own ways of governing itself and making decisions. Just as Canadian residents expect Liberal, NDP, Bloc Québécois, and Conservative candidates to compete for public offices, residents of the People's Republic of China and Cuba are accustomed to one-party rule by the Communist party. In this section, we will examine a number of important aspects of political behaviour within Canada.

Political Socialization

Do your political views coincide with those of your parents? Did you vote in the last election? Did you register to vote, or do you plan to do so? The process by which you acquire political attitudes and develop patterns of political behaviour is known as ***political socialization.*** This involves not only learning the prevailing beliefs of a society but also coming to accept the political system, whatever its limitations and problems.

One of the functional prerequisites that a society must fulfil to survive is teaching recruits to accept the values and customs of the group. In a political sense, this function is crucial; each succeeding generation must be encouraged to accept a society's basic political values and its particular methods of decision making. The principal institutions of political socialization are those that also socialize us to other cultural norms: the family, schools, and the media.

pp. 103–104

Many observers see the family as playing a particularly significant role in the process. Parents pass on their political attitudes and evaluations to their sons and daughters through discussions at the dinner table and also through the example of their political involvement or apathy. Early socialization does not always determine a person's political orientation; there are changes over time and between generations. Yet research on political socialization continues to show that parents' views have an important impact on their children's outlook (Jennings and Niemi 1981).

Schools provide young people with information and analysis of the political world. Unlike the family and peer groups, schools are easily susceptible to centralized and uniform control. In democratic and totalitarian societies alike, political education will generally reflect the norms and values of the prevailing political order.

Participation and Apathy

In theory, a representative democracy will function most effectively and fairly if an informed and active electorate communicates its views to government leaders. Unfortunately, this is hardly the case in Canada. Many citizens are familiar with the basics of the political process, however, decreasing numbers of Canadians tend to identify with a political party (see Figure 13-1), and only a small minority (often members of the higher social classes) actually participate in political organizations on a provincial or territorial or federal level. Only a small minority of Canadians belong to a political party.

The failure of most citizens to become involved in political parties diminishes the democratic process. Within the political system of Canada, the political party serves as an intermediary between people and government. Through competition in regularly scheduled elections, the major parties provide for challenges to public policies and for an orderly transfer of power. An individual dissatisfied with the state of the country, province, territory, or local community can become involved in the political process in many ways, such as by joining a political party, supporting candidates for public office, or working to change the party's position on controversial issues.

By the 1980s, it became clear that many people in Canada were beginning to be turned off by political parties, politicians, and government. The most dramatic

FIGURE 13-1

The Evolution of Party Identification

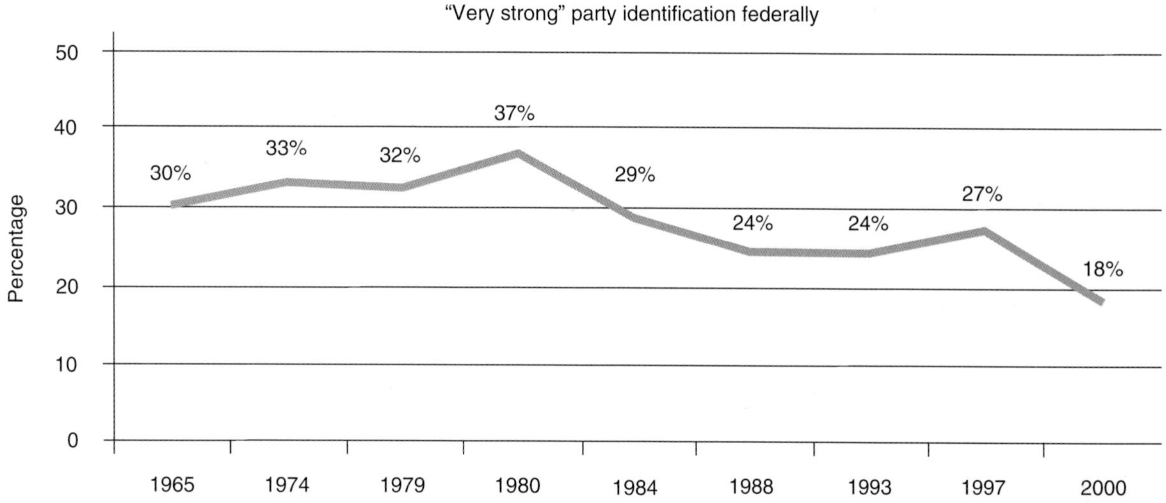

Source: Mendelsohn 2002. Data from Canadian Elections Studies.

Think about It

Why do so many Canadian voters no longer strongly identify themselves with a political party?

indication of this growing alienation comes from voting statistics. Voters of all ages appear to be less enthusiastic than ever about elections, particularly provincial or territorial and federal. For example, 75 percent of eligible voters in Canada went to the polls in the federal election of 1988. Yet by the 2000 election, turnout had fallen to 61 percent of all eligible voters. Voter turnout for provincial and territorial elections between 1980 and 2003 also generally declined, with the exception of PEI, where the turnout rate increased, and Alberta, where the turnout rate declined only slightly.

Although a few nations still command high voter turnout, it is increasingly common to hear national leaders of other countries complain of voter apathy. Japan typically enjoyed 70 percent turnout in its Upper House elections in the 1950s through mid-1980s, but by 1998 turnout was closer to 58 percent. In 2001, only 59 percent of British voters participated in the general elections. The same year, just 55 percent of Swiss voters went to the polls to decide a highly controversial referendum on membership in the European Union (*Facts on File Weekly News Report* 2001a, 2001b; Masaki 1998).

Political participation makes government accountable to the voters. If participation declines, government can operate with less of a sense of accountability to society. This issue is most serious for the least powerful individuals and groups within Canada. Voter turnout has been particularly low among Canadians of particular age groups and among Canadians living in particular regions. Elections Canada statistics revealed that voter turnout for the 2000 federal election was strikingly lower for younger Canadians, part of the trend that has contributed to lower overall turnout rates in Canada over the past decade. The number of younger people, those between the ages of 18 and 30, who did not vote far outnumbered those who did. For example, 78 percent of 18- to 20-year-olds and 73 percent of 21- to 24-year-olds did not vote in the 2000 federal election (Elections Canada 2005a). In terms of regional patterns, Newfoundland and Labrador, which has historically been economically disadvantaged, has one of the lowest turnouts for federal elections of all provinces and territories. During the 1960s, 69 percent of the province's residents voted in federal elections. By the 1990s, that number had dropped to 56 percent. In the 2004 election, only 49 percent of people voted. Nunavut had the lowest voter turnout in the 2004 federal election, with only 43 percent casting ballots, followed by the Northwest Territories at 47 percent (Elections Canada 2005b). The low turnout found among these provinces and territories is explained, at least in part, by their common feeling of powerlessness. Yet these low statistics encourage political power brokers to continue to ignore the interests of those who feel alienated from the dominant culture (Casper and Bass 1998).

Canadians are socialized to see freedom of expression as an essential part of the democratic process. These people are protesting against a visit by U.S. President George W. Bush in 2004.

Women in Politics

Women continue to be dramatically underrepresented in the halls of government. As mentioned in Chapter 10, most women in Canada (with the most notable exception of Aboriginal women) were granted the right to vote in federal elections by 1918. It wasn't until 1929, however, that women in Canada were considered "persons" under the law, making them eligible for appointment to the Canadian Senate.

p. 230

Sexism has been the most serious barrier to women interested in holding office. Female candidates continue to attempt to overcome the prejudices of both men and women regarding women's fitness for leadership. Although Canada has had one female prime minister, Kim Campbell in 1993, she did not obtain her position through a federal election. She earned it through her party's nomination of her to replace the retiring prime minister, Brian Mulroney. Currently, approximately 20 percent of members of the House of Commons are female, even though women make up 51 percent of the Canadian population. There are no female provincial or territorial premiers in Canada today. Moreover, women often encounter prejudice, discrimination, and abuse *after* they are elected.

Female politicians may be enjoying more electoral success now than in the past, but there is evidence that the media cover them differently from men. A content analysis of newspaper coverage showed that reporters wrote more often about a female candidate's personal life, appearance, or personality than a male candidate's and less often about her political positions and voting record. Furthermore, when political issues were raised in newspaper articles, reporters were more likely to illustrate them with statements made by male candidates than by female candidates (Devitt 1999).

Although the proportion of women in legislatures has increased in Canada and many other nations, women still do not account for half the members of the national legislature in any country. Rwanda ranks the highest, with 48.8 percent. Overall, Canada in 2005 ranked 34th among 184 nations in the proportion of women serving as national legislators (Inter-Parliamentary Union 2005). To remedy this situation, many countries—including the world's largest democracy, India—have reserved a minimum number of legislative seats for women.

A gender gap becomes apparent when we examine the relationship between gender and politics. In the 2004 Canadian federal election, for example, the largest number of female candidates running for elected office represented the New Democratic Party (NDP), followed by (in descending order), the Green Party of Canada, the Liberal Party, the Conservative party, the Marxist-Leninist Party, and the Bloc Québécois. Of the four major political parties in Canada (Liberal, Conservative, Bloc Québécois, and NDP), the NDP had the largest percentage of women elected as members of Parliament in 2004.

A gender gap has also emerged in relation to voting patterns in Canada. Between 1993 and 2000, Canadian men tended to support more conservative, right-wing political parties, while Canadian women did not. Research suggests that gender differences in values and beliefs have contributed to corresponding gender differences in terms of party support (Gidengil et al. 2003). Canadian women were less likely to support cutting taxes, doing less for minorities, and reducing expenditures on government-sponsored welfare programs, policies, and proposals, which tend to be advocated more by conservative political parties (Gidengil et al. 2003).

Use Your Sociological Imagination

Imagine a world in which women, not men, held the majority of elective offices. What kind of world would it be?

MODELS OF POWER STRUCTURE IN CANADA

Who really holds power in Canada? Do the people genuinely run the country through elected representatives? Or is it true that, behind the scenes, a small elite controls both the government and the economic system? It is sometimes difficult to determine the location of power in a society as complex as Canada's. In exploring this critical question, social scientists have developed two basic views of the power structure of capitalist countries: the power elite and the pluralist models.

Power Elite Models

Karl Marx believed that nineteenth-century representative democracy was essentially a sham. He argued that industrial societies were dominated by relatively small numbers of people who owned factories and controlled natural resources. In Marx's view, government officials and military leaders were essentially servants of this capitalist class and followed their wishes. Therefore, any key decisions made by politicians inevitably reflected the interests of the dominant bourgeoisie. Like others who hold an ***elite model*** of power relations, Marx believed that society is ruled by a small group of individuals who share a common set of political and economic interests.

Mills's Model

Sociologist C. Wright Mills took this model a step further in his pioneering work *The Power Elite* (1956). Mills described a small group of military, industrial, and governmental leaders who controlled the fate of a country—the ***power elite.*** Power rested in the hands of a few, both inside and outside government,

A pyramid illustrates the power structure of Mills's model (see Figure 13-2a). At the top are the corporate rich, leaders of the executive branch of government, and heads of the military (whom Mills called the "warlords"). Directly below are local opinion leaders, members of the legislative branch of government, and leaders of special-interest groups. Mills contended that such individuals and groups would basically follow the wishes of the dominant power elite. At the bottom of the pyramid are the unorganized, exploited masses.

This power elite model is, in many respects, similar to the work of Karl Marx. The most striking difference is that Mills believed that the economically powerful coordinate their manoeuvres with other elites to serve their common interests. Yet, reminiscent of Marx, Mills argued that the corporate rich were perhaps the most powerful element of the power elite (first among "equals"). There is a further dramatic parallel between the work of these conflict theorists. The powerless masses at the bottom of Mills's power elite model certainly bring to mind Marx's

FIGURE 13-2

Power Elite Models

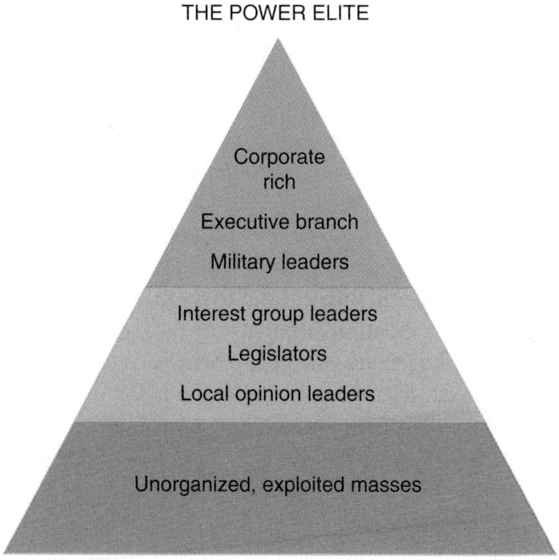

a. C. Wright Mills's model, 1956

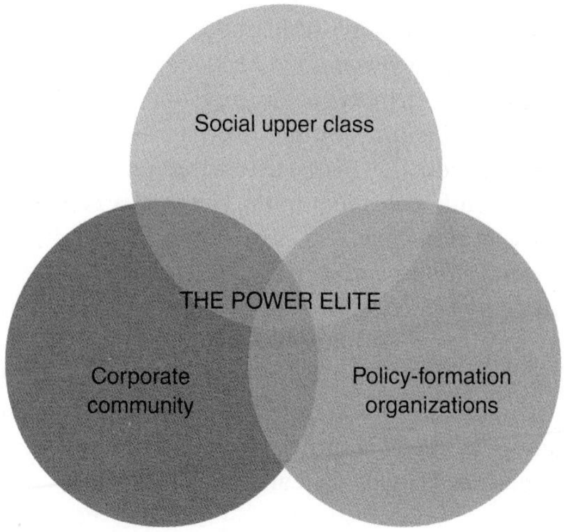

b. William Domhoff's model, 1998

Source: Domhoff 2001, p. 96.

portrait of the oppressed workers of the world, who have "nothing to lose but their chains."

A fundamental element in Mills's thesis is that the power elite not only includes relatively few members but also operates as a self-conscious, cohesive unit. Although not necessarily diabolical or ruthless, the elite comprises similar types of people who regularly interact with one another and have essentially the same political and economic interests. Mills's power elite is not a conspiracy but rather a community of interest and sentiment among a small number of influential people (Hacker 1964).

Admittedly, Mills failed to clarify when the elite opposes protests and when it tolerates them; he also failed to provide detailed case studies that would substantiate the interrelationship among members of the power elite. Nevertheless, his challenging theories forced scholars to look more critically at the democratic political system of capitalist societies, such as Canada. Fox and Ornstein (1986) did reveal the existence of extensive networks linking corporations with the federal cabinet, Senate, and federal bureaucracy in Canada, as well the growth of these links over the three decades of the examination period.

Fox and Ornstein found that, in Canada, links between the corporate world and government were far greater at the federal level than at the provincial or territorial level.

Domhoff's Model

More recently, sociologist G. William Domhoff (2001), coauthor of *Diversity in the Power Elite,* has agreed with Mills that a powerful elite runs the capitalist societies of the developed world. He finds that it is still largely white, male, and upper class, as he wrote in his book with Richard L. Zweigenhaft (1998). But Domhoff stresses the role played both by elites of the corporate community and by the leaders of policy-formation organizations, such as chambers of commerce and labour unions. Many of the people in both groups are also members of the social upper class.

Although these groups overlap, as Figure 13-2b shows, they do not necessarily agree on specific policies. Domhoff notes that in the electoral arena two different coalitions have exercised influence. A *corporate-conservative coalition* has played a large role in political parties and has generated support for particular candidates through direct-mail appeals. But there is also a *liberal-labour coalition* based in unions, local environmental organizations, a segment of the minority group community, liberal churches, and the university and arts communities (Zweigenhaft and Domhoff 1998).

Pluralist Model

Several social scientists insist that power in capitalist countries, such as Canada, is more widely shared than the elite models indicate. In their view, a pluralist model more accurately describes the nation's political system. According to the ***pluralist model,*** many conflicting groups within the community have access to government, so that no single group is dominant.

The pluralist model suggests that a variety of groups play a significant role in decision making. Typically, pluralists make use of intensive case studies or community studies based on observation research. One of the most famous was reported by Robert Dahl in his book *Who Governs?* (1961). Dahl found that although the number of people involved in any important decision was rather small, community power was nonetheless diffuse. Few political actors exercised decision-making power on all issues. One individual or group might be influential in a battle over urban renewal but at the same time have little impact on educational policy. Several other studies of local politics further document that monolithic power structures do not operate on the level of local government.

The pluralist model, however, has not escaped serious questioning. Domhoff (1978, 2001) reexamined Dahl's study of decision making and argued that Dahl and other pluralists had failed to trace how local elites prominent in decision making were part of a larger national ruling class. In addition, studies of community power, such as Dahl's work, can examine decision making only on issues that become part of the political agenda. This focus fails to address the possible power of elites to keep certain matters entirely *out* of the realm of government debate.

Many sociologists and political scientists have criticized the pluralist model for failing to account for the exclusion of disadvantaged groups (women, the poor, Aboriginal peoples) from the political process. Although Canada prides itself on its multicultural character, what it is to be multicultural is open to many different interpretations. In general terms, multiculturalism is a process through which Canadians come to be engaged in their society as different from yet equal to one another (Fleras and Kunz 2001). Levels of engagement in the political process, however, do not reflect the racial and ethnic diversity of Canada. The pluralist claim that diverse and conflicting groups—whether they are based on gender, occupation, ethnicity, or race—have access to government, with no one group being dominant, is seriously flawed. Members of Parliament, for example, do not reflect the characteristics of the Canadian population in terms of race, ethnicity, class, education, or gender (Dyck 2006). Members of Parliament tend to be better educated and from higher-status occupational groups than the overall Canadian population. Since 1984, the two largest occupational groups have been educators and people with business backgrounds, followed by lawyers and administrators (Dyck 2006). In

Sociology in the Global Community

13-2 Terrorist Violence

For people in the United States, the moment that a hijacked commercial airliner slammed into the World Trade Center on the morning of September 11, 2001, terrorism became a frightening reality—something that no longer took place only in "foreign" countries.

It was, of course, not the first terrorist attack on the United States, or even on the World Trade Center. Just six years earlier, the U.S. federal building in Oklahoma City had been truck-bombed by terrorist Timothy McVeigh, who was born and raised in the United States; 168 people died in the blast. And in 1993, terrorists had succeeded in destroying the lower levels of the World Trade Center. But the collapse of the two towers and the loss of nearly three thousand lives in 2001 seared the nation's psyche in a way the earlier attacks had not.

When letters purporting to contain anthrax spores began arriving at abortion clinics shortly after the attacks and a U.S. citizen was taken into custody by the FBI for sending them, Americans could no longer escape the fact that terrorism had become a home-grown as well as an imported phenomenon.

Such acts of terror, whether perpetrated by a few or by many people, can also be a powerful political force. Formally defined, ***terrorism*** is the use or threat of violence against random or symbolic targets in pursuit of political aims. An essential aspect of contemporary terrorism involves use of the media. Terrorists may want to keep secret their individual identities, but they want their political messages and goals to receive as much publicity as possible. Drawing on Erving Goffman's dramaturgical approach, sociologist Alfred McClung Lee has likened terrorism to the theatre, where certain scenes are played out in a predictable fashion. Whether through calls to the media, anonymous manifestos, or other means, terrorists typically admit responsibility for and defend their violent acts.

For terrorists, the end justifies the means. The status quo is viewed as oppressive; desperate measures are believed essential to end the suffering of the deprived. Convinced that working through the formal political process will not bring about desired political change, terrorists insist that illegal actions—often directed against innocent people—are needed. Ultimately, terrorists hope to intimidate society and thereby create a new political order.

Some political commentators have argued that terrorism defies definition because one person's "terrorist" is another person's "freedom fighter." To many people around the world, for example, Osama bin Laden and the terrorists who destroyed the World Trade Center were heroes. In this view of terrorism, we carry our biases into our evaluation of terrorist incidents and criticize only those perpetrated by groups who do not share our political goals.

Sociologists reject this critique, countering that even in warfare there are accepted rules outlawing the use of certain tactics. For example, civilian noncombatants are supposedly immune from deliberate attack and are not to be taken prisoner. If we are to set objective standards regarding terrorism, then we should condemn *any and all people* who are guilty of certain actions, no matter how understandable or even admirable some of their goals may be.

Applying Theory

1. Have you ever lived in a place where the threat of terrorism was a part of daily life or known someone who did? What was it like?
2. Can any goal, no matter how noble, justify terrorist activity?

Sources: Eisler 2000; Herman and O'Sullivan 1990; A. Lee 1983; Lewin 2001; McCoy and Cauchon 2001; R. Miller 1988.

terms of gender representation in the federal Parliament, in 2000 only 62 of 301 seats were filled by women, up slightly from 1993, when women filled 53 of 295 seats.

Historically, pluralists have stressed ways in which a diversity of people could participate in or influence governmental decision making. New communications technologies, like the Internet, are increasing the opportunity to be heard, not just in such countries as Canada but also in developing countries the world over. One common point of the elite and pluralist perspectives stands out, however: Power in the political system of Canada is unequally distributed. All citizens may be equal in theory, yet those high in the nation's power structure are "more equal." New communications technology may or may not change that distribution of power. Sometimes, people try to change the balance by means of terrorist acts (see Box 13-2).

THE CHANGING ECONOMY

As advocates of the power elite model point out, the trend in capitalist societies has been toward concentration of ownership by giant corporations, especially pp. 184–186

transnational ones. For example, in 1998, there were 3882 mergers in the United States alone, involving $1.4 trillion in business. The nature of national economies is changing in important ways, in part because each nation's economy is increasingly intertwined with and dependent on the global economy.

In the following sections, we will examine the economy and the nature of work from four theoretical perspectives: conflict, functionalism, feminism, and interactionism. We will also examine developments in the global economy that have interested sociologists: the changing face of the workforce, deindustrialization, the emergence of e-commerce, and the rise of a contingency or nonstandard workforce. As these trends show, any change in the economy inevitably has social and political implications and soon becomes a concern of policymakers.

Conflict View

Conflict theorists view the economy as the central institution of a society and as the institution that defines the character of the entire society and, correspondingly, the quality of people's lives. In 1887, Karl Marx laid the foundation for the conflict perspective in his critique of capitalism. According to Marx's framework of economic determinism, the economy was the base of society, determining the character of all other institutions: the family, religion, the education system, the legal system, and the mass media. In capitalist societies, according to Marx, the economy is based on a division of classes: those who own the means of production (i.e., the factories and the workplaces), called the bourgeoisie, and those who work for the owners of the means of production, the proletariat. These classes are in conflict with each other, as the owning class exploits the workers to maximize profits. The nature of work, therefore, in capitalist societies is one in which workers experience great inequality, exploitation, and alienation. Work, for Marx, was central to human happiness and fulfilment; however, the conditions inherent in the capitalist economy denied workers the actualization of this basic human desire. The alienation of the proletariat from the product that was being produced, from the way in which it was produced, from themselves, and from their fellow workers, for Marx, was rooted in the nature of the capitalist economy.

Today, conflict thinkers still maintain the view that the interests of the dominant economic class and the working class are opposed and, for the most part, incompatible. Conflict theorist Richard Edwards (1979) has called the workplace in capitalist economies "contested terrain" in which struggle and competition between these two groups is inevitable.

Functionalist View

Although conflict thinkers view the capitalist economy as the basis for inequality, and thus as an institution requiring radical change, functional thinkers view the economy in an uncritical fashion. The economy, for functionalists, is an integral part of the whole society in which the various institutions (family, religion, education, and so on) contribute to the functioning of that society through their interdependence and interrelationships. Functionalists believe that the economy, with workplaces containing diverse jobs and occupations, serves to provide order and regulation.

Functional sociologists Kingsley Davis and Wilbur Moore (1945), in their classic argument on the function of social stratification, maintain that an economy based on inequality, such as the capitalist economy, ensures that the best people reach the top positions of the workplace. Critics of this view, such as Melvin Tumin (1953), maintain that those who are disadvantaged because of ascribed characteristics, such as class, race, and gender, may, in fact, be the "best," but because of the barriers they face in hiring and employment practices (e.g., the glass ceiling), they rarely make it to the top positions in the economy. Today, when we examine who makes it to the highest positions of the Canadian economy, clearly the economy is more "functionally" beneficial to some Canadians rather than to others.

Feminist Views

Although feminist perspectives are diverse, many point to the economy as a source of gender inequality. As with conflict thinkers, Marxist feminists, for example, maintain that the principle of private ownership, central to capitalist economies, creates massive inequalities between those who own and those who work. Marxist feminists believe that at the heart of gender inequality is the fact that it is men who own the means of production and women who are used as a reserve of surplus labour—labour to be included or excluded at the whim of the owning class. Marxist feminists believe, therefore, that the root of women's opposition lies in the nature of the capitalist economy, where women's work in the paid workforce constitutes exploited labour and work done in the home goes unpaid.

In contrast to the Marxist feminists' view, socialist feminists maintain that because the capitalist economy and patriarchy are inextricably connected, both must be eliminated to bring about gender equality. For example, socialist feminists state that the economy could change from being privately owned to publicly owned; however, this would not ensure the elimination of patriarchal values, beliefs, and norms, which perpetuate sexism.

Liberal feminism, which tends to be moderate in its recommendations for change, suggests how the economy could be tweaked, rather than overhauled, to provide women with greater access to jobs and economic power.

Interactionist View

Interactionist sociologists examine the meaning that people give to work and the economy. Using this theoretical perspective allows us to see not only what work means to people but also why they work, why they choose to retire, how they view being unemployed, and how they view work relative to other aspects of their lives. Do people work only because they need money to feed and house themselves and their families? Or do they also work for intrinsic reasons, such as self-fulfilment and a sense of identity? Sociologist Robert Wuthnow (1996) found that although people said that the most important reason for working was for the money, when asked what they preferred about their jobs, 48 percent said "a feeling of accomplishment." Work also may provide people with a social network, a feeling of engagement in the larger society, or a sense of attachment to a community.

The Face of the Workforce

The workforce in Canada is constantly changing. During World War II, when men were mobilized to fight abroad, women entered the workforce in large numbers. During the postwar years, however, many women retreated to the private sphere, where domesticity and family life took primacy over paid employment. During the 1970s, a trend began that proved to be one of the most significant forces of social change in the latter half of the twentieth century—the changing role of women in Canadian society. From 1980 to 1985 and from 1985 to 1990, women accounted for 14.7 percent and 29.6 percent, respectively, of increases in full-time, full-year workers. This compares with the increases of 1.7 percent and 10.6 percent for men during the same periods (Statistics Canada 1998). Figure 13-3 shows the increases in the percentage of women aged 15 and over in the workforce. In addition, the federal government's Employment Equity Act of 1986 established the existence of four "target groups": women, people of Aboriginal descent, people with disabilities, and members of visible minorities. It was the government's plan to increase the representation of these groups in the Canadian workforce.

Although predictions are not always reliable, sociologists and labour specialists foresee a workforce increasingly comprising women and members of racial and ethnic minorities. In 1960 there were twice as many men in the paid labour force as women. Today, women constitute slightly less than half of all Canadians 15 years of age and older in the paid labour force. It's likely that by 2015 the total numbers of male and female workers will be the same.

The Canadian workforce increasingly reflects the diversity of the population as ethnic and visible minority immigrants enter the labour force. All immigrants, however, do not face the same treatment when entering the Canadian workforce. Visible minority immigrants experience greater inequality in income and employment than do those immigrants whose identities are not racialized. The "double jeopardy" of being a member of a visible minority and female compounds the effects of inequality in the workforce, resulting in lower incomes and fewer employment opportunities. The impact of this changing labour force is not merely statistical. A more diverse workforce means that relationships between workers are more likely to cross gender, racial, and ethnic lines. Interactionists

pp. 201–203

FIGURE 13-3

Employment of Canadian Women Aged 15 and over, 1976–2000, Selected Years

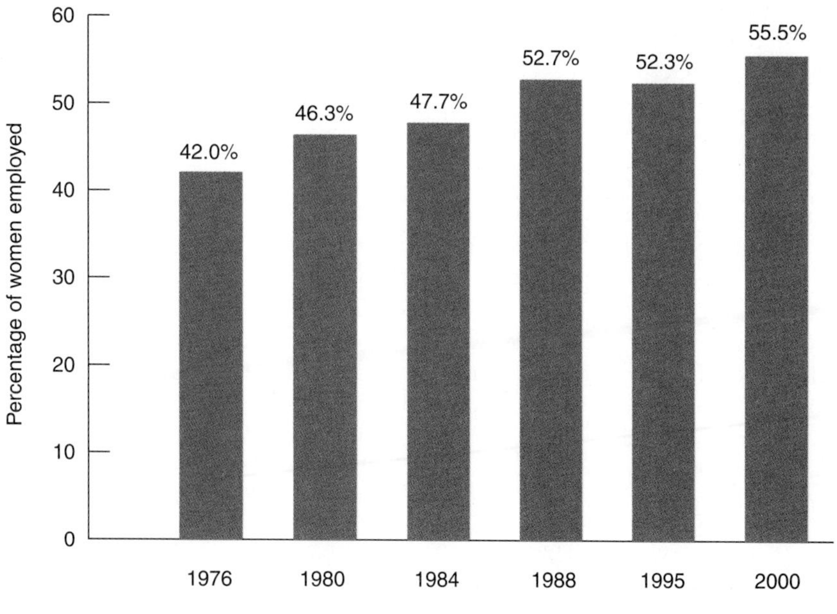

Source: Adapted by the author from Statistics Canada 2003g.

note that people will find themselves supervising and being supervised by people very different from them. In response to these changes, 75 percent of businesses had instituted some type of cultural diversity training programs by 2000 (Melia 2000).

Deindustrialization

What happens when a company decides it is more profitable to move its operations out of an established community to another part of the country or out of the country altogether? People lose jobs; stores lose customers; the local government's tax base declines and it cuts services. This devastating process has occurred again and again in the past decade or so.

When North American plants deindustrialize at home, they often move their investment in manufacturing outside the country to take advantage of low wages. Shown here is a U.S. AT&T telephone repair plant located in Nuevo Laredo, Mexico.

The term ***deindustrialization*** refers to the systematic, widespread withdrawal of investment in basic aspects of productivity, such as factories and plants. Giant corporations that deindustrialize are not necessarily refusing to invest in new economic opportunities. Rather, the targets and locations of investment change, and the need for permanent or standard labour decreases as technology continues to automate production. First, there may be a relocation of plants from central cities to the suburbs. The next step may be relocation from suburban areas to jurisdictions where labour laws place more restrictions on unions. Finally, a corporation may simply relocate *outside* Canada to a country, such as Mexico, with a lower rate of prevailing wages. General Motors, for example, decided to build a multibillion-dollar plant in Spain rather than in Kansas City (Bluestone and Harrison 1982; Rifkin 1995).

Although deindustrialization may involve relocation, in some instances it takes the form of corporate restructuring, as companies seek to reduce costs in the face of growing worldwide competition. When such restructuring occurs, the impact on the bureaucratic hierarchy of formal organizations can be significant. A large corporation may choose to sell off or entirely abandon less productive divisions and eliminate layers of management viewed as unnecessary. Wages and salaries may be frozen and fringe benefits cut—all in the name of "restructuring." Increasing reliance on automation also spells the end of work as we have known it.

The term ***downsizing*** was introduced in 1987 to refer to reductions in a company's workforce. Downsizing contributed to the elimination of 60 percent of the workforce in British Columbia's sawmills between 1979 and 1998. According to the Economic Council of Canada, between 1988 and 1995, the manufacturing sector lost 400 000 jobs—17 percent of its workforce. The deindustrialization of Canada contributed to lower levels of job creation: job creation rates fell from 2 percent per year in the 1980s to 1 percent per year in the 1990s. Overall, though, from 1975 to 1995, there was a net increase of 2.8 million jobs in Canada. These jobs, however, were in the service sector, where wages are typically lower, benefits are fewer, and part-time work is more common. Two-thirds of these new jobs went to women, which only serves to perpetuate the "pink ghetto" phenomenon, in which women are overrepresented in areas of employment that provide fewer rewards, opportunities, and benefits.

Viewed from a conflict perspective, the unprecedented attention given to downsizing in the mid-1990s reflected the continuing importance of social class in Canada. Conflict theorists note that job loss, affecting factory workers in particular, has long been a feature of deindustrialization. But when large numbers of middle-class managers and other white-collar employees with substantial incomes began to be laid off, suddenly there was great concern in the media over downsizing. By mid-2000, downsizing was being applied to dot-com companies, the sector of the economy that had flown high in the 1990s (Richtel 2000; Safire 1996; R. Samuelson 1996a, 1996b).

The social costs of deindustrialization and downsizing cannot be minimized. Plant closings, such as the carpet factory in Hawkesbury, Ontario, in 1999, lead to substantial unemployment in a community; this can have a devastating impact on both the microlevel and the macrolevel. On the microlevel, the unemployed person and his or her family must adjust to a loss of spending power. Both marital happiness and family cohesion may suffer as a result. Although many dismissed workers eventually reenter the paid labour force, they often must accept less desirable positions with lower salaries and fewer benefits. Unemployment and underemployment are tied into many of the social problems discussed throughout this textbook, among them the need for child care, the controversy over welfare, and immigration issues.

On the societal, or macro-, level, the impact on a community of a plant closing can be as difficult as it is for an individual worker and his or her family. As noted earlier, the community will experience a significant loss of tax revenues. It then becomes more difficult to support police and fire protection, schools, parks, and other public services. Moreover, rising unemployment in a community leads to a reduced demand for goods and services. Sales by retail firms and other businesses fall off, and this can lead to further layoffs.

E-commerce

Another development following close on the heels of deindustrialization was the emergence of e-commerce, as online businesses compete with bricks-and-mortar establishments. ***E-commerce*** refers to the numerous ways that people with access to the Internet can do business from their computers. Amazon.com, for example, began in 1995 as a supplier of books but soon became the prototype for online businesses, branching into selling a variety of merchandise, including toys and hardware equipment. By 2002, Amazon.com boasted customers in 220 countries. The growth of e-commerce means jobs in a new line of industry as well as growth for related industries, such as warehousing, packing, and shipping. However, the industry is volatile, and many e-commerce companies have yet to turn a profit. In 2000, when the speculative dot-com bubble burst, hundreds of companies failed and thousands of unsuspecting employees lost their jobs.

Although e-commerce will not immediately overwhelm traditional businesses, it has brought new social dynamics to the retail trade. Consider the impact on traditional retail outlets and on face-to-face interaction with local store owners. Even established companies, such as Chapters, Indigo, A&B Sound, and Mattel, have their own online "stores," bypassing the retail outlets that they courted for years in order to directly reach customers with their merchandise. Megamalls once replaced personal ties to stores for many shoppers; the growth of e-commerce with its "cybermalls" is just the latest change in the economy.

Some observers note that e-commerce offers more opportunities to consumers in rural areas (assuming they have the necessary high-tech infrastructure) and those with disabilities. To its critics, however, e-commerce signals more social isolation, more alienation, and greater disconnect for the poor and disadvantaged who are not a part of the new information technology (Amazon.com 2001; Drucker 1999; Stoughton and Walker 1999).

The Contingency Workforce

In the past, the term *temp* typically conjured up images of a replacement receptionist or a worker covering for someone on vacation. However, along with the deindustrialization and downsizing described above, contingency work—work that is considered atypical or nonstandard—has emerged.

The downsizing of both the public and the private sectors in the 1980s was accompanied by the growth of nonstandard work in Canada. Nonstandard work is contingent on the employer's needs; it can include part-time and temporary work, work that is contracted or outsourced, and self-employment. In 1990, the Economic Council of Canada released a report making the distinction between "good jobs" (i.e., work that is done on an ongoing basis and provides some degree of continuity and security) and "bad jobs" (i.e., work that is nonstandard). Grant Schellenberg and Christopher Clark (1996) wrote a report for the Canadian Council for Social Development in which they argue that new forms of employment are one of the strategies used by corporations to achieve flexibility in a changing economic environment—an environment greatly transformed by free trade, global markets, new technologies, and shifting customer demands. Incidentally, this so-called flexibility also allows for employees to hire workers without having to provide benefits, such as pensions, health care, dental plans, and disability insurance. The private sector is not alone in its shift toward nonstandard work; the public sector has increased its rates of nonstandard work as well. In 1981, this type of work made up 12.4 percent of the total employment sector; by 1997, it was 19 percent.

Nonstandard jobs are most often filled by women and younger people. These jobs are part-time or temporary, contracted or outsourced, and often in self-employment areas.

Both unemployed workers and entrants to the paid labour force accept positions as temporary or part-time workers. Some do so for flexibility and control over their work time, but others accept these jobs because they are the only ones available. Young people and women are especially likely to fill nonstandard positions (Johanis and Meguerditchian 1996).

During the 1970s and 1980s, temporary workers typically held low-skill positions at fast-food restaurants, telemarketing firms, and other service industries. Today, the contingent workforce is evident at virtually *all* skill levels and in *all* industries. Clerical "temps" handle word processing and filing duties, managers are hired on a short-term basis to reorganize departments, freelance writers prepare speeches for corporate executives, and blue-collar workers fill in for a few months when a factory receives an unusually high number of orders. A significant minority of temporary employees are contract workers who are being "rented" for specific periods of time by the companies that previously downsized them—and are now working at lower salary levels without benefits or job security (Kirk 1995; Uchitelle 1996).

Use Your Sociological Imagination

What will the Canadian workforce look like in 2020? Consider workers' ages, genders, races, and ethnicities. How much education will workers need? Will they work full time or part time? What will be the most common occupations?

SOCIAL POLICY AND GOVERNMENT AND THE ECONOMY

Gender Equality

The Issue

Despite the reality that more than one-half of the Canadian population is female, Canadian women are considered a minority group. As discussed in Chapter 9, members of a minority group experience unequal treatment compared with members of dominant groups; membership in a minority group is not voluntary—people are born into this group; and members of minority groups share physical or cultural characteristics that distinguish them from the dominant group.

Because of systemic discrimination and cultural attitudes concerning their "essential" nature, Canadian women have been underrepresented—in varying degrees based on age, race, ethnicity, sexual orientation, and physical disability—in decision-making positions in Canadian society. These decision-making positions may include those of elected politics: provincial or territorial premiers, the prime minister of Canada, members of provincial or territorial legislatures, members of the House of Commons, and federal cabinet ministers, to name a few. As well, women are often underrepresented in other nonelected decision-making positions in government, such as senior bureaucratic posts in federal and provincial or territorial government departments, such as finance, education, health, foreign affairs, and trade and industry. The underrepresentation of women in top decision-making positions is even more pronounced in the private sector than in the public sector: fewer than 2 percent of the CEOs of major companies in Canada are female.

In 1995, in the Canadian government's policy initiative *Setting the Stage for the Next Century: The Federal Plan for Gender Equality*, Shiela Finestone, then the secretary of state for the status of women, wrote:

> There is no question that women—and men—are living in a better Canada because of advances in gender equality. These advances have created change in the workplace, in public policy and public attitudes, and in our individual lives. (Status of Women Canada 1995)

Finestone reaffirmed Canada's commitment to advancing the goal of gender equality first established in law in the Charter of Rights and Freedoms ten years earlier. Employment equity, a federal Act, attempts to eliminate barriers found by minority group members (women being one group) in the area of employment. The objectives of both documents (the *Federal Plan for Gender Equality* and the Charter) make it clear that there is a commitment to advancing women's full participation in Canadian society.

The Setting

The struggle for gender equality in Canada is one involving an ongoing effort by thousands of women over many decades. Table 13-1 traces the "progress" of women's rights in Canada—progress that has included some women while excluding others.

Most notably, although Alberta, Saskatchewan, and Manitoba were the first provinces to give women the vote in 1916, they did not include Aboriginal women. Before 1960, only those Aboriginals people (women and men) who gave up their Indian status were entitled to vote. Aboriginal women who married white men were automatically "enfranchised" (i.e., given the right to vote) (Ng 1988).

The progress of women's rights in Canada since the early twentieth century can be grouped into three stages (Mossman 1998):

1. Those involving the right to vote for *some* women in the early twentieth century
2. Those involving important "test case" legal claims during the second wave of feminism in the 1960s and 1970s
3. Those involving equality claims and the Canadian Charter of Rights and Freedoms since the mid-1980s

Sociological Insights

Sociologists, depending on their theoretical perspective, differ in the degree to which they emphasize the role of gender in the public realms of the economy and politics. As might be expected, feminist perspectives tend to address the ways in which both public and private spheres are gendered, the reasons for gender inequality, and the strategies for social change. What also might be expected is that there is great diversity among feminist thinkers concerning the underpinnings of gender inequality in society

Table 13-1 Progress of Women's Rights in Canada

1916 —	First provinces give women right to vote—Alberta, Saskatchewan, and Manitoba
1918 —	Women are given full federal right to vote
1920 —	Women are given right to be elected to Parliament
1921 —	First woman elected to the House of Commons
1928 —	Supreme Court of Canada decides that women are not "persons" and cannot be appointed to the Senate of Canada
1929 —	British Privy Council overturns Supreme Court decision
1930 —	First woman Senator
1952 —	First province enacts equal pay legislation—Ontario
1955 —	Restrictions on the employment of married women in the federal public service are removed
1956 —	Legislation is enacted guaranteeing equal pay for equal work within federal jurisdiction
1957 —	First woman Cabinet Minister
1961 —	Canadian Bill of Rights is passed
1977 —	Canadian Human Rights Act forbids discrimination on the basis of sex and ensures equal pay for work of equal value for women; Canadian Labour Code is similarly amended and provides for 17 weeks of maternity leave
1978 —	Canadian Labour Code is amended, eliminating pregnancy as a basis for lay-off or dismissal
1982 —	Canadian Charter of Rights and Freedoms, Section 28, is enacted—Charter guarantees apply equally to men and women
1983 —	Canadian Human Rights Act is amended to prohibit sexual harassment and to ban discrimination on the basis of pregnancy and family or marital status
1984 —	First woman Governor General
1984 —	Canadian Constitution is amended to affirm that Aboriginal and treaty rights are guaranteed equally to both men and women
1985 —	Section 15 of the Canadian Charter of Rights and Freedoms comes into effect, guaranteeing equality for all Canadians before and under law and equal protection and benefit of law
1985 —	Court Challenges Program expanded to address equality rights cases
1985 —	Indian Act is amended, restoring status and right to band membership to Indian women who had lost such status through marriage to a non-Indian
1986 —	Employment Equity Act is introduced, applicable to Crown corporations and federally regulated business, aimed at redressing historic and systemic discrimination of "larger group" populations
1993 —	Guidelines on women refugee claimants are instituted for the Immigration and Refugee Board
1994 —	Funding for equality test cases is reinstated as Charter Law Development Program
1995 —	Gender-based analysis of legislation and policies is adopted by the federal government

Source: Status of Women Canada 1995.

in general and in the economy and politics in particular, and the appropriate remedies for its eradication.

Radical feminists view gender inequality through the prism of the omnipresence of patriarchy, such that the laws, policies, and legislation of the public sphere will reflect patriarchal priorities and values. Thus, to achieve gender equality in such realms as the economy and politics, patriarchy's grip on society must be removed.

Liberal or equality feminists differ from radical feminists in that they advocate making incremental alterations to the public sphere through policies and legislation, with the goal of providing women with greater access to employment, education, and greater overall participation in the public sphere. Unlike radical feminists, who would consider this approach fruitless because of the persistence of patriarchy, liberal feminists tend to be more conservative in their approach to addressing gender inequality. As well, liberal feminists, who were among the reformers who struggled to achieve suffrage for *some* women during the first wave of feminism, were white, heterosexual, middle-class women. Critical of the universal manner in which women's perspectives are presented by liberal, radical, and other feminist perspectives, standpoint or antiracism perspectives emphasize the need to include the specificity and diversity of women's experiences; for example, the effects of racism and heterosexism need to be included in analyses of gender inequality in the economic and political spheres.

Although it may seem counterintuitive, not all feminist perspectives advocate women's full participation in political and economic life. Anarchist feminist Emma Goldman, for example, believed that the right to vote (i.e., female suffrage), access to higher education, and overall greater participation in public life were *not* desirable goals and would *not* improve the quality of life for many women:

> Goldman's rejection of female suffrage, higher education and careerism was not, as many liberal reformers thought, based on a rejection of women as equal partners with men in the public sphere or a claim that women were not "fit" for public life. Rather, Goldman rejected these feminist goals because she believed that public or "State" life was "unfit" for women and not worthy of their participation. (Haaland 1993:47)

Policy Initiatives

Canada's 1995 *Federal Plan for Gender Equality* was to set "the stage for the next century." The plan, among other elements, provides an opportunity to change the ways in which government legislation and policies are analyzed, increasing the government's ability to address the issue of gender equality. The stated intention of the plan is to recognize the diverse realities of women's lives, realities shaped by not only gender but also by age, race, class, national origin, mental and physical disability, region, religion, and language (Status of Women 1995). The federal plan for gender equality is organized around eight objectives (Status of Women 1995):

1. Implementing gender-based analysis throughout federal departments and agencies to inform and guide the legislation and policy process
2. Improving women's economic autonomy and well-being through such efforts as promoting women's equitable participation in the paid and unpaid labour force
3. Improving women's physical and psychological well-being through a women's health strategy and in research, policy development, and practices in health care
4. Reducing violence in society, particularly violence against women and children
5. Promoting gender equality in all aspects of Canada's cultural life
6. Incorporating women's perspectives into governance
7. Promoting global gender equality
8. Advancing gender equality for employees of federal departments

Applying Theory

1. Do you think it is more important for women to gain equality within the home or in the workplace? Do you think that they can be separated?
2. Do you think employment equity policies will reach their goals in your lifetime?
3. If Marxist feminists could draft a law that would provide equality for women in Canadian society, what provisions would it include?

CHAPTER RESOURCES

Summary

The ***economic system*** of a society has an important influence on social behaviour and on other social institutions. Each society must have a ***political system*** to establish procedures for the allocation of valued resources.

1. As the Industrial Revolution proceeded, a new form of social structure emerged: the industrial society.
2. Economic systems of capitalism vary in the degree to which the government regulates private ownership and economic activity, but all emphasize the profit motive.
3. The basic objective of a socialist economic system is to eliminate economic exploitation and meet people's needs.
4. Marx believed that ***communism*** would naturally evolve out of the socialism stage.
5. There are three basic sources of power within any political system: coercion, ***influence,*** and ***authority.***
6. Max Weber identified three ideal types of authority: ***traditional, legal-rational,*** and ***charismatic.***
7. The principal institutions of ***political socialization*** in Canada are the family, schools, and the media.
8. Political participation makes government accountable to its citizens, but there is a great deal of apathy in both Canada and other countries.
9. Women are still underrepresented in office but are becoming more successful at winning elections to public office.
10. Advocates of the ***elite model*** of the power structure of Canada see the country as being ruled by a small group of individuals who share common political and economic interests (a ***power elite***), whereas advocates of a ***pluralist model*** believe that power is more widely shared among conflicting groups.
11. The nature of the Canadian economy is changing. Sociologists are interested in the changing face of the workforce, the effects of ***deindustrialization,*** increased use of a contingency workforce, and the emergence of e-commerce.
12. The struggle for women's equality in Canada has been ongoing over the last century. Over the past 40 years there have been improvements in women's access to political and economic opportunities, partly because of employment equity programs, but the goal of a gender equity has not yet been achieved. Through its federal plan to achieve gender equality, Canada has begun to work for this goal at home and in other parts of the world.

Critical Thinking Questions

1. How are the decision makers of Canada different from those whose lives are being affected by their decisions?
2. Who really holds power at the university you attend? Describe the distribution of power at your school, drawing on the elite and pluralist models where they are relevant.
3. Do you vote during provincial or territorial or federal elections? If not, why not? What do you think the implications of growing political apathy might be?
4. If you had the power to change the way in which electoral politics work, how would you increase the diversity of those elected to represent Canadians?

Key Terms

Authority Power that has been institutionalized and is recognized by the people over whom it is exercised. (page 304)

Charismatic authority Power made legitimate by a leader's exceptional personal or emotional appeal to his or her followers. (305)

Communism As an ideal type, an economic system under which all property is communally owned and no social distinctions are made on the basis of people's ability to contribute to the economy. (302)

Deindustrialization The systematic, widespread withdrawal of investment in basic aspects of productivity, such as factories and plants. (314)

Downsizing Reductions taken in a company's workforce as part of deindustrialization. (314)

E-commerce Numerous ways that people with access to the Internet can do business from their computer. (315)

Economic system The structures and processes through which goods and services are produced, distributed, and consumed. (300)

Elite model A view of society as controlled by a small group of individuals who share a common set of political and economic interests. (309)

Force The actual or threatened use of coercion to impose a person's will on others. (303)

Influence The exercise of power through a process of persuasion. (303)

Informal economy Transfers of money, goods, or services that are not reported to the government. (303)

Laissez-faire A form of capitalism under which people compete freely, with minimal government intervention in the economy. (301)

Legal-rational authority Power made legitimate by law. (305)

Monopoly Control of a market by a single business firm. (301)

Pluralist model A view of society in which many competing groups within the community have access to government so that no single group is dominant. (310)

Political socialization The process by which individuals acquire political attitudes and develop patterns of political behaviour. (306)

Political system The structures and processes used for implementing and achieving society's goals. (300)

Politics In Harold D. Lasswell's words, "who gets what, when, and how." (303)

Power elite A small group of military, industrial, and government leaders who control the fate of the every major capitalistic country. (309)

Socialism An economic system under which the means of production and distribution are collectively owned. (302)

Terrorism The use or threat of violence against random or symbolic targets in pursuit of political aims. (311)

Traditional authority Legitimate power conferred by custom and accepted practice. (305)

Suggested Readings

Dyck, Rand. 2006. *Canadian Politics,* concise 3rd ed. Toronto: Nelson Thompson. A comprehensive overview of Canadian politics that includes coverage of political culture, socialization, and participation, as well as the mass media and public opinion polls.

Knuttila, Murray, and Wendee Kubik. 2000. *State Theories: Classical, Global, and Feminist Perspectives,* 3rd ed. Halifax: Fernwood Publishers. A review of various perspectives on the state.

Tremblay, Manon, and Caroline Andrews, eds. 1998. *Women and Political Representation in Canada.* Ottawa: Ottawa University Press. A collection of writings addressing a variety of issues related to women and politics in Canada.

Online Learning Centre

Visit the *Sociology: A Brief Introduction* Online Learning Centre at www.mcgrawhill.ca/college/schaefer to access quizzes, interactive exercises, video clips, and other research and study tools related to this chapter.

Reel Society Interactive Movie CD-ROM 2.0

Reel Society 2.0 can be used to spark discussion about the following topics from this chapter:

- Power and authority
- Economic systems
- The changing economy

chapter 14

POPULATION, AGING, AND HEALTH

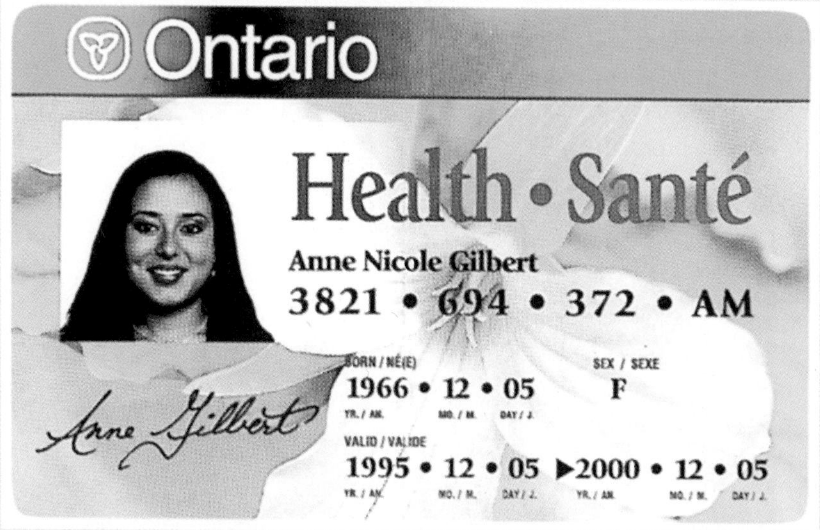

The condition of medicare has become a major concern for Canadians, with public debates and private discussions focusing on whether the present system requires restructuring or dismantling. The Ontario health card, necessary for health care in that province, can also be used in other provinces, illustrating the Canada Health Act's principle of portability.

Good workers are always hard to find, but just wait till boomers start retiring. Smart businesses are already preparing for the crunch. Here's how John Murphy has done the math, and it doesn't look good: over the next five years, his company will likely need to replace more than a quarter of its 11,000 employees. Murphy, executive vice-president of human resources at Ontario Power Generation, the Crown corporation that manages provincial electricity supply, says there isn't much he can do to avoid it. The average age of OPG's workforce is 45, its ranks filled with baby boomers who have their sights set on retirement. Many of those leaving the corporation in the next few years will be senior engineers and managers who, after decades on the job, will give up their desks for good—taking valuable skills and experience with them. . . .

This year, the oldest members of the Canadian baby boom generation—those born from 1947 to 1966—will turn 57, an age at which most people are downshifting their careers, if not pulling out of the rat race altogether. In 2011, nearly one-fifth of boomers will be 61, and the proportion of the population 65 years or older will begin to expand rapidly, reinforced by a low birth rate and longer life expectancy. What does this mean for Canada's labour force? In 2001, the baby boom generation made up 47% of the labour force, and by the end of the last decade 15% of working Canadians were within 10 years of retirement age. It follows that by 2010, some occupations will begin to experience shortages. In fact, according to a 2001 Conference Board of Canada report, sectors like manufacturing, construction, technology, health care and financial services are already experiencing skill shortages, some due to retiring boomers. One survey of medium-sized and large companies revealed that 83% experienced shortages of skilled labour, and more than 60% expected them to become more pronounced in the future.

The changing demographics have many subtleties. For instance, some argue that changing policies to make it easier for immigrant professionals to gain acceptable Canadian accreditation could help. Then there's the so-called echo generation, born between 1980 and 1995, that's starting to enter the job market. But the echoes are a smaller cohort than their boomer parents and, more importantly, they won't be able to step into the senior-level jobs the oldest boomers vacate. Theoretically, younger boomers now in their late 30s and early 40s might be available for those assignments, but, corporations shed many of those Gen X employees during restructuring—they were stuck in dead-end jobs behind the older boomers anyway—and many turned away from corporate-ladder climbing in favour of entrepreneurial career paths. And there aren't nearly enough people in the "bust" generation between the boomers and their children. "There are some significant demographic situations in Canada, particularly companies that have a mature labour force," says Robert Scott, a consultant at PricewaterhouseCoopers. "They're looking at the longer-term plan for replacing those skills as people start to retire." *(Wahl 2004)* ■

Andrew Wahl, in his article "Leaders Wanted: Skills Shortage Dead Ahead," describes the problem facing many Canadian CEOs: a looming job crunch. He relates the expected shortage of skilled workers in workplaces across Canada to population factors or demographics. According to Wahl, much of the shortage will be due to the population issue of aging and the age structure of the population. The generation closest to retirement is the baby boom generation—those born between 1947 and 1966—who make up more than 33 percent of the Canadian population. Wahl addresses the impact that this generation's retirement will have on workplaces and various employment sectors and suggests strategies to deal with the demand for skilled workers.

Sociologists who study population issues, such as aging, have a key role in policymaking on these issues.

This chapter takes a sociological overview of certain aspects of the population as well as the population-related issues of health, illness, and medicine as a social institution. We will begin with Thomas Robert Malthus's controversial analysis of population trends and Karl Marx's critical response to it. A brief overview of world population history follows. We'll pay particular attention to the current problem of overpopulation and the prospects for and potential consequences of stable population growth in Canada and the United States.

In the second half of the chapter we will examine how functionalists, conflict theorists, interactionists, feminist, and labelling theorists look at health-related issues. Then we will study the distribution of diseases in a society by gender, social class, race and ethnicity, and age. We'll also look at the evolution of the health care system of Canada. Sociologists are interested in the roles that people play within the health care system and the organizations that deal with issues of health and sickness. Therefore, we will analyze the interactions among doctors, nurses, and patients; the role of government in providing health services; and alternatives to traditional health care. Finally, the social policy section will explore the issue of how to finance health care worldwide. ■

Use Your Sociological Imagination www.mcgrawhill.ca/college/schaefer

Does mandatory retirement make sense given that Canadians are living healthier and longer lives while, at the same, Canada needs skilled workers? How long would you like to work—until you are 55, 65, or maybe 70?

DEMOGRAPHY: THE STUDY OF POPULATION

The study of population issues engages the attention of both natural and social scientists. The biologist explores the nature of reproduction and casts light on factors that affect ***fertility***, the level of reproduction among women of childbearing age. The medical pathologist examines and analyzes trends in the causes of death. Geographers, historians, and psychologists also have distinctive contributions to make to our understanding of population. Sociologists, more than these other researchers, focus on the *social* factors that influence population rates and trends.

In their study of population issues, sociologists are keenly aware that various elements of population—such as fertility and *mortality* (the amount of death)—are profoundly affected by the norms, values, and social patterns of a society. Fertility is influenced by people's age of entry into sexual unions and by their use of contraception—both of which, in turn, reflect the social and religious values that guide a particular culture. Mortality is shaped by a nation's level of nutrition, acceptance of immunization, and provisions for sanitation, as well as its general commitment to health care and health education. Migration from one country to another can depend on marital and kinship ties, the relative degree of racial and religious tolerance in various societies, and people's evaluations of employment opportunities.

Demography is the scientific study of population. It draws on several components of population, including size, composition, and territorial distribution, to understand the social consequences of population. Demographers study geographical variations and historical trends in their effort to develop population forecasts. They also analyze the structure of a population—the age, gender, race, and ethnicity of its members. A key figure in this type of analysis was Thomas Malthus.

Malthus's Thesis and Marx's Response

The Reverend Thomas Robert Malthus (1766–1834) was educated at Cambridge University and spent his life teaching history and political economy. He strongly criticized two major institutions of his time—the church and slavery—yet his most significant legacy for contemporary scholars is his still-controversial *Essays on the Principle of Population,* published in 1798.

Essentially, Malthus held that the world's population was growing more rapidly than the available food supply. Malthus argued that the food supply increases in an arithmetic progression (1, 2, 3, 4, and so on), whereas the population expands by a geometric progression (1, 2, 4, 8, and so on). According to his analysis, the gap between the food supply and the population will continue to grow over time. Even though the food supply will increase, it will not increase nearly enough to meet the needs of an expanding world population.

Malthus advocated population control to close the gap between the rising population and the food supply, yet he explicitly denounced artificial means of birth control because they were not sanctioned by religion. For Malthus, the appropriate way to control population was to postpone marriage. He argued that couples must take responsibility for the number of children they choose to bear; without such restraint, the world would face widespread hunger, poverty, and misery (Malthus, Huxley, and Osborn 1960, original edition 1824; Petersen 1979).

Karl Marx strongly criticized Malthus's views on population. Marx pointed to the nature of economic relations in Europe's industrial societies as the central problem. He could not accept the Malthusian notion that a rising world population, rather than capitalism, was the cause of social ills. In Marx's opinion, there was no special relationship between world population figures and the supply of resources (including food). If society were well ordered, increases in population should lead to greater wealth, not to hunger and misery.

Of course, Marx did not believe that capitalism operated under these ideal conditions. He maintained that capitalism devoted its resources to the financing of buildings and tools rather than to more equitable distribution of food, housing, and other necessities of life. Marx's work is important to the study of population because he linked overpopulation to the unequal distribution of resources—a topic that will be taken up again later in this chapter. His concern with the writings of Malthus also testifies to the importance of population in political and economic affairs.

The insights of Malthus and Marx regarding population issues have come together in what is termed the *neo-Malthusian view.* Best exemplified by the work of Paul Ehrlich (1968; Ehrlich and Ehrlich 1990), author of *The Population Bomb,* neo-Malthusians agree with Malthus that world population growth is outstretching natural resources. However, in contrast to the British theorist, they insist that birth control measures are needed to regulate population increases. Neo-Malthusians have a Marxist flavour in their condemnation of developed nations that, despite their low birthrates, consume a disproportionately large share of world resources. Although rather pessimistic about the future, these theorists stress that birth control and sensible use of resources are essential responses to rising world population (Tierney 1990; Weeks 1999; for a critique, see Commoner 1971).

Studying Population Today

The relative balance of births and deaths is no less important today than it was during the lifetime of Malthus and Marx. The suffering that Malthus spoke of is certainly a reality for many people of the world who are hungry and poor. Malnutrition remains the largest contributing factor to illness and death among children in the developing countries. Almost 18 percent of these children will die before age five—a rate more than 11 times higher than in developed nations. Warfare and large-scale migration intensify problems of population and food supply. For example, strife in Bosnia, Iraq, and Sudan caused very uneven distribution of food supplies, leading to regional concerns about malnutrition and even starvation. Combatting world hunger may require reducing human births, dramatically increasing the world's food supply, or perhaps both at the same time. The study of population-related issues seems to be essential today (World Bank 2000b:277).

In Canada and most other countries, the census is the primary mechanism for collecting population information. A ***census*** is an enumeration or counting of a population. The Constitution Act of Canada requires that a census be held every ten years to determine representation in the House of Commons. The five-year census, which is mandated by Statistics Canada, provides the basis for government policies and decision making for social programs, such as housing, health care, day care, and federal–provincial/territorial transfer payments (Flanders 2001). The questions asked on the census reflect changing social and political patterns that reveal the dynamic nature of Canadian society. Table 14-1 shows some of the milestones of the Canadian census that reflect changing values and attitudes on such matters as unpaid work, common-law and same-sex partnerships, and fertility of those who have mental illnesses. As well, the study of our population is supplemented by vital statistics; these records of births, deaths, marriages, and divorces are gathered through a registration system maintained by governments. In addition, Statistics

Canada provides up-to-date information based on surveys of such topics as educational trends, the status of women, children, racial and ethnic minorities, agricultural crops, medical care, and time spent on leisure and recreational activities, to name only a few.

In administering a nationwide census and conducting other types of research, demographers employ many of the skills and techniques described in Chapter 2, including questionnaires, interviews, and sampling. The precision of population projections depends on the accuracy of a series of estimates that demographers must make. First, they must determine past population trends and establish a base population as of the date for which the forecast began. Next, birthrates and death rates must be established, along with estimates of future fluctuations. In making projections for a nation's population trends, demographers must consider migration as well, since a significant number of individuals may enter and leave a country.

Elements of Demography

Demographers communicate population facts with a language derived from the basic elements of human life—birth and death. The ***birthrate*** (or, more specifically, the *crude birthrate*) is the number of live births per 1000 population in a given year. In 2005, for example, there were an estimated 10.84 live births per 1000 people in Canada. The birthrate provides information on the actual reproductive patterns of a society.

One way demography can project future growth in a society is to make use of the ***total fertility rate (TFR)***. The TFR is the average number of children born alive to any woman, assuming that she conforms to current fertility rates. The TFR estimated for Canada in 2000 was 1.6 live births per woman, as compared with more than 3.66 births per woman in a developing country, such as Kenya.

Mortality, like fertility, is measured in several different ways. The ***death rate*** (also known as the *crude death rate*) is the number of deaths per 1000 population in a given year. In 2005, Canada had an estimated death rate of 7.73 per 1000 population. The ***infant mortality rate*** is the number of deaths of infants under one year of age per 1000 live births in a given year. This particular measure serves as an important indicator of a society's level of health care; it reflects prenatal nutrition, delivery procedures, and infant screening measures. The infant mortality rate also functions as a useful indicator of future population growth, since those infants who survive to adulthood will contribute to further population increases.

Nations vary widely in the rate of death of newborn children. In 2005, the estimated infant mortality rate for Canada was 4.75 deaths per 1000 live births, whereas for the world as a whole it was an estimated 50.11 deaths per 1000 live births. At the same time, some nations have lower rates of infant mortality than Canada, including Switzerland, Japan, and Sweden (see Figure 14-3 on page 340).

A general measure of health used by demographers is ***life expectancy***, the median number of years a person

Table 14-1 Selected Milestones in the History of the Census in Canada

1921:	The population questions no longer include those on "insanity and idiocy" and fertility.
1931:	Questions are added to gauge the extent and severity of unemployment, and to analyze its causes.
1956:	The first five-year national census is conducted. It is introduced to monitor the rapid economic growth and urbanization that took place during the postwar years.
1971:	The majority of respondents now complete the census questionnaire themselves, a process called *self-enumeration*. Under the new Statistics Act, it becomes a statutory requirement to hold censuses of population and of agriculture every five years.
1986:	The Census of Population contains a question on disability, which is also used to establish a sample of respondents for the first post-censal survey on activity limitation. Also for the first time, the Census of Agriculture asks a question on computer use for farm management.
1991:	For the first time, the census asks a question on common-law relationships.
1996:	A question on unpaid work is included in the census.
2001:	The definition of "common-law" is expanded to include both opposite-sex and same-sex partners. Also, the Census of Agriculture asks about production of certified organic products.

Source: Adapted from Flanders 2001:4.

can be expected to live under current mortality conditions. Usually the figure is reported as life expectancy *at birth*. At present, Japan reports a life expectancy at birth of 81 years, slightly higher than Canada's figure of 79 years. By contrast, life expectancy at birth is less than 45 years in several developing nations, including Gambia.

The ***growth rate*** of a society is the difference between births and deaths, plus the difference between *immigrants* (those who enter a country to establish permanent residence) and *emigrants* (those who leave a country permanently) per 1000 population. For the world as a whole, the growth rate is simply the difference between births and deaths per 1000 population, since worldwide immigration and emigration must of necessity be equal. In 2005, Canada had an estimated growth rate of 0.9 percent, compared with an estimated 1.14 percent for the entire world (*World Fact Book* 2005).

WORLD POPULATION PATTERNS

One important aspect of demographic work involves study of the history of population. But how is this possible? After all, official national censuses were relatively rare before 1850. Researchers interested in early population must turn to archeological remains of settlements, burial sites, baptismal and tax records, and oral history sources.

On October 13, 1999, in a maternity clinic in Sarajevo, Bosnia-Herzegovina, Helac Fatina gave birth to a son, who has been designated as the six billionth person on this planet. Yet until modern times, there were relatively few humans living in the world. One estimate placed the world population of a million years ago at only 125 000 people. As Table 14-2 indicates, the population has exploded in the past 200 years and continues to accelerate rapidly (World Health Organization 2000:3).

Demographic Transition

The phenomenal growth of the world population in recent times can be accounted for by changing patterns of births and deaths. Beginning in the late eighteenth century—and continuing until the middle of the twentieth century—there was a gradual reduction in death rates in Northern and Western Europe. People were able to live longer because of advances in food production, sanitation, nutrition, and public health care. Although death rates fell, birthrates remained high; as a result, there was unprecedented population growth during this period of European history. However, by the late nineteenth century, the birthrates of many European countries began to decline, and the rate of population growth also decreased (Bender and Smith 1997).

The changes in birthrates and death rates in nineteenth-century Europe serve as an example of demographic transition. Demographers use this term to describe an observed pattern in changing vital statistics. Specifically, ***demographic transition*** is the change from high birthrates and death rates to relatively low birthrates and death rates. This concept, which was introduced in the 1920s, is now widely used in the study of population trends.

As illustrated in Figure 14-1, demographic transition is typically viewed as a three-stage process:

1. *Pretransition stage:* high birthrates and death rates with little population growth
2. *Transition stage:* declining death rates, primarily the result of reductions in infant deaths, along with high to medium fertility—resulting in significant population growth
3. *Posttransition stage:* low birthrates and death rates with little population growth

Table 14-2 Estimated Time for Each Successive Increase of One Billion People in World Population

Population Level	Time Taken to Reach New Population Level	Year of Attainment
First billion	Human history before 1800	1804
Second billion	123 years	1927
Third billion	33 years	1960
Fourth billion	14 years	1974
Fifth billion	13 years	1987
Sixth billion	12 years	1999
Seventh billion	14 years	2013
Eighth billion	15 years	2028
Ninth billion	26 years	2054
Tenth billion	129 years	2183

Source: United Nations Population Division 2001.
Note: Data for 2013 through 2054 are projections.

FIGURE 14-1

Demographic Transition

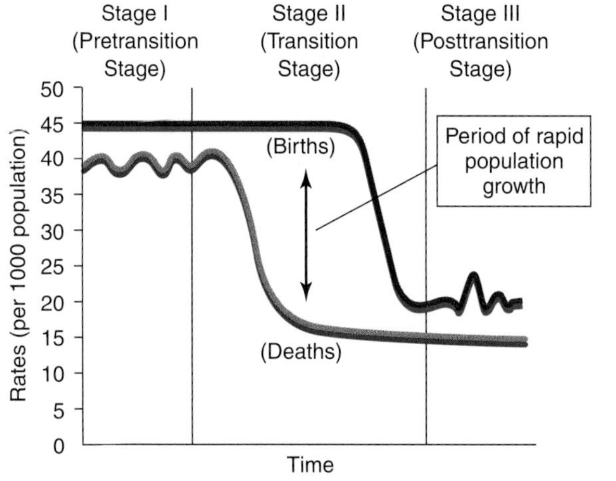

Demographers use the concept of *demographic transition* to describe changes in birthrates and death rates during stages of a nation's development. This graph shows the pattern that took place in developed nations. In the first stage, both birthrates and death rates were high, so that there was little population growth. In the second stage, the birthrate remained high while the death rate declined sharply, which led to rapid population growth. By the last stage, which many developing countries have yet to enter, the birthrate also declined, and there was again little population growth.

Demographic transition should be regarded not as a "law of population growth" but rather as a generalization of the population history of industrial nations. This concept helps us understand the growth problems faced by the world in the 1990s. About two-thirds of the world's nations have yet to pass fully through the second stage of demographic transition. Even if such nations make dramatic advances in fertility control, their populations will nevertheless increase greatly because of the large base of people already at prime childbearing age.

The pattern of demographic transition varies from nation to nation. One particularly useful distinction is the contrast between the transition now occurring in developing nations—which include about two-thirds of the world's population—and that that occurred over almost a century in more industrialized countries. Demographic transition in developing nations has involved a rapid decline in death rates without adjustments in birthrates.

Specifically, in the post–World War II period, the death rates of developing nations began a sharp decline. This revolution in "death control" was triggered by antibiotics, immunization, insecticides (such as DDT, used to strike at malaria-bearing mosquitoes), and largely successful campaigns against such fatal diseases as smallpox. Substantial medical and public health technology was imported almost overnight from more developed nations. As a result, the drop in death rates that had taken a century in Europe was telescoped into two decades in many developing countries.

Birthrates scarcely had time to adjust. Cultural beliefs about the proper size of families could not possibly change as quickly as the falling death rates. For centuries, couples had given birth to as many as eight or more children, knowing that perhaps only two or three would survive to adulthood. Consequently, whereas Europeans had had several generations to restrict their birthrates, peoples of developing nations needed to do the same in less than a lifetime. Many did not, as is evident from the astronomical "population explosion" that was already under way by the mid-twentieth century. Families were more willing to accept technological advances that prolonged life than to abandon fertility patterns that reflected centuries of tradition and religious training (Crenshaw, Christenson, and Oakey 2000; McFalls 1998).

The Population Explosion

Apart from war, rapid population growth has been perhaps the dominant international social problem of the past 30 years. Often this issue is referred to in emotional terms as the "population bomb" or the "population explosion." Such striking language is not surprising,

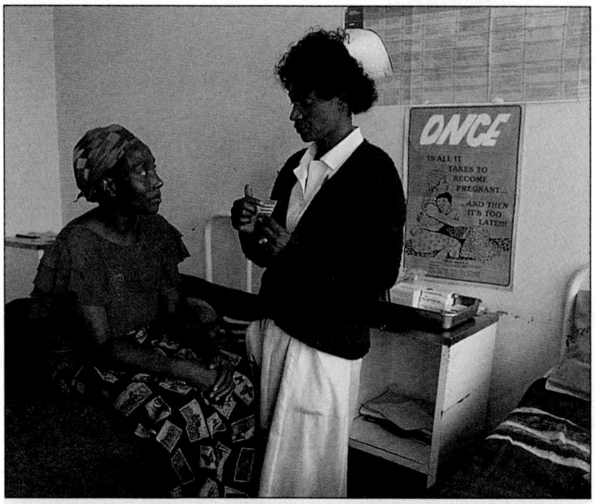

A nurse in Zambia, Africa, instructs a client in how to use birth control pills. Family planning clinics have helped to slow the population growth rate in developing countries.

Sociology in the Global Community

14-1 Population Policy in China

In a residential district in Shanghai, a member of the local family planning committee knocks on the door of a childless couple. Why, she inquires, have they not started a family?

Such a question would have been unthinkable in 1979, when family planning officials, in an attempt to avoid a looming population explosion, began resorting to sterilization to enforce the government rule of one child per family. Since then, the government has quietly begun to grant exceptions to the one-child policy to adults who are only children themselves. In 2002 it extended the privilege to all families, but at a price. A new family planning law imposes "social compensation fees" to cover the cost to society of an additional child. The fee, which is substantial, is equivalent to 20 years' worth of a rural farm family's income.

Chinese families are beset, too, by the unforeseen results of their attempts to circumvent the one-child policy. In the past, in an effort to ensure that their one child would be a male capable of perpetuating the family line, many couples chose to abort female fetuses, or quietly allowed female infants to die of neglect. As a result, among children one to four years old, China's sex ratio (the ratio of males to females) is now about 121 to 100—well above the normal rate at birth of 106 to 100. The difference in birthrates translates into 1.7 million fewer female births per year than normal—and down the line, to many fewer childbearers than normal.

Chinese women have borne the brunt not just of the government's population policy but also of the economic dislocation caused by recent market reforms and the redistribution of rural farmland. On rural farms, women struggle to cope without their husbands, many of whom have gone to work in city factories. The female suicide rate in rural China is now the highest in the world. Experts think this alarming statistic reflects a fundamental lack of self-esteem among rural Chinese women. The social patterns of centuries, unlike birthrates, cannot be changed in a generation.

Finally, the one-child policy has caused a shortage not just of rural workers, but of caretakers for the elderly. Coupled with improvements in longevity, the generation-long decline in births has greatly increased the ratio of dependent elders to able-bodied children. The migration of young adults to other parts of China has further compromised their ability to care for their elders. To compound the crisis, barely one in four of China's elders receives any pension at all. No other country in the world faces the prospect of caring for such a large population of seniors with so little available social support.

Applying Theory

1. How would a conflict perspective contribute to your understanding of the one-child policy in China?
2. What issues or topics might you raise as a sociologist examining this policy?

Sources: Glenn 2004; Kahn 2004; *Migration News* 2003; N. Riley 2004.

given the staggering increases in world population during the last two centuries (refer to Table 14-2). The population of our planet rose from 1 billion around the year 1800 to 6.1 billion by 2000 (Haub and Cornelius 2000).

By the middle 1970s, demographers had observed a slight decline in the growth rate of many developing nations. These countries were still experiencing population increases, yet their *rates* of increase had declined as death rates could not go much lower and birthrates began to fall. It appears that family planning efforts have been instrumental in this demographic change. Beginning in the 1960s, governments in certain developing nations sponsored or supported campaigns to encourage family planning. For example, in good part as the result of government-sponsored birth control campaigns, Thailand's total fertility rate fell from 6.1 births per woman in 1970 to only 2.0 in 1998. And China's strict one-child policy resulted in a *negative* growth rate in some urban areas; see Box 14-1.

Through the efforts of many governments (among them Canada's) and private agencies (among them Planned Parenthood), the fertility rates of many developing countries have declined. However, some critics, reflecting a conflict orientation, have questioned why Canada and other industrialized nations are so enthusiastic about population control in the developing world. In line with Marx's response to Malthus, they argue that large families and even population growth are not the causes of hunger and misery. Rather, the unjust economic domination by the developed states of the world results in an unequal distribution of world resources and in widespread poverty in exploited developing nations (Fornos 1997).

Even if family planning efforts are successful in reducing fertility rates, the momentum toward a growing world population is well established. The developing nations face the prospect of continued population growth, since a substantial proportion of their population is approaching childbearing years. This is evident in Figure 14-2, comparing the population structures of Kenya and Canada.

A ***population pyramid*** or population structure is a special type of bar chart that distributes the population by gender and age; it is generally used to illustrate the population structure of a society. As Figure 14-2 shows, a substantial portion of the population of Kenya consists of children under the age of 15, whose childbearing years are still to come. Thus, the built-in momentum for population growth is much greater in Kenya (and in many developing countries in other parts of the world) than in Western Europe or Canada.

Consider, also, India, which in 2000 surpassed one billion in population. Sometime between the years 2040 and 2050 India's population will surpass China's. The substantial momentum for growth built into India's age structure means that the nation will face a staggering increase in population in the coming decades—even if its birthrate declines sharply (Mann 2000).

Population growth is not a problem in all nations. A handful of countries are even adopting policies that *encourage* growth. One of them is Japan, where the total fertility rate has fallen sharply. Nevertheless, a global perspective underscores the serious consequences that could result from overall continued population growth.

A tragic new factor has emerged in the last 15 years that will restrict worldwide population growth: the spread of AIDS. Presently, about 39 million people around the world are infected with the HIV virus. According to the United Nations, 4.9 million people were newly infected with the virus in 2004. Of that number, 47 percent were women. In sub-Saharan Africa, the hardest-hit region with 25.4 million people infected, 57 percent are women between the ages of 15 and 49. Women are disproportionately affected because of such factors as sexual violence, less access to education, and lack of power to refuse sexual contact or insist on condom use (United Nations 2004). As a result of the increasing number of implications for women, the reality of the "feminization of AIDS" has been acknowledged by academics, politicians, and journalists alike.

pp. 109–111

FERTILITY PATTERNS IN CANADA

During the past four decades, Canada and other industrial nations have passed through two different patterns

FIGURE 14-2

Population Structure of Kenya and Canada, 2005 (estimated)

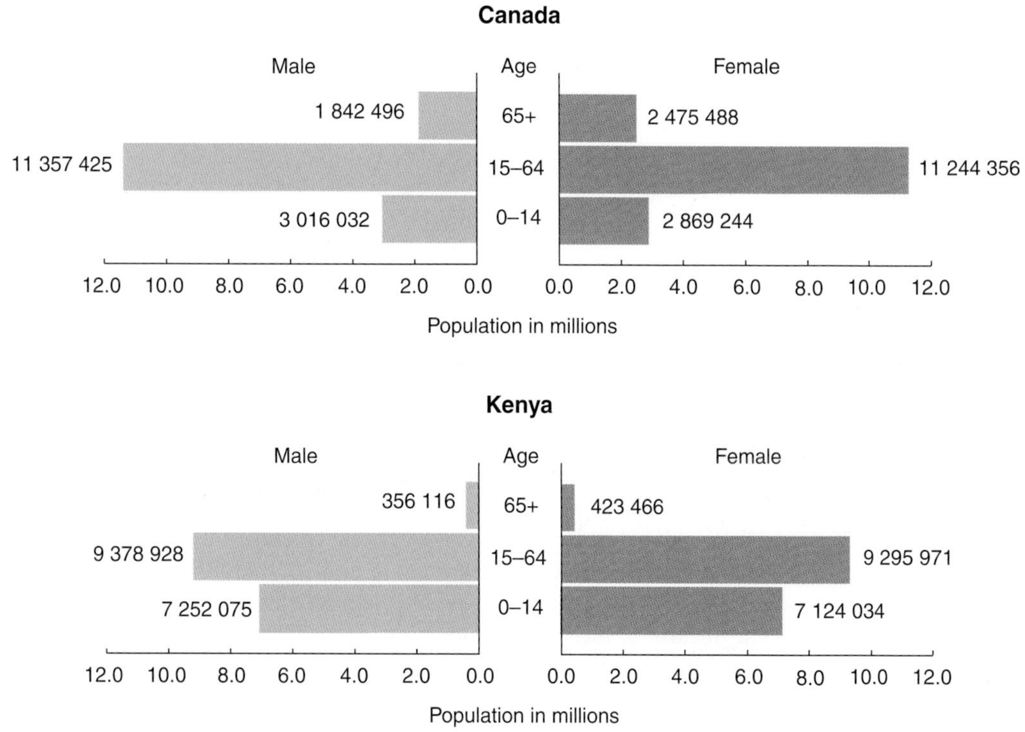

Source: World Fact Book 2005.

of population growth—the first marked by high fertility and rapid growth (stage II in the theory of demographic transition), the second marked by declining fertility and little growth (stage III). Sociologists are keenly aware of the social impact of these fertility patterns.

The Baby Boom

The most recent period of high fertility in Canada has often been referred to as the *baby boom.* The return of soldiers after World War II, high wages, and general prosperity during the postwar period encouraged many married couples to have children and purchase homes. In addition, several sociologists—as well as feminist author Betty Friedan (1963)—have noted that there were pervasive pressures on women during the 1950s to marry and become mothers and homemakers (Bouvier 1980).

The dramatic increase in births between 1946 and 1966 produced an age cohort in Canada that made up approximately one-third of the population. By the end of the boom in 1966, the age structure reflected a young, dependent population with a high percentage of Canadians under 15 years of age. As the baby boomers have aged, society has responded to their needs in education, recreation, consumer preferences, housing, and so on. Now, a significant challenge to society is to meet the needs of aging baby boomers as they begin to require greater medical attention at a time when health care resources are severely strained.

Use Your Sociological Imagination

You are living in a country that is so heavily populated that basic resources, such as food, water, and living space, are running short. What will you do? How will you respond to the crisis if you are a government social planner? a politician?

Stable Population Growth

Although the total fertility rate of Canada has remained low in the past two decades, the nation continues to grow in size because of two factors: the momentum built into our age structure by the postwar population boom and immigration. The 2001 census revealed that Canada's fertility rate was 1.5 children, below the 2.1 children needed to sustain the population (Armstrong 2002). Despite low levels of fertility, Canada's population grew 4 percent between 1996 and 2001. Because of the upsurge of births beginning in the late 1940s—in 1956 the fertility rate in Canada was four children per woman—there were more people in their childbearing years than in older age groups (where most deaths occur). This growth of population represented a demographic "echo" of the baby boom generation, many of whom are now parents. Based on the 2001 rate of population growth, beginning as soon as 2011 Canada will stop growing (Armstrong 2002). This prediction is based on current fertility rates and assumes that immigration rates will remain stable.

Despite these trends, in the 1980s and early 1990s, some analysts projected that there would be relatively low fertility levels and moderate net migration over the coming decades. As a result, it seemed possible that Canada might reach ***zero population growth (ZPG).*** ZPG is the state of a population in which the number of births plus immigrants equals the number of deaths plus emigrants. Thirty countries, most of them in Europe, are now at or approaching ZPG. In the recent past, although some nations have achieved ZPG, it has been relatively short-lived. However, given the current international concern over world population, more nations may attempt to maintain ZPG in the early twenty-first century (Kent 1999; McFalls 1998; McFalls, Jones, and Gallegher 1984; Population Reference Bureau 1978).

What would a society with stable population growth be like? In demographic terms, it would be quite different from the Canada of the 1990s. There would be relatively equal numbers of people in each age group, and the median age of the population would be higher. Based on 2001 census data, by 2035 the percentage of Canadians 65 and older will double to 25 percent from the current 12 percent (Armstrong 2002). As a result, the population pyramid of Canada would look more like a rectangle.

There would also be a much larger proportion of older people, especially age 75 and over. They would place a greater demand on the nation's social service programs and health care institutions. On a more positive note, the economy would be less volatile under ZPG, since the number of entrants into the paid labour force would remain stable. ZPG would also lead to changes in family life. With fertility rates declining, women would devote fewer years to child rearing and to the social roles of motherhood; the proportion of married women entering the labour force would continue to rise (Spengler 1978; Weeks 1999).

According to the latest United States Census Bureau projections, however, that country is *not* moving toward ZPG. Instead, the nation's population is growing faster than was expected. Previous projections indicated that the American population would stabilize between 290 million and 300 million by the middle of this century, but demographers now believe that by 2050, the population of the United States will reach 391 million.

In contrast, for the first time in 100 years Canada is growing more slowly than the United States, whose growth rate was 5.4 percent between 1995 and 2000 (Armstrong 2002). Canada's rate of growth remains ahead of such countries as Japan and Germany and behind such countries as Mexico, whose population grew 8.5 percent between 1995 and 2000.

In Canada over the next five to fifteen years, it is expected that, because of low or nonexistent rates of growth and an older population, labour shortages will occur. Occupations that are likely to be in demand include skilled and technical trades workers, teachers, health care workers, information technology experts, and academics (Armstrong 2002). As you can see, population growth owes much to the age structure of a given region or country. In the next part of this chapter, we will look at aging from a sociological perspective.

AGING AND SOCIETY

The meanings of youth and old age are socially constructed by the society in which we live. Older Sherpas, living in Nepal, value their independence and prefer not to live with their children. Among the Fulani of Africa, however, older men and women move to the edge of the family homestead. Since this is where people are buried, the elderly sleep over their own graves, for they are already viewed as socially dead. Like gender stratification, age stratification varies from culture to culture. One society may treat older people with great reverence, while another sees them as unproductive and "difficult" (M. Goldstein and Beall 1981; Stenning 1958; Tonkinson 1978).

It is understandable that all societies have some system of age stratification and associate certain social roles with distinct periods in a person's life (see Box 14-2). Some of this age differentiation seems inevitable; it would make little sense to send young children off to war or to expect most older citizens to handle physically demanding tasks, such as loading goods at shipyards. However, as is the case of the social construction of gender, age stratification in North America goes far beyond the physical constraints of human beings at different ages.

"Being old" is a master status that commonly overshadows all others in our society. The insights of labelling theory help us analyze the consequences of aging. Once people are labelled "old," this designation has a major impact on how others perceive them and even on how they view themselves. Negative stereotypes of the elderly contribute to their position as a minority group subject to discrimination, as we'll see later in the chapter.

pp. 96–97

The model of five basic properties of a minority or subordinate group (introduced in Chapter 9) can be applied to older people in Canada to clarify their subordinate status:

pp. 195–196

1. The elderly experience unequal treatment in employment and may face prejudice and discrimination.
2. The elderly share physical characteristics that distinguish them from younger people. In addition, their cultural preferences and leisure-time activities often differ from those of the rest of society.
3. Membership in this disadvantaged group is involuntary.
4. Older people have a strong sense of group solidarity, as is reflected in the growth of senior citizens' centres, retirement communities, and advocacy organizations.
5. Older people generally are married to others of comparable age.

There is one crucial difference between older people and other subordinate groups, such as racial and ethnic minorities or women: *All* of us who live long enough will eventually assume the ascribed status of being an older person (Barron 1953; Levin and Levin 1980; Wagley and Harris 1958).

This elderly woman in the central region of China is honoured among her people for her age. Older people in many other cultures in which youth is prized are not granted the same honour.

Sociology in the Global Community

14-2 Aging Worldwide: Issues and Consequences

An electric water kettle is wired so that people in another location can determine if it has been used in the previous 24 hours. This may seem a zany use of modern technology, but it symbolizes a change taking place around the globe—the growing needs of an aging population. The Japanese Welfare Network Ikebukuro Honcho has installed these wired hot pots so that volunteers can monitor whether the elderly have used the devices to prepare their morning tea. An unused pot will trigger personal contact to see if the older person needs help. This technological monitoring system is an indication of the tremendous growth of Japan's elderly population, and particularly significant, the increasing numbers who live *alone*.

Around the world, there are more than 442 million people aged 65 or over, representing about 7 percent of the world's population. In an important sense, the aging of the world's population represents a major success story that unfolded during the latter years of the twentieth century. Through the efforts of both national governments and international agencies, many societies have drastically reduced the incidence of diseases and the rates of death. Consequently, these nations—especially the industrialized countries of Europe and North America—now have increasingly higher proportions of older members.

The overall population of Europe is older than that of any other continent. As the proportion of older people in Europe continues to rise, many governments that have long prided themselves on their pension programs have reduced benefits and raised the age at which retired workers can receive benefits. By 2050, Europe's population is projected to have a median age of over 52.

In most developing countries, people over 60 are likely to be in poorer health than their counterparts in industrialized nations. Yet few of those countries are in a position to offer extensive financial support to the elderly. Ironically, modernization of the developing world, while bringing with it many social and economic advances, has undercut the traditionally high status of the elderly. In many cultures, the earning power of younger adults now exceeds that of older family members.

Worldwide, governments are beginning to pay attention to population aging and the permanent social transformation it represents. In 1940, of the 227 nations with a population of at least five thousand, only 33 had some form of old-age disability or survivors' program. By 2001 the number stood at 167, or 74 percent of those 227 nations.

Applying Theory

1. How do the effects of aging differ according to gender, race, class, and nationality?
2. Using symbolic interactionism as a framework within which to study aging, what differences might emerge among various cultures' views on aging?

Sources: American Association of Retired Persons 2004; Bernstein 2003; Hani 1998; Haub 2003; Kinsella and Velkoff 2001; R. Samuelson 2001.

Explaining the Aging Process

Aging is one important aspect of socialization—the lifelong process through which an individual learns the cultural norms and values of a particular society. There are no clear-cut definitions for different periods of the aging cycle in Canada. *Old age* has typically been regarded as beginning at 65, which corresponds to the retirement age for many workers, but not everyone in our society accepts this definition. With life expectancy being extended, writers are beginning to refer to people in their 60s as the "young old" to distinguish them from those in their 80s and beyond (the "old old").

The particular problems of the elderly have become the focus for a specialized area of research and inquiry known as gerontology. ***Gerontology*** is the scientific study of the sociological and psychological aspects of aging and the problems of the aged. It originally developed in the 1930s, as an increasing number of social scientists became aware of the plight of the elderly.

Gerontologists rely heavily on sociological principles and theories to explain the impact of aging on the individual and society. They also draw on the disciplines of psychology, anthropology, physical education, counselling, and medicine in their study of the aging process. Two influential views of aging—disengagement theory and activity theory—can be best understood in terms of the sociological perspectives of functionalism and interactionism, respectively. The conflict and feminist perspectives also contribute to our sociological understanding of aging.

Functionalist Approach: Disengagement Theory

Elaine Cumming and William Henry (1961) introduced ***disengagement theory*** to explain the impact of aging during the life course. This theory, based on a study of elderly people in good health and relatively comfortable economic circumstances, contends that society and the aging individual mutually sever many of their relationships. In keeping with the functionalist perspective, disengagement theory emphasizes that passing social roles on from one generation to another ensures social stability.

According to this theory, the approach of death forces people to drop most of their social roles—including those of worker, volunteer, spouse, hobby enthusiast, and even reader. Younger members of society then take on these functions. The aging person, it is held, withdraws into an increasing state of inactivity while preparing for death. At the same time, society withdraws from the elderly by segregating them residentially (retirement homes and communities), educationally (programs designed solely for senior citizens), and recreationally (senior citizens' social centres). Implicit in disengagement theory is the view that society should *help* older people to withdraw from their accustomed social roles.

Since it was first outlined more than three decades ago, disengagement theory has generated considerable controversy. Some gerontologists have objected to the implication that older people want to be ignored and "put away"—and even more to the idea that they should be encouraged to withdraw from meaningful social roles. Critics of disengagement theory insist that society *forces* the elderly into an involuntary and painful withdrawal from the paid labour force and from meaningful social relationships. Rather than voluntarily seeking to disengage, older employees find themselves pushed out of their jobs—in many instances, even before they are entitled to maximum retirement benefits (Boaz 1987).

Although functionalist in its approach, disengagement theory ignores the fact that postretirement employment has been *increasing* in recent decades. Some employees move into a "bridge job"—employment that bridges the period between the end of a person's career and his or her retirement. Unfortunately, the elderly can easily be victimized in such "bridge jobs." Psychologist Kathleen Christensen (1990), warning of "bridges over troubled water," emphasizes that older employees do not want to end their working days as minimum-wage jobholders engaged in activities unrelated to their career jobs (Doeringer 1990; Hayward, Grady, and McLaughlin 1987).

Interactionist Approach: Activity Theory

Often seen as an opposing approach to disengagement theory, ***activity theory*** argues that the elderly person who remains active and socially involved will be best adjusted. Proponents of this perspective acknowledge that a 70-year-old person may not have the ability or desire to perform various social roles that he or she had at age 40. Yet they contend that old people have essentially the same need for social interaction as any other group.

The improved health of older people—sometimes overlooked by social scientists—has strengthened the arguments of activity theorists. Illness and chronic disease are no longer quite the scourge of the elderly that they once were. The recent emphasis on fitness, the availability of better medical care, greater control of infectious diseases, and the reduction of fatal strokes and

These "silver surfers" still enjoy life to the fullest, just as they did when they were young. Staying active and involved has been shown to be healthy for the older population.

heart attacks have combined to mitigate the traumas of growing old. Accumulating medical research also points to the importance of remaining socially involved. Among those who decline in their mental capacities later in life, deterioration is most rapid in old people who withdraw from social relationships and activities (Liao et al. 2000; National Institute on Aging 1999).

Admittedly, many activities open to the elderly involve unpaid labour, for which younger adults may receive salaries. Such unpaid workers include hospital volunteers (versus aides and orderlies), drivers for charitable organizations (versus chauffeurs), tutors (as opposed to teachers), and craftspeople for charity bazaars (as opposed to carpenters and dressmakers). However, some companies have recently initiated programs to hire retirees for full-time or part-time work. For example, about 130 of the 600 reservationists at the Days Inn motel chain are over 60 years of age.

Disengagement theory suggests that older people find satisfaction in withdrawal from society. Functionally speaking, they conveniently recede into the background and allow the next generation to take over. Proponents of activity theory view such withdrawal as harmful for both the elderly and society and focus on the potential contributions of older people to the maintenance of society. In their opinion, aging citizens will feel satisfied only when they can be useful and productive in society's terms—primarily by working for wages (Civic Ventures 1999; Dowd 1980; Quadagno 1999).

The Conflict Approach

Conflict theorists have criticized both disengagement theory and activity theory for failing to consider the impact of social structure on patterns of aging. Neither approach, they say, attempts to question why social interaction "must" change or decrease in old age. In addition, these perspectives, in contrast to the conflict perspective, often ignore the impact of social class on the lives of the elderly.

The privileged position of the upper class generally leads to better health and vigour and to a lower likelihood of dependency in old age. Affluence cannot forestall aging indefinitely, but it can soften the economic hardships faced in later years. Although pension plans, retirement packages, and insurance benefits may be developed to assist older people, those whose wealth allows them access to investment funds can generate the greatest income for their later years.

By contrast, working-class jobs often carry greater hazards to health and a greater risk of disability; aging will be particularly difficult for those who suffer job-related injuries or illnesses. Working-class people also depend more heavily on government and private pension programs. During inflationary times, their relatively fixed incomes from these sources barely keep pace with escalating costs of food, housing, utilities, and other necessities (Atchley 1985).

Conflict theorists have noted that the transition from agricultural economies to industrialization and capitalism has not always been beneficial for the elderly. As a society's production methods change, the traditionally valued role of older people within the economy tends to erode. Their wisdom is no longer relevant.

According to the conflict approach, the treatment of older people in Canada reflects the many divisions in our society. The low status of older people is seen in prejudice and discrimination against them, age segregation, and unfair job practices—none of which is directly addressed by either disengagement or activity theory.

Feminist Approaches

Feminist frameworks view aging in women from a variety of perspectives. However, feminist researchers have frequently challenged two biases in the study of women's aging: (1) an androcentricity in the discussion of the life course (assuming that generalizations on the male life course can be applied to women) and (2) a lack of diversity in identifying the stages and central issues that mark women's lives (C. Jones, Marsden, and Tepperman 1990). In sociological research in previous decades, women's aging was seen almost exclusively in the context of marriage and family development (A. Nelson and Robinson 1999). This perspective, to a large degree, implies women's biological determinism; that is, that their life course is largely shaped by reproduction and nurturing of children. Moreover, studies on family life often contain an *ageist* bias; they adopt the perspective of middle-aged adults while regarding the aged as passive members of families (Eichler 2001). This bias also results in a failure to recognize that aging family members, particularly women, not only receive care but also give care to the younger members. Thus, they are not solely dependent but are interdependent members of the family (Connidis 1989).

Perhaps most importantly, feminist perspectives have drawn attention to how aging affects women of diverse backgrounds and characteristics. Aging does not manifest itself in all women in a universal, uniform manner, but rather intersects with class, race and ethnicity, and sexual orientation to produce diverse patterns and conditions.

The four perspectives considered here take different views of the elderly. Functionalists portray them as socially isolated with reduced social roles; interactionists see older people as involved in new networks of people in a change of social roles; conflict theorists regard older people as victimized by social structure, with their social roles relatively unchanged but devalued; and feminist perspectives have challenged the androcentricity and biological determinism implicit in many explanations of women's aging. Feminist perspectives also draw attention to how aging intersects with class, race and ethnicity, and sexual orientation. Table 14-3 summarizes these perspectives.

An Aging Canadian Population

As an index of aging, the United Nations uses the proportion of individuals 65 years of age and older to classify a population as "young," "mature," or "aged" (McVey and Kalbach 1995). A population is "young" if its proportion of older adults is under 4 percent; it is considered "mature" if its proportion of those 65 years of age and older is between 4 and 8 percent; and it is considered "aged" if this age group makes up 8 percent or more (McVey and Kalbach 1995). Canada became an "aged" population according to census data by 1971, when 8.1 percent of Canadians were 65 years of age and older. By 2001, 13 percent of the population was 65 years of age and older, following a steady increase of the proportion of this group in the total population (Statistics Canada 2002c). According to Health Canada (2000), by 2016, approximately 20 percent of our population will be in this age group.

National averages of aging, however, mask great diversity within Canada as it relates to such factors as region, gender, and race and ethnicity. There is a vast variation among regions in the percentage of the older age group, resulting in some regions being classified as "aged" populations while others are considered "young." Saskatchewan, for example, has the oldest population, with 14.1 percent of its population 65 years of age or older, while Yukon Territory and the Northwest Territories have the youngest population, with only 3.2 percent of their residents 65 years of age or older. Although the overall trend in Canada is toward the aging of the population, regional responses in the form of specialized housing, health care, caregiving services, and other social services may vary.

Gender differences sharply punctuate overall rates of aging in Canadian society. The proportion of older women in Canada has been increasing steadily since 1961. Given women's greater life expectancy, they constitute a disproportionate number of the aged. Because of women's lower average incomes and overall financial security, they are more likely to experience poverty than their male counterparts. The feminization of poverty, then, is accentuated by an aging population of which women make up a disproportionately high number. Although some may view their greater life expectancy as a positive gain, for many women, particularly immigrants, women of colour, Aboriginal women, and those of lower social class, living longer means an even greater chance of living in poverty. Aboriginal men and women, as will be discussed in the next section on health, are more likely to suffer from poor health and have lower life expectancies because of the prevailing conditions of poverty in their lives.

Ageism

It "knows no one century, nor culture, and is not likely to go away any time soon." This is how physician Robert Butler (1990:178) described prejudice and discrimination against the elderly, which he called ***ageism.*** Ageism reflects a deep uneasiness among young and middle-aged people about growing old. For many, old age symbolizes disease, disability, and death; seeing the elderly serves as a reminder that *they* may someday become old and infirm. The notion of ageism was popularized by Maggie Kuhn, a senior citizen who took up the cause of elder rights after she was forced to retire from her position at the United Presbyterian Church. Kuhn formed the Gray Panthers in 1971, a national organization dedicated to the fight against age discrimination (R. Thomas 1995).

With ageism all too common in North America, it is hardly surprising that older people are barely visible on

Table 14-3 Theories of Aging

Sociological Perspective	View of Aging	Social Roles	Portrayal of Elderly
Functionalist	Disengagement	Reduced	Socially isolated
Interactionist	Activity	Changed	Involved in new networks
Conflict	Competition	Relatively unchanged	Victimized, organized to confront victimization
Feminist	Challenges androcentric bias and assumptions of homogeneity	Socially constructed, diverse according to class, race and ethnicity, sexual orientation	Caught in a double-standard, men gain status and women lose status

television. A content analysis of 1446 American fictional television characters in the early 1990s revealed that only 2 percent were age 65 and over—even though this age group accounted for about 13 percent of the nation's population. A second study found older women particularly underrepresented on television (J. Robinson and Skill 1993; J. Vernon et al. 1990).

Feminist perspectives have drawn attention to the social construction of gender as it relates to ageism in North American society. Although men's aging is seen as a sign of wisdom and experience, women's aging is seen as a sign of decline and diminishing status. Standards of beauty in our society are based on women's youth and sexual attractiveness and are often narrowly defined and frequently impossible to achieve (Abu-Laban and McDaniel 1995). Aging women are therefore seen as a departure from our culture's norms of physical beauty and sexual attractiveness. The culture, through messages transmitted by mass media, encourages us to "steal beauty back from the ravages of time" (A. Nelson and Robinson 1999:464). Thus, a multibillion-dollar beauty industry of cosmetics, fashion, fitness, and cosmetic surgery is flourishing (N. Wolf 1991) among an aging population in the midst of an anti-aging culture.

Use Your Sociological Imagination

How might women be portrayed by the mass media if society's dominant culture revered age rather than youth?

SOCIOLOGICAL PERSPECTIVES ON HEALTH AND ILLNESS

From a sociological point of view, social factors contribute to the evaluation of a person as "healthy" or "sick." How, then, can we define health? We can imagine a continuum with health on one end and death on the other. In the preamble to its 1946 constitution, the World Health Organization defined ***health*** as a "state of complete physical, mental, and social well-being, and not merely the absence of disease and infirmity" (Leavell and Clark 1965:14). With this definition in mind, the "health" end of our continuum represents an ideal rather than a precise condition. Along the continuum, people define themselves as "healthy" or "sick" on the basis of criteria established by each individual, relatives, friends, coworkers, and medical practitioners. Because health is relative, we can view it in a social context and consider how it varies in different situations or cultures (Twaddle 1974; Wolinsky 1980).

Why is it that you may consider yourself sick or well when others do not agree? Who controls definitions of health and illness in our society, and for what ends? What are the consequences of viewing yourself (or being viewed) as ill or disabled? Drawing on four sociological perspectives—functionalism, conflict theory, interactionism, and feminist theories—we can gain greater insight into the social context shaping definitions of health and treatment of illness.

An Overview

As you know by now, the sociological approaches should not be regarded as mutually exclusive. In the study of health-related issues, they share certain common themes. First, any person's health or illness is more than an organic condition, since it is subject to the interpretation of others. Owing to the impact of culture, family and friends, and the medical profession, health and illness are not purely biological occurrences but are sociological occurrences as well. Second, since members of a society (especially industrial societies) share the same health delivery system, health is a group and societal concern. Although health may be defined as the complete well-being of an individual, it is also the result of his or her social environment. As we will see, such factors as a person's social class, race and ethnicity, gender, and age can influence the likelihood of contracting a particular disease (Cockerham 1998).

Functionalist Approach

Illness entails at least a temporary disruption in a person's social interactions both at work and at home. Consequently, from a functionalist perspective, "being sick" must be controlled so that not too many people are released from their societal responsibilities at any one time. Functionalists contend that an overly broad definition of illness would disrupt the workings of a society.

"Sickness" requires a person to take on a social role, even if temporarily. The ***sick role*** refers to societal expectations about the attitudes and behaviour of a person viewed as being ill. Sociologist Talcott Parsons (1951, 1972, 1975), well known for his contributions to functionalist theory (see Chapter 1), has outlined the behaviour required of people considered "sick." They are exempted from their normal, day-to-day responsibilities and generally are not blamed for their condition. Yet they are obligated to try to get well, and this may include seeking competent professional care. Attempting to get well is particularly important in the world's developing countries. In modern automated industrial societies, we can absorb a greater degree of illness or disability, but in horticultural or agrarian societies, the availability of workers is far more critical (Conrad 1997).

p. 12

According to Parsons's theory, physicians function as "gatekeepers" for the sick role, either verifying a patient's condition as "illness" or designating the patient as "recovered." The ill person becomes dependent on the doctor because the latter can control valued rewards (not only treatment of illness but also excused absences from work and school). Parsons suggests that the doctor–patient relationship is somewhat like that between parent and child. Like a parent, the physician helps the patient to return to society as a full and functioning adult (A. Segall 1976).

There have been a number of criticisms of the concept of the sick role. First, patients' judgments regarding their own state of health may be related to their gender, age, social class, and ethnic group. For example, younger people may fail to detect warning signs of a dangerous illness while the elderly may focus too much on the slightest physical malady. Second, the sick role may be more applicable to people experiencing short-term illnesses than to those with recurring, long-term illnesses. Finally, even simple factors, such as whether a person is employed or not, seem to affect willingness to assume the sick role—as does the impact of socialization into a particular occupation or activity. For example, beginning in childhood, athletes learn to define certain ailments as "sports injuries" and therefore do not regard themselves as "sick" (Curry 1993). Nonetheless, sociologists continue to rely on Parsons's model for functionalist analysis of the relationship between illness and societal expectations for the sick.

Midwives demonstrate in an effort to be included in the "legitimate" field of obstetrics in Canada. Physicians continue to exert control in the field, marginalizing the role of midwives.

Conflict Approach

Functionalists seek to explain how health care systems meet the needs of society as well as those of individual patients and medical practitioners, but conflict theorists take issue with this view. They express concern that the profession of medicine has assumed a preeminence that extends well beyond whether to excuse a student from school or an employee from work. Sociologist Eliot Freidson (1970:5) has likened the position of medicine today to that of state religions yesterday—it has an officially approved monopoly of the right to define health and illness and to treat illness. Conflict theorists use the term *medicalization of society* to refer to the growing role of medicine as a major institution of social control (Conrad and Schneider 1992; McKinlay and McKinlay 1977; Zola 1972, 1983).

Social control involves techniques and strategies for regulating behaviour in order to enforce the distinctive norms and values of a culture. Typically, we think of informal social control as occurring within families and peer groups, and formal social control as carried out by authorized agents, such as police officers, judges, school administrators, and employers. However, viewed from a conflict perspective, medicine is not simply a "healing profession"; it is a regulating mechanism as well.

pp. 136–142

How does it manifest its social control? First, medicine has greatly expanded its domain of expertise in recent decades. Physicians have become much more involved in examining a wide range of issues, among them sexuality (including homosexuality), old age, anxiety, obesity, child development, alcoholism, and drug addiction. Society tolerates such expansion of the boundaries of medicine because we hope that these experts can bring new "miracle cures" to complex human problems as they have to the control of certain infectious diseases. The social significance of medicalization is that once a problem is viewed using a *medical model*—once medical experts become influential in proposing and assessing relevant public policies—it becomes more difficult for "common people" to join the discussion and exert influence on decision making. It also becomes more difficult to view these issues as being shaped by social, cultural, or psychological factors, rather than simply by physical or medical factors (Caplan 1989; Conrad and Schneider 1992; P. Starr 1982).

Second, medicine serves as an agent of social control by retaining absolute jurisdiction over many health care procedures. It has even attempted to guard its jurisdiction by placing such health care professionals as chiropractors and nurse-midwives outside the realm of acceptable medicine. Despite the fact that midwives first brought professionalism to child delivery, they have been portrayed as having invaded the "legitimate" field of obstetrics in North America. Nurse-midwives have sought licensing as a way to achieve professional respectability, but physicians continue to exert power to ensure that midwifery remains a subordinate occupation (Friedland 2000).

The medicalization of society is but one concern of conflict theorists as they assess the workings of health care institutions. As we have seen throughout this textbook, when analyzing any issue, conflict theorists seek to determine who benefits, who suffers, and who dominates at the expense of others. Viewed from a conflict perspective, there are glaring inequities in health care delivery within Canada. For example, northern and rural areas tend to be underserved because medical services concentrate where people are numerous or wealthy.

Similarly, from a global perspective, there are obvious inequities in health care delivery. In 2003, Canada had about 2.1 physicians per 1000 people, while African nations have fewer than 1 per 1000. This situation is only worsened by the "brain drain"—the immigration to industrialized nations of skilled workers, professionals, and technicians who are desperately needed by their home countries. As part of this brain drain, physicians and other health care professionals have come to developed countries from developing countries, such as India, Pakistan, and various African states. Conflict theorists view such emigration out of the developing world as yet another way in which the world's core industrialized nations enhance their quality of life at the expense of developing countries (World Bank 2000a:190–91).

In another example of global inequities in health care, multinational corporations based in industrialized countries have reaped significant profits by "dumping" unapproved drugs on unsuspecting consumers in the developing world. In some cases, fraudulent capsules and tablets are manufactured and marketed as established products in developing countries. These "medications" contain useless ingredients or perhaps one-tenth of the needed dosage of a genuine medication. Even when the drugs dumped on developing countries are legitimate, the information available to physicians and patients is less likely to include warnings of health hazards and more likely to include undocumented testimonials than in industrialized nations (Silverman, Lydecker, and Lee 1990).

Conflict theorists emphasize that inequities in health care resources have clear life-and-death consequences. For example, in 2005, the infant mortality rate in Sierra Leone is estimated to be 143.64 infant deaths per 1000 live births. By contrast, Japan's infant mortality rate was only 3.26 deaths per 1000 live births and Sweden's was 2.77. From a conflict perspective, the dramatic differences in infant mortality rates around the world (see Figure 14-3) reflect, at least in part, unequal distribution of health care resources based on the wealth or poverty of various communities and nations.

FIGURE 14-3

Infant Mortality Rates, 2005

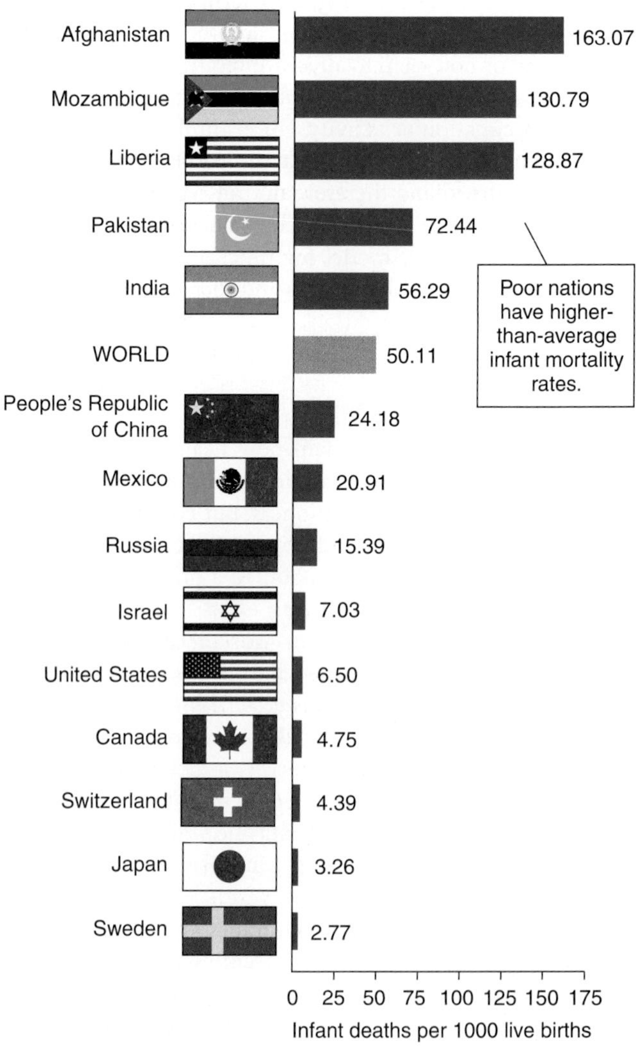

Source: World Fact Book 2005.

In 2005, the United States had a rate of 6.5 infant deaths per 1000 live births (although it is estimated that the rate in some poor, inner-city neighbourhoods in that country exceeds 30 deaths per 1000 live births). Yet, despite the wealth of the United States, at least 22 nations have lower infant mortality rates, among them Canada, Great Britain, and Japan. Conflict theorists point out that, unlike the United States, Canada and these other countries offer some form of government-supported health care for all citizens, which typically leads to greater availability and greater use of prenatal care than is the case in the United States. (We will examine government's role in health care in greater detail in the social policy section of this chapter.)

Interactionist Approach

In examining health, illness, and medicine as a social institution, interactionists generally focus on microlevel study of the roles played by health care professionals and patients. They emphasize that the patient should not always be viewed as passive, but instead as an actor who often shows a powerful intent to see the physician (Alonzo 1989; Zola 1983).

Sometimes patients play an active role in health care by *failing* to follow a physician's advice. For example, some patients stop taking medications long before they should, some take an incorrect dosage on purpose, and others never even fill their prescriptions. Such non-compliance results in part from the prevalence of self-medication in our society; many people are accustomed to self-diagnosis and self-treatment. Conversely, patients' active involvement in their health care can sometimes have very *positive* consequences. Some patients read books about preventive health care techniques, attempt to maintain healthful and nutritious diets, carefully monitor any side effects of medication, and adjust dosage based on such perceived side effects.

Labelling theorists suggest that the designation "healthy" or "ill" generally involves social definition by others. Just as police officers, judges, and other regulators of social control have the power to define certain people as criminals, health care professionals (especially physicians) have the power to define certain people as "sick."

An example from history illustrates the labelling of women by the medical profession as fragile and possessing a limited source of energy. During the early years of the last century, women who expended energy pursuing intellectual activities (such as advanced education) were perceived to be endangering their womanhood. The medical establishment viewed the female body as a closed system of energy in which use of the brain would leave less energy to be used in other parts, such as the reproductive system. Women's brains and ovaries, according to doctors of the time, competed for the same supply of energy. Women who spent too much energy in intellectual pursuits were labelled "unhealthy" and unwomanly:

> A young woman . . . who consumed her vital force in intellectual activities was necessarily diverting these energies from the achievement of true womanhood. She would become weak and nervous, perhaps sterile . . . capable of bearing only sickly and neurotic children. . . . The brain and ovary could not develop at the same time. (Smith-Rosenberg and Rosenberg 1974:340)

Patriarchical views of women's health during this period even went so far as to suggest that male semen had a therapeutic and soothing effect on the female reproductive organs (Smith-Rosenberg 1986).

By the late 1980s, the power of a label—"person with AIDS"—had become quite evident. This label often functions as a master status that overshadows all other aspects of a person's life. Once someone is told that he or she has tested positive for HIV, the virus associated with AIDS, that person is forced to confront immediate and difficult questions: Should I tell my family members, my sexual partner(s), my friends, my co-workers, my employer? How will these people respond? People's intense fear of this disease has led to prejudice and discrimination—even social ostracism—against those who have (or are suspected of having) AIDS. Consequently, a person who has AIDS must deal with not only the serious medical consequences of the disease but also the distressing social consequences associated with the label.

p. 97

According to labelling theorists, we can view a variety of life experiences as illnesses or not. Recently, premenstrual syndrome, posttraumatic disorders, and hyperactivity have been "labelled" as medically recognized disorders. Disagreements continue in the medical community over whether chronic fatigue syndrome constitutes a medical illness. Following the 1991 Gulf War against Iraq, more than 21 000 American soldiers and other personnel reported a variety of symptoms ranging from fatigue and rashes to respiratory disorders. These symptoms have come to be called the Gulf War syndrome (or illness), although the government has yet to officially recognize a clear link between the combat situation and subsequent symptoms.

Probably the most noteworthy recent medical example of labelling is the case of homosexuality. For years, psychiatrists classified being gay or lesbian as a mental disorder subject to treatment. This official sanction by the psychiatry profession became an early target of the growing gay and lesbian rights movement in North America. In 1974, members of the American Psychiatric Association voted to drop homosexuality from the standard manual on mental disorders (Adam 1995; Charmaz and Paterniti 1999; Monteiro 1998).

Interactionist perspectives attempt to illuminate the "social meaning" of illness, as well as how these meanings affect a person's self-concept and relationships with others. For example, in the case of someone suffering from a mental illness, such as depression, interactionist approaches might shed light on the social stigma of the illness. In addition, these approaches might focus on how the stigma of the illness affects the individual's interpersonal relationships with family, friends, and co-workers. The interactionist perspective has been especially helpful in unravelling cultural differences that affect health care in a multicultural society, such as that of Canada. For example, regular exercise is not part of the culture of some ethnic groups; attitudes on diet, smoking, drinking, and body image and fatalistic views of illness may be culturally specific (Levy and Hawks 1996). Cultural sensitivity is necessary at all levels of health care delivery in order to effectively treat a diverse patient population where many face language barriers, racism, social isolation, and inequality. Determining the different cultural meanings that individuals might attach to a doctor's report, referral to a medical specialist, or a health survey are examples of how interactionists might approach the study of health and illness.

Feminist Approaches

Many feminist approaches to health and illness have pointed to a historical pattern of concentrating on women's reproductive potential, overshadowing a diversity of concerns related to health and illness. Early research on women focused on their roles as mothers and wives as they related to women's mental health, while comparable studies on men focused more on their physical health and job conditions. This bias still can be found in the research literature, even though most women now work in the paid labour force.

Other feminist perspectives point out the need to recognize that patterns of women's health and illness are as diverse as Canadian women themselves and that this diversity (e.g., poor women, immigrants, refugees, women of colour, lesbians, disabled women) must not be masked by talking about "women" as a universal category. As one feminist sociologist argues:

> Women are often discussed as a single group defined chiefly by their biological sex, members of an abstract universal (and implicitly white) category. In reality, we are a mixed lot, our gender roles and options shaped by history, culture and deep divisions across class and colour lines. . . . Traditionally women as a group are defined by this reproductive potential. Usually ignored are the many ways that gender as a social reality gets into the body and transforms our biology. (Krieger and Fee 1994:18)

Sociological investigations of women's health must, many feminist theories argue, shift the focus from reproduction potential and roles as mothers and wives to women's health and illness, which reflect the diversity of Canadian women.

SOCIAL EPIDEMIOLOGY AND HEALTH

Social epidemiology is the study of the distribution of disease, impairment, and general health status across a population. Epidemiology initially concentrated on the scientific study of epidemics, focusing on how they started and spread. Contemporary social epidemiology is much broader in scope, concerned not only with epidemics but also with nonepidemic diseases, injuries, drug addiction and alcoholism, suicide, and mental illness. Epidemiology draws on the work of a wide variety of scientists and researchers, among them physicians, sociologists, public health officials, biologists, veterinarians, demographers, anthropologists, psychologists, and meteorologists.

Researchers in social epidemiology commonly use two concepts: incidence and prevalence. ***Incidence*** refers to the number of *new* cases of a specific disorder occurring within a given population during a stated period of time, usually a year. For example, the incidence of AIDS in Canada in 2002 was 174 cases. By contrast, ***prevalence*** refers to the total number of cases of a specific disorder that exist at a given time. The prevalence of AIDS in Canada in 2002 was about 18 000 cases (Health Canada 2003).

When incidence figures are presented as rates, or as the number of reports per 100 000 people, they are called ***morbidity rates***. (The term ***mortality rate***, you will recall, refers to the incidence of *death* in a given population.) Sociologists find morbidity rates useful because they reveal that a specific disease occurs more frequently among one segment of a population than another. As we will see, social class, race, ethnicity, gender, and age can all affect a population's morbidity rates.

Social Class

Social class is clearly associated with differences in morbidity and mortality rates. Studies in Canada and other countries have consistently shown that people in the lower classes have higher rates of mortality and disability. Health Canada has identified 12 determinants of health, which include income and social status, employment, education, gender, and culture (see Table 14-4).

Although available data do suggest the relationship between health and social class, they mask the vast diversity within Canada. For example, because social class, race, and gender intersect, Aboriginal women are affected

Table 14-4 Twelve Determinants of Health Identified by Health Canada

- Income and social status
- Employment and working conditions
- Education
- Social environments
- Physical environments
- Healthy child development
- Personal health practices and coping skills
- Health services
- Social support networks
- Biology and genetic endowment
- Gender
- Culture

Source: Health Canada 2002.

by poor health to a much greater degree than non-Aboriginal women. Aboriginal women who, on average, have lower incomes, were almost three times as likely to report a heart problem in 1997 as were all Canadian women in general. As well, Aboriginal women between the ages of 25 and 34 have rates of suicide four times as high as those of non-Aboriginal women (Statistics Canada 2000a).

Numerous studies document the impact of social class on health. An examination of data from 11 countries in North America and Europe found strong associations between household income and health, and between household income and life expectancy, when comparing families of similar size. Researchers from the Harvard School of Public Health found that higher overall mortality rates—as well as higher incidence of infant mortality and deaths from coronary heart disease, cancer, and homicide—were associated with lower incomes.

Why is class linked to health? Crowded living conditions, substandard housing, poor diet, and stress all contribute to the ill health of many low-income people in Canada. In certain instances, limited education and literacy may lead to a lack of awareness of measures necessary to maintain good health.

Another factor in the link between class and health is evident at the workplace: the occupations of people in the working and lower classes of Canada tend to be more dangerous than those of more affluent citizens. Miners, for example, must face the possibility of injury or death from explosions and cave-ins; they are also likely to develop respiratory diseases, such as black lung. Workers in textile mills may contract a variety of illnesses caused by exposure to toxic substances, including one disease commonly known as *brown lung disease* (R. Hall 1982). In recent years, the nation has learned of the perils of asbestos poisoning, a particular worry for construction workers.

In the view of Karl Marx and other contemporary conflict theorists, capitalist societies, such as Canada, would be seen as caring more about maximizing profits than about the health and safety of industrial workers. As a result, government agencies do not take forceful action to regulate conditions in the workplace, and workers suffer many preventable, job-related injuries and illnesses.

Research also shows that the lower classes are more vulnerable to environmental pollution than the affluent; this is the case not only where the lower classes work but also where they live (Moffatt 1995).

Sociologists Link and Phelan maintain that socioeconomic status is "a fundamental cause of disease" since it is linked to access to resources "that can be used to avoid risks or minimize the consequences of disease once it occurs . . . resources that include money, knowledge, power, prestige and kinds of interpersonal resources embodied in the concepts of social support and social network" (Link and Phelan 1995:87).

Race and Ethnicity

Health profiles of many racial and ethnic minorities reflect the social inequality evident in Canada. The most glaring examples of the relationship between race and ethnicity and health can be found within Canada's Aboriginal communities. The health of Aboriginal people reflects patterns of exclusion, past and present, that have limited and continue to limit their access to many of the social determinants of health—such determinants as income, employment, education, and literacy. Aboriginal people not only experience a lack of material resources but also face limited opportunities, isolation, discrimination, and racism.

A 1996 study prepared at the request of the Canadian Task Force on the Periodic Health Examination concluded that Aboriginal people "sustain a disproportionate share of the burden of physical disease and mental illness" (MacMillan, Offord, and Dingle 1996: 1569). Many Aboriginal populations have an increased risk of death from alcoholism, homicide, suicide, and pneumonia; overall death rates for both men and women are higher among the Aboriginal population than their counterparts in the overall Canadian population

(MacMillan et al. 1996). Rates of tuberculosis (TB) between 1984 and 1989 among registered Aboriginal and Inuit were approximately nine times the Canadian average (MacMillan et al. 1996). Aboriginal communities have identified such problems as substance abuse, unemployment, suicide, and family violence as concerns affecting their members' health. A study in Ontario found that 80 percent of the Aboriginal women in its sample had been victims of family violence (Stout 1996). The health of Aboriginal people as well as that of other disadvantaged ethnic and racial minorities is interwoven with the conditions of poverty. In the case of Aboriginal people, this interrelationship is one that few studies have assessed (MacMillan et al. 1996).

Gender

A large body of research indicates that, in comparison with men, women experience a higher prevalence of many illnesses, though they tend to live longer. Females born in 2000 have a life expectancy of approximately 82 years; males born at the same time are expected to live for about 77 years. The difference in life expectancy between Canadian men and women has been attributed to such factors as risk-taking behaviour, such as drinking and dangerous driving on the part of males; levels of danger associated with male-dominated occupations, such as mining and construction; and women's tendency to use health care services more often and at earlier stages of their illness. The difference in life expectancy between men and women has decreased to a gap of 5.2 years in 2000 from a gap of 7.4 years in 1976 (Statistics Canada 2003l). This has been attributed to a reduction of deaths because of cardiovascular disease in men, contributed to by a decrease in smoking. Smoking rates for women, however, have been increasing steadily for about three decades, contributing to higher rates of lung cancer and heart disease (Lem 2000). The narrowing of the gender gap in life expectancy is predicted to continue in this century because of women's changing roles and their exposure to stress, and the general aging of the population (McVey and Kalbach 1995).

Recent studies suggest that the genuine differences in morbidity between women and men may be less pronounced than previously assumed (Macintyre, Hunt, and Sweeting 1996). Using the 1994 National Population Health Survey (NPHS) data, Canadian sociologists found no "clear excess of ill-health among women" (McDonough and Walters 2000:3). The researchers concluded that there is a need to further examine gender differences rather than to operate on the widely held assumption that women experience greater ill-health even though they live longer. The authors also concluded that although existing gender differences should not be minimized, for many age groups the health of women and men is more similar than previously assumed. Other researchers argue that women are much more likely than men to seek treatment, to be diagnosed as having diseases, and thus to have their illnesses reflected in data examined by epidemiologists.

From a conflict perspective, women have been particularly vulnerable to the medicalization of society, with everything from birth to beauty treated in an increasingly medical context. Such medicalization may contribute to women's higher morbidity rates as compared with those of men. Ironically, although women have been especially affected by medicalization, medical researchers have often excluded women from clinical studies. Female physicians and researchers charge that sexism is at the heart of such research practices and insist that there is a desperate need for studies with female subjects.

Moreover, many feminist researchers state the need for greater investigation into the health effects of discrimination as a function of gender, race, sexual orientation, or disability, as well as how these variables interact to produce varying levels of health and disease. They argue that since gender is not a uniform category, research approaches are needed that will lead to a better understanding of the "dynamics of diversity" among and within the various groups of Canadian women (Vissandjee 2001:3).

Research on the relationship between culture and gender as they relate to health reveals that immigrant women's experiences differ from those that are depicted to be the Canadian "norm" (Repper et al. 1996). Certain immigrant women, for example, are less likely to participate in cancer screening programs (e.g., mammograms and pap smears), while others with concerns arising from female genital mutilation are reluctant to consult health care providers (Vissandjee 2001).

Despite renewed attention to women's health, recent studies confirm that women still are sometimes neglected by the medical establishment. In the United States, for example, even federally funded clinical research ignores the requirement since 1993 that their data be analyzed to see if women and men respond differently. Similarly, a content analysis of medical journals in the 1990s found that even the most recent published research focuses primarily on men: no studies excluded men, 20 percent excluded women, and another 30 percent failed to report the findings from female participants (General Accounting Office 2000; Vidaver et al. 2000).

Age

Health is the overriding concern of the elderly. Most older people in Canada report having at least one chronic illness, but only some of these conditions are potentially life threatening or require medical care. At the same time, health problems can affect the quality of life of older people in important ways. Arthritis and visual or hearing impairments can interfere with the performance of everyday tasks.

As the Canadian population ages, led by the baby boom generation, to which roughly one-third of all Canadians belong, our society will experience a greater prevalence of particular types of diseases. The Vancouver Brain Research Centre predicts that in 20 years, brain diseases, such as Alzheimer's and Parkinson's diseases, to which older people are more prone, will be the leading cause of death and disability among Canadians (Fong 2001). In Canada today, approximately 300 000 people have Alzheimer's disease, while another 100 000 have Parkinson's disease. Since the likelihood of contracting these diseases increases with age, it is predicted that 750 000 Canadians will be afflicted with Alzheimer's disease and 300 000 will have Parkinson's disease by 2020 (Fong 2001). The incidence of diseases related to vision (e.g., glaucoma and macular degeneration) as well as stroke is currently on the increase and will continue to rise as the baby boomers make their way into the senior years. Overall, these diseases will surpass heart disease and cancer, which currently are the leading causes of death and disability. Gender is of particular importance in the study of health and aging, since women on average live longer lives. Living longer means older women are at increased risk of disease, and thus greater life expectancy can actually be viewed as a threat to women's health (Rodin and Ickovics 1990). Despite the fact that women make up a greater proportion of the elderly and therefore have greater health care needs, they receive little research attention (M.L. Weber 1998).

Social support is a key factor related to the health of both older men and women. In older women, research reveals that depression is more strongly related to social support than to physical health (Albarracin, Fishbein, and Goldstein de Muchinik 1997). Older people tend to visit doctors more frequently and require hospitalization more often than do their younger counterparts (Canadian Institute for Health Information 2000). Given the demographic shift toward an older population accentuated by baby boomers, it is obvious that the disproportionate use of the health care system in Canada by older people is a critical factor in all discussions about the cost of health care and possible reforms of the health care system (Bureau of the Census 1999: 134, 138).

Sexual Orientation

Since heterosexuality is assumed to be the norm in Canadian society, there is a lack of attention paid to gay and lesbians in health research (M.L. Weber 1998). There does, however, tend to be more research carried out on gays than on lesbians (Lynch and Ferri 1997). Lesbians, then, face the combined effects of sexism and sexual orientation as they relate to health research and provision of health care. Research on health is conducted using mainly white, middle-class women, which results in a lack of knowledge about the health of bisexual women, older lesbians, lesbians of colour, and lesbians from rural areas (Hart 1995).

The assumption of diversity is, however, being integrated into some health care systems, such as the Vancouver/Richmond Health Board, which represents the needs of lesbian, gay, bisexual, and transgender patients as well as other groups who traditionally have not been well served by the health care system. As well, there have been concerns expressed over the curricula of Canadian medical schools regarding gay, lesbian, and bisexual issues. Medical schools are being prompted to ensure that the doctors they graduate are competently trained to care for *all* Canadians (Robinson and Cohen 1996).

In sum, to achieve the goal of 100 percent access and zero health disparities, public health officials must overcome inequities that are rooted not just in age but in social class, race and ethnicity, gender, and sexual orientation. If that were not enough, they must also deal with a geographical disparity in health care resources. Dramatic differences in the availability of physicians, hospitals, and nursing homes also exist between urban and rural areas within the same province or territory. In the next section we will look more closely at issues surrounding the delivery of health care in Canada.

HEALTH CARE IN CANADA

In 1947 Swift Current, Saskatchewan, became the first region in North America to embrace a public hospital insurance program, in which all of its citizens were provided access to hospital services without direct payment. The following year, Saskatchewan Premier Tommy Douglas introduced a program for the entire province, based largely on the Swift Current model. Ten years later, the federal government followed suit by introducing the first national hospital insurance plan in North America. In 1962, Saskatchewan was again at the forefront of public health care when it introduced North America's first medicare program, which would cover doctor's fees incurred outside hospitals. The program sparked the highly profiled Saskatchewan doctors' strike, which saw many doctors threatening to leave the province if this perceived threat to "free enterprise" in medical care went through. Critics of the medicare plan accused the government of "communist" and "socialist" tendencies, and of attempting to destroy the private relationship between physicians and patients.

The doctors' strike, which lasted three weeks, became the focus of media attention not only in Canada but also in the United States. The American Medical Association supported the dissenting Saskatchewan doctors in their attempt to resist the public administration of medical care and to preserve "free enterprise."

In 1968, the public administration of medical care became national policy, after the provinces and territories moved to implement their own insurance plans for in-hospital care. Justice Emmett Hall, after carrying out a review of the Canadian health care system in 1979, reported it to be among the best in the world. He did, however, warn that the system was being weakened by extra billing by doctors and that user fees were creating a "two-tiered" system. These unresolved issues still pose a threat to the principles of accessibility, universality, and public administration, which, as discussed in a later section, are cornerstones of Canadian medicare.

Physicians, Nurses, and Patients

The preeminence of physicians within the health care system of Canada, whose fees made up approximately 13 percent of total health care spending in 2001 (Canadian Institute for Health Information 2001), has traditionally given them a position of dominance in their dealings with governments, patients, nurses, and other health professionals. The functionalist and interactionist perspectives combine to offer a framework for understanding the professional socialization of physicians as it relates to patient care. Functionalists suggest that established physicians and medical school professors serve as mentors or role models who transmit knowledge, skills, and values to the passive learner—the medical student. Interactionists emphasize that students are moulded by the medical school environment as they interact with their classmates.

Both approaches argue that the typical training of physicians in Canada leads to rather dehumanizing physician–patient encounters. As Dr. Lori Arviso Alvord writes in *The Scalpel and the Silver Bear,* "I had been trained by a group of physicians who placed much more emphasis on their technical abilities and clinical skills than on their abilities to be caring and sensitive" (Alvord and Van Pelt 1999:13). Despite many efforts to formally introduce a humanistic dimension of patient care into the medical school curriculum, patient overload and underfunding of hospitals tend to undercut positive relations.

Interactionists have closely examined how compliance and negotiation occur between physician and patient. They concur with Talcott Parsons's view that the relationship is generally asymmetrical, with doctors holding a position of dominance and control of rewards.

p. 233

Just as physicians have maintained dominance in their interactions with patients, doctors have similarly controlled interactions with nurses. Despite their training and professional status, nurses commonly take orders from physicians. Traditionally, the relationship between doctors and nurses has paralleled the male dominance of North America: Most physicians have been male, whereas virtually all nurses have been female.

Like other women in subordinate roles, nurses have been expected to perform their duties without challenging the authority of men. Psychiatrist Leonard Stein (1967) refers to this process as the *doctor–nurse game.* According to the rules of this "game," the nurse must never disagree openly with the physician. When she has recommendations concerning a patient's care, she must communicate them indirectly in a deferential tone. For example, if asked by a hospital's medical resident, "What sleeping medication has been helpful to Mrs. Brown in the past?" (an indirect request for a recommendation), the nurse will respond with a disguised recommendation statement, such as "Pentobarbital 100 mg was quite effective night before last." Her careful response allows the physician to authoritatively restate the same prescription as if it were *his* idea.

Like nurses, female physicians have traditionally found themselves in a subordinate position because of gender. Although enrolments in medical schools across Canada are approaching or have approached gender equity, faculty in medical schools are still predominantly male.

A study of male and female medical residents suggests that the increasing number of female physicians may alter the traditional doctor–patient relationship. Male residents were found to be more focused on the intellectual challenges of medicine and the prestige associated with certain medical specialties. By contrast, female residents were more likely to express a commitment to caring for patients and devoting time to them. In terms of the functionalist analysis of gender stratification offered by sociologists Talcott Parsons and Robert Bales, male residents took the *instrumental,* achievement-oriented role, while female residents took the *expressive,* interpersonal-oriented role. As women continue to enter and move higher in the hierarchies of the medical profession, there will surely be sociological studies to see if these apparent gender differences persist (Geckler 1995).

p. 225

Patients have traditionally relied on medical personnel to inform them of health care issues, but increasingly they are now turning to the media for health care information. Recognizing this change, pharmaceutical firms are advertising their prescription drugs directly to potential customers through television and magazine advertisements. The Internet is also a growing source for patient information.

Medical professionals are understandably suspicious of these new sources of information. The American Academy of Pediatrics published a study in 1998 that investigated Web sites with information on treating childhood diarrhea. They found that only 20 percent of the sources of information conformed to current recommended medical practices. The study noted that even if the source of information was a major medical centre, it did not improve the likelihood of compliance. Reflecting its professional stake in the issue, the Academy concluded that patients need to be "warned" not to use Internet medical information. However, there is little doubt that Web research is transforming an increasing proportion of patient–physician encounters, as patients arrive for their doctor's appointments armed with the latest printout from the Internet (Kolata 2000; McClung, Murray, and Heiflinger 1998).

Health Care Alternatives

Canada, along with most Western, industrialized countries, follows a medical model of illness. This model, dominated by doctors who are graduates of Western medical schools, is based on the assumption that when specific body parts break down, they can be treated according to a neutral scientific process (Weitz 1996). The cause of illness, then, is viewed to be largely biological. The medical model considers illness to be a deviation from the norm and advocates "treatment" of the specific body part considered to be the cause of illness.

Polls suggest that 60 percent to 70 percent of Canadians have used some form of alternative therapy in the last six months (Canadian Institute for Health Information 2001). In recent decades, there has been growing interest in *holistic* (this term is also spelled *wholistic*) medical principles first developed in China. ***Holistic medicine***, also referred to as integrative, alternative, or complementary medicine, refers to therapies in which the health care practitioner considers the person's physical, mental, emotional, and spiritual characteristics. The individual is regarded as a totality, rather than as a collection of interrelated organ systems. Treatment methodologies include massage, chiropractic medicine, acupuncture (which involves the insertion of fine needles into surface points), respiratory exercises, and the use of herbs as remedies. Nutrition, exercise, and visualization may also be used to treat ailments generally treated through medication or hospitalization (Sharma and Bodeker 1998).

Canada's ethnic and racial diversity and recent waves of immigration have provided Canadians greater exposure to alternative forms of medical treatment. Because of the monopoly of the Western medical model, these forms of treatment have remained outside of the boundaries of government-sponsored health care. However, in 1996, the Vancouver Hospital and Health Science Centre in British Columbia opened the Tzu Chi Institute for Complementary and Alternative Medicine, whose mandate was to integrate traditional Asian therapies and Western medicare. As well, various postsecondary institutions across Canada now offer credit courses in alternative therapies, such as acupuncture. The recent resurgence of holistic medicine comes amid a widespread recognition of the value of nutrition and the dangers of overreliance on prescription drugs (especially those used to reduce stress, such as Valium).

The medical establishment—professional organizations, research hospitals, and medical schools—has generally served as a stern protector of traditionally accepted health care techniques. However, a major breakthrough occurred in 1992 when the American government's National Institutes of Health—that nation's major funding source for biomedical research—opened an Office of Alternative Medicine, empowered to accept grant requests. Possible areas of study include herbal medicine, mind–body control techniques, and the use of electromagnetism to heal bones. A national study published in *The Journal of the American Medical Association* indicates that 46 percent of the general public uses alternative medicine. Most of it is not covered by insurance. In fact, out-of-pocket expenses for alternative medicine match all out-of-pocket expenses for traditional physician services (Eisenberg et al. 1998; Stolberg 2000).

Although many observers applaud the use of alternative medical procedures, conflict theorists note the difference between those who can afford to use alternatives *in addition to* conventional medicine and those who have no choice. For example, Cubans have recently begun to rely more on traditional cures, such as sitting on cobalt blocks to ease circulatory problems, in response to a shortage of government resources. Likewise, in low-income neighbourhoods in the United States, people often rely on alternative care techniques out of necessity, not choice (Kovaleski 1999).

In some cases, movements for political change have generated health care alternatives. For example, as part of the larger feminist movement beginning in the 1960s, women became more vocal in their dissatisfaction with the North American health care system. The appearance of the book *Our Bodies, Ourselves* (Boston Women's Health Book Collective 1969, 1992) marked the emergence of the contemporary women's health movement. Women realized that they are by far the most frequent users of health services for themselves, their children, and other dependent family members. Activists agree that women should assume more responsibility for decisions concerning their health. The movement therefore has taken many forms, including organizations working for changes in the health care system, women's clinics, and "self-help" groups.

The goals of the women's health movement are ambitious, but the health care system has proved to be fairly resistant to change. Conflict theorists point out that physicians, medical schools, hospitals, and drug companies all have a vested interest in keeping women in a rather dependent and uninformed position as health care consumers. Despite an increase in the number of female doctors, women remain underrepresented in all key decision-making positions in the health care system of Canada.

The Role of Government

In 1984, the federal government's Canada Health Act became the basis for the administration of our health care system, known as *medicare*. The Act set out to ensure (in theory) that all Canadians receive access to hospital and doctors' services on the basis of need, not on the ability to pay. It also sets the conditions and criteria under which the provinces and territories receive transfer payments—payments that are then used to finance health care services in their respective jurisdictions. The principles of the Canada Health Act are as follows (Health Canada 2001):

1. *Public administration*: health care in a province or territory must be carried out by public institutions on a nonprofit basis.
2. *Comprehensiveness*: all services carried out by hospitals and doctors and deemed to be medically necessary must be insured.
3. *Universality*: all residents of a province or territory are entitled to uniform health coverage.
4. *Portability*: health coverage must be maintained when a person moves to or travels across provinces and territories or outside Canada.
5. *Accessibility*: reasonable access to necessary medical services should be available to all Canadians.

In many respects the principles of public administration, comprehensiveness, universality, portability, and accessibility represent Max Weber's idea of "ideal types"; that is, they act as abstract measuring rods against which we are able to compare our perceptions of reality. For example, most Canadians would be able to give an example of how our health care system today may not measure up to at least one of these principles. Whether the concern is waiting lists for surgery; access to specialists in remote locations; the growth of private, fee-for-service clinics; long waits in hospital emergency wards; waiting lists for specialized tests, such as MRIs; the closing of rural hospitals; the reduction of beds in urban hospitals; or the shortage of nurses nation-wide, Canadians consider the delivery of health care services a concern of top priority (Canadian Institute for Health Information 2001). Canadians living in northern or rural areas, or outside major metropolitan areas, immigrants, those with low incomes, Aboriginal persons, and people with disabilities represent some of the groups vulnerable to the so-called "crisis" in the Canadian health care system. We will look further into government's role in health care in the social policy section of this chapter.

SOCIAL POLICY AND HEALTH — Financing Health Care Worldwide

The Issue

In many developing nations of the world, health care issues centre on very basic needs of primary care. The goals established at the U.N.'s World Health Assembly in 1981 were modest by North American standards: safe water in the home or within 15 minutes' walking distance; immunization against major infectious diseases; availability of essential drugs within an hour's walk or travel; and the presence of trained personnel for pregnancy and childbirth. Although significant progress has been made in some areas, many developing countries have seen little improvement; in some places, health care has deteriorated (World Bank 1997). The focus of this social policy section, however, is on those industrialized (or developed) nations where the availability of health care is really not an issue. The question is more one of accessibility and affordability. What steps are being taken to make the available services reachable and affordable?

The Setting

The Canadian health care system, despite its flaws, is the envy of other countries. Many Americans, in particular, praise the Canadian system for its universality and accessibility. At a Canadian Medical Association conference in 1995, Dr. Theodore Marmor of the Yale School of

Management praised medicare as "Canada's postwar miracle," arguing that claims of it being a "fundamentally troubled and gravely threatened system" are distorted (1995:1505).

Contrast what you have learned about the Canadian health care system thus far in this chapter with the situation in the United States and elsewhere in the developed world.

The United States is now the only Western industrial democracy that does not treat health care as a basic right. According to the United States Bureau of the Census in 2000, some 44 million people in the United States had no health insurance the entire year. The uninsured typically include self-employed people with limited incomes, illegal immigrants, and single mothers who are the sole providers for their families. Black Americans, Asian Americans, and Hispanics are less likely than whites to carry private health insurance. Although people with lower incomes are least likely to be covered, substantial numbers of households at all income levels go without coverage for some or most of any given year (Mills 2000).

National health insurance is a general term for legislative proposals that focus on ways to provide the entire population with health care services. First discussed by government officials in the United States in the 1930s, it has come to mean many different things, ranging from narrow health insurance coverage with minimal public subsidies to broad coverage with large-scale public funding.

Opponents of national health insurance insist that it would be extremely costly and would lead to significant tax increases. Defenders counter, however, that Canada and other countries have maintained broad governmental health coverage for decades:

- Great Britain's National Health Service is almost totally tax-supported, and health care services are free to all citizens.
- Under Sweden's national health system, medical care is delivered primarily by publicly funded hospitals and clinics, while a national health insurance system sets fees for health care services and reimburses providers of health care.
- Although Canadians rely on private physicians and hospitals for day-to-day treatment, health care is guaranteed as a right for all citizens. Income taxes finance public medical insurance and medical fees are set by the government.

Ironically, although these countries offer extensive health coverage for all citizens, the United States has higher health care costs than any other nation: an average annual cost of U.S.$4499 per person, compared with U.S.$2058 in Canada and only U.S.$1747 in Great Britain. As Figure 14-4 shows, most industrial nations finance a substantially larger share of health care costs

FIGURE 14-4

Government Expenditures for Health Care, Selected Countries

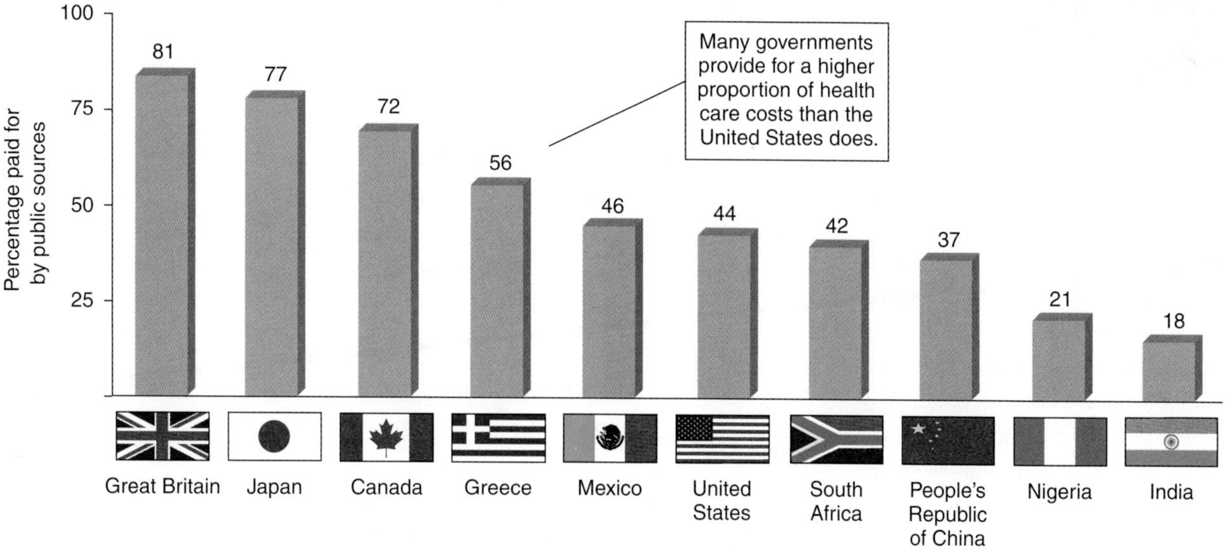

Source: World Bank 2003:92–94.

through public expenditures than does the United States (World Bank 2003:92–94).

Sociological Insights

As conflict theorists suggest, the United States health care system, like other social institutions, resists basic change. In general, those who receive substantial wealth and power through the workings of an existing institution will have a strong incentive to keep things as they are. In this case, private insurance companies are benefiting financially from the current system and have a clear interest in opposing certain forms of national health insurance. In addition, the American Medical Association (AMA), one of Washington's most powerful lobbying groups, has been successfully fighting national health insurance since the 1930s. Overall, there are more than 200 political action committees (PACs) that represent the medical, pharmaceutical, and insurance industries. These PACs contribute millions of dollars each year to members of Congress and use their influence to block any legislation that would threaten their interests (Dolbeare 1982; Kemper and Novak 1991).

Those who look at the system from the conflict perspective are disturbed by the possibility that illness may be exploited for profit. Moreover, in Canada, defenders of publicly funded health care argue that the growth of private, for-profit hospitals and fee-for-service clinics will create a two-tiered system. Such hospitals and clinics, critics argue, would accentuate the have–have not status of Canadians, making some medical services more accessible to those who can afford them. Obviously, conflict thinkers would argue that a postal clerk, for example, should have the same access to an MRI as a highly paid, professional hockey player. With private clinics, the hockey player may be able to afford the fee for the diagnostic test, while the postal clerk, who may not be able to afford the cost of the test, may be forced to wait until time is available in the publicly funded system. The increasing costs of Canadian medicare have led many to question the sustainability of its present structure (see Figure 14-5). Critics of the corporatization of health care worry that the growing pressures on physicians and other health care providers to make cost-effective decisions may lead to inadequate and even life-threatening patient care (Sherrill 1995).

Policy Initiatives

With the increasing cost of health care accelerated by the cost of technology and the demographic pressures of an aging population, it is doubtful, given current levels of funding, whether our present system of health care can be sustained over the long term. The strain in the current system has manifested itself in hospital overcrowding and long waiting lists for specialists, surgery, and specialized diagnostic tests. In 2000, in response to some of these pressures in publicly funded health care, the province of Alberta introduced the controversial Bill 11—a bill that would provide for the regulation of

FIGURE 14-5

Health Expenditures by Source of Finance, Canada, 1975–2004

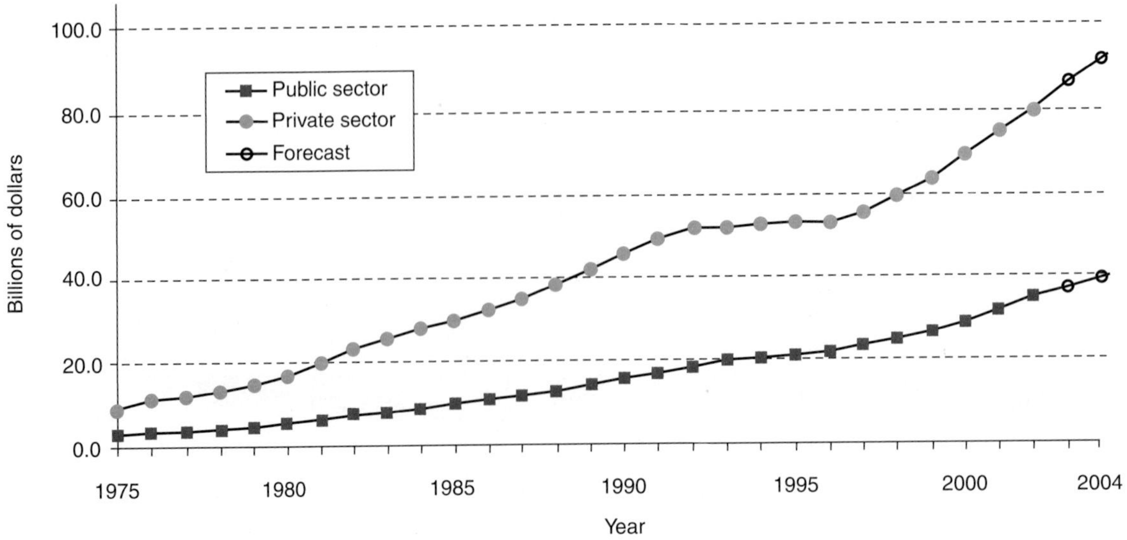

Source: Copyright © CIHI 2005.

This demonstrator is protesting against for-profit hospitals in Canada.

contracting surgical services to private, for-profit facilities. The Canadian Nurses Association was one of many professional organizations to oppose the bill, claiming that privatized health care is not what is needed to alleviate the current strain in the system. Rather, the association argued, adequate funding for the public health care system is the solution. In 2000, the prime minister established a royal commission on the future of Canada's health care system, asking Roy Romanow, the former premier of Saskatchewan, to be its head. Mr. Romanow has been investigating all aspects of the system, considering various options for the delivery of health care in this country, including private, for-profit facilities. Some social scientists argue that the way in which health care is delivered—publicly or privately—may affect a society's social cohesion. A two-tiered system that provides unequal access to and unequal quality of health care (based on people's ability to pay) may lead to a diminished sense of trust in the community (Drache and Sullivan 1999). In 2005, the Supreme Court of Canada ruled that Quebec's health insurance law banning two-tier medical coverage violated that province's Charter of Human Rights and Freedoms. See Figure 14-6 for public and private health spending in Canada in 1998.

Many industrial countries are paying greater attention to unequal health care delivery. Addressing this problem, however, often creates difficulties. Great Britain, for example, in attempting to meet the needs of

FIGURE 14-6

Public and Private Shares of Total Health Expenditure, by Use of Funds, Canada, 2004

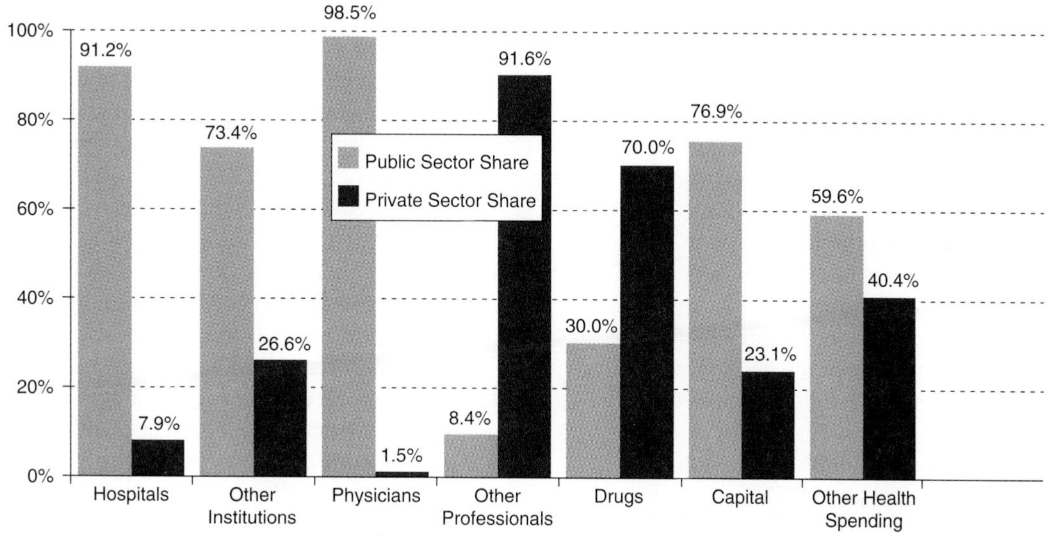

Although hospitals and physicians are almost totally publicly funded, "other" health care professionals, such as chiropractors, are not.

Source: Copyright © CIHI 2005.

previously underserved rural areas, has closed facilities in London and other metropolitan areas and tried to reassign medical staff to rural areas. In addition to concerns about quality and availability of medical care, the National Health Service remains underfunded (Moseley 2000).

As governments throughout the world take greater responsibility for health care and as care becomes increasingly expensive, governments can be expected to give more and more attention to controlling expenditures.

Applying Theory

1. How would a conflict sociologist view the way health care in Canada is delivered?
2. Do you believe that the principles of the Canada Health Act (i.e., public administration, comprehensiveness, universality, portability, and accessibility) should be maintained? At what cost?
3. Should health care be a basic right of all people?

CHAPTER RESOURCES

Summary

Sociologists focus on the social factors that influence population rates and trends. The meanings of ***health,*** sickness, and disease are also shaped by social definitions of behaviour. This chapter considered sociological perspectives on various aspects of population, the current problems of overpopulation, health and illness, the distribution of diseases in a society, and the evolution of the health care system as a social institution.

1. Thomas Robert Malthus suggested that the world's population was growing more rapidly than the available food supply and that this gap would increase over time. However, Karl Marx saw capitalism, rather than a rising world population, as the cause of social ills.
2. The primary mechanism for obtaining population information in Canada and most other countries is the ***census.***
3. Roughly two-thirds of the world's nations have yet to pass fully through the second stage of ***demographic transition***, and thus they continue to experience significant population growth.
4. The developing nations face the prospect of continued population growth, since a substantial portion of their population is approaching the childbearing years. Some of the developed nations, however, have begun to stabilize population growth.
5. According to Talcott Parsons's functionalist perspective, physicians function as "gatekeepers" for the ***sick role***, either verifying a person's condition as "ill" or designating the person as "recovered."
6. Conflict theorists use the term *medicalization of society* to refer to medicine's growing role as a major institution of social control.
7. Like other forms of stratification, age stratification varies from culture to culture.
8. "Being old" is a master status that seems to overshadow all others in North America.
9. The particular problems of the aged have become the focus for a specialized area of research and inquiry known as ***gerontology***.
10. ***Disengagement theory*** implicitly suggests that society should help older people withdraw from their accustomed social roles, whereas ***activity theory*** argues that the elderly person who remains active and socially involved will be best adjusted.
11. From a conflict perspective, the low status of older people is reflected in prejudice and discrimination against them and in unfair job practices.
12. An increasing proportion of the population of Canada comprises older people.
13. ***Ageism*** reflects a deep uneasiness on the part of younger people about growing old.
14. Labelling theorists suggest that the designation of a person as "healthy" or "ill" generally involves social definition by others. These definitions affect how others see us and how we view ourselves.
15. Contemporary ***social epidemiology*** is concerned not only with epidemics but also with nonepidemic diseases, injuries, drug addiction and alcoholism, suicide, and mental illness.
16. Studies have consistently shown that people in the lower classes have higher rates of ***mortality*** and disability.

17. Racial and ethnic minorities have higher rates of ***morbidity*** and ***mortality*** than do the dominant groups. Older people are especially vulnerable to brain diseases, like Alzheimer's disease.
18. The preeminent role of physicians within Canada's health care system has given them a position of dominance in their dealings with nurses and patients.
19. Many people seek alternative health care techniques, such as ***holistic medicine*** and self-help groups.
20. In the developed world, an aging population and technological breakthroughs have made health care both more extensive and more costly. At the same time, developing nations struggle to provide primary care for a burgeoning population. Throughout the world, an important issue is who is to pay for this care.

Critical Thinking Questions

1. Some European nations are now experiencing population declines. Their death rates are low and their birthrates are even lower than in stage III of the demographic transition model. Does this pattern suggest that there is now a fourth stage in the demographic transition? Even more important, what are the implications of negative population growth for an industrialized nation in the twenty-first century?
2. How would you characterize the relationship between you and your doctor? How does the dimension of power play into that relationship?
3. Relate what you have learned about ageism to the ways in which our society socially constructs "old age." How is ageism evident in the mass media in Canada? How is gender related to ageism?
4. Are there gender implications for the predicted wave of retirements in the Canadian workforce? If so, what are they?
5. In your view, should mandatory retirement continue to be the norm in Canada? Whose interests would be best served if mandatory retirement were to be abolished?

Key Terms

Activity theory An interactionist theory of aging that argues that elderly people who remain active and socially involved will be best adjusted. (page 335)

Ageism Prejudice and discrimination against the elderly. (337)

Birthrate The number of live births per 1000 population in a given year. Also known as the *crude birthrate.* (327)

Census An enumeration, or counting, of a population. (326)

Death rate The number of deaths per 1000 population in a given year. Also known as the *crude death rate.* (327)

Demographic transition A term used to describe the change from high birthrates and death rates to relatively low birthrates and death rates. (328)

Demography The scientific study of population. (325)

Disengagement theory A functionalist theory of aging that contends that society and the aging individual mutually sever many of their relationships. (334)

Fertility The amount of reproduction among women of childbearing age. (325)

Gerontology The scientific study of the sociological and psychological aspects of aging and the problems of the aged. (334)

Growth rate The difference between births and deaths, plus the differences between immigrants and emigrants, per 1000 population. (328)

Health As defined by the World Health Organization, a state of complete physical, mental, and social well-being, and not merely the absence of disease and infirmity. (338)

Holistic medicine A means of health maintenance using therapies in which the health care practitioner considers the person's physical, mental, emotional, and spiritual characteristics. (347)

Incidence The number of *new* cases of a specific disorder occurring within a given population during a stated period. (342)

Infant mortality rate The number of deaths of infants under one year of age per 1000 live births in a given year. (327)

Life expectancy The median number of years a person can be expected to live under current mortality conditions. (327)

Morbidity rates The incidence of diseases in a given population. (342)

Mortality rate The incidence of death in a given population. (342)

Population pyramid A special type of bar chart that shows the distribution of population by gender and age. (331)

Prevalence The total number of cases of a specific disorder that exist at a given time. (342)

Sick role Societal expectations about the attitudes and behaviour of a person viewed as being ill. (338)

Social epidemiology The study of the distribution of disease, impairment, and general health status across a population. (342)

Total fertility rate (TFR) The average number of children born alive to a woman, assuming that she conforms to current fertility rates. (327)

Zero population growth (ZPG) The state of a population with a growth rate of zero, achieved when the number of births plus immigrants is equal to the number of deaths plus emigrants. (332)

Additional Readings

Cockerham, William C. 1999. *Health and Social Change in Russia and Eastern Europe.* New York: Routledge. An examination of the sociological causes of the decline in life expectancy—unusual in an industrialized society—that began in the 1960s in the countries of the former Soviet Union.

Decter, Michael. 2004. *Healing Medicare: Managing Health Care System Change the Canadian Way.* Toronto: McGilligan Books. This book provides a plan for the reform of the Canadian health care system, offering suggestions on how to ensure the system remains affordable and high quality.

Kalipeni, Ezekiel, Susan Craddock, Joseph Oppong, and Jayati Ghosh, eds. 2004. *HIV and AIDS in Africa: Beyond Epidemiology.* Oxford: Blackwell Publishing. An edited work covering a vast scope of HIV/AIDs–related topics and their impact on African Nations.

McTeer, Maureen A. 1999. *Tough Choices: Living and Dying in the 21st Century.* Toronto: Irwin Law. The author examines the ways in which science and technology are influencing medical practice and our society's choices about life and death.

Online Learning Centre

Visit the *Sociology: A Brief Introduction* Online Learning Centre at www.mcgrawhill.ca/college/schaefer to access quizzes, interactive exercises, video clips, and other research and study tools related to this chapter.

Reel Society Interactive Movie CD-ROM 2.0

Reel Society 2.0 can be used to spark discussion about the following topics from this chapter:

- Demography: The study of population

chapter 15

COMMUNITIES AND THE ENVIRONMENT

In India, pollution is becoming a controversial political issue. This billboard graphically suggests the harmful effect of pollution on public health.

Tent City is not a city and we don't live in tents. We live in shacks and shanties on the edge of Canada's largest metropolis where the river meets the lake. There's a fence dividing these 27 acres from the rest of Toronto, and on this side we've built what dwellings we can with the rubble of a scrapyard, a no-man's landfill caught in confusion between the city and private business. Sometimes it seems like a community and sometimes like chaos. Junk Town would be a better name.

Picture a dump, littered with the cast-outs of the last millennium. Refrigerators, stuffed animals, shoes, original paintings on torn canvasses, photo albums, three hundred broken bicycles and toboggans and hockey sticks, TVs and microwaves, lamps and cash registers, headless Cabbage Patch Kids and enough books to start a library or a bookstore or your own education.

SHAUGHNESSY BISHOP-STALL
DOWN TO THIS
SQUALOR AND SPLENDOUR
IN A BIG-CITY SHANTYTOWN
"Nothing less than a masterpiece." National Post
"Some writers go to great lengths to write a book. They climb Mount Everest, follow armies into war zones, go undercover with a professional sports team or travel around the world on a motorbike. . . . Shaughnessy Bishop-Stall has more guts than any of those writers." Edmonton Journal

Now picture dozens of the country's thieves and drug addicts, vagabonds and ex-cons. They're drunk, hungry and tired of running. It's getting old and getting cold, and one night they find themselves in this place, with the rest of the discards, on the edge of the world but smack in the middle of it all.

They look around and realize that everything they've been hustling for is right here: stereos and VCRs, room to move, a perfect hideout and waterfront property. They aren't way out in the lonesome countryside or the goddamn suburbs or trapped in the same old city. In fact, the city looks perfect from here—the lake, the downtown high-rises, the sun setting beneath the tallest free-standing structure in the world—it's like a picture postcard. And best of all, there are no laws and no cops—as long as they stay this side of the fence. It's all private property. No one can tell them what to do, no one but Home Depot, the company that owns this land.

So they dig into a corner of the rubble for something they can use to build. There's so much, they could make anything. But for now they just throw together a few shelters using tarps and old office furniture. They buy some beer, light a fire, call it Tent City and decide to stay. The smoke rises for everyone to see, like a warning or an invitation. They drink and wait.

For almost four years people have been squatting here, and now some days the population reaches sixty or so. The singularity of this place has drawn media attention from all over the world, as well as a flood of well-meaning, but mostly redundant, donations—if only salvation could be bought with wool hats and toothbrushes. This remains, as much as such a thing is possible, a society of anarchy.

The rules are made up nightly. Repercussions are rarely considered in advance, or recorded for future reference. It is a useful, using and sometimes useless place. The castoffs of the megacity are snatched up, played with, eaten, worn, painted over and tossed into the mud. China plates are disposable, pillowcases never washed. If this place has a credo, it is: Grab what you can, stay drunk and mind your own damn business.

The protocol for moving into Tent City is one of invitation or recommendation. I unknowingly broke protocol. I came without a clue and nothing to lose, to learn about this place, write a book and live rent free. During the month I've spent so far, I've realized there is no one way to live here and a hundred possible stories to be written. Some people beg, some squeegee windows, some steal, some work jobs, some sell themselves, sell others, sell drugs. Most do drugs, some do nothing at all. I don't yet know what I'm going to do. *(Bishop-Stall 2005)* ■

This selection from Shaughnessy Bishop-Stall's *Down to This: Squalor and Splendour in a Big-City Shantytown* highlights the coexistence of wealth and poverty within a confined urban area—in this particular case, Toronto. The former "Tent City," as it was known, was littered with the excesses and throwaways of our consumer culture—children's toys, bikes, and electronics—and was inhabited by people drawn there for a variety of reasons. All the residents, however, shared the condition of being marginalized by the larger society. Some were dealing drugs, begging, or squeegeeing windows, and some were working in low-paying jobs. The residents formed their own community on land owned by Home Depot and filled it with shacks and shanties on the edge of what social commentators have often called "Toronto the Good."

As this excerpt shows, communities and their environments are intimately connected. Environmental issues, in fact, can make or break a community because they determine how safe, healthy, and satisfying our living conditions are. This chapter explores the important role that communities of all sorts, from rural towns to suburbs and big-city neighbourhoods, play in people's lives. Communities give people the feeling that they are a part of something larger than themselves. In sociological terms, a ***community*** may be formally defined as a spatial or political unit of social organization that gives people a sense of belonging. That sense of belonging can be based either on shared residence in a particular city or neighbourhood or on a common identity, like that of gays and lesbians (Dotson 1991; see also Hillery 1955).

Anthropologist George Murdock (1949) has observed that there are only two truly universal units of human social organization: the family and the community. This chapter looks at the importance of communities from a sociological perspective. We will begin with the successive development of early communities, preindustrial cities, and industrial and postindustrial cities. We will examine the dramatic urbanization evident around the world and contrast two different views of urban growth. Then we'll look at the three types of communities found in Canada: central cities, suburbs, and rural areas. We will also consider a new type of community brought about by technological change: the online community. Later in the chapter, we will examine the environmental problems facing the world and will draw on the functionalist, conflict, feminist, and interactionist perspectives to better understand environmental issues. Finally, in the social policy section, we will analyze the distressing phenomenon of homelessness in Canada and elsewhere. ■

Use Your Sociological Imagination www.mcgrawhill.ca/college/schaefer

Do you think that squatter communities, such as Tent City, are an inevitable part of big-city neighbourhoods? How do you think such communities affect the quality of the environment?

HOW DID COMMUNITIES ORIGINATE?

As we noted in the chapter opening, a *community* is a spatial or political unit of social organization that gives people a sense of belonging. The nature of community has changed greatly over the course of history—from early hunting and gathering societies to highly modernized postindustrial cities, as we will now see.

Early Communities

For most of human history, people used very basic tools and knowledge to survive. They satisfied their need for an adequate food supply through hunting, foraging for fruits or vegetables, fishing, and herding. In comparison with later industrial societies, early civilizations were much more dependent on the physical environment and much less able to alter that environment to their advantage. The emergence of horticultural societies, in which people actually cultivated food rather than merely gathering fruits and vegetables, led to many dramatic changes in human social organization.

pp. 107–108

It was no longer necessary to move from place to place in search of food. Because people had to remain in specific locations to cultivate crops, more stable and enduring communities began to develop. As agricultural techniques became more and more sophisticated, a co-operative division of labour involving both family members and others developed. It gradually became possible for people to produce more food than they actually needed for themselves. They could then provide food, perhaps as part of an exchange, to others who might be involved in nonagricultural labour. This transition from subsistence to surplus represented a critical step in the emergence of cities.

Eventually, people produced enough goods to cover both their own needs and those of people not engaged in agricultural tasks. Initially, the surplus was limited to agricultural products, but it gradually evolved to include all types of goods and services. Residents of a city came to rely on community members who provided craft products and means of transportation, gathered information, and so forth (Nolan and Lenski 1999).

With these social changes came an even more elaborate division of labour, as well as a greater opportunity for differential rewards and privileges. As long as everyone was engaged in the same tasks, stratification was limited to such factors as gender, age, and perhaps the ability to perform the task (a skilful hunter could win unusual respect from the community). However, the surplus allowed for expansion of goods and services, leading to greater differentiation, a hierarchy of occupations, and social inequality. Therefore, surplus was a precondition not only for the establishment of cities but also for the division of members of a community into social classes (see Chapter 8). The ability to produce goods for other communities marked a fundamental shift in human social organization.

Preindustrial Cities

It is estimated that, beginning about 10 000 BC, permanent settlements free from dependence on crop cultivation emerged. Yet, by today's standards of population, these early communities would barely qualify as cities. The ***preindustrial city,*** as it is termed, generally had only a few thousand people living within its borders and was characterized by a relatively closed class system and limited mobility. Status in these early cities was usually based on ascribed characteristics, such as family background, and education was limited to members of the elite. All the residents relied on perhaps 100 000 farmers and their own part-time farming to provide them with the needed agricultural surplus. The Mesopotamian city of Ur had a population of about 10 000 and was limited to roughly 90 hectares (220 acres) of land, including the canals, the temple, and the harbour.

Why were these early cities so small and relatively few in number? Several key factors restricted urbanization:

- **Reliance on animal power (both humans and beasts of burden) as a source of energy for economic production.** This limited people's ability to make use of and alter the physical environment.
- **Modest levels of surplus produced by the agricultural sector.** Between 50 and 90 farmers may have been required to support one city resident (Davis [1949] 1995).
- **Problems in transportation and storage of food and other goods.** Even an excellent crop could easily be lost as a result of such difficulties.
- **Hardships of migration to the city.** For many peasants, migration was both physically and economically impossible. A few weeks of travel was out of the question without more sophisticated techniques of food storage.
- **Dangers of city life.** Concentrating a society's population in a small area left it open to attack from outsiders, as well as more susceptible to extreme damage from plagues and fires.

Gideon Sjoberg (1960) examined the available information on early urban settlements of medieval Europe, India, and China. He identified three preconditions of city life: a favourable physical environment, a well-developed social organization, and advanced technology in both agricultural and nonagricultural areas.

For Sjoberg, the criteria for defining a "favourable" physical environment are variable. Proximity to coal and iron helps only if a society knows how to *use* these natural resources. Similarly, proximity to a river is particularly beneficial only if a culture has the means to transport water efficiently to the fields for irrigation and to the cities for consumption.

A sophisticated social organization is also an essential precondition for urban existence. Specialized social roles bring people together in new ways through the exchange of goods and services. A well-developed social organization ensures that these relationships are clearly defined and generally acceptable to all parties. Admittedly, Sjoberg's view of city life is an ideal type, since inequality did not vanish with the emergence of urban communities.

Industrial and Postindustrial Cities

Imagine how life could change by harnessing the energy of air, water, and other natural resources to power society's tasks. Advances in agricultural technology led to dramatic changes in community life, but so did the process of industrialization. The *industrial revolution,* p. 108 which began in the middle of the eighteenth century, focused on the application of nonanimal sources of power to labour tasks. Industrialization had a wide range of effects on people's lifestyles as well as on the structure of communities. Emerging urban settlements became centres not only of industry but also of banking, finance, and industrial management.

The factory system that developed during the industrial revolution led to a much more refined division of labour than was evident in preindustrial cities. The many new occupations that were created produced a complex set of relationships among workers. Thus, the ***industrial city*** was not merely more populous than its preindustrial predecessors; it was also based on very different principles of social organization. Sjoberg outlined the contrasts between preindustrial and industrial cities, as summarized in Table 15-1.

In comparison with preindustrial cities, industrial cities have a more open class system and more mobility. After initiatives in industrial cities by women's rights groups, labour unions, and other political activists, formal education gradually became available to many children from poor and working-class families. Although ascribed characteristics, such as gender, race, and ethnicity, remained important, a talented or skilled individual had a greater opportunity to better his or her social position. In these and other respects, the industrial city is genuinely a "different world" from the preindustrial urban community.

In the latter part of the twentieth century, a new type of urban community emerged. The ***postindustrial city*** is a city in which global finance and the electronic flow of information dominate the economy. Production is decentralized and often takes place outside urban centres, but control is centralized in multinational corporations whose influence transcends urban and even national boundaries. Social change is a constant feature of the postindustrial city. Economic restructuring and spatial change seem to occur each decade, if not more frequently. In the postindustrial world, cities are forced into increasing competition for economic opportunities, which deepens the plight of the urban poor (Phillips 1996; Smith and Timberlake 1993).

p. 108

Table 15-1 Comparing Types of Cities

Preindustrial Cities (through eighteenth century)	Industrial Cities (eighteenth through mid-twentieth century)	Postindustrial Cities (beginning late twentieth century)
Closed class system—pervasive influence of social class at birth	Open class system—mobility based on achieved characteristics	Wealth based on ability to obtain and use information
Economic realm controlled by guilds and a few families	Relatively open competition	Corporate power dominates
Beginnings of division of labour in creation of goods	Elaborate specialization in manufacturing of goods	Sense of place fades, transitional networks emerge
Pervasive influence of religion on social norms	Influence of religion limited to certain areas as society becomes more secularized	Religion becomes more fragmented; greater openness to new religious faiths
Little standardization of prices, weights, and measures	Standardization enforced by custom and law	Conflicting views of prevailing standards
Population largely illiterate, communication by word of mouth	Emergence of communication through posters, bulletins, and newspapers	Emergence of extended electronic networks
Schools limited to elites and designed to perpetuate their privileged status	Formal schooling open to the masses and viewed as a means of advancing the social order	Professional, scientific, and technical personnel are increasingly important

Sources: Based on Phillips 1996:132–135; Sjoberg 1960:323–328.

Use Your Sociological Imagination

What would the ideal city of the future look like? Describe its architecture, public transportation, neighbourhoods, schools, and workplaces. What kinds of people would live and work there?

URBANIZATION

The 2001 census showed that 79.4 percent of Canadians live in urban centres, compared with 78.5 percent in 1996. The 2001 census also revealed that 51 percent of Canada's population is concentrated in four broad urban areas: Southern Ontario, Montreal and environs, the lower mainland of British Columbia and southern Vancouver Island, and the Calgary–Edmonton corridor.

Urbanization can be seen throughout the rest of the world, too. In 1900, only 10 percent of the world's people lived in urban areas, but by 2000, that proportion had risen to around 50 percent. By the year 2025, the number of city dwellers could reach five billion (Koolhaas et al. 2001:3).

During the nineteenth and early twentieth centuries, rapid urbanization occurred primarily in European and North American cities. Since World War II, however, there has been an urban "explosion" in the world's developing countries (see Figure 15-1). Such rapid population growth is evident in the rising number of ***squatter settlements***, areas occupied by the very poor on the fringe of cities, described in Box 15-1.

Some metropolitan areas have spread so far that they have connected with other urban centres. Such a densely populated area, containing two or more cities and their suburbs, has become known as a ***megalopolis.*** An example is the so-called Golden Horseshoe region of Southern Ontario, which encompasses such communities as Hamilton, Burlington, and the Greater Toronto Area. Even when it is divided into autonomous political jurisdictions, the megalopolis can be viewed as a single economic entity. The megalopolis is also evident in Great Britain, Germany, Italy, Egypt, India, Japan, and China. Table 15-2 compares the 10 largest megalopolises in the world in 1970 with the projected 10 largest in 2015.

Table 15-2 The 10 Most-Populous Megalopolises in the World, 1970 and 2015 (in millions)

1970		2015 (Projected)	
1. Tokyo	16.5	1. Bombay (India)	28.2
2. New York	16.2	2. Tokyo	26.4
3. Shanghai (China)	11.2	3. Lagos (Nigeria)	23.2
4. Osaka (Japan)	9.4	4. Dhaka (Bangladesh)	23.0
5. Mexico City	9.1	5. São Paulo (Brazil)	20.4
6. London	8.6	6. Karachi (Pakistan)	19.8
7. Paris	8.5	7. Mexico City	19.2
8. Buenos Aires	8.4	8. Delhi (India)	17.8
9. Los Angeles	8.4	9. New York	17.4
10. Beijing	8.1	10. Jakarta (Indonesia)	17.3

Source: United Nations, quoted in Brockerhoff 2000:10.

Think about It
What trend does this table suggest?

Functionalist View: Urban Ecology

Human ecology is concerned with the interrelationships between people and their environment. Human ecologists have long been interested in how the physical environment shapes people's lives (for example, rivers can serve as a barrier to residential expansion) and also how people influence the surrounding environment (air-conditioning has accelerated growth of major metropolitan areas in the American Southwest). ***Urban ecology*** focuses on such relationships as they emerge in urban areas. Although the urban ecological approach examines social change in cities, it is nevertheless functionalist in its orientation because it emphasizes that different elements in urban areas contribute to stability.

Early urban ecologists, such as Robert Park (1916, 1936) and Ernest Burgess (1925), concentrated on city life but drew on the approaches used by ecologists who studied plant and animal communities. With few exceptions, urban ecologists trace their work back to the

FIGURE 15-1

Urbanization around the World, 2000

Mapping Life WORLDWIDE

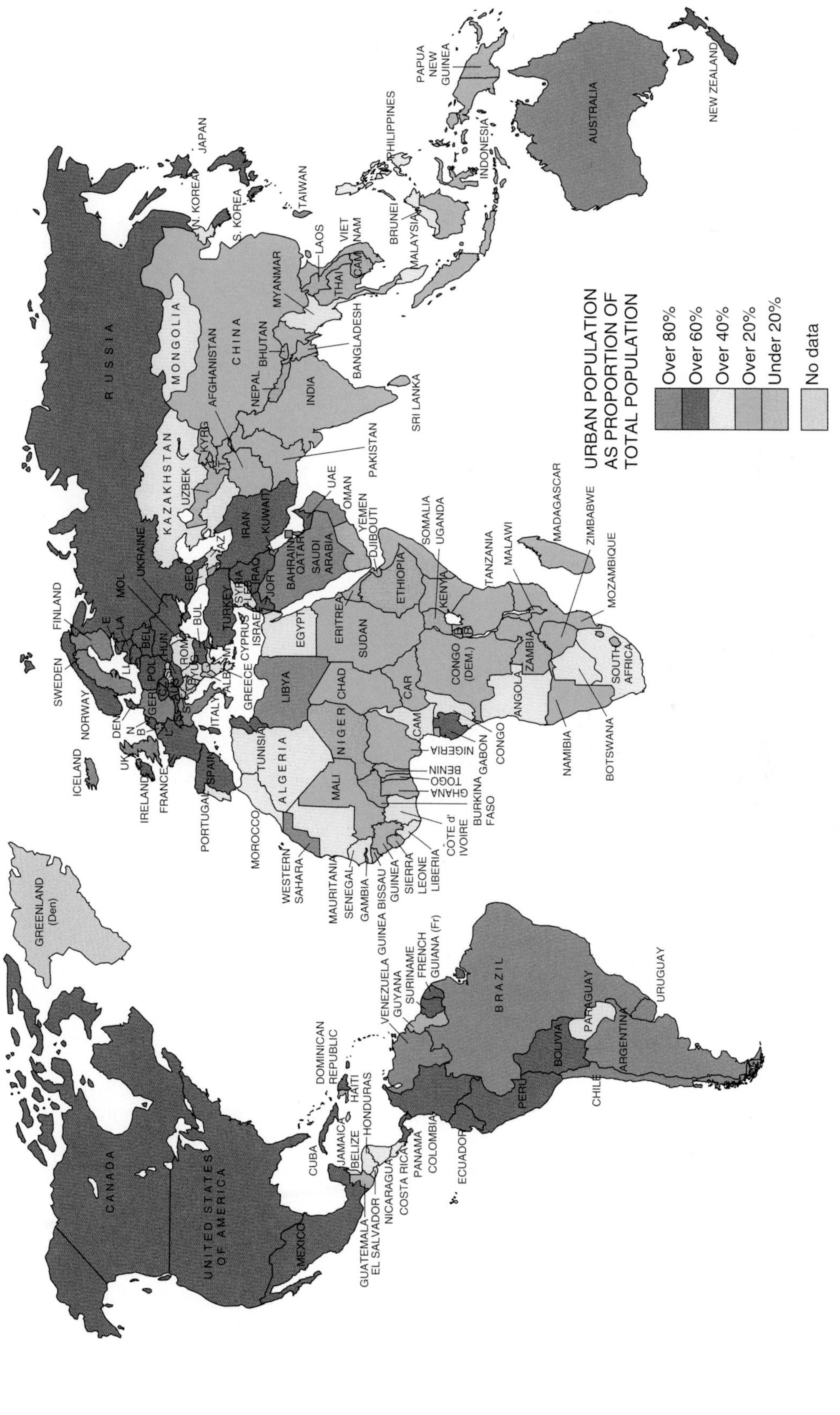

Source: Based on data in Haub 2002.

Sociology in the Global Community

15-1 Squatter Settlements

Bariadas, favelas, bustees, kampungs, and *bidonvilles:* The terms vary depending on the nation and language, but the meaning is the same—"squatter settlements." In squatter settlements, areas occupied by the very poor on the fringe of cities, housing is constructed by the settlers themselves from discarded material, including crates from loading docks and loose lumber from building projects. Although the term "squatter settlement" has wide use, many observers prefer to use a less pejorative term, such as "autonomous settlements."

This type of settlement is very typical of cities in the world's developing nations. In such countries, new housing has not kept pace with the combined urban population growth resulting from births and migration from rural areas. In addition, squatter settlements swell when city dwellers are forced out of housing by astronomical jumps in rent. By definition, squatters living on vacant land are trespassers and can be legally evicted. However, given the large number of poor people who live in such settlements (by U.N. estimates, 40 percent or 50 percent of inhabitants of cities in many developing nations), governments generally look the other way.

Obviously, squatters live in substandard housing, yet this is only one of the many problems they face. Residents do not receive most public services, since their presence cannot be legally recognized. Police and fire protection, paved streets, and sanitary sewers are virtually nonexistent. In some countries, squatters may have trouble voting or enrolling their children in public schools.

Despite such conditions, squatter settlements are not always as bleak as they may appear from the outside. You can often find a well-developed social organization rather than disorganized collections of people. A thriving "informal economy" typically develops: residents establish small, home-based businesses, such as grocery stores, jewellery shops, and the like. Rarely, however, can any but the most ambitious entrepreneurs climb out of poverty through success in this underground economy.

Local churches, men's clubs, and women's clubs are often established in specific neighbourhoods within the settlements. In addition, certain areas may form governing councils or membership associations. These governing bodies may face the usual problems of municipal governments, including charges of corruption and factional splits. Yet, in many cases, they seem to serve their constituents effectively. In Peru, squatters hold annual elections, whereas the rest of the nation has not held local elections for more than 70 years.

Squatter settlements remind us that respected theoretical models of social science in some cultures may not directly apply to others. The various ecological models of urban growth, for example, would not explain metropolitan expansion that locates the poorest people on the urban fringes. Furthermore, solutions that are logical for a highly industrialized nation may not be relevant in the developing nations. Planners in developing nations, rather than focusing on large-scale solutions to urban problems, must think in terms of basic amenities, such as providing water taps or electrical power lines to the ever-expanding squatter settlements.

Applying Theory

1. Do you know of any "squatters" in your own community? If so, describe them and the place where they live.
2. Given the number of homeless people in Canada, why aren't there more squatters? How would a conflict thinker answer this question?

Sources: Castells 1983; Patton 1988; Yap 1998.

concentric-zone theory devised in the 1920s by Burgess (see Figure 15-2a). Using Chicago as an example, Burgess proposed a theory for describing land use in industrial cities. At the centre, or nucleus, of such a city is the central business district. Large department stores, hotels, theatres, and financial institutions occupy this highly valued land. Surrounding this urban centre are succeeding zones that contain other types of land use and that illustrate the growth of the urban area over time.

Note that the creation of zones is a *social* process, not the result of nature alone. Families and business firms compete for the most valuable land; those possessing the most wealth and power are generally the winners. The concentric-zone theory proposed by Burgess also represented a dynamic model of urban growth. As urban growth proceeded, each zone would move even farther from the central business district.

Because of its functionalist orientation and its emphasis on stability, the concentric-zone theory tended to understate or ignore certain tensions apparent in metropolitan areas. For example, the growing use by the affluent of land in a city's peripheral areas was uncriti-

FIGURE 15-2

Comparison of Ecological Theories of Urban Growth

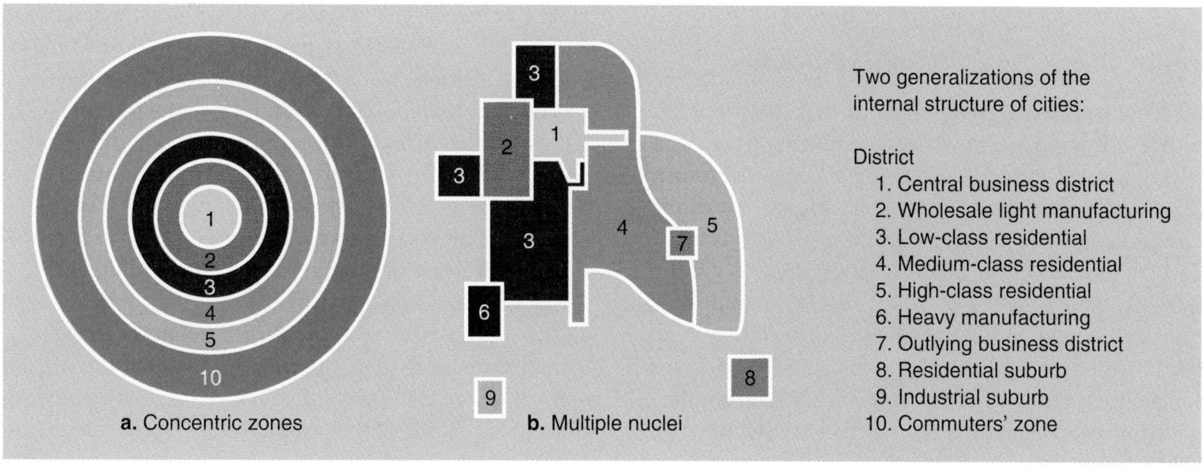

Source: C. Harris and Ullmann 1945:13.

cally approved, while the arrival of visible minorities in white neighbourhoods has been described by some sociologists in such terms as "invasion" and "succession." Moreover, the urban ecological perspective gave little thought to gender inequities, such as the establishment of men's softball and golf leagues in city parks without any programs for women's sports. Consequently, the urban ecological approach has been criticized for its failure to address issues of gender, race, and class.

By the middle of the twentieth century, urban populations had spilled beyond the traditional city limits. No longer could urban ecologists focus exclusively on *growth* in the central city, for large numbers of urban residents were abandoning the cities to live in suburban areas. As a response to the emergence of more than one focal point in some metropolitan areas, Chauncy D. Harris and Edward Ullman (1945) presented the ***multiple-nuclei theory*** (see Figure 15-2b). In their view, not all urban growth radiates outward from a central business district. Instead, a metropolitan area may have many centres of development, each of which reflects a particular urban need or activity. Thus, a city may have a financial district, a manufacturing zone, a waterfront area, an entertainment centre, and so forth. Certain types of business firms and certain types of housing will naturally cluster around each distinctive nucleus (Schwab 1993).

The rise of suburban shopping malls is a vivid example of the phenomenon of multiple nuclei within metropolitan areas. Initially, all major retailing in cities was located in the central business district. Each residential neighbourhood had its own grocers, bakers, and butchers, but people travelled to the centre of the city to make major purchases at department stores. However, as major metropolitan areas expanded and the suburbs became more populous, an increasing number of people began to shop nearer their homes. Today, the suburban mall is a significant retailing and social centre for communities across Canada.

In a refinement of multiple-nuclei theory, contemporary urban ecologists have begun to study what journalist Joel Garreau (1991) has called "edge cities." These communities, which have grown up on the outskirts of major metropolitan areas, are economic and social centres with identities of their own. By any standard of measurement—height of buildings, amount of office space, presence of medical facilities, presence of leisure-time facilities, or, of course, population—edge cities qualify as independent cities rather than as large suburbs.

Whether they include edge cities or multiple nuclei, more and more metropolitan areas are characterized by spread-out development and unchecked growth. A David Suzuki Foundation report, called *Understanding Sprawl,* argues that, in some parts of Canada, urban sprawl is the largest contributor of greenhouse gas emissions, as it segregates houses from stores and workplaces, forcing residents to rely on cars to get around (Gurin 2003). Large corporations are capitalizing on this so-called sprawl by building store and services that depend on the use of the automobile. Recently, the CEO of Starbucks stated that the suburbs and small towns in the United States will be the focus of growth for his company; allowing people to stay in their cars by increasingly using drivethroughs is one the company's goals. Orin Smith states, "We know from our studies that the reason our most frequent users—and as well our most infrequent users—don't use us more is because there are not enough of us and we're not convenient enough. . . . Americans don't want to walk, so if you have to go more than two blocks, they don't go" (*Vancouver Sun* 2004).

Conflict View: New Urban Sociology

Contemporary sociologists point out that metropolitan growth is not governed by waterways and rail lines, as a purely ecological interpretation might suggest. From a conflict perspective, communities are human creations that reflect people's needs, choices, and decisions—but some people have more influence over these decisions than others do. Drawing on conflict theory, an approach that has come to be called the ***new urban sociology*** considers the interplay of local, national, and worldwide forces and their effect on local space, with special emphasis on the impact of global economic activity (Gottdiener and Hutchison 2000).

New urban sociologists note that ecological approaches typically have avoided examining the social forces, largely economic in nature, that have guided urban growth. For example, central business districts may be upgraded or abandoned, depending on whether urban policymakers grant substantial tax exemptions to developers. The suburban boom in the post–World War II era was fuelled by highway construction and by federal housing policies that channelled investment capital into the construction of single-family homes rather than into affordable rental housing in the cities. Similarly, although some observers suggest that the growth of sun-belt cities in the United States is due to a "good business climate," new urban sociologists counter that this term is actually a euphemism for hefty state and local government subsidies and antilabour policies intended to draw manufacturers (Gottdiener and Feagin 1988; M. Smith 1988).

The new urban sociology draws generally on the conflict perspective and more specifically on sociologist Immanuel Wallerstein's world systems analysis. Wallerstein argues that certain industrialized nations (among them, the United States, Japan, and Germany) hold a dominant position at the *core* of the global economic system. At the same time, the poor developing countries of Asia, Africa, and Latin America are on the *periphery* of the global economy, where they are controlled and exploited by core industrialized nations. Through use of world systems analysis, new urban sociologists consider urbanization from a global perspective. They view cities not as independent and autonomous entities but rather as the outcome of decision-making processes directed or influenced by a society's dominant classes and by core industrialized nations. New urban sociologists note that the rapidly growing cities of the world's developing countries were shaped first by colonialism and then by a global economy controlled by core nations and multinational corporations (Gottdiener and Feagin 1988; Smith 1995).

p. 181

The urban ecologists of the 1920s and 1930s were aware of the role that the larger economy played in urbanization, but their theories emphasized the impact of local rather than national or global forces. By contrast, through a broad, global emphasis on social inequality and conflict, new urban sociologists are interested in such topics as the existence of an underclass, the power of multinational corporations, deindustrialization, homelessness, and residential segregation.

pp. 185–187

Developers, builders, and investment bankers are not especially interested in urban growth when it means providing housing for middle- or low-income people. This lack of interest contributes to the problem of homelessness. These urban elites counter that the nation's housing shortage and the plight of the homeless are not

Though the African country of Kenya is mostly rural, Nairobi, a city with almost a million residents, is a modern urban area with international business connections. According to world systems analysis, the cities of developing nations exist on the periphery of the global economy, controlled and exploited by the more powerful industrialized nations.

their fault—and insist that they do not have the capital needed to construct and support such housing. But affluent people *are* interested in growth and *can* somehow find capital to build new shopping centres, office towers, and ballparks.

Why, then, can't they provide the capital for affordable housing, ask new urban sociologists? Part of the answer is that developers, bankers, and other powerful real estate interests view housing in quite a different manner from tenants and most homeowners. For a tenant, an apartment is shelter, housing, a home. But for developers and investors—many of them large (and sometimes multinational) corporations—an apartment is simply a housing investment. These financiers and owners are primarily concerned with maximizing profit, not with solving social problems (Feagin 1983; Gottdiener and Hutchison 2000).

As we have seen throughout this textbook—in studying such varied issues as deviance, race and ethnicity, and aging—no single theoretical approach necessarily offers sociologists the only valuable perspective. As is shown in Table 15-3, urban ecology and new urban sociology offer significantly different ways of viewing urbanization that enrich our understanding of this complex phenomenon.

TYPES OF COMMUNITIES

Communities vary substantially in the degree to which their members feel connected and share a common identity. Ferdinand Tönnies ([1887]1988) used the term *Gemeinschaft* to describe a close-knit community in which social interaction among people is intimate and familiar. It is the kind of place where people in a coffee shop will stop talking when anyone enters, because they are sure to know whoever walks through the door. A shopper at the small grocery store in this town would expect to know every employee and probably every other customer as well. By contrast, the ideal type of *Gesellschaft* describes modern urban life, in which people feel little in common with others. Their social relationships often are a result of interactions focused on immediate tasks, such as purchasing a product. Contemporary city life in Canada generally resembles a *Gesellschaft*.

pp. 106–107

The following sections will examine different types of communities found in Canada, focusing on the distinctive characteristics and problems of central cities, suburbs, and rural communities.

Interactionist View

Sociologist Louis Wirth (1928, 1938) argued that a relatively large and permanent settlement leads to distinctive patterns of behaviour, which he called ***urbanism.*** He identified three critical factors contributing to urbanism: the size of the population, the population density, and the heterogeneity (variety) of the population. A frequent result of urbanism, according to Wirth, is that we become insensitive to events around us and restrict our attention to the primary groups to which we are emotionally attached.

Wirth suggested that urbanization brings with it a way of life resulting from such factors as the spatial segregation of people according to class, race and ethnicity,

Table 15-3 Comparing Approaches to Urbanization

	Urban Ecology	New Urban Sociology
Theoretical Perspective	Functionalist	Conflict
Primary Focus	Relationship of urban areas to their spatial setting and physical environment	Relationship of urban areas to global, national, and local forces
Key Source of Change	Technological innovations, such as new methods of transportation	Economic competition and monopolization of power
Initiator of Actions	Individuals, neighbourhoods, communities	Real estate developers, banks and other financial institutions, multinational corporations
Allied Disciplines	Geography, architecture	Political science, economics

and occupation. In this way of life, human interaction changes from being based on primary relationships (i.e., face to face, personal, and ongoing) to secondary relationships (i.e., detached, impersonal, and fragmented). Although people in urban areas, according to Wirth, gain greater autonomy, independence, and freedom from community norms and sanctions, they also lose the sense of intimacy, connection, and support that accompany primary forms of interaction.

Urban life is noteworthy for its diversity, so it would be a serious mistake to see all city residents as being alike. Sociologist Herbert J. Gans (1991) has distinguished among five types of people found in cities:

1. *Cosmopolites.* These residents remain in cities to take advantage of unique cultural and intellectual benefits. Writers, artists, and scholars fall into this category.
2. *Unmarried and childfree people.* Such people choose to live in cities because of the active nightlife and varied recreational opportunities.
3. *Ethnic villagers.* These urban residents prefer to live in their own tight-knit communities. Typically, immigrant groups isolate themselves in such neighbourhoods to avoid resentment from well-established urban dwellers.
4. *The deprived.* Very poor people and families have little choice but to live in low-rent, and often run-down, urban neighbourhoods.
5. *The trapped.* Some city residents want to leave urban centres but cannot because of their limited economic resources and prospects. Gans includes the "downward mobiles" in this category—people who once held higher social positions but who are forced to live in less prestigious neighbourhoods owing to loss of a job, death of a wage earner, or old age. Both elderly individuals living alone and families may feel "trapped" in part because they resent changes in their communities. Their desire to live elsewhere may reflect their uneasiness with unfamiliar immigrant groups who have become their neighbours.

These categories remind us that the city represents a choice (even a dream) for certain people and a nightmare for others. Gans's work underscores the importance of neighbourhoods in contemporary urban life. Ernest Burgess, in his study of life in Chicago in the 1920s, gave special attention to the ethnic neighbourhoods of that city. Many decades later, residents in such districts as Chinatown or Greektown continue to feel attached to their own ethnic communities rather than to the larger unit of a city. Even outside ethnic enclaves, a special sense of belonging can take hold in a neighbourhood.

In a more recent study in Chicago, Gerald Suttles (1972) coined the term ***defended neighbourhood*** to refer to people's definitions of their community boundaries. Neighbourhoods acquire unique identities because residents view them as geographically separate—and socially different—from adjacent areas. The defended neighbourhood, in effect, becomes a sentimental union of similar people. Neighbourhood phone directories, community newspapers, school and parish boundaries, and business advertisements all serve to define an area and distinguish it from nearby communities.

Feminist Views

Feminist perspectives outlining the ways in which gender intersects with the conditions of city life have long been absent from the sociological literature. Studies on urban life have generally neglected the impact of industrialization and urbanization on the lives of women—women in the private sphere caring for their children and those, as has increasingly been the case, also employed in workplaces in urban areas. Recently, urban studies have highlighted the ways in which patriarchy underpins how social life is organized, both in private and in public spheres or urban centres (Garber and Turner 1995).

As is consistent with the research in Chapter 10 on female students' feelings of safety on Canadian university campuses (DeKeseredy and Schwartz 1998), safety is a major concern for women living in urban centres. In 1993, Statistics Canada revealed that 80 percent of women feared entering a parking garage, 76 percent worried about using public transportation after dark, and 60 percent were afraid to walk in their neighbourhoods after dark (Speirs 1993). Clearly, as far as gender representation goes, there has been a lag between social change and the sociological research on urban spaces.

Central Cities

In terms of land mass, Canada is the second-largest nation in the world. Yet approximately two-thirds of the population is concentrated metropolitan centres on a mere fraction of the nation's land area. As previously mentioned, about half of Canada's population is heavily concentrated in four urban regions, most of which are in narrow strips close to border with the United States. Even those who live outside central cities, such as residents of suburban and rural communities, find that urban centres heavily influence their lifestyles.

Urban Dwellers

Many urban residents are the descendants of European immigrants—Irish, Italians, Jews, Poles, and others—who came to Canada in the nineteenth and early twentieth

Many racial and ethnic minority group members live in communities that are urban and close knit. Above is an Indo-Canadian community in Vancouver.

centuries. With a "vertical mosaic" firmly entrenched in Canada, the cities socialized newcomers to the norms, values, and language of their new homeland and gave them unequal opportunity to work their way up the economic ladder. In addition, a substantial number of Canadians of European descent came to the cities from rural farming areas in the period following World War II.

Cities in Canada are the destinations of immigrants from around the world, particularly those from China, India, the Philippines, and Hong Kong. Yet, unlike those who came to this country one hundred years ago, current immigrants are arriving at a time of rapidly increasing housing costs in the larger cities. This makes it more difficult for them to find decent housing.

Some urban planners argue that the federal government in Canada has failed to disperse recent immigrants to areas outside the cities in which these ethnic neighbourhoods are located. Larry Bourne, a University of Toronto geographer, states that "we're turning a half-dozen cities into intensely multicultural and multilingual places and creating these fantastically vibrant but under-serviced cities while the rest of the country remains homogeneous with a declining and aging population" (Jimenez and Lunman 2004).

Issues Facing Cities

People and neighbourhoods vary greatly within any city in Canada. Yet all residents of a central city—regardless of social class, racial, and ethnic differences—face certain common problems. Crime, air pollution, noise, crumbling infrastructures, congested roads and freeways, inadequate public transportation—these unpleasant realities and many more are an increasing feature of contemporary urban life.

A critical problem for the cities is mass transportation. In 1992, there were 13.3 million passenger cars in Canada—nearly one car for every two people in the country. By 2000, the number of cars/light trucks had increased to 16.8 million. Next to the United States, Canada has the highest rate of car ownership in the world. Growing traffic congestion in metropolitan areas has led many cities to recognize a need for safe, efficient, and inexpensive mass transit systems. However, the federal government has traditionally given much more assistance to highway programs than to public transportation. Conflict theorists note that such a bias favours the relatively affluent (automobile owners) as well as corporations, such as auto manufacturers, tire makers, and oil companies. Meanwhile, low-income residents of metropolitan areas, who are much less likely to own cars than are members of the middle and upper classes, face higher fares on public transit along with deteriorating service (Mason 1998).

Suburbs

The term *suburb* derives from the Latin *sub urbe,* meaning "under the city." Until recent times, most suburbs were just that—tiny communities totally dependent on urban centres for jobs, recreation, and even water.

Today, the term ***suburb*** defies any simple definition. The term generally refers to any community near a large city or any territory within a metropolitan area that is not included in the central city. Large cities and the suburbs that surround them make up a metropolitan area in which people live in one part of the area and work or go to school in another (e.g., living in Delta, British Columbia, and working in Vancouver). In the 2001 census, Statistics Canada considered Census Metropolitan Areas (CMAs) to be urban, suburban, and rural areas of more than 100 000 people that are socially and economically integrated.

Three social factors differentiate suburbs from cities. First, suburbs are generally less dense than cities; in the newest suburbs, there are often no more than four dwellings on a hectare of land. Second, the suburbs consist almost exclusively of private space. Private ornamental lawns replace common park areas for the most part. Third, suburbs have more exacting building design codes than cities, and these codes have become increasingly precise in the last decade. Although the suburbs may be diverse in population, such design standards give the impression of uniformity.

It can also be difficult to distinguish between suburbs and rural areas. Certain criteria generally define suburbs: Most people work at urban (as opposed to rural) jobs, and local governments provide services, such as water supply, sewage disposal, and fire protection. In rural areas, these services are less common, and a greater proportion of residents is employed in farming and related activities.

Suburbanization was the most dramatic population trend in Canada throughout the twentieth century. The exacting building design codes often give the impression of uniformity.

Suburban Expansion

Whatever the precise definition of a suburb, it is clear that suburbs have expanded. In fact, suburbanization was the most dramatic population trend in Canada throughout the twentieth century. Suburban areas grew at first along railroad lines, then at the termini of streetcar tracks, and by the 1950s along the nation's growing systems of freeways and expressways. The suburban boom has been especially evident since World War II.

According to University of Toronto demographer David Foot, increased urbanization was arguably the most controversial finding of the 2001 census. However, he believes that the real trend was suburbanization, not urbanization (Foot 2002). For example, the City of Toronto has grown by 4 percent since 1996, while the Greater Toronto Area's growth was twice that number. Foot notes that similar patterns occurred in Edmonton, Montreal, Calgary, and Vancouver. Foot contends that during the 1980s and 1990s, the baby boom generation moved to the suburbs to raise their children (what he refers to as the "echo boom"). When considering whether this trend will continue, Foot states, "Migration to these urban clusters from the rest of the country will, undoubtedly, continue to contribute to this suburban growth. And most aging boomers will not immediately sell their suburban homes because they are hoping that their future grandchildren will come and visit" (Foot 2002: A17).

Diversity in the Suburbs

In Canada, race and ethnicity remain the most important factors distinguishing cities from suburbs. Nevertheless, the common assumption that suburbia includes only prosperous whites is far from correct. The last 20 years have witnessed the diversification of suburbs in terms of race and ethnicity. For example, by 2001, more than 40 percent of the people living in the Vancouver suburb of Richmond were Chinese, a suburb that also has a significant South Asian population. Like the rest of the nation, members of racial and ethnic minorities are becoming suburban dwellers (El Nasser 2001; Frey 2001).

The term *ethnoburbia* was coined in the 1990s by geographer Wei Li. Ethnoburbia refers to the growing trend toward *ethnoburbs*—suburbs that are ethnically diverse and contain a wide variety of income groups whose members are white collared and well educated. The ethnoburb serves not only as an ethnic residential suburb but also as a community centre and place of business (Li 1999). In the United States, a study of suburban residential patterns in 11 metropolitan areas found that Asian Americans and Hispanics tend to reside in equivalent socioeconomic areas with whites—that is, affluent Hispanics live alongside affluent whites, poor Asians near poor whites, and so on. However, the case for African Americans is quite distinct. Suburban blacks live in poorer suburbs than whites do, even after taking into account differences in individuals' income, education, and homeownership.

Again, in contrast to prevailing stereotypes, the suburbs include a significant number of low-income people from diverse backgrounds—visible minority and non-visible-minority groups. Poverty is not conventionally associated with the suburbs, partly because the suburban poor tend to be scattered among more affluent people. In some instances, suburban communities intentionally hide social problems, such as homelessness, so they can maintain a "respectable image." Soaring housing costs have contributed to suburban poverty, which is expected to rise at a faster rate than city poverty through 2010 (El Nasser 1999).

Some urban and suburban residents are moving to communities even more remote from the central city or to rural areas altogether. Initial evidence suggests that this move to rural areas is only intensifying the racial disparities in our metropolitan areas (Bureau of the Census 1997b; Holmes 1997).

Rural Communities

As we have seen, the people of Canada live mainly in urban areas. Yet, in 2001, 20 percent of the population lived in rural areas and small towns, outside commuting distance to larger cities (Statistics Canada 2002e). As is true of the suburbs, it would be a mistake to view rural communities as fitting into one set image. Grain farms, coal mining towns, cattle ranches, and gas stations along the TransCanada highway are all part of the rural landscape of Canada.

The historic stereotype of the farmer is a white male. Yet women have long played a significant role in agriculture, both in Canada and throughout the world. Women participate actively in agriculture—on large and small farms and in profitable and failing family businesses. Farming women are almost always married and generally have families. In Canada, the percentage of farms operated exclusively by women increased from 3.9 percent in 1991 to 5 percent in 2001 (Statistics Canada 2002e). Segregation by gender is typical of farm labour: Men are more likely to be engaged in field work, while women serve their farms as accountants, personnel and equipment managers, and purchasing agents. Many studies have documented the high degree of stress that farming women experience as they attempt to fulfil many demanding social roles (Keating and Munro 1988).

A study by Statistics Canada released in 2004 using data from the 2001 census showed that a disproportionately high number of self-employed Canadians live in rural areas and small towns, outside the commuting distances to larger cities. In 2001, some 620 000 self-employed Canadians lived in rural areas, accounting for one in every four self-employed workers in the country (Statistics Canada 2004j). Between 1981 and 2001, rates of self-employment through farming declined substantially, while rates of nonfarm self-employment were steady from 1981 to 1986 and increased throughout the 1990s. Provinces and territories heavily dependent on farming have seen their farming workforce rates decline, with many farm families leaving the rural areas for the larger cities. In 1976 in Saskatchewan, for example, 25 percent of the province's workforce was in farming, as opposed to only 11 percent in 2001.

Religious Jews pray in the locker room at a kosher meat-processing plant near Postville, Iowa. When the plant first opened, the rural Christians hired to work there were unfamiliar with Orthodox Jewish culture and faith, but members of the two groups soon learned to work together.

In 2004, the Government of Canada appointed a Canada research chair in the new rural economy. The appointee will study the linkages between technological change and economic growth in rural areas. The focus of this research on rural life will include an examination of how information and knowledge-intensive technologies will play a role in the sustainability of rural areas in Canada.

In smaller communities, the construction of large businesses, such as Wal-Mart, Target, Home Depot, or Costco, can create its own problems. Although many residents

Research in Action 15-2 Store Wars

No organization exists in a vacuum, especially not a corporate giant. Executives of Wal-Mart know that. The epitome of the superstore, Wal-Mart has become the centre of controversy in towns and cities across North America, despite the familiar smiley-face logo and its red, white, and blue corporate image. The reason: a new Wal-Mart can have powerfully negative effects on the surrounding community.

Wal-Mart was founded in 1962 by Sam Walton, whose strategy was to locate new stores in rural communities, where competition from other retailers was weak and unions were not organized. Over the years, as the enormously successful discount chain expanded, Wal-Mart began to move into the fringes of metropolitan areas as well. But the residents of the communities Wal-Mart moved into did not always welcome their new neighbour.

Residents of smaller communities worried that Wal-Mart would destroy the small-town atmosphere they treasured. Would their cozy grocery store, known for its personal service, survive the discount giant's competition? Would their quaint and charming Main Street fall into decline? Would full-time jobs with full benefits give way to part-time employment? (Studies have shown that superstores ultimately *reduce* employment.) Community grassroots opposition to Wal-Mart, chronicled in the PBS documentary *Store Wars*, ultimately lost its battle because of Wal-Mart's promised low prices and increased tax revenues. But citizens in many other communities have won, at least temporarily.

On the urban fringes, too, residents have mobilized to stop new superstores, with environmentalists raising alarms over a proposed Wal-Mart superstore to be located next to a marsh that sheltered endangered wildlife.

But the issue is more complicated in these areas, because communities on the urban fringe are hardly untouched by economic development. New houses that dot the suburbs surrounding new stores, built on lots carved out of farmland or forest, have had an environmental impact themselves. In fact, the trend toward the superstore seems to parallel the emergence of the megalopolis, whose boundaries push farther and farther outward, eating up open space in the process. Recognizing the drawbacks of urban sprawl, some planners are beginning to advocate "smart growth"— restoring the central city and its older suburbs rather than abandoning them for the outer rings.

In his book *Wal-Mart: Template for Twenty-First Century Capitalism* (2005), labour historian Nelson Lichtenstein states that Wal-Mart rules suburbia and smaller centres across both Canada and the United States; the company's next move, however, will be to infiltrate the urban market, where it is significantly less dominant. In British Columbia, for example, Wal-Mart has 30 stores, but none in the City of Vancouver.

Wal-Mart executives are unapologetic about the chain's rapid expansion. They argue that their aggressive competition has lowered prices and raised working people's standard of living. And they say they have given back to the communities where their stores are located by donating money to educational institutions and local agencies.

Applying Theory

1. Is there a Wal-Mart, Home Depot, or some other superstore near you? If so, was its opening a matter of controversy in your community?
2. What do you think of the "smart growth" movement? Should communities attempt to redirect business and residential development, or should developers be free to build wherever and whatever they choose? What insights might some feminist sociologists provide to this movement?

Sources: Ibata 2001; Kaufman 2000; Lichtenstein 2005; *Maine Times* 2001; PBS 2001; Simon 2001; Smart Growth 2001; Wal-Mart 2001; Wal-Mart Watch 2000.

welcome the new employment opportunities and the convenience of one-stop shopping, local merchants see their longtime family businesses endangered by formidable 200 000-square-foot competitors with national reputations. Even when such discount stores provide a boost to a town's economy (and they do not always do so), they can undermine the town's sense of community and identity. Box 15-2 chronicles the "store wars" that often ensue.

Rural communities that do survive may feel threatened by provincial and territorial governments that, in the name of fiscal responsibility, have cut such services as health care, education, legal and court services, and various other social programs in rural areas. Many rural residents must now travel to larger urban areas to seek medical treatment or counselling or to attend court hearings.

On a more positive note, advances in electronic communication have allowed some people in Canada to work wherever they want. For those who are concerned about quality-of-life issues (e.g., clean environment, affordable housing, community cohesion, lack of congestion), working at home in a rural area that has access to the latest high-tech services is the perfect arrangement. No matter where people make their homes—whether in the city, the suburbs, or a rural village—economic and technological change will have an impact on their quality of life.

Use Your Sociological Imagination

You have fast-forwarded to a future in which there are no central cities—just sprawling suburbs and isolated rural communities. What are the economic and social effects of the disappearance of the downtown area?

THE ENVIRONMENT

Decisions made in the economic and political spheres, as well as in local communities, often have environmental consequences. We can see signs of despoliation almost everywhere. Our air, our water, and our land are being polluted. Whether we live in Toronto, Mexico City, or Lagos, Nigeria, environmental degradation tends to accompany the increasing size of cities. In the following section, we will survey these problems and see what sociologists have to say about them.

Environmental Problems: An Overview

In recent decades, the world has witnessed serious environmental disasters. For example, Love Canal, near Niagara Falls in New York State, was declared a disaster area in 1978 because of chemical contamination. In the 1940s and 1950s, a chemical company had disposed of waste products on the site where a housing development and a school were subsequently built. The metal drums that held the chemical wastes eventually rusted out, and toxic chemicals with noxious odours began seeping into the residents' yards and basements. Subsequent investigations revealed that the chemical company knew as early as 1958 that toxic chemicals were seeping into homes and a school playground. After repeated protests in the late 1970s, 239 families living in Love Canal had to be relocated.

In 1986, a series of explosions set off a catastrophic nuclear reactor accident at Chernobyl, a part of Ukraine (in what was then the Soviet Union). This accident killed at least 32 000 people. Some 300 000 residents had to be evacuated, and the area became uninhabitable for 30 kilometres (19 miles) in any direction. High levels of radiation were found as far as 50 kilometres (30 miles) from the reactor site, and radioactivity levels were well above normal as far away as Sweden and Japan. According to one estimate, the Chernobyl accident and the resulting nuclear fallout may ultimately result in 100 000 additional cases of cancer worldwide (Shcherbak 1996).

Although Love Canal, Chernobyl, and other environmental disasters understandably grab headlines, it is the silent, day-to-day deterioration of the environment that ultimately poses a devastating threat to humanity. It is impossible to examine all our environmental problems in detail, but three broad areas of concern stand out: air pollution, water pollution, and contamination of land.

Air Pollution

More than one billion people on the planet are exposed to potentially health-damaging levels of air pollution (World Resources Institute 1998). Unfortunately, in cities around the world, residents have come to accept smog and polluted air as "normal." Air pollution in urban areas is caused primarily by emissions from automobiles and secondarily by emissions from electric power plants and heavy industries. Urban smog not only limits visibility but can also lead to health problems as uncomfortable as eye irritation and as deadly as lung cancer. Such problems are especially severe in developing countries. The World Health Organization estimates that up to 700 000 premature deaths *per year* could be prevented if pollutants were brought down to safer levels (Carty 1999).

Because transportation is the greatest source of air pollution in Canada, in 2001 the federal government included goals for cleaner-running engines and cleaner-burning fuels as part of its Clean Air Strategy. Under the Canadian Environmental Protection Act and the Emissions Control program, strategies were developed to reduce emissions from cars, trucks, construction equipment, gasoline utility engines, outboard marine engines, and personal watercraft.

Water Pollution

Throughout North America, dumping of waste materials by both industries and local governments has polluted streams, rivers, and lakes. Consequently, many bodies of water have become unsafe for drinking, fishing, and swimming. Around the world, the pollution of the oceans is an issue of growing concern. Such pollution results regularly from waste dumping and is made worse by fuel leaks from shipping and occasional oil spills. In a dramatic accident in 1989, the oil tanker *Exxon Valdez* ran aground in Prince William Sound, Alaska. The tanker's cargo of 50 million litres (11 million gallons) of crude oil spilled into the sound and washed onto the shore, contaminating 2065 kilometres (1285 miles) of shoreline. About 11 000 people joined in a cleanup effort that cost more than $2 billion.

Less dramatic than large-scale accidents or disasters, but more common in many parts of the world, are problems with the basic water supply. The most serious case

Rusty barrels leak chemicals into a lake near a city east of Moscow. Throughout the word, industrial pollutants have rendered many bodies of water unsafe for fishing, drinking, or swimming.

of water contamination in Canadian history occurred in Walkerton, Ontario, in 2000. Seven people died and 2300 became ill from *E. coli* after consuming contaminated water from the town's supply. Worldwide, more than a billion people lack safe and adequate drinking water, and nearly half of the world's population has no acceptable means of sanitation—a problem that further threatens the quality of water supplies. The health costs of unsafe water are enormous (World Health Organization 2000).

Contamination of Land

The former site of ICI Canada in Shawinigan, Quebec, has now been remediated. The earth around and under the plant had been soaking up contaminates for nearly 50 years. More than 650 000 litres of solvents that were trapped in the soil under the water table were pumped out and recycled or disposed of, and tonnes of soil were excavated.

A significant part of land contamination comes from the tremendous demand for landfills to handle the nation's waste. Recycling programs aimed at reducing the need for landfills are perhaps the most visible aspect of environmentalism. How successful have such programs been? In 1980, about 10 percent of urban waste was recycled; the proportion increased steadily throughout the 1980s but started to level off at about 29 percent in 1998. Experts are beginning to revise their goals for recycling campaigns, which now appear overambitious. Still, a new way to be green has developed: the Internet. For example, over-the-Net commercial transactions allow the downloading of new software, reducing the need for wasteful packaging and shipping materials, including fuel for delivery trucks. And the availability of email and electronic networking encourages people to work at home rather than contribute to the pollution caused by commuting (Belsie 2000; Booth 2000).

What are the basic causes of our growing environmental problems? Some observers, such as Paul Ehrlich and Anne Erhlich, see the pressure of world population growth as the central factor in environmental deterioration. They argue that population control is essential in preventing widespread starvation and environmental decay. Barry Commoner, a biologist, counters that the primary cause of environmental ills is the increasing use of technological innovations that are destructive to the world's environment—among them plastics, detergents, synthetic fibres, pesticides, herbicides, and chemical fertilizers. In the following sections, we will examine the functionalist, conflict, feminist, and interactionist approaches to the study of environmental issues (Commoner 1971, 1990; P. Ehrlich 1968; P. Ehrlich and Ehrlich 1990; P. Ehrlich and Ellison 2002).

Functionalism and Human Ecology

Human ecology is concerned with the interrelationships between people and their environment. Environmentalist Barry Commoner (1971:39) has stated that "everything is connected to everything else." Human ecologists focus on how the physical environment shapes people's lives and also on how people influence the surrounding environment.

In an application of the human ecological perspective, sociologist Riley Dunlap suggests that the natural environment serves three basic functions for humans, as it does for the many animal species (Dunlap 1993; Dunlap and Catton 1983):

1. *The environment provides the resources essential for life.* These include air, water, and materials used to create shelter, transportation, and needed products. If human societies exhaust these resources—for example, by polluting the water supply or cutting down rain forests—the consequences can be dire.

2. *The environment serves as a waste repository.* More so than other living species, humans produce a huge quantity and variety of waste products—bottles, boxes, papers, sewage, garbage, to name just a few. Various types of pollution have become more common because human societies are generating more wastes than the environment can safely absorb.
3. *The environment "houses" our species.* It is our home, our living space, the place where we reside, work, and play. At times we take this for granted, but not when day-to-day living conditions become unpleasant and difficult. If our air is "heavy," if our tap water turns brown, if toxic chemicals seep into our neighbourhood, we remember why it is vital to live in a healthful environment.

Dunlap (1993) points out that these three functions of the environment actually compete with one another. Human use of the environment for one of these functions will often strain its ability to fulfil the other two. For example, with world population continuing to rise, we have an increasing need to raze forests or farmland and build housing developments. But each time we do so, we are reducing the amount of land providing food, lumber, or habitat for wildlife.

The tension among the three essential functions of the environment brings us back to the human ecologists' view that "everything is connected to everything else." In facing the environmental challenges of the twenty-first century, government policymakers and environmentalists must determine how they can fulfil human societies' pressing needs (for example, for food, clothing, and shelter) while at the same time preserving the environment as a source of resources, a waste repository, and our home.

Conflict View of Environmental Issues

In Chapter 8, we drew on world systems analysis to show how a growing share of the human and natural resources of the developing countries is being redistributed to the core industrialized nations. This process only intensifies the destruction of natural resources in poorer regions of the world. From a conflict perspective, less affluent nations are being forced to exploit their mineral deposits, forests, and fisheries to meet their debt obligations. The poor turn to the only means of survival available to them: They plow mountain slopes, burn plots in tropical forests, and overgraze grasslands (Livernash and Rodenburg 1998).

Brazil exemplifies this interplay between economic troubles and environmental destruction. Each year more than 28 500 square kilometres (11 000 square miles) of the Amazon rain forest are cleared for crops and livestock through burning. The elimination of the rain forest affects worldwide weather patterns, heightening the gradual warming of Earth.

These socioeconomic patterns, with harmful environmental consequences, are evident not only in Latin America but also in many regions of Africa and Asia. Conflict theorists are well aware of the environmental implications of land use policies in the developing world, but they contend that such a focus on the developing countries can contain an element of ethnocentrism. Who, they ask, is more to blame for environmental deterioration: the poverty-stricken and "food-hungry" populations of the world or the "energy-hungry" industrialized nations (G.T. Miller 1972:117)?

Conflict theorists point out that Western industrialized nations account for only 25 percent of the world's population but are responsible for 85 percent of worldwide consumption. Take the United States alone: A mere 5 percent of the world's people consume more than half the world's nonrenewable resources and more than one-third of all the raw materials produced. Such data led conflict theorists to charge that the most serious threat to the environment comes from "affluent megaconsumers and megapolluters" (Bharadwaj 1992; G.T. Miller 1972).

Allan Schnaiberg (1994) further refines this analysis by criticizing the focus on affluent consumers as the cause of environmental troubles. In his view, a capitalist system creates a "treadmill of production" because of its inherent need to build ever-expanding profits. This treadmill necessitates creating an increasing demand for products, obtaining natural resources at minimal cost, and manufacturing products as quickly and as cheaply as possible—no matter what the long-term environmental consequences of this approach.

Environmental Justice

Kennedy Heights, a new subdivision of Houston, attracted buyers in the late 1960s with its tidy brick façade homes and bucolic street names. But what the mostly black buyers were not told was that the developers had constructed these homes on oil pits abandoned by Gulf Oil decades earlier. In 1997 after experiencing periodic contaminated water supplies and a variety of illnesses, including a large incidence of cancer and lupus, Kennedy Heights residents filed a class-action suit against Chevron, the company that acquired Gulf Oil. This case of environmental pollution is compounded by charges of "environmental racism," based on Gulf Oil documents in 1967 that targeted the area "for Negro residential and commercial development" (Verhovek 1997).

The first trial in the Kennedy Heights residents' case resulted in a mistrial. In 1999, Chevron decided to settle with the residents, even though it had no legal obligation to do so. The company maintained that the oil stored on the property in the 1920s never posed a health or safety risk to the Kennedy Heights residents. Chevron also contended that race played no part in its decisions and that the land was sold to the developer 30 years before homes were built. But there are signs that some headway is being made in establishing ***environmental justice (EJ),*** a legal strategy based on claims that racial minorities are subjected disproportionately to environmental hazards. In 1998, Shintech, a chemical company, dropped plans to build a plastics plant in an impoverished black community in Mississippi. Opponents of the plant had filed a civil rights complaint with the Environmental Protection Agency (EPA). EPA administrator Carol Browner praised Shintech's decision: "The principles applied to achieve this solution should be incorporated into any blueprint for dealing with environmental justice issues in communities across the nation" (Associated Press 1998:18).

Following reports from the EPA and other organizations documenting discriminatory locating of hazardous waste sites, then-President Bill Clinton issued an Executive Order in 1994 that requires all federal agencies to ensure that low-income and minority communities have access to better information about their environment and have an opportunity to participate in shaping government policies that affect their communities' health. Initial efforts to implement the policy have aroused widespread opposition because of the delays it imposes in establishing new industrial sites. Some observers question the wisdom of an order that slows economic development coming to areas in dire need of employment opportunities. However, there are those who point out that such businesses employ few unskilled or less skilled workers and only make the environment less livable for those left behind (Cushman 1998; Goldman and Fitton 1994).

As is evident from the above discussion, much of the literature on environmental justice (EJ) is based on U.S. studies and cases (Bryant and Mohai 1992; Bullard 1990; Hofrichter 1993). In 2001, however, Alice Nabalamba published a Canadian study using 1996 census data in which she investigated the links among socioeconomic status, visible minority group status, and the location of pollution sources in Toronto, Hamilton, and the Niagara region. Nabalamba's findings suggest that poorer people are more likely than the general population to live in neighbourhoods near sources of pollution and industrial land use. Nabalamba predicts that future use of land for industrial discharges, waste treatment, disposal, storage, and so on, will continue to affect those Canadians of lower socioeconomic status—those who have, obviously, less political clout to fight back (Nabalamba 2001).

Feminist View: Eco-feminism

None of the various feminist perspectives addresses the links between gender and the environment as directly as eco-feminism does. Eco-feminism forges an alliance between the environmental movement and the feminist movement, between ecology and feminist principles. Central to the core tenants of eco-feminism is the belief that, historically, men have dominated and exploited both nature and women. Androcentric thinking, rooted in principles of dualism and hierarchy, has justified activities that have led to men's domination over nature and women. Eco-feminists reject this way of thinking and acting and the harm that it has caused the environment. Instead, they argue that women inherently have a closer, more intimate, and nonexploitive connection to nature. Women's relationships with nature, eco-feminists contend, are not ones of domination, control, and exploitive self-interest but rather of protection and nurturance. Critics of eco-feminism suggest that arguing that women have inherent qualities of nurturance reduces their position to a form of biological determinism. Biological determinism has long been used as a justification for the separation, exclusion, and oppression of women, because their differences, in an adrocentric world, have been interpreted as inferiorities.

Interactionist View

The symbolic interactionist perspective focuses on the meaning or symbolic significance that people attribute to one another's actions. Through social interaction, "human beings interpret or 'define' each other's actions instead of merely reacting to each other's actions" (Blumer 1969:79). Symbolic interactionism, therefore, may concentrate on the meaning we give to one another's actions as they relate to environmental practices. For example, your neighbour's use of a "blue box" for recycling might be interpreted as a sign that he or she is a good citizen, with the blue box as a symbol of concern for the environmental sustainability of the local community, or simply as an opportunity to meet or chat with other neighbours as they place their blue boxes at the roadside for pickup. The interactionist perspective encompasses the phenomenon of social constructionism, in which individuals continually construct and reconstruct their meaning of environmental practices. Sociologists Clay Schoenfeld, Robert Meir, and Robert Griffin (1979) studied how environmental issues become the concerns of everyday citizens and how concern for an environmental issue one year (e.g., child labour or deforestation) may be supplanted by a different environmental concern the next year (e.g., public transportation or genetically modified foods). The meaning we give to human interaction is continually reconstructed; thus, different environmental issues may emerge as being of a higher profile than others are.

Use Your Sociological Imagination

Your community is designated as a site for the burial of toxic waste. How would you react? Would you organize a protest? Or would you make sure the authorities carry the project out safely? How can such sites be chosen fairly?

SOCIAL POLICY AND COMMUNITIES: Seeking Shelter Worldwide

The Issue

A chance meeting brought two old classmates together. In late 1997, England's Prince Charles encountered Clive Harold during a tour of the offices of a magazine sold by the homeless in London. But while Prince Charles can call several palaces home, Harold is homeless. This modern-day version of the "The Prince and the Pauper" intrigued many people with its message that "it can happen to anyone." Harold had been a successful author and journalist until his marriage fell apart and alcohol turned his life inside out (*Chicago Tribune* 1997).

The issue of inadequate shelter manifests itself in many ways, for all housing problems can be considered relative. For a middle-class family in Canada, it may mean a somewhat smaller house than they need because that is all they can afford. For a single working adult in Tokyo, it may mean having to commute two hours to a full-time job. For many people worldwide, however, the housing problem consists of merely finding shelter of any kind that they can afford, in a place where anyone would reasonably want to live. Prince Charles of Buckingham Palace and Clive Harold, homeless person, are extreme examples of a continuum present in many communities in all societies. What can be done to ensure adequate shelter for those who can't afford it?

The Setting

Homelessness is evident in both industrialized and developing countries. According to the 2004 report of the National Anti-Poverty Organization, a conservative estimate of the number of homeless in Canada exceeds 200 000. Compiling an accurate list of the homeless is both difficult and expensive.

In Great Britain, some 175 000 people are accepted as homeless by the government and are given housing. An even larger number, perhaps one million people, are turned away from government assistance or are sharing a household with relatives or acquaintances but want separate accommodations. Although an accurate figure is not available, it is estimated that 1 percent of Western Europeans are homeless; they sleep in the streets, depend on night shelters and hostels, or live in precarious accommodations (B. Lee 1992; Platt 1993; Stearn 1993).

In Japan, the problem of homelessness is just as serious. A single protest drew roughly six thousand homeless people to Tokyo in 1998. The Japanese usually hide such misfortune, thinking it shameful, but a severe economic downturn had victimized many formerly prosperous citizens, swelling the numbers of the homeless. A chronic space shortage in the heavily populated island nation, together with opposition to the establishment of homeless shelters in residential neighbourhoods, compounds the problem (Hara 2000).

In developing countries, rapid population growth has outpaced the expansion of housing by a wide margin, leading to a rise in homelessness. For example, estimates of homelessness in Mexico City range from 10 000 to 100 000, and these estimates do not include the many people living in caves or squatter settlements (see Box 15-1). In 1998, in urban areas alone, 600 million people around the world were either homeless or inadequately housed (G. Goldstein 1998; Ross 1996).

Sociological Insights

Both in Canada and around the world, being homeless functions as a master status that largely defines a person's position within society. In this case, homelessness tends to mean that in many important respects, the individual is *outside* society. Without a home address and telephone, it is difficult to look for work or even pp. 97–98, 143 apply for public assistance. Moreover, the master status of being homeless carries a serious stigma and can lead to prejudice and discrimination. Poor treatment of people suspected of being homeless is common in stores and restaurants, and many communities have reported acts of random violence against homeless people.

Twenty years ago, most homeless people were older white males, often alcoholics, living in skid-row areas. Today, homeless people are comparatively younger.

The profile of homelessness has changed significantly during the last 20 years. In the past, homeless people were primarily older white males living as alcoholics in skid-row areas. However, best estimates suggest that today's homeless people are comparatively younger. As with counting the overall number of homeless Canadians, calculating their age in any precise way is impossible.

Changing economic and residential patterns account for much of this increase in homelessness. In recent decades, the process of urban renewal has included a noticeable boom in gentrification. In some instances, city governments have promoted gentrification by granting lucrative tax breaks to developers who convert low-cost rental units into luxury apartments and condominiums. Conflict theorists note that although the affluent may derive both financial and emotional benefits from gentrification and redevelopment, the poor often end up being thrown out on the street.

There is an undeniable connection between the nation's growing shortage of affordable housing and the rise in homelessness (M. Elliott and Krivo 1991). Yet sociologist Peter Rossi (1989, 1990) cautions against focusing too narrowly on the housing shortage while ignoring structural factors, such as the decline in the demand for manual labour in cities and the increasing prevalence of chronically unemployed young men among the homeless. Rossi contends that structural changes have put everyone in extreme poverty at higher risk of becoming homeless—especially poor people with an accumulation of disabilities (such as drug abuse, bad health, unemployment, and criminal records). Having a disability in this manner forces the individual to rely on family and friends for support, often for a prolonged period. If the strain on this support network is so great that it collapses, homelessness may result. Although many researchers accept Rossi's theory, the general public often prefers to "blame the victim" for becoming homeless (B. Lee 1992).

Homeless women often have additional problems that distinguish them from homeless men. Homeless women report a larger number of recent injuries or acute illnesses, as well as a greater number of chronic health problems, than do homeless men (Liebow 1993).

Sociologists attribute homelessness in developing nations not only to income inequality but also to population growth and an influx of people from rural areas and areas experiencing natural disaster, famine, or warfare. A major barrier to constructing decent, legal, and affordable housing in the urban areas of these developing nations is the political power of large-scale landowners and small-scale land speculators—anyone buying a few lots as an investment. In the view of conflict theorists, these groups conspire to enhance their own financial investment by making the supply of legally buildable land scarce. (This problem is not unknown in the cities of North America, but a World Bank survey shows that the increase in the cost of land is twice as great in developing nations as in industrial countries.) In many cases, residents who can afford building materials have no choice but to become squatters. Those who can't are likely to become homeless.

Policy Initiatives

Thus far, policymakers have often been content to steer the homeless toward large, overcrowded, unhealthy shelters. Many neighbourhoods and communities have resisted plans to open large shelters or even smaller residences for the homeless, often raising the familiar cry of "not in my backyard!"

The Government of Canada's Homeless Initiative was announced in 1999 and funded with $753 million over the next three years. The goal of the program was to create partnerships with local governments in the 10 Canadian cities with a "documented" and "significant absolute homeless problem," to develop affordable, stable housing alternatives. Those 10 urban centres contain 80 percent of the nation's homeless population. The main program associated with the initiative has as its goals (1) to ensure that no one is forced to live on the street, (2) to reduce the number of Canadians dependent on shelters and transition and supportive housing, and (3) to help the homeless achieve self-sufficiency.

Even though media portrayals tend to stereotype the homeless as middle-aged men with addictions, the actual population is much more diverse. For instance, a 2002 report by researchers from the Canadian Housing and Renewal Association revealed that girls and young women make up one-third to one-half of the young homeless (aged 12 to 24 years). Within this group, certain subgroups tend to be overrepresented: Aboriginals, lesbians, those in and from government care, and (in Toronto) recent refugees and immigrants (Status of Women 2002). The report recommended general and city-specific services, programs, and policies—affordable housing, transitional and supportive housing projects, and longer-term intervention—as well as gender-specific services and programs. Overall, the report emphasized the necessity of the government implementing macrolevel policies to alleviate poverty and to provide affordable housing to address the underlying causes of homelessness (Status of Women 2002).

Despite occasional media spotlights on the homeless and the booming economy, affordable housing has become harder to find. Two out of three low-income renters receive no housing allowance, and most spend a disproportionately large share of their income to maintain their shelter. Research shows that this worsening of affordable housing stems from a substantial drop in the number of unsubsidized, low-cost rental housing units in the private market and a growing number of low-income renter households.

Developing nations have special problems. They have understandably given highest priority to economic productivity as measured by jobs with living wages. Unfortunately, even the most ambitious economic and social programs may be overwhelmed by minor currency fluctuations, a drop in the value of a nation's major export, or an influx of refugees from a neighbouring country. Some of the reforms implemented have included promoting private (as opposed to government-controlled) housing markets, allowing dwellings to be places of business as well, and loosening restrictions on building materials.

All three of these short-term solutions have shortcomings. Private housing markets invite exploitation; mixed residential and commercial use may only cause good housing to deteriorate faster; and the use of marginal building materials leaves low-income residential areas more vulnerable to calamities, such as floods, fires, and earthquakes. Large-scale rental housing under government supervision, the typical solution in North America and Europe, has been successful only in economically advanced city-states, like Hong Kong and Singapore (Strassman 1998).

In sum, homeless people both in Canada and abroad are not getting the shelter they need, and they lack the political clout to corral the attention of policymakers.

Applying Theory

1. Have you ever worked as a volunteer in a shelter or soup kitchen? If so, were you surprised by the people who lived or ate there? Have you or anyone you know ever had to move into a shelter?
2. How might a conflict sociologist analyze the problem of gentrification of low-income housing?
3. What kind of assistance is available to homeless people in the community where you live? Does the help come from the government, from private charities, or from both? What about housing assistance for people with low incomes, such as rent subsidies—is it available?

CHAPTER RESOURCES

Summary

A ***community*** is a spatial or political unit of social organization that gives people a sense of belonging. This chapter explained how communities originated and analyzed the process of urbanization from functionalist, feminist, interactionist, and conflict perspectives. It described various types of communities, including central cities, the ***suburbs***, and rural communities, and it introduced the new concept of an electronic community. The functionalist, feminist, interactionist, and conflict perspectives were also used to explore environmental issues.

1. Stable communities began to develop when people stayed in one place to cultivate crops; surplus production enabled cities to emerge.
2. Gideon Sjoberg identified three preconditions of city life: advanced technology in both agricultural and nonagricultural areas, a favourable physical environment, and a well-developed social organization.
3. There are important differences among the ***preindustrial city***, the ***industrial city***, and the ***postindustrial city***.
4. Urbanization is evident not only in Canada but also throughout the world; by 2000, 45 percent of the world's population lived in urban areas.
5. The ***urban ecological*** approach is functionalist because it emphasizes that different elements in urban areas contribute to stability.
6. Drawing on conflict theory, ***new urban sociology*** considers the interplay of a community's political and economic interests as well as the impact of the global economy on communities in Canada and other countries.
7. Many urban residents are immigrants from other nations and tend to live in ethnic neighbourhoods.
8. In the last three decades, cities have confronted an overwhelming array of economic and social problems, including crime, unemployment, and the deterioration of schools and public transit systems.
9. Suburbanization was the most dramatic population trend in Canada throughout the twentieth century. In recent decades, suburbs have witnessed increasing diversity in race and ethnicity.
10. Farming, mining, and logging have all been in decline in the rural communities of Canada.
11. Technological advances, like electronic information networks, are changing the economy, the distribution of population, and even the concept of community.
12. Three broad areas of environmental concern are air pollution, water pollution, and contamination of land.
13. Using the human ecological perspective, sociologist Riley Dunlap suggests that the natural environment serves three basic functions: It provides essential resources, it serves as a waste repository, and it "houses" our species.
14. Conflict theorists charge that the most serious threat to the environment comes from Western industrialized nations.
15. Eco-feminism forges an alliance between the environmental movement and the feminist movement and between ecology and feminist principles.
16. The symbolic interactionist perspective on the environment reveals the meaning that humans give to human interaction; thus, different environmental issues may emerge as being higher profile than others are.
17. ***Environmental justice*** is concerned with the disproportionate subjection of minorities to environmental hazards.
18. Soaring housing costs, unemployment, cutbacks in public assistance, and rapid population growth have all contributed to rising homelessness around the world. Most social policy is directed toward sending the homeless to large shelters.

Critical Thinking Questions

1. How can the functionalist and conflict perspectives be used in examining the growing interest among policymakers in privatizing public services presently offered by cities and other communities?
2. How has your home community (your city, town, or neighbourhood) changed over the years you have lived there? Have there been significant changes in the community's economic base and in its racial and ethnic profile? Have the community's

social problems intensified or lessened over time? Is unemployment currently a major problem? What are the community's future prospects?

3. Imagine that you have been asked to study the issue of air pollution in the largest city in your province or territory. How might you draw on surveys, observation research, experiments, and existing sources to help you study this issue?
4. How would you explain the existence of a tent city in the midst of a major city in a country as rich and full of resources as Canada?

Key Terms

Community A spatial or political unit of social organization that gives people a sense of belonging, based either on shared residence in a particular place or on a common identity. (page 357)

Concentric-zone theory A theory of urban growth that sees growth in terms of a series of rings radiating from the central business district. (362)

Defended neighbourhood A neighbourhood that residents identify through defined community borders and a perception that adjacent areas are geographically separate and socially different. (366)

Environmental justice (EJ) A legal strategy based on claims that members of visible minority groups are disproportionately subjected to environmental hazards. (374)

Human ecology An area of study concerned with the interrelationships between people and their spatial setting and physical environment. (360)

Industrial city A city characterized by relatively large size, open competition, an open class system, and elaborate specialization in the manufacturing of goods. (359)

Megalopolis A densely populated area containing two or more cities and their surrounding suburbs. (360)

Multiple-nuclei theory A theory of urban growth that views growth as emerging from many centres of development, each of which may reflect a particular urban need or activity. (363)

New urban sociology An approach to urbanization that considers the interplay of local, national, and worldwide forces and their effect on local space, with special emphasis on the impact of global economic activity. (364)

Postindustrial city A city in which global finance and the electronic flow of information dominate the economy. (359)

Preindustrial city A city with only a few thousand people living within its borders and characterized by a relatively closed class system and limited mobility. (358)

Squatter settlements Areas occupied by the very poor on the fringes of cities, in which housing is often constructed by the settlers themselves from discarded material. (360)

Suburb Any territory within a metropolitan area that is not included in the central city. (367)

Urban ecology An area of study that focuses on the interrelationships between people and their environment in urban areas. (360)

Urbanism Distinctive patterns of social behaviour evident among city residents. (365)

Additional Readings

Burdon, Roy. 2003. *The Suffering Gene: Environmental Threats to Our Health.* Montreal: McGill-Queen's University Press. An examination of the effects of a toxic environment on human genes.

Fitzpatrick, Kevin, and Mark LaGory. 2000. *Unhealthy Places: The Ecology of Risk in the Urban Landscape.* New York: Routledge. Two sociologists take a spatial view of urban ecology and raise the concept of the "urban health penalty"—the effect of place on an individual's access to health resources.

Hessing, Melody, Rebecca Ragion, and Catriona Sandilands. 2004. *This Elusive Land: Women and the Canadian Environment.* Vancouver: UBC Press. An interdisciplinary anthology that introduces readers to women's experiences and perceptions of the natural environment.

Online Learning Centre

Visit the *Sociology: A Brief Introduction* Online Learning Centre at www.mcgrawhill.ca/college/schaefer to access quizzes, interactive exercises, video clips, and other research and study tools related to this chapter.

Reel Society Interactive Movie CD-ROM 2.0

Reel Society 2.0 can be used to spark discussion about the following topics from this chapter:

- The environment

chapter 16

SOCIAL MOVEMENTS, SOCIAL CHANGE, AND TECHNOLOGY

"Yahoo!—A nice place to stay on the Internet." A traveller just 20 years ago would not have known what to make of this ad for Yahoo!, an Internet service provider. This is one manifestation of the fast pace of social change and technology in the last two decades. New technology today has a major impact on our daily lives and the ways we interact.

Chuck D is an unlikely hero of the digital age. With hit albums such as *Yo! Bum Rush the Show* and *Fear of a Black Planet,* the founder of the rap group Public Enemy would seem to inhabit a world far removed from the more conspicuous pioneers of cyberspace, from the Netscapes and Yahoos! and AOLs. In 1998, however, Chuck D stormed into cyberspace. Rather than giving his latest songs to Def Jam, the label that had produced his music for over a decade, the rap artist instead released his music directly onto the Internet, at www.public-enemy.com. It shouldn't have been such a big deal, really: one artist, a handful of songs, and a funky distribution method that probably reached several thousand fans. But in the music business this was very big news. For Chuck D had taken one of the industry's most sacred practices and thrown it, quite literally, into space. With just a couple of songs, he challenged how music was sold and, even more fundamentally, how it was owned. "This is the beginning," proclaimed the rapper, "of the end of domination."

As far as Chuck D was concerned, putting music online was a matter of power, of using new technologies to right old wrongs and give recording artists the influence and money that was rightfully theirs. To the recording industry, however, it was heresy. . . .

Had Chuck D been an isolated case, the studios most likely could have looked the other way. They could have dismissed Chuck D as a simple renegade, a rapper gone bad, and forgotten him and his web site. But the problem was that Chuck D, potentially, was everywhere. In cyberspace, any recording artist could distribute his or her music online; any musician could become a mini-studio, circumventing the record labels and their complex, clunky rules. . . .

Matters reached a head in 1999, when a nineteen-year-old college dropout named Shawn Fanning joined Chuck D in storming the frontier. Backed by his uncle in Boston, Fanning created Napster, a revolutionary system that allowed thousands—even millions—of users to trade their music online. Within months of its release, Napster had become a social phenomenon and a massive commercial threat. Universities complained that Napster was suddenly consuming huge chunks of their Internet bandwidth, and the music industry condemned it as piracy of the most blatant sort: "STEALING," as one music lawyer described it, "in big letters." Ironic foes such as Prince and the rock band Metallica joined the labels in pursuit of these new pirates, while prophets predicted the death of the recorded music industry. "A revolution has occurred in the way music is distributed," wrote one observer, "and the big record companies are in a state of panic." *(Spar 2001:327–329)* ■

In this selection from *Ruling the Waves: Cycles of Discovery, Chaos, and Wealth from the Compass to the Internet,* political scientist Debora L. Spar describes the economic repercussions of a recent change in the way popular music is distributed. To students, the advent of Napster meant that suddenly, free music was available to them over the Internet. But to recording artists and record companies, Napster was a revolutionary new technology with the potential to shift the balance of power from the corporate giants that produced popular music to the artists who created and performed it. The distribution of digitized music via the Internet, then, changed both the way people behaved—how they selected, obtained, and listened to music—and the cultural institution that is the music business.

The invention of the personal computer and its integration into people's day-to-day lives is another example of the social change that often follows the introduction of a new technology. ***Social change*** has been defined as significant alteration over time in behaviour patterns and culture (W. Moore 1967). But what constitutes a "significant" alteration? Certainly the dramatic rise in formal education documented in Chapter 12 represents a change that has had profound social consequences. Other social changes that have had long-term and important consequences include the emergence of slavery as a system of stratification (see Chapter 8), the industrial revolution (Chapters 5 and 13), the increased participation of women in the paid labour forces of Canada and Europe (Chapter 10), and the worldwide population explosion (Chapter 14). As we will see, social movements have played an important role in promoting social change.

How do social movements emerge? How does social change happen? Why do some people resist social change? What changes are likely to follow the technologies of the future? And what have been the negative effects of the sweeping technological changes of the last century?

This chapter examines social movements and the process of social change, with special emphasis on the impact of technological advances. Efforts to explain long-term social changes have led to the development of theories of change; we will consider the evolutionary, functionalist, feminist, interactionist, and conflict approaches to change. We will see how vested interests attempt to block changes that they see as threatening. We'll also look at various aspects of our technological future, such as telecommuting, the Internet, biotechnology, and technological accidents. We will examine the effects of technological advances on culture and social interaction, social control, and social stratification and inequality. Taken together, the impact of these technological changes may be approaching a level of magnitude comparable to that of the industrial revolution. Finally, in the social policy section we will discuss the ways in which technological advances have intensified concerns over privacy and censorship. ■

Use Your Sociological Imagination **www.mcgrawhill.ca/college/schaefer**

Do you see the "Napsterization" of music as reinforcing a generation gap between a younger generation that thinks music should be common property and an older generation that views it as private property?

SOCIAL MOVEMENTS

Although such factors as the physical environment, population, technology, and social inequality serve as sources of change, it is the *collective* effort of individuals organized in social movements that ultimately leads to change. Sociologists use the term ***social movements*** to refer to collective activities organized to bring about or resist fundamental change in an existing group or society (Benford 1992). Herbert Blumer (1955:19) recognized the special importance of social movements when he defined them as "collective enterprises to establish a new order of life."

In many nations, including Canada, social movements have had a dramatic impact on the course of history and the evolution of social structure. Consider the actions of environmentalists, animal rights activists, women's groups, and fair trade activists. Members of each social movement stepped outside traditional channels for bringing about social change and yet had a noticeable influence on public policy. Equally dramatic collective efforts in Eastern Europe helped to topple communist regimes in a largely peaceful manner, in nations that many observers had felt were "immune" to such social change (Ramet 1991).

Social movements imply the existence of conflict, but we can also analyze their activities from a functionalist, a feminist, and an interactionist perspective. Even when unsuccessful, social movements contribute to the formation of public opinion. Initially, the ideas of Margaret Sanger and other early advocates of birth control were viewed as "radical," yet contraceptives are now widely available in North America. Moreover, functionalists view social movements as training grounds for leaders of the political establishment. Such heads of state as Cuba's Fidel Castro and South Africa's Nelson Mandela came to power after serving as leaders of revolutionary movements. Poland's Lech Walesa, Russia's Boris Yeltsin, and Czech playwright Vaclav Havel all led protest movements against communist rule and subsequently became leaders of their countries' governments.

How and why do social movements emerge? Obviously, people are often discontented with the way things are. But what causes them to organize at a particular moment in a collective effort to work for change? Sociologists rely on two explanations for why people mobilize: the relative-deprivation and resource-mobilization approaches.

Two views on abortion among social movements in France: In the top photo, members of the pro-choice movement take to the streets. One sign states, "A child if I want it, when I want it." In the bottom photo, a member of the pro-life movement wears a T-shirt that states, "To abort is to kill."

Relative Deprivation

Those members of a society who feel most frustrated and disgruntled by the social and economic conditions of their lives are not necessarily "worst off" in an objective sense. Social scientists have long recognized that what is most significant is how people *perceive* their situation. Karl Marx pointed out that although the misery of the workers was important in reflecting their oppressed state, so was their position *relative* to the capitalist ruling class (Marx and Engels [1847] 1955).

The term ***relative deprivation*** is defined as the conscious feeling of a negative discrepancy between legitimate expectations and present actualities (J. Wilson 1973). In other words, things aren't as good as you hoped they would be. Such a state may be characterized by scarcity rather than complete lack of necessities (as we saw in the distinction between absolute and relative poverty in

p. 175

Chapter 8). A relatively deprived person is dissatisfied because he or she feels downtrodden relative to some appropriate reference group. Thus, blue-collar workers who live in two-family houses on small plots—though hardly at the bottom of the economic ladder—may nevertheless feel deprived in comparison with corporate managers and professionals who live in lavish and exclusive suburbs.

In addition to the feeling of relative deprivation, two other elements must be present before discontent will be channelled into a social movement. People must feel that they have a *right* to their goals, that they deserve better than what they have. For example, the struggle against European colonialism in Africa intensified when growing numbers of Africans decided that it was legitimate for them to have political and economic independence. At the same time, the disadvantaged group must perceive that it cannot attain its goals through conventional means. This belief may or may not be correct. Whichever is the case, the group will not mobilize into a social movement unless there is a shared perception that it can end its relative deprivation only through collective action (Morrison 1971).

p. 181

Critics of this approach have noted that people don't have to feel deprived to be moved to act. In addition, this approach fails to explain why certain feelings of deprivation are transformed into social movements, whereas in other similar situations, there is no collective effort to reshape society. Consequently, in recent years, sociologists have given increasing attention to the forces needed to bring about the emergence of social movements (Alain 1985; Finkel and Rule 1987; Orum 1989).

Resource Mobilization

It takes more than desire to start a social movement. It helps to have money, political influence, access to the media, and workers. The term ***resource mobilization*** refers to the ways in which a social movement utilizes such resources. The success of a movement for change will depend in good part on what resources it has and how effectively it mobilizes them (see also Gamson 1989; Staggenborg 1989a, 1989b).

Sociologist Anthony Oberschall (1973:199) has argued that to sustain social protest or resistance, there must be an "organizational base and continuity of leadership." As people become part of a social movement, norms develop to guide their behaviour. Members of the movement may be expected to attend regular meetings of organizations, pay dues, recruit new adherents, and boycott "enemy" products or speakers. An emerging social movement may give rise to special language or new words for familiar terms. In recent years, social movements have been responsible for such new terms of self-reference as *blacks* and *African Americans* (used to replace *Negroes*), *senior citizens* (used to replace *old folks*), *gays* (used to replace *homosexuals*), and *people with disabilities* (used to replace *the handicapped*).

Leadership is a central factor in the mobilization of the discontented into social movements. Often, a movement will be led by a charismatic figure, such as Dr. Martin Luther King, Jr. As Max Weber described it in 1904, *charisma* is that quality of an individual that sets him or her apart from ordinary people. Of course, charisma can fade abruptly; this helps account for the fragility of certain social movements (A. Morris 2000).

p. 305

Yet many social movements do persist over long periods because their leadership is well organized and ongoing. Ironically, as Robert Michels (1915) noted, political movements fighting for social change eventually take on some of the aspects of bureaucracy they were organized to protest. Leaders tend to dominate the decision-making process without directly consulting followers. The bureaucratization of social movements is not inevitable, however. More radical movements that advocate major structural change in society and embrace mass actions tend not to be hierarchical or bureaucratic (Fitzgerald and Rodgers 2000).

pp. 125–126

Why do certain individuals join a social movement whereas others who are in similar situations do not? Some of them are recruited to join. Karl Marx recognized the importance of recruitment when he called on workers to become *aware* of their oppressed status and develop a class consciousness. In agreement with the contemporary resource-mobilization approach, Marx held that a social movement (specifically, the revolt of the proletariat) would require leaders to sharpen the awareness of the oppressed. They must help workers to overcome feelings of false consciousness, or attitudes that do not reflect workers' objective position, in order to organize a revolutionary movement. Similarly, one of the challenges faced by women's liberation activists of the late 1960s and early 1970s was to convince women that they were being deprived of their rights and of socially valued resources.

pp. 168–169

Today's technology facilitates a new way to mobilize resources. The Internet brings us together in an electronic global village to act and to react. Box 16-1 shows how virtual social movements can develop on the Web.

New Social Movements

Beginning in the late 1960s, European social scientists observed a change in both the composition and the targets of emerging social movements. Previously, traditional social movements had focused on economic issues,

Research in Action 16-1 Virtual Social Movements

We are accustomed to thinking of social movements in terms of protest marches and door-to-door petition drives. But the World Wide Web allows for alternative ways to organize people and either bring about fundamental change or resist it. The Internet itself has often been referred to as a "virtual community," and as in any community, there are people who seek to persuade others to their point of view. Furthermore, the Internet serves to "bring people together"—say, by transforming the cause of the Mexican Zapatistas into an international lobbying effort, by linking environmentalists on every continent through Greenpeace International, or by emailing information and news from abroad to dissidents in China.

Sociologists have begun to call such electronic enhancements of social movements *computer-mediated communication (CMC)*. Electronic communication strengthens a group's solidarity, allowing the fledgling social movement to grow and develop faster than it might otherwise. Thus, face-to-face contact, which was once critical to a social movement, is no longer necessary.

People can engage in their own virtual community with little impact on their everyday lives. On the Internet, for example, anyone can mount a petition drive to free a death row inmate without taking days and weekends away from a job and the family. Dissidents can communicate with one another using computers in Internet cafés, with little concern about being traced or monitored by the government.

Two studies by Matthew Zook and research by sociologist Roberta Garner examined Web sites that express ideological points of view that are contentious or hostile to existing institutions. Garner looked at 542 Web sites that could be regarded as "ideological postings"; some reflect the interests of a particular group or organization and some are only the opinions of isolated individuals. Among the sites were postings that reflected extreme patriotic views, white racism, attachment to cults, regional separatism and new forms of nationalism, and expression of militant environmentalism.

Although the Garner sample was not random and therefore may not be representative of all ideological postings, the hundreds of sites did show some consistencies, many of them also noted by Zook:

- Like conventional social movements, these sites serve as an alternative source of information, bypassing mainstream sources of opinion found in newspaper editorials.
- These nonmainstream movements enjoy legitimacy because no gatekeeper keeps them off the Web. By virtue of being on a Web site, even an unsophisticated one, the information has the appearance of being legitimate.
- The sites rely heavily on written documents, in the form of either manifestos or established documents such as the Constitution or the Bible. Written testimonials (such as "How I Became a Conservative") also proliferate on these Web sites.

often led by people who shared the same occupation or by labour unions. However, many social movements that have become active in recent decades—including the contemporary women's movement, the peace movement, and the environmental movement—did not have the social class roots typical of the labour protests over the preceding one hundred years (Tilly 1993).

The term ***new social movements*** refers to organized collective activities that promote autonomy and self-determination as well as improvements in the quality of life. These movements may be involved in developing collective identities, have complex agendas that go beyond a single issue, and cross national boundaries. Educated, middle-class people are significantly represented in some of these new social movements, such as the women's movement and the movement for lesbian and gay rights. However, marginalized people also take part in new social movements. For example, in 1986, a group of single mothers started Low Income Families Together in response to the Government of Ontario's review of social assistance. Today, members are actively seeking social change through such activities as systemic advocacy and workshops on rights, policy development, and access to media, government, and nonprofit organizations.

New social movements typically do not view government as their ally in the struggle for a better society. Although they generally do not seek to overthrow the government, they may criticize, protest, or harass public officials. Researchers have found that members of new social movements show little inclination to accept established authority, even scientific or technical authority. This is especially evident in the environmental and anti–nuclear power movements, where movement activists

- The presentations are still fairly unsophisticated. Although there are glossy animated Web sites, most sites look like a printed page.
- Unlike conventional social movements, these virtual sites are generally not geared for action. Despite expressions of concern or foreboding (such as the site "Are You Ready for Catastrophic Natural Disasters?"), there are few calls to do anything. Sites, such as "Glory to the Cuban Revolution," seek to inform visitors, serve as a resource, and, perhaps, bring people around to their point of view.

Zook as well as Garner and her student researchers found that these sites often seem to define themselves by their choice of links on the Web. In other words, with whom do they want to be associated? This is particularly true of well-established social movements that have expanded to use the Internet. For example, both the leading abortion rights groups and antiabortion organizations feature links to other groups, but only to those that are like-minded.

The entire process of "links" is very important in the Internet network. How someone defines his or her ideology determines how a site may be located and who makes links. For example, the Web site of a female national socialist from Sweden boldly encourages visitors to establish a link from their Web sites to hers as long as they are a part of the "white aryan movement on the Net." Using the term "militia" as opposed to "patriotic" would bring different people to a site. The terms used are important since Web pages act as recruiting tools to attract new members to a movement and may, in fact, be the only realistic way that some groups will attract followers.

People in conventional social movements commonly try to infiltrate other groups holding opposing views to learn their strategy or even disrupt their ability to function. There is a parallel to that emerging on the Internet. The term *hactivists* (a merging of "hackers" with "activists") refers to people who invade computer systems electronically, placing embarrassing information on their enemies' Web pages or, at the very least, defacing them. During the height of the 1999 NATO attacks on Yugoslavia, movements opposed to the military action bombarded the official NATO Web site with requests meant to overload it and paralyze its operation.

Research into virtual social movements is still exploratory. Social movement researchers, such as Garner and Zook, are interested in establishing the relationship between ideological Web sites and "real" organizations. Do these sites merely reflect a single posting? Or are they the visible manifestation of a broader consensus? And sociologists will be interested in examining a more representative sample of such sites to determine how often they explicitly call for social change.

Applying Theory

1. What are some of the advantages of having a virtual social movement on the Internet? What might be some disadvantages?
2. If you were to create a Web page designed to attract followers to a feminist movement, what would it be like?

Sources: Calhoun 1998; Castells 1996; Diani 2000; Garner 1999; Rosenthal 2000; Van Slambrouck 1999; Zook 1996.

present their own experts to counter those of government or big business (Garner 1996; Scott 1990).

The environmental social movement is one of many new movements with a worldwide focus. For example, Greenpeace, which began in Vancouver in the mid-1970s, today has offices in approximately 40 countries. In their efforts to reduce air and water pollution, curtail global warming, and protect endangered animal species, environmental activists have realized that strong regulatory measures within a single country are not sufficient. Similarly, labour union leaders and human rights advocates cannot adequately address exploitative sweatshop conditions in a developing country if a multinational corporation can simply move the factory to another country where it pays workers even less.

Founded in 1985, the Council of Canadians today has 100 000 members across the country. The Council was formed as a citizens' group to watch over environmental concerns, to safeguard social programs, to promote economic justice, to advance alternatives to corporate-style free trade, and to assert Canadian sovereignty. Using a poll conducted by Ipsos-Reid in 2004 as its basis for action today, the Council of Canadians pledged to pressure the government to ensure that its policies reflect the concerns of Canadians: public health, Canadian sovereignty, clean water, fair trade, and safe food (Council of Canadians 2004). In 2005, the group focused its activities on stopping the bid to introduce genetically engineered wheat into Canada through its Safe Food team, fighting to stop commercial water exports in Quebec, building an international coalition for a U.N. convention on water as a human right, and gearing up for trade talks in the Americas and globally.

Whereas traditional views of social movements tended to emphasize resource mobilization on a local level, new social movement theory offers a broader, global perspective on social and political activism.

Use Your Sociological Imagination

Try to imagine a society without any social movements. Under what conditions could such a society exist? Would you want to live in it?

THEORIES OF SOCIAL CHANGE

We defined *social change* as significant alteration over time in behaviour patterns and culture. Such explanations are clearly a challenge in the diverse and complex world we inhabit today. Nevertheless, theorists from several disciplines have sought to analyze social change. In some instances, they have examined historical events to arrive at a better understanding of contemporary changes. We will review five theoretical approaches to change—evolutionary, functionalist, conflict, feminist, and interactionist theory—and then take a look at global change today.

Evolutionary Theory

Charles Darwin's (1809–1882) pioneering work in biological evolution contributed to nineteenth-century theories of social change. According to his approach, there has been a continuing progression of successive life forms. For example, since human beings came at a later stage of evolution than reptiles, we represent a more complex form of life. Social theorists sought an analogy to this biological model and originated ***evolutionary theory,*** which views society as moving in a definite direction. Early evolutionary theorists generally agreed that society was inevitably progressing to a higher state. As might be expected, they concluded in ethnocentric fashion that their own behaviour and culture were more advanced than those of earlier civilizations.

p. 7

August Comte (1798–1857), a founder of sociology, was an evolutionary theorist of change. He saw human societies as moving forward in their thinking from mythology to the scientific method. Similarly, Émile Durkheim ([1893]1933) maintained that society progressed from simple to more complex forms of social organization.

The writings of Comte and Durkheim are examples of ***unilinear evolutionary theory.*** This approach contends that all societies pass through the same successive stages of evolution and inevitably reach the same end. English sociologist Herbert Spencer (1820–1903) used a similar approach: Spencer likened society to a living body with interrelated parts that were moving toward a common destiny. However, contemporary evolutionary theorists, such as Gerhard Lenski, are more likely to picture social change as multilinear than to rely on the more limited unilinear perspective. ***Multilinear evolutionary theory*** holds that change can occur in several ways and that it does not inevitably lead in the same direction (Haines 1988; Turner 1985).

Multilinear theorists recognize that human culture has evolved along a number of lines. For example, the theory of demographic transition graphically demonstrates that population change in developing nations has not necessarily followed the model evident in industrialized nations. Sociologists today hold that events do not necessarily follow in a single or several straight lines but instead are subject to disruptions—a topic we will consider later in the discussion of global social change.

Functionalist Theory

Functionalist sociologists focus on what *maintains* a system, not on what changes it. This might seem to suggest that functionalists can offer little of value to the study of social change. Yet, as the work of sociologist Talcott Parsons demonstrates, functionalists have made a distinctive contribution to this area of sociological investigation.

Parsons (1902–1979), a leading proponent of functionalist theory, viewed society as naturally being in a state of equilibrium. By "equilibrium," he meant that society tends toward a state of stability or balance. Parsons would view even prolonged labour strikes or civilian riots as temporary disruptions in the status quo rather than as significant alterations in social structure. Therefore, according to his equilibrium model, as changes occur in one part of society, there must be adjustments in other parts. If this does not take place, the society's equilibrium will be threatened and strains will occur.

p. 12

Reflecting an evolutionary approach, Parsons (1966) maintained that four processes of social change are inevitable. The first, *differentiation,* refers to the increasing complexity of social organization. A change from "medicine man" to physician, nurse, and pharmacist is an illustration of differentiation in the field of health. This process is accompanied by *adaptive upgrading,* whereby social institutions become more specialized in their purposes. The division of labour among physicians into obstetricians, internists, surgeons, and so forth, is an example of adaptive upgrading.

The third process identified by Parsons is the *inclusion* into society of groups that were previously excluded because of such factors as gender, race, and social class background. Medical schools have practised inclusion by admitting increasing numbers of women and blacks. Finally, Parsons contends that societies experience *value generalization,* the development of new values that tolerate and legitimate a greater range of activities. The acceptance of preventive and alternative medicine is an example of value generalization; our society has broadened its view of health care. All four processes identified by Parsons stress consensus—societal agreement on the nature of social organization and values (B. Johnson 1975; Wallace and Wolf 1980).

African Americans are now accepted in many exclusive golf clubs that were previously restricted, illustrating the process of *inclusion* described by Talcott Parsons. The phenomenal success of pro golfer Tiger Woods has helped the process along.

Parsons's approach explicitly incorporates the evolutionary notion of continuing progress. However, the dominant theme in his model is balance and stability. Society may change, but it remains stable through new forms of integration. For example, in place of the kinship ties that provided social cohesion in the past, there are laws, judicial processes, and new values and belief systems.

Functionalists assume that social institutions will not persist unless they continue to contribute to the overall society. This leads functionalists to conclude that drastically altering institutions will threaten societal equilibrium. Critics note that the functionalist approach virtually disregards the use of coercion by the powerful to maintain the illusion of a stable, well-integrated society (Gouldner 1960).

Conflict Theory

The functionalist perspective minimizes change. It emphasizes the persistence of social life and sees change as a means of maintaining the equilibrium (or balance) of a society. By contrast, conflict theorists contend that social institutions and practices persist because powerful groups have the ability to maintain the status quo. Change has crucial significance, since it is needed to correct social injustices and inequalities.

Karl Marx accepted the evolutionary argument that societies develop along a particular path. However, unlike Comte and Spencer, he did not view each successive stage as an inevitable improvement over the previous one. History, according to Marx, proceeds through a series of stages, each of which exploits a class of people. Ancient society exploited slaves; the estate system of feudalism exploited serfs; modern capitalist society exploits the working class. Ultimately, through a socialist revolution led by the proletariat, human society will move toward the final stage of development: a classless communist society, or "community of free individuals" as Marx described it in *Das Kapital* in 1867 (see Bottomore and Rubel 1956:250).

As we have seen, Karl Marx had an important influence on the development of sociology. His thinking offered insights into such institutions as the economy, the family, religion, and government. The Marxist view of social change is appealing because it does not restrict people to a passive role in responding to inevitable cycles or changes in material culture. Rather, Marxist theory offers a tool for those who want to seize control of the historical process and gain their freedom from injustice. In contrast to functionalists' emphasis on stability, Marx argues that conflict is a normal and desirable aspect of social change. In fact, change must be encouraged as a means of eliminating social inequality (Lauer 1982).

pp. 8–9

One conflict sociologist, Ralf Dahrendorf (1958), has noted that the contrast between the functionalist perspective's emphasis on stability and the conflict perspective's focus on change reflects the contradictory nature of society. Human societies are stable and long-lasting, yet they also experience serious conflict. Dahrendorf found that the functionalist approach and the conflict approach were ultimately compatible despite their many areas of disagreement. Indeed, Parsons spoke of new functions that result from social change, and Marx recognized the need for change so that societies could function more equitably.

Feminist Theories

Unlike other sociological perspectives, social change is the hallmark of feminist perspectives. Feminist sociologists, diverse as they are, share a desire to deepen their understanding of society in order to change the world; it is their desire to make it more just and humane (Lengermann and Niebrugge-Brantley 1998). Confronting social injustice in order to promote change for those groups in society who are disadvantaged by their "social location"—their class, race, ethnicity, sexual preference, age, or global location—is a key feature of feminist perspectives. As feminist sociologist Patricia Hill Collins (1998:xiv) explains, change is sought for "people differently placed in specific political, social, and historic contexts characterized by injustice."

Increasingly, feminist perspectives advance the view that acknowledging women's differences must be paramount in guiding the direction of social change. The interests of white, middle-class women, for example, must not be assumed to represent the interests of all women. Social change must be inclusive of the interests of women of diverse backgrounds. As feminist theorists Rosemary Hennessy and Chrys Ingraham ask, "What are the consequences of this way of thinking for transforming the inequities in women's lives?" and "How is this way of explaining the world going to improve life for all women?" (Lengermann and Niebrugge-Brantley 1998: 445)

Interactionist Theory

The symbolic interactionist perspective sees people as active agents or actors and the social world as being active, so constant adjustment and change occur through social interaction. People give meaning to events as they interpret their own "social reality." Movements for social change, therefore, are not the results of external or objective factors, but rather a social construction based on the meaning or interpretation the participants give to their actions. As Herbert Blumer (1969:180) notes, and as mentioned in Chapter 15, "human beings interpret or 'define' each other's actions instead of merely reacting to each other's actions. Their response is not made directly to the actions of one another but instead is based on the meaning which they attach to such actions. Thus, human interaction is mediated by the use of symbols, by interpretation, or by ascertaining the meaning of one another's actions." Recent theories, founded on the principles of symbolic interactionism, are based on the assumption that social movements involve participants, opponents, and bystanders engaged in a process that is interactive, symbolically defined, and negotiated (Buechler 2000). Using the work of Goffman, who suggested that our interpretation of events depends on the way we "frame" them, theories, such as that of Steven M. Buechler (2000:41), articulate the relationship between this framing and social movement theory:

> In the context of social movements, framing refers to the interactive, collective ways that movement actors assign meaning to their activities in the conduct of social movement activism. The concept of framing is designed for discussing the social construction of grievances as a fluid and variable process of social interaction.

Social movements may modify or re-create their frames to advance their goals. An example would be an environmental group whose frame was global deforestation but who reframes it to air quality and the health effects on children (e.g., increasing rates of childhood asthma).

Global Social Change

Sociologists point out that gender is an important element in understanding social movement development. In our male-dominated society, women find it more difficult to assume leadership positions in social movement organizations. And although women often disproportionately serve as volunteers in these movements, their work is not always recognized and their voices are not as easily heard as men's. Moreover, gender bias causes the real extent of women's influence to be overlooked. Traditional examination of the sociopolitical system tends to focus on such male-dominated corridors of power as legislatures and corporate boardrooms to the neglect of more female-dominated domains, such as households and community-based groups. But efforts to influence what goes on in households, schools, and communities are clearly significant to a culture and society (Ferree and Merrill 2000; Noonan 1995).

Scholars of social movements now realize that gender can affect even the way we view organized efforts to bring about or resist change. For example, an emphasis on using masculinist values, such as objectivity, to achieve goals helps to obscure the importance of passion and subjectivity in successful social movements. It would be difficult to find any movement—from labour battles to voting rights to animal rights—in which passion was not part of the consensus-building force. Yet calls for a more serious study of the role of subjectivity are frequently seen as applying only to the women's movement, because subjectivity is traditionally thought of as feminine (Ferree and Merrill 2000; Taylor 1995).

We are at a truly dramatic time in history to consider global social change. Terrorism in various parts of the world, the war in Iraq, revolution and famine in Africa, the spread of AIDS, and the computer revolution are reminders that change is a constant.

In this era of massive social, political, and economic change on a global scale, is it possible to predict change? Some technological changes seem obvious, but the collapse of communist governments in the former Soviet Union and Eastern Europe in the early 1990s took people by surprise. However, before the Soviet collapse, sociologist Randall Collins (1986, 1995), a conflict theorist, had observed a crucial sequence of events that most observers had missed.

In seminars as far back as 1980, and in a book published in 1986, Collins had argued that Soviet expansionism had resulted in an overextension of resources, including disproportionate spending on military forces. Such an overextension strains a regime's stability. Moreover, geopolitical theory suggests that nations in the middle of a geographic region, such as the Soviet Union, tend to fragment into smaller units over time. Collins predicted that the coincidence of social crises on several frontiers would precipitate the collapse of the Soviet Union.

And that is just what happened. In 1979, the success of the Iranian revolution had led to an upsurge of Islamic fundamentalism in nearby Afghanistan, as well as in the Soviet republics with substantial Muslim populations. At the same time, resistance to communist rule was growing both throughout Eastern Europe and within the Soviet Union itself. Collins had predicted that the rise of a dissident form of communism within the Soviet Union might facilitate the breakdown of the regime. Beginning in the late 1980s, Soviet leader Mikhail Gorbachev chose not to use military power and other types of repression to crush dissidents in Eastern Europe, offered plans for democratization and social reform of Soviet society, and seemed willing to reshape the Soviet Union into a loose federation of somewhat autonomous states. But, in 1991, six republics on the western periphery declared their independence, and within months the entire Soviet Union had formally disintegrated into Russia and a number of other independent nations now called the Commonwealth of Independent States.

The president of the American Sociological Association, Maureen Hallinan (1997), cautioned that we need to move beyond the restrictive models of social change—the linear view of evolutionary theory and the assumptions about equilibrium within functionalist theory. She and other sociologists have looked to "chaos theory," advanced by mathematicians to consider erratic events as a part of change. Hallinan noted that upheavals and major chaotic shifts do occur and that sociologists must learn to predict their occurrence, as Collins did with the Soviet Union. Imagine the dramatic nonlinear social change that will result from major innovations in the areas of communications and biotechnology, a topic we will discuss later in the chapter.

RESISTANCE TO SOCIAL CHANGE

Efforts to promote social change are likely to meet with resistance. In the midst of rapid scientific and technological innovations, many people are frightened by the demands of an ever-changing society. Moreover, certain individuals and groups have a stake in maintaining the existing state of affairs.

Social economist Thorstein Veblen (1857–1929) coined the term ***vested interests*** to refer to those people or groups that will suffer in the event of social change. For example, the Canadian Medical Association (CMA) has taken strong stands against the professionalization of midwifery. pp. 339–340 A rise in the status of midwives could threaten the preeminent position of doctors as the nation's deliverers of babies. In general, those with a disproportionate share of society's wealth, status, and power, such as members of the Canadian Medical Association, have a vested interest in preserving the status quo (Starr 1982; Veblen 1919).

Economic and Cultural Factors

Economic factors play an important role in resistance to social change. For example, it can be expensive for manufacturers to meet high standards for the safety of products and workers and for protection of the environment. Conflict theorists argue that, in a capitalist economic system, many firms are not willing to pay the price of meeting strict safety and environmental standards. They may resist social change by cutting corners within their plants or by pressuring the government to ease regulations.

Communities, too, protect their vested interests, often in the name of "protecting property values." The abbreviation "NIMBY" stands for "not in my backyard," a cry often heard when people protest landfills, prisons, nuclear power facilities, and even bike trails and group homes for people with developmental disabilities. The targeted community may not challenge the need for the facility but may simply insist that it be located elsewhere. The "not in my backyard" attitude has become so common that it is almost impossible for policymakers to find acceptable locations for such facilities as dump sites for hazardous wastes (Jasper 1997).

Like economic factors, cultural factors frequently shape resistance to change. William F. Ogburn (1922) distinguished between material and nonmaterial p. 52 aspects of culture. *Material culture* includes inventions, artifacts, and technology;

nonmaterial culture encompasses ideas, norms, communications, and social organization. Ogburn pointed out that no one can devise methods for controlling and utilizing new technology before the introduction of a technique. Thus, nonmaterial culture typically must respond to changes in material culture. Ogburn introduced the term culture lag to refer to the period of maladjustment during which the nonmaterial culture is still adapting to new material conditions. One example is the Internet. Its rapid uncontrolled growth raises questions about whether to regulate it and, if so, how much (see the social policy section in this chapter).

In certain cases, changes in material culture can add strain to the relationships between social institutions. For example, new means of birth control have been developed in recent decades. Large families are neither economically necessary nor commonly endorsed by social norms. But the leaders of certain religious faiths, among them Roman Catholicism, continue to extol large families and to disapprove of methods of limiting family size, such as contraception and abortion. This represents a lag between aspects of material culture (technology) and nonmaterial culture (religious beliefs). Conflicts may emerge between religion and other social institutions, such as government and the educational system, over the dissemination of birth control and family-planning information (Riley, Kahn, and Foner 1994a, 1994b).

Aboriginal drummers participate in a protest over the dumping of garbage from Toronto into the Adams Mine pit in Northern Ontario in 2000.

Resistance to Technology

Technological innovations are examples of changes in material culture that have often provoked resistance. The *industrial revolution,* which took place largely in England from 1760 to 1830, was a scientific revolution focused on the application of nonanimal sources of power to labour tasks. As this revolution proceeded, societies relied on new inventions that facilitated agricultural and industrial production and on new sources of energy, such as steam. In some industries, the introduction of power-driven machinery reduced the need for factory workers and made it easier to cut wages.

p. 358

Strong resistance to the industrial revolution emerged in some countries. In England, beginning in 1811, masked craft workers took extreme measures: They conducted nighttime raids on factories and destroyed some of the new machinery. The government hunted these rebels, known as ***Luddites,*** and ultimately banished some while hanging others. In a similar effort in France, some angry workers threw their wooden shoes *(sabots)* into factory machinery to destroy it, thereby giving rise to the term *sabotage.* Although the resistance of the Luddites and the French workers was short-lived and unsuccessful, they have come to symbolize resistance to technology over the previous two centuries.

Are we now in the midst of a second industrial revolution, with a contemporary group of Luddites engaged in resistance? Many sociologists believe that we are now living in a *postindustrial society.* It is difficult to pinpoint exactly when this era began. Generally, it is viewed as having begun in the 1950s, when for the first time the majority of workers in industrial societies became involved in services rather than in the actual manufacturing of goods (D. Bell 1999; Fiala 1992).

p. 359

Just as the Luddites resisted the industrial revolution, people in many countries have resisted postindustrial technological changes. The term *neo-Luddites* refers to those who are wary of technological innovations and who question the incessant expansion of industrialization, the increasing destruction of the natural and agrarian world, and the "throw it away" mentality of contemporary capitalism with its resulting pollution of the environment. Neo-Luddites insist that whatever the presumed benefits of industrial and postindustrial technology, such technology has distinctive social costs and may represent a danger to the future of the human species and our planet (Bauerlein 1996; Rifkin 1995; Sale 1996; Snyder 1996).

Such concerns are worth remembering as we turn now to examine aspects of our technological future and their possible impact on social change.

TECHNOLOGY AND THE FUTURE

Technology is information about how to use the material p. 51 resources of the environment to satisfy human needs and desires. Technological advances—the airplane, the automobile, the television, the atomic bomb, and, more recently, the computer, the fax machine, and the cellular phone—have brought striking changes in our cultures, our patterns of socialization, our social institutions, and our day-to-day social interactions. Technological innovations are, in fact, emerging and being accepted with remarkable speed. For example, scientists at Monsanto estimated in 1998 that the amount of genetic information used in practical applications will double every year. Part of the reason for this explosion in using new technology is that it is becoming cheaper. In 1974, it cost $2.5 million to determine the chemical structure of a single gene; less than 25 years later that cost was $150 (Belsie 1998).

The technological knowledge with which we work today represents only a tiny portion of the knowledge that will be available in the year 2050; we are witnessing an information explosion as well. Individuals, institutions, and societies will face unprecedented challenges in adjusting to the technological advances still to come (Cetron and Davies 1991; Wurman 1989).

In the following sections, we will examine various aspects of our technological future and consider their overall impact on social change, including the strains they will bring. We will focus in particular on recent developments in computer technology and biotechnology.

Computer Technology

The last decade has witnessed an explosion of computer technology in Canada and around the world. Its effects are particularly noteworthy in the areas of telecommuting and the Internet.

Telecommuting

As the industrial revolution proceeded, the factory and the office replaced the home as the typical workplace. But the postindustrial revolution has brought people home again. In 2001, the Canadian Telework Association estimated the number of Canadian telecommuters to be 1.5 million. Telecommuters are employees who work full-time or part-time at home rather than in an outside office. They are linked to their supervisors and colleagues through computer terminals, phones, and fax machines.

In our postindustrial society, computers are in use almost everywhere imaginable.

As part of a shift toward postindustrial societies linked within a global economy, telecommuting can even cross national boundaries, oceans, and continents (Hall 1999).

Telecommuting has many advantages. It facilitates communication among a company's employees who work in different locations, including those who work at home. Telecommuting also reduces time and money spent on transportation and can be helpful in a family's child care arrangements. At the same time, working at home can be isolating and stressful—and even more stressful if a parent must attempt to combine working at home and caring for children. Moreover, companies still need to encourage face-to-face communication in staff meetings and social settings (Marklein 1996).

The rise of telecommuting is especially beneficial for p. 98 one marginalized group in Canada: people with disabilities. Computer terminals lend themselves to ancillary devices that make them adaptable to most types of physical impairments. For example, people who are blind can work at home using word processors that read messages in a computer voice or that translate the messages into Braille text (J. Nelson 1995).

The Internet

The Internet is the world's largest computer network. By 2003, it was estimated to have reached some 763 million computer users—20 times the number in 1998 (Global Reach 2002).

Sociology in the Global Community

16-2 Global Disconnect

Students in colleges and universities in North America expect to be able to use the Internet or leave messages through voice mail. They complain when the computer is "slow" or the electronic mailbox is "full." Despite their complaints, they take these services for granted and generally do not even pay directly for them. But in much of the world, it is very different.

The United Nations has tried for years to assist the nation of Madagascar to upgrade its telephone system to be able to handle a 300-baud communication device—the slowest speed available. At this glacial rate, it would take about two minutes to transmit this page without the colour and without the graphics. By comparison, in Canada, most people are *discarding* systems 50 times faster and turning to devices that transmit information 180 times faster. The irony is that it costs more per minute to use a telephone in Madagascar and much of Africa than in Canada, so we have a continent paying more per minute to transmit information much more slowly.

This is but one example of the haves and have-nots in the information age. The Internet is virtually monopolized by North America and Europe and a few other industrial nations. As of 1999, 95.1% of Internet computers were controlled by high-income countries (Fleras 2003). They have the most *Internet hosts,* computers directly connected to the worldwide network of interconnected computer systems. In contrast, in 2001, three countries had no Internet service provider at all: Guyana in South America, Guinea-Bissau in Africa, and North Korea.

This inequality is not new. We also find dramatic differences in the presence of newspapers, telephones, televisions, and even radios throughout the world. For example, in Madagascar, there are 3 telephone lines per 1000 people, and for all low-income nations the average is 16. In Canada, there are more than 600 lines per 1000 people; for all high-income nations the average is 552. Often in developing nations, and especially their rural areas, radio and television transmission is sporadic, and the programming may be dominated by recycled information from the United States.

The consequences of the global disconnect for developing nations are far more serious than not being able to "surf the Net." Today we have the true emergence of what sociologist Manuel Castells refers to as a "global economy" because the world has the capacity to work as a single unit in real time. However, if large numbers of people and, indeed, entire nations are disconnected from the information economy, their slow economic growth will continue, with all the negative consequences it has for people. The educated and skilled will immigrate to labour markets that are a part of this global economy, deepening the impoverishment of the nations on the periphery.

Applying Theory

1. What factors might contribute to the global disconnect in developing nations?
2. What are some of the social and economic consequences for nations that are not "connected"? What groups are particularly vulnerable to not being connected?

Sources: Castells 1996, 2000; Fleras 2003; Matrix.Net 2000; World Bank 2000a; Wresch 1996.

The Internet actually evolved from a computer system built in 1962 by the U.S. Defense Department to enable scholars and military researchers to continue to do government work even if part of the nation's communications system was destroyed by a nuclear attack. Until recently, it was difficult to gain access to the Internet without holding a position at a university or a government research laboratory. Today, however, virtually anyone can reach the Internet with a phone line, a computer, and a modem. And it is possible to buy and sell cars, trade stocks, auction items, research new medical remedies, vote, and track down long-lost friends—to mention just a few of the thousands of online possibilities (Reddick and King 2000).

As we saw in Chapter 8, not everyone is able to get on the information highway, especially the less affluent.

p. 181

Moreover, this pattern of inequality is global. The core nations that Immanuel Wallerstein describes in his *world systems analysis* have a virtual monopoly on information technology while the developing nations of Asia, Africa, and Latin America are on the periphery, depending on the industrial giants for both the technology and the information it provides. Box 16-2 explores this "global disconnect."

Biotechnology

Sex selection of fetuses, genetically engineered organisms, cloning of sheep and cows—these have been among the significant and yet controversial scientific advances in

pp. 51–52

the field of biotechnology in recent years. George Ritzer's concept of McDonaldization applies to the entire area of biotechnology. Just as the fast-food concept has permeated society, it seems there is now no phase of life exempt from therapeutic or medical intervention. Biotechnology holds itself out as totally beneficial to human beings, but ultimately it reveals itself as in constant need of monitoring and adjustment. As we will see in the following sections, biotechnological advances have raised many difficult ethical and political decisions (D. Weinstein and Weinstein 1999).

Sex Selection

Advances in reproductive and screening technology have brought us closer to effective techniques for sex selection. In Canada, the prenatal test of amniocentesis has been used for more than 25 years to ascertain the presence of certain defects that require medical procedures prior to birth. Such tests can also identify the sex of the fetus, as can ultrasound scans. This outcome has had profound social implications.

In some societies, young couples planning to have only one child may want to ensure that this child is a boy because their culture may place a premium on a male heir. In some instances, advances in fetal testing may lead to abortion if the fetus is found to be female. Kuckreja Sohoni, a social scientist from India, notes that many parents in India are "mortally afraid" of having baby girls. Well aware of the pressure on Indian women to produce sons, Sohoni (1994:96), the mother of three teenage girls, admits, "had ultrasound been available when I was having children, I shudder to think how easily I would have been persuaded to plan a sex-selected family."

The preference for a male child is hardly limited to people from India. In one U.S. study, when asked what sex they would prefer for an only child, 86 percent of men and 59 percent of women wanted a boy. Moreover, fetal testing to determine the sex of a child is becoming more accepted in the United States (Hall 1993; Sohoni 1994). In Canada, a voluntary moratorium has been established on these types of reproductive and genetic practices.

From a functionalist perspective, we can view sex selection as an adaptation of the basic family function of regulating reproduction. However, some feminist theorists emphasize that sex selection may intensify the male dominance of our society and contribute to a further devaluation of the female.

Genetic Engineering

Even more grandiose than sex selection—and not necessarily improbable—is altering human behaviour through genetic engineering. Fish and plant genes have already been mixed to create frost-resistant potato and tomato crops; more recently, human genes have been implanted in pigs to provide humanlike kidneys for organ transplants.

One of the latest developments in genetic engineering is gene therapy. Geneticists in Japan have managed to disable genes in a mouse fetus that carry an undesirable trait and replace them with genes carrying a desirable trait. Such advances raise staggering possibilities for altering animal and human life forms. Still, gene therapy remains highly experimental and must be assessed as a long, long shot (Kolata 1999).

The debate on genetic engineering escalated in 1997 when scientists in Scotland announced that they had cloned a sheep. After many unsuccessful attempts, scientists finally were able to replace the genetic material of a sheep's egg with DNA from an adult sheep and thereby create a lamb that was a clone of the adult. The very next year, Japanese researchers successfully cloned cows. These developments raised the possibility that, in the near future, we may be able to clone human beings.

TECHNOLOGY AND SOCIETY

An ATM that identifies a person by facial structure, a small device that sorts through hundreds of odours to ensure the safety of a chemical plant, a cell phone that recognizes its owner's voice: these are real-life examples of technologies that were purely science fiction a few decades ago. Today's computer chip cannot just think but it can also see, smell, and hear too (Salkever 1999).

Technological advances can dramatically transform the material culture. Word processing programs, the pocket calculator, the photocopier, and the compact disc player have largely eliminated use of the typewriter, the adding machine, the mimeograph machine, and the turntable—all of which were themselves technological advances.

Technological change also can reshape *nonmaterial* culture. In the following sections, we will examine the effects of technological advances on culture and social interaction, social control, and stratification and inequality.

Culture and Social Interaction

In Chapter 3, we emphasized that language is the foundation of every culture. From a functionalist perspective, language can bring together members of a society and promote cultural integration. However, from a conflict perspective, the use of language can intensify divisions between groups and societies—just look at the battles over language in Canada, the United States, and other societies.

The Internet has often been lauded as a democratizing force that will make huge quantities of information available to great numbers of people around the world. However, although the Internet and its World Wide Web open up access to most societies, close to half of the material is transmitted in English (see Figure 16-1). According to Augie Fleras in *Mass Communication in Canada,* global Internet use is "unevenly distributed partly because of cultural bias toward American values and language" (2003:255). In 1999, only 0.2 percent of Internet-connected computers were controlled by low-income countries (Fleras 2003). Fleras states that there is a double-edged aspect to Internet use. Although, in rhetoric, its goal is egalitarian, in reality, it reinforces the divide between the "e-have-nots" and the "e-haves." In rhetoric, the scope of the Internet is globalizing with everyone online and no one in control; in reality, it leads to greater Americanization through the reproduction of capitalism and liberalism.

How will social interaction *within* a culture be transformed by the growing availability of electronic forms of communication? Will people turn to email, Web sites, and faxes rather than to telephone conversations and face-to-face meetings? Certainly, the technological shift to telephones reduced the use of letter writing as a means of maintaining kinship and friendship ties. For this reason, some people worry that computers and other forms of electronic communication may be socially isolating. Sociologist Sherry Turkle (1999) has warned that some individuals may become so gratified by their online lives that they lose touch with their families, friends, and work responsibilities.

Yet Turkle (1995, 1999) has found positive effects of Internet usage as well. Over a 10-year period, she made anonymous visits to chat rooms and multiuser domains (MUDs), which allow people to assume new identities in role-playing games. She also conducted face-to-face interviews with more than one thousand people who communicate by electronic mail and participate actively in MUDs. Distinguishing between users' on-screen personae and their real identities, Turkle concluded that many MUD users' lives were enhanced by the opportunity to engage in role-playing and "become someone else." A new sense of self had emerged, she wrote, that was "decentred and multiple." In making this observation, Turkle was expanding on George Herbert Mead's notion of self (Nass and Moon 2000).

p. 75

One obvious form of online role-playing is gender switching. In a 1999 study, researchers found that 40 percent of their subjects had presented themselves online as a member of the opposite sex. Yet gender switching does not appear to dominate online communication. Even among the gender-switched, the majority of subjects spent only about 10 percent of their time online disguised as the opposite sex (L. Roberts and Parks 1999).

If electronic communication can facilitate social interaction within a community—if it can create ties among people in different communities or even countries who "meet" in chat rooms or MUDs—then is there genuinely a new interactive world known as "cyberspace"? The term *cyberspace* was introduced in 1984 by William Gibson, a Canadian science fiction writer. He came up with this term after he walked by a video arcade and noticed the intensity of the players hunched over their screens. Gibson felt that these video game enthusiasts "develop a belief that there's some kind of actual space behind the screen. Some place that you can't

FIGURE 16-1

Estimated Language Use on the Internet, 2004

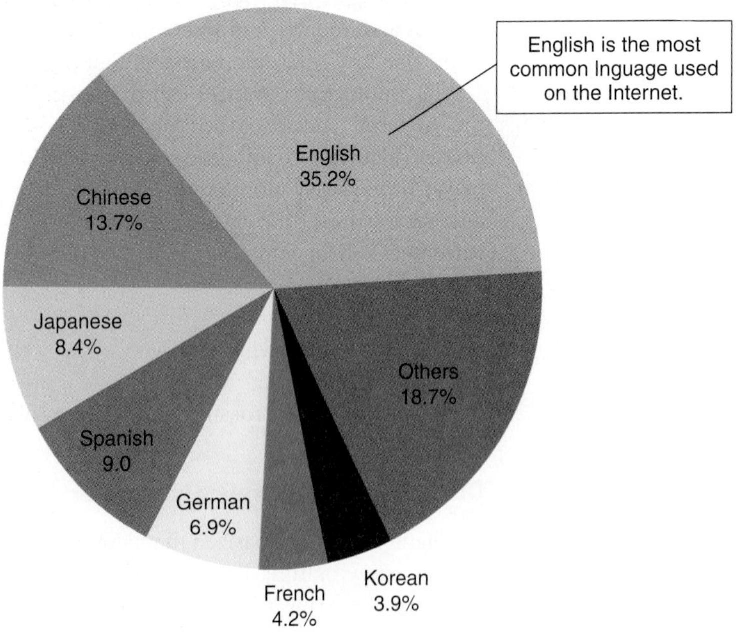

Source: Global Reach 2004.

Think about It
Why do you think Chinese is the second most common language on the Internet?

"Keystroke! . . . Keystroke! . . . Keystroke!"

see but you know is there" (Elmer-DeWitt 1995:4; see also Shields 1996; Wellman et al. 1996).

The emergence of cyberspace can be viewed as yet another step away from Ferdinand Tönnies's concept of the familiar, intimate *Gemeinschaft* to the comparatively impersonal *Gesellschaft,* and as yet another way in which social cohesion is being eroded in contemporary society. Critics of electronic communication question whether nonverbal communication, voice inflections, and other forms of interpersonal interaction will be lost as people turn to email and chat rooms (P. Schaefer 1995; Schellenberg 1996).

But whereas some conclude that by opening up the world to cyberspace interaction, we may have reduced face-to-face interaction, others have reached different conclusions. One study surveyed more than two thousand households in the United States to assess the impact of the Internet on the everyday lives of its users. It found that parents report that they often surf the Web together with their children and that the Internet has had little effect on their children's interactions with friends. This study concludes that about two-thirds of the population in the United States are using the Internet more than ever and without sacrificing their social lives (Cha 2000; Howard, Rainie, and Jones 2001; Nie 2001).

Social Control

A data entry employee pauses to say hello to a colleague. A checker at the supermarket takes a moment to banter with a customer. A customer service telephone representative takes too much time helping callers. Each of these situations is subject to computer surveillance. Given the absence of strong protective legislation, many employees are subject to increasing and pervasive supervision by computers.

Supervisors have always scrutinized the performance of their workers, but with so much work now being handled electronically, the possibilities for surveillance have risen dramatically. According to a 2001 study, one-third of the online workforce is under continuous electronic surveillance. With Big Brother watching and listening in more and more, there is a danger that electronic monitoring will become a substitute for effective management or lead to perceptions of unfairness and intrusiveness (J. Lee 2001; Schulman 2001).

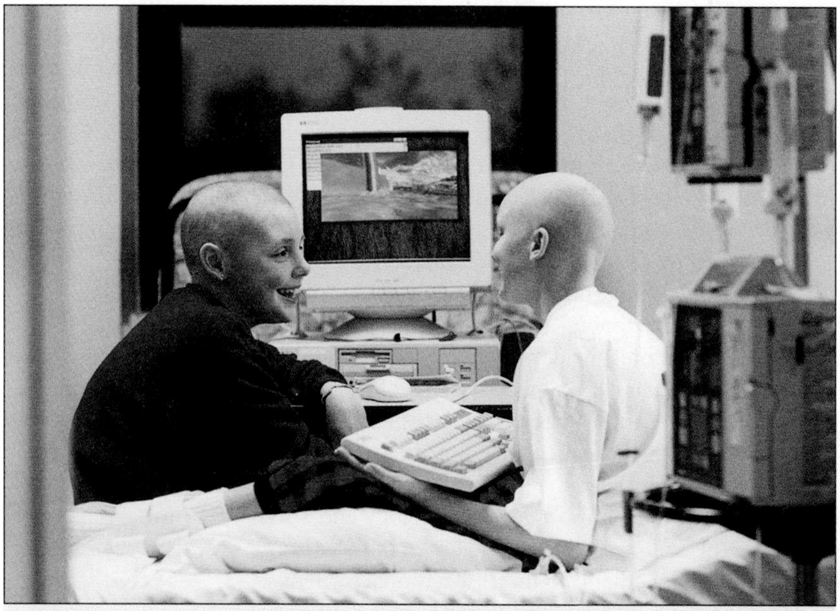

Two young patients at a New York City hospital communicate electronically with peers at a hospital in California. Electronic communication has proved useful in promoting social interaction among children who are seriously ill. The new technology, known as Starbright World, was developed with the assistance of director Steven Spielberg.

In recent years, a new type of corporate surveillance has emerged. A number of Internet sites are highly critical of the operations of various corporations. On McSpotlight are attacks on nutritional practices at McDonald's; on Up Against the Wal is advice on how to fight plans to open new Wal-Mart stores in a community. The Internet sites of such "anticorporate vigilantes" are being carefully monitored by powerful corporations in an attempt to counteract the activities of their critics (Neuborne 1996).

Technological advances have also created the possibility for a new type of white-collar crime: computer crime. It is now possible to gain access to a computer's inventory without leaving home and to carry out embezzlement or electronic fraud without leaving a trace. One report released in 2000 put cybercrime losses by big businesses at $10 billion in the United States alone. Typically, discussions of computer crime focus on computer theft and on problems caused by computer "hackers," but widespread use of computers has facilitated many new ways of participating in deviant behaviour. Consequently, greatly expanded police resources may be needed to deal with online child molesters, prostitution rings, software pirates, con artists, and other types of computer criminals. There is now a cybercrime unit of the RCMP. The consensus of the heads of these types of units is that these cases are increasing and becoming more difficult (Piller 2000).

pp. 135–136, 152–153

Not all the technological advances relevant to social control have been electronic in nature. DNA data banks have given police a powerful weapon in solving crimes; they have also opened the way to free wrongfully convicted citizens. Arguably, the most famous Canadian case involving DNA evidence was that of David Milgaard. Milgaard spent 28 years in prison for the murder of Gail Miller in Saskatoon in the 1960s. Finally, DNA evidence proved, conclusively, that Milgaard was not the killer. He was subsequently released from prison. The Government of Saskatchewan provided monetary compensation to Milgaard for the wrongful conviction. Although appropriate safeguards must be devised, the expansion of such DNA data banks has the potential to revolutionize law enforcement in Canada—especially in the area of sex crimes, where biological evidence is telling (Butterfield 1996; Death Penalty Information Center 2000).

Another connection between technology and social control is the use of computer databases and electronic verification of documents to increase national security in Canada, the United States, and Europe since September 11, 2001. Although concerned about the issue of national security, many visible minority groups, particularly in the United States, but also in Canada, believe that *their* privacy is most likely to be infringed by government authorities (Brandon 1995). The next section looks more fully at how technological changes can intensify stratification and inequality based on race, ethnicity, and other factors.

Stratification and Inequality

The unfettered access to technology of some members of society, coexisting with limited access on the part of others, has been referred to as the "digital divide" (Gates 1999: A15). An important continuing theme in sociology is stratification among people. Thus far, there is little evidence to suggest that technology will reduce inequality; in fact, it may only intensify it. Technology is costly, and it is generally impossible to introduce advances to everyone simultaneously. So who gets this access first? Conflict theorists contend that as we travel further and further along the electronic frontier through such advances as telecommuting and the Internet, the disenfranchised poor may be isolated from mainstream society in an "information ghetto," just as racial and ethnic minorities have traditionally been subjected to residential segregation (Ouellette 1993).

According to Statistics Canada (2004f), in 2003, the number of Internet users in Canada had increased by 5 percent from 2002. The Household Internet Use Survey revealed that Internet use was highest at home—nearly 55 percent of Canadian households had at least one member who used the Internet regularly at home in 2003. This general statistic, however, masks the unequal pattern of Internet access in Canada, which varies greatly according to income, education, family type, and region.

Dividing Canadian households into four income groups or quartiles (each group represents 25 percent of the income spectrum) the study demonstrated the importance of income as it relates to Internet access at home. In 2003, 82 percent, or four out of five, of the highest-income households had a member who used the Internet on a regular basis at home (see Figure 16-2), more than double that group's use five years earlier. In contrast, only 27 percent of the lowest-income households had a member who used the Internet on a regular basis at home.

Access to the Internet is also related to education: The higher the level of education in the household, the greater is the use of the Internet. Almost 77 percent of households in which one person had a university degree used the Internet on a regular basis at home; this percentage contrasts sharply with households in which the highest educational attainment was less than high school. In these households, only 12 percent had a member who used the Internet on a regular basis at home.

Internet use in Canada also varies according to family type, with families with children under the age of 18 living at home having the greatest rate of usage. Eighty-seven

FIGURE 16-2

The Importance of Income to Internet Access at Home, 2003

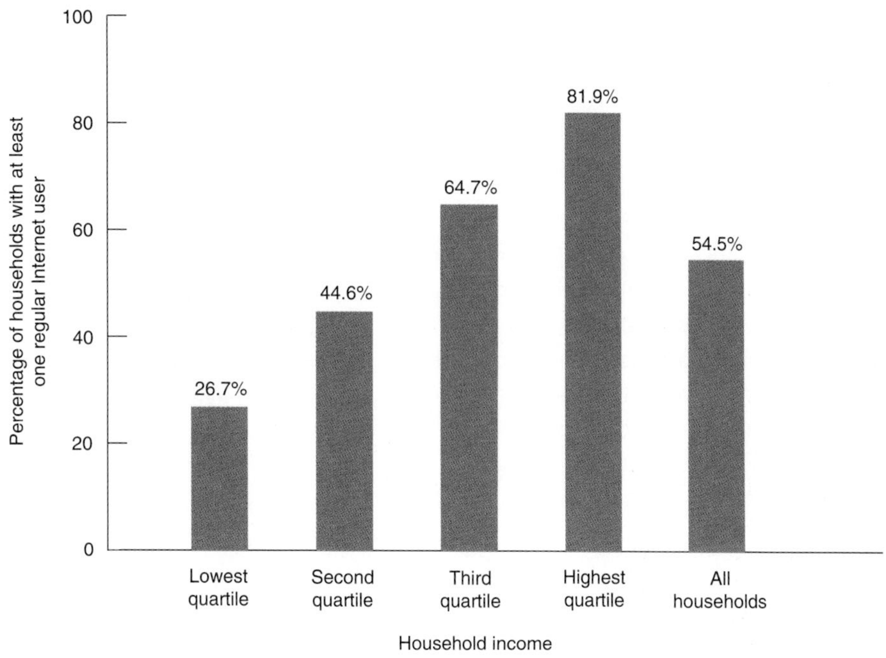

Source: Statistics Canada 2003n.

percent of households who had never used the Internet were families without children or were one-person households.

In terms of regional variations, British Columbia, Ontario, and Alberta led the way, with approximately 60 percent of households connected to the Internet, surpassing the national average of 55 percent. In 2003, the Atlantic provinces had the lowest rates of Internet connection from home; however, they also experienced the greatest proportional increases in usage over 2002 (Statistics Canada 2004e).

The issue of technology and inequality is especially sensitive when viewed in a cross-cultural perspective. Although industrialization has dramatically improved the standard of living of many workers, it has allowed elites to amass untold wealth. Moreover, the activities of multinational corporations have increased the inequality between industrialized core nations (such as the United States, Germany, and Japan) and the periphery of developing countries.

Use Your Sociological Imagination

One hundred years from now, how might society have changed? Will the differences among social classes be more or less pronounced than they are now? What about the differences among nations, races, and ethnic groups?

SOCIAL POLICY AND TECHNOLOGY — Privacy and Censorship in the Digital Village

The Issue

Imagine discovering that a complete stranger has been able to construct a profile of your identity; she or he has been able to find your social insurance number, the number of bedrooms in your home, the names of your former partners, the restaurants you frequent, and the number of vacations you take each year. Such invasions do occur, which has prompted the Canadian government to take action. To protect Canadian citizens from invasions of their privacy and unwanted use of their personal information, and to create trust and confidence in using the Internet to conduct business, the federal government has recently established new rules to protect Canadians' personal information.

In the past, Canadian privacy laws have had loopholes and were so patchy that it is often difficult to distinguish between data that are obtained legally and data that are gathered illicitly. The other side of the coin is the fear that government might restrict the flow of electronic information too much, stepping over the border into censorship. Some observers, however, feel the government is fully justified in restricting pornographic information. The whole issue of privacy and censorship in this technological age is another case of culture lag, in which the material culture (the technology) is changing faster than the nonmaterial culture (norms controlling the technology).

p. 53

The Setting

The typical consumer in Canada is included in dozens of marketing databases. These lists may seem innocent enough at first. Does it really matter if companies can buy lists for marketing with our names, addresses, and telephone numbers? Part of the problem is that computer technology has made it increasingly easy for any individual, business firm, or government agency to retrieve more and more information about any of us. For decades, information from motor vehicle offices, voter registration lists, and credit bureaus has been electronically stored, yet the incompatibility of different computer systems used to prevent access from one system to another. Today, having some information about a person has made it much easier to get other and perhaps more sensitive information.

The question of how much free expression should be permitted on the Internet relates to the issue of censorship. Some X-rated material is perfectly legal, if inappropriate for children who use the Net. Some of the sites are clearly illegal, such as those that serve the needs of pedophiles who prey on young children. Some are morally and legally elusive, such as the "upskirt" sites (sites that post images taken by video cameras aimed under the skirts of unsuspecting women in public places) or the site that, in 2005, featured the exposed thong underwear of unsuspecting female students at the University of Victoria in British Columbia. This is another area in which we can see the results of culture lag.

Sociological Insights

Functionalists can point to the manifest function of the Internet in its ability to facilitate communications. They also can identify the latent function of providing a forum for groups with few resources to communicate with literally tens of millions of people. Poorly financed groups ranging from hate organizations to special interest groups can vie against powerful wealthy interests. Thus, the functionalist perspective would see many aspects of technology fostering communication. The issue of censorship depends on how we view the content of the message, and the issue of privacy hinges on how information is used.

Viewed from a conflict perspective, however, there is the ever-present danger that a society's most powerful groups will use technological advances to invade the privacy of the less powerful and thereby maintain or intensify various forms of inequality and injustice. For example, in 1989, the People's Republic of China used various types of technology to identify protestors who had participated in pro-democracy demonstrations at Tiananmen Square and elsewhere. Some protestors identified in this manner received long prison terms because of their activism. During the same period, the Chinese government intercepted the news reports, telephone calls, and facsimile messages of foreign journalists covering the demonstrations. Although encouraging e-commerce, the government began in 2000 to undertake a "security certification" of all Internet content and service providers in China. Conflict theorists argue that control of technology in almost any form remains in the hands of those who already wield the most power, usually at the expense of the powerless and poor (Pomfret 2000).

Some feminist theorists have pointed out that technology is not neutral but rather is bound to masculinist belief systems and practices (Gill and Grint 1995). Sociologists Rosalind Gill and Keith Grint (1995) note that because technology has historically been associated with masculinity, gendered patterns of technological creation, use, and control have been constructed that continue today. Although these gendered patterns have often led to the separation of women from technology, feminist theorists, such as eco-feminists, argue that women are intrinsically closer to nature and that technology can be an intrusion into that relationship. Despite their differences, feminist positions draw our attention to the cultural separation between women and technology—philosophically and practically—thus prompting us

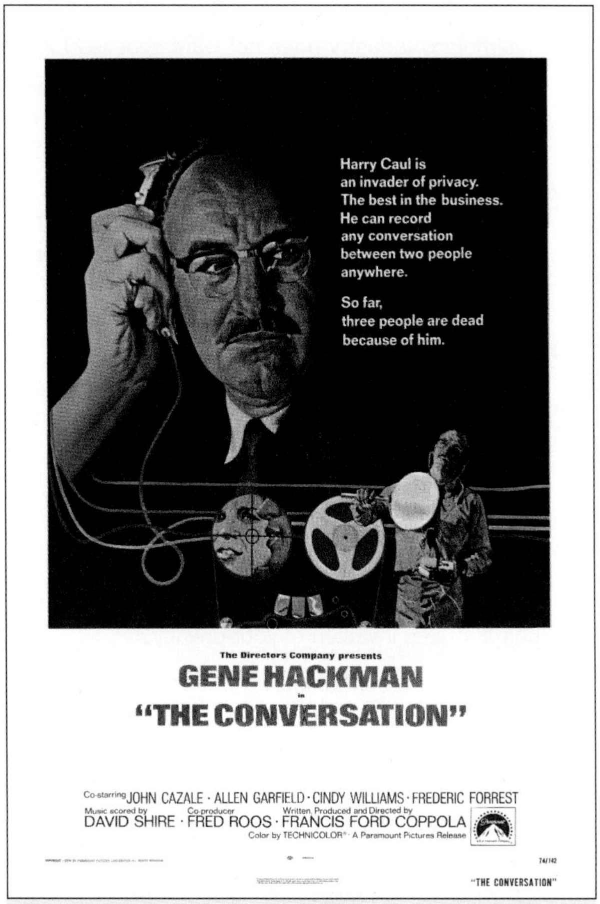
Harry Caul is
an invader of privacy.
The best in the business.
He can record
any conversation
between two people
anywhere.
So far,
three people are dead
because of him.
The Directors Company presents
GENE HACKMAN
"THE CONVERSATION"
Co-starring JOHN CAZALE · ALLEN GARFIELD · CINDY WILLIAMS · FREDERIC FORREST
Music scored by DAVID SHIRE · Co-producer FRED ROOS · Written, Produced and Directed by FRANCIS FORD COPPOLA
Color by TECHNICOLOR® · A Paramount Pictures Release
"THE CONVERSATION"

The 1974 motion picture *The Conversation,* in which Gene Hackman eavesdropped on other characters' conversations in their homes and in the park, raised an alarm among viewers concerned about their privacy. A generation later, citizens wonder how much of their electronic communication is monitored and for what purposes.

to question the vulnerability of women when it comes to the application of technology (i.e., issues of protection of privacy) to their everyday lives.

Interactionists view the privacy and censorship debate as one that parallels concerns people have in any social interaction. Just as we may disapprove of some associations that relatives or friends have with other people, we also express concern over controversial Web sites and attempt to monitor people's social interactions. Obviously, the Internet facilitates interactions with a broad range of people, with minimal likelihood of detection compared with face-to-face interactions. Moreover, anyone can easily move a Web site from one country to another, avoiding not only detection but also prosecution.

Policy Initiatives

To protect the privacy and personal information of Canadians in the digital economy, the federal government implemented the Personal Information Protection and Electronic Documents Act (PIPEDA) in 2004. PIPEDA sets out 10 key principles that organizations must follow when collecting, using, and disclosing Canadians' personal information. Central to the law are the following provisions:

- Organizations must seek the consent of individuals before collecting, using, or disclosing their personal information.
- Organizations must protect personal information with security safeguards according to the sensitivity of the information.
- Individuals may access personal information about themselves and have it corrected if necessary.
- The purposes for which the information is collected must be identified by the organization at the time of its collection.

PIPEDA provides a consistent set of provisions to protect Canadians' personal information and privacy, regardless of what province or territory they live in. It also allows Canadian companies to seamlessly do business with the European Union (EU), which has implemented an Act called the European Union Data Protection Directive.

Privacy and censorship are also global issues. In Myanmar (or Burma), the government has ruled that fax machines and computer modems are illegal. In Saudi Arabia, access to the Internet was banned until 1999. Now all Internet connections are routed through a government hub where computers block access to thousands of sites catalogued on a rapidly expanding censorship list—for example, all gambling sites, all free-wheeling chat rooms, and all sites critical of the ruling Saudi family. By contrast, the openness of the Internet in other parts of the Middle East allows scattered Palestinian refugees to communicate with one another and establish Web sites that provide a history of Palestinian settlements. Although China encourages expansion of the Internet, it has been wary of facilitating communication that it regards as disruptive. From time to time it shuts down Internet search engines, such as Google. Meanwhile, the British government is constructing an Internet spy centre that is geared to watch all online activity in Great Britain. It will be able to track every Web site a person visits (Africa News Service 1998; Jehl 1999; MacLeod 2000; E. Rosenthal 1999, 2000; Wilkinson 1999).

Although some people chastise government efforts to curb technology, others decry their *failure* to limit certain aspects of technology. Unlike Canada, the United States has developed an international reputation of being opposed to efforts to protect people's privacy. For example, the Center for Public Integrity, a nonpartisan research organization, issued a report in 1998 that critiques the U.S. government for failing to approve legislation protecting the confidentiality of medical records. In another case, America Online revealed to a U.S. Navy investigator the identity of a sailor who had described his marital status online as gay. In 1998, both the Navy and America Online were forced to reach settlements for violating the privacy of the sailor. At the same time, the United States has been vocal in opposing the European Union Data Protection Directive designed to protect citizens from computer-age invasions of privacy. The U.S. technology industry does not want access to information blocked, since information is vital to global commerce. Such cases as these illustrate the fine line between safeguarding privacy and stifling the electronic flow of information (Fleras 2003).

The conflict over privacy and censorship is far from over. As technology continues to advance in the twenty-first century, there are sure to be new battlegrounds.

Applying Theory

1. How might interactionists study the ways that people can obtain information about other people?
2. Taking a conflict perspective, do you think corporations and employers have a right to monitor employees' email and phone calls?
3. Are you more concerned about government censorship of electronic communication or about unauthorized invasion of your privacy?

CHAPTER RESOURCES

Summary

A ***social movement*** is an organized collective activity to promote or resist change. ***Social change*** is significant alteration over time in behaviour patterns and culture, including norms and values. Technology is information about how to use the material resources of the environment to satisfy human needs and desires. This chapter examined origins and types of social movements, sociological theories of social change, resistance to change, and the impact of technology on society's future and on social change.

1. A group will not mobilize into a social movement unless there is a shared perception that its ***relative deprivation*** can be ended only through collective action.
2. The success of a social movement will depend in good part on how effectively it mobilizes its resources.
3. ***New social movements*** tend to focus on more than just economic issues and often cross national boundaries.
4. Early advocates of the ***evolutionary theory*** of social change believed that society was progressing inevitably toward a higher state.
5. Talcott Parsons, a leading advocate of functionalist theory, viewed society as being in a natural state of equilibrium or balance.
6. Conflict theorists see change as having crucial significance, since it is needed to correct social injustices and inequalities.
7. In general, those with a disproportionate share of society's wealth, status, and power have a ***vested interest*** in preserving the status quo, and will resist change.
8. Feminist sociologists, despite their diversity, share a desire to deepen their understanding of the ways in which gender acts as an organizing principle in order to bring about social change.
9. Symbolic interactionist perspectives view people as active agents or actors in their social world, therefore viewing change as being constituted through human interaction.

10. The period of maladjustment when a nonmaterial culture is still adapting to new material conditions is known as culture lag.
11. In the computer age, telecommuters are linked to their supervisors and colleagues through computer terminals, phone lines, and fax machines.
12. The Internet is the world's largest computer network, used by hundreds of millions. Yet access to it is not equal.
13. Advances in biotechnology have raised difficult ethical questions about the sex selection of fetuses and genetic engineering.
14. English has become the dominant language of the Internet and the international language of commerce and communication.
15. Computer and video technology have facilitated supervision, control, and even domination of workers and citizens by employers and the government.
16. Conflict theorists fear that the disenfranchised poor may be isolated from mainstream society in an "information ghetto," just as racial and ethnic minorities have been subjected to residential segregation.
17. Computer technology has made it increasingly easy for any individual, business firm, or government agency to retrieve more and more information about any of us, thereby infringing on our privacy. How much government should restrict access to electronic information and how much it should censor such content are important policy issues.

Critical Thinking Questions

1. Select one social movement that is currently working for change in Canada. Analyze that movement, drawing on the concepts of relative deprivation, resource mobilization, and false consciousness.
2. In the last few years we have witnessed phenomenal growth in the use of cellular phones in all parts of the world. Analyze this example of material culture from the point of view of culture lag. Consider how usage, government regulation, and privacy issues are being worked out to keep up with the new technology.
3. In what ways has social interaction in your university community been affected by the kinds of technological advances examined in this chapter? Are there particular subcultures that are more likely or less likely to employ new forms of electronic communication?
4. Officials in the music industry have condemned the downloading of music, calling it "stealing." Do you agree with this assessment? Why?

Key Terms

Evolutionary theory A theory of social change that holds that society is moving in a definite direction. (page 388)

Luddites Rebellious craft workers in nineteenth-century England who destroyed new factory machinery as part of their resistance to the industrial revolution. (392)

Multilinear evolutionary theory A theory of social change that holds that change can occur in several ways and does not inevitably lead in the same direction. (388)

New social movements Organized collective activities that promote autonomy and self-determination as well as improvements in the quality of life. (386)

Relative deprivation The conscious feeling of a negative discrepancy between legitimate expectations and present actualities. (384)

Resource mobilization The ways in which a social movement utilizes such resources as money, political influence, access to the media, and personnel. (385)

Social change Significant alteration over time in behaviour patterns and culture, including norms and values. (383)

Social movement An organized collective activity to promote or resist change in an existing group or society. (383)

Unilinear evolutionary theory A theory of social change that holds that all societies pass through the same successive stages of evolution and inevitably reach the same end. (388)

Vested interests Those people or groups who will suffer in the event of social change, and who have a stake in maintaining the status quo. (391)

Additional Readings

Gurstein, Penny. 2002. *Wired to the World, Chained to the Home.* Vancouver: UBC Press. An examination of how technology has allowed people to work from home and the impact this has on people's activity patterns, social networks, and working spaces.

Kline, Stephen, Nick Dyer-Witherford, and Greig dePeuter. 2003. *Digital Play: The Interaction of Technology, Culture, and Marketing.* Montreal: McGill-Queen's University Press. This book offers a critical analysis of interactive media, focusing on the growth of video gaming.

Simard, Rene. 2000. *Reaching Out: Canada, International Science and Technology, and the Knowledge-Based Economy.* Ottawa: Industry Canada. Simard examines the attempt by Canada to create a new place for itself in the new global economy. How well can Canada compete in the knowledge-based marketplace of the twenty-first century?

Online Learning Centre

Visit the *Sociology: A Brief Introduction* Online Learning Centre at www.mcgrawhill.ca/college/schaefer to access quizzes, interactive exercises, video clips, and other research and study tools related to this chapter.

Reel Society Interactive Movie CD-ROM 2.0

Reel Society 2.0 can be used to spark discussion about the following topics from this chapter:

- Theories of social change

GLOSSARY

Numbers following the definitions indicate pages where the terms were identified. Consult the index for further page references.

A

Absolute poverty In developed countries, a standard of poverty based on a minimum level of subsistence below which families should not be expected to exist. (174)

Achieved status A social position attained by a person largely through his or her own efforts. (97)

Activity theory An interactionist theory of aging that argues that elderly people who remain active will be best adjusted. (335)

Adoption In a legal sense, a process that allows for the transfer of the legal rights, responsibilities, and privileges of parenthood to a new legal parent or parents. (256)

Ageism A term coined by Robert N. Butler to refer to prejudice and discrimination against the elderly. (337)

Agrarian society The most technologically advanced form of preindustrial society. Members are primarily engaged in the production of food but increase their crop yield through such innovations as the plow. (108)

Alienation The condition of being estranged or disassociated from the surrounding society. (123)

Anomie Durkheim's term for the loss of direction felt in a society when social control of individual behaviour has become ineffective. (8)

Anomie theory of deviance A theory developed by Robert Merton that explains deviance as an adaptation either of socially prescribed goals or of the norms governing their attainment, or both. (145)

Anticipatory socialization Processes of socialization in which a person "rehearses" for future positions, occupations, and social relationships. (80)

Apartheid The former policy of the South African government designed to maintain the separation of blacks and other nonwhites from the dominant whites. (207)

Argot Specialized language used by members of a group or subculture. (61)

Ascribed status A social position "assigned" to a person by society without regard for the person's unique talents or characteristics. (96)

Assimilation The process by which a person forsakes his or her own cultural tradition to become part of a different culture. (206)

Authority Power that has been institutionalized and is recognized by the people over whom it is exercised. (304)

B

Bilateral descent A kinship system in which both sides of a person's family are regarded as equally important. (247)

Birthrate The number of live births per 1000 population in a given year. Also known as the crude birthrate. (327)

Bourgeoisie Karl Marx's term for the capitalist class, comprising the owners of the means of production. (168)

Bureaucracy A component of formal organization in which rules and hierarchical ranking are used to achieve efficiency. (122)

Bureaucratization The process by which a group, organization, or social movement becomes increasingly bureaucratic. (125)

C

Capitalism An economic system in which capital, primarily in the form of currency, is used as a tool to create wealth, the means of production are largely in private hands, and the main incentive for economic activity is the accumulation of profits. (168)

Castes Hereditary systems of rank, usually religiously dictated, that tend to be fixed and immobile. (164)

Causal logic The relationship between a condition or variable and a particular consequence, with one event leading to the other. (28)

Census An enumeration, or counting, of a population. (326)

Charismatic authority Max Weber's term for power made legitimate by a leader's exceptional personal or emotional appeal to his or her followers. (305)

Class A term used by Max Weber to refer to a group of people who have a similar level of wealth and income. (169)

Class consciousness In Karl Marx's view, a subjective awareness held by members of a class regarding their common vested interests and need for collective political action to bring about social change. (169)

Classical theory An approach to the study of formal organizations that views workers as being motivated almost entirely by economic rewards. (126)

Class system A social ranking based primarily on economic position in which achieved characteristics can influence mobility. (165)

Closed system A social system in which there is little or no possibility of individual mobility. (179)

Coalition A temporary or permanent alliance geared toward a common goal. (120)

Code of ethics The standards of acceptable behaviour developed by and for members of a profession. (37)

Cognitive theory of development Jean Piaget's theory explaining how children's thinking progresses through four stages. (78)

Cohabitation The practice of living together as a couple without marrying. (260)

Colonialism The maintenance of political, social, economic, and cultural dominance over a people by a foreign power for an extended time. (181)

Communism As an ideal type, an economic system under which all property is communally owned and no social distinctions are made on the basis of people's ability to contribute to the economy. (302)

Community A spatial or political unit of social organization that gives people a sense of belonging, based either on shared residence in a particular place or on a common identity. (357)

Concentric-zone theory A theory of urban growth that sees growth in terms of a series of rings radiating from the central business district. (362)

Conflict perspective A sociological approach that assumes that social behaviour is best understood in terms of conflict or tension between competing groups. (13)

Conformity Going along with our peers, individuals of a person's own status, who have no special right to direct our behaviour. (138)

Contact hypothesis An interactionist perspective that states that interracial contact between people of equal status in cooperative circumstances will reduce prejudice. (205)

Content analysis The systematic coding and objective recording of data, guided by some rationale. (37)

Control group Subjects in an experiment who are not introduced to the independent variable by the researcher. (35)

Control theory A view of conformity and deviance that suggests that our connection to members of society leads us to systematically conform to society's norms. (141)

Control variable A factor held constant to test the relative impact of an independent variable. (31)

Correlation A relationship between two variables whereby a change in one coincides with a change in the other. (28)

Correspondence principle A term used by Bowles and Gintis to refer to the tendency of schools to promote the values expected of individuals in each social class and to prepare students for the types of jobs typically held by members of their class. (287)

Counterculture A subculture that deliberately opposes certain aspects of the larger culture. (62)

Creationism A literal interpretation of the Bible regarding the creation of man and the universe used to argue that evolution should not be presented as established scientific fact. (293)

Crime A violation of criminal law for which formal penalties are applied by some governmental authority. (151)

Cultural imperialism The influence or imposition of the material or non-material elements of a culture on another culture or cultures. (63)

Cultural relativism The viewing of people's behaviour from the perspective of their own culture. (64)

Cultural transmission A school of criminology that argues that criminal behaviour is learned through social interactions. (147)

Cultural universals General practices found in every culture. (50)

Culture The totality of learned, socially transmitted behaviour. (49)

Culture lag Ogburn's term for a period of maladjustment during which the non-material culture is still adapting to new material conditions. (53)

Culture shock The feeling of surprise and disorientation that is experienced when people witness cultural practices different from their own. (62)

D

Death rate The number of deaths per 1000 population in a given year. Also known as the crude death rate. (327)

Defended neighbourhood A neighbourhood that residents identify through defined community borders and through a perception that adjacent areas are geographically separate and socially different. (366)

Degradation ceremony An aspect of the socialization process within total institutions, in which people are subjected to humiliating rituals. (80)

Deindustrialization The systematic, widespread withdrawal of investment in basic aspects of productivity, such as factories and plants. (314)

Demographic transition A term used to describe the change from high birthrates and death rates to relatively low birthrates and death rates. (328)

Demography The scientific study of population. (325)

Denomination A large, organized religion not officially linked with the state or government. (279)

Dependency theory An approach that contends that industrialized nations continue to exploit developing countries for their own gain. (181)

Dependent variable The variable in a causal relationship that is subject to the influence of another variable. (28)

Deviance Behaviour that violates the standards of conduct or expectations of a group or society. (142)

Differential association A theory of deviance proposed by Edwin Sutherland that holds that violation of rules results from exposure to attitudes favourable to criminal acts. (147)

Diffusion The process by which a cultural item is spread from group to group or society to society. (51)

Discovery The process of making known or sharing the existence of an aspect of reality. (51)

Discrimination The process of denying opportunities and equal rights to individuals and groups because of prejudice or other arbitrary reasons. (201)

Disengagement theory A functionalist theory of aging introduced by Cumming and Henry that contends that society and the aging individual mutually sever many of their relationships. (334)

Domestic partnership Two unrelated adults who have chosen to share one another's lives in a relationship of mutual caring, who reside together, and who agree to be jointly responsible for their dependents, basic living expenses, and other common necessities. (262)

Dominant ideology A set of cultural beliefs and practices that helps to maintain powerful social, economic, and political interests. (59)

Downsizing Reductions taken in a company's workforce as part of deindustrialization. (314)

Dramaturgical approach A view of social interaction, popularized by Erving Goffman, that examines people as if they were theatrical performers. (16)

Dyad A two-member group. (119)

Dysfunction An element or a process of society that may disrupt a social system or lead to a decrease in stability. (13)

E

Ecclesia A religious organization that claims to include most or all of the members of a society and is recognized as the national or official religion. (279)

E-commerce Numerous ways that people with access to the Internet can do business from their computers. (315)

Economic system The structures and processes through which goods and services are produced, distributed, and consumed. (300)

Education A formal process of learning in which some people consciously teach while others adopt the social role of learners. (271)

Egalitarian family An authority pattern in which the adult members of the family are regarded as equals. (248)

Elite model A view of society as controlled by a small group of individuals who share a common set of political and economic interests. (309)

Employment equity A federal Act that attempts to eliminate barriers faced in the area of employment. (203)

Endogamy The restriction of mate selection to people within the same group. (251)

Environmental justice (EJ) A legal strategy based on claims that members of visible minority groups are disproportionately subjected to environmental hazards. (374)

Equilibrium model Talcott Parsons's functionalist view of society as tending toward a state of stability or balance. (12)

Esteem The reputation that a particular individual has earned within an occupation. (172)

Ethnic group A group that is set apart from others because of its national origin or distinctive cultural patterns. (195)

Ethnocentrism The tendency to assume that our own culture and way of life are superior to all others. (64)

Ethnography The study of an entire social setting through extended systematic observation. (35)

Evolutionary theory A theory of social change that holds that society is moving in a definite direction. (388)

Exogamy The requirement that people select mates outside certain groups. (251)

Experiment An artificially created situation that allows the researcher to manipulate variables. (35)

Experimental group Subjects in an experiment who are exposed to an independent variable introduced by a researcher. (35)

Exploitation theory A Marxist theory that views racial subordination, such as that in the Canada and the United States, as a manifestation of the class system inherent in capitalism. (204)

Expressiveness A term used by Parsons and Bales to refer to concern for maintenance of harmony and the internal emotional affairs of the family. (225)

Extended family A family in which relatives—such as grandparents, aunts, or uncles—live in the same home as parents and their children. (246)

F

Face-work A term used by Erving Goffman to refer to the efforts of people to maintain the proper image and avoid embarrassment in public. (77)

False consciousness A term used by Karl Marx to describe an attitude held by members of a class that does not accurately reflect its objective position. (169)

Family A set of people related by blood, marriage (or some other agreed-on relationship), or adoption who share the primary responsibility for reproduction and caring for members of society. (244)

Feminist perspectives Various diverse streams of sociological analysis having in common the attempt to explain, understand, and change the ways in which gender socially organizes our public and private lives in such a way as to produce inequality between men and women. (14)

Fertility The amount of reproduction among women of childbearing age. (325)

Folkways Norms governing everyday social behaviour whose violation raises comparatively little concern. (56)

Force The actual or threatened use of coercion to impose a person's will on others. (303)

Formal norms Norms that generally have been written down and that specify strict rules for punishment of violators. (56)

Formal organization A special-purpose group designed and structured for maximum efficiency. (121)

Formal social control Social control carried out by authorized agents, such as police officers, judges, school administrators, and employers. (140)

Functionalist perspective A sociological approach that emphasizes the way that parts of a society are structured to maintain its stability. (12)

G

Gemeinschaft A term used by Ferdinand Tönnies to describe close-knit communities, often found in rural areas, in which strong personal bonds unite members. (106)

Gender roles Expectations regarding the proper behaviour, attitudes, and activities of males and females. (82)

Gender socialization An aspect of socialization through which we learn the attitudes, behaviours, and practices associated with being male and female according to our society and social groups within it. (82)

Generalized others A term used by George Herbert Mead to refer to the child's awareness of the attitudes, viewpoints, and expectations of society as a whole that a child takes into account in his or her behaviour. (16)

Genocide The deliberate, systematic killing of or blatant disregard for an entire people or nation. (205)

Gerontology The scientific study of the sociological and psychological aspects of aging and the problems of the aged. (334)

Gesellschaft A term used by Ferdinand Tönnies to describe communities, often urban, that are large and impersonal with little commitment to the group or consensus on values. (106)

Glass ceiling An invisible barrier that blocks the promotion of a qualified individual in a work environment because of the individual's gender, race, or ethnicity. (201)

Globalization The worldwide integration of government policies, cultures, social movements, and financial markets through trade and the exchange of ideas. (183)

Goal displacement Overzealous conformity to official regulations within a bureaucracy. (124)

Group Any number of people with similar norms, values, and expectations who interact meaningfully with one another on a regular basis. (101)

Growth rate The difference between births and deaths, plus the difference between immigrants and emigrants, per 1000 population. (328)

H

Hawthorne effect The unintended influence that observers or experiments can have on their subjects. (36)

Health As defined by the World Health Organization, a state of complete physical, mental, and social well-being, and not merely the absence of disease and infirmity. (338)

Hidden curriculum Standards of behaviour that are deemed proper by society and are taught subtly in schools. (286)

Holistic medicine A means of health maintenance using therapies in which the health care practitioner considers the person's physical, mental, emotional, and spiritual characteristics. (347)

Horizontal mobility The movement of an individual from one social position to another of the same rank. (179)

Horticultural societies Preindustrial societies in which people plant seeds and crops rather than subsist merely on available foods. (108)

Human ecology An area of study concerned with the interrelationships between people and their spatial setting and physical environment. (360)

Human relations approach An approach to the study of formal organizations that emphasizes the role of people, communication, and participation within a bureaucracy and tends to focus on the informal structure of the organization. (127)

Hunting-and-gathering society A preindustrial society in which people rely on whatever foods and fibre are readily available in order to live. (107)

Hypothesis A speculative statement about the relationship between two or more variables. (28)

I

Ideal type A construct or model that serves as a measuring rod against which specific cases can be evaluated. (8)

Impression management A term used by Erving Goffman to refer to the altering of the presentation of the self in order to create distinctive appearances and satisfy particular audiences. (76)

Incest taboo The prohibition of sexual relationships between certain culturally specified relatives. (251)

Incidence The number of new cases of a specific disorder occurring within a given population during a stated time. (342)

Income Salaries and wages and monies brought in by investments. (162)

Independent variable The variable in a causal relationship that, when altered, causes or influences a change in a second variable. (28)

Industrial city A city characterized by relatively large size, open competition, an open class system, and elaborate specialization in the manufacturing of goods. (359)

Industrial society A society that depends on mechanization to produce its economic goods and services. (108)

Infant mortality rate The number of deaths of infants under one year of age per one thousand live births in a given year. (327)

Influence The exercise of power through a process of persuasion. (303)

Informal economy Transfers of money, goods, or services that are not reported to the government. (303)

Informal norms Norms that generally are understood but are not precisely recorded. (56)

Informal social control Social control carried out by people casually through such means as laughter, smiles, and ridicule. (139)

In-group Any group or category to which people feel they belong. (120)

Innovation The process of introducing new elements into a culture through either discovery or invention. (51)

Institutional discrimination The denial of opportunites and equal rights to individuals and groups that results from the normal operations of a society. (202)

Instrumentality A term used by Parsons and Bales to refer to emphasis on tasks, focus on more distant goals, and a concern for the external relationship between one's family and other social institutions. (225)

Interactionist perspective A sociological approach that generalizes about fundamental or everyday forms of social interaction. (15)

Intergenerational mobility Changes in the social position of children relative to their parents. (179)

Interview A face-to-face or telephone questioning of a respondent to obtain desired information. (32)

Intragenerational mobility Changes in a person's social position within his or her adult life. (179)

Invention The combination of existing cultural items into a form that did not previously exist. (51)

Iron law of oligarchy A principle of organizational life developed by Robert Michels under which even democratic organizations will become bureaucracies ruled by a few individuals. (125)

K

Kinship The state of being related to others. (247)

L

Labelling theory An approach to deviance that attempts to explain why certain people are viewed as deviants while others engaging in the same behaviour are not. (149)

Labour unions Organized workers who share either the same skill or the same employer. (129)

Laissez-faire A form of capitalism under which people compete freely, with minimal government intervention in the economy. (301)

Language An abstract system of word meanings and symbols for all aspects of culture. It also includes gestures and other nonverbal communication. (53)

Latent functions Unconscious or unintended functions; hidden purposes. (13)

Law Governmental social control. (56)

Legal-rational authority Max Weber's term for power made legitimate by law. (305)

Liberal feminism The stream of feminism that asserts that women's equality can be obtained through the extension of the principles of equality of opportunity and freedom. (14)

Liberation theology Use of a church, primarily Roman Catholicism, in a political effort to eliminate poverty, discrimination, and other forms of injustice evident in a secular society. (275)

Life chances Max Weber's term for people's opportunities to provide themselves with material goods, positive living conditions, and favourable life experiences. (177)

Life expectancy The median number of years a person can be expected to live under current mortality conditions. (327)

Looking-glass self A concept used by Charles Horton Cooley that emphasizes the self as the product of our social interactions with others. (74)

Luddites Rebellious craft workers in nineteenth-century England who destroyed new factory machinery as part of their resistance to the Industrial Revolution. (392)

M

Macrosociology Sociological investigation that concentrates on large-scale phenomena or entire civilizations. (10)

Manifest functions Open, stated, and conscious functions. (13)

Marxist feminism The stream of feminist sociological approaches that place the system of capitalism at fault for the oppression of women and hold that women are not oppressed by sexism or patriarchy, but rather by a system of economic production that is based on unequal gender relations in the capitalist economy. (14)

Master status A status that dominates other statuses and thereby determines a person's general position within society. (97)

Material culture The physical or technological aspects of our daily lives. (52)

Matriarchy A society in which women dominate in family decision making. (248)

Matrilineal descent A kinship system that favours the relatives of the mother. (247)

McDonaldization The process by which the principles of the fast-food restaurant have come to dominate certain sectors of society, both in Canada and throughout the world. (117)

Megachurches Large worship centres affiliated only loosely, if at all, with existing denominations. (280)

Megalopolis A densely populated area containing two or more cities and their surrounding suburbs. (360)

Microsociology Sociological investigation that stresses study of small groups and often uses laboratory experimental studies. (10)

Minority group A subordinate group whose members have significantly less control or power over their own lives than the members of a dominant or majority group have over theirs. (196)

Modernization The far-reaching process by which a society moves from traditional or less developed institutions to those characteristic of more developed societies. (186)

Modernization theory A functionalist approach that proposes that modernization and development will gradually improve the lives of people in peripheral nations. (186)

Monogamy A form of marriage in which one woman and one man are married only to each other. (247)

Monopoly Control of a market by a single business firm. (301)

Morbidity rates The incidence of diseases in a given population. (342)

Mores Norms deemed highly necessary to the welfare of a society. (56)

Mortality rate The incidence of death in a given population. (342)

Multiculturalism A policy that promotes cultural and racial diversity and full and equal participation of individuals and communities of all origins as a fundamental characteristic of Canadian identity. (63)

Multilinear evolutionary theory A theory of social change that holds that change can occur in several ways and does not inevitably lead in the same direction. (388)

Multinational corporations Commercial organizations that are headquartered in one country but do business throughout the world. (184)

Multiple-nuclei theory A theory of urban growth that views growth as emerging from many centres of development, each of which may reflect a particular urban need or activity. (363)

N

Natural science The study of the physical features of nature and the ways in which they interact and change. (4)

Negotiated order A social structure that derives its existence from the social interactions through which people define and redefine its character. (96)

Negotiation The attempt to reach agreement with others concerning some objective. (96)

Neocolonialism Continuing dependence of former colonies on foreign countries. (181)

New religious movement (NRM) or **cult** A generally small, secretive religious group that represents either a new religion or a major innovation of an existing faith. (281)

New social movements Organized collective activities that promote autonomy and self-determination as well as improvements in the quality of life. (386)

New urban sociology An approach to urbanization that considers the interplay of local, national, and worldwide forces and their effect on local space, with special emphasis on the impact of global economic activity. (364)

Nonmaterial culture Cultural adjustments to material conditions, such as customs, beliefs, patterns of communication, and ways of using material objects. (52)

Nonverbal communication The sending of messages through the use of posture, facial expressions, and gestures. (16)

Norms Established standards of behaviour maintained by a society. (56)

Nuclear family A married couple and their unmarried children living together. (246)

O

Obedience Compliance with higher authorities in a hierarchical structure. (138)

Objective method A technique for measuring social class that assigns individuals to classes on the basis of criteria, such as occupation, education, income, and place of residence. (172)

Observation A research technique in which an investigator collects information through direct participation in or observation of a group, tribe, or community. (33)

Open system A social system in which the position of each individual is influenced by his or her achieved status. (179)

Operational definition An explanation of an abstract concept that is specific enough to allow a researcher to measure the concept. (27)

Organized crime The work of a group that regulates relations between various criminal enterprises involved in the smuggling and sale of drugs, prostitution, gambling, and other activities. (152)

Out-group A group or category to which people feel they do not belong. (120)

P

Patriarchy A society in which men dominate family decision making. (248)

Patrilineal descent A kinship system that favours the relatives of the father. (247)

Personality In everyday speech, a person's typical patterns of attitudes, needs, characteristics, and behaviour. (71)

Peter principle A principle of organizational life, originated by Laurence J. Peter, according to which each individual within a hierarchy tends to rise to his or her level of incompetence. (124)

Pluralist model A view of society in which many competing groups within the community have access to governmental officials so that no single group is dominant. (310)

Political socialization The process by which individuals acquire political attitudes and develop patterns of political behaviour. (306)

Political system The structures and processes used for implementing and achieving society's goals. (300)

Politics In Harold D. Lasswell's words, "who gets what, when, and how." (303)

Polyandry A form of polygamy in which a woman can have several husbands at the same time. (247)

Polygamy A form of marriage in which an individual can have several husbands or wives simultaneously. (247)

Polygyny A form of polygamy in which a husband can have several wives at the same time. (247)

Population pyramid A special type of bar chart that shows the distribution of the population by gender and age. (354)

Postindustrial city A city in which global finance and the electronic flow of information dominate the economy. (359)

Postindustrial society A society whose economic system is primarily engaged in the processing and control of information. (108)

Postmodern society A technologically sophisticated society that is preoccupied with consumer goods and media images. (16)

Power The ability to exercise our will over others. (170)

Power elite A term used by C. Wright Mills for a small group of military, industrial, and government leaders who control the fate of the United States and every other major capitalist country. (309)

Preindustrial city A city with only a few thousand people living within its borders and characterized by a relatively closed class system and limited mobility. (358)

Prejudice A negative attitude toward an entire category of people, such as a racial or ethnic minority. (199)

Prestige The respect and admiration that an occupation holds in a society. (172)

Prevalence The total number of cases of a specific disorder that exist at a given time. (342)

Primary group A small group characterized by intimate, face-to-face association and cooperation. (117)

Profane The ordinary and commonplace elements of life, as distinguished from the sacred. (273)

Professional criminal A person who pursues crime as a day-to-day occupation, developing skilled techniques and enjoying a certain degree of status among other criminals. (151)

Proletariat Karl Marx's term for the working class in a capitalist society. (168)

Protestant ethic Max Weber's term for the disciplined work ethic, this-worldly concerns, and rational orientation to life emphasized by John Calvin and his followers. (275)

Q

Qualitative research Research that relies on what is seen in the field or naturalistic settings more than on statistical data. (33)

Quantitative research Research that collects and reports data primarily in numerical form. (33)

Questionnaire A printed research instrument employed to obtain desired information from a respondent. (32)

R

Racial group A group that is set apart from others because of obvious physical differences. (195)

Racial or ethnic profiling The use of a social construct of race as a consideration in suspect profiling in law enforcement and national security practices. (202)

Racism The belief that one race is supreme and all others are innately inferior. (201)

Radical feminism The stream of feminism that maintains that the root of all oppression of women is embedded in patriarchy. (15)

Random sample A sample for which every member of the entire population has the same chance of being selected. (29)

Reference group Any group that people use as a standard in evaluating themselves and their own behaviour. (121)

Relative deprivation The conscious feeling of a negative discrepancy between legitimate expectations and present actualities. (384)

Relative poverty A floating standard of deprivation by which people at the bottom of a society, whatever their lifestyles, are judged to be disadvantaged in comparison with the nation as a whole. (175)

Reliability The extent to which a measure provides consistent results. (29)

Religion According to Émile Durkheim, a unified system of beliefs and practices relative to sacred things. (273)

Religious beliefs Statements to which members of a particular religion adhere. (277)

Religious experience The feeling or perception of being in direct contact with the ultimate reality, such as a divine being, or of being overcome with religious emotion. (278)

Religious rituals Practices required or expected of members of a faith. (277)

Research design A detailed plan or method for obtaining data scientifically. (31)

Resocialization The process of discarding former behaviour patterns and accepting new ones as part of a transition in life. (80)

Resource mobilization The ways in which a social movement utilizes such resources as money, political influence, access to the media, and personnel. (385)

Rites of passage Rituals marking the symbolic transition from one social position to another. (79)

Role conflict Difficulties that occur when incompatible expectations arise from two or more social positions held by the same person. (99)

Role exit The process of disengagement from a role that is central to self-identity and reestablishment of an identity in a new role. (100)

Role strain Difficulties that result from the differing demands and expectations associated with the same social position. (99)

Role taking The process of mentally assuming the perspective of another, thereby enabling you to respond from that imagined viewpoint. (75)

Routine activities theory The notion that criminal victimization increases when there is a convergence of motivated offenders and suitable targets. (148)

S

Sacred Elements beyond everyday life that inspire awe, respect, and even fear. (273)

Sample A selection from a larger population that is statistically representative of that population. (28)

Sanctions Penalties and rewards for conduct concerning a social norm. (57)

Sapir-Whorf hypothesis A hypothesis concerning the role of language in shaping cultures. It holds that language is culturally determined and serves to influence our mode of thought. (55)

Science The body of knowledge obtained by methods based upon systematic observation. (4)

Scientific management approach Another name for the classical theory of formal organizations. (126)

Scientific method A systematic, organized series of steps that ensures maximum objectivity and consistency in researching a problem. (26)

Secondary analysis A variety of research techniques that make use of publicly accessible information and data. (36)

Secondary group A formal, impersonal group in which there is little social intimacy or mutual understanding. (118)

Sect A relatively small religious group that has broken away from some other religious organization to renew what it views as the original vision of the faith. (280)

Secularization The process through which religion's influence on other social institutions diminishes. (271)

Segregation The act of physically separating two groups; often imposed on a minority group by a dominant group. (206)

Self According to George Herbert Mead, the sum total of people's conscious perceptions of their own identity as distinct from others. (74)

Self-segregation The situation that arises when members of a minority deliberately develop residential, economic, or social network structures that are separate from those of the majority population. (207)

Serial monogamy A form of marriage in which a person can have several spouses in his or her lifetime but only one spouse at a time. (247)

Sexism The ideology that one sex is superior to the other. (230)

Sick role Societal expectations about the attitudes and behaviour of a person viewed as being ill. (338)

Significant others A term used by George Herbert Mead to refer to those individuals who are most important in the development of the self, such as parents, friends, and teachers. (16)

Single-parent families Families in which there is only one parent present to care for children. (257)

Slavery A system of enforced servitude in which people are legally owned by others and in which enslaved status is transferred from parents to children. (164)

Small group A group small enough for all members to interact simultaneously, that is, to talk with one another or at least be acquainted. (118)

Social change Significant alteration over time in behaviour patterns and culture, including norms and values. (383)

Social constructionist perspective An approach to deviance that emphasizes the role of culture in the creation of the deviant identity. (149)

Social control The techniques and strategies for preventing deviant human behaviour in any society. (136)

Social epidemiology The study of the distribution of disease, impairment, and general health status across a population. (342)

Social inequality A condition in which members of a society have different amounts of wealth, prestige, or power. (162)

Social institutions Organized patterns of beliefs and behaviour centred on basic social needs. (103)

Social interaction The ways in which people respond to one another. (94)

Socialism An economic system under which the means of production and distribution are collectively owned. (302)

Socialist feminism The stream of feminism that maintains gender relations are shaped by both patriarchy and capitalism, and thus equality for women implies that both the system of capitalism and the ideology of patriarchy must be challenged and eliminated. (14)

Socialization The process whereby people learn the attitudes, values, and actions appropriate for individuals as members of a particular culture. (71)

Social mobility Movement of individuals or groups from one position of a society's stratification system to another. (178)

Social movement An organized collective activity to promote or resist change in an existing group or in society. (383)

Social network A series of social relationships that links a person directly to others and therefore indirectly to still more people. (101)

Social role A set of expectations of people who occupy a given social position or status. (97)

Social science The study of various aspects of human society. (4)

Social structure The way in which a society is organized into predictable relationships. (94)

Societal-reaction approach Another name for labelling theory. (149)

Society A fairly large number of people who live in the same territory, are relatively independent of people outside it, and participate in a common culture. (49)

Sociobiology The systematic study of the biological bases of social behaviour. (74)

Sociocultural evolution The process of change and development in human societies that results from cumulative growth in their stores of cultural information. (107)

Sociological imagination Awareness of the relationship between an individual and the wider society. (3)

Sociology The systematic study of social behaviour and human groups. (3)

Squatter settlements Areas occupied by the very poor on the fringes of cities, in which housing is often constructed by the settlers themselves from discarded material. (360)

Standpoint feminism The stream of feminism that takes into account women's diversity and maintains that no one standpoint will represent all women's lives. (15)

Status A term used by sociologists to refer to any of the full range of socially defined positions within a large group or society. (96)

Status group A term used by Max Weber to refer to people who have the same prestige or lifestyle, independent of their class positions. (170)

Stereotypes Unreliable generalizations about all members of a group that do not recognize individual differences within the group. (198)

Stigma A label used to devalue members of deviant social groups. (143)

Stratification A structured ranking of entire groups of people that perpetuates unequal economic rewards and power in a society. (162)

Subculture A segment of society that shares a distinctive pattern of mores, folkways, and values that differs from the pattern of the larger society. (61)

Suburbs Any territory within a metropolitan area that is not included in the central city. (367)

Survey A study, generally in the form of interviews or questionnaires, that provides sociologists and other researchers with information concerning how people think and act. (32)

Symbols The gestures, objects, and language that form the basis of human communication. (75)

T

Teacher-expectancy effect The impact that a teacher's expectations about a student's performance may have on the student's actual achievements. (288)

Technology Information about the ways in which the material resources of the environment can be used to satisfy human needs and desires. (52)

Telecommuters Employees who work full-time or part-time at home rather than in an outside office and who are linked to their supervisors and colleagues through computer terminals, phone lines, and fax machines. (128)

Terrorism The use or threat of violence against random or symbolic targets in pursuit of political aims. (311)

Theory A template containing definitions and relationships used to organize and understand the social world. A theory may have explanatory power, predictive power, or both. (6)

Total fertility rate (TFR) The average number of children born alive to a woman, assuming that she conforms to current fertility rates. (327)

Total institutions A term coined by Erving Goffman to refer to institutions that regulate all aspects of a person's life under a single authority, such as prisons, the military, mental hospitals, and convents. (80)

Tracking The practice of placing students in specific curriculum groups on the basis of test scores and other criteria. (286)

Traditional authority Legitimate power conferred by custom and accepted practice. (305)

Trained incapacity The tendency of workers in a bureaucracy to become so specialized that they develop blind spots and fail to notice obvious problems. (123)

Triad A three-member group. (120)

U

Underclass Long-term poor people who lack training and skills. (177)

Unilinear evolutionary theory A theory of social change that holds that all societies pass through the same successive stages of evolution and inevitably reach the same end. (388)

Urban ecology An area of study that focuses on the interrelationships between people and their environment. (360)

Urbanism Distinctive patterns of social behaviour evident among city residents. (365)

V

Validity The degree to which a scale or measure truly reflects the phenomenon under study. (29)

Value neutrality Max Weber's term for objectivity of sociologists in the interpretation of data. (39)

Values Collective conceptions of what is considered good, desirable, and proper—or bad, undesirable, and improper—in a culture. (58)

Variable A measurable trait or characteristic that is subject to change under different conditions. (28)

Verstehen The German word for "understanding" or "insight"; used by Max Weber to stress the need for sociologists to take into account people's emotions, thoughts, beliefs, and attitudes. (8)

Vertical mobility The movement of a person from one social position to another of a different rank. (179)

Vested interests Veblen's term for those people or groups who will suffer in the event of social change and who have a stake in maintaining the status quo. (391)

Victimization surveys Questionnaires or interviews used to determine whether people have been victims of crime. (154)

Victimless crime A term used by sociologists to describe the willing exchange among adults of widely desired, but illegal, goods and services. (153)

Visible minority Canadians who are non-white or are identified as being physically different from white Canadians of European descent, who compose the dominant group. (196)

Voluntary associations Organizations established on the basis of common interest, whose members volunteer or even pay to participate. (127)

W

Wealth An inclusive term encompassing all of a person's material assets, including land and other types of property. (162)

White-collar crime Crimes committed by affluent individuals or corporations in the course of their daily business activities. (152)

World systems analysis Immanuel Wallerstein's view of the global economic system as divided between certain industrialized nations that control wealth and developing countries that are controlled and exploited. (181)

X

Xenocentrism The belief that the products, styles, or ideas of one's society are inferior to those that originate elsewhere. (64)

Z

Zero population growth (ZPG) The state of a population with a growth rate of zero, achieved when the number of births plus immigrants is equal to the number of deaths plus emigrants. (332)

REFERENCES

A

American Association of Retired Persons (AARP). 2004. *Global Report on Aging.* Washington, DC: AARP.

ABC News. 1992. *Primetime Live: True Colors.* Transcript of November 26 episode.

Abercrombie, Nicholas, Bryan S. Turner, and Stephen Hill, eds. 1990. *Dominant Ideologies.* Cambridge, MA: Unwin Hyman.

Abercrombie, Nicholas, Stephen Hill, and Bryan S. Turner. 1980. *The Dominant Ideology Thesis.* London: George Allen and Unwin.

Aberle, David F., A.K. Cohen, A.K. Davis, M.J. Leng, Jr., and F.N. Sutton. 1950. "The Functional Prerequisites of a Society." *Ethics* 60(January):100–111.

Abrahams, Ray G. 1968. "Reaching an Agreement over Bridewealth in Labwor, Northern Uganda: A Case Study." Pp. 202–215 in *Councils in Action,* edited by Audrey Richards and Adam Kuer. Cambridge: Cambridge University Press.

Abrahamson, Mark. 1978. *Functionalism.* Englewood Cliffs, NJ: Prentice-Hall.

Abu-Laban, Sharon M., and Susan A. McDaniel. 1995. "Ageing Women and Standards of Beauty." Pp. 97–122 in *Feminist Issues: Race, Class and Sexuality,* edited by Nancy Mandell. Scarborough, ON: Prentice Hall Canada.

Acharya, Menna. 2000. *Labor Market Developments and Poverty: With Focus on Economic Opportunities for Women.* Kathmandu, Nepal: Tanka Prasad Acharya Foundation/FES.

Adam, Barry D. 1995. *The Rise of a Gay and Lesbian Movement.* Rev. ed. New York: Twayne.

Adamson, Nancy, Linda Briskin, and Margaret McPhail. 1998. *Feminist Organizing for Change: The Contemporary Women's Movement in Canada.* Toronto: Oxford University Press.

Adler, Patricia A., and Peter Adler. 1998. *Peer Power: Preadolescent Culture and Identity.* New Brunswick, NJ: Rutgers University Press.

Adler, Patricia A., Peter Adler, and John M. Johnson. 1992. "Street Corner Society Revisited: New Questions about Old Issues." *Journal of Contemporary Ethnography* 21(April):3–10.

Adler, Patricia A., Steven J. Kless, and Peter Adler. 1992. "Socialization to Gender Roles: Popularity among Elementary School Boys and Girls." *Sociology of Education* 65(July): 169–187.

Africa News Service. 1998. "CPJ's 10 Enemies of the Press." Retrieved October 8, 2000 (http://www.elibrary.com).

AIDS Alert. 1999. "AIDS Complacency Leads Back to Risk Behavior." November 14, 127–128.

Akers, Ronald L. 1997. *Criminological Theories: Introduction and Evaluation.* 2nd ed. Los Angeles, CA: Roxbury Publishing Co.

Alain, Michel. 1985. "An Empirical Validation of Relative Deprivation." *Human Relations* 38(8):739–749.

Albarracin, Dolores, Martin Fishbein, and Eva Goldstein de Muchinik. 1997. "Seeking Social Support in Old Age as a Reasoned Action: Structural and Volitional Determinants in a Middle-Aged Sample of Argentinean Women." *Journal of Applied Social Psychology* 27:463–476.

Albas, Daniel, and Cheryl Albas. 1988. "Aces and Bombers: The Post-exam Impression Management Strategies of Students." *Symbolic Interaction* 11(Fall):289–302.

Albrecht, Gary L., Katerine D. Steelman, and Michael Bury. 2001. *Handbook of Disabilities Study.* Thousand Oaks, CA: Sage.

Alfino, Mark, John S. Carpeto, and Robin Wyngard. 1998. *McDonaldization Revisited: Critical Essays on Consumer Culture.* Westport, CT: Praeger.

Allen, Bem P. 1978. *Social Behavior: Fact and Falsehood.* Chicago: Nelson-Hall.

Allen, John L. 2001. *Student Atlas of World Geography.* 2nd ed. Chicago: McGraw-Hill/ Dushkin.

———. 2003. *Student Atlas of World Geography.* 3rd ed. New York: McGraw-Hill.

Allport, Gordon W. 1979. *The Nature of Prejudice.* 25th anniversary ed. Reading, MA: Addison-Wesley.

Alonzo, Angelo A. 1989. "Health and Illness and the Definition of the Situation: An Interactionist Perspective." Presented at the annual meeting of the Society for the Study of Social Problems, Berkeley, CA.

Alvord, Lori Arviso, and Elizabeth Cohen Van Pelt. 1999. *The Scalpel and the Silver Bear.* New York: Bantam.

Amato, Paul, and Alan Booth. 1997. *A Generation at Risk.* Cambridge, MA: Harvard University Press.

Amazon.com. 2001. "About Amazon.com." Retrieved September 20, 2001 (http://www.amazon.com).

Ambert, Anne-Marie. 2002. "The Changing Experience of Childhood." *Canadian Journal of Sociology* 27(2). Retrieved February 1, 2003 (http://www.cjsonline.ca/backiss/cjsjan feb.03.html).

American Bar Association. 1999. "Commission on Domestic Violence." Retrieved July 20, 1999 (http://www.abanet.org/domviol/stats.html).

American Humane Association. 1999. "Child Abuse and Neglect Data." Retrieved July 20, 1999 (http://www.Americanhumane.org/cpfactdata.htm).

American Society of Plastic Surgeons. 2002. "National Clearinghouse of Plastic Surgery Statistics." Retrieved February 1, 2002 (http://www.plasticsurgery.org/mediactr/stats_ncs.htm).

———. 2005. "National Plastic Surgery Statistics: Cosmetic and Reconstructive Procedure Trends." Retrieved October 23, 2005 (http://www.plasticsurgery.org/public_education/2004Statistics.cfm).

Anderssen, Erin, Michael Valpy, et al. 2004. *The New Canada: A Globe and Mail Report on the Next Generation.* Toronto: McClelland and Stewart.

Andersen, Margaret. 1997. *Thinking about Women: Sociological Perspectives on Sex and Gender.* 4th ed. Boston: Allyn and Bacon.

Anderson, Elijah, and Molly Moore. 1993. "The Burden of Womanhood." *Washington Post National Weekly Edition,* March 22–28, 6–7, 33–45.

Angier, Natalie. 1998. "Drugs, Sports, Body Image and G.I. Joe." *New York Times,* December 22, D1, D3.

Appelbaum, Richard, and Peter Dreier. 1999. "The Campus Anti-sweatshops Movement." *The American Prospect* (September–October): 71–78.

Armer, J. Michael, and John Katsillis. 1992. "Modernization Theory." Pp. 1299–1304 in *Encyclopedia of Sociology.* Vol. 4, edited by Edgar F. Borgatta and Marie L. Borgatta. New York: Macmillan.

Armstrong, Jane. 2002. "Canada Is 30 Million, but Will That Last?" *The Globe and Mail,* March 13, A1, A7.

Aronowitz, Stanley, and William Di Fazio. 1994. *The Jobless Future: Sci-Tech and Dogma of Work.* Minneapolis: University of Minneapolis.

Aronson, Elliot. 1999. *The Social Animal.* 8th ed. New York: Worth.
Ashley, David, and Michael Orenstein. 1998. *Sociological Theory.* 4th ed. Boston: Allyn and Bacon.
Associated Press. 2001. "Member of the Dwindling Shaker Sect." *Chicago Tribune,* June 20, 11.
———. 1998. "Environmental Test Case Averted." *Christian Science Monitor,* September 21, p. 18.
Association of Universities and Colleges of Canada. 2001. "About Canada's Universities." Retrieved July 28, 2001 (http://www.aucc.ca/en/acuindex.html).
Atchley, Robert C. 1985. *The Social Forces in Later Life: An Introduction to Social Gerontology.* 4th ed. Belmont, CA: Wadsworth.
Augustine, Noah. 2000. "Grandfather Was a Knowing Christian." *Toronto Star,* August 9, A17.
Axtell, Roger E. 1990. *Do's and Taboos around the World.* 2nd ed. New York: John Wiley and Sons.
Azumi, Koya, and Jerald Hage. 1972. *Organizational Systems.* Lexington, MA: Heath.

B

Bachrach, Christine A. 1986. "Adoption Plans, Adopted Children, and Adoptive Mothers." *Journal of Marriage and the Family* 48(May): 243–253.
Baer, Douglas, James Curtis, and Edward Grabb. 2000. "Has Voluntary Association Activity Declined? A Cross-National Perspective." Paper presented at the annual meeting of the American Sociological Association, Washington, DC.
Bainbridge, William Sims. 1999. "Cyberspace: Sociology's Natural Domain." *Contemporary Sociology* 28(November):664–667.
Baker, Maureen. 2001. "The Future of Family Life." Pp. 285–302 in *Families: Changing Trends in Canada.* 4th ed., edited by Maureen Baker. Toronto: McGraw-Hill Ryerson.
Baker, Therese L. 1999. *Doing Social Research.* 3rd ed. New York: McGraw-Hill.
Barron, Milton L. 1953. "Minority Group Characteristics of the Aged in American Society." *Journal of Gerontology* 8:477–482.
Basso, Keith H. 1972. "Ice and Travel among the Fort Norman Slave: Folk Taxonomies and Cultural Rules." *Language in Society* 1(March):31–49.
Bauerlein, Monika. 1996. "The Luddites Are Back." *Utne Reader* (March–April), pp. 24, 26.
Bauman, Kurt J. 1999. "Extended Measures of Well-Being: Meeting Basic Needs." *Current Population Reports,* ser. P70, no. 67. Washington, DC: U.S. Government Printing Office.
Beach, Charles M., and Christopher Worswick. 1993. "Is There a Double-Negative Effect on the Earnings of Immigrant Women?" *Canadian Public Policy* 19(1):36–53.
Beaujot, Roderic, Ellen M. Gee, Fernando Rajulton, and Zenaida R. Ravanera. 1995. *Family over the Life Course.* Ottawa: Minister of Industry.
Becker, Anne E. 1995. *Body, Self, and Society: The View from Fiji.* Philadelphia: University of Pennsylvania Press.
Becker, Anne E., and R.A. Burwell. 1999. "Acculturation and Disordered Eating in Fiji." Presented at the annual meeting of the American Psychiatric Association.
Becker, Howard S. 1952. "Social Class Variations in the Teacher–Pupil Relationship." *Journal of Educational Sociology* 25(April):451–465.
———. 1963. *The Outsiders: Studies in the Sociology of Deviance.* New York: Free Press.
———, ed. 1964. *The Other Side: Perspectives on Deviance.* New York: Free Press.
———. 1973. *The Outsiders: Studies in the Sociology of Deviance.* Rev. ed. New York: Free Press.
Beeghley, Leonard. 1978. *Social Stratification in America: A Critical Analysis of Theory and Research.* Santa Monica, CA: Goodyear Publishing.
Begley, Sharon. 1998. "Why Wilson's Wrong." *Newsweek,* June 22, 61–62.
———. 1999. "Designer Babies." *Newsweek,* November 9, 61–62.
Bélanger, Alain. 1999. *Report of the Demographic Situation in Canada 1997.* Ottawa: Minister of Industry.
Bell, Daniel. 1999. *The Coming of Post-industrial Society: A Venture in Social Forecasting.* With new foreword. New York: Basic Books.
Belsie, Laurent. 2000. "Strange Webfellows." *Christian Science Monitor,* March 2, 15–16.
———. 1998. "Genetic Research Data Will Double Annually." *Christian Science Monitor,* July 30, B4.
Bender, William, and Margaret Smith. 1997. "Population, Food, and Nutrition." *Population Bulletin* 51(February).
Bendix, B. Reinhard. 1968. "Max Weber." Pp. 493–502 in *International Encyclopedia of the Social Sciences,* edited by David L. Sills. New York: Macmillan.
Benford, Robert D. 1992. "Social Movements." Pp. 1880–1887 in *Encyclopedia of Sociology.* Vol. 4, edited by Edgar F. Borgatta and Marie L. Borgatta. New York: Macmillan.
Berger, Peter, and Thomas Luckmann. 1966. *The Social Construction of Reality.* New York: Doubleday.
Berkeley Wellness Letter. 1990. "The Nest Refilled." 6(February):1–2.
Bernstein, Anne C. 1988. "Unraveling the Tangles: Children's Understanding of Stepfamily Kinship." Pp. 83–111 in *Relative Strangers: Studies of Step-Family* Press, edited by W.R. Beer. Totowa, NJ: Rowan and Liten Field.
Bernstein, Richard. 2003. "An Aging Eruope May Find Itself on the Sidelines." *New York Times,* June 29, 3.
Berlin, Brent, and Paul Kay. 1991. *Basic Color Terms: Their Universality and Evolution.* Berkeley, CA: University of California Press.
Best, Fred, and Ray Eberhard. 1990. "Education for the 'Era of the Adult.'" *The Futurist* 21(May–June):23–28.
Bharadwaj, Lakshmik. 1992. "Human Ecology." Pp. 848–867 in *Encyclopedia of Sociology.* Vol. 2, edited by Edgar F. Borgatta and Marie L. Borgatta. New York: Macmillan.
Bianchi, Suzanne M., and Daphne Spain. 1996. "Women, Work, and Family in America." *Population Bulletin* 51(December).
Bibby, Reginald W. 1990. *Mosaic Madness.* Toronto: Stoddart.
———. 1995. *The Bibby Report: Social Trends Canadian Style.* Toronto: Stoddart.
———. 2004. "Ethos versus Ethics: Canada and the U.S. and Homosexuality." Annual meeting of the Pacific Sociological Association, San Francisco, April 2004.
Bielby, William T., and Denise D. Bielby. 1992. "I Will Follow Him: Family Ties, Gender-Role Beliefs, and Reluctance to Relocate for a Better Job." *American Journal of Sociology* 97(March):1241–1267.
Bielby, Denise D., and William T. Bielby. 2002. "Hollywood Dreams, Harsh Realities: Writing for Film and Television." *Contexts* 1(Fall/Winter):21–25.
Bishop-Stall, Shaughnessy. 2004. *Down to This: Squalor and Splendour in a Big-City Shantytown.* Toronto: Random House of Canada.
Black, Donald. 1995. "The Epistemology of Pure Sociology." *Law and Social Inquiry* 20 (Summer):829–870.
Black, Naomi. 1993. "The Canadian Women's Movement: The Second Wave." Pp. 151–176 in *Changing Patterns: Women in Canada.* 2nd ed., edited by Sandra Burt, Lorraine Code, and Lindsay Dorney. Toronto: McClelland and Stewart.
Blanc, Ann Klimas. 1984. "Nonmarital Cohabitation and Fertility in the United States and Western Europe." *Population Research and Policy Review* 3:181–193.
Blanchard, Fletcher A., Teri Lilly, and Leigh Ann Vaughn. 1991. "Reducing the Expression of Racial Prejudice." *Psychological Science* 2(March):101–105.
Blanco, Robert. 1998. "The Disappearance of Mom and Dad." *USA Today,* December 17, D1.
Blau, Peter M., and Marshall W. Meyer. 1987. *Bureaucracy in Modern Society.* 3rd ed. New York: Random House.
Blauner, Robert. 1972. *Racial Oppression in America.* New York: Harper and Row.
Bluestone, Barry, and Bennett Harrison. 1982. *The Deindustrialization of America.* New York: Basic Books.
Blumer, Herbert. 1969. *Symbolic Interactionism: Perspective and Method.* Englewood Cliffs, NJ: Prentice-Hall.

———. 1955. "Collective Behavior." Pp. 165–198 in *Principles of Sociology.* 2nd ed., edited by Alfred McClung Lee. New York: Barnes and Noble.

Boaz, Rachel Floersheim. 1987. "Early Withdrawal from the Labor Force." *Research on Aging* 9(December):530–547.

Bobo, Lawrence. 1991. "Social Responsibility, Individualism, and Redistribution Policies." *Sociological Forum* 6:71–92.

Booth, William. 2000. "Has Our Can-Do Attitude Peaked?" *Washington Post National Weekly Edition,* February 7, 29.

Bornschier, Volker, Christopher Chase-Dunn, and Richard Rubinson. 1978. "Cross-National Evidence of the Effects of Foreign Investment and Aid on Economic Growth and Inequality: A Survey of Findings and a Reanalysis." *American Journal of Sociology* 84(November): 651–683.

Boston Women's Health Book Collective. 1969. *Our Bodies, Ourselves.* Boston: New England Free Press.

———. 1992. *The New Our Bodies, Ourselves.* New York: Touchstone.

Bottomore, Tom, and Maximilien Rubel, eds. 1956. *Karl Marx: Selected Writings in Sociology and Social Philosophy.* New York: McGraw-Hill.

Bouvier, Leon F. 1980. "America's Baby Boom Generation: The Fateful Bulge." *Population Bulletin* 35(April).

Bowles, Samuel, and Herbert Gintis. 1976. *Schooling in Capitalist America: Educational Reforms and the Contradictions of Economic Life.* New York: Basic Books.

Bowles, Scott. 1999. "Fewer Violent Fatalities in Schools." *USA Today,* April 28, 4A.

Boyd, Monica. 1992. "Gender, Visible Minority, and Immigrant Earnings Inequality: Reassessing Employment Equity Premise." Pp. 279–321 in *Deconstructing a Nation: Immigration, Multiculturalism and Racism in '90s Canada,* edited by Vic Satzewch. Halifax: Fernwood Publishing.

———. 1984. "At a Disadvantage: The Occupational Attainments of Foreign-Born Women in Canada." *International Migration Review* 18(4):1091–1119.

Boyd, Monica, and Edward Pryor. 1990. "Young Adults Living in Their Parents' Home." Pp. 188–191 in *Canadian Social Trends,* edited by C. McKie and K. Thompson. Toronto: Thompson Educational Press.

Brand, Dionne. 1993. "A Working Paper on Black Women In Toronto: Gender, Race, and Class." Pp. 220–241 in *Returning the Gaze: Essays on Racism, Feminism and Politics,* edited by Himani Bannerji. Toronto: Sister Vision Press.

Brandon, Karen. 1995. "Computer Scrutiny Adds to Furor over Immigrants." *Chicago Tribune,* December 5, 1, 16.

Brannigan, Augustine. 1992. "Postmodernism." Pp. 1522–1525 in *Encyclopedia of Sociology.* Vol. 3, edited by Edgar F. Borgatta and Marie L. Borgatta. New York: Macmillan.

Brannon, Robert. 1976. "Ideology, Myth, and Reality: Sex Equality in Israel." *Sex Roles* 6:403–419.

Brasfield, Charles R. 2001. "Residential School Syndrome." *BC Medical Journal* 43(2):78–81.

Braxton, Greg, and Dana Calvo. 2002. "Networks Come under the Gun as Watchdogs Aim for Diversity." *Chicago Tribune,* June 4, sec. 5, p. 2.

Bray, James H., and John Kelly. 1999. *Stepfamilies: Love, Marriage, and Parenting in the First Decade.* New York: Broadway Books.

Brint, Steven. 1998. *Schools and Societies.* Thousand Oaks, CA: Pine Forge Press.

Brockerhoff, Martin P. 2000. "An Urbanizing World." *Population Bulletin* 55(September).

Brown, Robert McAfee. 1980. *Gustavo Gutierrez.* Atlanta: John Knox.

Brundtland, Gro Harlem. 2001. "Affordable AIDS Drugs Are Within Reach." *International Herald Tribune.* Retrieved March 1 (http://www.who.int/inf-pr-2001/en/note2001-02.html).

Bruni, Frank. 1998. "A Small-but-Growing Sorority Is Giving Birth to Children for Gay Men." *New York Times,* June 25, A12.

Bryant, Adam. 1999. "American Pay Rattles Foreign Partners." *New York Times,* January 17, 1, 4.

Bryant, Bunyan, and Paul Mohai, eds. 1992. *Race and the Incidence of Environmental Hazards.* Boulder, CO: Westview Press.

Buckley, Stephen. 1997. "Left Behind Prosperity's Door." *Washington Post National Weekly Edition,* March 24, 8–9.

Buechler, Steven M. 2000. *Social Movements in Advanced Capitalism: The Political Economy and Cultural Construction of Social Activism.* New York: Oxford University Press.

Bula, Francis. 2000. "This Is an International Crisis." *Vancouver Sun,* November 21, A1, A6.

Bullard, Robert. 1990. *Dumping in Dixie: Race, Class, and Environmental Quality.* Boulder, CO: Westview Press.

Bulle, Wolfgang F. 1987. *Crossing Cultures? Southeast Asian Mainland.* Atlanta: Centers for Disease Control.

Bunzel, John H. 1992. *Race Relations on Campus: Stanford Students Speak.* Stanford, CA: Portable Stanford.

Bureau of Labor Statistics. 2001. *Highlights of Women's Earnings in 2000 Report.* Washington, DC: U.S. Government Printing Office.

Bureau of the Census. 1975. *Historical Statistics of the United States, Colonial Times to 1970.* Washington, DC: U.S. Government Printing Office.

———. 1997a. *Statistical Abstract of the United States, 1997.* Washington, DC: U.S. Government Printing Office.

———. 1997b. "Geographical Mobility: March 1995 to March 1996." *Current Population Reports,* ser. P-20, no. 497. Washington, DC: U.S. Government Printing Office.

———. 1999. *Statistical Abstract of the United States, 1996.* Washington, DC: U.S. Government Printing Office.

———. 2000. "National Population Projections." Retrieved May 11, 2000 (http://www.census.gov/population/www/projection/natsum-T3html).

Burgess, Ernest W. 1925. "The Growth of the City." Pp. 47–62 in *The City,* edited by Robert E. Park, Ernest W. Burgess, and Roderick D. McKenzie. Chicago: University of Chicago Press.

Butterfield, Fox. 1996. "U.S. Has Plan to Broaden Availability of DNA Testing." *New York Times,* June 14, A8.

Butler, Daniel Allen. 1998. *"Unsinkable:" The Full Story.* Mechanicsburg, PA: Stackpole Books.

Butler, Robert N. 1990. "A Disease Called Ageism." *Journal of American Geriatrics Society* 38(February):178–180.

C

Calhoun, Craig. 1998. "Community without Propinquity Revisited." *Sociological Inquiry* 68(Summer):373–397.

Calhoun, David B. 2000. "Learning at Home." P. 193 in *Yearbook of the Encyclopedia Britannica 2000.* Chicago: Encyclopedia Britannica.

Calliste, Agnes. 2001. "Black Families in Canada. Exploring the Interconnections of Race, Class and Gender." Pp. 401–419 in *Family Patterns, Gender Relations,* edited by Bonnie J. Fox. Toronto: Oxford University Press.

Campaign 2000. 2004. "Poor Jobs, Modest Social Investments Drive up Child Poverty in Canada." Retrieved November 24, 2004 (http://action.web.ca/home/c2000/alerts.shtml?x=70077).

Camus, Albert. 1948. *The Plague.* New York: Random House.

Canadian Broadcasting Corporation (CBC). 2000. *Stockwell Day's New Alliance.* Retrieved April 5, 2002 (http://www.cbc.ca/insidecbc/newsinreview/Sep2000/stockwell/separation.htm).

———. 2005. "Police Stop More Blacks, Ont. Study Finds." Retrieved May 27, 2005 (http://www.cbc.ca/story/canada/national/2005/05/26/race050526.html).

Canada Citizens' Forum on Canada's Future. 1991. *Report to the People and Government of Canada.* Ottawa: Minister of Supply and Services Canada.

Canadian Education Statistics Council (CESC). 2000. *Education Indicators in Canada: Report of the Pan-Canadian Education Indicators Program 1999.* Ottawa: Statistics Canada and Council of Ministers of Education Canada.

Canadian Institute for Health Information (CIHI). 1999. *Supply and Distribution of Registered Nurses in Canada.* Ottawa: Canadian Institute for Health Information.

———. 2000. *Health Care in Canada 2000: First Annual Report.* Retrieved April 20, 2000 (http://secure.cihi.ca/cihiweb/products/Healthreport2000.pdf).

———. 2001. *Health Care in Canada 2001.* Retrieved January 27, 2002 (http://www.cihi.ca/HealthReport2001.pdf).

———. 2005. *Health Expenditures by Source of Finance, Canada 1975 to 2004.* Retrieved September 26, 2005 (http://secure.cihi.ca/cihiweb/en/media).

Caplan, Ronald L. 1989. "The Commodification of American Health Care." *Social Science and Medicine* 28(11):1139–1148.

Carey, Anne R., and Elys A. McLean. 1997. "Heard It through the Grapevine?" *USA Today,* September 15, B1.

Carey, Anne R., and Jerry Mosemak. 1999. "Big on Religion." *USA Today,* April 1, D1.

Carty, Win. 1999. "Greater Dependence on Cars Leads to More Pollution in World's Cities." *Population Today* 27(December):1–2.

Casper, Lynne M., and Loretta E. Bass. 1998. "Voting and Registration in the Election of November 1996." *Current Population Reports,* ser. P-20, no. 504. Washington, DC: U.S. Government Printing Office.

Castells, Manuel. 1983. *The City and the Grass Roots.* Berkeley: University of California Press.

———. 1996. *The Information Age: Economy, Society and Culture.* Vol. 1 of *The Rise of the Network Society.* London: Blackwell.

———. 1997. *The Power of Identity.* Vol. 1 of *The Information Age: Economy, Society and Culture.* London: Blackwell.

———. 1998. *End of Millennium.* Vol. 3 of *The Information Age: Economy, Society and Culture.* London: Blackwell.

———. 2000. *The Information Age: Economy, Society and Culture* (3 vols.). 2nd. ed. Oxford and Malden, MA: Blackwell.

———. 2001. *The Internet Galaxy: Reflections on the Internet, Business, and Society.* New York: Oxford University Press.

Catalyst. 1998. *The Catalyst Census of Women Board Directors in Canada.* Toronto: Catalyst.

CBS News. 1979. Transcript of *Sixty Minutes* segment "I Was Only Following Orders." March 31, pp. 2–8.

———. 1998. "Experimental Prison." *Sixty Minutes.* June 30.

Centers for Disease Control and Prevention. 2002. "Need for Sustained HIV Prevention among Men Who Have Sex with Men." Retrieved January 23, 2004 (http://www.cdc.gov/hiv/pubs/facts/msm.htm).

Cetron, Marvin J., and Owen Davies. 1991. "Trends Shaping the World." *Futurist* 20 (September–October):11–21.

Cha, Ariena Eunjung. 2000. "Painting a Portrait of Dot-Camaraderie." *Washington Post,* October 26, E1, E10.

Chaddock, Gail Russell. 1998. "The Challenge for Schools: Connecting Adults with Kids." *Christian Science Monitor,* August 4, p. B7.

Chalfant, H. Paul, Robert E. Beckley, and C. Eddie Palmer. 1994. *Religion in Contemporary Society.* 3rd ed. Itasca, IL: F.E. Peacock.

Chambliss, William. 1972. "Introduction." Pp. ix–xi in *Box Man,* by Henry King. New York: Harper and Row.

———. 1973. "The Saints and the Roughnecks." *Society* 11(November–December):24–31.

Chan, R.W., B. Rayboy and C.J. Patterson. 1998. "Psychological Adjustment among Children Conceived via Donor Insemination by Lesbian and Heterosexual Mothers." *Child Development* 69:443–457.

Charmaz, Kathy, and Debora A. Paterniti, eds. 1999. *Health, Illness, and Healing: Society, Social Context, and Self.* Los Angeles, CA: Roxbury.

Charter, David, and Jill Sherman. 1996. "Schools Must Teach New Code of Values." *London Times,* January 15, p. 1.

Chase-Dunn, Christopher, and Peter Grimes. 1995. "World-Systems Analysis." Pp. 387–417 in *Annual Review of Sociology, 1995,* edited by John Hagan. Palo Alto, CA: Annual Reviews.

Chase-Dunn, Christopher, Yukio Kawano, and Benjamin D. Brewer. 2000. "Trade Globalization since 1795: Waves of Integration in the World System." *American Sociological Review* 65 (February):77–95.

Cheng, Wei-yuan, and Lung-li Liao. 1994. "Women Managers in Taiwan." Pp. 143–159 in *Competitive Frontiers: Women Managers in a Global Economy,* edited by Nancy J. Adler and Dafna N. Izraeli. Cambridge, MA: Blackwell Business.

Cherlin, Andrew J. 1999. *Public and Private Families: An Introduction.* 2nd ed. New York: McGraw-Hill.

Cherlin, Andrew J., and Frank Furstenberg. 1992. *The New American Grandparent: A Place in the Family, A Life Apart.* Cambridge, MA: Harvard University Press.

Chiang, Frances. 2001. "The Intersection of Class, Race, Ethnicity, Gender, and Migration: A Case Study of Hong Kong Chinese Immigrant Women Entrepreneurs in Richmond, British Columbia." Unpublished Ph.D. thesis, University of British Columbia.

Chicago Tribune. 1997. "In London, Prince Meets a Pauper, an Ex-Classmate." December 5, p. 19.

Childcare Resource and Research Unit. 2000. *Early Childhood Care and Education in Canada, Provinces and Territories 1998.* Toronto: Centre for Urban and Community Studies, University of Toronto.

Children Now. 2002. *Fall Colors: 2001–02 Prime Time Diversity Report.* Los Angeles: Children Now.

Christensen, Kathleen. 1990. "Bridges over Troubled Water: How Older Workers View the Labor Market." Pp. 175–207 in *Bridges to Retirement,* edited by Peter B. Doeringer. Ithaca, NY: IRL Press.

Citizenship and Immigration Canada. 2001. *Pursuing Canada's Commitment to Immigration: The Immigration Plan for 2002.* Cat. no. Ci51-105/2001. October. Ottawa: Minister of Works and Government Services.

Civic Ventures. 1999. *The New Face of Retirement: Older Americans, Civic Engagement, and the Longevity Revolution.* Washington, DC: Peter D. Hart Research Associates.

Clark, Andy. 2005. "Making Poverty History?" Radio Netherlands. Retrieved November 10, 2005 (http://www2.rnw.nl/rnw/en/features/amsterdamforum/050618af?view=standard).

Clark, Burton, and Martin Trow. 1966. "The Organizational Context." Pp. 17–70 in *The Study of College Peer Groups,* edited by Theodore M. Newcomb and Everett K. Wilson. Chicago: Aldine.

Clark, Campbell. 2005. "G8 Boosts Africa Aid by $25-Billion." *The Globe and Mail,* July 9. Retrieved July 9, 2005 (http://www.globeandmail.com).

Clark, Thomas. 1994. "Culture and Objectivity." *The Humanist* 54(August):38–39.

Cleveland, Gordon, and Michael Krashinsky. 1998. *The Benefit and Costs of Good Child Care.* Toronto: Childcare Resource and Research Unit, Univeristy of Toronto.

Cloward, Richard A. 1959. "Illegitimate Means, Anomie, and Deviant Behavior." *American Sociological Review* 24(April):164–176.

Cockerham, William C. 1998. *Medical Sociology.* 7th ed. Upper Saddle River, NJ: Prentice-Hall.

Code, Lorraine. 1993. "Feminist Theory." Pp. 19–57 in *Changing Patterns: Women in Canada.* 2nd ed., edited by Sandra Burt, Lorraine Code, and Lindsay Dorney. Toronto: McClelland and Stewart.

Cohen, David, ed. 1991. *The Circle of Life: Ritual from the Human Family Album.* San Francisco: Harper.

Cohen, Lawrence E., and Marcus Felson. 1979. "Social Change and Crime Rate Trends: A Routine Activities Approach." *American Sociological Review* 44:588–608.

Cole, Elizabeth S. 1985. "Adoption, History, Policy, and Program." Pp. 638–666 in *A Handbook of Child Welfare,* edited by John Laird and Ann Hartman. New York: Free Press.

Cole, Mike. 1988. *Bowles and Gintis Revisited: Correspondence and Contradiction in Educational Theory.* Philadelphia: Falmer.

Collier, Jane, Michelle Rosaldo, and Sylvia Yanagisako. 2001. "Is There a Family? New Anthropological Views." Pp. 11–21 in *Family Patterns, Gender Relations.* 2nd ed., edited by Bonnie J. Fox. Toronto: Oxford University Press.

Collins, Gail. 1998. "Why the Women Are Fading Away." *New York Times,* October 25, 54–55.

Collins, Patricia Hill. 1998. *Fighting Words: Black Women and the Search for Justice.* Minneapolis: University of Minnesota.

Collins, Randall. 1975. *Conflict Sociology: Toward an Explanatory Sociology.* New York: Academic.

———. 1980. "Weber's Last Theory of Capitalism: A Systematization." *American Sociological Review* 45(December):925–942.

Comack, Elizabeth. 1996. *Women in Trouble.* Halifax: Fernwood Publishing.

Commoner, Barry. 1971. *The Closing Circle.* New York: Knopf.

———. 1990. *Making Peace with the Planet.* New York: Pantheon.

Communications Canada. 2001. "Facts on Canada." Retrieved April 11, 2001 (http://www.infocan.gc.ca/facts/multi_e.html).

ComQuest Research Group. 1993. *Lifestyles Television Focus Group Report.* Vancouver: Bureau of Broadcast Measurement.

Comstock, P., and M.B. Fox. 1994. "Employer Tactics and Labor Law Reform." Pp. 90–109 in *Restoring the Promise of American Labor Law,* edited by S. Friedman, R.W. Hurd, R.A. Oswald, and R.L. Seeber. Ithaca, NY: ILR Press.

Connidis, Ingrid A. 1989. *Family Ties and Ageing.* Toronto: Butterworths.

Conrad, Peter, ed. 1997. *The Sociology of Health and Illness: Critical Perspectives.* 5th ed. New York: St. Martin's.

Conrad, Peter, and Joseph W. Schneider. 1992. *Deviance and Medicalization: From Badness to Sickness.* Expanded ed. Philadelphia: Temple University Press.

Cooley, Charles H. 1902. *Human Nature and the Social Order.* New York: Scribner.

Corak, Miles, and Andrew Heisz. 1996. *The Intergenerational Income Mobility of Canadian Men.* Analytical Studies branch no. 89. Ottawa: Statistics Canada.

Coser, Lewis A. 1956. *The Functions of Social Conflict.* New York: Free Press.

———. 1977. *Masters of Sociological Thought: Ideas in Historical and Social Context.* 2nd ed. New York: Harcourt, Brace and Jovanovich.

Côté, James E., and Anton L. Allahar. 1994. *Generation on Hold: Coming of Age in the Late Twentieth Century.* Toronto: Stoddart.

Couch, Carl. 1996. *Information Technologies and Social Orders.* Edited with an introduction by David R. Maines and Shing-Ling Chien. New York: Aldine de Gruyter.

Council of Canadians. 2004. *Annual Report, 2004.* Ottawa: Council of Canadians. Retrieved January 9, 2006 (http://www.canadians.org/documents/wcp05_pg9.pdf).

Cox, Kevin. 2001. "Nova Scotia Gay Couple Given Legal Recognition." *The Globe and Mail,* June 5, A5.

Cox, Oliver C. 1948. *Caste, Class and Race: A Study in Social Dynamics.* Detroit: Wayne State University Press.

Creese, Gillian. 1999. *Contracting Masculinity: Gender, Class and Race in a White-Collar Union, 1944–1994.* Toronto: Oxford Univeristy Press.

Creese, Gillian, Neil Guppy, and Martin Meissner. 1991. *Ups and Downs on the Ladder of Success: Social Mobility in Canada.* Ottawa: Statistics Canada.

Crenshaw, Edward M., Matthew Christenson, and Doyle Ray Oakey. 2000. "Demographic Transition in Ecological Focus." *American Sociological Review* 65(June):371–391.

Cressey, Donald R. 1960. "Epidemiology and Individual Contact: A Case from Criminology." *Pacific Sociological Review* 3(Fall):47–58.

Cromwell, Paul F., James N. Olson, and D'Aunn Wester Avarey. 1995. *Breaking and Entering: An Ethnographic Analysis of Burglary.* Newbury Park, CA: Sage.

Crouse, Kelly. 1999. "Sociology of the Titanic." *Teaching Sociology Listserv.* May 24.

Cuff, E.C., W.W. Sharrock, and D.W. Francis, eds. 1990. *Perspectives in Sociology.* 3rd ed. Boston: Unwin Hyman.

Cullen, Francis T., Jr., and John B. Cullen. 1978. *Toward a Paradigm of Labeling Theory,* ser. 58. Lincoln: University of Nebraska Studies.

Cumming, Elaine, and William E. Henry. 1961. *Growing Old: The Process of Disengagement.* New York: Basic Books.

Currie, Elliot. 1985. *Confronting Crime: An American Challenge.* New York: Pantheon.

———. 1998. *Crime and Punishment in America.* New York: Metropolitan Books.

Curry, Timothy Jon. 1993. "A Little Pain Never Hurt Anyone: Athletic Career Socialization and the Normalization of Sports Injury." *Symbolic Interaction* 26(Fall):273–290.

Cushman, John H., Jr. 1998. "Pollution Policy Is Unfair Burden, States Tell E.P.A." *New York Times,* May 10, 1, 20.

Cussins, Choris M. 1998. In *Cyborg Babies: From Techno-Sex to Techno-Tots,* edited by Robbie Davis-Floyd and Joseph Dumit. New York: Routledge.

D

Dahl, Robert A. 1961. *Who Governs?* New Haven, CT: Yale University Press.

Dahrendorf, Ralf. 1958. "Toward a Theory of Social Conflict." *Journal of Conflict Resolution* 2(June):170–183.

———. 1959. *Class and Class Conflict in Industrial Sociology.* Stanford, CA: Stanford University Press.

Daley, Suzanne. 2000. "French Couples Take Plunge That Falls Short of Marriage." *New York Times,* April 18, A1, A4.

Dalfen, Ariel, K. 2000. "Cyberaddicts in Cyberspace? Internet Addiction Disorder." *Wellness Options* (Winter):38–39.

Daniels, Arlene Kaplan. 1987. "Invisible Work." *Social Problems* 34 (December):403–415.

———. 1988. *Invisible Careers.* Chicago: University of Chicago Press.

Davies, Christie. 1989. "Goffman's Concept of the Total Institution: Criticisms and Revisions." *Human Studies* 12(June):77–95.

Davis, Darren W. 1997. "The Direction of Race of Interviewer Effects among African-Americans: Donning the Black Mask." *American Journal of Political Science* 41 (January):309–322.

Davis, James Allan, and Tom W. Smith. 1999. *General Social Surveys, 1972–1998.* Storrs, CT: The Roper Center.

———. 2001. *General Social Surveys, 1972–2000.* Storrs, CT: The Roper Center.

Davis, James A., Tom W. Smith, and Peter V. Marsden. 2003. *General Social Surveys, 1972–2002: Cumulative Codebook.* Chicago: NORC.

Davis, Kingsley. 1937. "The Sociology of Prostitution." *American Sociological Review* 2(October):744–755.

———. 1940. "Extreme Social Isolation of a Child." *American Journal of Sociology* 45(January):554–565.

———. 1947. "A Final Note on a Case of Extreme Isolation." *American Journal of Sociology* 52(March):432–437.

———. [1949] 1995. *Human Society.* Reprint. New York: Macmillan.

Davis, Kingsley, and Wilbert E. Moore. 1945. "Some Principles of Stratification." *American Sociological Review* 10(April):242–249.

Davis, Nanette J. 1975. *Sociological Constructions of Deviance: Perspectives and Issues in the Field.* Dubuque, IA: Wm. C. Brown.

Day, David M., Carol A. Golench, Jyl MacDougall, and Cheryl A. Beals-Gonzaléz. 1995. *School-Based Violence Prevention in Canada: Results of A National Survey of Policies and Programs.* Ottawa: Ministry of the Solicitor General: Supply and Services Canada. Retrieved December 16, 2001 (http://www.eurowrc.org/os/education/education_en/os.edu_en.html).

Deardorff, Kevin E., and Lisa M. Blumerman. 2001. "Evaluation Components of International Migration: Estimates of the Foreign-Born Population by Migrant States in 2000." Working Paper Series No. 58. Retrieved January 8, 2002 (http://www.census.gov/population/www/documentation/twps0058.html).

Death Penalty Information Center. 2000. "The Death Penalty in 1999: Year End Report." Retrieved February 13, 2000 (http://www.essential.org/dpic/yrendrpt99.html).

DeKeseredy, Walter S. 2001. "Patterns of Family Violence." Pp. 238–266 in *Families: Changing Trends in Canada.* 4th ed., edited by Maureen Baker. Toronto: McGraw-Hill Ryerson.

DeKeseredy, Walter S., and Martin D. Schwartz. 1998. *Woman Abuse on Campus: Results from the Canadian National Survey.* Thousand Oaks, CA: Sage Publications.

DePalma, Anthony. 1999. "Rules to Protect a Culture Make for Confusion." *New York Times,* July 14, B1, B2.

Department of Education. 1999. *Report on State Implementation of the Gun-Free Schools Act. School Year 1997–98.* Rockville, MD: Westat.

Department of Health and Human Services. 2000. *Total Numbers of Families and Recipients for 1st Quarter FY2002.* Retrieved June 14, 2002 (http://www.acf.dhhs.gov/news/stats/tanf.htm).

———. 2002. *Percent Change in AFDC/TANF Families and Recipients, August 1996-September 2002.* Retrieved June 14, 2002 (http://www.acf.dhhs.gov/news/stats/afdc.htm).

Derouin, Jodey Michael. 2004. "Asians and Multiculturalism in Canada's Three Major Cities: Some Evidence from the Ethnic Diversity Survey." Pp. 58–62 in *Our Diverse Cities.* Number 1, edited by Caroline Andrew. Ottawa: Metropolis Project.

DeSimone, Bonnie. 2000. "Gold Tendency." *Chicago Tribune Magazine,* February 20, pp. 9–19.

Devine, Don. 1972. *Political Culture of the United States: The Influence of Member Values on Regime Maintenance.* Boston: Little, Brown.

Devitt, James. 1999. *Framing Gender on the Campaign Trail: Women's Executive Leadership and the Press.* New York: Women's Leadership Conference.

Diani, Marie. 2000. "Social Movement Networks: Virtual and Real." *Information, Communication and Society.* Retrieved October 14, 2001 (http://www.infosoc.co.uk).

Dionne, Annette, Cecile, and Yvonne. 1997. "Letter." *Time,* December 1, p. 39.

Directors Guild of America. 2002. *Diversity Hiring Special Report.* Los Angeles: DGA.

Doeringer, Peter B., ed. 1990. *Bridges to Retirement: Older Workers in a Changing Labor Market.* Ithaca, NY: ILR Press.

Dolbeare, Kenneth M. 1982. *American Public Policy: A Citizen's Guide.* New York: McGraw-Hill.

Domhoff, G. William. 1978. *Who Really Rules? New Haven and Community Power Reexamined.* New Brunswick, NJ: Transaction.

———. 2001. *Who Rules America?* 4th ed. New York: McGraw-Hill.

Donohue, Elizabeth, Vincent Schiraldi, and Jason Ziedenberg. 1998. *School House Hype: School Shootings and Real Risks Kids Face in America.* New York: Justice Policy Institute.

Dorai, Frances. 1998. *Insight Guide: Singapore.* Singapore: Insight Media, APA Publications.

Doress, Irwin, and Jack Nusan Porter. 1977. *Kids in Cults: Why They Join, Why They Stay, Why They Leave.* Brookline, MA: Reconciliation Associates.

Dornbusch, Sanford M. 1989. "The Sociology of Adolescence." Pp. 233–259 in *Annual Review of Sociology, 1989,* edited by W. Richard Scott and Judith Blake. Palo Alto, CA: Annual Reviews.

Dotson, Floyd. 1991. "Community." P. 55 in *Encyclopedic Dictionary of Sociology.* 4th ed. Guilford, CT: Dushkin.

Dougherty, Kevin, and Floyd M. Hammack. 1992. "Education Organization." Pp. 535–541 in *Encyclopedia of Sociology.* Vol. 2, edited by Edgar F. Borgatta and Marie L. Borgatta. New York: Macmillan.

Douglas, Jack D. 1967. *The Social Meanings of Suicide.* Princeton, NJ: Princeton University Press.

Douthitt, Robin A., and Joanne Fedyk. 1990. *The Cost of Raising Children in Canada.* Toronto: Butterworths.

Dowd, James J. 1980. *Stratification among the Aged.* Monterey, CA: Brooks/Cole.

Downie, Andrew. 2000. "Brazilian Girls Turn to a Doll More Like Them." *Christian Science Monitor.* January 20. Retrieved January 20, 2000 (http://www.csmonitor.com/durable/2000/01/20/fpls3-csm.shtml).

Doyle, James A. 1995. *The Male Experience.* 3rd ed. Dubuque, IA: Brown & Benchmark.

Doyle, James A., and Michele A. Paludi. 1998. *Sex and Gender: The Human Experience.* 4th ed. New York: McGraw-Hill.

Drache, Daniel, and Terrence J. Sullivan, eds. 1999. "Health, Health Care and Social Cohesion." *Public Success, Private Failures: Market Limits in Health Reform.* Toronto: Routledge. Retrieved August 1, 2001 (http://www.founders.ner/fn/papers).

Drucker, Peter F. 1999. "Beyond the Information Revolution." *Atlantic Monthly* 284(October): 42–57.

Dua, Enakshi. 1999. "Introduction: Canadian Anti-racist Feminist Thought: Scratching the Surface of Racism." Pp. 7–31 in *Scratching the Surface: Canadian Anti-racist Feminist Thought,* edited by Enakshi Dua and Angela Robertson. Toronto: Women's Press.

Duberman, Lucille. 1976. *Social Inequality: Class and Caste in America.* Philadelphia: Lippincott.

Dugger, Celia W. 1999. "Massacres of Low-Born Touch off a Crisis in India." *New York Times,* March 15, A3.

Dumas, Jean. 1994. *Report on the Demographic Situation in Canada 1993.* Catalogue No. 91-209E. Ottawa: Statistics Canada.

Duneier, Mitchell. 1994a. "On the Job, but Behind the Scenes." *Chicago Tribune,* December 26, 1, 24.

———. 1994b. "Battling for Control." *Chicago Tribune,* December 28, 1, 8.

Dunlap, Riley E. 1993. "From Environmental to Ecological Problems." Pp. 707–738 in *Introduction to Social Problems,* edited by Craig Calhoun and George Ritzer. New York: McGraw-Hill.

Dunlap, Riley E., and William R. Catton, Jr. 1983. "What Environmental Sociologists Have in Common." *Sociological Inquiry* 53(Spring): 113–135.

Dupuis, Dave. 1998. "What Influences People's Plans to Have Children?" *Canadian Social Trends* Spring:2–5

Durkheim, Émile. [1893] 1933. *Division of Labor in Society.* Translated by George Simpson. Reprint, New York: Free Press.

———. [1912] 1947. *The Elementary Forms of the Religious Life.* Reprint, Glencoe, IL: Free Press.

———. [1897] 1951. *Suicide.* Translated by John A. Spaulding and George Simpson. Reprint, New York: Free Press.

———. [1895] 1964. *The Rules of Sociological Method.* Translated by Sarah A. Solovay and John H. Mueller. Reprint, New York: Free Press.

Durrant, Joan E., and Linda Rose-Krasnor. 1995. *Corporal Punishment Research Review and Policy Development.* Ottawa: Ontario Health Canada and Department of Justice Canada.

Dworkin, Rosalind J. 1982. "A Woman's Report: Numbers Are Not Enough." Pp. 375–400 in *The Minority Report,* edited by Anthony Dworkin and Rosalind Dworkin. New York: Holt.

Dyck, Rand. 2006. *Canadian Politics.* 3rd ed. Toronto: Nelson.

E

Eayrs, Caroline B., Nick Ellis, and Robert S. P. Jones. 1993. "Which Label? An Investigation into the Effects of Terminology on Public Perceptions of and Attitudes toward People with Learning Difficulties." *Disability, Handicap, and Society* 8(2):111–127.

Ebaugh, Helen Rose Fuchs. 1988. *Becoming an Ex: The Process of Role Exit.* Chicago: University of Chicago Press.

The Economist. 1995. "Home Sweet Home." 336(September 9):25–26, 29, 32.

Edmonton Social Planning Council. 1999. *Often Hungry, Sometimes Homeless.* Edmonton: Edmonton Social Planning Council and the Edmonton Food Bank.

Edwards, Richard. 1979. *Contested Terrain: The Transformation of the Workplace in America.* New York: Basic Books.

Efron, Sonni. 1997. "In Japan, Even Tots Must Make the Grade." *Los Angeles Times,* February 16, A1, A17.

———. 1998. "Japanese in Quandary on Fertility." *Los Angeles Times,* July 27, A1, A6.

Ehrenreich, Barbara. 2001. *Nickel and Dimed: On (Not) Getting by in America.* New York: Metropolitan.

Ehrenreich, Barbara, and Frances Fox Piven. 2002. "Without a Safety Net." *Mother Jones* 27 (May/June):34–41.

Ehrlich Martin, Susan. 1984. "Sexual Harassment: The Link between Gender Stratification, Sexuality, and Women's Economic Status." In *Women: A Feminist Perspective.* 3rd ed., edited by J. Freeman. Palo Alto, CA: Mayfield.

Ehrlich, Paul R. 1968. *The Population Bomb.* New York: Ballantine.

Ehrlich, Paul R., and Anne H. Ehrlich. 1990. *The Population Explosion.* New York: Simon and Schuster.

Ehrlich, Paul R., and Katherine Ellison. 2002. "A Looming Threat We Won't Face." *Los Angeles Times,* January 20, M6.

Eichler, Margrit. 1984. "Sexism in Research and Its Policy Implications." Pp. 17–39 in *Taking Sex into Account: The Policy Implications of Sexist Research,* edited by J. McCella Vickers. Ottawa: Carelton Univeristy Press.

———. 1997. *Family Shifts: Families, Policies, and Gender Equality.* Toronto: Oxford University Press.

———. 2001. "Biases in Family Literature." Pp. 51–66 in *Families: Changing Trends in Canada.* 4th ed., edited by Maureen Baker. Toronto: McGraw-Hill Ryerson.

Eisenberg, David M., Roger B. Davis, Susan L. Ettner, Scott Appel, Sonja Wilkey, Maria Van Rompay, Ronald C. Kessler. 1998. "Trends in Alternative Medicine Use in the United States, 1990–1997: Results of a Follow-up National Survey." *Journal of the American Medical Association* 280(November 11): 1569–1575.

Eisler, Peter. 2000. "This Is Only a Test, but Lives Are at Stake." *USA Today,* June 30, 219–220.

Ekman, Paul, Wallace V. Friesen, and John Bear. 1984. "The International Language of Gestures." *Psychology Today* 18(May): 64–69.

Ekos Research Associates. 2001. "Canadians and Working from Home." Retrieved November 27, 2005 (http://www.ekos.com/admin/articles/telework4.pdf).

El-Badry, Samira. 1994. "The Arab-American Market." *American Demographics* 16(January):21–27, 30.

El Nasser, Haya. 1999. "Soaring Housing Costs Are Culprit in Suburban Poverty." *USA Today,* April 28, A1, A2.

———. 2001. "Minorities Reshape Suburbs." *USA Today,* July 9, 1A.

Elections Canada. 2005a. *Young Voters.* Retrieved September 26, 2005 (http://www.elections.ca).

———. 2005b. *Voter turnout for 2004, 2000, 1997, and 1993 General Elections,* Table 4. Retreived November 12, 2005 (http://www.elections.ca/scripts/OVR2004/23/table4.html).

Elias, Marilyn. 1996. "Researchers Fight Child Consent Bill." *USA Today,* January 2, A1.

Elliot, Patricia, and Nancy Mandell. 1998. "Feminist Theories." Pp. 2–25 in *Feminist Issues: Race, Class, and Sexuality.* 2nd ed., edited by Nancy Mandell, Scarborough, ON: Prentice Hall Allyn and Bacon Canada.

Elliott, Helene. 1997. "Having an Olympic Team Is Their Miracle on Ice." *Los Angeles Times,* March 25, Sports section, 5.

Elliott, Marta, and Lauren J. Krivo. 1991. "Structural Determinants of Homelessness in the United States." *Social Problems* 38(February): 113–131.

Elliott, Michael. 1994. "Crime and Punishment." *Newsweek* 123(April 18):18–22.

Elmer-DeWitt, Philip. 1995. "Welcome to Cyberspace." *Time* 145(Special Issue, Spring):4–11.

Ely, Robin J. 1995. "The Power of Demography: Women's Social Construction of Gender Identity at Work." *Academy of Management Journal* 38(3):589–634.

Engels, Friedrich. 1884. "The Origin of the Family, Private Property and the State." Pp. 392–394, excerpted in *Marx and Engels: Basic Writings on Politics and Philosophy,* edited by Lewis Feuer. Garden City, NY: Anchor, 1959.

Entine, Jon, and Martha Nichols. 1996. "Blowing the Whistle on Meaningless 'Good Intentions.'" *Chicago Tribune,* June 20, 21.

Erikson, Kai. 1966. *Wayward Puritans: A Study in the Sociology of Deviance.* New York: Wiley.

Etzioni, Amitai. 1964. *Modern Organization.* Englewood Cliffs, NJ: Prentice-Hall.

———. 1985. "Shady Corporate Practices." *New York Times,* November 15, A35.

———. 1990. "Going Soft on Corporate Crime." *Washington Post,* April 1, C3.

———. 1996. "Why Fear Date Rape?" *USA Today,* May 20, 14A.

Evans, Peter. 1979. *Dependent Development.* Princeton, NJ: Princeton University Press.

F

Facts on File Weekly News Report. 2001a. "Switzerland: Votes Solidly Reject EU Membership." Retrieved March 2 (http://www.facts.com).

———. 2001b. "Great Britain: British Elections, 1997 and 2001." Retrieved June 14 (http://www.facts. com).

Fager, Marty, Mike Bradley, Lonnie Danchik, and Tom Wodetski. 1971. *Unbecoming Men.* Washington, NJ: Times Change.

Faludi, Susan. 1999. *Stiffed: The Betrayal of the American Man.* New York: William Morrow.

Farhi, Paul, and Megan Rosenfeld. 1998. "Exporting America." *Washington Post National Weekly Edition,* November 30, 6–7.

Farr, Grant M. 1999. *Modern Iran.* New York: McGraw-Hill.

———. 1989. *Minority Group Issues in Higher Education: Learning from Qualitative Research.* Norman, OK: Center for Research on Minority Education, University of Oklahoma.

Feagin, Joe R. 1983. *The Urban Real Estate Game: Playing Monopoly with Real Money.* Englewood Cliffs, NJ: Prentice-Hall.

———. 1989. *Minority Group Issues in Higher Education: Learning from Qualitative Research.* Norman, OK: Center for Research on Minority Education, University of Oklahoma.

Feagin, Joe R., Harnán Vera, and Nikitah Imani. 1996. *The Agony of Education: Black Students at White Colleges and Universities.* New York: Routledge.

Federman, Joel. 1998. *1998 National Television Violence Study: Executive Summary.* Santa Barbara: University of California, Santa Barbara.

Feketekuty, Geza. 2001. "Globalization—Why All the Fuss?" P. 191 in *2001 Britannica Book of the Year.* Chicago: Encyclopedia Britannica.

Felson, Marcus. 1998. *Crime and Everyday Life: Insights and Implications for Society.* 2nd ed. Thousand Oaks, CA: Pine Forge Press.

Ferree, Myra Marx, and David A. Merrill. 2000. "Hot Movements, Cold Cognition: Thinking about Social Movements in Gendered Frames." *Contemporary Society* 29(May): 454–462.

Feuer, Lewis S., ed. 1959. *Karl Marx and Friedrich Engels: Basic Writings on Politics and Philosophy.* Garden City, NY: Doubleday.

Fiala, Robert. 1992. "Postindustrial Society." Pp. 1512–1522 in *Encyclopedia of Sociology.* Vol. 3, edited by Edgar F. Borgatta and Marie L. Borgatta. New York: Macmillan.

Fields, Jason. 2003. "Children's Living Arrangements and Characteristics: March 2002." *Current Population Reports,* ser. P-20, no. 547. Washington, DC: U.S. Government Printing Office.

Fine, Gary Alan. 1984. "Negotiated Orders and Organizational Cultures." Pp. 239–262 in *Annual Review of Sociology, 1984,* edited by Ralph Turner. Palo Alto, CA: Annual Reviews.

Finkel, Alvin, and Margaret Conrad with Veronica Stong-Boag. 1993. *History of the Canadian Peoples: 1867 to Present.* Toronto: Copp Clark Putnam.

Finkel, Steven E., and James B. Rule. 1987. "Relative Deprivation and Related Psychological Theories of Civil Violence: A Critical Review." *Research in Social Movements* 9:47–69.

Finnie, Ross. 1993. "Women, Men and the Economic Consequences of Divorce: Evidence from Canadian Longitudinal Data." *Canadian Review of Sociology and Anthropology* 30(2): 205–241

Firestone, Shulamith. 1970. *The Dialectic of Sex: The Case for Feminist Revolution.* New York: Bantam.

Fisher, Ian. 1999. "Selling Sudan's Slaves into Freedom." *New York Times,* April 25, A6.

Fitzgerald, Kathleen J., and Diane M. Rodgers. 2000. "Radical Social Movement Organization: A Theoretical Model." *The Sociological Quarterly* 41(4):573–592.

Fitzpatrick, Eleanor. 1994. *Violence Prevention: A Working Paper and Proposal for Action.* St. John's: Avalon Consolidated School Board.

Flanders, John. 2001. "Getting Ready for the 2001 Census." *Canadian Social Trends* (Spring) Statistics Canada. Catalogue No. 11-008. Ottawa: Minister of Industry.

Flavin, Jeanne. 1998. "Razing the Wall: A Feminist Critique of Sentencing Theory, Research, and Policy." Pp. 145–164 in *Cutting the Edge,* edited by Jeffrey Ross. Westport, CT: Praeger.

Fleras, Augie. 2003. *Mass Communication in Canada.* Scarborough, ON: Nelson.

Fleras, Augie, and Jean Leonard Elliott. 1992. *The Nations Within. Aboriginal-State Relations in*

Canada, the United States, and New Zealand. Toronto: Oxford University Press.

———. 1999. *Unequal Relations: An Introduction to Race, Ethnic and Aboriginal Dynamics.* Scarborough, ON: Prentice-Hall.

———. 2003. *Unequal Relations: An Introduction to Race, Ethnic, and Aboriginal Dynamics in Canada.* 4th ed. Scarborough, ON: Prentice Hall Canada.

———. 2001. *Media and Minorities: Representing Diversity in Multicultural Canada.* Toronto: Thompson Educational Publishing.

Fletcher, Connie. 1995. "On the Line: Women Cops Speak Out." *Chicago Tribune Magazine,* February 19, pp. 14–19.

Fong, Petti. 2001. "Brain Diseases 'Loom as Next Big Health Threat.'" *Vancouver Sun,* March 20, A3.

Foot, David K. 2002. "Boomers Blow up Census." *The Globe and Mail,* March 21, A17.

Form, William. 1992. "Labor Movements and Unions." Pp. 1054–1060 in *Encyclopedia of Sociology.* Vol. 3, edited by Edgar F. Borgatta and Marie L. Borgatta. New York: Macmillan.

Fornos, Werner. 1997. *1997 World Population Overview.* Washington, DC: The Population Institute.

Fortune. 2002. "Fortune's Global 500." August 12.

Fortin, Myriam, and Dominique Fleury. 2004. *A Profile of the Working Poor in Canada: Draft.* Ottawa: Social Development Canada.

Fox, Bonnie. 2001. "As Times Change: A Review of Trends in Personal and Family Life." Pp. 153–175 in *Family Patterns, Gender Relations.* 2nd ed., edited by Bonnie J. Fox. Toronto: Oxford University Press.

Fox, John, and Michael Ornstein. 1986. "The Canadian State and Corporate Enlites in the Post-war Period." *Canadian Review of Sociology and Anthropology* 23:481–506.

France, David. 2000. "Slavery's New Face." *Newsweek,* December 18, pp. 61–65.

Freeman, Linton C. 1958. "Marriage without Love: Mate Selection in Non-Western Countries." Pp. 20–30 in *Mate Selection,* edited by Robert F. Winch. New York: Harper and Row.

Freeze, Colin. 2001. "Women Outwork Men by Two Weeks Every Year." *The Globe and Mail,* March 13, A1.

Freidson, Eliot. 1970. *Profession of Medicine.* New York: Dodd, Mead.

Freire, Paulo. 1970. *Pedagogy of the Oppressed.* New York: Herder and Herder.

Fridlund, Alan. J., Paul Erkman, and Harriet Oster. 1987. "Facial Expressions of Emotion: Review of Literature 1970–1983." Pp. 143–224 in *Nonverbal Behavior and Communication.* 2nd ed., edited by Aron W. Seigman and Stanley Feldstein. Hillsdale, NJ: Lawrence Erlbaum Associates.

Friedan, Betty. 1963. *The Feminine Mystique.* New York: W.W. Norton.

Friedland, Jonathon. 2000. "An American in Mexico Champions Midwifery as a Worthy Profession." *Wall Street Monitor,* February 15, A1, A12.

Friedrichs, David O. 1998. "New Directions in Critical Criminology and White Collar Crime." Pp. 77–91 in *Cutting the Edge,* edited by Jeffrey Ross. Westport, CT: Praeger.

Frey, William H. 2001. *Melting Pot Suburbs: A Census 2000 Study of Suburban Diversity.* Washington, DC: The Brookings Institution.

Furstenberg, Frank, and Andrew Cherlin. 1991. *Divided Families: What Happens to Children When Parents Part.* Cambridge, MA: Harvard University Press.

G

Gabor, Andrea. 1995. "Crashing the 'Old Boy' Party." *New York Times,* January 8, 1, 6.

Gale Research Group. 2002. *Encyclopedia of Associations: National Organizations of the U.S.* Detroit: Gale Research Group.

Gallup. 2003. "The Gallup Poll of Baghdad." Retrieved November 25, 2004 (http://www.gallup.com).

Galt, Virginia. 1998. "Where the Boys Aren't: At the Top of the Class." *The Globe and Mail,* February 26, A6.

———. 2003. "The Future of Work." *The Globe and Mail,* September 23. Retrieved November 10, 2005 (http://www.suiteworks.ca/documents/GM%20Sep-23-2003.pdf).

Gamson, Josh. 1989. "Silence, Death, and the Invisible Enemy: AIDS Activism and Social Movement 'Newness.'" *Social Problems* 36(October):351–367.

Gans, Herbert J. 1991. *People, Plans, and Policies: Essays on Poverty, Racism, and Other National Urban Problems.* New York: Columbia University Press and Russell Sage Foundation.

Garber, Judith A., and Robyne S. Turner, eds. 1995. *Gender in Urban Research.* Thousand Oaks, CA: Sage.

Gardner, Carol Brooks. 1989. "Analyzing Gender in Public Places: Rethinking Goffman's Vision of Everyday Life." *American Sociologist* 20(Spring):42–56.

———. 1990. "Safe Conduct: Women, Crime, and Self in Public Places." *Social Problems* 37(August):311–328.

———. 1995. *Passing By: Gender and Public Harassment.* Berkeley: University of California Press.

Gardner, Marilyn. 1998. "Prime-Time TV Fare Rarely Shows Family Life as It's Really Lived." *Christian Science Monitor,* June 10, 13. Retrieved December 1, 2005 (http://csmonitor.com/cgi-bin/durableRedirect.pl?/durable/1998/06/10/p13s1.htm).

Garfinkel, Harold. 1956. "Conditions of Successful Degradation Ceremonies." *American Journal of Sociology* 61(March): 420–424.

Garner, Roberta. 1996. *Contemporary Movements and Ideologies.* New York: McGraw-Hill.

———. 1999. "Virtual Social Movements." Presented at Zaldfest: A Conference in Honor of Mayer Zald. September 17, Ann Arbor, MI.

Garreau, Joel. 1991. *Edge City: Life on the New Frontier.* New York: Doubleday.

Gartner, Rosemary, Myrna Dawson, and Maria Crawford. 2001. "Confronting Violence in Women's Lives." Pp. 473–490 in *Family Patterns, Gender Relations,* edited by Bonnie J. Fox. Toronto: Oxford University Press.

Garza, Melita Marie. 1993. "The Cordi-Marian Annual Cotillion." *Chicago Tribune,* May 7, sec. C, 1, 5.

Gaskell, Jane, Arlene McLaren, and Myra Novogrodsky. 1995. "What Is Worth Knowing?" Pp. 100–118 in *Gender in the 1990s: Images, Realities and Issues,* edited by Edna D. Nelson and Barrie W. Robinson. Scarborough, ON: Nelson Canada.

Gates, Henry Louis, Jr. 1999. "One Internet, Two Nations." *New York Times,* October 31, A15.

Gauette, Nicole. 1998. "Rules for Raising Japanese Kids." *Christian Science Monitor,* October 14, B1, B6.

Gearty, Robert. 1996. "Beware of Pickpockets." *Chicago Daily News,* November 19, 5.

Gecas, Viktor. 1982. "The Self-Concept." Pp. 1–33 in *Annual Review of Sociology, 1982,* edited by Ralph H. Turner and James F. Short, Jr. Palo Alto, CA: Annual Reviews.

———. 1992. "Socialization." Pp. 1863–1872 in *Encyclopedia of Sociology.* Vol. 4, edited by Edgar F. Borgatta and Marie L. Borgatta. New York: Macmillan.

Geckler, Cheri. 1995. *Practice Perspectives and Medical Decision-Making in Medical Residents: Gender Differences—A Preliminary Report.* Wellesley, MA: Center for Research on Women.

Gelles, Richard J., and Claire Pedrick Cornell. 1990. *Intimate Violence in Families.* 2nd ed. Newbury Park, CA: Sage.

Gelles, Richard J., and Murray A. Straus. 1988. *Intimate Violence: The Causes and Consequences of Abuse in the American Family.* New York: Simon and Schuster.

General Accounting Office. 2000. *Women's Health: NIH Has Increased Its Efforts to Include Women in Research.* Washington, DC: U.S. Government Printing Office.

General Social Survey. 1998. Ottawa: Statistics Canada.

Gerth, H.H., and C. Wright Mills. 1958. *From Max Weber: Essays in Sociology.* New York: Galaxy.

Geschwender, James A. 1994. "Married Women's Waged Labor and Racial/Ethnic Stratification in Canada." *Canadian Ethnic Studies* 26(3): 53–73.

Gest, Ted. 1985. "Are White-Collar Crooks Getting off Too Easy?" *U.S. News & World Report,* July 1, 43.

Gidengil, Elizabeth, Matt Hennigar, Andre Blais, Richard Nadeau and Neil Nevitte. 2003. "The Gender Gap in Support for The New Right: The Case of Canada." Paper prepared for the conference on Populisms in North America, South America, and Europe: Comparative and Historical, Bogliasco Italy, January.

Gifford, Allen L., William E. Cunningham, Kevin C. Heslin, Ron M. Andersen, Terry Nakazono, Dale K. Lieu, Martin F. Shapiro, Samuel A. Bozzette. 2002. "Participation in Research and Access to Experimental Treatments by HIV-Infected Patients." *New England Journal of Medicine* 346 (May):1400–1402.

Gill, Rosalind, and Keith Grist, eds. 1995. *The Gender-Technology Relation: Contemporary Theory and Research*. London: Taylor and Francis.

Giroux, Henry A. 1988. *Schooling and the Struggle for Public Life: Critical Pedagogy in the Modern Age.* Minneapolis: University of Minnesota Press.

Glenn, David. 2004. "A Dangerous Surplus of Sons?" *Chronicle of Higher Education* 50 (April 30): A14–A16, A18.

Global Alliance for Workers and Communities. 2001. *Workers' Voices: An Interim Report on Workers' Needs and Aspirations in Nine Nike Contract Factories in Indonesia.* Baltimore, MD: Global Alliance.

Global Reach. 2002. "Global Internet Statistics (by Language)." Retrieved June 24, 2002 (http://glreach.com/globstats/).

———. 2004. "Global Internet Statistics (by Language)." Retrieved October 13, 2005 (http://global-reach.biz/globestats/index.php3).

Globe and Mail. 2004a. "Canada's Wealthy Not Cheapskates, Poll Finds." August 20, B5.

———. 2004b. "Education System Failing Innu, Report Says." December 14. Retrieved December 14, 2004 (http://www.theglobeandmail.com/servlet/stroy/RTGAM.2004.winnu1214/BNStory/)

Goffman, Erving. 1959. *The Presentation of Self in Everyday Life.* New York: Doubleday.

———. 1961. *Asylums: Essays on the Social Situation of Mental Patients and Other Inmates.* Garden City, NY: Doubleday.

———. 1963a. *Stigma: Notes on Management of Spoiled Identity.* Englewood Cliffs, NJ: Prentice-Hall.

———. 1963b. *Behavior in Public Places.* New York: Free Press.

———. 1967. *Interaction Ritual: Essays in Face-to-Face Behavior.* New York: Doubleday.

———. 1971. *Relations in Public.* New York: Basic Books.

———. 1979. *Gender Advertisements.* New York: Harper and Row.

Goldman, Benjamin A., and Laura Fitton. 1994. *Toxic Wastes and Race Revisited: An Update of the 1987 Report on the Racial and Social Economic Characteristics of Communities with Hazardous Waste.* Washington, DC: Center for Policy Alternatives, United Church of Christ Commission for Racial Justice, and NAACP.

Goldman, Robert, and Stephen Papson. 1998. *Nike Culture: The Sign of the Swoosh.* London: Sage Publications.

Goldstein, Greg. 1998. "World Health Organization and Housing." Pp. 636–637 in *The Encyclopedia of Housing,* edited by Willem van Vliet. Thousand Oaks, CA: Sage Publications.

Goldstein, Melvyn C., and Cynthia M. Beall. 1981. "Modernization and Aging in the Third and Fourth World: Views from the Rural Hinterland in Nepal." *Human Organization* 40(Spring):48–55.

Gonnut, Jean Pierre. 2001. Interview. June 18, 2001.

Goode, William J. 1959. "The Theoretical Importance of Love." *American Sociological Review* 24(February):38–47.

Gordon, Jesse, and Knickerbocker. 2001. "The Sweat Behind the Shirt: The Labor History of a Gap Sweatshirt." *The Nation* 273 (September 3/10):14.

Gornick, Janet C. 2001. "Cancel the Funeral." *Dissent* (Summer):13–18.

Gottdiener, Mark, and Joe R. Feagin. 1988. "The Paradigm Shift in Urban Sociology." *Urban Affairs Quarterly* 24(December):163–187.

Gottdiener, Mark, and Ray Hutchison. 2000. *The New Urban Sociology*. 2nd ed. New York: McGraw-Hill.

Gottfredson, Michael, and Travis Hirschi. 1990. *A General Theory of Crime.* Palo Alto, CA: Stanford University Press.

Gough, E. Kathleen. 1974. "Nayar: Central Kerala." Pp. 298–384 in *Matrilineal Kinship,* edited by David Schneider and E. Kathleen Gough. Berkeley: University of California Press.

Gouldner, Alvin. 1960. "The Norm of Reciprocity." *American Sociological Review* 25(April): 161–177.

———. 1970. *The Coming Crisis of Western Sociology.* New York: Basic Books.

Gove, Walter R., ed. 1987. "Sociobiology Misses the Mark: An Essay on Why Biology but Not Sociobiology Is Very Relevant to Sociology." *American Sociologist* 18(Fall):258–277.

Government of Canada. 2002. "Sustainable Development: A Canadian Perspective. Canada at the World Summit on Sustainable Development." Retrieved February 25, 2005 (http://www.sdinfo.gc.ca/canadian_perspective/pg027_e.cfm).

Gram, Karen. 2001. "Hard Times in the Good Ol' Days." *Vancouver Sun,* May 5, A21.

Gramsci, Antonio. 1929. *Selections from the Prison Notebooks.* Edited and introduced by Quintin Hoare and Geoffrey Nowell-Smith. London: Lawrence and Wishort.

Grant, Judith. 1993. *Fundamental Feminism: Contesting the Core Concepts of Feminist Theory.* New York and London: Routledge.

Graydon, Shari. 2001. "The Portrayal of Women in Media: The Good, the Bad, and the Beautiful." Pp. 179–195 in *Communications in Canadian Society.* 5th ed., edited by Craig McKie and Benjamin D. Singer. Toronto: Thompson Educational Publishing.

Greaves, Lorraine. 1996. *Smoke Screen: Women's Smoking and Social Control.* Halifax: Fernwood Publishing.

Greeley, Andrew M. 1989. "Protestant and Catholic: Is the Analogical Imagination Extinct?" *American Sociological Review* 54(August):485–502.

Grossman, David C., H.J. Neckerman, Thomas D. Koepsell, P.Y. Liu, K. Asher, Kathy Beland, Karen S. Frey, and Frederick P. Rivara. 1997. "Effectiveness of a Violence Prevention Curriculum among Children in Elementary School." *Journal of the American Medical Association* 277(May 28):1605–1617.

Groza, Victor, Daniela F. Ileana, and Ivor Irwin. 1999. *A Peacock or a Crow: Stories, Interviews, and Commentaries on Romanian Adoptions.* Euclid, OH: Williams Custom Publishing.

Guardian Unlimited. 2005. "Eight Women, One Voice." Retrieved July 9, 2005 (http://www.guardian.co.uk/africa8).

Guppy, Neil, and Scott Davies. 1998. *Education in Canada: Recent Trends and Future Challenges.* Ottawa: Statistics Canada.

Gurin, David. 2003. *Understanding Sprawl.* Vancouver: David Suzuki Foundation.

Guterman, Lila. 2000. "Why the 25-Year-Old Battle over Sociology Is More Than Just 'an Academic Sideshow.'" *Chronicle of Higher Education,* July 7, A17–A18.

Gutierrez, Gustavo. 1990. "Theology and the Social Sciences." Pp. 214–225 in *Liberation Theology at the Crossroads: Democracy or Revolution?* edited by Paul E. Sigmund. New York: Oxford University Press.

Gwynne, S.C., and John F. Dickerson. 1997. "Lost in the E-mail." *Time,* April 21, pp. 88–90.

H

Ha, Tu Thanh. 2004. "Pregnant Woman Called Him 'Papa,' Sperm Donor's Court Petition Says." *The Globe and Mail,* September 14. Retrieved November 27, 2004 (http://www.theglobeandmial.com).

Haaland, Bonnie. 1993. *Emma Goldman: Sexuality and the Impurity of the State.* Black Rock: Montreal.

Haas, Michael, ed. 1999. *The Singapore Puzzle.* Westport, CT: Praeger.

Hacker, Andrew. 1964. "Power to Do What?" Pp. 134–146 in *The New Sociology,* edited by Irving Louis Horowitz. New York: Oxford University Press.

Hacker, Helen Mayer. 1951. "Women as a Minority Group." *Social Forces* 30(October): 60–69.

———. 1974. "Women as a Minority Group, Twenty Years Later." Pp. 124–134 in *Who Discriminates against Women?*, edited by Florence Denmark. Beverly Hills, CA: Sage.

Haines, Valerie A. 1988. "Is Spencer's Theory an Evolutionary Theory?" *American Journal of Sociology* 93(March):1200–1223.

Halbfinger, David M. 1998. "As Surveillance Cameras Peer, Some Wonder If They Also Pry." *New York Times,* February 22, A1.

Hall, Kay. 1999. "Work from Here." *Computer User* 18(November):32.

Hall, Mimi. 1993. "Genetic-Sex-Testing a Medical Mine Field." *USA Today,* December 20, 6A.

Hall, Robert H. 1982. "The Truth about Brown Lung." *Business and Society Review* 40(Winter 1981–82):15–20.

Hallinan, Maureen T. 1997. "The Sociological Study of Social Change." *American Sociological Review* 62(February):1–11.

Hani, Yoko. 1998. "Hot Pots Wired to Help the Elderly." *Japan Times Weekly International Edition,* April 13, 16.

Hank, Karsten. 2001. "Changes in Child Care Could Reduce Job Options for Eastern German Mothers." *Population Today* 29 (April):3, 6.

Hara, Hiroko. 2000. "Homeless Desperately Want Shelter, Jobs." *Japan Times International* January 16, 14.

Harap, Louis. 1982. "Marxism and Religion: Social Functions of Religious Belief." *Jewish Currents* 36(January):12–17, 32–35.

Harlow, Harry F. 1971. *Learning to Love.* New York: Ballantine.

Harrington, Michael. 1980. "The New Class and the Left." Pp. 123–138 in *The New Class,* edited by B. Bruce-Briggs. Brunswick, NJ: Transaction.

Harris, Chauncy D., and Edward Ullman. 1945. "The Nature of Cities." *Annals of the American Academy of Political and Social Science* 242(November):7–17.

Harris, Judith Rich. 1998. *The Nurture Assumption: Why Children Turn out the Way They Do.* New York: Free Press.

Harris, Marvin. 1997. *Culture, People, Nature: An Introduction to General Anthropology.* 7th ed. New York: Longman.

Harrison, Trevor W., and John W. Friesen. 2004. *Canadian Society in the Twenty-First Century.* Toronto: Pearson Prentice Hall.

Hart, Stacey. 1995. *(Re)searching Lesbian Health Care: Methodological Considerations for Future Directions.* Retrieved April 18, 2002 (http://www.usc.edu/isd/archives/queer frontiers/queer/papers/hart.html).

Hartjen, Clayton A. 1978. *Crime and Criminalization.* 2nd ed. New York: Praeger.

Hartman, Chris, and Jake Miller. 2001. *Bail outs That Work For Everyone.* Boston: United for a Fair Economy.

Harvey, Bob. 2004. "Women Poised to Match Men on the Protestant Pulpits." *National Post.* August 7.

Haub, Carl. 2002. *2002 World Population Report Data Sheet.* Washington, DC: Population Reference Bureau.

———. 2003. *World Population Data Sheet, 2003.* Washington, DC: Population Reference Bureau.

Haub, Carl, and Diana Cornelius. 2000. *2000 World Population Data Sheet.* Washington, DC: Population Reference Bureau.

———. 2001. *2001 World Population Data Sheet.* Washington, DC: Population Reference Bureau.

Haviland, William A. 1999. *Cultural Anthropology (Case Studies in Cultural Anthropology).* 9th ed. Ft. Worth: Harcourt Brace.

Hayward, Mark D., William R. Grady, and Steven D. McLaughlin. 1987. "Changes in the Retirement Process." *Demography* 25(August): 371–386.

Health Canada. 2000. "The Changing Face of Heart Disease and Stroke in Canada 2000." Retrieved January 30, 2002 (http://www.hc-sc.gc.ca/hpb/lcdc/bcrdd/hdsc2000/index.html/).

———. 2001. *Canada Health Act Annual Report 1999–2000.* Ottawa: Queen's Printers.

———. 2002. "Women's Health Strategy." Ottawa: Health Canada, Women's Health Bureau. Retrieved April 4, 2002 (http://www.hc-sc.gc.ca/english/women/womenstrat.htm).

———. 2003. *HIV and AIDS in Canada. Surveillance Report to June 30, 2003.* Ottawa: Surveillance and Risk Assessment Division, Centre for Infections, Disease Prevention and Control, Health Canada.

Heckert, Druann, and Amy Best. 1997. "Ugly Duckling to Swan: Labeling Theory and the Stigmatization of Red Hair." *Symbolic Interaction* 20(4):365–384.

Hedley, R. Alan. 1992. "Industrialization in Less Developed Countries." Pp. 914–920 in *Encyclopedia of Sociology.* Vol. 2, edited by Edgar F. Borgatta and Marie L. Borgatta. New York: Macmillan.

Heikes, E. Joel. 1991. "When Men Are the Minority: The Case of Men in Nursing." *Sociological Quarterly* 32(3):389–401.

Heilman, Madeline E. 2001. "Description and Prescription: How Gender Stereotypes Prevent Women's Ascent up the Organizational Ladder." *Journal of Social Issues* 57(4): 657–674.

Heise, Lori, M. Ellseberg, and M. Gottemuelle. 1999. "Ending Violence against Women." *Population Reports,* ser. L, no. 11. Baltimore: Johns Hopkins University School of Public Health.

Henley, Nancy, Mykol Hamilton, and Barrie Thorne. 1985. "Womanspeak and Manspeak: Sex Differences and Sexism in Communication, Verbal and Nonverbal." Pp. 168–185 in *Beyond Sex Roles.* 2nd ed., edited by Alice G. Sargent. St. Paul, MN: West.

Henly, Julia R. 1999. "Challenges to Finding and Keeping Jobs in the Low-Skilled Labor Market." *Poverty Research News* 3(No. 1):3–5.

Henneberger, Melinda. 1995. "Muslims Continue to Feel Apprehensive." *New York Times,* April 14, B10.

Henry, Francis, C. Tator, W. Mattis, and T. Reese. 1995. *The Colour of Democracy: Racism in Canadian Society.* Toronto: Harcourt Brace.

Henry, Mary E. 1989. "The Function of Schooling: Perspectives from Rural Australia." *Discourse* 9(April):1–21.

Herman, Edward S., and Noam Chomsky. 1988. *Manufacturing Consent: The Political Economy of the Mass Media.* New York: Pantheon Books.

Herman, Edward S., and Gerry O' Sullivan. 1990. *The "Terrorism" Industry: The Experts and Institutions That Shape Our View of Terror.* New York: Pantheon.

Hickman, Jonathan. 2002. "America's 50 Best Corporations for Minorities." *Fortune,* July 8, pp. 110–120.

Hillery, George A. 1955. "Definitions of Community: Areas of Agreement." *Rural Sociology* (2):111–123.

Hirschi, Travis. 1969. *Causes of Delinquency.* Berkeley: University of California Press.

Hochschild, Arlie Russell. 1973. "A Review of Sex Role Research." *American Journal of Sociology* 78(January):1011–1029.

———. 1990. "The Second Shift: Employed Women Are Putting in Another Day of Work at Home." *Utne Reader* 38(March–April): 66–73.

Hochschild, Arlie Russell, with Anne Machung. 1989. *The Second Shift: Working Parents and the Revolution at Home.* New York: Viking Penguin.

Hodge, Robert W., and Peter H. Rossi. 1964. "Occupational Prestige in the United States, 1925–1963." *American Journal of Sociology* 70(November):286–302.

Hoebel, E. Adamson. 1949. *Man in the Primitive World: An Introduction to Anthropology.* New York: McGraw-Hill.

Hoffman, Adonis. 1997. "Through an Accurate Prism." *Los Angeles Times,* August 8, M1.

Hoffman, Lois Wladis. 1985. "The Changing Genetics/Socialization Balance." *Journal of Social Issues* 41(Spring):127–148.

Hofrichter, Richard, ed. 1993. *Toxic Struggles: The Theory and Practise of Environmental Justice.* Philadelphia: New Society.

Holden, Constance. 1980. "Identical Twins Reared Apart." *Science* 207(March 21):1323–1328.

———. 1987. "The Genetics of Personality." *Science* 257(August 7):598–601.

Hollingshead, August B. 1975. *Elmtown's Youth and Elmtown Revisited.* New York: Wiley.

Holmes, Steven A. 1997. "Leaving the Suburbs for Rural Areas." *New York Times,* October 19, 34.

Holmes, Tracy. 2000. "Performance Anxiety." *Peace Arch News,* February 2, 11.

Homans, George C. 1979. "Nature versus Nurture: A False Dichotomy." *Contemporary Sociology* 8(May):345–348.

Hondagneu-Sotelo, Pierette. 2001. *Domestica: Immigrant Workers Cleaning and Caring in the Shadows of Affluence.* Berkeley: University of California Press.

Horgan, John. 1993. "Eugenics Revisited." *Scientific American* 268(June):122–128, 130–133.

Horowitz, Helen Lefkowitz. 1987. *Campus Life.* Chicago: University of Chicago Press.

Horowitz, Irving Louis. 1983. *C. Wright Mills: An American Utopia.* New York: Free Press.

Horsey, Jen. 2004. "Canada's Rich Getting Richer." *The Globe and Mail,* December 5. Retrieved December 6, 2004 (http://www.theglobeandmail.com).

Howard, Judith A. 1999. "Border Crossings between Women's Studies and Sociology." *Contemporary Sociology* 28(September): 525–528.

Howard, Michael C. 1989. *Contemporary Cultural Anthropology.* 3rd ed. Glenview, IL: Scott, Foresman.

Howard, Philip E., Lee Rainie, and Steve Jones. 2001. "Days and Nights on the Internet." *American Behavioral Scientist* 45(November): 383–404.

Howell, Nancy, Patricia Albanese, and Kwaku Obusu-Mensah. 2001. "Ethnic Families." Pp. 116–142 in *Families: Changing Trends in Canada.* 4th ed., edited by Maureen Baker. Toronto: McGraw-Hill Ryerson.

Hua, Anh. 2003. "Critical Race Feminism." Presented at the Canadian Critical Race Conference 2003: Pedagogy and Practice. University of British Columbia, Vancouver, May 2–4.

Huang, Gary. 1988. "Daily Addressing Ritual: A Cross-Cultural Study." Presented at the annual meeting of the American Sociological Association, Atlanta.

Huddy, Leonie, Joshua Billig, John Bracciodieta, Lois Hoeffler, Patrick J. Moynihan, and Patricia Pugliani. 1997. "The Effect of Interviewer Gender on the Survey Response." *Political Behavior* 19(September):197–220.

Hughes, Everett. 1945. "Dilemmas and Contradictions of Status." *American Journal of Sociology* 50 (March):353–359.

Hunt, Geoffrey, Stephanie Riegel, Tomas Morales, and Dan Waldorf. 1993. "Changes in Prison Culture: Prison Gangs and the Case of the 'Pepsi Generation.'" *Social Problems* 40(3): 398–409.

Hunter, Herbert, ed. 2000. *The Sociology of Oliver C. Cox: New Perspectives: Research in Race and Ethnic Relations.* Vol. II. Stanford, CT: JAI Press.

Hurn, Christopher J. 1985. *The Limits and Possibilities of Schooling.* 2nd ed. Boston: Allyn and Bacon.

I

Ibata, David. 2001. "Greener Pastures Devoured by Sprawl." *Chicago Tribune,* March 18, 1, 18.

Inglehart, Ronald, and Wayne E. Baker. 2000. "Modernization, Cultural Change, and the Persistence of Traditional Values." *American Sociological Review* 65(February):19–51.

Institute for Social Research. 1994. *World Values Survey, 1990–1993.* Ann Arbor: The Regents of the University of Michigan.

Institute of International Education. 1998. "Foreign Students in U.S. Institutions 1997–98." *Chronicle of Higher Education* 45(December 11):A67.

Instituto del Tercer Mundo. 1999. *The World Guide 1999/2000.* Oxford, Eng.: New International Publications.

International Monetary Fund. 2000. *World Economic Outlook: Asset Prices and the Business Cycle.* Washington, DC: International Monetary Fund.

Inter-Parlimentary Union. 2005. "Women in National Parliaments." Retrieved October 30, 2005 (http://www.ipu.org/wmn-e/world.htm).

J

Jackson, Elton F., Charles R. Tittle, and Mary Jean Burke. 1986. "Offense-Specific Models of the Differential Association Process." *Social Problems* 33(April):335–356.

Jackson, Philip W. 1968. *Life in Classrooms.* New York: Holt.

Jacobs, Charles A. 2001. "Slavery in the 21st Century." Pp. 310–311 in *Britannica Book of the Year 2001.* Chicago: Encyclopedia Britannica.

Jacobson, Jodi. 1993. "Closing the Gender Gap in Development." Pp. 61–79 in *State of the World,* edited by Lester R. Brown. New York: Norton.

Jagger, Alison M., and Paula S. Rothenberg. 1984. *Feminist Frameworks.* 2nd ed. New York: McGraw-Hill.

Jasper, James M. 1997. *The Art of Moral Protest: Culture, Biography, and Creativity in Social Movements.* Chicago: University of Chicago Press.

Jehl, Douglas. 1999. "The Internet's 'Open Sesame' Is Answered Warily." *New York Times,* March 18, A4.

Jenkins, Richard. 1991. "Disability and Social Stratification." *British Journal of Sociology* 42(December):557–580.

Jennings, M. Kent, and Richard G. Niemi. 1981. *Generations and Politics.* Princeton, NJ: Princeton University Press.

Jimenez, Marina, and Kim Lunmann. 2004. "Canada's Biggest Cities See Influx of New Immigrants." *The Globe and Mail,* August 19, A5.

Jobtrak.com. 2000. "79% of College Students Find the Quality of an Employer's Website Important in Deciding Whether or Not to Apply for a Job." Retrieved on June 29, 2000 (http://static.jobtrak.com/mediacenter/press_polls/polls_061200.html).

Johanis, Paul, and Albert Meguerditchian. 1996. *A Framework for Statistics on Employment in the Services Sector.* Ottawa: Statistics Canada.

Johnson, Anne M., Jane Wadsworth, Kaye Wellings, and Julie Field. 1994. *Sexual Attitudes and Lifestyles.* Oxford: Blackwell Scientific.

Johnson, Benton. 1975. *Functionalism in Modern Sociology: Understanding Talcott Parsons.* Morristown, NJ: General Learning.

Johnson, George. 1999. "It's a Fact: Faith and Theory Collide over Evolution." *New York Times,* August 15, 1, 12.

Johnson, Harry M. 1960. *Sociology: A Systematic Introduction.* New York: Harcourt, Brace and World.

Johnson, Holly. 1996. *Dangerous Domains: Violence against Women in Canada.* Scarborough, ON: Nelson Canada.

Johnson, Patrick. 1983. *Native Children and the Child Welfare System.* Toronto: Canadian Council on Social Development in association with James Lorimer Publishing.

Johnston, David Cay. 1996. "The Divine Write-Off." *New York Times,* January 12, D1, D6.

Jolin, Annette. 1994. "On the Backs of Working Prostitutes: Feminist Theory and Prostitution Policy." *Crime and Delinquency* 40(No. 2): 69–83.

Jones, Charles, Lorna Marsden, and Lorne Tepperman. 1990. *Lives of Their Own.* Toronto: Oxford University Press.

Jones, Stephen R. G. 1992. "Was There a Hawthorne Effect?" *American Journal of Sociology* 98(November):451–568.

K

Kahn, Joseph. 2004. "The Most Populous Nation Faces a Population Crisis." *New York Times,* May 30, 1.

Kaiser Family Foundation. 2001. *Few Parents Use V-Chip to Block TV Sex and Violence.* Menlo Park: Kaiser Family Foundation.

Kalb, Claudia. 1999. "Our Quest to Be Perfect." *Newsweek,* August 9, pp. 52–59.

Kang, Mee-Eun. 1997. "The Portrayal of Women's Images in Magazine Advertisements: Goffman's Gender Analysis Revisited." In *Sex Roles* 37(December):979–996.

Katovich, Michael A. 1987. Correspondence. June 1.

Kaufman, Leslie. 2000. "As Biggest Business, Wal-Mart Propels Changes Elsewhere." *New York Times,* October 27, A1, A24.

Kazemipur, Abdie. 2002. "The Intersection of Socio-Economic Status and Race/Ethnicity/Official Language/Religion." Prepared for the Intersections of Diversity Seminar, Draft, March 8.

Keating, Noah and Brenda Munro. 1988. "Farm Women/Farm Work." *Sex Roles* 19(August): 155–168.

Kelly, Katherine, and Walter S. DeKeseredy. 1993. "The Incidence and Prevalence of Woman Abuse in Canadian University and College Dating Relationships." *Journal of Human Justice* 4(2):25–52.

Kelsoe, John R., E.I. Ginns, J.A. Egeland, D.S. Gerhard, A.M. Goldstein, S.J. Bale, D.L. Pauls, R.T. Long, K.K. Kidd, G. Conte, D.E. Housman, and S.M. Paul. 1989. "Reevaluation of the Linkage Relationship between Chromosome 11p Loci and the Gene for Bipolar Affective Disorder in the Old Order Amish." *Nature* 342(November 16):238–243.

Kemper, Vicki, and Viveca Novak. 1991. "Health Care Reform: Don't Hold Your Breath." *Washington Post National Weekly Edition,* October 28, 28.

Kent, Mary Mederios. 1999. "Shrinking Societies Favor Procreation." *Population Today* 27(December):4–5.

Kerbo, Harold R. 2000. *Social Stratification and Inequality: Class Conflict in Historical, Comparative, and Global Perspective.* New York: McGraw-Hill.

Kessler R.C. 1998. "Sex Differences in DSM-III-R Psychiatric Disorders in the United States: Results from the National Comorbidiy Survey." *Journal of American Medical Woman's Association* 53:148–158.

Kilborne, Jean. 1999. *Deadly Persuasions: Why Women and Girls Must Fight the Addictive Power of Advertising.* New York: The Free Press.

King, Leslie. 1998. "'France Needs Children': Pronatalism, Nationalism, and Women's Equity." *Sociological Quarterly* 39(Winter): 33–52.

Kinkade, Patrick T., and Michael A. Katovich. 1997. "The Driver Adaptations and Identities in the Urban Worlds of Pizza Delivery Employees." *Journal of Contemporary Ethnography* 25 (January):421–448.

Kinsella, Kevin and Victoria A. Velkoff. 2001. "An Aging World: 2001." *Current Population Reports,* ser. 95. no. 01-1. Washington, DC: U.S. Government Printing Office.

Kinsey, Alfred C., Wardell B. Pomeroy, and Clyde E. Martin. 1948. *Sexual Behavior in the Human Male.* Philadelphia: Saunders.

Kinsey, Alfred C., Wardell B. Pomeroy, and Paul H. Gebhard. 1953. *Sexual Behavior in the Human Female.* Philadelphia: Saunders.

Kirk, Margaret O. 1995. "The Temps in the Gray Flannel Suits." *New York Times,* December 17, F13.

Kitchener, Richard F. 1991. "Jean Piaget: The Unknown Sociologist." *British Journal of Sociology* 42(September):421–442.

Klinger, Scott, Chris Hartman, Sarah Anderson, and John Cavanagh. 2002. *Executive Excess 2002: CEOs Cook the Books, Skewer the Rest of Us.* Boston, MA: Institute for Policy Studies and United for a Fair Economy.

Kohn, Alfie. 1988. "Girltalk, Guytalk." *Psychology Today* 22(February):65–66.

Kohn, Melvin L. 1970. "The Effects of Social Class on Parental Values and Practices." Pp. 45–68 in *The American Family: Dying or Developing,* edited by David Reiss and H.A. Hoffman. New York: Plenum.

Kohn, Melvin L., Kazimierz M. Slomeznsky, and Carrie Schoenbach. 1986. "Social Stratification and the Transmission of Values in the Family: A Cross-National Assessment." *Sociological Forum* 1, 1:73–102.

Kolata, Gina. 1998. "Infertile Foreigners See Opportunity in U.S." *New York Times,* January 4, 1, 12.

———. 1999. *Clone: The Road to Dolly and the Path Beyond.* New York: William Morrow.

———. 2000. *Clone. The Road to Dolly, and the Path Ahead.* New York: William Morrow.

Koolhaas, Rem, et al. 2001. *Mutations.* Barcelona, Spain: Actar.

Kortenhaus, Carole M., and Jack Demarest. 1993. "Gender Role Stereotyping in Children's Literature: An Update." *Sex Roles* 28(3–4):219–232.

Kovaleski, Serge F. 1999. "Choosing Alternative Medicine by Necessity." *Washington Post National Weekly Edition,* April 5, 16.

Krieger, Nancy, and Elizabeth Fee. 1994. "Man-Made Medicine and Women's Health." Pp. 11–29 in *Women's Health Politics and Power: Essays on Sex/Gender, Medicine and Public Health,* edited by Elizabeth Fee and Nancy Krieger. Amityville, NY: Baywood Publications.

Kristof, Nicholas D. 1998. "As Asian Economies Shrink, Women Are Squeezed Out." *New York Times,* June 11, A1, A12.

Kunkel, Dale, et al. 2001. *Sex on TV2.* Menlo Park, CA: Kaiser Family Foundation.

Kyodo News International. 1998a. "More Japanese Believe Divorce Is Acceptable." *Japan Times,* January 12, B4.

L

Labaree, David F. 1986. "Curriculum, Credentials, and the Middle Class: A Case Study of a Nineteenth Century High School." *Sociology of Education* 59(January):42–57.

Lakshimi, Rama. 2001. "Gender Prejudice in India Still against Daughters." *The Globe and Mail,* April 4, A10.

Lampkin, Lorna. 1985. *Visible Minorities in Canada.* Research paper for the Abella Royal Commission on Equality in Employment. Ottawa: Ministry of Supply and Services.

Landtman, Gunnar. 1968. *The Origin of Inequality of the Social Class.* New York: Greenwood.

Lang, Eric. 1992. "Hawthorne Effect." Pp. 793–794 in *Encyclopedia of Sociology.* Vol. 2, edited by Edgar F. Borgatta and Marie L. Borgatta. New York: Macmillan.

Langman, L. 1987. "Social Stratification." Pp. 211–249 in *Handbook of Marriage and the Family,* edited by Marvin B. Sussman and Suzanne K. Steinmetz. New York: Plenum.

Larsen, Elena. 2000. *Wired Churches, Wired Temples: Taking Congregations and Missions into Cyberspace.* Washington, DC: Pew Internet and American Life Project.

Lasch, Christopher. 1977. *Haven in a Heartless World: The Family Besieged.* New York: Basic Books.

Lasswell, Harold D. 1936. *Politics: Who Gets What, When, How.* New York: McGraw-Hill.

Lauer, Robert H. 1982. *Perspectives on Social Change.* 3rd ed. Boston: Allyn and Bacon.

Laumann, Edward O., John H. Gagnon, and Robert T. Michael. 1994a. "A Political History of the National Sex Survey of Adults." *Family Planning Perspectives* 26(February): 34–38.

Laumann, Edward O., John H. Gagnon, and Robert T. Michael, and Stuart Michaels. 1994b. *The Social Organization of Sexuality: Sexual Practices in the United States.* Chicago: University of Chicago Press.

Lautard, Hugh E., and Donald J. Loree. 1984. "Ethnic Stratification in Canada, 1931–1971." *Canadian Journal of Sociology* 9:333–343.

Lautard, Hugh, and Neil Guppy. 1999. "Revisiting the Vertical Mosaic: Occupational Stratification among Canadian Ethnic Groups." Pp. 219–252 in *Race and Ethnic Relations in Canada.* 2nd ed., edited by Peter S. Li. Toronto: Oxford University Press.

Leacock, Eleanor. 2001. "Women in an Egalitarian Society: The Montagnais-Naskapi of Canada." Pp. 55–66 in *Family Patterns, Gender Relations.* 2nd ed., edited by Bonnie J. Fox. Toronto: Oxford University Press.

Leacock, Eleanor Burke. 1969. *Teaching and Learning in City Schools.* New York: Basic Books.

Leavell, Hugh R., and E. Gurney Clark. 1965. *Preventive Medicine for the Doctor in His Community: An Epidemiologic Approach.* 3rd ed. New York: McGraw-Hill.

Le Bourdais, Celine, and Nicole Marcil-Gratton. 1994. "Quebec's Proactive Approach to Family Policy: 'Thinking and Acting Family.'" *Canada's Changing Families: Challenges to Public Policy,* edited by Maureen Baker. Ottawa: Vanier Institute of the Family.

Lee, Alfred McClung. 1983. *Terrorism in Northern Ireland.* Bayside, NY: General Hall.

Lee, Barrett A. 1992. "Homelessness." Pp. 843–847 in *Encyclopedia of Sociology.* Vol. 2, edited by Edgar F. Borgatta and Marie L. Borgatta. New York: Macmillan.

Lee, Jennifer A. 2001. "Tracking Sales and the Cashiers." *New York Times,* June 11, C1, C6.

Lehne, Gregory K. 1995. "Homophobia among Men: Supporting and Defining the Male Role." Pp. 325–336 in *Men's Lives,* edited by Michael S. Kimmel and Michael S. Messner. Boston: Allyn and Bacon.

Lem, Sharon. 2000. "Life Expectancy Gender Gap Narrowing." *Toronto Sun,* June 7. Retrieved July 30, 2001 (http://www.canoe.ca/Health 0003-6/07_men.html).

Lengermann, Patricia Madoo, and Jill Niebrugge-Brantley. 1996. "Contemporary Feminist Theory." Pp. 436–486 in *Sociological Theory.* 4th ed., edited by George Ritzer. New York: McGraw-Hill.

———. 1998. *The Women Founders: Sociology and Social Theory, 1830–1930.* Boston: McGraw-Hill.

Lenski, Gerhard. 1966. *Power and Privilege: A Theory of Social Stratification.* New York: McGraw-Hill.

Lenski, Gerhard, Jean Lenski, and Patrick Nolan. 1995. *Human Societies: An Introduction to Macrosociology.* 7th ed. New York: McGraw-Hill.

Leo, John. 1987. "Exploring the Traits of Twins." *Time,* January 12, p. 63.

Levin, Jack, and William C. Levin. 1980. *Ageism.* Belmont, CA: Wadsworth.

Levine, Felice. 2001. "Deja Vu All over Again—The Tiahrt Amendment." *Footnotes* 29(May/June).

Levinson, Arlene. 1984. "Laws for Live-In Lovers." *Ms.,* June, p. 101.

Levy, R., and J. Hawks. 1996. "Multicultural Medicine and Pharmacy Management: Part One: New Opportunities for Managed Care." *Drug Benefit Trends* 7(3):27–30.

Lewin, Tamar. 2000. "Differences Found in Care with Stepmothers." *New York Times,* August 17, A16.

———. 2001. "Anthrax Is Familiar Threat at Nation's Abortion Clinics." *New York Times,* November 7, B7.

Lewis, Anthony. 1999. "Abroad at Home: Something Rich and Strange," *New York Times,* October 12.

Li, Peter S. 1988. *Ethnic Inequality in a Class Society.* Toronto: Wall and Thompson.

———. 1992. "Race and Gender as Bases of Class Fractions and Their Effects on Earnings." *Canadian Review of Sociology and Anthropology* 29(4):488–510.

———. 2000. "Earning Disparities between Immigrants and Native-Born Canadians." *Canadian Review of Sociology and Anthropology* 37(3).

———. 2003. "Social Inclusion of Visible Minorities and Newcomers: The Articulation of "Race" and "Racial" Difference in Canadian Society." Presented at the Conference on Social Inclusion, Ottawa, March 27–28.

Li, W. 1999. "Building Ethnoburbia: The Emergence and Manifestation of the Chinese Ethnoburb in Los Angeles's San Gabriel Valley." *Journal of Asian American Studies* 2(1):1–28.

Lian, Jason Z., and David Ralph Matthews. 1998. "Does the Vertical Mosaic Still Exist? Ethnicity and Income in Canada, 1991." *Canadian Review of Sociology and Anthropology* 35(4): 461–481.

Liao, Youlian, Daniel L. McGee, Guichan Cao, and Richard S. Cooper. 2000. "Quality of the Last Year of Life of Older Adults: 1986–1993." *Journal of American Medical Association* 283(January 26):512–518.

Lichtenstein, Nelson. 2005. *Wal-Mart: Template for Twenty-First Century Capitalism.* New York: New Press.

Liebow, Elliot. 1993. *Tell Them Who I Am: The Lives of Homeless Women.* New York: Free Press.

Light, Ivan. 1999. "Comparing Incomes of Immigrants." *Contemporary Sociology* 28(July): 382–384.

Liker, Jeffrey K., Carol J. Hoddard, and Jennifer Karlin. 1999. "Perspectives on Technology and Work Organization." Pp. 575–596 in *Annual Review of Sociology 1999,* edited by Karen S. Cook and John Hagen. Palo Alto, CA: Annual Reviews.

Lillard, Margaret. 1998. "Olympics Put Spotlight on Women's Hockey." *Rocky Mountain News,* February 1, 8C.

Lin, Na, and Wen Xie. 1988. "Occupational Prestige in Urban China." *American Journal of Sociology* 93(January):793–832.

Lin, Nan. 1999. "Social Networks and Status Attainment." Pp. 467–487 in *Annual Review of Sociology 1999,* edited by Karen S. Cook and John Hagen. Palo Alto, CA: Annual Reviews.

Lindbergh, Anne Morrow. 1955. *Gift from the Sea.* Reprint. New York: Pantheon.

Lindholm, Charles. 1999. "Isn't It Romantic?" *Culture Front Online* Spring:1–5.

Lindner, Eileen, ed. 1998. *Yearbook of American and Canadian Churches, 1998.* Nashville: Abingdon Press.

———, ed. 2000. *Yearbook of American and Canadian Churches.* Nashville: Abingdon Press.

Link, Bruce G., and Jo Phelan. 1995. "Social Conditions as Fundamental Causes of Disease." *Journal of Health and Social Behaviour* (Extra Issue):80–94.

Linton, Ralph. 1936. *The Study of Man: An Introduction.* New York: Appleton-Century.

Lips, Hilary M. 1993. *Sex and Gender: An Introduction.* 2nd ed. Mountain View, CA: Mayfield.

Lipset, Seymour Martin. 1996. *American Exceptionalism: A Double-Edged Sword.* New York: Norton.

Lipson, Karen. 1994. "'Nell' Not Alone in the Wilds." *Los Angeles Times,* December 19, F1, F6.

Liska, Allen E., and Steven F. Messner. 1999. *Perspectives on Crime and Deviance.* 3rd ed. Upper Saddle River, NJ: Prentice-Hall.

Little, Kenneth. 1988. "The Role of Voluntary Associations in West African Urbanization." Pp. 211–230 in *Anthropology for the Nineties: Introductory Readings,* edited by Johnnetta B. Cole. New York: Free Press.

Livernash, Robert, and Eric Rodenburg. 1998. "Population Change, Resources, and the Environment." *Population Bulletin* 53(March).

Livingstone, David. 1999. *The Education-Jobs Gap: Underemployment or Economic Democracy?* Toronto: Garamond Press.

Livingstone, D.W., and Meg Luxton. 1989. "Gender Consciousness at Work: Modification of the Male Breadwinning Norm among Steelworkers and Their Spouses." *Canadian Review of Sociology and Anthropology* 26:240–275.

Lofland, Lyn H. 1975. "The 'Thereness' of Women: A Selective Review of Urban Sociology." Pp. 144–170 in *Another Voice,* edited by M. Millman and R.M. Kanter. New York: Anchor/Doubleday.

Longworth, R.C. 1993. "UN's Relief Agendas Put Paperwork before People." *Chicago Tribune,* September 14, 1, 9.

Lorber, Judith. 1994. *Paradoxes of Gender.* New Haven, CT: Yale University Press.

Lowman, John, and Ted Palys. 2000. "Ethics and Institutional Conflict of Interest: The Research Confidentiality Controversy at Simon Fraser University." *Sociological Practice: A Journal of Clinical and Applied Sociology* 2(4):245–264.

Lukacs, Georg. 1923. *History and Class Consciousness.* London: Merlin.

Luker, Kristin. 1984. *Abortion and the Politics of Motherhood.* Berkeley: University of California Press.

———. 1996. *Dubious Conceptions: The Politics of Teenage Pregnancy.* Cambridge, MA: Harvard University Press.

Lundy, Colleen. 1991. "Women and Alcohol: Moving Beyond Disease Theory." Pp. 57–73 in *Health Futures: Alcohol and Drugs,* edited by Douglas J. McCready. Waterloo: Interdisciplinary Research Committee, Wilfred Laurier University.

Luo, Michael. 1999. "Megachurches Search for Ideas to Grow Again." *Los Angeles Times,* June 7, B1, B3.

Luster, Tom, Kelly Rhoades, and Bruce Haas. 1989. "The Relation between Parental Values and Parenting Behavior: A Test of the Kohn Hypothesis." *Journal of Marriage and the Family* 51(February):139–147.

Luxton, Meg. 1980. *More Than a Labour of Love: Three Generations of Women's Work in the Home.* Toronto: Women's Press.

———. 2001. "Husbands and Wives." Pp. 176–198 in *Family Patterns, Gender Relations.* 2nd ed., edited by Bonnie J. Fox. Toronto: Oxford University Press.

Lynch, Margaret, and Richard Ferri. 1997. "Health Needs of Lesbian Women and Gay Men." *Clinicians Reviews* 7(1):85–88, 91–92, 95, 98–102, 105–107, 108–115, 117–118.

Lyotard, Jean François. 1993. *The Postmodern Explained: Correspondence, 1982–1985.* Minneapolis: University of Minnesota Press.

M

Macintyre, Sally, Kate Hunt, and Helen Sweeting. 1996. "Gender Differences in Health: Are Things Really As Simple As They Seem?" *Social Science and Medicine* 42:617–624.

Mack, Raymond W., and Calvin P. Bradford. 1979. *Transforming America: Patterns of Social Change.* 2nd ed. New York: Random House.

Mackie, Richard. 2001. "Ontario Opposed School Subsidies before Courts, UN." *The Globe and Mail,* June 13. Retrieved June 15, 2001 (http://www.globeandmail.com).

MacKinnon, Catharine A. 1987. *Feminism Unmodified: Discourses on Life and Law.* Cambridge, MA: Harvard University Press.

MacLeod, Alexander. 2000. "UK Moving to Open All (E-)Mail." *The Christian Science Monitor,* May 5, pp. 1, 9.

MacMillan, Angus B., David R. Offord and Jennifer L. Dingle. 1996. "Aboriginal Health." *Canadian Medical Association Journal* 155(11):1569–78.

MacMillan, H. L., J.E. Fleming, N. Trocme, M.H. Boyle, M. Wong, Y.A. Racine, W.R. Beardslee, and D.R. Offord. 1997. "Prevalence of Child Physical and Sexual Abuse in the Community: Results from the Ontario Health Supplement." *Journal of the American Medical Association* 278:131–135.

Maguire, Brendan. 1988. "The Applied Dimension of Radical Criminology: A Survey of Prominent Radical Criminologists." *Sociological Spectrum* 8(2):133–151.

Mahbub ul Haq Human Development Centre. 2000. *Human Development in South Asia 2000.* Oxford, England: Oxford University Press for Mahbub ul Haq Human Deveopment Centre.

Maine Times. 2001. Article on Wal-Mart's Plan to Build near the Penja. January 4.

Maines, David R. 1977. "Social Organization and Social Structure in Symbolic Interactionist Thought." Pp. 235–259 in *Annual Review of Sociology, 1977,* edited by Alex Inkles. Palo Alto, CA: Annual Reviews.

———. 1982. "In Search of Mesostructure: Studies in the Negotiated Order." *Urban Life* 11(July):267–279.

Malcolm X, with Alex Haley. 1964. *The Autobiography of Malcolm X.* New York: Grove.

Malthus, Thomas Robert. 1798. *Essays on the Principle of Population.* New York: Augustus Kelly, Bookseller; reprinted in 1965.

Malthus, Thomas Robert, Julian Huxley, and Frederick Osborn. [1824] 1960. *Three Essays on Population.* Reprint, New York: New American Library.

Mandell, Nancy, ed. 1998. *Feminist Issues.* 2nd ed. Scarborough, ON: Prentice Hall Allyn and Bacon.

Manitoba Human Rights Commission. 2004. "The Fighting Spirit of Lee Williams." *Connections* 4(2):1–2.

Mann, Jim. 2000. "India: Growing Implications for U.S." *Los Angeles Times,* May 17, A5.

Manson, Donald A. 1986. *Tracking Offenders: White-Collar Crime.* Bureau of Justice Statistics Special Report. Washington, DC: U.S. Government Printing Office.

Maracle, Lee. 1996. *I A Woman: A Native Perspective on Sociology and Feminism.* Vancouver: Press Gang Publishers.

Marchak, M. Patricia. 1975. *Ideological Perspectives on Canada.* Toronto: McGraw-Hill Ryerson.

Marcil-Gratton, Nicole. 1999. "Growing up with Mom and Dad? Canadian Children Experience Shifting Family Structures." *Transition* 29(1):4–7.

Marklein, Mary Beth. 1996. "Telecommuters Gain Momentum." *USA Today,* June 18, 6E.

Marmor, Theodore. 1995. P. 1505 in "Medicare 'Canada's Postwar Miracle,' US Management Expert Tells CMA Conference," by J. Rafuse. *Canadian Medical Association Journal* 152(9).

Marshall, Kathleen. 1999. *The Gambling Industry: Raising the Stakes.* Ottawa: Minister of Industry.

Martin, Philip, and Elizabeth Midgley. 1999. "Immigrants to the United States." *Population Bulletin* 54(June):1–42.

Martin, Philip, and Jonas Widgren. 1996. "International Migration: A Global Challenge." *Population Bulletin* 51(April).

Martin, Susan E. 1994. "Outsider within the Station House: The Impact of Race and Gender on Black Women Politics." *Social Problems* 41(August):383–400.

Martineau, Harriet. 1896. "Introduction" to the translation of *Positive Philosophy* by Auguste Comte. London: Bell.

———. [1837] 1962. *Society in America.* Edited, abridged, with an introductory essay by Seymour Martin Lipset. Reprint, Garden City, NY: Doubleday.

Martyna, Wendy. 1983. "Beyond the He/Man Approach: The Case for Nonsexist Language." Pp. 25–37 in *Language, Gender and Society,* edited by Barrie Thorne, Cheris Kramorae, and Nancy Henley. Rowley, MA: Newly House.

Marx, Karl, and Friedrich Engels. [1847] 1955. *Selected Work in Two Volumes.* Reprint. Moscow: Foreign Languages Publishing House.

———. [1848] 1969. "Communist Manifesto." Pp. 98–137 in *Selected Works, Volume 1.* Translated by Samuel Moore. Reprint. Moscow, Russia: Progress Publishers.

Masaki, Hisane. 1998. "Hashimoto Steps Down." *Japan Times,* July 20, 1–5.

Masland, Tom. 1992. "Slavery." *Newsweek,* May 4, pp. 30–32, 37–39.

Mason, J.W. 1998. "The Buses Don't Stop Here Anymore." *American Prospect* 37(March): 56–62.

Matrix.Net. 2000. "State of the Internet, January 2000." MMQ 701. Retrieved October 14, 2001 (http://www.mids.org).

Matsushita, Yoshiko. 1999. "Japanese Kids Call for a Sympathetic Ear." *Christian Science Monitor,* January 20, p. 15.

Matthews, Jay. 1999. "A Home Run for Home Schooling." *Washington Post National Weekly Edition,* March 29, 34.

Mayer, Karl Ulrich, and Urs Schoepflin. 1989. "The State and the Life Course." Pp. 187–209 in *Annual Review of Sociology, 1989,* edited by W. Richard Scott and Judith Blake. Palo Alto, CA: Annual Reviews.

McClung, H. Juhling, Robert D. Murray, and Leo A. Heitlinger. 1998. "The Internet as a Source for Current Patient Information." *Pediatrics* 10(June 6). Retrieved November 27, 2005 (http://pediatrics.aappublications.org/cgi/content/full/101/6/e2).

McCoy, Kevin, and Dennis Cauchon. 2001. "The Business Side of Terror." *USA Today,* October 16, 1B, 3B.

McCreary Centre Society. 2001. *No Place to Call Home.* Burnaby, BC: McCreary Centre Society.

McCreary, D. 1994. "The Male Role and Avoiding Femininity." *Sex Roles* 31:517–531.

McDonough, Peggy, and Vivienne Walters. 2000. "Gender, Work and Health: An Analysis of the 1994 National Population Health Survey." *Centres of Excellence for Women's Health Research Bulletin* 1(1):3–4.

McFalls, Joseph A., Jr. 1998. "Population: A Lively Introduction." *Population Bulletin* 53(September).

McFalls, Joseph A., Jr., Brian Jones, and Bernard J. Gallegher III. 1984. "U.S. Population Growth: Prospects and Policy." *USA Today,* January, 30–34.

McGue, Matt, and Thomas J. Bouchard Jr. 1998. "Genetic and Environmental Influence on Human Behavioral Differences." Pp. 1–24 in *Annual Review of Neurosciences.* Palo Alto, CA: Annual Reviews.

McGuire, Meredith B. 1981. *Religion: The Social Context.* Belmont, CA: Wadsworth.

———. 1992. *Religion: The Social Context.* 3rd ed. Belmont, CA: Wadsworth.

McIntosh, Peggy. 1988. "White Privilege and Male Privilege: A Personal Account of Coming to See Correspondence through Work and Women's Studies." Working Paper No. 189, Wellesley College Center for Research on Women, Wellesley, MA.

McKenna, Barrie. 2004. "Unions Starting to Make Inroads at Wal-Mart." *The Globe and Mail,* August 23, B1, B12.

McKinlay, John B., and Sonja M. McKinlay. 1977. "The Questionable Contribution of Medical Measures to the Decline of Mortality in the United States in the Twentieth Century." *Milbank Memorial Fund Quarterly* 55(Summer):405–428.

McKinley, James C., Jr. 1999. "In Cuba's New Dual Economy, Have-Nots Far Exceed Haves." *New York Times,* February 11, A1, A6.

McLane, Daisann. 1995. "The Cuban-American Princess." *New York Times Magazine,* February 26, pp. 42–43.

McTeer, Maureen A. 1999. *Tough Choices: Living and Dying in the 21st Century.* Toronto: Irwin Law.

McVey, Wayne W., Jr., and Warren Kalbach. 1995. *Canadian Population.* Scarborough, ON: Nelson Canada.

Mead, George H. 1934. *Mind, Self and Society,* edited by Charles W. Morris. Chicago: University of Chicago Press.

———. 1964a. *On Social Psychology,* edited by Anselm Strauss. Chicago: University of Chicago Press.

———. 1964b. "The Genesis of the Self and Social Control." Pp. 267–293 in *Selected Writings: George Herbert Mead,* edited by Andrew J. Reck. Indianapolis: Bobbs-Merrill.

Mead, Margaret. [1935] 1963. *Sex and Temperament in Three Primitive Societies.* Reprint, New York: Morrow.

———. 1973. "Does the World Belong to Men—Or to Women?" *Redbook,* October, pp. 46–52.

Meisel, John. 2001. "Stroking the Airwaves: The Regulation of Broadcasting by the CRTC." Pp. 217–232 in *Communications in Canada.* 5th ed., edited by Craig McKie and Benjamin D. Singer. Toronto: Thompson Educational Publishing.

Melia, Marilyn Kennedy. 2000. "Changing Times." *Chicago Tribune,* January 2, 12–15.

Mendez, Jennifer Bickham. 1998. "Of Mops and Maids: Contradictions and Continuities in Bureaucratized Domestic Work." *Social Problems* 45(February):114–135.

Mendelsohn, Matthew. 2002. *Canadian Public Opinion on Representative Democracy.* Ottawa: Canadian Centre for Management Development.

Mensah, Joseph. 2002. *Black Canadians: History, Experiences, Social Conditions.* Halifax: Fernwood.

Merton, Robert K. 1968. *Social Theory and Social Structure.* New York: Free Press.

Merton, Robert K., and Alice S. Kitt. 1950. "Contributions to the Theory of Reference Group Behavior." Pp. 40–105 in *Continuities in Social Research: Studies in the Scope and Method of the American Soldier,* edited by Robert K. Merton and Paul L. Lazarsfeld. New York: Free Press.

Messner, Michael A. 1997. *Politics of Masculinities: Men in Movements.* Thousand Oaks, CA: Sage.

Meyers, Thomas J. 1992. "Factors Affecting the Decision to Leave the Old Order Amish." Presented at the annual meeting of the American Sociological Association, Pittsburgh.

Michels, Robert. 1915. *Political Parties.* Glencoe, IL: Free Press (reprinted 1949).

Mifflin, Lawrie. 1999. "Many Researchers Say Link Is Already Clear on Media and Youth Violence." *New York Times,* May 9, 23.

Migration News. 2003. "China: Economy, Migrants." January. Retreived August 23, 2003 (http://migration.ucdavis.edu).

Milgram, Stanley. 1963. "Behavioral Study of Obedience." *Journal of Abnormal and Social Psychology* 67(October):371–378.

———. 1975. *Obedience to Authority: An Experimental View.* New York: Harper and Row.

Miller, George A., and Oleg I. Gubin. 2000. "The Structure of Russian Organizations." *Sociological Inquiry* 70 (Winter):74–87.

Miller, G. Tyler, Jr. 1972. *Replenish the Earth: A Primer in Human Ecology.* Belmont, CA: Wadsworth.

Miller, Reuben. 1988. "The Literature of Terrorism." *Terrorism* 11(1):63–87.

Millet, Kate. 1971. *Sexual Politics.* New York: Avon Books.

Mills, C. Wright. 1956. *The Power Elite.* New York: Oxford University Press.

Mills, Robert J. 2000. "Health Insurance Coverage." *Current Population Reports,* ser. P60, no. 211. Washington, DC: U.S. Government Printing Office.

Miner, Horace. 1956. "Body Ritual among the Nacirema." *American Anthropologist* 58(June): 503–507.

Mingle, James R. 1987. *Focus on Minorities.* Denver: Education Commission of the States and the State Higher Education Executive Officers.

Mitchell, Alanna. 1999. "Home Schooling Goes AWOL." *The Globe and Mail,* February 2, A1, A6.

Mitnick, Kevin D., and William L. Simon. 2005. *The Art of Intrusion: The Real Stories behind the Exploits of Hackers, Intruders and Deceivers.* New York: John Wiley and Sons.

Moffatt, Susan. 1995. "Minorities Found More Likely to Live Near Toxic Sites." *Los Angeles Times,* August 30, B1, B3.

Mogelonsky, Marcia. 1996. "The Rocky Road to Adulthood." *American Demographics* 18(May):26–29, 32–35, 56.

Monteiro, Lois A. 1998. "Ill-Defined Illnesses and Medically Unexplained Symptoms Syndrome." *Footnotes* 26(February):3, 6.

Moore, Oliver. 2004. "Ontario Liberals Focus on School Violence." *The Globe and Mail,* December 14. Retrieved December 14, 2004 (http://www.theglobeandmail.com/Servlet/story/RTGAM.20041214.wskul1214/BNStory/)

Moore, Wilbert E. 1967. *Order and Change: Essays in Comparative Sociology.* New York: Wiley.

———. 1968. "Occupational Socialization." Pp. 861–883 in *Handbook of Socialization Theory and Research,* edited by David A. Goslin. Chicago: Rand McNally.

Morin, Richard. 2000. "Will Traditional Polls Go the Way of the Dinosaur?" *Washington Post National Weekly Edition,* May 15, 34.

Morris, Aldon. 2000. "Reflections on Social Movement Theory: Criticisms and Proposals." *Contemporary Sociology* 29(May): 445–454.

Morris, Bonnie Rothman. 1999. "You've Got Romance! Seeking Love on Line." *New York Times,* August 26, D1.

Morrison, Denton E. 1971. "Some Notes toward Theory on Relative Deprivation, Social Movements, and Social Change." *American Behavioral Scientist* 14(May–June):675–690.

Moseley, Ray. 2000. "Britons Watch Health Service Fall to Its Knees." *Chicago Tribune,* January 22, 1, 2.

Mossman, M.J. 1994. "Running Hard to Stand Still: The Paradox of Family Law Reform." *Dalhousie Law Journal* 17(5).

Mossman, Mary Jane. 1998. "The Paradox of Feminist Engagement with Law." Pp. 180–206 in *Feminist Issues: Race, Class, and Sexuality.* 2nd ed., edited by Nancy Mandell. Scarborough, ON: Prentice Hall Allyn and Bacon Canada.

MOST. 1999. *MOST Quarterly.* Internet vol. 1. Retrieved July 19, 1999 (http://www.most online.org/qtrly/qtrly-index.htm).

Murdock, George P. 1945. "The Common Denominator of Cultures." Pp. 123–142 in *The Science of Man in the World Crisis,* edited by Ralph Linton. New York: Columbia University Press.

———. 1949. *Social Structure.* New York: Macmillan.

———. 1957. "World Ethnographic Sample." *American Anthropologist* 59(August):664–687.

Murphy, Caryle. 1993. "Putting aside the Veil." *Washington Post National Weekly Edition,* April 12–18, 10–11.

Murphy, Dean E. 1997. "A Victim of Sweden's Pursuit of Perfection." *Los Angeles Times,* September 2, A1, A8.

N

Nader, Laura. 1986. "The Subordination of Women in Comparative Perspective." *Urban Anthropology* 15(Fall–Winter):377–397.

Naiman, Joanne. 2004. *How Societies Work: Class Power and Change in the Canadian Context.* 3rd ed. Toronto: Nelson.

Nakao, Keiko, and Judith Treas. 1990. *Computing 1989 Occupational Prestige Scores.* Chicago: NORC.

———. 1994. "Updating Occupational Prestige and Socio-economic Scores: How the New Measures Measure Up." Pp. 1–72 in *Sociological Methodology, 1994,* edited by Peter V. Marsden. Oxford: Basil Blackwell.

Nabalamba, Alice. 2001. *Locating Risk: A Multivariate Analysis of the Spatial and Socio-demographic Characteristics of Pollution.* Unpublished Ph.D. dissertation, University of Waterloo, Ontario.

Nanda, Serena. 1991. *Cultural Anthropology.* Belmont, CA: Wadsworth Publishing Company.

Nash, Manning. 1962. "Race and the Ideology of Race." *Current Anthropology* 3(June):285–288.

Nass, Clifford, and Youngme Moon. 2000. "Machines and Mindlessness: Social Responses to Computers." *Journal of Social Issues* 56(1):81–103.

National Advisory Commission on Criminal Justice. 1976. *Organized Crime.* Washington, DC: U.S. Government Printing Office.

National Center for Educational Statistics. 1999. *Digest of Education Statistics, 1998.* Washington, DC: U.S. Government Printing Office.

National Center on Elder Abuse. 1998. *The National Elder Abuse Incidence Study.* Washington, DC: American Public Human Services Association.

National Council of Welfare. 1999. *Poverty Profile 1997.* Ottawa: National Council of Welfare.

National Homeschool Association. 1999. *Homeschooling Families: Ready for the Next Decade.* Retrieved November 19, 2000 (http://www.n-h-a.org/decade.htm).

National Institute on Aging. 1999. *The Declining Disability of Older Americans.* Washington, DC: U.S. Government Printing Office.

National Partnership for Women and Families. 1998. *Balancing Acts: Work/Family Issues on Prime-Time TV. Executive Summary.* Washington, DC: The National Partnership for Women and Families.

Navarro, Mireya. 2002. "Trying to Get Beyond the Role of the Maid." *New York Times,* May 16, E1, E4.

Neft, Naomi, and Ann D. Levine. 1997. *Where Women Stand: An International Report on the Status of Women in 140 Countries.* New York: Random House.

Nelson, Adie, and Augie Fleras. 1995. *Social Problems in Canada: Issues and Challenges.* Scarborough, ON: Prentice-Hall Canada.

———. 1998. *Social Problems in Canada: Conditions and Consequences.* 2nd ed. Scarborough, ON: Prentice-Hall.

Nelson, Adie, and Barrie W. Robinson. 1999. *Gender in Canada.* Scarborough, ON: Prentice Hall.

———. 2002. *Gender in Canada.* 2nd ed. Toronto: Pearson Education Canada.

Nelson, Jack. 1995. "The Internet, the Virtual Community, and Those with Disabilities." *Disability Studies Quarterly* 15(Spring): 15–20.

Neuborne, Ellen. 1996. "Vigilantes Stir Firms' Ire with Cyberantics." *USA Today,* February 28, A1, A2.

Newman, William M. 1973. *American Pluralism: A Study of Minority Groups and Social Theory.* New York: Harper and Row.

Newsday. 1997. "Japan Sterilized 16,000 Women." September 18, A19.

New York Times. 1998. "2 Gay Men Fight Town Hall for a Family Pool Pass Discount." July 14, B2.

Ng, Roxanna. 1988. *The Politics of Community Services: Immigrant Women, Class and the State.* Toronto: Garamond Press.

Nguyen, S. D. 1982. "The Psycho-social Adjustment and Mental Health Needs of Southeast Asian Refugees." *Psychiatric Journal of the University of Ottawa* 7(1):6–34.

Nie, Norman H. 1999. "Tracking Our Techno-Future." *American Demographics* (July): 50–52.

———. 2001. "Sociability, Interpersonal Relations, and the Internet." *American Behavioral Scientist* 45 (November):420–435.

Nielsen, Joyce McCarl, Glenda Walden, and Charlotte A. Kunkel. 2000. "Gendered Heteronormativity: Empirical Illustrations in Everyday Life." *Sociological Quarterly* 41(2):283–296.

Nixon, Howard L., II. 1979. *The Small Group.* Englewood Cliffs, NJ: Prentice-Hall.

Nolan, Patrick, and Gerhad Lenski. 1999. *Human Societies: An Introduction to Macrosociology.* New York: McGraw-Hill.

Noonan, Rita K. 1995. "Women against the State: Political Opportunities and Collective Action Frames in Chile's Transition to Democracy." *Sociological Forum* 10:81–111.

NORC (National Opinion Research Center). 1994. *General Social Surveys 1972–1994.* Chicago: National Opinion Research Center.

O

O'Donnell, Mike. 1992. *A New Introduction to Sociology.* Walton-on-Thames, UK: Thomas Nelson and Sons.

Oberschall, Anthony. 1973. *Social Conflict and Social Movements.* Englewood Cliffs, NJ: Prentice-Hall.

Organisation for Economic Co-operation and Development (OECD). 2003. *Education at a Glance: OECD Indicators.* Paris: OECD.

———. 2004. *Early Childhood Education and Care Policy: Canada Country Note October 2004.* Retrieved October 28, 2004 (http://www.11.sdc.go.ca/en/cs/sp/socpol/publications/reports/2004-002619/page00.shtml).

Office of Justice Programs. 1999. "Transnational Organized Crime." *NCJRS Catalog* 49(November/December):21.

Ogburn, William F. 1922. *Social Change with Respect to Culture and Original Nature.* New York: Huebsch (reprinted 1966, New York: Dell).

Ogburn, William F., and Clark Tibbits. 1934. "The Family and Its Functions." Pp. 661–708 in *Recent Social Trends in the United States,* edited by Research Committee on Social Trends. New York: McGraw-Hill.

O'Hanlan, Kate. 2002. "Lesbian Health and Homophobia: Perspectives for Treating Obstetrician/Gynecologist." Retrieved April 4, 2002 (http://www.ohanlan.com/lhr.htm).

Okano, Kaori, and Motonori Tsuchiya. 1999. *Education in Contemporary Japan: Inequality and Diversity.* Cambridge: Cambridge University Press.

Oliver, Melvin L., and Thomas M. Shapiro. 1995. *Black Wealth/White Wealth: New Perspectives on Racial Inequality.* New York: Routledge.

Orum, Anthony M. 1989. *Introduction to Political Sociology: The Social Anatomy of the Body Politic.* 3rd ed. Englewood Cliffs, NJ: Prentice-Hall.

Orwell, George. 1949. *1984.* New York: Harcourt Brace Jovanovich.

Ostling, Richard N. 1993. "Religion." *Time International,* July 12, p. 38.

Ouellette, Laurie. 1993. "The Information Lockout." *Utne Reader,* September–October, pp. 25–26.

P

Pagani, Steve. 1999. "End the 'Culture of Death,' Pope Tells America." Reuters Wire Service, January 23.

Page, Charles H. 1946. "Bureaucracy's Other Face." *Social Forces* 25(October):89–94.

Palmer Patterson, E. 1972. *The Canadian Indian: A History Since 1500.* New York: Collier-Macmillan of Canada Ltd.

Paquet, Laura Byrne. 2003. *The Urge to Splurge: A Social History of Shopping.* Toronto: ECW Press.

Park, Robert E. 1916. "The City: Suggestions for the Investigation of Human Behavior in the Urban Environment." *American Journal of Sociology* 20(March):577–612.

———. 1936. "Succession, an Ecological Concept." *American Sociological Review* 1(April):171–179.

Park, Steve. 1997. "In the Spirit of Jerry Maguire, I Submit This to the Hollywood Community." *Social Culture.* Korean newsgroups 48:17. Retrieved August 17, 2005 (http://www.dpg.devry.edu/~akim/sck/ho1.html).

Parsons, Talcott. 1951. *The Social System.* New York: Free Press.

———. 1966. *Societies: Evolutionary and Comparative Perspectives.* Englewood Cliffs, NJ: Prentice-Hall.

———. 1972. "Definitions of Health and Illness in the Light of American Values and Social Structure." Pp. 166–187 in *Patients, Physicians and Illness,* edited by Gartley Jaco. New York: Free Press.

———. 1975. "The Sick Role and the Role of the Physician Reconsidered." *Milbank Medical Fund Quarterly, Health and Society* 53(Summer):257–278.

Parsons, Talcott, and Robert Bales. 1955. *Family, Socialization, and Interaction Process.* Glencoe, IL: Free Press.

Pate, Antony M., and Edwin E. Hamilton. 1992. "Formal and Informal Deterrents to Domestic Violence: The Dade County Spouse Assault Experiment." *American Sociological Reviews* 57(October):691–697.

Patton, Carl V., ed. 1988. *Spontaneous Shelter: International Perspectives and Prospects.* Philadelphia: Temple University Press.

Paulson, Amanda. 2000. "Where the School Is Home." *Christian Science Monitor,* October 10, pp. 18–21.

PBS. 2001. "Store Wars: When Wal-Mart Comes to Town." Retrieved August 24, 2001 (http://www.pbs.org).

Pear, Robert. 1996. "Clinton Endorses the Most Radical of Welfare Trials." *New York Times*, May 19, 1, 20.

———. 1997a. "New Estimate Doubles Rate of HIV Spread." *New York Times*, November 26, A6.

———. 1997b. "Now, the Archenemies Need Each Other." *New York Times*, June 22, 1, 4.

Pearlstein, Steven. 2001. "Coming Soon (Maybe): Worldwide Recession." *Washington Post National Weekly Edition*, November 12, 18.

Pelton, Tom. 1994. "Hawthorne Works' Glory Now Just So Much Rubble." *Chicago Tribune*, April 18, pp. 1, 6.

Pendakur, Krishna, and Ravi Pendakur. 1998. "The Colour of Money: Earnings Differentials across Ethnic Groups in Canada." *Canadian Journal of Economics* 31(3):518–548.

———. 2002. "Colour My World: Have Earnings Gaps for Canadians-Born Ethnic Minorities Changed over Time?" *Canadian Public Policy* 28(4):489–512.

Perrow, Charles. 1986. *Complex Organizations*. 3rd ed. New York: Random House.

Peter, Laurence J., and Raymond Hull. 1969. *The Peter Principle*. New York: Morrow.

Petersen, William. 1979. *Malthus*. Cambridge, MA: Harvard University Press.

Philip, Margaret. 2001. "Teens' Dilemma: Cash or Class." *The Globe and Mail*, March 27, A7.

Phillips, E. Barbara. 1996. *City Lights: Urban–Suburban Life in the Global Society*. New York: Oxford University Press.

Piaget, Jean. 1954. *The Construction of Reality in the Child*. Translated by Margaret Cook. New York: Basic Books.

Piller, Charles. 2000. "Cyber-Crime Loss at Firms Doubles to $10 Billion." *Los Angeles Times*, May 22, C1, C4.

Platt, Steve. 1993. "Without Walls." *Statesman and Society* 6(April 2):5–7.

Pleck, J.H., and E. Corfman. 1979. "Married Men: Work and Family." *Families Today: A Research Sampler on Families and Children* 1:387–411.

Plomin, Robert. 1989. "Determinants of Behavior." *American Psychologist* 44(February): 105–111.

Polk, Barbara Bovee. 1974. "Male Power and the Women's Movement." *Journal of Applied Behavioral Science* 10:415–431.

Pomfret, John. 2000. "A New Chinese Revolution." *Washington Post National Weekly Edition*, February 21, 17–19.

Ponczek, Ed. 1998. "Are Hiring Practices Sensitive to Persons with Disabilities?" *Footnotes* 26(3):5.

Poniewozik, James. 2001. "What's Wrong with This Picture?" *Time*, May 28, pp. 80–81.

Population Reference Bureau. 1978. "World Population: Growth on the Decline." *Interchange* 7(May):1–3.

———. 1996. "Speaking Graphically." *Population Today* 24(June/July).

Porter, John. 1965. *The Vertical Mosaic: An Analysis of Social Class and Power in Canada*. Toronto: University of Toronto Press.

Power, Carla. 1998. "The New Islam." *Newsweek* 131(March 16):34–37.

Powers, Mary G., and Joan J. Holmberg. 1978. "Occupational Status Scores: Changes Introduced by the Inclusion of Women." *Demography* 15(May):183–204.

Princeton Religion Research Center. 2000. "Nearly Half of Americans Describe Themselves as Evangelicals." *Emerging Trends* 22(April):5.

Proctor, Bernadette D., and Joseph Dalaker. 2002. "Poverty in the United States: 2001." *Current Population Reports*, ser. P-60, no. 219. Washington, DC: U.S. Government Printing Office.

Q

Quadagno, Jill. 1999. *Aging and the Life Course: An Introduction to Social Gerontology*. New York: McGraw-Hill.

Quinney, Richard. 1970. *The Social Reality of Crime*. Boston: Little, Brown.

———. 1974. *Criminal Justice in America*. Boston: Little, Brown.

———. 1979. *Criminology*. 2nd ed. Boston: Little, Brown.

———. 1980. *Class, State and Crime*. 2nd ed. New York: Longman.

R

Rainie, Lee, and Dan Pakel. 2001. *More Online, Doing More*. Washington, DC: Pew Internet and American Life Project.

Ramet, Sabrina. 1991. *Social Currents in Eastern Europe: The Source and Meaning of the Great Transformation*. Durham, NC: Duke University Press.

Rau, William, and Ann Durand. 2000. "The Academic Ethic and College Grades: Does Hard Work Help Students to 'Make the Grade?'" *Sociology of Education* 73(January):19–38.

Reddick, Randy, and Elliot King. 2000. *The Online Student: Making the Grade on the Internet*. Fort Worth: Harcourt Brace.

Rees, Ruth. 1990. *Women and Men in Education: A National Survey of Gender Distribution in School Systems*. Toronto: Canadian Education Association.

Reese, William A., II, and Michael A. Katovich. 1989. "Untimely Acts: Extending the Interactionist Conception of Deviance." *Sociological Quarterly* 30(2):159–184.

Reinharz, Shulamit. 1992. *Feminist Methods in Social Research*. New York: Oxford University Press.

Reitz, Jeffrey. 1980. *The Survival of Ethnic Groups*. Toronto: McClelland and Stewart.

Religion Watch. 1995. "European Dissenting Movement Grows among Laity Theologians." 10(October):6–7.

Remnick, David. 1998. "Bad Seeds." *New Yorker* 74(July 20):28–33.

Rennison, Callie. 2002. *Criminal Victimization 2001. Changes 2000–01 with Trends 1993–2001*. Washington, DC: U.S. Government Printing Office.

Rennison, Callie Marie, and Sarah Welchans. 2000. *Intimate Partner Violence*. Washington, DC: U.S. Government Printing Office.

Repper, J., R. Perkins, S. Owen, D. Deighton, and J. Robinson. 1996. "Evaluating Services for Women with Serious and Ongoing Mental Health Problems: Developing an Appropriate Research Method." *Journal of Psychiatric and Mental Health Nursing* 3:39–46.

Rheingold, Harriet L. 1969. "The Social and Socializing Infant." Pp. 779–790 in *Handbook of Socialization Theory and Research*, edited by David A. Goslin. Chicago: Rand McNally.

Richard, Amy O'Neill. 2000. *International Trafficking in Women to the United States: A Contemporary Manifestation of Slavery and Organized Crime*. Washington, DC: Center for the Study of Intelligence, CIA.

Richardson, Diane, and Victoria Robinson. 1993. *Thinking Feminist: Key Concepts in Women's Studies*. New York: The Guildford Press.

Richardson, James T., and Barend van Driel. 1997. "Journalists' Attitudes toward New Religious Movements." *Review of Religious Research* 39(December):116–136.

Richtel, Matt. 2000. "www.layoffs.com." *New York Times*, June 22, C1, C12.

Riding, Alan. 1998. "Why 'Titanic' Conquered the World." *New York Times*, April 26, 1, 28, 29.

Rifkin, Jeremy. 1995. *The End of Work: The Decline of the Global Labor Force and the Dawn of the Post-Market Era*. New York: Tarcher/Putnam.

———. 1996. "Civil Society in the Information Age." *The Nation* 262(February 26):11–12, 14–16.

———. 1998. *The Biotech Century: Harnessing the Gene and Remaking the World*. New York: Tarcher/Putnam.

Riley, Matilda White, Robert L. Kahn, and Anne Foner. 1994a. *Age and Structural Lag*. New York: Wiley Inter-Science.

Riley, Matilda White, Robert L. Kahn, and Anne Foner, in association with Karin A. Mock. 1994b. "Introduction: The Mismatch between People and Structures." Pp. 1–36 in *Age and Structural Lag*, edited by Matilda White Riley, Robert L. Kahn, and Ann Foner. New York: Wiley Inter-Science.

Riley, Nancy E. 2004. "China's Population: New Trends and Challenges." *Population Bulletin* 59(June).

Ritzer, George. 1995a. *Modern Sociological Theory*. 4th ed. New York: McGraw-Hill.

———. 1995b. *The McDonaldization of Society*. Rev. ed. Thousand Oaks, CA: Pine Forge Books.

———. 2000. *The McDonaldization of Society*. New century ed. Thousand Oaks, CA: Pine Forge Press.

Robb, N. 1993. "School of Fear." *OH&S Canada:* 43–48.

Roberts, D. F, Lisa Henriksen, Peter G. Christenson, and Marcy Kelly. 1999. "Substance Abuse in Popular Movies and Music." Washington, DC: Office of Juvenile Justice. Retrieved October 19, 2000 (http://www.whitehouse drugpolicy. gov/news/press/042899.html).

Roberts, Keith A. 1995. *Religion in Sociological Perspective.* 3rd ed. Belmont, CA: Wadsworth.

Roberts, Lynne D., and Malcolm R. Parks. 1999. "The Social Geography of Gender-Switching in Virtual Environments on the Internet." *Information, Communication and Society* 2(Winter).

Robertson, Roland. 1988. "The Sociological Significance of Culture: Some General Considerations." *Theory, Culture, and Society* 5(February):3–23.

Robinson, Gregory, and May Cohen. 1996. "Gay, Lesbian and Bisexual Health Care Issues and Medical Curricula. *Canadian Medical Association Journal* 155:709–711. Retrieved April 4, 2002 (http://www.cma.ca/cmaj/vol-155/issue-06/0709.htm).

Robinson, James D., and Thomas Skill. 1993. "The Invisible Generation: Portrayals of the Elderly on Television." Unpublished paper. University of Dayton.

Rocks, David. 1999. "Burger Giant Does as Europeans Do." *Chicago Tribune*, January 6, 1, 4.

Rodberg, Simon. 1999. "Woman and Man at Yale." *Culturefront Online*. Retrieved September 9, 1999 (http://www.culturefront.org/culturefront/magazine/99/spring/article.5.html).

Rodgers, M. 1993. "Helping Students, Families, and Schools of the Niagara Region Resolve Conflict." *Brock Education* 3(1):12–14.

Rodin, Judith, and Jeanette R. Ickovics. 1990. "Women's Health: Review and Research Agenda as We Approach the 21st Century." *American Psychologist* 45:1018–1034.

Roethlisberger, Fritz J., and W.J. Dickson. 1939. *Management and the Worker.* Cambridge, MA: Harvard University Press.

Roher, Eric M. 1993. "Violence in a School Setting." *Brock Education* 3(1):1–4.

Rollins, Judith. 1985. *Between Women: Domestics and Their Employers.* Philadelphia: Temple University Press.

Rose, Arnold. 1951. *The Roots of Prejudice.* Paris: UNESCO.

Rose, Peter I., Myron Glazer, and Penina Migdal Glazer. 1979. "In Controlled Environments: Four Cases of Intense Resocialization." Pp. 320–338 in *Socialization and the Life Cycle,* edited by Peter I. Rose. New York: St. Martin's.

Rosen, Laurel. 2001. "If U Cn Rd Ths Msg, U Cn B Txtin W/Millions in Europe and Asia." *Los Angeles Times,* July 3, A5.

Rosenbaum, Lynn. 1996. "Gynocentric Feminism: An Affirmation of Women's Values and Experiences Leading Us toward Radical Social Change." *SSSP Newsletter* 27(1):4–7.

Rosenberg, Douglas H. 1991. "Capitalism." Pp. 33–34 in *Encyclopedic Dictionary of Sociology.* 4th ed., edited by Dushkin Publishing Group. Guilford, CT: Dushkin.

Rosenthal, Elizabeth. 1999. "Web Sites Bloom in China, and Are Waded." *New York Times,* December 23, A1, A10.

———. 2000. "China Lists Controls to Restrict the Use of E-Mail and Web." *New York Times,* January 27, A1, A10.

———. 2001. "College Entrance in China: 'No' to the Handicapped." *New York Times,* May 23, A3.

Rosenthal, Robert, and Elisha Y. Babad, and Lenore Jacobson. 1968. *Pygmalion in the Classroom.* New York: Holt.

Rosman, Abraham, and Paula G. Rubel. 1994. *The Tapestry of Culture: An Introduction to Cultural Anthropology.* 5th ed. Chapter 1, Map, p. 35. New York: McGraw-Hill.

Ross, John. 1996. "To Die in the Street: Mexico City's Homeless Population Booms as Economic Crisis Shakes Social Protections." *SSSP Newsletter* 27(Summer):14–15.

Rossi, Alice S. 1968. "Transition to Parenthood." *Journal of Marriage and the Family* 30(February):26–39.

———. 1984. "Gender and Parenthood." *American Sociological Review* 49(February):1–19.

Rossi, Peter H. 1989. *Down and Out in America: The Origins of Homelessness.* Chicago: University of Chicago Press.

———. 1990. "The Politics of Homelessness." Presented at the annual meeting of the American Sociological Association, Washington, DC.

Rotella, Sebastin. 1999. "A Latin View of American-Style Violence." *Los Angeles Times,* November 25, p. A1.

Royal Commission Status of Women. 1970. *Report of the Royal Commission on the Status of Women in Canada.* Ottawa: The Commission

Russell, Cheryl. 1995. "Murder Is All-American." *American Demographics* 17(September):15–17.

Russo, Nancy Felipe. 1976. "The Motherhood Mandate." *Journal of Social Issues* 32:143–153.

Ryan, William. 1976. *Blaming the Victim.* Rev. ed. New York: Random House.

S

Saad, Lydia. 2003. "What Form of Government for Iraq?" Retrieved September 26 (http://www.gallup.com).

Sadker, Myra Pollack, and David Sadker. 1985. "Sexism in the Schoolroom of the '80s." *Psychology Today* 19(March):54–57.

Sadker, Myra, and David Sadker. 1994. *Failing at Fairness: How America's Schools Cheat Girls.* New York: Scribner.

———. 1995. *Failing at Fairness: How America's Schools Cheat Girls.* 2nd ed. New York: Touchstone.

Safire, William. 1996. "Downsized." *New York Times Magazine,* May 26, pp. 12, 14.

Sagarin, Edward, and Jose Sanchez. 1988. "Ideology and Deviance: The Case of the Debate over the Biological Factor." *Deviant Behavior* 9(1):87–99.

Sale, Kirkpatrick. 1996. *Rebels against the Future: The Luddites and Their War on the Industrial Revolution* (with a new preface by the author). Reading, MA: Addison-Wesley.

Salkever, Alex. 1999. "Making Machines More Like Us," *Christian Science Monitor,* December 20.

Samuelson, Paul A., and William D. Nordhaus. 1998. *Economics.* 16th ed. New York: McGraw-Hill.

———. 2001. *Economics.* 17th ed. New York: McGraw-Hill.

Samuelson, Robert J. 1996a. "Are Workers Disposable?" *Newsweek* 127, February 12, p. 47.

———. 1996b. "Fashionable Statements," *Washington Post National Weekly Edition,* March 18, 5.

———. 2001. "The Specter of Global Aging." *Washington Post National Weekly Edition,* March 11, 27.

Sandberg, Jared. 1999. "Spinning a Web of Hate." *Newsweek,* July 19, pp. 28–29.

Sassen, Saskia. 1999. *Guests and Aliens.* New York: The New Press.

Saukko, Paula. 1999. "Fat Boys and Goody Girls." In *Weighty Issues: Fatness and Thinness as Social Problems,* edited by Jeffrey Sobal and Donna Maurer. New York: Aldine de Gruyter.

Sawyer, Tom. 2000. "Antiretroviral Drug Costs." Correspondence to author from Roxane Laboratories, Cincinnati, OH, January 19.

Schaefer, Peter. 1995. "Destroy Your Future." *Daily Northwestern*, November 3, 8.

Schaefer, Richard T. 2004. *Racial and Ethnic Relations.* 9th ed. Upper Saddle River, NJ: Prentice-Hall.

Schaefer, Sandy. 1996. "Peaceful Play." Presentation at the annual meeting of the Chicago Association for the Education of Young Children, Chicago.

Schaller, Lyle E. 1990. "Megachurch!" *Christianity Today* 34(March 5):10, 20–24.

Schellenberg, Grant, and Christopher Clark. 1996. *Temporary Employment in Canada: Profiles, Patterns and Policy Considerations.* Ottawa: Canadian Council on Social Development.

Schellenberg, Kathryn, ed. 1996. *Computers in Society.* 6th ed. Guilford, CT: Dushkin.

Schlenker, Barry R., ed. 1985. *The Self and Social Life.* New York: McGraw-Hill.

Schmetzer, Uli. 1999. "Modern India Remains Shackled to Caste System." *Chicago Tribune,* December 25, p. 23.

Schmid, Carol. 1980. "Sexual Antagonism: Roots of the Sex-Ordered Division of Labor." *Humanity and Society* 4(November):243–261.

Schmidt, Sarah. 2004. "Older Men Kick Tradition, Opt for Cosmetic Surgeries." *Vancouver Sun*, October 29, A8.

Schnaiberg, Allan. 1994. *Environment and Society: The Enduring Conflict.* New York: St. Martin's.

Schnaiberg, Lynn. 1999. "Study Finds Home Schoolers Are Top Achievers on Tests." *Education Week* 18(March 31):5.

Schoenfeld, A. Clay, Robert F. Meier, and Robert J. Griffin. 1979. "Constructing a Social Problem: The Press and the Environment." *Social Problems*, 27:38–61.

Schur, Edwin M. 1965. *Crimes without Victims: Deviant Behavior and Public Policy.* Englewood Cliffs, NJ: Prentice-Hall.

———. 1968. *Law and Society: A Sociological View.* New York: Random House.

———. 1983. *Labelling Women Deviant: Gender, Stigma and Social Control.* Philadelphia: Temple University Press.

———. 1985. "'Crimes without Victims': A 20-Year Reassessment." Paper presented at the annual meeting of the Society for the Study of Social Problems.

Schulman, Andrew. 2001. *The Extent of Systematic Monitoring of Employee E-mail and Internet Users.* Denver, CO: Workplace Surveillance Project, Privacy Foundation.

Schwab, William A. 1993. "Recent Empirical and Theoretical Developments in Sociological Human Ecology." Pp. 29–57 in *Urban Sociology in Transition,* edited by Ray Hutchison. Greenwich, CT: JAI Press.

Scott, Alan. 1990. *Ideology and the New Social Movements.* London: Unwin Hyman.

Segall, Alexander. 1976. "The Sick Role Concept: Understanding Illness Behavior." *Journal of Health and Social Behavior* 17(June):163–170.

Segall, Rebecca. 1998. "Sikh and Ye Shall Find." *Village Voice* 43(December 15):46–48, 53.

Segerstråle, Ullica. 2000. *Defense of the Truth: The Battle for Science in the Sociobiology Debate and Beyond.* New York: Oxford University Press.

Seidman, Steven. 1994. "Heterosexism in America: Prejudice against Gay Men and Lesbians." Pp. 578–593 in *Introduction to Social Problems,* edited by Craig Calhoun and George Ritzer. New York: McGraw-Hill.

Shaheen, Jack G. 1999. "Image and Identity: Screen Arabs and Muslims." In *Cultural Diversity: Curriculum, Classrooms, and Climate Issues,* edited by J.Q. Adams and Janice R. Welsch. Macomb, IL: Illinois Staff and Curriculum Development Association.

Shapiro, Joseph P. 1993. *No Pity: People with Disabilities Forging a New Civil Rights Movement.* New York: Times Books.

Sharma, Hari M., and Gerard C. Bodeker. 1998. "Alternative Medicine." Pp. 228–229 in *Britannica Book of the Year 1998.* Chicago: Encyclopaedia Britannica.

Shcherbak, Yuri M. 1996. "Ten Years of the Chernobyl Era." *Scientific American* 274(April): 44–49.

Sheehy, Gail. 1999. *Understanding Men's Passages: Discovering the New Map of Men's Lives.* New York: Ballantine Books.

Shenon, Philip. 1995. "New Zealand Seeks Causes of Suicides by Young." *New York Times,* July 15, 3.

Sherman, Lawrence W., Patrick R. Gartin, and Michael D. Buerger. 1989. "Hot Spots of Predatory Crime: Routine Activities and the Criminology of Place." *Criminology* 27:27–56.

Sherrill, Robert. 1995. "The Madness of the Market." *The Nation* 260(January 9–16):45–72.

Shields, Rob, ed. 1996. *Cultures of Internet: Virtual Spaces, Real Histories, Living Bodies.* London: Sage.

Shinkai, Hiroguki, and Ugljesa Zvekic. 1999. "Punishment." Pp. 89–120 in *Global Report on Crime and Justice*, edited by Graeme Newman. New York: Oxford University Press.

Shupe, Anson D., and David G. Bromley. 1980. "Walking a Tightrope." *Qualitative Sociology* 2:8–21.

Sigelman, Lee, Timothy Bledsoe, Susan Welch, and Michael W. Combs. 1996. "Making Contact? Black–White Social Interaction in an Urban Setting." *American Journal of Sociology* 5(March):1306–1332.

Silicon Valley Cultures Project. 1999. "The Silicon Valley Cultures Project Website." Retrieved July 30, 1990 (http://www.sjsu.edu/depts/anthrology/svcp).

Silver, Cynthia, Cara Williams, and Trish McOrmond. 2001. "Learning on Your Own." *Canadian Social Trends* (Spring). Statistics Canada. Catalogue No. 11-008. Ottawa: Minister of Industry.

Silver, Ira. 1996. "Role Transitions, Objects, and Identity." *Symbolic Interaction* 19(1):1–20.

Simmel, Georg. 1950. *Sociology of Georg Simmel.* Translated by K. Wolff. Glencoe, IL: Free Press (originally written in 1902–1917).

Simmons, Ann M. 1998. "Where Fat Is a Mark of Beauty." *Los Angeles Times*, September 30, A1, A12.

Simon, Bernard. 2001. "Canada Warms to Wal-Mart." *New York Times,* November 1, B1, B3.

Simons, Marlise. 1997. "Child Care Sacred as France Cuts Back the Welfare State." *New York Times*, December 31, A1, A6.

Simpson, Sally. 1993. "Corporate Crime." Pp. 236–256 in *Introduction to Social Problems,* edited by Craig Calhoun and George Ritzer. New York: McGraw-Hill.

Sjoberg, Gideon. 1960. *The Preindustrial City: Past and Present.* Glencoe, IL: Free Press.

Smart, Barry. 1990. "Modernity, Postmodernity, and the Present." Pp. 14–30 in *Theories of Modernity and Postmodernity,* edited by Bryan S. Turner. Newbury Park, CA: Sage.

Smart Growth. 2001. "About Smart Growth." Retrieved August 24, 2001 (http://www.smartgrowth.org).

Smeeding, Timothy, Lee Rainwater, and Gary Burtless. 2001. "United States Poverty in a Cross-National Context." *Focus* 21 (Spring): 50–54.

Smelser, Neil. 1963. *The Sociology of Economic Life.* Englewood Cliffs, NJ: Prentice-Hall.

Smith, Christian. 1991. *The Emergence of Liberation Theology: Radical Religion and Social Movement Theory.* Chicago: University of Chicago Press.

Smith, David A. 1995. "The New Urban Sociology Meets the Old: Rereading Some Classical Human Ecology." *Urban Affairs Review* 20(January):432–457.

Smith, David A, and Michael Timberlake. 1993. "World Cities: A Political Economy/Global Network Approach." Pp. 181–207 in *Urban Sociology in Transition,* edited by Ray Hutchison. Greenwich, CT: JAI Press.

Smith, Dorothy. 1987. *The Everyday World as Problematic: A Feminist Sociology.* Toronto: University of Toronto Press.

Smith, Kristin. 2000. "Who's Minding the Kids? Child Care Arrangements." *Current Population Reports,* ser. P-70, no. 70. Washington, DC: U.S. Government Printing Office.

Smith, Michael Peter. 1988. *City, State, and Market.* New York: Basil Blackwell.

Smith, Tom W. 2001. "Measuring Inter-racial Friendships: Experimental Comparisons." *Public Opinion Quarterly,* forthcoming.

Smith-Rosenburg, Carroll. 1986. *Disorderly Conduct: Visions of Gender in America.* Toronto: Oxford University Press.

Smith-Rosenberg, Carroll, and Charles Rosenberg. 1974. "The Female Animal: Medical and Biological Views of Woman and Her Role in Nineteenth-Century America." *Journal of American History* 60(March):332–356.

Snyder, Thomas D. 1996. *Digest of Education Statistics 1996.* Washington, DC: U.S. Government Printing Office.

Sohoni, Neera Kuckreja. 1994. "Where Are the Girls?" *Ms.,* July–August, p. 96.

Sørensen, Annemette. 1994. "Women, Family and Class." Pp. 27–47 in *Annual Review of Sociology, 1994,* edited by Annemette Sørensen. Palo Alto, CA: Annual Reviews.

Soriano, Cesar G. 2001. "Latino TV Roles Shrank in 2000, Report Finds." *USA Today,* August 26, 3rd.

Sorokin, Pitirim A. 1959. *Social and Cultural Mobility.* New York: Free Press (original edition 1927, New York: Harper).

Spar, Debora. 2001. *Ruling the Waves: Cycles of Discovery, Chaos, and Wealth from the Compass to the Internet.* Toronto: Harcourt.

Specter, Michael. 1998. "Doctors Powerless as AIDS Rakes Africa." *New York Times,* August 6, A1, A7.

Speirs, Rosemary. 1993. "Violence Affects Half of Women, Study Says." *Toronto Star* November 19, A1, A29.

Spengler, Joseph J. 1978. *Facing Zero Population Growth: Reactions and Interpretations, Past and Present.* Durham, NC: Duke University Press.

Spindel, Cheywa, Elisa Levy, and Melissa Connor. 2000. *With an End in Sight.* New York: United Nations Development Fund for Women.

Spitzer, Steven. 1975. "Toward a Marxian Theory of Deviance." *Social Problems* 22(June): 641–651.

Spradley, James P., and David W. McCurdy. 1980. *Anthropology: The Cultural Perspective.* 2nd ed. New York: Wiley.

Staggenborg, Suzanne. 1989a. "Stability and Innovation in the Women's Movement: A Comparison of Two Movement Organizations." *Social Problems* 36(February):75–92.

———. 1989b. "Organizational and Environmental Influences on the Development of the Pro-Choice Movement." *Social Forces* 68(September):204–240.

Stammer, Larry B. 1999. "Former Baptists Leader Seeks a Dialogue with Gay Church." *Los Angeles Times,* July 27, B1, B5.

Stark, Rodney, and William Sims Bainbridge. 1979. "Of Churches, Sects, and Cults: Preliminary Concepts for a Theory of Religious Movements." *Journal for the Scientific Study of Religion* 18(June):117–131.

———. 1985. *The Future of Religion.* Berkeley: University of California Press.

Stark, Rodney, and Laurence R. Iannaccone. 1992. "Sociology of Religion." Pp. 2029–2037 in *Encyclopedia of Sociology.* Vol. 4, edited by Edgar F. Borgatta and Marie L. Borgatta. New York: Macmillan.

Starr, Kevin. 1999. "Building from Within." *Los Angeles Times,* March 7, 1.

Starr, Paul. 1982. *The Social Transformation of American Medicine.* New York: Basic Books.

Statistics Canada. 1996. "Sexual Activity and Contraceptive Use." *National Population Health Survey 1994/1995.* Retrieved February 15, 2002 (http://www.statcan.ca/english/kits/preg/preg3c.htm).

———. 1997a. "1996 Census: Marital Status, Common-Law Unions and Families." *The Daily,* October 14. Retrieved April 23, 2002 (http://www.statcan.ca/Daily/English/971014/d971014.htm).

———. 1997b. "Divorces, 1995." *Divorces.* Catalogue No. 84-213-XPB.

———. 1998. "1996 Census." *The Daily,* March 17. Retrieved November 27, 2005 (http://www.statcan.ca/Daily/English/980317/d980317.htm#ART2).

———. 1999a. *Earnings of Men and Women.* Catalogue No. 13-217-XIB. Ottawa: Minister of Industry.

———. 1999b. *Overview of the Time Use of Canadians in 1998.* Catalogue No. 12F0080XIE. Ottawa: Minister of Industry. Retrieved November 27, 2005 (http://www.statcan.ca/english/freepub/12F0080XIE/12F0080XIE1999001.pdf).

———. 1999c. "Survey of Labour and Income Dynamics: The Wage Gap between Men and Women." *The Daily,* December 20. Retrieved April 21, 2002 (http://www.statcan.ca/Daily/English/991220/d991220a.htm).

———. 2000a. *Women in Canada: A Gender-Based Statistical Report.* Catalogue No. 89-503-XPE. Ottawa: Ministry of Industry, p. 115.

———. 2000b. "Attending Religious Services." *The Daily,* December 12. Retrieved April 21, 2002 (http://www.statcan.ca/Daily/English/001212/d001212b.htm).

———. 2001a. *The Assets and Debts of Canadians: An Overview of the Results of the Survey of Financial Security.* Catalogue No. 13-595-XIE. Retrieved August 15, 2001 (http://www.statcan.ca/cgi_bin/downpub/research.cgi).

———. 2001b. "Crime Statistics." *The Daily,* July 19. Retrieved August 15, 2001 (http://www.statcan.ca/Daily/English/010719/d010719b.htm).

———. 2001c. "Family Income, 1999." *The Daily,* November 6. Retrieved May 5, 2002 (http://www.statcan.ca/Daily/English/011106/d011106b.htm).

———. 2001d. *Family Violence in Canada: A Statistical Profile.* Catalogue No. 85-224-XIE. Retrieved January 19, 2002 (http://www.statcan.ca/english/freepub/85-224-XIE/0100085-224-XIE.pdf).

———. 2002a. "Profile of Canadian Families and Households: Diversification Continues." *2001 Census (Analysis Series).* September 25, 2003 (http://www.12statcan.ca/english/census01/Products/Analytic/companion/fam/contents.cfm).

———. 2002b. "Divorces, 1999 and 2000." *The Daily,* December 2. Retrieved September 25, 2003 (http://www.statcan.ca/Daily/English/021202/d021202f.htm).

———. 2002c. "Profile of Canadian Population by Age and Sex: Canada Ages." *2001 Census (Analysis Series).* Catalogue No. 96F0030XIE2001002.

———. 2002nd. *A Profile of the Canadian Population: Where We Live, 2001 Census.* Catalogue No. 96F0030XIE2001001. Retrieved November 27, 2005 (http://geodepot.statcan.ca/Diss/Highlights/Index_e.cfm).

———. 2002e. "Census of Agriculture: Profile of Farm Operators." *The Daily,* November 20. Retrieved November 27, 2005 (http://www.statcan.ca/Daily/English/021120/d021120a.htm).

———. 2003a. *Family Income and Participation in Post-secondary Education. Analytical Studies Branch Research Paper Series.* Catalogue No. 11F0019M1E. Retrieved November 27, 2005 (http://www.statcan.ca/english/research/11F0019MIE/11F0019MIE2003210.pdf).

———. 2003b. "Crime Statistics." *The Daily,* July 24. Retrieved November 27, 2005 (http://www.statcan.ca/Daily/English/030724/d030724a.htm).

———. 2003c. *Income of Canadian Families, 2001 Census.* Catalogue No. 96F0030XIE2001014. Retrieved May 13, 2003 (http://www12.statcan.ca/english/census01/products/analytic/companion/inc/contents.cfm).

———. 2003d. *Canada's Ethnocultural Portrait: The Changing Mosaic, 2001 Census.* Catalogue No. 96F0030X2001008. Retrieved November 27, 2005 (http://www12.statcan.ca/english/census01/products/analytic/companion/etoimm/contents.cfm).

———. 2003e. *Ethnic Diversity Survey: Portrait of a Multicultural Society.* Catalogue No. 89-593-XIE. Retrieved November 27, 2005 (http://www.statcan.ca/english/freepub/89-593-XIE/89-593-XIE2003001.pdf).

———. 2003f. *Earnings of Canadians, 2001 Cenus.* Catalogue No. 96F0030. Retrieved November 27, 2005 (http://www.statcan.ca/bsolc/english/bsolc?catno=97F0019X2001057).

———. 2003g. *Women in Canada: Work Chapter Updates.* 89F0133XIE. Retrieved November 27, 2005 (http://www.statcan.ca/english/freepub/89F0133XIE/89F0133XIE00001.pdf).

———. 2003h. "Aboriginal Peoples of Canada." *2001 Census (Analysis Series).* Retrieved September 15, 2003 (http://www12.statcan.ca/english/census01/products/analytic/companion/abor/contents.cfm). Catalogue No. 96F003XIE2001007.

———. 2003i. "Family Violence." *The Daily,* June 23. Retrieved December 1, 2005 (http://www.statcan.ca/Daily/English/030623/d030623c.htm).

———. 2003j. "Religions in Canada," *2001 Census (Analysis Series).* Catalogue No. 96F0030XIE2001015. Retrieved November 27, 2005 (http://www12.statcan.ca/english/census01/Products/Analytic/companion/rel/canada.cfm).

———. 2003k. "University Enrolment by Age Groups." *The Daily,* April 17. Accessed September 24, 2003 (http://www.statcan.ca/daily/english/030417/d030417b.htm).

———. 2003l. "Deaths." *The Daily,* April 2. Accessed September 24, 2003 (http://www.statcan.ca/daily/english/030402/d030402b.htm).

———. 2003m. "Marriages, 2000." *The Daily,* June 2. Retreived November 27, 2005 (http://www.statcan.ca/Daily/English/030602/d030602a.htm).

———. 2003n. *Characteristics of Household Internet Users, by Location of Access (Home).* CANSIM tables 358-0003, 358-0004, 358-0005, and 358-0017. Retrieved November 27, 2005 (http://www40.statcan.ca/l01/cst01/comm10b.htm).

———. 2004a. "Study: The Union Movement in Transition." *The Daily,* August 31. Retrieved November 4, 2004 (http://www.statcan.ca/Daily/English/040831/d040831b.htm).

———. 2004b. *Immigrants to Canada, by Country of Last Permanent Residence, Canada.* Retrieved January 28, 2005 (http://www.statcan.ca/english/Estat/guide/track.htm).

———. 2004c. "Crime Statistics," *The Daily,* July 28. Retrieved November 27, 2005 (http://www.statcan.ca/Daily/English/040728/d040728a.htm).
———. 2004d. "Study: Trends in the Use of Social Assistance," *The Daily,* August 19. Retrieved January 17, 2005 (http://www.statcan.ca/Daily/English/040819/d040819e.htm).
———. 2004e. "E-commerce: Household Shopping on the Internet." *The Daily,* September 23. Retrieved September 23, 2004 (http://www.stat.ca/Daily/English/040923/d040923a.htm).
———. 2004f. "Household Internet Use Survey." *The Daily,* July 8. Retrieved February 26, 2005 (http://www.statcan.ca/Daily/English/040708/d040708a.htm).
———. 2004g. *Immigrants in Canada's Census Metropolitan Areas.* Catalogue No. 89-613-MIE. Retrieved November 27, 2005 (http://www.statcan.ca/english/research/89-613-MIE/2004003/89-613-MIE2004003.pdf).
———. 2004h. "Divorces, 2001 and 2002." *The Daily,* May 4. Retrieved November 27, 2005 (http://www.statcan.ca/Daily/English/040504/d040504a.htm).
———. 2004i. "Marriages, 2002." *The Daily,* December 21. Retrieved November 27, 2005 (http://www.statcan.ca/Daily/English/041221/d041221d.htm).
———. 2004j. "Study: Self-Employment Activity in Rural Canada." *The Daily,* July 23. Retrieved November 27, 2005 (http://www.statcan.ca/Daily/English/040723/d040723c.htm).
———. 2005a. *Health Reports* 16(3). Catalogue No. 82-003-XIE2004003.
———. 2005b. *Population by Selected Origins, Canada, 2001 Census.* Retrieved November 25, 2005 (http://www40.statcan.ca/l01/cst01/demo26a.htm?sdi=population%20selected%20origins).
———. 2005c. "Census Family." *Definitions, Data Sources and Methods: Statistical Units.* Retrieved July 4, 2005 (http://dissemination.statcan.ca/English/concepts/definitions/cen-family.htm).
Status of Women Canada. 1995 *Setting the Stage for the Next Century: The Federal Plan for Gender Equality*. Ottawa: Status of Women Canada.
———. 2000. "National Day of Remembrance and Action on Violence against Women." News Release. December 5. Retrieved April 22, 2002 (http://www.swc-cfc.gc.ca/news2000/1205-e.html).
———. 2002. *On Her Own: Young Women and Homelessness in Canada.* Ottawa: Status of Women Canada.
Stearn, J. 1993. "What Crisis?" *Statesmen and Society* 6(April 2):7–9.
Stedman, Nancy. 1998. "Learning to Put the Best Shoe Forward." *New York Times,* October 27.
Steffenhagen, Janet. 2001. "City Streets Draw Non-B.C. Youths." *Vancouver Sun,* March 26, A3.
Stein, Leonard. 1967. "The Doctor–Nurse Game." *Archives of General Psychiatry* 16:699–703.
Steinhauer, Jennifer. 2000. "The New Landscape of AIDS." *New York Times,* June 25, 1, 15.
Stenning, Derrick J. 1958. "Household Viability among the Pastoral Fulani." Pp. 92–119 in *The Developmental Cycle in Domestic Groups,* edited by John R. Goody. Cambridge, Eng.: Cambridge University Press.
Sternberg, Steve. 1999. "Virus Makes Families Pay Twice." *USA Today,* May 24, 6D.
Stevenson, David, and Barbara L. Schneider. 1999. *The Ambitious Generation: America's Teenagers, Motivated but Directionless.* New Haven: Yale University Press.
Stolberg, Sheryl Gay. 2000. "Alternative Care Gains a Foothold." *New York Times,* January 31, A1, A16.
Stoughton, Stephanie, and Leslie Walker. 1999. "The Merchants of Cyberspace." *Washington Post National Weekly Edition,* February 15, 18.
Stout, Madeline Dion. 1996. *Aboriginal Canada: Women and Health: A Canadian Perspective.* Paper prepared for the Canada–USA Forum on Women's Health. Ottawa: Health Canada.
Straus, Murray A. 1994. "State-to-State Differences in Social Inequality and Social Bonds in Relation to Assaults on Wives in the United States." *Journal of Comparative Family Studies* 25(Spring):7–24.
Strauss, Anselm. 1977. *Negotiations: Varieties, Contexts, Processes, and Social Order.* San Francisco: Jossey Bass.
Strassman, W. Paul. 1998. "Third-World Housing." Pp. 589–592 in *The Encyclopedia of Housing,* edited by Willem van Vliet. Thousand Oaks, CA: Sage.
Stuckey, Johanna H. 1998. "Women and Religion: Female Spirituality, Feminist Theology, and Feminist Goddess Worship." In *Feminist Issues: Race, Class, and Sexuality.* 2nd ed., edited by Nancy Mandell. Scarborough, ON: Pearson Canada.
Sugimoto, Yoshio. 1997. *An Introduction to Japanese Society.* Cambridge, Eng.: Cambridge University Press.
Sumner, William G. 1906. *Folkways.* New York: Ginn.
Sutherland, Edwin H. 1937. *The Professional Thief.* Chicago: University of Chicago Press.
———. 1940. "White-Collar Criminality." *American Sociological Review* 5(February):1–11.
———. 1949. *White Collar Crime.* New York: Dryden.
———. 1983. *White Collar Crime: The Uncut Version.* New Haven, CT: Yale University Press.
Sutherland, Edwin H., and Donald R. Cressey. 1978. *Principles of Criminology.* 10th ed. Philadelphia: Lippincott.
Suttles, Gerald D. 1972. *The Social Construction of Communities.* Chicago: University of Chicago Press.
Sweet, Kimberly. 2001. "Sex Sells a Second Time." *Chicago Journal* 93(April):12–13.

T

Talbot, Margaret. 1998. "Attachment Theory: The Ultimate Experiment." *New York Times Magazine,* May 24, pp. 4–30, 38, 46, 50, 54.
Tannen, Deborah. 1990. *You Just Don't Understand: Women and Men in Conversation.* New York: Ballantine.
———. 1994a. *Talking from 9 to 5.* New York: William Morris.
———. 1994b. *Gender and Discourse.* New York: Oxford University Press.
Taylor, Verta. 1995. "Watching for Vibes: Bringing Emotions into the Study of Feminist Organizations." Pp. 223–233 in *Feminist Organizations: Harvest of the New Women's Movement,* edited by Myra Marx Ferree and Patricia Yancy Martin. Philadelphia: Temple University Press.
Terry, Sara. 2000. "Whose Family? The Revolt of the Child-Free." *Christian Science Monitor,* August 29, pp. 1, 4.
Theberge, Nancy. 1997. "'It's Part of the Game'—Physicality and the Production of Gender in Women's Hockey." *Gender and Society* 11(February):69–87.
Third World Institute. 2001. *The World Guide 2001–2002.* Oxford, Eng.: New Internationalist Publishers.
Thomas, Jim. 1984. "Some Aspects of Negotiating Order: Loose Coupling and Mesostructure in Maximum Security Prisons." *Symbolic Interaction* 7(Fall):213–231.
Thomas, Robert McG., Jr. 1995. "Maggie Kuhn, 89, the Founder of the Gray Panthers, Is Dead." *New York Times,* April 23, 47.
Thomas, William I. 1923. *The Unadjusted Girl.* Boston: Little, Brown.
Thomson, Elizabeth, and Ugo Colella. 1992. "Cohabitation and Marital Stability: Quality or Commitment?" *Journal of Marriage and the Family* 54(May):259–267.
Thornton, Russell. 1987. *American Indians Holocaust and Survival: A Population History Since 1492.* Norman: University of Oklahoma Press.
Tidmarsh, Lee. 2000. "If I Shouldn't Spank, What Should I Do? Behaviour Techniques for Disciplining Children." *Canadian Family Physician* 46:1119–1123.
Tierney, John. 1990. "Betting the Planet." *New York Times Magazine,* December 2, pp. 52–53, 71, 74, 76, 78, 80–81.
Tilly, Charles. 1993. *Popular Contention in Great Britain 1758–1834.* Cambridge, MA: Harvard University Press.
Tolbert, Kathryn. 2000. "In Japan, Traveling Alone Begins at Age 6." *Washington Post National Weekly Edition* May 15, 17.
Tong, Rosemary. 1989. *Feminist Theory: A Comprehensive Introduction.* Boulder, CO: Westview.

Tonkinson, Robert. 1978. *The Mardudjara Aborigines.* New York: Holt.

Tönnies, Ferdinand. [1887] 1988. *Community and Society.* Rutgers, NJ: Transaction.

Touraine, Alain. 1974. *The Academic System in American Society.* New York: McGraw-Hill.

Treiman, Donald J. 1977. *Occupational Prestige in Comparative Perspective.* New York: Academic.

Trimble, Linda, and Jane Arscott. 2003. *Still Counting: Women in Politics across Canada.* Peterborough, ON: Broadview Press.

Tuchman, Gaye. 1992. "Feminist Theory." Pp. 695–704 in *Encyclopedia of Sociology.* Vol. 2, edited by Edgar F. Borgatta and Marie L. Borgatta. New York: Macmillan.

Tuck, Bryan, Jan Rolfe, and Vivienne Adair. 1994. "Adolescents' Attitudes toward Gender Roles within Work and Its Relationship to Gender, Personality Type and Parental Occupations." *Sex Roles* 31(9–10):547–558.

Tumin, Melvin M. 1953. "Some Principles of Stratification: A Critical Analysis." *American Sociological Review* 18(August):387–394.

———. 1985. *Social Stratification.* 2nd ed. Englewood Cliffs, NJ: Prentice-Hall.

Turkle, Sherry. 1995. *Life on the Screen: Identity in the Age of the Internet.* New York: Simon and Schuster.

———. 1999. "Looking toward Cyberspace: Beyond Grounded Sociology." *Contemporary Sociology* 28(November):643–654.

Turner, Bryan S., ed. 1990. *Theories of Modernity and Postmodernity.* Newbury Park, CA: Sage.

Turner, J.H. 1985. *Herbert Spencer: A Renewed Application.* Beverly Hills, CA: Sage.

Twaddle, Andrew. 1974. "The Concept of Health Status." *Social Science and Medicine* 8(January):29–38.

U

Uchitelle, Louis. 1996. "More Downsized Workers Are Returning as Rentals." *New York Times,* December 8, 1, 34.

UNAIDS. 2004. "UNAIDS 2004 Report on the Gobal Epidemic." Retrieved November 28, 2004 (http://www.unaids.org/bangkok2004/epi_graphics.html).

UNESCO. 2002. *Education for All 2002.* Paris, France: UNESCO.

UNICEF. 2004. *Report: The State of the World's Children, 2004.* New York: UNICEF.

———. 2005. *Report: Child Poverty in the Rich Countries, 2005.* New York: UNICEF.

Union of B.C. Indian Chiefs. 1991. Published by Technical Support Section, Surveys and Resources Mapping Branch, Ministry of Environment, Lands and Parks, Victoria, B.C.

United Nations. 1995. *The World's Women, 1995: Trends and Statistics.* New York: United Nations.

———. 2004. *AIDS Epidemic Update.* New York: United Nations

United Nations Development Programme. 1995. *Human Development Report 1995.* New York: Oxford University Press.

———. 2001. *Human Development Report 2001.* Making New Technologies Work for Human Development. New York: UNDP.

———. 2002. *Human Development Report 2002: Deepening Democracy in a Fragmented World.* New York: Oxford University Press.

United Nations Population Division. 1998. *World Abortion Policies.* New York: Department of Economic and Social Affairs, UNPD.

———. 2001. "World Marriage Patterns 2000." Retrieved September 13, 2002 (http://www.undp.org/popin/wdtrends/worldmarriage.patters2000.pdf).

United Nations Population Fund. 2000. *State of World Population 2000: Lives Together, Worlds Apart: Men and Women in a Time of Change.* New York: United Nations Population Fund.

U.S. Bureau of Labour Statistics. 2004. Press release. Retrieved on June 13 (http://www.bls.gov/news.release/union2.nrO.htm).

Uttley, Alison. 1993. "Who's Looking at You, Kid?" *Times Higher Education Supplement* 30(April 30):48.

V

Valdez, Enrique. 1999. "Using Hotlines to Deal with Domestic Violence: El Salvador." Pp. 139–142 in *Too Close to Home,* edited by Andrew R. Morrison and Maria Loreto Biehl. Washington, DC: Inter-American Development Bank.

Vallas, Steven P. 1999. "Rethinking Post-Fordism: The Meaning of Workplace Flexibility." *Sociological Theory* 17(March):68–101.

Vancouver Sun. 2000. "Youth Violence in Canada." December 2, B4.

———. 2004a. "Smarter Doesn't Always Equal Richer." September 3, B3.

———. 2004b. "Not Enough Starbucks in the World, CEO Says." October 15, H4.

van den Berghe, Pierre. 1978. *Race and Racism: A Comparative Perspective.* 2nd ed. New York: Wiley.

Van der Gaag. 2004. *The No-Nonsense Guide to Women's Rights.* Toronto: New International Publications.

Vanier Institute of the Family. 1999. *Profiling Canadian Families.* Ottawa: Vanier Institute of the Family.

Vanneman, Reeve, and Lynn Weber Cannon. 1987. *The American Perception of Class.* Philadelphia: Temple University Press.

Van Slambrouck, Paul. 1999. "Netting a New Sense of Connection." *Christian Science Monitor,* May 4, pp. 1, 4.

van Veucht, Tijssen Lieteke. 1990. "Women between Modernity and Postmodernity." Pp. 147–163 in *Theories of Modernity and Postmodernity,* edited by Bryan S. Turner. London: Sage.

Veblen, Thorstein. 1919. *The Vested Interests and the State of the Industrial Arts.* New York: Huebsch.

Venkatesh, Sudhir Alladi. 2000. *American Project: The Rise and Fall of a Modern Ghetto.* Cambridge, MA: Harvard University Press.

Verhovek, Sam Howe. 1997. "Racial Tensions in Suit Slowing Drive for 'Environmental Justice,'" *New York Times,* September 7, 1, 16.

Vernon, Glenn. 1962. *Sociology and Religion.* New York: McGraw-Hill.

Vernon, JoEtta A., Allen Williams, Terri Phillips, Janet Wilson. 1990. "Media Stereotyping: A Comparison of the Way Elderly Women and Men Are Portrayed on Prime-Time Television." *Journal of Women and Aging* 2(4):55–68.

Vidaver, R.M., B. LaFleur, C. Tong, R. Bradshaw, and S.A. Marts. 2000. "Women Subjects in NIH-funded Clinical Research Literature: Lack of Progress in Both Representation and Analysis by Sex. *Journal of Women's Health Gender Based Medicine* 9(June):495–504.

Vissandjee, Bilkis. 2001. "The Consequences of Cultural Diversity." *The Canadian Women's Health Network* 4(2):3–4.

Vladimiroff, Christine. 1998. "Food for Thought." *Second Harvest Update* (Summer):2.

Vobejda, Barbara, and Judith Havenmann. 1997. "Experts Say Side Income Could Hamper Reforms." *Washington Post,* November 3, A1.

W

Wages for Housework Campaign. 1999. *Wages for Housework Campaign.* Circular. Los Angeles.

Wagley, Charles, and Marvin Harris. 1958. *Minorities in the New World: Six Case Studies.* New York: Columbia University Press.

Wahl, Andrew. 2004. "Leaders Wanted: Skills Shortage Dead Ahead." *Canadian Business.* Retrieved March 1, 2004 (http://www.canadianbusiness.com/article.jsp?content=20040301_58657_58657&page=1).

Wake, Bev. 2000. "Home Schooling Gets Top Marks: More Parents are Home Schooling their Children because of Better Internet Access and the Availability of Educational Material." *Ottawa Citizen,* September 7, C3.

Wallace, Ruth A., and Alison Wolf. 1980. *Contemporary Sociological Theory.* Englewood Cliffs, NJ: Prentice-Hall.

Wallerstein, Immanuel. 1974. *The Modern World System.* New York: Academic Press.

———. 1979a. *Capitalist World Economy.* Cambridge, Eng.: Cambridge University Press.

———. 1979b. *The End of the World as We Know It: Social Science for the Twenty-First Century.* Minneapolis: University of Minnesota Press.

———. 2000. *The Essential Wallerstein.* New York: The New Press.

Wallerstein, Judith S., Judith M. Lewis, and Sandra Blakeslee. 2000. *The Unexpected Legacy of Deviance.* New York: Hyperion.

Wallis, Claudia. 1987. "Is Mental Illness Inherited?" *Time,* March 9, p. 67.

Wal-Mart. 2001. "Wal-Mart News: Our Commitment to Communities." Retrieved August 24, 2001 (http://www.walmartstores. com).

Wal-Mart Watch. 2000. "Riverside, California Swats Wal-Mart Away." Retrieved August 24, 2001 (http://www.Walmartwatch.com).

Walzer, Susan. 1996. "Thinking about the Baby: Gender and Divisions of Infant Care." *Social Problems* 43(May):219–234.

Wanner, Richard A. 1998. "Book review of *The Vertical Mosaic Revisited* by Rick Helmes-Hayes and James Curtis." *CJS* Online (December). Retrieved May 12, 2005 (http://www.arts.ualberta.ca/cjcopy/reviews/vmrevisited.html).

Weber, Martha L. 1998. "She Stands Alone: A Review of the Recent Literature on Women and Social Support." *Prairie Women's Health Centre of Excellence.* Winnipeg: Prairie Women's Health Centre of Excellence.

Weber, Max. [1922] 1947. *The Theory of Social and Economic Organization.* Translated by A. Henderson and T. Parsons. New York: Free Press.

———. [1904] 1949. *Methodology of the Social Sciences.* Translated by Edward A. Shils and Henry A. Finch. Glencoe, IL: Free Press.

———. [1904] 1958a. *The Protestant Ethic and the Spirit of Capitalism.* Translated by Talcott Parsons. New York: Scribner.

———. [1916] 1958b. *The Religion of India: The Sociology of Hinduism and Buddhism.* New York: Free Press.

Weedon, Chris. 1999. *Feminism, Theory and the Politics of Difference.* Oxford: Blackwell Publishers.

Weeks, John R. 1999. *Population: An Introduction to Concepts and Issues.* 7th ed. Belmont, CA: Wadsworth.

———. 2002. *Population: An Introduction to Concepts and Issues.* 8th ed. Belmont, CA: Wadsworth.

Weinfeld, M. 1994. "Ethnic Assimilation and the Retention of Ethnic Cultures." Pp. 238–266 in *Ethnicity and Culture in Canada: The Research Landscape,* edited by J.W. Berry and J.A. Laponce. Toronto: University of Toronto Press.

Weinstein, Deena. 1999. *Knockin' The Rock: Defining Rock Music as a Social Problem.* New York: McGraw-Hill/Primis.

———. 2000. *Heavy Metal: The Music and Its Culture.* Cambridge, MA: Da Capo.

Weinstein, Deena, and Michael A. Weinstein. 1999. "McDonaldization Enframed." Pp. 57–69 in *Resisting McDonaldization,* edited by Barry Smart. London: Sage.

Weinstein, Henry, Michael Finnegan, and Teresa Watanabe. 2001. "Racial Profiling Gains Support as Search Tactic." *Los Angeles Times,* September 24, A1, M9.

Weiss, Rick. 1998. "Beyond Test-Tube Babies." *Washington Post National Weekly Edition,* February 16, 6–7.

Weitz, Rose. 1996. *The Sociology of Health, Illness and Health Care: A Critical Approach.* Belmont, CA: Wadsworth.

Wellman, Barry, J. Salaff, D. Dimitrova, L. Garton, M. Gulia, and C. Haythornthwaite. 1996. "Computer Networks as Social Networks: Collaborative Work, Telework, and Virtual Community." Pp. 213–238 in *Annual Review of Sociology, 1996,* edited by John Hagan. Palo Alto, CA: Annual Reviews.

West, Candace, and Don H. Zimmerman. 1983. "Small Insults: A Study of Interruptions in Cross Sex Conversations between Unacquainted Persons." Pp. 86–111 in *Language, Gender, and Society,* edited by Barrie Thorne, Cheris Kramarae, and Nancy Henley. Rowley, MA: Newbury House.

———. 1987. "Doing Gender." *Gender and Society* 1(June):125–151.

West, William G. 1993. "Violence in the Schools/Schooling in Violence: Escalating Problem or Moral Panic? A Critical Perspective." *Orbit* 24(1):6–7.

Whyte, William Foote. 1981. *Street Corner Society: Social Structure of an Italian Slum.* 3rd ed. Chicago: University of Chicago Press.

Wickman, Peter M. 1991. "Deviance." Pp. 85–87 in *Encyclopedic Dictionary of Sociology.* 4th ed. Guilford, CT: Dushkin.

Wilford, John Noble. 1997. "New Clues Show Where People Made the Great Leap to Agriculture." *New York Times,* November 18, B9, B12.

Wilkinson, Tracy. 1999. "Refugees Forming Bonds on Web." *Los Angeles Times,* July 31, A2.

Willett, Jeffrey G., and Mary Jo Deegan. 2000. "Liminality and Disability: The Symbolic Rite of Passage of Individuals with Disabilities." Presented at the annual meeting of the American Sociological Association, Washington, DC.

Williams, Carol J. 1995. "Taking an Eager Step Back." *Los Angeles Times,* June 3, A1, A14.

Williams, Christine L. 1992. "The Glass Escalator: Hidden Advantages for Men in the 'Female' Professions." *Social Problems* 39(3):253–267.

———. 1995. *Still a Man's World: Men Who Do Women's Work.* Berkeley: University of California Press.

Williams, Robin M., in collaboration with John P. Dean and Edward A. Suchman. 1964. *Strangers Next Door: Ethnic Relations in American Communities.* Englewood Cliffs, NJ: Prentice-Hall.

Williams, Simon Johnson. 1986. "Appraising Goffman." *British Journal of Sociology* 37(September):348–369.

Williams, Wendy M. 1998. "Do Parents Matter? Scholars Need to Explain What Research Really Shows." *Chronicle of Higher Education* 45(December 11):B6–B7.

Wilson, David. 2000. "Residential Schools: Bearing History's Burden." *The United Church Observe.* Retrieved August 16, 2005 (http://www.ucobserver.org/archives/nov00_cvst-part1.htm).

Wilson, Edward O. 1975. *Sociobiology: The New Synthesis.* Cambridge, MA: Harvard University Press.

———. 1978. *On Human Nature.* Cambridge, MA: Harvard University Press.

Wilson, John. 1973. *Introduction to Social Movements.* New York: Basic Books.

Wilson, Jolin J. 2000. *Children as Victims.* Washington, DC: U.S. Government Printing Office.

Wilson, Susannah. 2001. "Intimacy and Commitment in Family Formation." Pp. 144–63 in *Families: Changing Trends in Canada.* 4th ed., edited by Maureen Baker. Toronto: McGraw-Hill Ryerson.

Wilson, Warner, Larry Dennis, and Allen P. Wadsworth, Jr. 1976. "Authoritarianism Left and Right." *Bulletin of the Psychonomic Society* 7(March):271–274.

Wilson, William Julius. 1980. *The Declining Significance of Race: Blacks and Changing American Institutions.* 2nd ed. Chicago: University of Chicago Press.

———. 1987. *The Truly Disadvantaged: The Inner City, the Underclass and Public Policy.* Chicago: University of Chicago Press.

———, ed. 1989. *The Ghetto Underclass: Social Science Perspectives.* Newbury Park, CA: Sage.

———. 1996. *When Work Disappears: The World of the New Urban Poor.* New York: Knopf.

———. 1999. *The Bridge over the Racial Divide: Rising Inequality and Coalition Politics.* Berkeley: University of California Press.

Winter, J. Alan. 1977. *Continuities in the Sociology of Religion.* New York: Harper and Row.

Wirth, Louis. 1928. *The Ghetto.* Chicago: University of Chicago Press.

———. 1938. "Urbanism as a Way of Life." *American Journal of Sociology* 44(July):1–24.

Withers, Edward J., and Robert S. Brown. 2001. "The Broadcast Audience: A Sociological Perspective." Pp. 121–150 in *Communications in Canadian Society.* 5th ed., edited by Craig McKie and Benjamin D. Singer. Toronto: Thompson Educational Publishing.

Wolf, Charles, Jr. 2001. "China's Capitalists Join the Party." *New York Times,* August 13, A21.

Wolf, Naomi. 1991. *The Beauty Myth.* New York: Anchor Books.

———. 1992. *The Beauty Myth: How Images of Beauty Are Used against Women.* New York: Anchor.

Wolf, Richard. 1996. "States Can Expect Challenges after Taking over Welfare." *USA Today,* October 1, 8A.

Wolff, Edward N. 2002. *Top Heavy.* Updated ed. New York: New Press.

Wolinsky, Fredric P. 1980. *The Sociology of Health.* Boston: Little, Brown.

Women's International Network. 1995. "Working Women: 4 Country Comparison." *WIN News* 21(September 9):82.

Wood, Daniel B. 2000. "Minorities Hope TV Deals Don't Just Lead to 'Tokenism.'" *Christian Science Monitor*, January 19.

Woodard, Colin. 1998. "When Rate Learning Fails against the Test of Global Economy." *Christian Science Monitor*, April 15, p. 7.

Wooden, Wayne. 1995. *Renegade Kids, Suburban Outlaws: From Youth Culture to Delinquency.* Belmont, CA: Wadsworth.

Woolf, Virigina. 1977. *A Room of One's Own.* San Diego, CA: Harvest/HBJ.

World Bank. 1995. *World Development Report 1994: Workers in an Integrating World.* New York: Oxford University Press.

———. 1997. *World Development Report 1997: The State in a Changing World.* New York: Oxford University Press.

———. 2000a. *World Development Indicators 2000.* Washington, DC: World Bank.

———. 2000b. *World Development Report 2000/2001.* New York: Oxford University Press.

———. 2002. *World Development Indicators 2002.* Washington, DC: World Bank.

———. 2003. *World Development Report 2003: Sustainable Development in a Dynamic World.* Washington, DC: World Bank.

World Fact Book. 2005. U.S. Department of Commerce Technical Administration, Springfield, Virginia.

World Health Organization. 2000. *The World Health Report 2000. Health Systems: Improving Performance.* Geneva, Switzerland: WHO.

World Resources Institute. 1998. *1998–99 World Resources: A Guide to the Global Environment.* New York: Oxford University Press.

Wresch, William. 1996. *Disconnected: Haves and Have-Nots in the Information Age.* New Brunswick, NJ: Rutgers University Press.

Wright, Eric R., William P. Gronfein, and Timothy J. Owens. 2000. "Deinstitutionalization, Social Rejection, and the Self-Esteem of Former Mental Patients." *Journal of Health and Social Behavior* (March).

Wright, Erik Olin, David Hachen, Cynthia Costello, and Joy Sprague. 1982. "The American Class Structure." *American Sociological Review* 47(December):709–726.

Wu, Zheng. 1999. "Premarital Cohabitation and the Timing of First Marriage." *Canadian Review of Sociology and Anthropology* 36(1): 109–127.

Wu, Zheng, and Michael S. Pollard. 2000. "Economic Circumstances and the Stability of Nonmarital Cohabitation." *Journal of Family Issues* 21(3):303–328.

Wurman, Richard Saul. 1989. *Information Anxiety.* New York: Doubleday.

Wuthnow, Robert. 1996. *Poor Richard's Principle: Recovering the American Dream through the Moral Dimension of Work, Business, and Money.* Princeton, N.J.: Princeton University Press.

Y

Yamagata, Hisashi, Kuang S. Yeh, Shelby Stewman, and Hiroko Dodge. 1997. "Sex Segregation and Glass Ceilings: A Comparative Statistics Model of Women's Career Opportunities in the Federal Government over a Quarter Century." *American Journal of Sociology* 103(November):566–632.

Yap, Kioe Sheng. 1998. "Squatter Settlements." Pp. 554–556 in *The Encyclopedia of Housing,* edited by Willem van Vliet. Thousand Oaks, CA: Sage.

Yinger, J. Milton. 1970. *The Scientific Study of Religion.* New York: Macmillan.

———. 1974. "Religion, Sociology of." Pp. 604–613 in *Encyclopaedia Britannica.* Vol. 15. Chicago: Encyclopedia Britannica.

Young, K. 1988. " The Social Relations of Gender." In *Gender in Caribbean Development*, edited by P. Mohammed and C. Shepard. Mona, Jamaica: Women and Development Studies Group.

Z

Zelizer, Gerald L. 1999. "Internet Offers Only Fuzzy Cyberfaith, Not True Religious Experiences." *USA Today*, August 19, 13A.

Zellner, William M. 1978. "Vehicular Suicide: In Search of Incidence." Unpublished M.A. thesis. Western Illinois University, Macomb.

———. 1995. *Counter Cultures: A Sociological Analysis.* New York: St. Martin's Press.

———. 2001. *Extraordinary Groups: An Examination of Unconventional Lifestyles.* 7th ed. New York: Worth.

Zimbardo, Philip G. 1972. "Pathology of Imprisonment." *Society* 9(April):4, 6, 8.

———. 2004. "Power Turns Good Soldiers into 'Bad Apples.'" *Boston Globe*, May 9.

Zimbardo, Philip G., Craig Haney, W. Curtis Banks, and David Jaffe. 1974. "The Psychology of Imprisonments: Privation, Power, and Pathology." In *Doing unto Others: Joining, Molding, Conforming, Helping, and Loving*, edited by Zick Rubin. Englewood Cliffs, NJ: Prentice-Hall.

Zimmer, Lynn. 1988. "Tokenism and Women in the Workplace." *Social Problems* 35(February): 64–77.

Zola, Irving K. 1972. "Medicine as an Institution of Social Control." *Sociological Review* 20(November):487–504.

———. 1983. *Socio-Medical Inquiries.* Philadelphia: Temple University Press.

Zook, Matthew A. 1996. "The Unorganized Militia Network: Conspiracies, Computers, and Community." *Berkeley Planning Journal* 11:1–15.

Zuckerman, Laurence. 2001. "Divided, An Airline Stumbles." *New York Times*, March 14, C1, C6.

Zuckerman, M.J. 2000. "Criminals Hot on Money Trail to Cyberspace." *USA Today*, March 21, 8A.

Zweigenhaft, Richard L., and G. William Domhoff. 1998. *Diversity in the Power Elite: Have Women and Minorities Reached the Top?* New Haven: Yale University Press.

ACKNOWLEDGEMENTS

Chapter 1

P. 2: Quotation from Paquet, Laura Byrne. *The Urge to Splurge: A Social History of Shopping.* Toronto: ECW Press, 2003.

P. 20: Quotation in Box 1-2 from Carol Brooks Gardner. 1989. "Analyzing Gender in Public Places," *American Sociologist* 20 (Spring): 42–56. Reprinted by permission of Transaction Publishers. Copyright © 1989 by Transaction Publishers.

Chapter 2

P. 25: Quotation from James E. Côté and Anton L. Allahar. *Generation on Hold: Coming of Age in the Late Twentieth Century*. Copyright © 1995. Reproduced by permission of James Côté.

P. 31: Figure 2-3: Adapted from the Statistics Canada publication, *Analytical Studies Branch Research Paper Series*, Catalogue No. 11F0019MIE, No. 210, October 3, 2003, p. 33.

P. 34: Unnumbered figure in Box from William Rau and Ann Durand. 2000. "The Academic Ethic and College Grades: Does Hard Work Help Students to 'Make the Grade?'" *Sociology of Education* 73(January):26. Used by permission of the American Sociological Association and the authors.

P. 37 Canadian Sociology and Anthropology Association (CSAA), *Statement of Professional Ethics*. www.csaa.ca/structure/Code.htm.

P. 41: Figure 2-4 from Henry J. Kaiser Family Foundation. 2001. Executive Summary of *Sex on TV 2:* 2. This information was printed with permission of the Henry J. Kaiser Family Foundation of Menlo Park, CA. The Kaiser family Foundation is an independent health care philanthropy and is not associated with Kaiser Permanente or Kaiser Industries.

P. 42: Table 2-2 adapted from the Statistics Canada publication "Health Reports," Catalogue 82-003, Vol. 16, No. 3, May 2005.

Chapter 3

P. 48: Quotation from Horace Miner. 1956. "Body Ritual among the Nacirema." *American Anthropologist* 58(3). Reprinted by permission of the American Anthropological Association.

P. 54: Figure 3-2 from John L. Allen. 2001. *Student Atlas of World Geography*, 2nd ed. Copyright © 2001 by The McGraw-Hill Companies, Inc. Reprinted by permission of McGraw-Hill /Dushkin, a division of the McGraw-Hill Companies, Guilford, CT 06437.

P. 59: Figure 3-3 from Erin Anderssen, Michael Valpy, and others. 2004. *The New Canada: A Globe and Mail Report on the Next Generation.* Toronto: McClelland & Stewart. Used by permission of McClelland & Stewart Ltd and Ipsos-Reid.

P. 61: Figure 3-4 illustration by Jim Willis. 1996. "The Argot of Pickpockets," *New York Daily News* (November 19):5. © New York Daily News, L.P. Reprinted by permission.

P. 64: Figure 3-5 from Reginald Bibby. 1995. *The Bibby Report: Social Trends Canadian Style.* Toronto: Stoddart Publishing Company Limited, p. 49. Reprinted with permission.

Chapter 4

P. 70: Quotation reprinted and edited with the permission of The Free Press, a Division of Simon & Schuster Adult Publishing Group, from *DEADLY PERSUASION: Why Women and Girls Must Fight the Addictive Power of Advertising* by Jean Kilbourne. Copyright ©1999 by Jean Kilbourne. All rights reserved.

P. 76: Quotation from Daniel Albas and Cheryl Albas. 1988. "Aces and Bombers: The Post-Exam Impression Management Strategies of Students." *Symbolic Interaction* 11(Fall):289–302. © 1988 by JAI Press. Reprinted by permission of University of CA Press and the authors. UC Press Journals, 2000 Center St., Suite 303, Berkeley, CA 94704-1223, (510) 642-6188.

Chapter 5

P. 93: Quotation from Philip G. Zimbardo. 1972. "Pathology of Imprisonment," *Society,* 9(April):4. Reprinted by permission of Copyright Clearance Center. And from Philip G. Zimbardo, C. Haney, W. C. Banks, & D. Jaffe. 1974. "The Psychology of Imprisonment: Privation, Power, and Pathology." Pp. 61–73 in *Doing Unto Others: Explorations in Social Behavior,* edited by Z. Rubin. Englewood Cliffs: Prentice-Hall. Reprinted by permission of Philip G. Zimbardo, Stanford University.

P. 110: Figure 5-2 Reproduced by permission of UNAIDS, www.unaids.org.

Chapter 6

P. 116: Quotation from George Ritzer. 1996–2000. *The McDonaldization of Society,* new century edition:1–4, 10. Copyright © 1996, 2000. Reprinted by permission of Pine Forge Press, a Division of Sage Publications.

P. 130: Figure 6-1 data adapted in part from the Statistics Canada publication "Perspectives on Labour and Income," Catalogue 75-001, Vol. 5, No. 8, *The Union Movement in Transition*, August 2004.

Chapter 7

P. 135: Quotation from Kevin D. Mitnick and William L. Simon. *The Art of Intrusion: The Real Stories Behind the Exploits of Hackers, Intruders, and Deceivers.* New York: John Wiley and Sons, 2005. Reprinted by permission.

P. 143: Table 7-1 © 1989 by JAI Press. Reprinted by permission of University of California Press. Reprinted from *The Sociological Quarterly* 30(2), Summer 1989, pp. 159–184 by permission.

P. 143: Table 7-2 data from the American Society of Plastic Surgeons, 2002, 2005.

P. 146: Table 7-3 adapted with permission of The Free Press, copyright renewed 1985 by Robert K. Merton.

P. 154: Figure 7-1 adapted with permission of The Free Press, copyright renewed 1985 by Robert K. Merton.

Chapter 8

P. 161: Quotation from Robert Goldman and Stephen Papson. 1998. *Nike Culture: The Sign of the Swoosh:*2, 6–8, 184. Reprinted by permission of Sage Publications Ltd.

P. 163: Figure 8-1 from Jesse Gordon and Knickerbocker. 2001. "The Sweat Behind the Shirt: The Labor History of a Gap Sweatshirt," *The Nation* 273 (September 3/10, 2001):14. Reprinted with permission of *The Nation.*

P. 166: Figure 8-2 from Towers Perrin in Adam Bryant. 1999: Section 4, p. 1. "American Pay Rattles Foreign Partners," *New York Times,* January 17: p. D1. Copyright © 1999 by The New York Times Co. Reprinted by permission.

P. 173: Figure 8-3 adapted from the Statistics Canada "2001 Census: Analysis Series, Income of Canadian Families," Catalogue 96F0030XIE2001014, May 13, 2003, and from the Statistics Canada publication "The Daily," Catalogue 11-001, *Study: Trends in the Use of Social Assistance*, Thursday, August 19, 2004.

P. 174: Figure 8-4 Adapted from the Statistics Canada publication "The Daily," Catalogue 11-001, *Study: Trends in the Use of Social Assistance,* Thursday, August 19, 2004.

P. 175: Figure 8-5 from Timothy Smeeding, Lee Rainwater, and Gary Burtless. 2001. "United States Poverty in a Cross-National Context." *Focus*, newsletter for the Institute for Research on Poverty, 21(Spring):51. Used by permission of Institute for Research on Poverty.

P. 176: Table 8-2 adapted from Statistics Canada, *2001 Census: Analysis Series, Income of Canadian Families,* Catalogue No. 96F0030XIE2001014, May 13, 2003.

P. 182: Figure 8-6 adapted in part from John R. Weeks. 2002. *Population: An Introduction to Concepts and Issues,* 8th ed.:22–23. Belmont, CA: Wadsworth © 2002. Reprinted with permission of Wadsworth, a division of Thomson Learning, www.thomson rights.com. Fax (800) 730-2215; and adapted in part from Carl Haub. 2002. *World Population Data Sheet 2002.* Used by permission of Population Reference Bureau.

P. 183: Quotation in Box 8-2 from "Eight Woman One Voice," a Gideon Mendel/ActionAid project. This part is spoken by Rutica Banda. Her complete part can be read at www.guardian.co.uk/africa8/0,16068, 1501265,00.html.

P. 185: Table 8-3 adapted in part from *Fortune.* 2002. "Fortune's Global 500," *Fortune*, August 12. © 2002 Time Inc. All rights reserved. And adapted in part from United Nations Development Programme. 2002. *Human Development Report 2002: Deepening Democracy in a Fragmented World:*190–193. Copyright © 2002 by the United Nations Development Programme. Used by permission of Oxford University Press, Inc.

P. 187: Figure 8-7 based on data from World Bank. 2002a. *2002 World Development Indicators:*74–76; Table 2-8. © World Bank 2002. Used by permission of World Bank.

Chapter 9

P. 194: "Excerpt" and cover from *The New Canada: A Globe and Mail Report on the Next Generation* by Erin Anderssen and Michael Valpy. Used by permission of McClelland & Stewart Ltd.

P. 197: Figure 9-1 adapted from the Statistics Canada "2001 Census: Analysis Series, Canada's Ethnocultural Portrait: The Changing Mosaic," Catalogue 96F0030XIE2001008, January 21, 2003, available at http://www12.statcan.ca/english/census01/products/analytic/companion/etoimm/contents.cfm.

P. 199 Table 9-1 adapted from the Statistics Canada website at http://www40.statcan.ca/l01/cst01/demo28a.htm.

P. 208: Quotation in Box 9-1 from Augie Fleras and Jean Lock Kunz. 2001. *Media and Minorities: Representing Diversity in a Multicultural Canada*. Toronto: Thompson Educational Publishing: 30–31.

P. 210 Figure 9-2 copyright © Province of British Columbia. All rights reserved. Reprinted with permission of the Province of British Columbia. www.ipp.gov.bc.ca.

P. 213: Figure 9-3 adapted from the Statistics Canada "Ethnic Diversity Survey: Portrait of a Multicultural Society," 2002, Catalogue 89-593, September 29, 2003, available at http://www.statcan.ca/english/freepub/89-593-XIE/89-593-XIE2003001.pdf.

P. 215: Figure 9-4 adapted from the Statistics Canada website at http://www.statcan.ca/english/Estat/guide/track.htm.

P. 215: Figure 9-5 data adapted from the Statistics Canada publication "Immigrants in Canada's Census Metropolitan Areas," Catalogue 89-613, No. 03, August 2004, available at http://www.statcan.ca/english/research/89-613-MIE/89-613-MIE2004003.htm.

Chapter 10

P. 220: Quotation from Sarah Schmidt. 2004. "Older Men Kick tradition, Opt for Cosmetic Surgeries," *Vancouver Sun*, October 29: p. A8

P. 223: Table 10-1 from Joyce McCarl Nielsen, Glenda Walden, and Charlotte A. Kunkel. 2000. "Gendered Heteronormalinity: Empirical Illustrations in Everyday Life," *Sociological Quarterly* 41(2):283–296. ©2000 by The Midwest Sociological Society. Reprinted by permission.

P. 229: Table 10-2 adapted from the Statistics Canada publication "Earnings of Canadians, 2001 Census," Catalogue 97F0019XIE2001057, July 24, 2003, available at http://www.statcan.ca/bsolc/english/bsolc?catno=97F0019X2001057.

P. 232: Figure 10-2 adapted from the Statistics Canada publication "Women in Canada: work chapter updates," 2002, Catalogue 89F0133XIE, May 5, 2003, available at http://www.statcan.ca/english/freepub/89F0133XIE/free.htm.

P. 232: Table 10-3 adapted from the Statistics Canada publication "Women in Canada: work chapter updates," 2002, Catalogue 89F0133XIE, May 5, 2003, available at http://www.statcan.ca/english/freepub/89F0133XIE/free.htm.

P. 235: Figure 10-3 adapted from the Statistics Canada publication "Women in Canada: a gender-based statistical report," Catalogue 89-503, September 14, 2000

Chapter 11

P. 243: Quotation from Tu Thanh Ha, "Pregnant woman called him 'Papa,' sperm donor's court petition says," which appeared on www.globeandmail.com on Sept. 14, 2004. Reprinted with permission from *The Globe and Mail.*

P. 245: Figure 11-1 adapted from the Statistics Canada "2001 Census: Analysis Series, Profile of Canadian families and households: Diversification continues," Catalogue 96F0030XIE2001003, October 22, 2003, available at http://www12.statcan.ca/english/census01/products/analytic/companion/fam/contents.cfm.

P. 252: Figure 11-2 from United Nations Population Division. 2001. *World Marriage Patterns 2000.* Accessed August 2, 2002, at www.undp.org/popin/wdtrends/worldmarriagepatterns2000.pdf. Used by permission of United Nations Population Division.

P. 255: Figure 11-3 adapted from the Statistics Canada "2001 Census: Analysis Series, Profile of Canadian families and households: Diversification continues," Catalogue 96F0030XIE2001003, October 22, 2002, available at http://www12.statcan.ca/english/census01/products/analytic/companion/fam/contents.cfm.

P. 259: Figure 11-4 Adapted from the Statistics Canada publication "The Daily," Catalogue 11-001, *Divorces*, Monday, December 2, 2002, and *Marriages*, Monday, June 2, 2003, available at http://www.statcan.ca/Daily/English/021202/d021202f.htm and http://www.statcan.ca/Daily/English/030602/d030602a.htm; the Statistics Canada publication "The Daily," *Divorces, 2001 and 2002*, May 4, 2004, available at http://www.statcan.ca/Daily/English/040504/d040504a.htm; the Statistics Canada publication "The Daily," *Marriages, 2002*, December 21, 2004, available at http://www.statcan.ca/Daily/English/041221/d041221d.htm; also from the publication entitled "Divorces," 1995, Catalogue 84-213, January 15, 1997;

Chapter 12

P. 270: Quotation from Noah Augustine. "Grandfather was a Knowing Christian." *Toronto Star,* August 9, 2000, A17. Reprinted with permission of Noah Augustine.

P. 272: Figure 12-1 from John L. Allen. 2003. *Student Atlas of World Geography*, 3rd ed. Copyright © 2003 by The McGraw-Hill Companies, Inc. All rights reserved. Reprinted by permission of McGraw-Hill Dushkin Publishing.

P. 277: Figure 12-2 from Ronald Inglehart and Wayne Baker. 2000. "Modernization, Cultural Change, and the Persistence of Traditional Values," *American Sociological Review* 65(February):19–51; Table 7, p. 47. Used by permission of the American Sociological Association and the authors.

P. 280: Table 12-1 adapted from the Statistics Canada "2001 Census: Analysis Series, Religions in Canada," Catalogue 96F0030XIE2001015, May 13, 2003, available at http://www12.statcan.ca/english/census01/products/analytic/companion/rel/contents.cfm.

P. 283: Figure 12-3 Copyright Organisation for Economic Co-operation and Development, 2003.

Chapter 13

P. 299: Quotation from Linda Trimble and Jane Arscott, "Chapter 3: The Electoral Glass Ceiling," copyright © 2003 by Linda Trimble and Jane Arscott, reprinted from *Still Counting: Women in Politics Across Canada*, by Linda Trimble and Jane Arscott, Ontario: Broadview Press, 2003, pp. 43–45. Reprinted by permission of Broadview Press.

P. 304: Unnumbered figure in box from S. Acharya. 2000. In Mahbub ul Haq Human Development Centre, *Human Development in South Asia 2000: The Gender Question:* 54. Oxford University Press, Karachi. Reprinted by permission.

P. 307: Figure 13-1 source: The graph entitled "The Evolution of Party Identification," including data taken from Canadian Election Studies, by Matthew Mendelsohn, 2002. Reproduced with the permission of the Canada School of Public Service, 2005. URL: www.cric.ca/pwp_re/youth_leadership/Appendix_A.ppt.

P. 309: Figure 13-2 from G. William Domhoff. 2001.*Who Rules America,* 4th ed.:96. Reproduced with permission of The McGraw-Hill Companies.

P. 313: Figure 13-3 from the Statistics Canada publication. *Women in Canada: Work Chapter Updates*, 2003. Catalogue No. 89F0133XIE, May 5, 2003, Available online at www.statcan.ca/english/freepub/89F0133XIE/free.htm.

P. 318: Table 13-1 from Status of Women Canada. 1995. *Setting the Stage for the Next Century: The Federal Plan for Gender Equality.* Reproduced with the permission of the Minister of Public Works and Government Services Canada, 2001. <http://www.swc-cfc.gc.ca>.

Chapter 14

P. 324: Quotation from Andrew Wahl, "Leaders Wanted: Skills Shortage Dead Ahead," *Canadian Business,* March 1, 2004. Reprinted by permission.

P. 327: Table 14-1 Adapted from Statistics Canada. 2001. *Canadian Social Trends* (Spring). Catalogue No. 11-008.

P. 331: Figure 14-2 *The World Fact Book.* 2005. CIA.

P. 340: Figure 14-3 *The World Fact Book.* 2005. CIA.

P. 349: Figure 14-4 from World Bank, 2003, *World Development Indicators 2003.* Published by the World Bank. Used by permission.

P. 350: Figure 14-5 data obtained at the CIHI website and referred to as "Health Expenditure by Use of Funds, by Year, by Source of Finance, by Province/Territory, Canada. 1975–2003 Current Dollars." Reprinted with permission.

P. 351: Figure 14-6 data obtained at the CIHI website and referred to as "Health Expenditure by Use of Funds, by Year, by Source of Finance, by Province/Territory, Canada. 1975–2003 Current Dollars." Reprinted with permission.

Chapter 15

P. 356: Quotation from *Down to This: Squalor and Splendour in a Big-City Shantytown* by Shaughnessy Bishop-Stall. Copyright © 2004 Shaughnessy Bishop-Stall. Reproduced by permission of Random House Canada.

P. 359: Table 15-1 based on Gideon Sjoberg. 1960. *The Preindustrial City: Past and Present.* New York: The Free Press:323–328. Copyright © 1960 by The Free Press, copyright renewed 1988 by Gideon Sjoberg. Adapted with permission of The Free Press, a division of Simon & Schuster Adult Learning Group. And based on E. Barbara Phillips. 1996. *City Lights: Urban-Suburban Life in the Global Society.* Oxford: Oxford University Press:132–135. Copyright © 1981 by E. Barbara Phillips and Richard T. LeGates, 1996 by E. Barbara Phillips. Used by permission of Oxford University Press, Inc.

P. 360: Table 15-2 data from United Nations, quoted in Martin Brockerhoff. 2000. "An Urbanizing World." *Population Bulletin* 55(3):10. Used by permission of Population Reference Bureau.

P. 361: Figure 15-1 based on data in Carl Haub and Diana Cornelius. 2001. *World Population Data Sheet 2001.* Washington, DC: Population Reference Bureau. Used by permission of Population Reference Bureau.

P. 363: Figure 15-2 from Chauncy Harris and Edward Ullmann. 1945. "The Nature of Cities." *Annals of the American Academy of Political and Social Science* 242(November):13. Reprinted by permission of American Academy of Political and Social Science, Philadelphia.

Chapter 16

P. 382: Quotation from Debora L. Spar. 2001. *Ruling the Waves: Cycles of Discovery, Chaos, and Wealth from the Compass to the Internet:* 327–329. Copyright © 2001 by Debora L. Spar, reprinted by permission of Harcourt, Inc.

P. 390: Quotation from Steven M. Buechler. 2000. *Social Movements in Advanced Capitalism: The Political Economy and Cultural Construction of Social Activism.* New York: Oxford University Press.

P. 396: Figure 16-1 from Global Reach. 2004. *Global Internet Statistics (by Language).* Available online at http://global-reach.biz/globstats/index.php3.

P. 399: Figure 16-2 Adapted from the Statistics Canada CANSIM database <http://cansim2.statcan.ca>, Tables 358-0003, 358-0004, 358-0005, and 358-0017.

PHOTO CREDITS

Chapter 1
Chapter opener: Empics
P. 5: CP/Tom Hanson
P. 7: Bettmann/Corbis
P. 9: Left: Bibliotheque Nationale, Paris
P. 9: Middle: Granger Collection
P. 9: Right: Archivo Iconografico, S.A./Corbis
P. 10: Keith Brofsky/Getty Images
P. 11: Courtesy UBC
P. 13: CP/Andre Forget

Chapter 2
Chapter opener: Statistics Canada, 2001 Census
P. 27: CP/Richard Lam
P. 29: Cartoon © The New Yorker Collection 1980 James Stevenson from cartoonbank.com. All rights reserved.
P. 30: The Gallup Poll
P. 32: © 1989 C.B. Trudeau. Reprinted with permission of Universal Press Syndicate. All rights reserved.
P. 32: Mireille Vautier/Woodfin Camp
P. 35: Rex Ziak/Getty
P. 36: Courtesy of AT&T
P. 36: Everett Collection
P. 38: Mark Reinstein/The Image Works
P. 40: Bob Daemmrich/The Image Works

Chapter 3
Chapter opener: Barry Dawson, Street Graphics India (New York: Thames & Hudson, 1999)
P. 48: Tom Montante/Picturequest
P. 50: Top: Peter Menzel/Stock Boston
P. 50: Bottom: D. Berbaun, Explorer/Photo Researchers
P. 51: AP/Wide World Photos
P. 52: Left: CP/Ryan Remiorz
P. 52: Right: AP Photo/Matt Sayles
P. 56: CP/Ryan Remiorz
P. 62: Cartoon by Sidney Harris. © 2004 by Sidney Harris. Used with permission.
P. 65: CP/Montreal Gazette/Phil Carpenter

Chapter 4
Chapter opener: Setagaya Volunteer Association, Tokyo, Japan
P. 72: Anthony Sau/Getty Images News
P. 75: Elizabeth Crews/The Image Works
P. 79: Thomas S. England/Photo Researchers
P. 83: Tom Wagner/Corbis Saba
P. 86: Mary Kate Denny/Photo Edit
P. 88: Svenne Nordlov/Tio Photo

Chapter 5
Chapter opener: Courtesy of interTREND Communications, Inc. Torrance, CA.
P. 93: AP/Wide World Photos
P. 95: CP/STF
P. 99: Sarah Leen
P. 100: ©Dick Hemingway
P. 100: Anna Clopet/Getty Images News
P. 101: Cartoon by Toles. © 2000 The Buffalo News. TOLES © The Buffalo News. Reprinted with permission of UNIVERSAL PRESS SYNDICATE. All rights reserved.
P. 104: CP/Jonathan Hayward
P. 105: Charles & Josette Lenars/Corbis
P. 106: Cartoon by Victor. © The New Yorker Collection 1986 Dean Victor from cartoonbank.com. All rights reserved.

Chapter 6
Chapter opener: Courtesy of Magic International
P. 118: Courtesy of Robin Berlyn
P. 120: CBS Photo Archive
P. 121: Cartoon © The New Yorker Collection 1979 Robert Weber from cartoonbank.com. All rights reserved.
P. 122: AP/Wide World Photos
P. 122: H. Mahidar, DPA/The Image Works
P. 124: AP Photo/Janet Durrans
P. 126: AP/Wide World Photos
P. 128: Rob Crandall/Stock Boston

Chapter 7
Chapter opener: Source: Health Canada
P. 138: © 1965 by Stanley Milgram from the film, "Obedience," distributed by Pennsylvania State University, PCR.
P. 141: Photodisc/Getty Images
P. 142: CP/Rick Rowell. ABC/Courtesy Everett Collection
P. 147: CP/Halifax Daily News-Darrell Oake
P. 148: Christina Beamish
P. 150: Photo by Elaine Briere
P. 152: Cartoon © 2000 by Sidney Harris

Chapter 8
Chapter opener: Courtesy of Unicef
P. 164: Hampton University Museum, Hampton, Virginia
P. 167: Bruno Herdt/Getty Images
P. 168: Paul A. Souders/Corbis
P. 170: L.D. Gordon/Image Bank
P. 175: Cartoon by Frank Cammuso. The Post Standard, Syracuse, NY. Used by permission.
P. 176: Thomas Hopker/Magnum
P. 178: AP/Wide World Photos
P. 180: Rita Tsang Canada's Top Woman Entrepreneur
P. 184: Catherine Karnow/Woodfin Camp

Chapter 9
Chapter opener: Canadian Race Relations Foundation
P. 194: Used by permission of McClelland & Stewart Ltd.
P. 197: Mark Richards/PhotoEdit
P. 198: Elliot Erwitt/Magnum
P. 202: Bob Daemmrich/The Image Works
P. 202: Cartoon by Rob Rogers. ©UFS. Reprinted by permission.
P. 203: CP/Montreal Gazette—John Mahoney
P. 205: Art Zamur/Getty Images News
P. 206: Alon Reininger/Contact Press Images
P. 209: CP/Joe Bryksa
P. 211: PBase.ca
P. 212: Vancouver Public Library, Special Collections, VPL 30625

Chapter 10
Chapter opener: Guerilla Girls
P. 220: Gordon Beck, The Gazette, (Montreal)
P. 222: Picture provided by Harrison G. Pope, Jr., adapted from *THE ADONIS COMPLEX* by Harrison G. Pope, Jr., Katherine Phillips, Roberto Olivardia. The Free Press, © 2000
P. 224: © Maria Lepowsky
P. 227: B. Mahoney/Image Works
P. 229: CP/Frank Gunn
P. 234: Cartoon by Ed Stein. Reprinted by permission of Ed Stein, Rocky Mountain News.
P. 235: Michael Newman/Photo Edit
P. 236: Courtesy of the Canadian Heritage Gallery

Chapter 11
Chapter opener: Genetica DNA Laboratories, Inc.
P. 245: Saola/Getty Images News
P. 248: Eastcott/Woodfin Camp
P. 251: Michael Newman/Photo Edit
P. 253: Bill Truslow/Liaison
P. 254: Blair Seitz/Photo Researchers
P. 256: Adam Crowley/Getty Images
P. 257: Jules Frazier/Getty Images
P. 261: John Bradley/Getty
P. 262: CP/Belleville Intelligencer-Derek Baldwin
P. 265: © Andy Warhol Foundation, Inc./Art Resource

Chapter 12
Chapter opener: Thomas Coex/Agence France Presse
P. 270: CP/Andrew Vaughan
P. 273: Rachel Epstein
P. 274: CP/Kevin Frayer
P. 278: Steve McCurry/Magnum Photos
P. 285: Mary Kate Denny/PhotoEdit
P. 287: Joe McNally/Corbis Sygma
P. 292: Marilyn Humphries/The Image Works

Chapter 13
Chapter opener: Courtesy of cbc.ca. Website created by: Mark Isfeld Secondary School, Courtenay, British Columbia. Team Members: Mike Allan (15), Eric Bigelow (16), Krista Isberg (16), Nick Knowlson (15), Sandra Morson (15), Stephanie Senay (15), Monika Currie (15), Alayna Lepack (16), Ben Williams (15), Mike Monast (16), Megan Oliver (15), Janine DeVault, Sam Wallace (15), Karli Stubbs (15)
P. 301: Jerry Ohlinger's Movie Material Store
P. 302: Reuters/Claro/Getty Images
P. 305: CP/Peter Bregg
P. 308: CP/Tobin Grimshaw
P. 314: Bob Daemmrich/Stock Boston

P. 315: Cartoon by Toles. The New Republic, in Washington Post National Weekly Edition, February 26, 2000, p. 28. TOLES © The Buffalo News. Reprinted with permission of UNIVERSAL PRESS SYNDICATE. All rights reserved.
P. 316: John A. Rizzo/Getty Images

Chapter 14

Chapter opener: ©Queen's Printer for Ontario, 2001. Reproduced with permission
P. 324: Geoff Manasse/Getty Images
P. 329: A. Ramey/Woodfin Camp
P. 333: Courtesy of Bonnie Haaland
P. 335: Catherine Karnow/Woodfin Camp
P. 339: CP/Toronto Star/Ron Bull
P. 351: CP/Edmonton Sun—Brendon Dlouhy

Chapter 15

Chapter opener: Barry Dawson, Street Graphics India (New York: Thames Hudson, 1999).
P. 356: Goran Petkovski
P. 364: M. J. Griffith/Photo Researchers
P. 367: ©Dick Hemingway
P. 368: Kent Knudson/PhotoLink/Getty Images
P. 369: Harry Baumert/The Des Moines Register and Tribune Company
P. 371: AP/Wide World Photos
P. 376: McGraw-Hill Companies, Inc./Gary He, photographer

Chapter 16

Chapter opener: Courtesy of Yahoo
P. 384: Top: Frederique Jouval/Corbis Sygma
P. 384: Bottom: Frederique Jouval/Corbis Sygma
P. 389: AP/Wide World Photos
P. 392: CP/Jonathan Hayward
P. 393: Joe Sohm/The Image Works
P. 397: Cartoon ©1985 Carol*Simpson. Reprinted by permission of Carol*Simpson Productions.
P. 397: Stan Godlewski
P. 401: ©1974 by Paramount Pictures Corporation. All rights reserved. Jerry Ohlinger's Movie Material Store.

NAME INDEX

C

D

K

L

M

N

O

P

Q

R

S

T

U

V

W

Y

Z

SUBJECT INDEX

D

E

F

G

H

M

N

O

P

Q

R

S

T

U

V